Policy-Making in the European Union

Develop your understanding of the European Union with our range of textbooks from the New European Union Series, created to give you clear and comprehensive coverage of a range of essential topics in EU politics.

THE NEW EUROPEAN UNION SERIES

Series Editors: John Peterson and Helen Wallace

The European Union is both the most successful modern experiment in international cooperation and a daunting analytical challenge to students of politics, economics, history, law, and the social sciences.

The EU of the twenty-first century continues to respond to expanding membership and new policy challenges—including the Eurozone crisis, climate change, energy security, and relations with Russia, Ukraine, and the Middle East—as well as the challenges to its legitimacy presented by the global financial crisis and the rise of Eurosceptic political parties in Europe. The result is an ever-evolving European Union that requires continuous reassessment.

THE NEW EUROPEAN UNION SERIES brings together the expertise of a community of leading scholars writing on major aspects of EU politics for an international readership. Build your knowledge with regularly updated editions on:

ORIGINS AND EVOLUTION OF THE
EUROPEAN UNION

POLICY-MAKING AND THE
EUROPEAN UNION

THE EUROPEAN UNION: HOW DOES
IT WORK?

THE INSTITUTIONS OF THE
EUROPEAN UNION

THE MEMBER STATES OF THE
EUROPEAN UNION

INTERNATIONAL RELATIONS AND
THE EUROPEAN UNION

For more information on the titles available in the New European Union Series visit the OUP website at
http://ukcatalogue.oup.com/category/academic/series/politics/neu.do

Make your voice heard: join the OUP politics student panel

To help us make sure we develop the best books for you, the student, we've set up a student panel.

To find out more visit www.oxfordtextbooks.co.uk/politics/studentpanel

Policy-Making in the European Union

SEVENTH EDITION

Edited by

Helen Wallace

Mark A. Pollack

Alasdair R. Young

OXFORD
UNIVERSITY PRESS

OXFORD

UNIVERSITY PRESS

Great Clarendon Street, Oxford, OX2 6DP,
United Kingdom

Oxford University Press is a department of the University of Oxford.
It furthers the University's objective of excellence in research, scholarship,
and education by publishing worldwide. Oxford is a registered trade mark of
Oxford University Press in the UK and in certain other countries

© Oxford University Press 2015

The moral rights of the authors have been asserted

Fourth Edition 2000
Fifth Edition 2005
Sixth Edition 2010

Impression: 1

Published in the United States of America by Oxford University Press
198 Madison Avenue, New York, NY 10016, United States of America

British Library Cataloguing in Publication Data

Data available

Library of Congress Control Number: 2014954277

ISBN 978–0–19–968967–5

Printed in Italy by
L.E.G.O. S.p.A.

■ OUTLINE CONTENTS

PART I Institutions, Process, and Analytical Approaches

PART II Policies

PART III **Conclusions**

▌ DETAILED CONTENTS

PART I   Institutions, Process, and Analytical Approaches

PART II Policies

▐ PREFACE

This is a new book which builds on six previous editions. It follows the pattern established in *Policy-Making in the European Communities* (1977), extended and developed in the second, third, fourth, fifth, and sixth editions of 1983, 1996, 2000, 2005, and 2010. All of the chapters have been rewritten, many extensively, with references to the earlier versions as appropriate. Readers who wish to understand the historical development of EU policies and policy-making in more detail are encouraged to refer back to earlier editions in order to gain a broader sense of how patterns of policy-making and institutional interaction have changed over the past three decades.

This volume is a study of policy-making, not of European integration as such. We do not therefore plunge into discussions of the broader political processes of the EU, although Chapter 2 by Mark Pollack introduces the key debates. Other dimensions of the EU are well covered in the companion volumes in *The New European Union Series*. Our aim here is to provide a detailed picture of the diversity of EU policy-making across a range of policy domains and to identify predominant patterns and characteristic styles and trends over time. Chapter 3 by Alasdair Young provides an overview of the literature on policy-making in the EU, while Chapter 4 by Helen Wallace and Christine Reh introduces the EU's key institutions, as well as how they interact in five ideal-type 'modes' of policy-making.

The fourteen case studies have been chosen both to cover the most important fields of EU activity and to illustrate the range of policy domains in which EU institutions now operate. Familiar issues of distribution and redistribution, the single market, agriculture, competition, external trade, monetary integration, and foreign policy have been covered in each of the previous six editions. The expansion of the EU's policy agenda since the early 1980s is reflected in the inclusion of case studies of energy policy, environmental regulation, the social dimension, employment policy, and justice and home affairs.

Sixteen of the eighteen authors of this volume contributed to the sixth edition, and the other two are welcome new conscripts, although we are very sorry that the untimely death of our long-time contributor and friend Dave Allen necessitated one of those changes. The authors come from a range of nationalities and intellectual traditions. This volume continues to benefit from informal ties and friendships among contributors since the first edition, sustained through exchanges of visits and children as well as through conferences and shared research.

We would like to thank Martha Bailes and Joanna Hardern for their patience, hard work, and encouragement as the book has taken shape at Oxford University Press, as well as John Peterson, series co-editor, for his constant vigilance and commitment. Cassandra Emmons has done a splendid job in editing and compiling the manuscript, while Joy Ruskin-Tompkins did a scrupulous copy-edit of the manuscript, Lesley Harris did likewise for the proofs, Yvonne Dixon helped to make possible our ever-growing index, and Moira Greenhalgh pulled together our tables of cases and legislation. A special debt is owed to Josef Falke and Stephan Leibfried for compiling the remarkable statistics on the caseloads of the European courts, which appear in the Appendix.

Figures 4.2 and 4.3 appear in *The Council of Ministers*, 3rd edition by Daniel Naurin, Fiona Hayes-Renshaw, and Helen Wallace, and are reproduced here with the kind permission of the authors and of Palgrave Macmillan. Table 5.1 is reproduced by kind permission of the Royal Institute of International Affairs. Figure 16.1 is reprinted by permission of the publishers from 'EU Policy making in trade and investment,' in *European Union Economic Diplomacy* by Stephen Woolcock (Farnham: Ashgate, 2012). Copyright © 2012.

HW, MAP, ARY
London, Philadelphia, and Atlanta
November 2014

▌ NEW TO THIS EDITION

- Detailed assessment of the implications for European policy-making of the global financial crisis, the ensuing Great Recession, and the sovereign debt crises that struck many member states
- Evaluation of the differential impact of the Lisbon Treaty across EU policies
- Analysis, one decade after the 'big bang' enlargement in 2004, of how expanded membership has affected policy-making
- Coverage of other major developments including the establishment of the European Stability Mechanism, the reforms of the common agricultural policy and cohesion policy, new initiatives to promote EU energy security, and relations with Russia and Ukraine

■ LIST OF FIGURES

▮ LIST OF BOXES

■ LIST OF TABLES

■ ABBREVIATIONS AND ACRONYMS

ACER	Agency for the Cooperation of Energy Regulators
ACP	African, Caribbean, and Pacific states
ACTA	Anti-Counterfeiting Trade Agreement
AFSJ	area of freedom, security, and justice
AGRI	Committee on Agriculture and Rural Development (of the EP)
AGS	Annual Growth Survey (Commission)
AIDCO	Directorate-General for EuropeAid
AKP	Islamist Justice and Development Party (Turkey)
ALDE	Alliance of Liberals and Democrats for Europe
AP	accession partnership
ASEAN	Association of South East Asian Nations
BATNA	best alternatives to negotiated agreement
Benelux	Belgium, the Netherlands, and Luxembourg
BEPA	Bureau of European Policy Advisers
BEPGs	Broad Economic Policy Guidelines
BKA	Bundeskartellamt
BRICs	Brazil, Russia, India, and China (emerging national economies)
BSE	bovine spongiform encephalopathy
CA	cabinets (Commission)
CAP	common agricultural policy
CARDS	Community Assistance for Reconstruction, Development, and Stabilization
CATS	Coordinating Committee for Police and Judicial Cooperation in Criminal Matters
CCS	carbon capture and storage
CEAS	common European asylum system
CEECs	countries of central and eastern Europe
CEEP	European Centre of Enterprises with Public Participation and of Enterprises of General Economic Interest
CEER	Council of European Energy Regulators
CEFIC	European Chemical Industry Council
CEN	Committee for European Norms (Standards)
CENELEC	Committee for European Electrical Norms (Standards)
CEPOL	European Police College

CET	common external tariff
CFI	Court of First Instance
CFSP	common foreign and security policy
CHODs	Chiefs of Defence of the member states
CIVCOM	Committee for Civilian Aspects of Crisis Management
CJEU	Court of Justice of the European Union
CMPD	Crisis Management and Planning Department
COGs	chiefs of government
COPA	Committee of Professional Agricultural Organizations (*Comité des Organisations Professionnelles Agricoles*)
COP	Conference of the Parties
COPS	Comité politique et de sécurité; French acronym for PSC
CoR	Committee of the Regions
Coreper	Committee of Permanent Representatives
COSAC	Conference of Parliamentary Committees for Union Affairs of Parliaments of the European Union, *Conférence des organes spécialisées aux affaires européennes*
COSI	Standing Committee on Internal Security
CPCC	Civilian Planning and Conduct Capability
CPCMU	Conflict Prevention and Crisis Management Unit
CSDP	common security and defence policy
CTEU	Consolidated Treaty of the European Union
CVM	cooperation and verification mechanism
DDA	Doha Development Agenda
DEU	Decision-Making in the European Union data-set
DG	Directorate-General (for European Commission, see Table 4.1)
DG AGRI	Directorate-General for Agriculture
DG BUDG	Directorate-General for Budget
DG CLIMA	Directorate-General for Climate Action
DG CNECT	Directorate-General for Communications Networks, Content and Technology (formerly INFSO)
DG COMM	Directorate-General for Communication
DG COMP	Directorate-General for Competition (formerly DG IV)
DG DEVCO	Directorate-General for Development and Cooperation—EuropeAid
DG DIGIT	Directorate-General for Informatics
DG EAC	Directorate General for Education and Culture
DG ECFIN	Directorate-General for Economic and Financial Affairs
DG ECHO	Directorate-General for International Cooperation, Humanitarian Aid, and Crisis Response
DG ELARG	Directorate-General for Enlargement

DG EMPL	Directorate-General for Employment, Social Affairs, and Inclusion
DG ENER	Directorate-General for Energy
DG ENTR	Directorate-General for Enterprise and Industry
DG ENV	Directorate-General for Environment
DG HOME	Directorate-General for Home Affairs
DG HR	Directorate-General for Human Resources and Security
DG JLS	Directorate-General for Justice, Liberty and Security (later DG HOME and DG JUST)
DG JUST	Directorate-General for Justice
DG MARE	Directorate-General for Maritime Affairs and Fisheries
DG MARKT	Directorate-General for Internal Market and Services
DG MOVE	Directorate-General for Mobility and Transport
DG OIB	Director-General for Infrastructure and Logistics (Brussels)
DG OIL	Director-General for Infrastructure and Logistics (Luxembourg)
DG REGIO	Directorate-General for Regional and Urban Policy
DG RELEX	Directorate-General for External Relations
DG RTD	Directorate-General for Research and Innovation
DG SANCO	Directorate-General for Health and Consumer Protection
DG SCIC	Directorate-General for Interpretation
DG TAXUD	Directorate-General for Taxation and Customs Union
DG TRADE	Directorate-General for Trade
DG TREN	Directorate-General for Energy and Transport (later DG ENER and DG MOVE)
DGT	Directorate-General for Translation
DRC	Democratic Republic of Congo
E3	France, Germany, and the UK, the three EU participants in the P5+1 negotiations with Iran over its nuclear programme
EA	Europe agreement
EACEA	Education, Audiovisual, and Culture Executive Agency
EAFRD	European Agricultural Fund for Rural Development
EAGGF	European Agricultural Guidance and Guarantee Fund
EaP	Eastern Partnership
EAP	Environmental Action Programme
EaPIC	Eastern Partnership cooperation programme
EASO	European Asylum Support Office
EAW	European arrest warrant
EBA	Everything But Arms
EBRD	European Bank for Reconstruction and Development
EC	European Community

ECB	European Central Bank
ECHA	European Chemicals Agency
ECHO	European Humanitarian Aid Office
ECHR	European Convention on Human Rights and Fundamental Freedoms
ECJ	European Court of Justice
ECN	European Competition Network
Ecofin	Council of Ministers for Economic and Financial Affairs
ECR	European Court of Justice Reports
ECSC	European Coal and Steel Community
ECT	Energy Charter Treaty
ECtHR	European Court of Human Rights
ecu	European currency unit
EDA	European Defence Agency
EDC	European Defence Community
EEA	European Economic Area
EEAS	European External Action Service
EEB	European Environment Bureau
EEC	European Economic Community
EEG	European Employment Guidelines
EES	European Employment Strategy
EET	European Employment Taskforce
EFA	ecological focus area
EFC	Economic and Financial Committee
EFF	European Fisheries Fund
EFSA	European Food Safety Authority
EFSF	European Financial Stability Facility
EFSM	European Financial Stability Mechanism
EFTA	European Free Trade Association
EIB	European Investment Bank
EIRO	European Industrial Relations Observatory
EMA	European Medicines Agency (formerly European Agency for the Evaluation of Medicinal Products)
EMCDDA	European Monitoring Centre for Drugs and Drug Addiction
EMCO	Employment Committee
EMS	European Monetary System
EMU	economic and monetary union
ENGO	environmental non-governmental organization

ENP	European neighbourhood policy
ENTSOE	European Network of Transmission System Operators for Electricity
ENTSOG	European Network of Transmission System Operators for Gas
ENVI	Committee on Environment, Public Health and Food Safety (of the EP)
EP	European Parliament
EPA	economic partnership agreement
EPC	European political cooperation
EPN	European Patrol Network
EPP	European People's Party
EPSCO	Employment, Social Policy, Health, and Consumer Affairs Council
EPSO	European Personnel Selection Office
ERDF	European Regional Development Fund
ERGEG	European Regulators Group for Electricity and Gas
ERM	exchange-rate mechanism
ERT	European Round Table of Industrialists
ESC	Economic and Social Committee
ESDC	European Security and Defence College
ESDP	European security and defence policy
ESF	European Services Forum
ESF	European Social Fund
ESM	European Stability Mechanism
ESRB	European Systemic Risk Board
ESRC	European Systemic Risk Council
ESS	European Security Strategy
ESTAT	Statistical Office of the European Union, Eurostat
ETS	emissions trading system
ETSO	European Transmission System Operators' Association
ETUC	European Trade Union Confederation
EU	European Union
EU15	Austria, Belgium, Denmark, France, Federal Republic of Germany, Finland, Greece, Ireland, Italy, Luxembourg, the Netherlands, Portugal, Spain, Sweden, the UK
EU25	EU15 plus Cyprus, Czech Republic, Estonia, Hungary, Latvia, Lithuania, Malta, Poland, Slovakia, Slovenia
EU28	EU25 plus Bulgaria, Croatia, Romania
EUFOR	European Union Force (rapid reaction force)
EUMC	European Monitoring Centre on Racism and Xenophobia (since superseded by FRA)
EUMC	European Union Military Committee

EUSR	EU special representative
Euratom	European Atomic Energy Community
euro (€)	name of the single currency for EMU
Eurodac	European system for collecting fingerprints from asylum-seekers (from French abbrev.)
Eurojust	EU body to coordinate investigation and prosecution of serious cross-border and organized crime
Europol	European Police Office
Eurosur	European Border Surveillance System
EWC	European works council
FAC	Foreign Affairs Council
FDI	foreign direct investment
FIFG	Financial Instrument for Fisheries Guidance
FoE	Friends of the Earth
FPI	foreign policy instruments
FRA	Fundamental Rights Agency
Frontex	European Agency for the management of Operational Cooperation at the External Borders of the Member States of the European Union
FTA	free-trade agreement
FTAA	Free Trade Area of the Americas
FTC	Federal Trade Commission
FYROM	former Yugoslav Republic of Macedonia
G5	Group of 5 EU countries for JHA: France, Germany, Italy, Spain, UK
G6	G5 plus Poland
G8	Group of 8 (western economic powers): Canada, France, Germany, Italy, Japan, Russia, UK, US
G20	A coalition of developing countries active in the Doha Round of multilateral trade talks
GAC	General Affairs Council
GAERC	General Affairs and External Relations Council
GATT	General Agreement on Tariffs and Trade
GDP	gross domestic product
GES	Growth and Employment Strategy
GNI	gross national income
GNP	gross national product
GPA	Government Purchasing Agreement
GSP	generalized system of preferences
HICP	harmonized index of consumer prices
HR/SG	High Representative/Secretary General
HR/VP	High Representative/Vice-President of the European Commission (formerly HR/SG)

IAS	Internal Audit Service
ICTY	International Criminal Tribunal for the former Yugoslavia
IEA	International Energy Agency
IGC	intergovernmental conference
ILO	International Labour Organization
IMCO	Internal Market and Consumer Protection Committee (of the EP)
IMF	International Monetary Fund
IMPEL	European Network for the Implementation and Enforcement of Environmental Law
INTA	International Trade Committee (of the EP)
IPA	Instrument for Pre-Accession Assistance
IR	international relations
ISPA	Instrument for Structural Policies for Pre-Accession
ITRE	Industry, Research and Energy Committee (of the EP)
JHA	justice and home affairs
JRC	Joint Research Centre
LNG	liquefied natural gas
MEA	multilateral environmental agreement
MEP	member of the European Parliament
MFF	multi-annual financial framework
Monuc	United Nations Mission in the Democratic Republic of the Congo
MOP	Meeting of the Parties
MTR	Mid-Term Review of Uruguay Round
NAMA	non-agricultural market access
NAP	national action plan/programme
Nato	North Atlantic Treaty Organization
NCA	national competition authority
NCB	national central bank
NGO	non-governmental organization
NPAA	national programme for the adoption of the *acquis*
NRP	National Reform Programme
NSRF	National Strategic Reference Framework
OCA	optimum currency area
OECD	Organisation for Economic Co-operation and Development
OFT	Office of Fair Trading (UK)
OLAF	European Anti-Fraud Office, *Office de la Lutte Anti-Fraude* (formerly UCLAF)
OMC	open method of coordination
OMT	outright monetary transactions

OP	Publications Office
OPEC	Organization of Petroleum Exporting Countries
OSCE	Organization for Security and Cooperation in Europe
OU	ownership unbundling
PCA	partnership and cooperation agreement
PCTF	European Police Chiefs' Task Force
Phare	Poland and Hungary: Assistance for the Restructuring of the Economy, *Pologne, Hongrie: assistance à la restructuration des économies* (extended to other CEECs)
PMO	Office for Administration and Payment
PNR	Passenger Name Record
PSC	Political and Security Committee
QMV	qualified majority voting
R&D	research and development
RABIT	Rapid Border Intervention Team
REACH	Registration, Evaluation, Authorization and Restriction of Chemicals
REFIT	Regulatory Fitness and Performance
REA	Research Executive Agency
S&D	Progressive Alliance of European Socialists and Democrats
SAA	stabilization and association agreement
SAAP	State Aid Action Plan
SACU	Southern Africa Customs Union
SAM	State Aid Modernization
SAP	stabilization and association process
SAPARD	Special Accession Programme for Agriculture and Rural Development
SCA	Special Committee on Agriculture
SCIFA	Strategic Committee on Immigration, Frontiers and Asylum
SEA	Single European Act
SEM	single European market
SFP(S)	single farm payment (scheme)
SG	Secretariat General
SGP	Stability and Growth Pact
SIC	Schengen Implementing Convention
SIS	Schengen Information System
SIS II	Second Generation Schengen Information System
SJ	Legal Service
SPC	Social Protection Committee
SSM	Single Supervisory Mechanism
SWIFT	Society for Worldwide Interbank Financial Telecommunication Agreements

T&E	European Federation for Transport and Environment
TACIS	Technical Aid to the Commonwealth of Independent States
TAIEX	Technical Assistance Information Exchange Office
TBT	technical barrier to trade
TCA	trade and cooperation agreement
TEC	Consolidated Treaty establishing the European Community, Revised Treaty of Rome
TEN	Trans-European Network
TEU	Treaty on European Union
TFEU	Treaty on the Functioning of the European Union
ToA	Treaty of Amsterdam
ToL	Treaty of Lisbon
ToN	Treaty of Nice
TPA	Trade Promotion Authority
TPC	Trade Policy Committee (formerly the 133 Committee)
Trevi	Terrorism, Radicalism, Extremism, Violence, Information (agreement on internal security cooperation)
TRIPs	Trade-Related Intellectual Property Rights
troika	grouping of three successive Council presidencies
troika	Commission, European Central Bank, and International Monetary Fund
TSO	transmission system operator
TTIP	Transatlantic Trade and Investment Partnership
UCLAF	Unité de coordination de la lutte anti-fraude, now OLAF
UEAPME	European Association of Craft, Small and Medium-Sized Enterprises, *union européenne de l'artisan et des petites et moyennes enterprises*
UK	United Kingdom
UN	United Nations
UNFCCC	United Nations Framework Convention on Climate Change
UNICE	Union of Industrial and Employers' Confederations of Europe (since 2007 BusinessEurope)
UNIFIL	United Nations Interim Force in Lebanon
Unprofor	United Nations Protection Force in Bosnia
US	United States
USTR	United States Trade Representative
VAT	value-added tax
VER	'voluntary' export restraint agreement
VIS	Visa Information System
WEU	Western European Union
WTO	World Trade Organization
WWF	World Wide Fund for Nature

■ LIST OF CONTRIBUTORS

IAN BACHE	University of Sheffield
DAVID BUCHAN	Oxford Institute for Energy Studies
BASTIAN GIEGERICH	International Institute for Strategic Studies
DERMOT HODSON	Birkbeck College
BRIGID LAFFAN	European University Institute
SANDRA LAVENEX	University of Geneva
STEPHAN LEIBFRIED	University of Bremen and Jacobs University Bremen
ANDREA LENSCHOW	University of Osnabrück
JOHANNES LINDNER	European Central Bank
MARK A. POLLACK	Temple University
CHRISTINE REH	University College London
MARTIN RHODES	University of Denver
CHRISTILLA ROEDERER-RYNNING	University of Southern Denmark
ULRICH SEDELMEIER	London School of Economics and Political Science
HELEN WALLACE	British Academy
STEPHEN WILKS	University of Exeter
STEPHEN WOOLCOCK	London School of Economics and Political Science
ALASDAIR R. YOUNG	Georgia Institute of Technology

▮ TABLE OF CASES

European Court of Justice Reports (ECR), are available on-line at http://www.curia.eu.int/en/content/juris/index.htm

▌ TABLE OF LEGISLATION

Regulations

Directives

Decisions

Recommendations

■ EDITORS' NOTE

A number of problems of dating, numbering, and nomenclature should be noted.

Generally in this volume for convenience we use the term European Union (EU) to embrace the family of arrangements under different treaties, even though it was not formally introduced until 1992. Where specifically relevant we refer to individual Communities or the European Community (EC).

Table 1.1 sets out the main agreements, including treaty revisions, and enlargements. Treaty reforms are dated to their year of signature by member governments, rather than to the completion of negotiations (often the year before), or ratification (often the year after). The well-intentioned renumbering of treaty articles, agreed as an afterthought to the Treaty of Amsterdam (ToA) and repeated in the Treaty of Lisbon (ToL), has created immense difficulties for all students of the EU. We generally quote treaty articles under the new numbering in the consolidated texts of the Treaty on European Union (TEU) and the Treaty on the Functioning of the European Union (TFEU). The ToL further complicated matters by renaming the EU's courts, with the European Court of Justice (ECJ) now referred to as the Court of Justice of the European Union (CJEU) and the former Court of First Instance becoming the General Court. For the convenience of our readers who are coming fresh to the study of the EU, we use the Lisbon nomenclature even when not historically accurate.

The ToL should not be confused with the so-called 'Lisbon Agenda' or 'Lisbon Strategy' for economic reform, adopted at the March 2000 European Council in Lisbon with the aim of making the EU 'the most competitive and dynamic knowledge-based economy in the world', and whose impact, and variable successes, are discussed in a number of the chapters of the volume.

As regards terminology, readers will notice that we frequently refer to 'member government' rather than 'member state'. Although, strictly speaking, it is 'states' that sign and are parties to treaties and conventions, it is the member 'governments' which negotiate policies and legislation, or implement them at home, acting not only as representatives of states, but as the domestically accountable executive authorities.

There is also an issue about how to refer to the thirteen member states that joined the EU in 2004, 2007, and 2013. While we appreciate that these states are very different, a central issue for this volume is how policy-making in the EU has been affected by the accessions of these states. It is therefore useful to have a shorthand for referring to them collectively. We are not aware of a more succinct way of referring to these states collectively than as the 'new' member states, even though at the time of writing (November 2014) those states that joined in 2004 have been members for ten years.

Gross domestic product (GDP) is the most commonly used measure of the value of production in the area concerned (a country or a region). Gross national product (GNP) is GDP plus net transfers of factor incomes, that is, the repatriated profits of member-state multinationals overseas, and less the profits of non-national multinationals operating in the member state. In most countries the difference between the two may be insignificant, but in countries such as Ireland the difference between the two may be as high as 25 per cent. Recently, gross national income (GNI) has become the more commonly used name for GNP.

Finally, we have faced a new nomenclature challenge in this seventh edition, namely how to refer to the crisis that has arisen, particularly since 2010, within the group of countries that use the euro, many of which have faced significant challenges in servicing their sovereign debt in the wake of the 2007–8 financial crisis. These national challenges, in turn, have led to a larger EU crisis, as EU member states and institutions have cast about for policy responses to prevent sovereign defaults and preserve the euro. This crisis, or set of crises, has been variously referred to in the press as the 'euro crisis', the 'sovereign debt crisis', the 'Eurozone crisis', and the 'euro area crisis'. We have resisted the simple 'euro crisis' for its lack of precision, and sovereign debt crisis is both unwieldy and such crises are hardly unique to the EU, so we have generally opted for 'euro area crisis' in the text, although inevitably other appellations for this ongoing challenge also appear in the various chapters of this volume. By any name, the euro area crisis has cast a long shadow over EU policy-making in many areas, and emerges as one of the most striking, overarching themes of this new edition.

PART I

Institutions, Process, and Analytical Approaches

CHAPTER 1

An Overview

Helen Wallace, Mark A. Pollack, and Alasdair R. Young

Introduction

The European Union (EU) is perhaps the most important agent of change in contemporary government and policy-making in Europe. EU decisions pervade the policy-making activities of individual European countries and the lives of European citizens, from the safety of food and the price of goods to the quality of water and the right to privacy. The euro area crisis that has unfolded since 2008 has shaken much of the Union's earlier confidence, yet it has also involved the EU ever more deeply in the fiscal policies of a number of member states. Moreover, given the size of the EU's market, its activities can profoundly affect the lives of people around the world. Given the importance and pervasiveness of EU policies, it is vital to understand how such policies are made, which is the key aim of this volume.

Beyond its real-world significance, the EU is particularly interesting to study, because it represents a remarkable, ongoing experiment in the collective governance of a multinational continent. The EU's member states, which have increased from the original six in the 1950s to twenty-eight in 2014, have periodically agreed to transfer authority in particular policy domains to the EU level (see Table 1.1). After seven decades of such transfers, the EU today is less than a state, but far more than a traditional international organization (W. Wallace 1983; Hix and Hoyland 2011), able to adopt and implement policies that go to the heart of its member states. The EU is also distinctive in that, in addition to being a forum for international relations, it is also an actor in international relations. There is a question about the extent to which the EU's institutions provide the main junction box through which connections are made between the country level and the global level, but there is little doubt that, in a growing number of areas from economic regulation to political and military affairs, the Union itself is an increasingly coherent and important actor on the world stage. The EU is, therefore, both a novel political arena and one that takes decisions of real import for the more than 500 million citizens of the EU, but also for individuals around the world.

This book, like its six predecessors, seeks to understand the processes that produce EU policies: that is, the decisions (or non-decisions) by EU public authorities facing choices between alternative courses of public action (Peterson and Bomberg 1999: 4). We do not advance any single theory of EU policy-making, although we do draw extensively on theories of European integration, international cooperation, comparative politics, and contemporary governance in our search for vocabulary to understand and explain our subject. Instead, we look to a variety of approaches, drawing on diverse theoretical traditions and from both comparative politics and international relations, in order explicitly to 'mainstream' the study of the EU by linking EU policy processes to comparable domestic and international processes, particularly in multi-layered polities. Our aim is not to prove or falsify any particular theory, but to use all available theoretical tools to understand EU policy-making in

TABLE 1.1 The main agreements and expanding membership

Year*	Agreement	Outcome	New Members
1951	Treaty of Paris	European Coal and Steel Community (ECSC)	Belgium, the Federal Republic of Germany, France, Italy, Luxembourg, and the Netherlands
1957	Treaty of Rome	European Economic Community (EEC)	
1957	Treaty of Rome	European Atomic Energy Community (Euratom)	
1965–6	Luxembourg crisis and compromise	Interrupts extension of qualified majority voting (QMV)	
1965	Merger Treaty	Combines institutions into single set	
1970	Budgetary Treaty	'Own resources' (i.e. revenue) created; some budgetary powers for European Parliament (EP)	
1973			Denmark, Ireland, and the UK
1975	Budgetary Treaty	More powers to EP; new Court of Auditors	
1978	Treaty revision	For direct elections to EP	
1981			Greece
1986			Portugal and Spain
1986	Single European Act (SEA)	More QMV in Council; some legislative power for EP; new Court of First Instance; introduces cohesion; expands policy scope, especially single European market (SEM)	
1992	Treaty on European Union (Maastricht) (TEU)	Three-pillar structure of European Union; common foreign and security policy (CFSP) and justice and home affairs (JHA); more QMV in Council; formalizes European Council; some co-decision for EP; new Committee of the Regions; expands policy scope, especially for economic and monetary union (EMU); introduces subsidiarity and citizenship; Social Protocol (UK opt-out)	

TABLE 1.1 (Continued)

1995			Austria, Finland, and Sweden
1997	Treaty of Amsterdam (ToA)	More legislative powers to EP, and stronger requirement for its 'assent' on (e.g.) enlargement and Commission appointments; introduces 'flexibility' (some member states cooperating without others); modest extra QMV in Council; incorporates Schengen and develops JHA; reverses UK social opt-out	
2001	Treaty of Nice (ToN)	Intended to streamline the EU institutions for further enlargement	
2004			Cyprus, Czech Republic, Estonia, Hungary, Latvia, Lithuania, Malta, Poland, Slovakia, and Slovenia
2004	Constitutional Treaty (CT)	Wide-ranging reorganization of treaties into three parts: I—main 'constitutional' provisions; II—The Charter of Fundamental Rights; III—The Policies and functioning of the Union, and some institutional changes. Not ratified after negative referendums in France and the Netherlands	
2007			Bulgaria and Romania
2007	Treaty of Lisbon (ToL)	Modified version of CT	
2013			Croatia

* Note: dates of signature of agreements.

all its complexity. Similarly, we make no effort to identify a single EU policy style, but instead classify and explore empirically the extraordinary and ever-increasing diversity of 'policy modes' whereby the preferences of national governments, sub-national actors, and supranational organizations are converted into common policies.

This chapter introduces the volume first by identifying the significant developments that have impacted EU policy-making since the sixth edition. Next, it summarizes our collective approach to understanding policy-making in the EU. It concludes by introducing the other chapters.

Policy-making under pressure

The financial crisis of 2007–8 has turned, since the sixth edition of this book, into the long-running Great Recession, placing severe strains on the budgets and the social fabric of the EU and its member states, and calling public support for the EU and its mission severely into question. The Great Recession, in turn, precipitated sovereign debt crises among some member states of the euro area (i.e. the 18 member states which use the single currency, the euro), requiring a nearly continuous series of emergency measures by the EU and raising the question whether the ongoing crisis will destroy the euro experiment or alternatively propel the members into closer economic integration. The repercussions of the Great Recession and the euro area debt crises have reverberated throughout EU policy-making by modifying ambitions, reducing capabilities (in terms of both finances and legitimacy), and realigning preferences. This is most obvious in the area of economic and monetary union (EMU; see Chapter 7), but the reality of a crisis-ridden, cash-strapped Europe has significant implications for virtually every area of EU policy, and our contributors have all set out to assess the impacts, for good or ill, of the Great Recession and the euro area crisis for all of the EU's various policies.

At the same time, the EU has been grappling with the implications of implementing the Treaty of Lisbon (ToL), which entered into effect just as the sixth edition went to press. The ToL introduced a number of important institutional changes, introducing new political offices and agencies, giving the Union new competences in a handful of issue areas, and changing the rules governing policy-making in other issue areas. The chapters in this volume provide a preliminary assessment of these changes.

A third set of changes, finally, has been wrought by the enlargement of the EU and the integration, over a period of a decade, of thirteen new member states, most from central and eastern Europe. That enlargement marked the transformation of the EU from a west European to a pan-European union, yet amid the celebrations over the EU's enlargement there was a general fear of indigestion as institutions originally built for six now operate with twenty-eight members of considerable diversity. Would the EU be able to operate as efficiently as in the past, or would sheer numbers, as well as the increased diversity of its expanded membership, condemn the EU policy process to paralysis? In the sixth edition of this book, we began to explore these questions in the light of the first few years of eastern membership; in this edition, with a full decade of experience following the 'big bang' enlargement of 2004, we return to that question more systematically.

Understanding EU policy-making

A contention in this volume is that the wide array of the EU's policy domains reflects not one, but several, modes of policy-making, as the case studies reveal. Moreover, the same EU institutions, and the same national policy-makers, have different characteristics, exhibit different patterns of behaviour, and produce different kinds of outcomes, depending on the policy domain and depending on the period. Thus, as we shall see, there is no single and catch-all way of capturing the essence of EU policy-making. All generalizations need to be nuanced, although, as will be seen in Chapter 4, five main variants (ideal types) of the policy process—the Community method, the regulatory mode, the distributive mode, policy coordination, and intensive transgovernmentalism—can be identified. One of the primary aims of the case study chapters is to assess which of these modes, or which combinations of modes, sometimes in hybrid form, best characterize policy-making in each issue area.

There have also been broad changes in the nature of EU policy-making over time. The proliferation of patterns of policy-making identified in the previous volume has continued and, if anything, accelerated. In some issue areas, such as the internal market (Chapter 5), the environment (Chapter 13), and energy (Chapter 14), the EU's supranational actors, such as the executive Commission, the European Parliament (EP), and the Court of Justice of the European Union (CJEU, formerly known as the European Court of Justice or ECJ) have become more important players over time, while the intergovernmental Council of the European Union has moved in most areas from the traditional unanimity voting to qualified majority voting (QMV). Yet in other areas, EU policy-making takes place outside the classical Community framework, with the Commission, the EP, and the CJEU playing a less central role, while the main dynamics have been found in the intensive network interactions among national policy-makers (Chapters 6, 12), and in new agencies, such as the European Central Bank (ECB) (see Chapter 7) and Europol (see Chapter 15). The investments being made in new institutional arrangements have been designed to underpin this structured transgovernmentalism rather than to incorporate them within the traditional Community procedures (communitarization). The case study chapters suggest that this may be a sustained pattern, not a mere staging post in the transition from nationally rooted policy to 'communitarization'.

Tempting though it is to interpret this as the triumph of 'intergovernmentalism' (a process in which traditional states predominate) over 'supranationalism' (a process in which new European institutions enjoy political autonomy and authority), we argue that the story is more nuanced, with the emergence of new, varied, and often hybrid policy modes emerging across our fourteen issue areas.

Moreover, as we shall see from several of the case studies in this volume, how those European policies operate varies a good deal from one EU member state to another. In other words, the EU policy process is one which has differentiated outcomes, with significant variations between countries. Hence, it is just as important to understand the national institutional settings as to understand the EU-level institutions in order to get a grip on the EU policy process as a whole (H. Wallace 1973, 1999).

The EU as a unique arena with familiar politics?

Most accounts of the EU policy process, as we have noted, concentrate on the EU's own institutions. Their main features and characteristics are set out in Chapter 4, and their roles in the policy process will be a recurrent theme in this volume. We shall observe general features that are present in most areas of EU policy, as well as features that are specific to particular sectors, issues, events, and periods.

But how far do the particular features of the EU's institutional system produce a distinctive kind of policy process? It has been commonplace for commentators on the EU to stress its distinctive features, and indeed often to argue that they result in a unique kind of politics. Whether such an assertion is warranted is a question to keep in mind in reading subsequent chapters. In forming an answer to the question it is important to reflect on what other political arrangements might be appropriately compared with those of the EU. Some would say loose-knit states, such as Canada or Switzerland, mostly confederal in character, or a federal state like the US, Belgium, or Germany. Others would say some multilateral regimes, especially those that focus on the political economy, such as the World Trade Organization (WTO), or the various regional customs unions and free trade areas elsewhere in the world. Depending on which comparators are chosen, different 'benchmarks' will be useful for evaluating the EU institutions and their performance.

As we shall see in Chapter 2, this issue has been one of the longest running sources of controversy among political analysts of the EU. On one side of the debate are those who see the EU as example, perhaps a particularly richly developed example, of an international organization. On the other side of the debate are those who view the EU as a kind of polity-in-the-making, and, in this sense, state-like. The analyses of the EU's institutions conducted in these two camps differ considerably. A third camp argues that contemporary politics in Europe are changing anyway, with traditional forms of politics and government being transformed in quite radical ways. The net result, it is argued, is that it is more appropriate to talk of 'governance' than of 'government'. The EU has, according to this view, emerged as part of a reconfigured pattern of European governance, with an evolution of institutional arrangements and associated processes that have interestingly novel characteristics.

Chapters 2, 3, and 4 explore these three perspectives with different emphases. Subsequent chapters reveal some policy sectors in which the EU has powers as extensive as those normally associated with country-level governance, while other chapters will describe much lighter and more fragile European regimes. The institutional patterns vary between these two kinds of cases. Chapter 4 provides an anatomical overview of the institutions together with a broad characterization of five main policy modes that vary across issue areas and across time. Subsequent case studies identify many of the variations of institutional patterns that are observable in specific areas of policy, along with the organic features of the institutional processes.

These variations make the EU policy process a challenging one to characterize and hence the subject of lively argument for both practitioners and analysts.

However distinctive and unusual the EU institutions might be argued to be, we should not forget that the people, groups, and organizations that are active within these institutions are for the most part going about their 'normal' business in seeking policy and political outcomes. There is no reason to suppose that their activities have different purposes simply because the institutional arena is different from the others in which they are involved. The politics of the EU are just that—normal politics, with whatever one thinks are the normal features of domestic politics, and by extension policy-making, in European countries. Nonetheless, we need to be alert to differences in behaviour, in opportunities, and in constraints that arise from being involved in a multi-level and multi-layered process. It is around this feature of the EU that much of the most interesting analytical debate takes place.

Outline of the volume

The volume is organized in three parts. In Part I, we sketch the broad contours of the EU policy process—or policy processes—and relevant analytical approaches for understanding that process. Chapter 2 surveys the many theories that have been put forward to explain both European integration as a process, and the EU as a political system. Chapter 3 situates EU policy-making in the wider literature on policy-making, drawing on theories developed in comparative politics and international relations. Chapter 4 introduces the various EU institutions through which policies are articulated and presents a classification of five 'policy modes', drawn from the scholarly literature and empirical practice, which serve as an analytic framework for the analysis of policy-making in specific sectors.

Part II consists of fourteen case studies, which cover the main policy domains in which the EU dimension is significant. We have included policies that have been core European business from the outset, such as competition policy, the common agricultural policy (CAP), and trade policy; policies that have become central to the EU as it has developed, such as the budget, the structural funds, the single European market (SEM), EMU, and the environment, as well as enlargement; policies that illustrate more recent areas of European engagement, such as common foreign and security policy (CFSP), justice and home affairs (JHA), and employment; and policies in which recent developments have given new content to old policy ambitions, such as energy and social policy. The policies are also selected to illustrate the wide variety of policy-making patterns, from extensive delegation to supranational institutions—as in competition policy, monetary policy, and trade policy—to relatively loose coordination among member states, as in defence, employment, and police and judicial cooperation, and everything in between. All of the case study chapters in Part II have been extensively revised and updated since the last edition, published in 2010. In particular, they assess the operation of the ToL, which entered into force in December 2009, just as the previous edition of this book was going to press, and consider the implications of enlargement and of the global financial crisis, the Great Recession, and the euro area crisis, which were unfolding as the sixth edition went to press.

Part III, the concluding chapter, summarizes the broad findings of the volume, identifying contemporary trends in EU policy-making and offering some observations about EU policy-making under the multiple stresses of enlargement, institutional change, and financial crisis. In addition, the Appendix contains valuable data on the cases adjudicated by the CJEU and the General Court, which indicate the pattern of cases over time and across sectors.

CHAPTER 2

Theorizing EU Policy-Making

Mark A. Pollack

▌ Summary

Our understanding of European Union (EU) policy-making and policy processes is shaped largely by the language of theory, and an understanding of the main currents of EU-related theories is therefore a useful starting point for the case studies in this volume. Three primary currents or strands of theory are identified and explored. First, we examine the various theories of European integration, which sought to explain the process of EU development from its origins to the present day. This body of theory initially pitted neo-functionalist models of integration through spill-over against intergovernmentalist models emphasizing the continuing dominance of national governments; later, this debate was largely supplanted by a second debate pitting rational-choice

(continued...)

theorists against constructivist analyses. Secondly, we survey the increasing number of studies that approach the EU through the lenses of comparative politics and comparative public policy, focusing on the federal or quasi-federal aspects of the EU and its legislative, executive, and judicial politics. Thirdly and finally, we examine the 'governance approach' to the EU, which theorizes the Union as an experiment in non-hierarchical, informal, and deliberative governance, and focuses in large part on the normative questions of the EU's democratic legitimacy. Taken together, these theories pose important questions and provide distinctive hypotheses about the key actors and the dominant processes in EU policy-making.

Introduction

This chapter sketches the theoretical background for the book, by surveying theories of European integration, comparative politics, and governance, laying out clearly the analytical concepts that will subsequently be employed by our contributors.[1] The chapter does not seek to come up with a single theory to explain EU integration or policy-making, a project beyond the scope of this volume. Indeed, a consistent theme of this book from its first edition onwards has been the need to guard against over-generalizing about 'the' EU policy process, but instead being open to the prospect that policy-making may differ considerably and systematically across issue areas. Nevertheless, theories of European integration and public policy-making are useful in providing us with the analytical tools with which to chart and explain variation in EU policy-making both across issue areas and over time, and these theories inform the language and the categories of analysis used in the subsequent chapters of the volume.

The chapter is organized in four parts. The first provides a brief overview of the most influential theories of European integration, namely neo-functionalism, intergovernmentalism, institutionalism, constructivism, and realism, paying particular attention to the implications of each theory for our specific focus on EU policy-making. The second section looks beyond the integration literature, drawing on rational-choice theories of comparative politics for a set of analytic categories that can be used to analyse the participants, processes, and policies that we observe in the EU. In doing so, we pay special attention to the concept of the EU as a political system, characterized by a vertical and a horizontal separation of powers, which, we argue, has implications for the nature of policy-making and the key actors in the EU policy process. (In Chapter 3, Alasdair Young similarly mines the literature on comparative public policy analysis, reviewing and applying theories of the 'policy cycle' to the EU policy process.) The third section examines the recent development of a 'governance approach' to the EU. The governance approach emphasizes a series of interrelated concepts, including: the non-hierarchical or 'network' character of EU policy-making; the emergence of 'multi-level governance' implicating sub-national, national, and supranational actors; the potential for the EU to influence or 'Europeanize' the policies and politics of member and candidate countries; the politicization of EU politics and the emergence of an identity-driven scepticism towards the Union; and the prospect for 'deliberative supranationalism' as a partial response to the challenge of democratic legitimacy beyond the nation-state. The fourth section concludes with a brief restatement of the primary theoretical debates in EU studies today, and the questions that they raise for the study of policy-making in the EU.

Theories of European integration

For many years, the academic study of the European Communities (EC), as they were then called, was virtually synonymous with the study of European *integration*. The initially modest and largely technocratic achievements of the EC seemed less significant than the potential that they represented for the gradual integration of the countries of western Europe into something else: a supranational polity. When the integration process was going well, as during the 1950s and early 1960s, neo-functionalists and other theorists sought to explain the process whereby European integration proceeded from modest beginnings to something broader and more ambitious. When things seemed to be going badly, as from the 1960s until the early 1980s, intergovernmentalists and others sought to explain why the integration process had not proceeded as smoothly as its founders had hoped. Regardless of the differences among these bodies of theory, we can say clearly that the early literature on the EC sought to explain the process of European *integration* (rather than, say, policy-making), and that in doing so it drew largely (but not exclusively) on theories of international relations (IR).

In the first edition of this volume, Carole Webb (1977) surveyed the debate among the then dominant schools of European integration, neo-functionalism and intergovernmentalism, drawing from each approach a set of implications and hypotheses about the nature of the EC policy process. Similarly, here we review neo-functionalism and its views about the EU policy process, and then the intergovernmentalist response, as well as the updating of 'liberal intergovernmentalism' by Andrew Moravcsik in the 1990s. In addition, we examine the development of other bodies of integration theory—institutionalism, constructivism, and realism—which offer very different views of the integration process and very different implications for EU policy-making.

Neo-functionalism

In 1958, on the eve of the establishment of the European Economic Community (EEC) and European Atomic Energy Community (Euratom), Ernst Haas published his seminal work, *The Uniting of Europe*, setting out a 'neo-functionalist' theory of regional integration. As elaborated in subsequent texts by Haas and other scholars (e.g. E. Haas 1961; Lindberg 1963; Lindberg and Scheingold 1970), neo-functionalism posited a process of 'functional spill-over', in which the initial decision by governments to place a certain sector, such as coal and steel, under the authority of central institutions creates pressures to extend the authority of the institutions into neighbouring areas of policy, such as currency exchange rates, taxation, and wages. Thus, neo-functionalists predicted, sectoral integration would produce the unintended and unforeseen consequence of promoting further integration in additional issue areas.

Complementing this functional spill-over, George (1991) identifies a second strand of the spill-over process, which he calls 'political' spill-over, in which both supranational actors (e.g. the Commission) and sub-national actors (interest groups or others within the member states) create additional pressures for further integration. At the sub-national level, Haas suggested that interest groups operating in an integrated sector would have to interact with supranational actors charged with the management of their sector. Over time, these groups would come to appreciate the benefits from integration, and would thereby transfer their demands, expectations, and even their loyalties from national governments to a new centre, thus becoming an important force for further integration. At the supranational level, moreover, bodies such as the Commission would encourage such a transfer of loyalties, promoting European policies and brokering bargains among the member states in order to 'upgrade the common interest'. As a result of such sectoral and political spill-over, neo-functionalists predicted sectoral integration would become self-sustaining, leading eventually to the creation of a new political entity with its centre in Brussels (for a revived, updated case for neo-functionalist theory in the twenty-first century, see Sandholtz and Stone Sweet 2012).

For our purposes in this volume, the most important contribution of neo-functionalists to the study of EU policy-making was their conceptualization of a 'Community method' of policy-making. As Webb pointed out, this ideal-type Community method was based largely on the observation of a few specific sectors (the common agricultural policy (CAP), see Chapter 8, and the customs union, see Chapter 16) during the formative years of the Community, and presented a distinct picture of EC policy-making as a process driven by an entrepreneurial Commission and featuring collective deliberation among member-state representatives in the Council. The Community method in this view was not just a legal set of policy-making institutions but a 'procedural code' conditioning the expectations and the behaviour of the Commission and the member governments as participants in the process.

This Community method, Webb suggested, characterized EEC decision-making during the period from 1958 to 1963, as the original six member states met alongside the Commission to put in place the essential elements of the EEC customs union and the CAP. By 1965, however, Charles de Gaulle, the French president, had precipitated the so-called 'Luxembourg crisis', insisting on the importance of state sovereignty and arguably violating the implicit procedural code of the Community method. The EEC, which had been scheduled to move to extensive qualified majority voting

(QMV) in 1966, continued to take most decisions de facto by unanimity, the Commission emerged weakened from its confrontation with de Gaulle, and the nation-state appeared to have reasserted itself. These tendencies were reinforced, moreover, by developments in the 1970s, when the intergovernmental aspects of the Community were strengthened by the creation in 1974 of the European Council, a regular summit meeting of EU heads of state and government. Similarly, empirical studies showed the importance of national gatekeeping institutions (H. Wallace 1973). Even some of the major advances of this period, such as the creation of the European Monetary System (EMS) in 1978 (see Chapter 7), were taken outside the structure of the EEC Treaty, and with no formal role for the Commission or other supranational EC institutions.

Intergovernmentalism

Reflecting these developments, a new 'intergovernmentalist' school of integration theory emerged, beginning with Stanley Hoffmann's (1966) claim that the nation-state, far from being obsolete, had proven 'obstinate'. Most obviously with de Gaulle, but later with the accession of new member states such as the UK, Ireland, and Denmark in 1973, member governments made clear that they would resist the gradual transfer of sovereignty to the Community, and that EC decision-making would reflect the continuing primacy of the nation-state. Under these circumstances, Haas himself (1975) pronounced the 'obsolescence of regional integration theory', while other scholars such as Paul Taylor (1983) and William Wallace (1982) argued that neo-functionalists had underestimated the resilience of the nation-state. At the same time, historical scholarship by Alan Milward and others (Milward and Lynch 1993; Milward 2000) supported the view that national governments, rather than supranational organizations, played the central role in the historical development of the EU and were strengthened, rather than weakened, as a result of the integration process. And indeed, the early editions of *Policy-Making in the European Communities* found significant evidence of intergovernmental bargaining as the dominant mode of policy-making in many (but not all) issue areas.

Liberal intergovernmentalism

The period from the mid-1960s through to the mid-1980s has been characterized as 'the doldrums era', both for the integration process and for scholarship on the EU (Keeler 2005; Jupille 2005). While a dedicated core of EU scholars continued to advance the empirical study of the EU during this period, much of this work either eschewed grand theoretical claims about the integration process or accepted with minor modifications the theoretical language of the neo-functionalist/intergovernmentalist debate.

With the 'relaunching' of the integration process in the mid-1980s, however, scholarship on the EU exploded, and the theoretical debate was revived. While some of this scholarship viewed the relaunching of the integration process as a vindica-tion of earlier neo-functionalist models (Sandholtz and Zysman 1989; Tranholm-Mikkelsen 1991), Andrew Moravcsik (1993*a*, 1998) argued influentially that these new steps forward could be accounted for by a revised intergovernmental model emphasizing the power and preferences of EU member states.

Moravcsik's 'liberal intergovernmentalism' is a three-step model, which combines: (1) a liberal theory of national preference formation with (2) an intergovernmental model of EU-level bargaining, and (3) a model of institutional choice emphasiz-ing the role of international institutions in providing 'credible commitments' for member governments. In the first or liberal stage of the model, national chiefs of government (COGs) aggregate the interests of their domestic constituencies, as well as their own interests, and articulate their respective national preferences towards the EU. Thus, national preferences are complex, reflecting the distinctive interests, parties, and institutions of each member state, and they are determined *domestically*, not shaped by participation in the EU as some neo-functionalists had proposed.

In the second or intergovernmental stage, national governments bring their pref-erences to the bargaining table in Brussels, where agreements reflect the relative power of each member state, and where supranational organizations such as the Commission exert little or no influence over policy outcomes. By contrast with neo-functionalists, who emphasized the entrepreneurial and brokering roles of the Commission and the upgrading of the common interest among member states in the Council, Moravcsik and other intergovernmentalists emphasized the hardball bargaining among member states and the importance of bargaining power, package deals, and 'side payments' as determinants of intergovernmental bargains on the most important EU decisions.

Thirdly and finally, Moravcsik puts forward a rational-choice theory of institu-tional choice, arguing that EU member states adopt particular EU institutions—pooling sovereignty through QMV, or delegating sovereignty to supranational actors like the Commission and the Court of Justice of the European Union (CJEU)—in order to increase the credibility of their mutual commitments. In this view, sovereign states seeking to cooperate among themselves invariably face a strong temptation to cheat or 'defect' from their agreements. Pooling and delegating sovereignty through international organizations, he argues, allows states to commit themselves credibly to their mutual promises, by monitoring state compliance with international agree-ments and filling in the blanks of broad international treaties, such as those that have constituted the EC/EU.

In empirical terms, Moravcsik (1998) argues that the EU's historic intergov-ernmental agreements, such as the 1957 Treaties of Rome and the 1992 Treaty on European Union (TEU), were not driven primarily by supranational entrepreneurs, unintended spill-overs from earlier integration, or transnational coalitions of interest groups, but rather by a gradual process of preference convergence among the most powerful member states, which then struck central bargains among themselves, of-fered side-payments to smaller member states, and delegated strictly limited powers to supranational organizations that remained more or less obedient servants of the member states.

Overarching the three steps of this model is a 'rationalist framework' of international cooperation. The relevant actors are assumed to have fixed preferences (for wealth, power, etc.), and to act systematically to achieve those preferences within the constraints posed by the institutions within which they act (Moravcsik 1998: 19–20; Moravcsik and Schimmelfennig 2009).

During the 1990s, liberal intergovernmentalism emerged as arguably the leading theory of European integration, yet its basic theoretical assumptions were questioned by IR scholars coming from two different directions. A first group of scholars, collected under the rubrics of rational-choice institutionalism and historical institutionalism, accepted Moravcsik's rationalist assumptions, but rejected his spare, institution-free model of intergovernmental bargaining as an accurate description of the EU policy process. By contrast, a second school of thought, drawing from sociological institutionalism and constructivism, raised more fundamental objections to the methodological individualism of rational-choice theory in favour of an approach in which national preferences and identities were shaped, at least in part, by EU norms and rules.

The 'new institutionalisms'

The rise of institutionalist analysis of the EU did not develop in isolation, but reflected a gradual and widespread reintroduction of institutions into a large body of theories (e.g. pluralism, Marxism, and neo-realism), in which institutions had been either absent or considered epiphenomenal, reflections of deeper causal factors or processes such as the distribution of power in domestic societies or in the international system. By contrast with these institution-free accounts of politics, which dominated much of political science between the 1950s and the 1970s, three primary 'institutionalisms' developed during the course of the 1980s and early 1990s, each with a distinct definition of institutions and a distinct account of how they 'matter' in the study of politics (March and Olsen 1989; Hall and Taylor 1996).

Rational-choice institutionalism began with the effort by American political scientists to understand the origins and effects of US Congressional institutions on legislative behaviour and policy outcomes. By contrast with early rational-choice models of US legislative behaviour, which depicted legislative politics as a series of simple-majority votes among Congressional representatives, institutionalists argued that Congressional institutions, and in particular the committee system, could shape legislative outcomes and make those outcomes durable in the face of subsequent challenges. Congressional institutions, in this view, could produce 'structure-induced equilibrium', by ruling some alternatives as permissible or impermissible, and by structuring the voting power and the veto power of various actors in the decision-making process (Shepsle 1979).

The subsequent development of the rational-choice approach to institutions produced a number of theoretical offshoots with potential applications to both comparative and international politics. For example, rational-choice institutionalists have examined in some detail the 'agenda-setting' power of Congressional committees, which can send draft legislation to the floor that is often easier to adopt than it is to amend. In another offshoot, students of the US Congress have developed 'principal–agent' models of Congressional delegation to regulatory bureaucracies and to courts, and they have problematized the conditions under which legislative principals are able— or unable—to control their respective agents (Moe 1984; Kiewiet and McCubbins 1991; Epstein and O'Halloran 1999; Huber and Shipan 2002).

Although originally formulated and applied in the context of American political institutions, rational-choice institutionalist insights 'travelled' to other domestic and international contexts, and were quickly taken up by students of the EU. Responding to the increasing importance of EU institutional rules, such as the cooperation and co-decision procedures, these authors argued that purely intergovernmental models of EU decision-making underestimated the causal importance of formal EU rules in shaping policy outcomes. In an early application of rational-choice theory to the EU, for example, Fritz Scharpf (1988) argued that the inefficiency and rigidity of the CAP and other EU policies was due not simply to the EU's intergovernmentalism, but also to specific institutional rules, such as unanimous decision-making and the 'default condition' in the event that the member states failed to agree on a common policy (see Chapter 8). By the mid-1990s, George Tsebelis, Geoffrey Garrett, and many others sought to model both the choice and the functioning of EU institutions in rational-choice terms. Many of these studies fall essentially into the comparative study of executive, legislative, and judicial politics, and are therefore reviewed in the second part of this chapter.

By contrast, sociological institutionalism and constructivist approaches in IR defined institutions much more broadly to include informal norms and conventions as well as formal rules. They argued that such institutions could 'constitute' actors, shaping their identities and hence their preferences in ways that rational-choice approaches could not capture (see next section).

Historical institutionalists took up a position between these two camps, focusing on the effects of institutions *over time*, in particular on the ways in which a given set of institutions, once established, can influence or constrain the behaviour of the actors who established them (Hall 1986; Thelen and Steinmo 1992). In perhaps the most sophisticated presentation of this thinking, Paul Pierson (2000) has argued that political institutions are characterized by what economists call 'increasing returns', insofar as they create incentives for actors to stick with and not abandon existing institutions, adapting them only incrementally in response to changing circumstances. Thus, politics should be characterized by certain interrelated phenomena, including: *inertia*, or 'lock-ins', whereby existing institutions may remain in equilibrium for extended periods despite considerable political change; a critical role for *timing and sequencing*, in which relatively small and contingent events at critical junctures early in a sequence shape events that occur later; and *path-dependence*, in which early decisions provide incentives for actors to perpetuate institutional and policy choices inherited from the past, even when the resulting outcomes are manifestly inefficient. In recent years, these insights have been applied increasingly to the development of the EU, with various authors emphasizing the temporal dimension of European integration (Armstrong and Bulmer 1998; Fioretos 2011).

Pierson's (1996) study of path-dependence in the EU, for example, seeks to understand European integration as a process that unfolds over time, and the conditions under which path-dependent processes are most likely to occur. Working from essentially rationalist assumptions, Pierson argues that, despite the initial primacy of member governments in the design of EU institutions and policies, 'gaps' may occur in the ability of member governments to control the subsequent development of institutions and policies, for four reasons. First, member governments in democratic societies may, because of electoral concerns, apply a high 'discount rate' to the future, agreeing to EU policies that lead to a long-term loss of national control in return for short-term electoral returns. Secondly, even when governments do not heavily discount the future, unintended consequences of institutional choices can create additional gaps, which member governments may or may not be able to close through subsequent action. Thirdly, the preferences of member governments are likely to change over time, most obviously because of electoral turnover, leaving new governments with new preferences to inherit an *acquis communautaire* negotiated by, and according to the preferences of, a previous government. Finally, EU institutions and policies can become locked-in not only as a result of change-resistant institutions from above, but also through the incremental growth of entrenched support for existing institutions *from below*, as societal actors adapt to and develop a vested interest in the continuation of specific EU policies.

In sum, for both rational-choice and historical institutionalists, EU institutions 'matter', shaping both the policy process and policy outcomes in predictable ways, and indeed shaping the long-term process of European integration. In both cases, however, the effects of EU institutions are assumed to influence only the incentives confronting the various public and private actors—the actors themselves are assumed to remain unchanged in their fundamental preferences and identities. Indeed, despite their differences on substantive issues, liberal intergovernmentalism, rational-choice institutionalism, and most historical institutionalism arguably constitute a shared rationalist research agenda—a community of scholars operating from similar basic assumptions and seeking to test hypotheses about the most important determinants of European integration.

Constructivism, and reshaping European identities and preferences

Constructivist theory, like rational choice, did not begin as a theory of European integration, but rather as a broader 'metatheoretical' orientation with potential implications for the study of the EU. As Risse (2009: 145–6) explains in an excellent survey:

it is probably most useful to describe constructivism as based on a social ontology which insists that human agents do not exist independently from their social environment and its collectively shared systems of meanings ('culture' in a broad sense). This is in contrast to the methodological individualism of rational choice according to which '[t]he elementary unit of social life is the individual human action'. The fundamental insight of the structure-agency debate, which lies at the heart of many social constructivist works, is not only that social structures and agents are mutually co-determined. The crucial point is that constructivists insist on the *constitutiveness* of (social) structures and agents. The social environment in which we find ourselves, defines (constitutes) who we are, our identities as social beings.

For constructivists, institutions are understood broadly to include not only formal rules but also informal norms, and these rules and norms are expected to 'constitute' actors, that is, to shape their identities and their preferences. Actor preferences, therefore, are not exogenously given and fixed, as in rationalist models, but *endogenous* to institutions, and individuals' identities are shaped and reshaped by their social environment. Taking this argument to its logical conclusion, constructivists generally reject the rationalist conception of actors as utility-maximizers operating according to a 'logic of consequentiality', in favour of March and Olsen's (1989: 160–2) conception of a 'logic of appropriateness'. In this view, actors confronting a given situation do not consult a fixed set of preferences and calculate their actions in order to maximize their expected utility, but look to socially constructed roles and institutional rules and ask what sort of behaviour is appropriate in that situation. Constructivism, therefore, offers a fundamentally different view of human agency from rational-choice approaches, and it suggests that institutions influence individual identities, preferences, and behaviour in more profound ways than those hypothesized by rational-choice theorists.

Consistent with these hypotheses, a growing number of scholars have suggested that EU institutions shape not only the behaviour, but also the preferences and identities, of individuals and member governments. This argument has been put most forcefully by Thomas Christiansen, Knud Erik Jørgensen, and Antje Wiener (1999: 529):

A significant amount of evidence suggests that, as a process, European integration has a transformative impact on the European state system and its constituent units. European integration itself has changed over the years, and it is reasonable to assume that in the process agents' identity and subsequently their interests have equally changed. While this aspect of change can be theorized within constructivist perspectives, it will remain largely invisible in approaches that neglect processes of identity formation and/or assume interests to be given exogenously.

Not surprisingly, such arguments were forcefully rebutted by rationalist theorists, resulting in a major 'metatheoretical debate' (Moravcsik 1999; Checkel and Moravcsik 2001).

Fortunately, constructivist scholars have not been limited to theoretical or metatheoretical debates, but have produced a spate of empirical work, seeking rigorously to test hypotheses about socialization, norm-diffusion, and collective-preference formation in the EU, using a range of qualitative and quantitative research methods. The results of these studies are somewhat mixed, with some scholars finding evidence of socialization among long-standing EU members (Lewis 2005) and/or new and candidate members (Gheciu 2005), but the predominant finding has been that EU socialization of both Commission (Hooghe 2005) and national officials has been less far-reaching than expected. In a series of rigorous studies, for example, students of EU enlargement examined the attitudes and policies of new and candidate members of the Union, finding only weak evidence of socialization, and arguing that EU 'conditionality' or 'external incentives', rather than socialization, provided the strongest explanation of these states' behaviour (Kelley 2004; Schimmelfennig and Sedelmeier 2005a). A collective research project on international socialization in Europe, led by Jeffrey Checkel (2005), produced similar findings, concluding that, 'while there are good conceptual reasons for expecting a predominance of international socialization in Europe, the empirical cases instead suggest that effects of socialization are often weak and secondary to dynamics at the national level' (Zürn and Checkel 2005: 1047). Outside the elite arena of EU policy-making, studies of mass public opinion tell a similar story, with national identities clearly predominating, although scholars have found stronger evidence of European identification among 'young, educated, and well-to-do Europeans' (Schimmelfennig 2012: 41; see Fligstein 2009; Risse 2010).

Although socialization of actors in the EU policy process is the most obviously relevant constructivist claim for our purposes here, constructivist scholars have also offered broader hypotheses and claims about the roles of ideas, identity, and discourse in European integration and EU governance (V. Schmidt 2008; Schimmelfennig 2012). With respect to the role of ideas, for example, Craig Parsons (2003) has offered an account of the EU's early history in which the supranational ideas of French elites played a fundamental role in the founding of the Union and the creation of its institutions. Similarly, Frank Schimmelfennig (2001) has argued that the decision by the EU's member states to pursue enlargement to the east after the fall of the Soviet Union was shaped in large part by the EU's own discourse (in a process he calls 'rhetorical entrapment'), and Berthold Rittberger (2005) has similarly argued that ideas and identities have fundamentally shaped the preferences of political actors with respect to the empowerment of the European Parliament. Outside political science, a wave of sociological scholarship has emerged over the past two decades, seeking to theorize and empirically map the emergence of new professional 'fields' linking actors at the European, national, and sub-national levels, in areas ranging from business and economic regulation to law to sports (see e.g. Fligstein 2009; Parsons 2012).

From these studies and others, Frank Schimmelfennig (2012: 42) argues in a recent review of the literature:

we find ample evidence that ideas and discourses shape integration preferences and the negotiated outcomes of European integration. By contrast, the effects of European integration on identities and public spheres appear to be weak. To be sure, the limited evidence for transformative effects of institutional integration does not contradict constructivist assumptions. It merely shows that national identities, discourses, and public spheres are entrenched and persistent, and that the conditions stipulated by constructivist approaches for their transformation may be lacking.

If both of these claims are correct—that is, if ideas and identities matter, and if national ideas and identities are deeply entrenched and resistant to change—then 'Adding identity to the picture shows that the prospects for European integration are more limited domestically' than other rationalist theories suggest (Schimmelfennig 2012: 43). Constructivism, in other words, is not necessarily an optimistic theory predicting ever-greater socialization and Europeanization of European elites and masses: the power of ideas, identity, and discourse may push in multiple directions, not all towards greater integration.

The return of realism

Realism is, according to a widespread conventional wisdom, the oldest and arguably dominant theory of international relations. In fact, realism is not a single theory but a family of theories, commonly traced back to 'classical' realist works by Thucydides, Machiavelli, and Hobbes, as well as twentieth-century realists like E. H. Carr, Hans Morgenthau, and George Kennan (Smith 1986). In the late-twentieth century, Kenneth Waltz sought to systematize realist thought, articulating a parsimonious and influential 'neo-realist' theory of international politics, premised on the primacy of states and on a structural analysis of an anarchic international system that required states to focus on security, power, and relative gains (Waltz 1979).

Generalizing about such a diverse theoretical tradition is therefore a fraught exercise, but all or most realist theories seem to share a few key features. First, they tend to agree that key actors in international politics are states, typically conceived of as unitary rational actors (represented as the realist 'statesman'), devising foreign policies that respond to the exigencies of international competition. Secondly, the anarchical nature of the international system means that each state must be concerned above all with its own security and must therefore seek what Morgenthau called 'the national interest defined in terms of power', both military and economic. Thirdly, and following from the first two, realist theories tend to be pessimistic about the prospects for international cooperation, international law, and international morality: even where states could in principle benefit from cooperation, realists argue that cooperation will be frustrated by fears of cheating and by concerns that other rival states will gain more, the so-called 'relative gains' problem. In this view, best exemplified by the 'offensive realism' of John Mearsheimer, international institutions hold out only the 'false promise' of mitigating the harsh effects of anarchy (Mearsheimer 1994–5).

By and large, realist theory has been peripheral to the study of the EU, with EU scholars taking the success of the Union as a rebuke to realists' pessimism, and with realists generally considering European integration as an aberration and an exception in an otherwise dog-eat-dog world. Waltz (1979: 70–1), for example, dedicated only a few pages in his landmark text to the then European Communities, the success of which he attributed to the fact that the US had emerged as the guarantor of west European security in the face of the Soviet threat, leaving the member states of the EC free to pursue integration without concerns about security threats.

In recent decades, however, realists have increasingly weighed in with revisionist accounts of the Union's past and its future. Mearsheimer (1990), for example, offered a realist analysis of the prospects for the EU *after* the cold war, predicting that the collapse of the Soviet Union and the departure of the US from the defence of continental Europe would lead to an increase in concerns about relative gains among EU member states, most notably with respect to a reunified Germany, and place a significant check upon the future course of European integration. This prediction, of course, was largely disconfirmed by subsequent experience, as the EU moved towards greater integration, not disintegration, with the adoption of the reforms in the Maastricht Treaty and its successors over the next two decades.

More recently, Sebastian Rosato (2011a, 2011b) has offered a revisionist, realist history of European integration, arguing that: (1) the early years of European integration in the 1950s were driven primarily by a desire by west European countries to balance against a Soviet threat; (2) the intervening decades have seen the EU undertake no fundamentally new initiatives, given the subsequent decline of the Soviet threat; and (3) the current crisis of the EU is driven in part by the loss of the Soviet threat as a glue holding the EU together against a common enemy, resulting in increasing tensions and rising rates of non-compliance with EU rules. Rosato's account has been disputed, however, by other EU scholars, both as a description of the historical founding of the Union, and as an empirical claim about the purported stagnation of the EU since the end of the cold war. Critics have argued, for example, that Rosato engages in a selective reading of the historical record, 'cherry-picking' sources to find support for a balance-of-power story about the origins of the EU, and ignoring evidence that most European statesmen of the era had other economic or ideological motivations (Moravcsik 2013: 777; Parsons 2013). Similarly, it seems clear that Rosato's claim that the EU has been largely stagnant since the end of the cold war ignores the substantial dynamism of institutional and policy reform during that period.

By contrast with Mearsheimer and Rosato, other 'defensive' realists predicted that post-cold war Europe might in fact be 'primed for peace', given that military technology in today's EU strongly favours defensive strategies (Van Evera 1990–1). Other defensive realists, like Joseph Grieco (1996), went further, seeking to account for success of the integration process in post-cold war Europe. In a widely cited article, Grieco posits a 'neorealist voice opportunities hypothesis'. When negotiating new international institutions, he argues, 'states—and especially relatively weak but still necessary partners—will seek to ensure that any cooperative arrangement they construct will include effective voice opportunities' (1996: 288). Grieco's thesis is arguably consistent with a very broad defensive realism, but its core insight—that states seek to increase their influence through institutions—is not distinctive to realist theory, as Legro and Moravcsik (1999) point out.

In recent years, realist theory has also been applied to explaining not only the course of European integration, but also and especially the Union's foreign policy. By contrast with constructivist ideas about a 'Normative Power Europe' championing a powerful moral agenda and acting as a global superpower (Manners 2002), sceptical realist analyses of EU foreign policy see the EU motivated by concrete material interests (Hyde-Price 2008), championing international law and institutions primarily in a rearguard effort to compensate for Europe's long-term demographic, economic, and military decline vis-à-vis the US and a rising Asia (Walt 1998–9; Kagan 2002; for a rebuttal, see Moravcsik 2009). Realism, therefore, remains as an influential theory of international politics and of the EU's role in the world, yet outside the sphere of EU foreign policy, realists have had little to say about the day-to-day realities of policy-making in today's EU.

Integration theory today

European integration theory is far more complex than it was in 1977 when the first edition of this volume was published. In place of the traditional neo-functionalist/intergovernmentalist debate, the past two decades have witnessed the emergence of a new dichotomy in integration theory, pitting rationalist scholars against constructivists. During the late 1990s, it appeared that this debate might well turn into a metatheoretical dialogue of the deaf, with rationalists dismissing constructivists as 'soft', and constructivists denouncing rationalists for their obsessive commitment to parsimony and formal models. The subsequent decade, however, witnessed the emergence of a more productive dialogue between the two approaches (Jupille, Caporaso, and Checkel 2003), and a steady stream of empirical studies allowing us to adjudicate between the competing claims of the two approaches. Furthermore, whereas the neo-functionalist/intergovernmentalist debate was limited almost exclusively to the study of European integration, the contemporary rationalist/constructivist debate in EU studies mirrors larger debates among those same schools in the broader field of IR theory. Indeed, not only are EU studies *relevant* to the wider study of international relations, they are in many ways the *vanguard* of IR theory, insofar as the EU serves as a laboratory for broader processes such as globalization, institutionalization, and socialization.

Despite these substantial indicators of progress, the literature on European integration has not produced any consensus on the likely future direction of the integration process. At the risk of overgeneralizing, more optimistic theorists tend to be drawn from the ranks of neo-functionalists and constructivists, who point to the potential for further integration, the former through functional and political spill-overs, and the latter through gradual Europeanization of both elite and mass preferences and identities. In this view, even crises, such as the ongoing sovereign debt crisis in the euro area, can serve as the source of functional pressure for deeper integration through initiatives like the creation of a European Stability Mechanism (ESM) and a European banking union (see Chapters 5 and 7). Intergovernmentalist and especially realist critics, on the other hand, tend to be sceptical regarding claims of both spill-over and socialization, pointing to the strains of EU enlargement, the difficulties of ratifying both the Constitutional Treaty and the subsequent Treaty of Lisbon, and the rise of 'Euroscepticism' in EU public opinion. For these scholars, the EU may well represent an 'equilibrium polity', one in which functional pressures for further integration are essentially spent, and in which the current level of institutional and policy integration is unlikely to change substantially for the foreseeable future (Moravcsik 2001: 163). At the extreme, some pessimistic scholars see the EU as a potentially self-undermining institution, whose past missteps have sown the seeds of public opposition and even the potential exit of long-time members such as Greece or the UK (Rosato 2011b). Hence, while the literature on European integration has advanced substantially over the past two decades, a consensus on the causes and the future of the integration process remains as elusive as ever.

The EU as a political system

Thus far we have examined the EU literature as one concerned overwhelmingly with the causes and the direction of European integration as a process, with its theoretical inspiration primarily from the study of IR. However, many scholars have approached the EU very differently, as a polity or political system akin to other *domestic* political systems. This tendency was initially most pronounced in the work of federalist writers, who explicitly compared the EU to federal and confederal systems in Germany, Switzerland, and the US (Pinder 1968; Capelletti, Seccombe, and Weiler 1986; Scharpf 1988; Sbragia 1992), as well as in the work of systems theorists like Lindberg and Scheingold (1970), who saw the EU as a political system characterized by political demands (inputs), governmental actors, and public policies (outputs). At the same time, an increasing number of EU scholars, not least the editors and authors of the first (1977) edition of *Policy-Making in the European Union*, deliberately sought to bracket the uncertain question of the EU's final destination, focusing instead on a better understanding of the EU policy process in all its complexity and diversity.

By the mid-1990s, the dominance of IR and of integration theory came under serious challenge, with a growing number of scholars seeking explicitly to understand the EU as a political system using the theoretical tools developed in the study of domestic polities. This perspective was championed most effectively by Simon Hix (1994, 1999, 2005), who issued a call to arms to comparativists. Previous studies of the EU, Hix argued, had neglected the *politics* of the Union, as well as its characteristics as a *political system*. The EU, he contended, was clearly less than a Weberian state, lacking in particular a monopoly on the legitimate use of force; yet he echoed Lindberg and Scheingold by suggesting that the EU could be theorized as a political system, with a dense web of legislative, executive, and judicial institutions that adopted binding public policies and hence influenced the 'authoritative allocation of values' in European society. Furthermore, Hix suggested that EU politics takes place in a two-dimensional space, with integration vs. nationalism representing one dimension, alongside a second dimension spanning the traditional left–right divide over the extent and nature of government intervention in the economy. At least in the European Parliament (EP), he suggested, these left–right issues increasingly dominated EU policy-making. Hence the EU could, and should, be studied using 'the tools, methods and cross-systemic theories from the general study of government, politics, and policy-making. In this way, teaching and research on the EU can be part of the political science mainstream' (Hix 1999: 2).

Hix's call to arms among comparativists has not escaped criticism, with a number of authors arguing that the aim of EU scholars should not be to reject IR in favour of comparative politics, but rather to understand the interactions between domestic and international politics (Hurrell and Menon 1996). Nevertheless, comparative political scientists *have* moved increasingly into EU studies, in part because the EU has intruded increasingly into what had previously been seen as exclusively 'domestic' arenas, and in part because an increasing number of scholars accepted Hix's claim that the EU could be theorized as a 'political system' (Jupille 2005).

Although such comparative work on the EU is extraordinarily diverse, much of it can fairly be characterized as comparative, rational-choice, and positivist in nature. First, much of the work on EU politics proceeds from the assumption that the EU is not a *sui generis* system of governance, but is a variant on existing political systems. It can therefore be studied and understood with the aid of 'off-the-shelf' models of policy-making in other (primarily national) contexts. Many of these theories have drawn from American politics, since the EU arguably resembles the US in possessing both a vertical and a horizontal separation of powers.

Secondly, most of the work reviewed in this section is either implicitly or explicitly rationalist, taking the assumption that actors (be they states, individuals, or supranational organizations) have fixed, exogenously determined preferences, and act systematically to maximize their utility within the constraints of the EU's institutional system. A growing subset draws not only on the language of rational choice (i.e. 'soft' rational choice), but also elaborates formal and game-theoretic models of EU decision-making.

Thirdly and finally, much of the work discussed here can be characterized as implicitly or explicitly 'positivist', adopting and adapting the standards of the natural sciences, seeking to test theory-driven hypotheses systematically, and often (though by no means always) using quantitative as well as qualitative methods (see e.g. Gabel, Hix, and Schneider 2002 and Kreppel 2012 on EU studies as 'normal science'). A complete survey of this literature would take us beyond the remit of this chapter, although many elements of it are addressed by Alasdair Young in Chapter 3. In this section, I focus narrowly on two dimensions that are most relevant to the study of policy-making, namely the vertical or 'federal' division of powers between the EU and member-state levels, and the horizontal separation of powers among the legislative, executive, and judicial branches of the Union.

The vertical separation of powers: the EU as a federal system

The EU did not begin life as a federal union, nor, in the view of most analysts, does it constitute a fully developed federation today. In political terms, the very term 'federal' was contentious and referred to obliquely as 'the f-word'; and in analytical terms some scholars question whether the EU can or should be accurately described as a federal state:

The contemporary EU is far narrower and weaker a federation than any extant national federation—so weak, indeed, that we might question whether it is a federation at all. . . . The EU was designed as, and remains primarily, a limited international institution to coordinate national regulation of trade in goods and services, and the resulting flows of economic factors. Its substantive scope and institutional prerogatives are limited accordingly. The EU constitutional order is not only barely a federal state; it is barely recognizable as a state at all.
(Moravcsik 2001: 163–4)

Nevertheless, federalism was a powerful *normative* ideal motivating many of the founders of the European movement and much of the early scholarship on the EU. Recognizing the strong resistance of national governments to directly federal proposals, Jean Monnet and his colleagues opted instead for a more sectoral and incremental approach, more accurately captured in neo-functionalist theory than in traditional federalist approaches. By the 1980s, however, the EC had developed features with analytical similarities to those of existing federations. Theories of federalism therefore took on greater importance, not just as a normative ideal motivating European integration, but as a positive theoretical framework, capable of explaining and predicting the workings of the EU as a political system.

The term federalism has been the subject of numerous overlapping definitions, but most rely on the three elements emphasized by R. Daniel Kelemen (2003: 185), who defines federalism as 'an institutional arrangement in which: (a) public authority is divided between state governments and a central government; (b) each level of government has some issues on which it makes final decisions; and (c) a federal high court adjudicates disputes concerning federalism'. In most federal systems, moreover, the structure of representation is twofold, with popular or functional interests represented directly through a directly elected lower house, while territorial units are typically represented in an upper house, whose members may be either directly elected (as in the US Senate) or appointed by state governments (as in the German

Bundesrat). In both of these senses, the EU *already* constitutes a federal system, with a constitutionally guaranteed separation of powers between the EU and member-state levels, and a dual system of representation through the EP and the Council of Ministers. Hence, the literature on comparative federalism provides a useful toolkit for thinking about policy-making in the EU.

Students of comparative federalism have, however, pointed to an exceptional aspect of the EU, namely the absence or at least the weakness of 'fiscal federalism', and the dominance of 'regulatory federalism' (Börzel and Hosli 2003: 180–1). Most federal systems engage in substantial fiscal transfers across state boundaries, but the EU budget has been capped at a relatively small 1.27 per cent of EU gross domestic product (GDP), predominantly devoted to agricultural and cohesion spending (see Chapters 8, 9, and 10). The EU is therefore unable to engage in substantial redistribution or macroeconomic stabilization through fiscal policy (see Chapter 7), and only indirectly influences the structure of European welfare states, which remain predominantly national (see Chapter 11). In contrast, the Union has engaged primarily in regulatory activity (see Chapters 5, 6, and 10–15), earning it the moniker of a 'regulatory state' (Majone 1996). The regulatory output of the Union, in Majone's view, has been driven by both demand and supply factors. On the demand side, the imperative of creating a single internal market has put pressure on EU member states to adopt common or harmonized EU-wide regulations, most notably on products, in order to ensure the free movement of goods, services, labour, and capital throughout the Union. On the supply side, an entrepreneurial European Commission has seen regulation as a viable way to enhance its own policy competence despite the financial limits imposed by the EU's strict budgetary ceiling.

In empirical terms, the Union has engaged in a vast EU-wide project of economic regulation, driven largely by the creation and maintenance of the internal market, and these EU regulations have been adopted according to a 'regulatory mode' of governance (see Chapter 4). As in other federal systems, the adoption of far-reaching central regulations has taken the Union into areas of regulation not originally envisaged by the framers of the treaties, generating significant controversy and increasing demands since the 1990s for adherence to the principle of 'subsidiarity'—the notion that the EU should govern as close as possible to the citizen and therefore that it should engage in regulation only where necessary to ensure the completion of the internal market and/or other fundamental aims of the treaties. Even in the regulatory field, therefore, the vertical separation of powers is not fixed but fluid, and the result resembles not so much a layer cake as a marble cake, in which EU and member-state authorities are concurrent, intermixed, and constantly in flux.

The horizontal separation of powers

Unlike the parliamentary states of western Europe, but like the US, the EU has a horizontal separation of powers in which three distinct branches of government take the leading role in the legislative, executive, and judicial functions, respectively.

This does not mean that any one institution enjoys sole control of any of these three functions; indeed, as Amie Kreppel (2002: 5) points out, the Madisonian conception of the separation of powers 'requires to a certain extent a co-mingling of powers in all three arenas (executive, legislative, and judicial)'. In the case of the EU, for example, the legislative function is today shared by the Council of the European Union and the EP, with an agenda-setting role for the Commission; the executive function is shared by the Commission, the member states, and (in some areas) independent regulatory agencies; and the judicial function is shared by the CJEU, the General Court, and a wide array of national courts bound directly to the CJEU through the preliminary reference procedure (see Chapter 4).

Reflecting this separation of powers, comparative-politics scholars have devoted extraordinary attention to theorizing, predicting, and explaining legislative, executive, and judicial behaviour using off-the-shelf theories of domestic politics. Many of these theories are reviewed in Chapter 3, where Alasdair Young provides comparative analysis of the EU 'policy cycle', from agenda-setting through to implementation. We focus here on some of the applications of comparative analysis to the legislative, executive, and judicial policies of the EU, demonstrating briefly the promise and limits of such applications.

Legislative politics: towards bicameralism

A first strand of the literature, most relevant to EU policy-making, is the large and growing literature on the EU legislative process. Drawing heavily on theories of legislative behaviour (i.e. the ways in which legislators vote) and legislative organization (the ways in which legislatures organize their business), scholars have sought to understand the legislative process in the EU, focusing on three major questions: legislative politics within the EP; voting power and voting patterns in the Council of the EU; and the respective powers of these two bodies in the EU legislative process (McElroy 2007).

The EP has been the subject of extensive theoretical modelling and empirical study over the past two decades, with a growing number of scholars studying the legislative organization of the EP and the voting behaviour of its members (MEPs). Early studies of the EP emphasized the striking fact that, in spite of the multinational nature of the Parliament, the best predictor of MEP voting behaviour is not nationality but an MEP's 'party group', with the various party groups demonstrating extraordinarily high measures of cohesion in roll-call votes. These MEPs, moreover, were shown to contest elections and cast their votes in a two-dimensional 'issue space', including not only the familiar nationalism/supranationalism dimension but also and especially the more traditional, 'domestic' dimension of left–right contestation. Perhaps most fundamentally, these scholars have shown that the EP can increasingly be studied as a 'normal parliament' whose members vote predictably and cohesively within a political space dominated by the familiar contestation between parties of the left and right (Tsebelis and Garrett 2000; Kreppel 2001; Hix, Noury, and Roland 2007; Hix and Hoyland 2013).

By contrast with this rich EP literature, the rational-choice literature on the Council until recently focused on the relatively narrow question of member-state voting power under different decision rules. In recent years, however, the study of the Council has undergone a renaissance, driven in part by the increasing public availability of Council voting records and data-sets such as the Decision-Making in the European Union (DEU) project (R. Thomson *et al.* 2006; R. Thomson 2011). This thriving literature has produced new theoretical conjectures, and new qualitative and quantitative empirical tests, on issues such as the relative power of EU member states in the Council; the coalition patterns among member states within the Council (which appear to break down largely on geographical or north–south lines, with a secondary east–west cleavage since the 2004 enlargement); the Council's tradition of consensus decision-making, rather than minimum-winning coalitions; and the as yet uneven evidence for the socialization of national officials in the Council and its subsidiary committees and working groups (see Mattila 2004; Hayes-Renshaw and Wallace 2006; Naurin and Wallace 2008; R. Thomson 2011).

Thirdly and finally, a large and ever-growing literature has attempted to model in rational-choice terms, and to study empirically, the inter-institutional relations among the Commission (as agenda-setter) and the Council and EP, under different legislative procedures. Over the course of the 1980s and the 1990s, the legislative powers of the EP have grown sequentially, from the relatively modest and non-binding 'consultation procedure' through the creation of the 'cooperation' and 'assent' procedures in the 1980s, and the creation and reform of a 'co-decision procedure' in the 1990s. This expansion of EP legislative power, and the complex nature of the new legislative procedures, has fostered the development of a burgeoning literature and led to several vigorous debates among rational-choice scholars about the nature and extent of the EP's and the Council's respective influence across the various procedures. Such studies have shown that the institutional power and impact of the EP on legislative outcomes has grown substantially over time with the move from consultation to cooperation to the co-decision procedure, which under the Treaty of Lisbon is now referred to as the 'ordinary legislative procedure' and governs the large majority of EU legislation (see e.g. Tsebelis *et al.* 2001; Hix, Noury, and Roland 2007; McElroy 2007; Hix and Hoyland 2013). Even today, the powers of the EP vary by issue and by the treaty basis for any particular policy, with the EP still enjoying fewer powers in areas such as common foreign and security policy and justice and home affairs. Nevertheless, EU policy-making in a growing number of areas now vindicates the claim that 'the Council and the Parliament are currently co-equal legislators and the EU's legislative regime is truly bicameral' (Tsebelis and Garrett 2000: 24).

Notwithstanding the insights into the EU legislative process generated by formal models based on the EU's formal decision-making rules, it is worth noting that a growing body of scholarship has cast doubt on the utility of formal models, which rest on the assumption that actors behave according to formal rules. Instead, many studies now suggest that Council bargaining is governed less by formal treaty rules, and more by informal norms and practices, than early models had predicted (Farrell and Héritier 2003; Christiansen and Piattoni 2004; R. Thomson *et al.* 2006). Similarly, legislative politics scholars have shown that the ordinary legislative procedure, although conducted 'in the shadow' of formal rules allowing for three full readings by each house, operates increasingly through informal procedures in which representatives of the Council and EP resolve their differences in a single reading behind closed doors in informal 'trilogues', thereby increasing the speed and efficiency but reducing the transparency of the legislative process (Reh *et al.* 2013). These developments have led Mareike Kleine (2013, 2014) to argue that previous scholarship has dramatically underemphasized the importance of 'informal governance' in the EU. Informal practices, she argues, do not simply operate in the absence of formal procedures, or to supplement formal procedures; rather, she suggests, the EU's informal practices can *persistently and systematically depart* from formal rules, reflecting implicit political agreements among policy-makers. If this is correct, then scholars seeking to understand EU policy-making will need to focus less on the formal rules set down in the treaties, and more on the informal norms and practices that actually govern the conduct of policy-makers.

Executive politics: delegation and discretion

The study of EU executive politics, and especially the role of the European Commission, is a perennial issue in European integration theory, with neo-functionalists and intergovernmentalists debating the causal role of the executive Commission for decades. Nevertheless, rational-choice and principal–agent analysis have emerged over the past two decades as the dominant approach to the study of the Commission and other executive actors such as the European Central Bank (ECB) and the growing body of EU agencies (Tallberg 2007).

These studies generally address two specific sets of questions. First, they ask why and under what conditions a group of (member-state) *principals* might delegate powers to (supranational) *agents*, such as the Commission, the ECB, and the CJEU. Simplifying considerably, such *transaction-cost* accounts of delegation argue that member-state principals, as rational actors, delegate powers to supranational organizations primarily to lower the transaction costs of policy-making, in particular by allowing member governments to commit themselves credibly to international agreements and to benefit from the policy-relevant expertise provided by supranational actors. Despite differences in emphasis, the empirical work of these scholars has collectively demonstrated that EU member governments do indeed delegate powers to the Commission, the ECB, and the CJEU largely to reduce the transaction costs of policy-making, in particular through the monitoring of member-state compliance, the filling-in of framework treaties ('incomplete contracts'), and the speedy and efficient adoption of implementing regulations that would otherwise have to be adopted in a time-consuming legislative process by the member governments themselves (Pollack 1997, 2003; Moravcsik 1998; Majone 2000a; Franchino 2004, 2007).

In addition to the question of delegation, rational-choice institutionalists have devoted greater attention to a second question posed by principal–agent models: what if an agent—such as the Commission, the ECB, or the CJEU—behaves in ways that diverge from the preferences of the principals? The answer to this question lies primarily in the administrative procedures that the principals may establish to define *ex ante* the scope of agency activities, as well as the oversight procedures that allow for *ex post* oversight and sanctioning of errant agents. Applied to the EU, principal–agent analysis therefore leads to the hypothesis that agency autonomy is likely to vary across issue areas and over time, as a function of the preferences of the member states, the distribution of information between principals and agents, and the decision rules governing the application of sanctions or the adoption of new legislation. By and large, empirical studies of executive politics in the EU have supported these hypotheses, pointing in particular to the significance of decision rules as a crucial determinant of executive autonomy (Pollack 2003; Tallberg 2000; Tsebelis and Garrett 2001; Franchino 2007).

Finally, students of executive politics in the EU have turned increasingly to the study of relatively new phenomena, notably the ECB and a diverse array of regulatory agencies at the EU level. The ECB, now the collective central bank of the euro area, is without doubt the most spectacular example of supranational delegation in the history of the EU. Indeed, both rational-choice scholars and EU practitioners have referred to the ECB as the most independent central bank in the world, due to the long and non-renewable terms of its members and the insulation of the Bank and its mandate, which can be altered only by a unanimous agreement of the member states (see Chapter 7). At the same time, the EU's member states have created a growing number of regulatory agencies, such as the European Medicines Agency (EMA) and the European Food Safety Authority (EFSA), among more than a dozen others, each with their own rules and their own powers and responsibilities in the EU policy process, raising important questions about the independence and accountability of these agencies as well (Rittberger and Wonka 2011*a*; Busuioc 2012).

Judicial politics and the CJEU

Rational-choice institutionalists have also engaged in increasingly sophisticated research into the nature of EU judicial politics and the role of the CJEU in the integration process. Geoffrey Garrett (1992) first drew on principal–agent analysis to argue that the court, as an agent of the EU's member governments, was bound to follow the wishes of the most powerful member states. These member states, Garrett claimed, had established the CJEU as a means to solve problems of incomplete contracting and monitoring compliance with EU obligations, and they rationally accepted CJEU jurisprudence, even when rulings went against them, because of their longer term interest in the enforcement of EU law. In such a setting, Garrett and Weingast (1993: 189) argued, the CJEU might identify 'constructed focal points' among multiple equilibrium outcomes, but the court was unlikely to rule against the preferences of powerful EU member states, as Burley and Mattli (1993) had suggested in a famous article drawing on neo-functionalist theory.

Other scholars have argued forcefully that Garrett's model overestimated the control mechanisms available to powerful member states and the ease of sanctioning an activist court, which has been far more autonomous than Garrett suggests. Such accounts suggest that the court has been able to pursue the process of legal integration far beyond the collective preferences of the member governments, in part due to the high costs to member states in overruling or failing to comply with CJEU decisions, and in part because the CJEU enjoys powerful allies in the form of individual litigants and national courts which refer hundreds of cases per year to the CJEU via the 'preliminary reference' procedure of Article 234 TEC (ex Art. 177 EEC) (Weiler 1994; Mattli and Slaughter 1995, 1998; Stone Sweet and Caporaso 1998; Stone Sweet and Brunell 1998a, 1998b; Alter 2001). According to Stone Sweet and Caporaso (1998: 129), 'the move to supremacy and direct effect must be understood as audacious acts of agency' by the court.

More recently, the literature on the CJEU and legal integration has increasingly moved from the traditional question of the CJEU's relationship with national governments, towards the study of the CJEU's other interlocutors, including most notably the national courts that bring the majority of cases before the CJEU, and the individual litigants who use EU law to achieve their aims within national legal systems (Conant 2007b). Such studies have problematized and sought to explain the complex and ambivalent relationship between the CJEU and national courts, as well as the varying litigation strategies of 'one-shot' litigants and 'repeat players' before the courts (Mattli and Slaughter 1998; Alter 2001; Conant 2002; Kelemen 2011). These and other studies have demonstrated the complexities of EU legal integration, the interrelationships among supranational, national, and sub-national political and legal actors, and the limits of EU law in national legal contexts (Stone Sweet 2010).

Towards normal science?

A growing number of EU scholars today approach the study of Union policy-making employing the theoretical tools of comparative politics, together with a positivist commitment to systematic empirical testing. The resulting literature, although sometimes highly technical and inaccessible to the general reader, has substantially advanced our understanding of EU policy-making, of the respective roles and influence of the Commission, Council, Parliament, and Court, and increasingly of the relationship between EU institutions and their national and sub-national interlocutors. Furthermore, with the creation and dissemination of a range of new databases, the scope for systematic testing and falsification of theories is certain to increase in the years to come, making the EU an increasingly promising arena for the practice of 'normal science'.

The governance approach: the EU as a polity

The reader might easily conclude from the chapter so far that the story of theorizing about the EU is a linear progression from IR theories to comparative politics theories dominating EU studies. Such a story, however, would be misleading. IR scholars continue to theorize about and carry out empirical research about the process of European integration, the workings of EU institutions, and the EU's role in the global order (see Chapter 18), alongside the comparativists. Just as importantly, these approaches now coexist with a third approach, typically labelled the 'governance approach', which draws on both IR and comparative politics and considers the EU as neither a traditional international organization *nor* as a domestic 'political system', but rather as a new and emerging system of 'governance without government'.

The governance approach is not a single theory of the EU or of European integration, but rather a cluster of related theories emphasizing common themes (Jachtenfuchs 2001, 2007; Jachtenfuchs and Kohler-Koch 2004). Hix (1998) has usefully contrasted the governance school to its rationalist/comparativist/positivist alternative, arguing that the governance approach constitutes a distinctive research agenda across four dimensions.

First, the governance approach theorizes EU governance as non-hierarchical, mobilizing networks of private as well as public actors, who engage in deliberation and problem-solving efforts guided as much by informal as by formal institutions. Secondly, the practitioners of the governance approach are suspicious of 'off-the-shelf' models, advocating the need for a new vocabulary to capture the distinctive features of EU governance (Schmitter 1996; Eriksen and Fossum 2000: 2; Bache and Flinders 2004: 2). Thirdly, students of EU governance often (although not always) emphasize the capacity of the EU to foster 'deliberation' and 'persuasion'—a model of policy-making in which actors are open to changing their beliefs and their preferences, and in which good arguments can matter as much as, or more than, bargaining power (Risse 2000). Fourthly, governance theorists frequently express a normative concern with the 'democratic deficit' in the EU, with many emphasizing the potential of the EU as a 'deliberative democracy' (Joerges 2001).

The literature on 'governance' thus defined has exploded in recent years (Jachtenfuchs 1995; Scharpf 1999; Jachtenfuchs 2001; Hooghe and Marks 2001; Jachtenfuchs and Kohler-Koch 2004; Bache and Flinders 2004; Jachtenfuchs 2007; Pagoulatos and Tsoukalis 2012). I focus here on five key issues: (1) the concept of 'governance'; (2) early applications to the EU, in the literatures on 'multi-level governance' and policy networks; (3) the growing literature on the 'Europeanization' of both existing member states and new and candidate members; (4) a substantial literature on the governance capacity of member states and of EU institutions, and the problems of legitimacy faced by the latter; and (5) a new and novel set of claims about the EU as a process of 'deliberative supranationalism' capable of resolving these normative dilemmas.

Governing without government

In Hix's (1998) critique, the governance approach is presented as a *sui generis* approach, treating the EU as fundamentally different from other polities and therefore requiring new—as opposed to off-the-shelf—theoretical approaches. Nonetheless, the EU governance literature draws heavily on the concept(s) of governance worked out by students of both comparative politics *and* IR.

Within the field of comparative politics, the term governance has appeared with increasing frequency, but with different definitions and different emphases (Rhodes 1996). At their most far-reaching, governance theorists put forward the radical claim that contemporary governments lack the knowledge and information required to solve complex economic and social problems, and that governance should therefore be conceived more broadly as the negotiated interactions of public and private actors in a given policy arena. In this view, modern society is 'radically decentred', and government features as only one actor among many in the larger process of socio-economic governance (Kooiman 1993). Hence, in Rhodes's (1996: 660) terms, governance—as distinct from government—takes place through organized networks of public and private actors which 'steer' public policy towards common ends.

IR scholars have also increasingly embraced the notion of 'governance without government', with Rosenau (1992: 4) and others suggesting that international affairs may be 'governed' by various different types of networks, including 'transgovernmental' networks of lower level government or judicial actors interacting across borders with their foreign counterparts (Slaughter 2004), and 'transnational' networks of private actors forming a sort of 'global civil society' (Wapner 1996). This approach to governance, emphasizing networks of public and private actors 'steering' EU public policy, has gained widespread acceptance in EU studies, most notably in the study of 'multi-level governance' and policy networks.

Multi-level governance and EU policy networks

By most accounts (Jachtenfuchs 2001; Bache and Flinders 2004: 3), the governance approach to the EU can be traced, at least in part, to Gary Marks's (1992, 1993) work on the making and implementation of the EU's structural funds. Writing in opposition to intergovernmentalists, Marks argued that the structural funds of the 1980s and 1990s provided evidence for a very different image of the EU, one in which central governments were losing control both to the Commission (which played a key part in designing and implementing the funds), and to local and regional governments inside each member state (which were granted a 'partnership' role in planning and implementation). In making this argument, Bache and Flinders (2004: 3) point out, Marks and his colleagues placed a dual emphasis, first on the 'multi-level' interdependence of territorial governments at the European, national, and sub-national level, and secondly on the development of new public–private policy networks transcending all three levels.

Later studies of the EU structural funds questioned Marks's far-reaching empirical claims, noting in particular that EU member governments played central roles in the successive reforms of the funds, and that these member states remained effective 'gatekeepers', containing the inroads of both the Commission and sub-national governments into the traditional preserve of state sovereignty (Pollack 1995; Bache 1998; see also Chapter 10). Following these challenges, proponents of the multi-level governance approach have conceded the more varied, nuanced influence of EU policies on territorial governance, documenting how national governments have maintained gatekeeping roles in some countries, such as the UK and Greece, while other countries have witnessed 'an immense shift of authority' from national governments to the European arena and to sub-national, regional governments in a substantial number of states such as France, Italy, Spain, and Belgium (Hooghe 1996a; Hooghe and Marks 2001; Bache and Flinders 2004; see also Chapter 10).

In a related development, many EU scholars have focused on the horizontal or network aspects of European integration, drawing on network theory to describe and explain the workings of transnational and transgovernmental networks that can vary from the relatively closed 'policy communities' of public and private actors in areas such as research and technological development to the more open and porous 'issue networks' prevailing in areas such as environmental regulation (Peterson and Bomberg 1999; Peterson 2009). This network form of governance, moreover, has been accentuated further over the past decade by the creation of formal and informal networks of national regulators, in areas such as financial regulation and competition policy (see Chapter 6; for a general discussion of policy networks in the EU, see Chapter 3).

More recently, Hooghe and Marks (2008) have sought to build on the multi-level governance approach, as well as on constructivist insights, proposing what they call a 'post-functionalist' theory of European integration. By contrast with existing theories, which had focused on insulated elites such as national governments and interest groups pursuing their goals through European integration in the face of a 'permissive consensus' in mass public opinion, the authors argued that such an image, if it was ever valid, had ceased to be so since the early 1990s, as European integration became more salient and Euroscepticism more widespread in public opinion. Henceforth, Hooghe and Marks argued, national and European elites pursuing further integration would need to do so in the face of what they called a 'constraining dissensus'. This phenomenon, they argued, explained the substantial difficulties that states encountered in securing the adoption of the Maastricht, Nice, and Lisbon treaties, as well as the demise of the Constitutional Treaty, signed in 2003 but abandoned following two failed referenda in France and the Netherlands. Henceforth, they argued, integration theories would have be more attentive to public opinion about the EU, and in particular to the role of *identity*, and not just economic interests, in shaping the future of the Union.

Europeanization

Another, increasingly significant offshoot from the multi-level governance tradition examines the phenomenon of 'Europeanization', the process whereby EU institutions and policies influence national institutions and policies within the various member states. In general terms, such studies date to the 1970s, when a small number of scholars examined how EU membership had influenced national political institutions and public policies (see e.g. H. Wallace 1973). Since then, the study of Europeanization has become a cottage industry, with a growing number of studies seeking to explain both the process of Europeanization and the significant variation in outcomes observed across both member states and issue areas. In one particularly influential formulation, Cowles, Caporaso, and Risse (2001) suggested that the extent of Europeanization should be the dual product of: (1) adaptational pressures resulting from the varying 'goodness of fit' between EU and national institutions and policies; and (2) domestic intervening variables, including the number of veto points and the organizational and political cultures embedded in existing national institutions. These theories, in turn, have informed a growing literature on the implementation of EU policies 'on the ground' in the various member states, which remains a disputed and understudied topic (see e.g. Falkner *et al.* 2005; Hartlapp and Falkner 2008; and Chapter 3).

Subsequently, scholars have sketched alternative rationalist and constructivist mechanisms whereby the EU might influence national politics—in the first instance by constraining national choices, in the second case by instilling new norms and reshaping national identities and preferences (Kelley 2004; Börzel and Risse 2007). Extending the study of Europeanization outwards from the existing members, Frank Schimmelfennig and Ulrich Sedelmeier (2002, 2005a) led teams of researchers who tested alternative rationalist and constructivist hypotheses about the effect of EU membership on candidate and new member states. They found some evidence of EU-led policy learning and socialization, as predicted by constructivist models, but the content and the timing of policy reforms in the new member states suggested that the greatest impact of the EU has resulted from explicit EU conditionality, a classic rationalist mechanism.

From a policy perspective, the findings of these studies were both encouraging and alarming. On the one hand, they suggested that the EU could exert remarkable leverage over candidate countries, nudging them in the direction of free markets, democracy, and human rights. On the other hand, however, these findings raised the disturbing prospect that, once the candidate countries had achieved their goal of EU membership, the Union would lose much of its leverage over those countries, which might be expected to relapse, failing to comply with either the EU's economic rules or with its political ideals of democracy and the rule of law (Epstein and Sedelmeier 2008: 796). Despite these concerns, studies of Europeanization in the early years after the 2004 and 2007 enlargements returned optimistic results, with scholars generally finding that new member states had avoided backsliding in terms of the EU's core economic policies (Sedelmeier 2008; Falkner and Treib 2008). With respect to political democracy and human rights, students of the region were similarly optimistic that the new member states have generally not fallen into recidivism after enlargement (Levitz and Pop-Eleches 2010: 459–60; see also Sasse 2008; Pridham 2008; Vachudova 2008).

In recent years, however, concerns about democracy and human rights in the new member states have increased, particularly in the light of the dramatic and controversial constitutional reforms pushed through by the governing Fidesz party of Prime Minister Victor Orbán in Hungary and similar events in Romania. Scholarly studies of these events suggest at best tempered optimism, pointing to the limits of EU leverage over member states, particularly when the reforms in question are gradual and calculated to fall below the threshold at which EU member states might take the extreme sanction of suspending a member state's voting rights under Article 7 TEU (Bánkuti, Halmai, and Scheppele 2012; Epstein and Jacoby 2014b; Sedelmeier 2014).[2] Concern about democracy and human rights in the new member states is therefore likely to remain high on the list of political and scholarly concerns in the EU in the years to come.

A democratic deficit?

The issue of democracy, in turn, points to another major branch of the governance approach, which has assessed and often criticized the democratic legitimacy of the EU itself. Much of this work analyses and undertakes a normative critique of an EU that purportedly undermines the autonomy and domestic governance capacity of the member states through 'negative integration', while failing to establish a governance capacity through 'positive integration' that is both substantial and democratically legitimate at the supranational EU level (Streeck 1998; Scharpf 1999). This critique is typically made in two stages.

First, it is argued, EU internal market regulations and CJEU decisions have increasingly eroded, invalidated, or replaced national social regulations, thereby thwarting the social aims and the democratically expressed preferences of national electorates and their legislatures. Moreover, even where EU legislation and CJEU jurisprudence leave national laws, taxation systems, and welfare programmes untouched, it is often argued that the free movement provisions of the Union may set in train a process of regulatory competition in which national governments face pressures to adjust national regulations in an effort to make them more attractive to mobile capital. This may lead to a 'race to the bottom', in which national governments compete to lower the tax burden and the regulatory burdens on businesses threatening to move to other jurisdictions. In the words of Claus Offe (2000), the *acquis communautaire* (the body of rules and legislation mandated by the EU) now threatens the *acquis nationale* of strong liberal democracy and well-developed welfare states. Since 2010, moreover, the issue of EU constraints on democratically adopted national policies has been sharpened and further politicized by the strict fiscal conditionality and austerity imposed on south European member states borrowing from the Union under the European Financial Stability Facility (EFSF) and its successor, the ESM (see Chapter 7). The extent and character of this purported race to the bottom remain a matter of dispute, with even critics of the EU conceding that the impacts of the EU on domestic policies vary systematically across issue areas (Scharpf 1999). But either way, the prospect of the undermining of national regulations and welfare states poses important analytic as well as normative challenges (see Chapter 11).

This challenge to national governance raises a second question: whether the race to the bottom might be averted, and democracy regained, at the EU level. On this score, many contributors to the debate are pessimistic, pointing to: the distant and opaque nature of EU decision-making; the strong role of indirectly elected officials in the Council and unelected officials in the Commission; the weakness of the EP and the second-order nature of its elections; and the bias in the treaties in favour of market liberalization over social regulation (Williams 1991; Scharpf 1999; Greven 2000). Furthermore, even if these institutional flaws in the EU treaties were to be addressed, for example through the successive empowerment of the EP, Joseph Weiler (1995) has suggested that Europe lacks a *demos*, a group of people united by a sense of community or 'we-feeling' that could provide the constituent basis for an EU-level democracy. Other scholars, writing from the perspectives of critical theory (Manners 2007) and feminist theory (Prügl 2007), raise additional challenges to the EU's legitimacy, questioning the locus of public power in the Union, the inclusion of the concerns of peoples of various classes, genders, and ethnicities, and negative as well as the positive impacts of the EU's public policies. For all these reasons, governance theorists argue, the EU faces a 'democratic deficit' and a profound crisis of legitimacy.

Responding to these concerns, a larger literature has arisen, given over to proposals for increasing the democratic accountability and the governance capacity of the Union. Whereas in the past EU institutions had relied primarily on 'output legitimacy' (i.e. the efficiency or popularity of EU policy outputs), today there are increased calls for reforms that would increase the 'input legitimacy' (i.e. the democratic accountability of EU institutions to the electorate). We can identify three distinct reform tracks in the literature: constitutionalization, parliamentarization, and deliberation. The first and most modest of these proposals is 'constitutionalization', the creation of overarching rules and procedural controls that would ensure minimum levels of transparency and public participation in EU policy-making. Andrew Moravcsik (2002), for example, has suggested that the EU treaties contain sufficient checks and balances to address concerns about the EU's democratic legitimacy within the circumscribed limits of its powers.

Critics of the EU's democratic legitimacy, however, argue that such procedural safeguards are insufficient to produce an EU that is open and responsive to its citizens. In this context, the second proposed reform track, parliamentarization, would involve *inter alia* the strengthening of the EP's legislative and budgetary powers; a strengthening of EU party groups; the increased salience of EU (rather than national) issues in European elections; and the subordination of the Commission to the Parliament as in the national parliamentary systems of Europe (Hix 2008b). Others, however, have cast doubt on the parliamentary model, suggesting that such an approach could exacerbate, rather than ameliorate, the EU's crisis of legitimacy by subjecting national communities, or *demoi*, to a long-term minority position in an EU of twenty-eight or more members (Weiler 1995), and by threatening the independence and neutrality of the European Commission (Majone 2000*b*).

For these reasons, an increasing number of authors have suggested a third model for the EU, namely a 'deliberative democracy' in which citizens, or at least their representatives, would collectively deliberate in search of the best solution to common problems.

Argument, persuasion, and the 'deliberative turn'

This emphasis on deliberation as a characteristic feature of EU policy-making derives largely from the work of Jürgen Habermas (1985, 1998), whose theory of communicative action has been adapted to the study of international relations and of EU governance. The core claim of the approach, as popularized by Risse (2000), is that there are not two but three 'logics of social action', namely: the logic of consequentiality (or utility maximization) emphasized by rational-choice theorists; the logic of appropriateness (or rule-following behaviour) associated with constructivist theory; and a 'logic of arguing' derived largely from Habermas's theory of communicative action.

In Risse's (2000: 7) logic of arguing, political actors do not simply bargain based on fixed preferences and relative power, they may also 'argue', questioning their own beliefs and interests and being open to persuasion and the power of a better argument. In the view of many democratic theorists, such argumentative processes lead to the promise of a normatively desirable 'deliberative democracy', in which societal actors engage in a sincere collective search for truth and for the best available public policy, and in which even the losers in such debates accept the outcome by virtue of their participation in the deliberative process and their understanding of the principled arguments put forward by their fellow citizens (Elster 1998; Bohman 1998).

Despite the purported benefits of such deliberative democracy, Risse (2000: 19–20) concedes that genuine argumentative rationality is likely only under a fairly restrictive set of preconditions, including notably:

- the existence of a common lifeworld provided by a high degree of international institutionalization in the respective issue area;
- uncertainty of interests and/or lack of knowledge about the situation among the actors; and
- international institutions based on non-hierarchical relations enabling dense interactions in informal, network-like settings.

These conditions are by no means satisfied everywhere in international politics. Where they are present, however, constructivist scholars predict that international actors will engage in arguing rather than bargaining.

The promise of deliberation has received extraordinary attention within the study of the EU in recent years, most notably among scholars looking for a new normative basis for a democratically legitimate EU (Joerges 2001; Eriksen and Fossum 2000, 2003). Empirical studies of deliberation face significant methodological hurdles in distinguishing between arguing and bargaining, or between genuine communicative action and 'cheap talk' (Checkel 2001; Magnette 2004: 208). Despite these challenges, EU scholars have identified the promise of deliberation in three EU-related fora: comitology committees, the Constitutional Convention of 2003–4, and the 'new governance' mechanisms of the EU's 'open method of coordination' (OMC). With regard to the first, Christian Joerges and Jürgen Neyer (1997a, 1997b) argue that EU comitology committees provide a forum in which national and supranational experts meet and *deliberate* in a search for the best or most efficient solutions to common policy problems, arguing on the basis of informal norms, good arguments, and a search for consensus. Critics, however, question both the empirical basis of this claim, noting that evidence of deliberation in such committees remains partial and sketchy (Pollack 2003: 114–45), as well as the normative value of committee deliberations that take place largely outside the public eye (Zürn 2000).

A second EU arena often identified as a promising venue for deliberation was the Convention on the Future of Europe, which met in 2003 to consider changes to the EU treaties and proposed a draft Constitution, although here again the evidence for genuine deliberation, as opposed to bargaining from fixed interests, remains unclear and controversial (Maurer 2003; Closa 2004; Magnette 2004).

Thirdly, the promise of deliberation has also been emphasized by students of the OMC, codified and endorsed by the European Council in Lisbon in March 2000. This is a non-binding form of policy coordination, based on the collective establishment of policy guidelines, targets, and benchmarks, coupled with a system of periodic 'peer review' in which member governments present their respective national programmes for consideration and comment by their EU counterparts (see Chapter 4). The OMC remains controversial both politically and in the academic community (see Chapter 12). For many commentators, the OMC offered a flexible means to address common policy issues without encroaching on sensitive areas of national sovereignty, representing a 'third way' between communitarization and purely national governance and a potential test case for Habermasian deliberation (Hodson and Maher 2001; Scott and Trubek 2002). Careful empirical work, however, has at least tempered the more far-reaching claims put forward by the supporters of the OMC. A number of scholars have argued that when it comes to politically sensitive questions, national representatives revert to a presentation of fixed national positions, engaging clearly in bargaining rather than arguing behaviour (see e.g. Jacobsson and Vifell 2003; Jobelius 2003; Borrás and Jacobsson 2004; De la Porte and Nanz 2004; and Chapter 12).

Despite such setbacks, students of 'experimentalist governance' have pointed to what Charles Sabel and Jonathan Zeitlin (2008: 278) call a 'Cambrian explosion' of institutional forms and policy processes in the contemporary EU, where governance of various sectors now takes place increasingly through networked independent agencies, open methods of coordination, and a dazzling variety of other institutional mechanisms, all of which seek in various ways to reconcile the imperatives of joint governance with respect for national control and subsidiarity. The debate over what Sabel and Zeitlin call 'experimentalist governance' will therefore continue, and we shall have occasion in this volume to search for the Cambrian explosion of institutional forms of which the authors write.

Legitimate governance?

The governance approach to the EU draws on comparative politics as well as international relations and asks analytically and normatively important questions about the workings of EU policy networks, the variable transformation and Europeanization of national institutions and politics, the democratic legitimacy of the EU as a political system, and the prospects for deliberative policy-making at the EU level. Certainly, the governance approach is not without its flaws or critics, and even its proponents concede that it remains a constellation of interrelated claims rather than a single, coherent theory. In empirical terms, moreover, one can argue that the analytical and normative elaboration of the governance approach has outpaced the empirical work needed to assess the plausibility of its claims. Nevertheless, students of EU governance have made significant progress in formulating a research agenda and in producing more empirical evidence and more nuanced claims about territorial change, Europeanization, and deliberation in an enlarged EU.

Conclusion

In 1972, Donald Puchala likened theorists of EU integration to blind men touching an elephant, each one feeling a different part of the elephant and purporting to describe a very different animal. Today, theories of the EU are even more diverse, comprising three distinct approaches with lively debates both within and across all three. Puchala's metaphor suggested the relative immaturity and weakness of integration theory and the partiality of its insights. Yet there is a more optimistic reading of the dizzying array of theories purporting to provide insights into the workings of the EU and the *telos* of European integration.

The past decade of scholarship in EU studies witnessed at least a partial retreat from grand theorizing about the integration process in favour of mid-range theorizing about a variety of topics including the workings of the EU's legislative, executive, and judicial processes; the prospects of socialization or deliberation in EU institutions; the effects of European integration on national institutions and policies; and a wide range of other questions. These more fine-grained questions, in turn, have prompted scholars to undertake increasingly sophisticated empirical testing of their various hypotheses, replacing sterile 'metatheoretical' debates with the careful and patient accumulation of empirical findings that allow us to adjudicate with increasing precision among contending theories from all three traditions. The implications of these theories for our understanding of the EU policy process are explored at length by Alasdair Young in Chapter 3.

NOTES

1   The author is grateful to Helen Wallace and Alasdair Young for excellent comments on this chapter. Any remaining flaws or omissions are the responsibility of the author.

2   For a continuing analysis of the Hungarian constitutional reforms, see e.g. 'Kim Lane Scheppele Monitors Constitutional Developments in Hungary', Princeton University, Program in Law and Public Affairs, available on *http://lapa.princeton.edu/newsview2*

FURTHER READING

Excellent introductions to European integration theories can be found in Rosamond (2000) and Saurugger (2013), and in the essays in Jørgensen, Pollack, and Rosamond (2007), Wiener and Diez (2009), and Jones *et al.* (2012). Keeler (2005) and Jupille (2005) provide illuminating and thorough analyses of trends in the literature, especially the US literature over five decades. E. Haas (2004 [1958]) remains the *locus classicus* on neo-functionalism, and Hoffmann (1966) the founding text on intergovernmentalism. For more recent developments, see Sandholtz and Stone Sweet (2012) on neo-functionalism; Moravcsik (1998) and Moravcsik and Schimmelfennig (2009) on liberal intergovernmentalism; Pollack (2009) on institutionalism; and Jupille *et al.* (2003), Risse (2009), and Schimmelfennig (2012) on constructivism. Hix and Hoyland (2011) deftly review and apply comparative-politics approaches to various aspects of EU policy-making. The governance literature remains extremely diverse, but useful overviews are provided by Scharpf (1999), Hooghe and Marks (2001), and Jachtenfuchs (2007).

Haas, E. B. (2004) [1958], *The Uniting of Europe* (Stanford, CA: Stanford University Press); reprinted in 2004 by Notre Dame University Press.

Hix, S., and Hoyland, B. (2011), *The Political System of the European Union*, 3rd edn. (Basingstoke: Palgrave Macmillan).

Hoffmann, S. (1966), 'Obstinate or Obsolete? The Fate of the Nation-State and the Case of Western Europe', *Daedalus*, 95/3: 862–915.

Hooghe, L., and Marks, G. (2001), *Multi-Level Governance and European Integration* (Lanham, MD: Rowman & Littlefield).

Jachtenfuchs, M. (2007), 'The European Union as a Polity (II)', in K. E. Jørgensen, M. A. Pollack, and B. Rosamond (eds.), *The Handbook of European Union Politics* (London: Sage), 159–73.

Jones, E., Menon, A., and Weatherill, S. (2012) (eds.), *The Oxford Handbook of the European Union* (Oxford: Oxford University Press).

Jørgensen, K. E., Pollack, M. A., and Rosamond, B. (2007) (eds.), *The Handbook of European Union Politics* (London: Sage).

Jupille, J. (2005), 'Knowing Europe: Metatheory and Methodology in EU Studies', in M. Cini and A. Bourne (eds.), *Palgrave Advances in European Union Studies* (Basingstoke: Palgrave Macmillan), 209–32.

Jupille, J., Caporaso, J. A., and Checkel, J. (2003), 'Integrating Institutions: Rationalism, Constructivism, and the Study of the European Union', *Comparative Political Studies*, 36/1–2: 7–40.

Keeler, J. T. S. (2005), 'Mapping EU Studies: The Evolution from Boutique to Boom Field 1960–2001', *Journal of Common Market Studies*, 43/3: 551–82.

Moravcsik, A. (1998), *The Choice for Europe: Social Purpose and State Power from Messina to Maastricht* (Ithaca, NY: Cornell University Press).

Moravcsik, A., and Schimmelfennig, F. (2009), 'Liberal Intergovernmentalism', in A. Wiener and T. Diez (eds.), *European Integration Theory*, 2nd edn. (Oxford: Oxford University Press), 67–87.

Pollack, M. A. (2009), 'The New Institutionalism and European Integration', in A. Wiener and T. Diez (eds.), *European Integration Theory*, 2nd edn. (Oxford: Oxford University Press), 125–43.

Risse, T. (2009), 'Social Constructivism and European Integration', in A. Wiener and T. Diez (eds.), *European Integration Theory*, 2nd edn. (Oxford: Oxford University Press), 144–61.

Rosamond, B. (2000), *Theories of European Integration* (Basingstoke: Palgrave Macmillan).

Sandholtz, W., and Stone Sweet, A. (2012), 'Neo-Functionalism and Supranational Governance', in E. Jones, A. Menon, and S. Weatherill (eds.), *The Oxford Handbook of the European Union* (Oxford: Oxford University Press), 18–33.

Saurugger, S. (2013), *Theoretical Approaches to European Integration* (Basingstoke: Palgrave Macmillan).

Scharpf, F. W. (1999), *Governing in Europe: Democratic and Effective?* (Oxford: Oxford University Press).

Schimmelfennig, F. (2012), 'Constructivist Perspectives', in E. Jones, A. Menon and S. Weatherill (eds.), *The Oxford Handbook of the European Union* (Oxford: Oxford University Press), 34–47.

Wiener, A., and Diez, T. (2009) (eds.), *European Integration Theory*, 2nd edn. (Oxford: Oxford University Press).

CHAPTER 3

The European Policy Process in Comparative Perspective

Alasdair R. Young

▌ Summary

Policy-making in the European Union (EU) is particularly complex and is distinctive. Nonetheless, it can be fruitfully studied by drawing upon insights from the analysis of policy-making within states and cooperation among states. This chapter sets out the stages of the policy-making process (agenda-setting, policy formation, decision-making, implementation, and feedback), introduces the prevailing approaches to analysing each of these stages, and discusses how these apply to studying policy-making in the EU. It argues that theories rooted in comparative politics and international relations (IR) can explain different phases of the EU's policy process. The chapter also helps to explain why policy-making varies across issue areas within the EU.

Introduction

Policy-making is extremely complex even within traditional states (Hurrell and Menon 1996; Scharpf 1997: 29; John 1998; Sabatier 1999).[1] It is even more so in the EU where institutional structures are more in flux, the allocation of authority is more contested, and multiple levels of governance engage a multitude of actors (Hurrell and Menon 1996; McCormick 2006). Nonetheless, this chapter echoes the central theme of this volume by contending that EU policy-making can be fruitfully studied using general tools of political science (see also Sbragia 1992a; Peterson and Bomberg 1999; Hix 2005). The chapter does not aim to provide an introduction to the wealth of literature on policy-making in all of its myriad forms; rather, it aims to introduce those analytical approaches and debates drawn from comparative politics and international relations that are most commonly deployed, implicitly or explicitly, to explain policy-making in the EU. This chapter therefore situates EU policy-making in a broad comparative perspective, drawing on both policy-making within states and cooperation among them.[2]

This chapter is intended to serve as a stepping stone between the grand theories of European integration and the different approaches to studying the EU discussed in Chapter 2 and the patterns of policy-making and roles of the key institutions developed in Chapter 4. It begins by introducing the policy cycle before making the case that there has been convergence between comparative politics and IR with regard to the analysis of at least certain aspects of the policy process. The chapter then introduces the literatures on the different phases of the policy cycle—agenda-setting, policy formation, decision-making, and implementation—and relates them to the study of the EU before examining policy feedback. It concludes by drawing out the implications for explaining policy-making in the EU.

Policy-making and the policy cycle

The policy-making process is commonly depicted heuristically as a 'policy cycle' (see Figure 3.1): a self-conscious simplification of a complex phenomenon in order to facilitate our understanding (John 1998: 23–7, 36; Sabatier 1999: 6–7; McCormick 2006: 13–14; Richardson 2006: 7; Hague and Harrop 2007: 378). The policy cycle is usually portrayed as commencing with an issue being put on the political agenda; that is, it becomes an issue of concern (agenda-setting). Once a decision has been taken to address a particular issue, it is necessary to formulate specific proposals for action (policy formulation) and decide what course of action to pursue, or not (policy decision). If a policy is adopted, then it must be put into effect (implementation). The policy cycle emphasizes that the story does not stop with policy implementation, but that the intended, inadequate, and unintended effects of policies often feed back into the policy process.

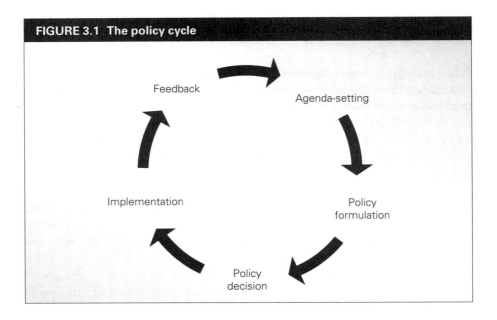

FIGURE 3.1 The policy cycle

The policy cycle has been criticized for being misleading (see Sabatier 1999: 7). First, the stages of the policy process are not as discrete as the heuristic implies. For instance, policy formulation may well occur as officials seek to implement vague legislation. Secondly, Kingdon (2003: 205–6) contends that problem identification (agenda-setting) and solution specification (policy formulation) do not necessarily occur in the sequence depicted in the policy cycle: policies are sometimes developed in advance of there being a specific problem to solve and these alternatives are advocated prior to an opportunity to push them on to the agenda. Thirdly, the cycle does not explicitly capture the interaction between multiple policies being pursued in a particular policy domain. This often comes up as the issue of policy coherence, namely whether different policies support or impede each other's objectives (see e.g. Streeck and Thelen 2005: 19–22). Although policy coordination is a problem for all political systems, it is a particular challenge for the EU as there are multiple actors operating in compartmentalized decision-making structures and multiple levels among which coordination must occur. Compartmentalization, while making it harder for the EU to pursue a strategic approach, can help to avoid direct confrontations among rival objectives (Peters 2012: 797–8). Fourthly, the heuristic can give the impression that there is a single policy cycle when in reality there are multiple, asynchronous policy cycles operating at different levels of governance. As a consequence, some have characterized the policy process as a 'garbage can', in which policies emerge in a manner much less predictable than that suggested by rational decision-making in response to an identified problem (Cohen *et al.* 1972; and, with specific reference to the EU, Richardson 2006: 24).

While these criticisms do not necessarily condemn the policy cycle as a heuristic device, they should caution against being seduced by its simplicity.

A more fundamental critique of the policy cycle is that it does not provide the basis for a causal theory of policy-making that applies across the policy cycle (Sabatier 1999: 7). Rather, different analytical approaches have been applied to try to explain each individual stage (see e.g. Peterson and Bomberg 1999; Richardson 2006: 7). There is, however, no agreement on a 'grand theory' of policy-making (Scharpf 1997: 19; John 1998: 195; Peterson and Bomberg 1999: 272; Sabatier 1999: 261; Richardson 2006: 7). This chapter does not seek to develop an overarching explanation of the policy process; rather, it highlights the analytical approaches that have been developed to explain the different stages of the policy process.

Convergence in the analysis of policy-making

Hurrell and Menon (1996) and Risse-Kappen (1996) have argued for drawing on insights from both comparative politics and IR in order to explain policy-making in the EU. Both contributions highlight developments in the IR literature—notably with regard to the implications of complex interdependence for state behaviour, attention to the roles of non-state actors, and the consequences of increasing institutionalization of international cooperation—that depict relations at the international level in ways increasingly analogous to those found at the domestic level (more generally see Milner 1998). The literature on international cooperation in particular is concerned with the central questions of policy-making: whether there should be cooperation (which conflates whether there should be action and by whom); what form it should take, including in terms of substance (see e.g. Rosenau and Czempiel 1992; O. R. Young 1999; Keohane and Nye 2001); and whether it results in the desired outcome (see e.g., Levy *et al.* 1993; Simmons 2010; Sedelmeier 2012*a*: 826).

This chapter points also to changes in how policy-making within states is analysed, particularly the decreased emphasis on hierarchy, that increase the resonance with analyses of international cooperation. These analytical changes are in response to and in recognition of real-world changes. Beginning in the 1980s, privatization, administrative reforms inspired by the New Public Management, changes in territorial politics (e.g. devolution in the UK), increased economic interdependence, and the development of policy-making beyond the state (not least by the EU) contributed to governing within European states being understood as occurring less through hierarchical authority structures and more through negotiation and persuasion within more decentralized networks (R. Rhodes 1997; Peters 2001; Kahler 2002: 58; Goodin *et al.* 2006: 11–12; Goetz 2008), although these changes have been more pronounced in some states than others (Bale 2013: 86). As a result of both of these shifts, approaches to analysing aspects of international cooperation and domestic policy-making have become more similar.

The players in the policy process

Before turning to ways of understanding the policy process, it is first necessary to identify the actors that engage in that process. Wherever policy-making occurs—within states, in the EU, or in the wider international arena—it involves the interaction of multiple actors that want different things and bring different resources and capabilities to the policy process.

The main actors in the policy processes of liberal democracies are politicians, bureaucrats, and interest groups. Politicians, either as legislators or as members of government, are the key decision-makers. Bureaucrats advise politicians in government, take some policy decisions, and implement policies. Interest groups seek to promote policies and to influence politicians' and bureaucrats' decisions and can play a role in implementing policy.

While politicians in government always matter in the policy process, how important legislators are depends on the distribution of power amongst political institutions (see the section on decision-making later in the chapter). Within political science, there are intense debates about how politicians do and should act. Some (e.g. Dahl 1961; Beer 1982; Baumgartner and Leech 1998; Grossman and Helpman 2001) depict them as being highly responsive to societal pressures, constituency demands, and/or interest-group lobbying. More typically, authors assume that politicians have their own preferences, informed by their own experiences and political beliefs, as well as being influenced by societal pressures (Derthick and Quirk 1986; Putnam 1988; Atkinson and Coleman 1989; Evans 1993).

Bureaucrats also tend to be depicted as having specific interests, which may be purposive (concerned with achieving policy goals, including greater European integration) or reflexive (concerned with enhancing the power and prestige of their particular branch of the bureaucracy) (Niskanen 1971; Peters 1992: 115–16; also Dunleavy 1997). The tendency for bureaucracies to have functionally determined preferences is captured by the aphorism popularized by Graham Allison (1969: 711) that 'where you stand depends on where you sit'.

Interest groups are associations of individuals or other organizations that are independent of governments that aggregate interests and inject them into the policy process (Keck and Sikkink 1998; Clark *et al.* 1998; Halliday 2001; Price 2003; Hawkins 2004). All interest groups must contend with the 'logic of collective action' (Olson 1965); that is, they must overcome the free-rider problem—that individuals or firms are able to enjoy the benefits of collective action (a policy) without incurring the costs of realizing it. The free-rider problem is more acute the more actors are involved (it is harder to identify free-riders with larger numbers) and the more diffuse the benefits of action (the lower the individual incentive to act). This implies that it is easier for producers to organize than for consumers or people concerned about the environment (for a critical discussion, see G. Jordan 1998). There are, however, ways for consumers and environmentalists to overcome the collective action problem, not least because members are motivated by non-material considerations (G. Jordan and Maloney 1996; A. R. Young 1998), but such groups tend to be fewer and more poorly resourced than producer interests. Moreover, many firms have the resources individually to participate in the policy process. Politicians and bureaucrats generally welcome the input of interest groups and firms into the policy process because they provide information, which helps to inform policy options and choices, and because many represent actors that are affected by the policies and compliance is likely to be better (and therefore policy effectiveness greater) if the affected actors have been part of the process (Lindblom 1977; Beer 1982). Producer interests tend to be particularly well equipped to provide these benefits to policy-makers, giving them a 'privileged position' in the policy process (Lindblom 1977).

These actors play roles in the EU process that are slightly different from those they perform at the national level. In the EU, the bureaucrats in the Commission have a greater role in agenda-setting and policy formulation and a lesser one in policy implementation than their counterparts within states. Members of the European Parliament (MEPs) are directly elected, but the European Parliament's (EP) role is somewhat more circumscribed than that of national parliaments (see Chapter 4). In those policy domains in which it is involved in legislation and exercises oversight, however, it is 'one of the world's most powerful parliaments' (Scully *et al.* 2012: 671). National ministers sit together in the Council of the European Union and play important roles in adopting legislation (see Chapter 4); overseeing the transposition of European decisions into national law; and, in some cases, directing implementation. European interest groups tend to be associations of national associations, which can present problems for agreeing common positions, although there are a growing number of European groups that have direct memberships (Greenwood and Young 2005). Producer groups enjoy privileged access to EU policy-makers, particularly focusing on the Commission, which combined with their organizational and information resources has led many analysts to characterize the EU as an 'élite pluralist environment' (see Coen 2007: 335).

Moreover, informed by the debate in integration theory between neo-functionalism and liberal intergovernmentalism (see Chapter 2), there is also a vigorous strand of the EU policy-making literature that considers the extent to which the EU's supranational institutions—the Commission, Court of Justice of the European Union (CJEU), and EP—influence the EU policy-making process. In this context they tend to be treated as distinctive, unitary actors, although each of these is a composite institution with complex internal politics (see Chapter 4).

Policy makes politics

Which interest groups, firms, and parts of the state engage in the policy process and how much autonomy the government has from societal actors vary with the type of policy at issue. In the EU, the policy in question also influences at what level of governance authority lies and which decision rules apply at the EU level. Theodore Lowi (1964, 1972: 299) contended that 'policy determines politics', identifying three main types of policy—distributive, regulatory, and redistributive—each characterized by a different type of politics.[3] Distributive policies, for which there are no visible losers within the polity because the individual costs are very small and are spread widely, such as 'pork-barrel' spending from the public purse, are characterized by supportive relations between interest groups and policy-makers and mutual non-interference among interest groups. Regulatory policy, which produces concentrated winners and losers, by contrast, leads to interest-group competition. Redistributive policies, such as those associated with the welfare state, which involve the transfer of resources from one diffuse group to another, are characterized by politics divided along class lines. In the EU contest, the most politicized division is between net-contributors to and net-beneficiaries from the EU budget (see Chapters 9 and 10). Despite its prominence and popularity, Lowi's scheme has been extensively criticized, particularly because the typology is difficult to apply to the messy reality of policy-making (Heidenheimer 1985: 455).

Wilson (1980) developed a more nuanced analysis grounded explicitly in the distribution of anticipated costs and benefits. Where the distribution of both costs and benefits is broad, majoritarian politics is likely to occur. Where benefits are diffuse and costs concentrated, such as in consumer and environmental protection (see Chapters 5 and 13), policy will be blocked by the vested interests that benefit from the status quo, unless a policy entrepreneur can mobilize latent public opinion in favour of policy change. Where anticipated costs and benefits are both concentrated, such as in economic regulation in which some firms gain at the expense of others, interest-group competition is expected (see Chapters 5 and 14). Policies that have narrow benefits and diffuse costs—such as economic regulations that shield producers from competition—are likely to be characterized by clientelistic politics (see Chapters 5 and 14). Redistributive policies, such as the budget (see Chapter 9) and cohesion policy (see Chapter 10) and increasingly agriculture (see Chapter 8), also involve explicit winners and losers, but mobilization occurs at state or sub-national level. The crucial insight to take away from this discussion, however, is straightforward—different types of policy are characterized by different types of politics, even if the precise contours are difficult to pin down (John 1998: 7).

Foreign policy has tended to be treated as distinct from domestic policy-making. In particular, policies that deal with the most basic concerns of the state (particularly security) are thought to be subject to 'high politics', in which heads of government are prominent and societal actors passive (see Chapter 18). Other policies, such as trade (see Chapter 16) and international environmental policies (see Chapter 13), however, have been depicted as subject to 'low politics', in which societal actors engage actively and which are addressed lower down the political hierarchy (Keohane and Nye 2001: 22–3; Hill 2003: 4), and thus look more similar to domestic politics. Governments are thus thought to have more autonomy from societal pressures when pursuing some types of foreign policy rather than others.

This high/low politics distinction is problematic, however. It assumes a hierarchy among issues that is not sustainable as non-military issues—including financial crises, pandemics, and environmental degradation (including climate change)—can have profound implications for states (Keohane and Nye 2001: 22–3; Hill 2003: 4). Moreover, foreign policy, even when its focus is security, often engages politicians, bureaucrats, and interest groups in ways similar to domestic politics (Allison 1971; Lowi 1972; Risse-Kappen 1991; Evans 1993; Hill 2003). In the late summer of 2013, for instance, there were vigorous, public debates within the western powers about whether they should intervene militarily in response to the alleged use of chemical weapons by the Syrian government against its own people, with the UK parliament voting against authorizing the government to commit troops to such action. In addition, foreign policy is arguably coming increasingly to resemble domestic policy (Hill 2003), particularly given the importance of police cooperation in combating cross-border terrorism (see Chapter 15). Conversely, there are claims that issues, such as energy (see Chapter 14), traditionally thought of as domestic, can be 'securitized'; that is, they can be 'presented as an existential threat, requiring emergency measures and justifying actions outside the normal bounds of political procedure' (Buzan *et al.* 1998: 24). It is, therefore, not easy and is probably unhelpful to designate certain issues as high or low politics *a priori*. This discussion, however, does draw attention to the variation in how much autonomy the government has with respect to societal actors when making policy choices.

Policy has particularly profound effects on politics in the EU (see Chapter 4). Whether competence (authority) resides with the member states or the EU or is shared between them varies across policy areas. Moreover, the roles of the institutions differ among policy areas at the EU level, as can the decision rule in the Council—a variation which contributes to the presence of different policy modes in EU policy-making (see Chapter 4).

Agenda-setting: deciding what to decide

Deciding what to decide is a crucial part of the policy-making process and one that often takes place in a context where there is a great deal of uncertainty. Deciding what to decide actually involves two steps in the policy cycle: agenda-setting and policy formation. Whether an issue attracts political attention in part reflects the character of the issue—how serious the problem is; whether there has been a change in the severity of the problem; whether it stands for a more general problem, such as the threatened extinction of a specific animal as emblematic of diminishing biodiversity; and whether it has emotional appeal, since some issues, such as those involving children or bodily harm, are more likely to garner sympathy from publics and policy-makers (Keck and Sikkink 1998: 26; Page 2006: 216).

There is, however, a significant degree of agency in agenda-setting, with policy entrepreneurs, be they interest groups, politicians, or others, identifying and exploiting opportunities to push a policy and presenting ('framing') it in a way that resonates politically (Kingdon 2003: 204–5; Price 2003: 583; Page 2006: 215). Framing an issue is most likely to be successful if it can be linked with existing widely held norms or concerns (Price 2003: 597; Hawkins 2004: 780).

An 'epistemic community' is a distinctive type of political entrepreneur. It is 'a network of professionals with recognized expertise and competence in a particular domain and an authoritative claim to policy-relevant knowledge within that domain or issue-area' (P. Haas 1992: 3). The members of an epistemic community share a set of normative and principled beliefs, causal beliefs, notions for weighing and evaluating knowledge, and a common set of problems to which they direct their expertise. The impact of epistemic communities tends to be particularly acute in highly technical areas, such as with respect to the environment (see Chapter 13; P. Haas 1992; Zito 2001) and economic and monetary union (EMU) (Verdun 1999; McNamara 2005). Epistemic communities affect the policy agenda by articulating cause-and-effect relationships and in doing so help to specify problems and propose solutions (P. Haas 1992: 14).

Events can also be crucial for creating opportunities for policy entrepreneurs to promote policies (Downs 1972: 39; Kingdon 2003: 197; Page 2006: 216). Crises can contribute to converting conditions that can be ignored into problems that need to be addressed (Kingdon 2003). For example, a series of regulatory failures concerning food safety in Europe during the 1980s, most notably bovine spongiform encephalopathy (BSE), contributed to the adoption of a more precautionary approach to regulating food safety (Vogel 2003: 568; Pollack and Shaffer 2010). The significance of events injects an important element of contingency into the policy-making process.

The agenda-setting literature, however, has been criticized for being too conditioned by the US political system in which it developed (Page 2006: 208–9). In particular, the US political system is relatively non-hierarchical: policy initiatives can come from many directions. In parliamentary democracies, the fusing of legislative and executive branches of government through party control tends to produce executive dominance, which means that there is one key audience that must be convinced if an issue is to get on the agenda (Page 2006: 208–9).

The EU combines pluralism with executive dominance. Its vertical and horizontal divisions of power create a great many access points (Beyers *et al.* 2008: 1112; Peters 1994; Richardson 2006: 5). In those policy areas in which the European Commission has the exclusive right of initiative, however, the Commission is the key audience that must be persuaded to put an issue forward (Majone 2005: 231; Daviter 2007: 655). Nevertheless, as the Commission's structure is highly fragmented with overlapping internal responsibilities, alternatives are available for a policy advocate looking for bureaucratic allies to develop a policy proposal (Peters 1994: 14). In addition, the Commission can be asked by the European Council or the EP to advance a policy initiative, and it is common for EU legislation to have built-in deadlines for reforms. Nonetheless, the Commission is the pre-eminent policy entrepreneur in the EU and it actively frames policy proposals in order to construct political support (Garrett and Weingast 1993; Jabko 2006; Daviter 2007: 659). The Commission, however, is constrained in that it needs external support from other EU institutional actors—either from influential member states, the EP, or the CJEU—if the agenda it is promoting is to have a realistic chance of adoption (Tallberg 2007: 204–5). In addition, because the Council and the EP can ask the Commission to advance proposals, it cannot act as a 'gatekeeper' and keep issues off the agenda (Schmidt and Wonka 2012: 341).

Policy formulation: what are the alternatives?

Before policy decisions can be taken, the range of alternatives must be narrowed. As discussed previously, this process does not necessarily neatly follow agenda-setting. Whatever the sequencing, the formulation of policy is seen as involving a different set of actors from those which participate in agenda-setting and is most commonly depicted as the product of policy networks (Peterson 1995; Richardson 2006: 7).

Policy networks are 'sets of formal institutional and informal linkages between governmental and other actors structured around shared if endlessly negotiated beliefs and interests in public policy-making and implementation' (R. Rhodes 2006: 426).[4] While most of the policy network literature focuses on domestic policy, it has been applied in foreign policy analysis (Risse-Kappen 1991; Hocking 2004) and IR (Keck and Sikkink 1998; Reinicke 1999–2000). Policy networks are seen as influencing policy choices by shaping which groups participate in the policy process (R. Rhodes 1997: 9; Peterson 2004). The term 'policy network' captures a variety of different types of relationship between public and private actors from tightly integrated 'policy communities' to loosely affiliated 'issue networks' (Peterson 2004: 120). Policy communities—which have stable memberships, exclude outsiders, and have members who depend heavily on each other for resources—are seen as having significant impacts on policy formulation and tend to promote policy continuity in the interests of the participating incumbents. Issue networks, by contrast, have open and unstable memberships, which tend to contain competing policy preferences (Peterson 2004: 120).

There are three actors within policy networks that warrant special attention: producers, epistemic communities, and advocacy coalitions. The resource dependencies at the heart of policy-network analysis are usually seen as privileging producer interests because it is often their behaviour that has to be changed, which means that they have detailed information about the costs and likely success of policy alternatives and they can either drag their feet on implementation or can lend their support to the initiative (Olson 1965; Lindblom 1977; Beer 1982). Epistemic communities are not only important in agenda-setting, but also advance solutions to identified policy problems (Peterson 2004; R. Rhodes 2006: 425). Sabatier and Jenkins-Smith (1993; Sabatier 1998) contend that policy networks tend to contain between one and four 'advocacy coalitions', 'each composed of actors from various governmental and private organizations who both (a) share a set of normative and causal beliefs and (b) engage in a non-trivial degree of co-ordinated activity over time' (Sabatier 1998: 103). Advocacy coalitions are thus networks within networks, which compete to advance their preferred policy solutions.

Policy network analysis is, however, seen by many as providing nothing more than a description of what is happening, rather than an explanation of how policy is made (John 1998: 86; Peterson 2004: 126–7). Dowding (1995: 137) contends that the metaphor of the network has no explanatory value, as the nature of the network and its impact on policy outcomes are both determined by the power relations among the actors involved. Further, Kingdon's (2003) 'policy streams' approach implies that policy formulation does not necessarily follow an issue being put on the agenda, as is implied in the policy-network approach.

There are also a number of criticisms of the policy-network approach that are particular to the EU. One is that EU policy-making is too fluid—with different focuses of authority and different constellations of actors involved in individual policy decisions even within the same policy area—to be captured by the network concept (Kassim 1994: 20–2). Further, because implementation of most EU rules is carried out by the member states, the Commission has a limited direct role in policy delivery, reducing the intensity of its engagement with societal actors and its dependence on them. Moreover, because there are public and private participants from twenty-eight member states as well as the EU-level participants, actors involved in the policy process have very different value systems and often have very different views of problems and possible solutions, which makes it difficult for groups to agree common positions that can be injected coherently into the policy process. Thus, it is relatively rare to find policy communities at the EU level, with the most notable exception being in agriculture, but even that policy community is eroding as agriculture is reframed as a trade and budgetary and environmental issue (see Chapter 8). Policy formulation, therefore, is a relatively open process in the EU (Richardson 2000: 1013), but, as with agenda-setting, the Commission is the pivotal actor in policy formation in those policy areas where it has sole right of initiative (Kassim 1994: 23). Crucially, its central role in agenda-setting and policy formulation give the Commission a significant say in many EU policies even if its role in decision-making is limited (Hix 2005: 74).

Decision-making: choosing what (not) to do

Although there is convergence between comparative-politics and IR approaches regarding agenda-setting and policy formulation, there is much less common ground with regard to decision-making. This is due in large part to decision-making within domestic contexts taking place through highly institutionalized procedures, including voting, while cooperative decision-making in international relations usually occurs through bargaining. Even in those international organizations in which binding decisions are taken by votes—such as the International Monetary Fund and the United Nations Security Council—decisions require super-majorities and powerful actors retain vetoes. Thus, the two sub-disciplines generally seek to explain decision-making in very different contexts.

These differences, however, are a boon when it comes to explaining decision-making in the EU because the context of policy-making varies extensively across policy areas (see Chapter 4), from unanimous decision-making among the member states, for example in foreign and security policy (Chapter 18), to decisions taken on the basis of qualified majority voting (QMV) amongst the member states in conjunction with the EP on a proposal from the European Commission, for example with regard to the single market (Chapter 5) and the environment (Chapter 13), with many combinations in between. Thus, some aspects of EU decision-making have features similar to the executive and legislative politics of domestic policy-making, while others are more similar to international negotiations.

The analysis of decision-making in the EU is rooted primarily in the 'new institutionalism': historical institutionalism, rational-choice institutionalism, and sociological institutionalism (Hall and Taylor 1996; Aspinwall and Schneider 1999; Peters 1999; Pollack 2004; and see Chapter 2). The historical and rational-choice variants have tended to be applied more frequently to studies of policy-making (Nugent 2006), particularly with regard to executive politics, primarily in the Commission, and legislative politics, focused on the EP. Both sociological and rational-choice institutionalist approaches, however, have been applied to analyses of decision-making in the Council of the European Union.

Executive politics: delegated decision-making

Executive politics is most often associated with providing political leadership, such as through agenda-setting and policy formation, and overseeing the implementation of legislation. Our focus here, however, is on the delegation of decision-making responsibility to executive bodies. Both comparative-politics and IR literatures consider the decision to delegate responsibilities, but it is the comparative-politics literature, particularly that on delegation by the US Congress to independent regulatory agencies, that focuses on the delegation of decision-making, rather than of agenda-setting or monitoring compliance (for a review see Pollack 2003: 20–34; and see Chapter 2). This literature is rooted in rationalism, particularly principal–agent analysis. A key insight is that the principal(s) and agent have different preferences and that the act of delegation gives the agent scope to pursue its own preferences, rather than those of the principal(s).

The benefits of delegating decision-making are considered to be particularly pronounced under certain circumstances, such as a significant need for policy-relevant expertise due to the technical or scientific complexity of a policy area (see Chapter 2). In the EU, the specialized agencies—such as the European Medicines Agency (EMA) and the European Food Safety Authority (EFSA) (see Chapter 5; Pollack and Shaffer 2010)—have been given the task of providing expert advice to the Commission, which formally takes decisions (at least under certain circumstances) (Krapohl 2004; Eberlein and Grande 2005). The delegation of decision-making is also more likely where doubts about politicians' commitment to a policy can undermine its effectiveness. The problem of commitments not being credible is likely to be pronounced when there is a conflict between short-run costs and long-run benefits (time inconsistency), such as in monetary policy (see Chapter 7), or a when policy delivers diffuse benefits, but imposes concentrated costs and therefore generates strong political pressure to abandon the policy, such as in competition policy (see Chapter 6). Decision-making may also be delegated in order to make it harder for successors to reverse the policy.

Alternatively, sociological institutionalists contend that delegation occurs not necessarily because it is efficient, but because it is perceived as a legitimate and appropriate institutional design. Thus, institutional designs are copied through processes of emulation and diffusion. In this view, the creation of a European Central Bank (ECB) was shaped by the acceptance of monetarist ideas and the view that independent central banks were appropriate (McNamara 2005).

Where decision-making is delegated, two different views of bureaucratic decision-making prevail. One view, rooted primarily in the analysis of independent regulatory agencies in the US, stresses the importance of technical expertise and legal mandates and sees value in insulating decision-makers from political pressures, so that decisions can be taken for the greater good rather than to benefit the powerful. Giandomenico Majone (1994: 94) has argued that the Commission, because it is pan-European and not democratically elected, is more insulated from political pressures and is therefore more likely to take difficult decisions and less likely to be captured by vested interests than national regulators.

A much messier view of bureaucratic politics comes primarily from the analysis of US foreign policy, not least Graham Allison's study of the Cuban Missile Crisis (Allison 1969, 1971; Allison and Zelikow 1999), which depicts bureaucratic politics as bargaining among different sections of the executive with different preferences (for a rare application to the EU, see Rosenthal 1975). In this view, decisions reflect compromise and consensus among the participants (Rosati 1981). While much of the European integration literature has treated the Commission as if it is a unitary actor and focused on its influence relative to the member states, the policy-making literature has pointed out vigorous differences within the Commission (see e.g. Chapter 13).

An important implication of the principal–agent approach, however, is that the bureaucratic agent is not completely free to take decisions, but is constrained by the principals' preferences. How constraining the principals' preferences are depends on how able they are to monitor the agent's behaviour and whether they are able to sanction behaviour they dislike, which in turn depends on whether some of the principals approve of what the agent is doing and are able to shield it (Pollack 2003). In this view, any analysis of Commission decision-making must consider what authority has been delegated to it and how its preferences relate to those of the member states on the issue in question.

Legislative politics or international negotiation?

Because of the separation of executive and legislative authority, the legislative politics of the EU, especially in the EP, is arguably more closely analogous to that of the US than to those of most EU member states (Hix 2005; McElroy 2007). Consequently, authors seeking to understand EU legislative politics have drawn extensively on theories developed to explain decision-making in the US Congress, particularly the House of Representatives. Care, however, is required when drawing such comparisons, not least because the connection between voters and representatives is much weaker in the EP than in the House of Representatives, because the powers of the Council and EP are not as equal as those of the Senate and the House, and because the executive–legislative division of powers is much less strict in the EU than in the US (McElroy 2007: 176). Moreover, despite its legislative role, interactions in the Council can appear similar to international negotiations, although the degree of bargaining relative to deliberation varies across policy areas (see Chapter 4).

'Pure' legislative politics in the European Parliament

The theory of 'minimum-winning coalitions' (Riker 1962) is particularly commonly applied to EU decision-making. A minimum-winning coalition, by involving the minimum number of votes needed to secure victory, means that there are fewer interests to accommodate and gives the members of the coalition, particularly those decisive in creating a winning majority, greater influence over the policy. It is more precise, however, to think in terms of 'minimum-connected-winning' coalitions among legislators or parties that have policy preferences that are relatively closely related (Axelrod 1970). In parliamentary systems such coalition-building dynamics are evident in the creation of coalition governments, rather than on individual policies (Swaan 1973; Felsenthal and Machover 2004). Contrary to these expectations, however, the EP has had a tendency to form oversized voting coalitions, ostensibly to increase the EP's influence relative to the Council. Recent studies, however, have pointed to a tentative retreat from oversized coalitions towards more 'normal' patterns of minimum-winning coalitions on the left or the right (Kreppel and Hix 2003; Hix and Noury 2009; Raunio 2012: 368). Ideological preferences, both left–right and pro-/anti-European integration, strongly influence the MEPs' attitudes (Scully *et al.* 2012: 678).

Given that the EP is a supranational legislature, in which electoral connections are notably weak, much attention has been paid to what motivates parliamentarians' voting behaviour (McElroy 2007: 177–8). Strikingly, the best predictor of MEP voting behaviour is not nationality, but an MEP's 'party group', with the centre-left Party of European Socialists, the centre-right European People's Party, and other smaller party groups demonstrating extraordinarily high measures of cohesion in empirical studies of roll-call votes (Kreppel 2001). MEPs, moreover, contest elections and cast their votes in a two-dimensional 'issue space', including not only the familiar nationalism/supranationalism dimension, but also and especially a more traditional, 'domestic' dimension of left–right contestation (Hix 2001; Hix et al. 2007; McElroy 2007; Scully et al. 2012: 678).[5]

Legislating, bargaining, or arguing? Decision-making in the Council

There is greater debate about how the Council takes decisions. Theories of coalition formation have also been extensively applied to the Council, at least when QMV applies.[6] A number of scholars have used increasingly elaborate formal models of Council voting to establish the relative bargaining power of various member states (Bueno de Mesquita and Stokman 1994; Hosli 1994; Felsenthal and Machover 1997). One implication of this analysis is that the relative preferences of member governments are relevant; governments with preferences close to the centre of the range of preferences on a given issue are more likely to be in a winning majority independent of their formal voting weight, while other governments may be 'preference outliers', and therefore more likely to be isolated in EU decision-making. There is also evidence that the member state holding the Council presidency has extra influence, through its capacity to shape the agenda (Tallberg 2006) and by exploiting its superior information about the positions of the other member states when the final decision is taken (Schalk et al. 2007; R. Thomson 2008) in order to shape outcomes to reflect more closely its own preferences. Strikingly, some smaller member states—Denmark, Finland, Ireland, Luxembourg, and Sweden—are better able to secure their objectives in the Council than larger member states, notably France and Germany (Golub 2012: 1312). It is possible that being able to develop high-quality negotiating positions in a timely fashion, pursue a range of negotiating strategies, and act as norm entrepreneurs enables these states to more than compensate for their lack of more tangible power attributes.

Historically, less than 20 per cent of legislative decisions are taken by ministers in the Council, with most reached by consensus among officials (Lewis 2012: 323; and see Chapter 4). Recently, however, the proportion of decisions taken by ministers has increased sharply to 40–50 per cent (see Chapter 4). Moreover, even when QMV applies, the Council tends to seek consensus whenever possible, although since 2008 the proportion of explicitly contested votes has also increased (see Chapter 4). Because of the lack of voting in the past, historically models of procedures, such as minimum-winning coalitions, provided a poor guide to understanding day-to-day practice in the Council even in those policies in which voting occurs (Hayes-Renshaw and Wallace 2006; Schneider et al. 2006). It is possible that, with the twin increases in the proportion of decisions taken by ministers and in the share of votes that are explicitly contested, these models may now have enhanced purchase.

Bargaining models, which have been extensively developed and applied to international negotiations, performed better at predicting decisions in the past (Schneider *et al.* 2006). In bargaining, policy is agreed through a process of identifying an outcome that makes none worse off—producing 'lowest common denominator' outcomes—or through the use of issue linkage, inducements, or threats (Putnam 1988). Bargaining outcomes, whether among states, among coalition partners, or in industrial relations, are expected to reflect the relative power of the actors, which, in turn, is shaped, by their 'best alternatives to negotiated agreement' (BATNA) (Fisher and Ury 1982; Garrett and Tsebelis 1996). The best alternative can involve being content with the status quo or having the capacity to realize objectives unilaterally or through cooperation with an alternative set of actors (Moravcsik 1998; Keohane and Nye 2001). The implication is that the actor that has the best alternative to an agreement will have the greatest say in the outcome.

An extreme variant of bargaining analysis is Fritz Scharpf's (1988: 239, 2006) 'joint-decision trap' in which there is no solution that all veto players prefer to the status quo. Scharpf (2006: 847) has stressed that the joint-decision trap is not a general condition of EU policy-making, but applies when institutions create an 'extreme variant of a multiple-veto player system' and where transaction costs are high, notably where the Commission does not have the right of initiative. Scharpf (2006: 851) argues, however, that agenda-setting by the Commission does not imply much softening of the pessimistic implications of the joint-decision trap because the diversity of the member states' preferences may still mean that there is no solution acceptable to all (or a qualified majority of) member states. The implication is that the 'logic of the joint decision trap' is 'strong' in an EU of twenty-eight member states (Scharpf 2006: 851).

Arguably, side-payments or package deals ('log-rolling') are ways of overcoming the joint-decision trap (Peters 1997), although Scharpf (2006) is sceptical about the availability of such bargaining techniques within the EU's fragmented policy-making process. In international negotiations in highly institutionalized settings, of which the EU is a prime example, however, cooperation is facilitated because the participants are aware that they will be interacting repeatedly in the future and as their experience of successful cooperation accumulates (Axelrod 1984; Peters 1997). This can generate 'diffuse reciprocity', in which governments acquiesce in the short run in the expectation of favourable consideration of their concerns at some point in the future (Keohane 1986: 4). Being able to accommodate diffuse reciprocity may be one of the key reasons why bargaining models are better at predicting policy-making in the EU than procedural models, which are blind to iteration (Schneider *et al.* 2006: 304–5).

In contrast to rationalist bargaining, constructivists contend that deliberation, argument, and persuasion—the 'logic of arguing'—can produce a reasoned consensus that is superior to a lowest-common-denominator outcome even in international negotiations (Risse 2000; and see Chapter 2). The policy-making literature in general now recognizes that reason-giving is important at all stages of the policy process (Goodin *et al.* 2006: 7). A key question is whether actors are simply trying to persuade others to change their positions by appeals to principle ('rhetorical action') or if they are genuinely open to being persuaded to change their own positions ('argumentative rationality') (Risse 2000: 7).

Argumentative rationality is thought to be most likely to occur under particular conditions (Risse 2000: 10–11; and see Chapter 2), which are particularly intense in the EU. The likelihood that argumentative rationality will apply depends also on the issue under consideration. It is most likely to occur—actors are most likely to be open to persuasion—under situations of uncertainty, where actors are not sure about their preferences and/or those of the other actors or are uncertain about the appropriate norm or how to resolve tensions among rules (Joerges and Neyer 1997b; Risse 2002: 601).

Rationalists also accept that persuasion, albeit of a more limited kind, can occur through exposure to new causal ideas (Goldstein and Keohane 1993; Sabatier and Jenkins-Smith 1993). New causal ideas can help to clarify the nature of problems confronted and/or introduce actors to new ways of realizing their objectives, including through presenting new policy alternatives ('policy learning').

Uncertainty is most likely to occur when issues are first identified; that is, during agenda-setting and policy formulation. Once the parameters of the problem have been agreed and responses formulated, the distributional implications of the alternatives become clearer, and even advocates of constructivism concede that bargaining may replace arguing (Joerges and Neyer 1997b; Risse 2000: 20, 2002: 607).

Decision-making in the Council, therefore, is clearly not purely power-based. It also reflects norms, most notably that solutions are found that all can live with, even if they do not get what they want (Lewis 2012: 321). Nonetheless, there is a great deal of uncertainty about how preferences translate into outcomes within the Council (Lewis 2012; Golub 2012).

Inter-institutional power dynamics

Although there are a few policy areas, such as foreign and security policy (Chapter 18) and a few remaining aspects of justice and home affairs (Chapter 15), in which the Council is essentially the sole decision-maker, in most areas of EU policy the Commission and EP have roles in decision-making. Most of the existing literature on interaction of the EU's institutions in decision-making, which is rooted in rationalist modelling, finds that the EP's influence is much greater under the co-decision procedure than under the cooperation procedure, arguably to the extent that it is a co-legislator with the Council (Schneider *et al.* 2006: 303; McElroy 2007: 186). The Commission, by contrast, is widely considered to have lost influence as the EP's has increased (Thomson and Hosli 2006: 414; see Chapter 4). The co-decision procedure, now known as the ordinary legislative procedure, has become, as the name implies, the dominant method for adopting significant legislation. Many specific implementing decisions—such as whether to approve a particular chemical or food additive—are adopted under comitology procedures, in which the Commission is central and the EP excluded.

The existing literature on inter-institutional politics, however, tends to treat the institutions as unitary actors, neglecting the competing preferences behind the common institutional positions (McElroy 2007: 186). Analyses of specific decisions, however, illustrate how actors within particular institutions, notably the Council, have been able to use the positions of the other institutions to shift legislation towards their preferences (Tsebelis 1994; A. R. Young and Wallace 2000).

The formal powers of the EU's institutions and the decision rules in the Council matter because the more actors there are that can block a decision—'veto players'— the harder it is to reach an agreement (Tsebelis 1995). If there is to be an agreement it must be acceptable to all veto players, which means that it must accommodate the concerns of the actor that is least enthusiastic about change. In the EU there are a great many veto players: under the ordinary legislative procedure, either the EP or the Council can block legislation; under unanimity, each member state is a veto player; and under QMV, a minority of states can block decisions. The need to accommodate so many veto players in order to adopt a policy led Simon Hix (2008a: 589) to characterize the EU as 'a hyper-consensus system of government'.

In such a highly consensual policy process, securing agreement requires a potent coalition across the key decision-makers. This often requires a coalition across two levels of governance: among European institutions and within member states. Such an advocacy coalition is evident in employment policy (see Chapter 12). Constructing such coalitions is difficult and demanding. Policy networks, which link officials and interest groups across the EU's member states and to the Commission, and epistemic communities, through persuading key actors in different institutions, can play vital roles in constructing such coalitions (Peters 1997; Zito 2001). Thus, cooperation among policy actors without formal roles in the policy process can be decisive to the adoption of policy.

Implementation: national legislative and executive politics

Once a decision has been taken, further steps are usually required in order to put it into effect. The difficulty of reaching agreement in the EU makes implementation particularly important because decisions often contain messy compromises and/or vague language, which leave significant room for discretion in how the policies are put into practice (Treib 2008). In addition, many of the most significant EU decisions—in the form of directives—must be incorporated ('transposed' in EU parlance) into national law before they are translated into practice by national bureaucracies (see Chapter 4). Thus, a very significant component of consequential decision-making occurs during the implementation phase of most EU policy-making.

The analysis of implementation in the EU context, as within states, is concerned primarily with the EU's internal policies, which occur within a legal hierarchy.[7] The literature on implementation includes discussions of how particular policies are carried out, most notably with regard to competition policy (see Chapter 6); cohesion and structural funds (see Chapter 10); the coordinating role of independent agencies in justice and home affairs (see Chapter 15); and the novel methods of implementation adopted in employment policy (see Chapter 12), as well as with respect to the common fisheries policy (Lequesne 2005). The academic literature on implementation in the EU has focused overwhelmingly on transposition, most notably in environmental and social policies (Treib 2008), although more attention is now being paid to whether EU decisions are actually implemented properly (see e.g. Börzel and Knoll 2012).

Different internal policies, moreover, target the behaviour of different types of actors and in different ways. For some policies, whether national or EU—such as setting interest rates (Chapter 7), approving/blocking mergers or imposing fines for anti-competitive behaviour (Chapter 6)—taking the decision and implementing it are essentially the same thing: no steps beyond taking the EU-level decision are required to put the policy into effect. There are other EU policies—such as budgetary policy (Chapter 9), aspects of justice and home affairs (Chapter 15), and the fiscal disciplines associated with EMU (Chapter 7)—in which the targets of policy are governments. Most EU policies, however, seek to influence the behaviour of individuals and firms within the member states. Although many such policies are implemented via 'regulations', which apply directly within the member states, the implementation literature focuses primarily on directives.

Because directives, except under limited circumstances, must be transposed into national law in order to have effect, they share some of the characteristics of international agreements. Consequently, there is a significant degree of overlap between explanations of 'implementation' and 'Europeanization' in the EU and IR explanations of 'compliance' (Sedelmeier 2012a: 826; and see Chapter 2). In both the EU-implementation (Treib 2008) and IR-compliance (A. R. Young 2009) literatures, there is increasing attention to the impact of domestic politics on whether and how international obligations are translated into policy change.

In these accounts, whether and how implementation (compliance) occurs depends on the preferences of key societal actors and the government regarding the new obligation relative to the status quo, and crucially whether any of those opposed to implementation are 'veto players' (for surveys see Treib 2008; A. R. Young 2009). Governments may leverage EU laws to overcome domestic opposition to a desired change (Sedelmeier 2012a: 829). Arguably, such a politicized approach to implementation is found only in some EU member states, with implementation being apolitical in some or accepted as appropriate, despite the costs, in yet others (Falkner et al. 2007). Moreover, whether implementation is politicized varies with the type of measure required—with legislation being more likely to produce contestation than administrative change (Steunenberg 2007)—and the political salience of the issue (Treib 2008; A. R. Young 2009). This broad level of agreement masks a degree of disagreement about the relative importance of rationalist or constructivist considerations (Börzel and Risse 2007; Sedelmeier 2012a: 829–30). In addition, these considerations address the will to implement EU rules, but there is also the issue of whether the member state has the administrative capacity to do so effectively.

Although most academic interest has focused on explaining transposition (Treib 2008), some scholars have begun to consider how national bureaucracies have changed in order to carry out EU policies and how variance among member states' administrative responses can be explained (Kassim et al. 2000; Knill 2001; A. Jordan 2003; Falkner et al. 2005; Toshkov 2007; Falkner and Treib 2008). A particular strand of this research examines the proliferation of (quasi-)independent agencies within the member states (Majone 2000b; Thatcher and Stone Sweet 2002; Kelemen 2002, 2004, 2012; Coen and Thatcher 2005) and how they are integrated into European networks (Eberlein and Grande 2005; Egeberg 2008). This literature, therefore, has been more concerned with the EU's impact on national institutions than with how national institutions actually implement and enforce EU policies (see Trondal 2007: 966–8 for a review).

The EU implementation literature, therefore, has largely neglected enforcement and implementation within the member states, how policy translates into action on the ground (Falkner et al. 2005: 17; Treib 2008: 14; an exception is Versluis 2007). In part this reflects the general neglect of implementation by political science (Goodin et al. 2006: 17; Hague and Harrop 2007: 382). A compounding cause is the difficulty of establishing systematically whether an EU law has been properly applied, particularly as there is extensive variation among member states and across policy areas concerning which and how many branches of the bureaucracy are involved, whether central, regional, or even local government is responsible, and whether enforcement is carried out by the state or private actors (see Falkner et al. 2005: 33–6 for a discussion). Some scholars have used the Commission's infringement proceedings—which capture complaints by other states, firms, and non-governmental organizations (NGOs) about improper implementation—to overcome this problem (Börzel and Knoll 2012).

Analyses of transposition and infringements both point to some member states being particularly assiduous in implementing EU law—Denmark, Finland, the Netherlands, Sweden, and the UK—and others being consistently poor, notably France, Greece, and Italy (Börzel and Knoll 2012; Falkner 2010). At least some of the newer member states—Czech Republic, Hungary, Slovakia, and Slovenia—seem to fall into the latter category, at least with respect to EU social standards (Falkner 2010). There is not, however, an uncontested explanation for this variation among states (Sedelmeier 2012a).

Nonetheless, three crucial implications emerge from the analysis of policy implementation in the EU. First, the impact of EU decisions, in terms of benefits, costs, and associated political and administrative challenges, varies among member states (Héritier et al. 2001: 9; Börzel and Risse 2007). Secondly, member states—due to differences in both legislative and executive politics, as well as local circumstances—adopt very different national policies in order to implement 'common' EU policies. Thirdly, member states, whether intentionally or not, do not always comply with EU rules.

Judicial politics: adjudicating disputes

It is with respect to how the EU deals with non-compliance that the Union differs most sharply from other international organizations. In the EU, the domestic political process of implementation is supervised by the Commission, aided and abetted by societal actors and member governments, and may be subject to adjudication before national or European courts (Tallberg 2003; Börzel and Knoll 2012; see Appendix Tables A.1 and A.2). Both rationalist and constructivist accounts recognize that the Commission, by threatening legal action, can create pressure for policy adaptation, although the outcomes may be less than intended (Börzel and Risse 2007: 492; for an analysis of how it performs this role, see Hartlapp 2007).

As much of the oversight of implementation occurs through (or with the threat of) legal action, how the EU's legal order functions is essential to understanding the implementation of many, but by no means all, EU policies. The European legal order is much more highly developed than those commonly found among states, and has consequently become the subject of debate between intergovernmentalists and neo-functionalists (see Chapter 2).

Beyond the integration-centric question of the independence of the CJEU (see Chapter 2), there are a number of aspects of judicial politics that are more common to comparative politics than international relations (Conant 2007a). One concerns which actors are most able to take advantage of the opportunities to challenge national (and European) policies under EU law. Although even relatively disenfranchised actors have made use of the European legal system, more politically powerful actors have tended to make more and better use of litigation to challenge (predominantly national) policies that they dislike (Conant 2007a).

The direct implications of court rulings tend to be quite narrow, requiring member state governments to accommodate only the specific requirements of the judgment (Conant 2007a), although governments may extend the implications to other similar circumstances. The implications of court judgments, however, may be developed and exploited by policy entrepreneurs, as the European Commission famously did in developing the concept of 'mutual recognition' on the basis of the CJEU's *Cassis de Dijon* ruling (Alter and Meunier-Aitsahalia 1994; and see Chapter 5). Nevertheless, even the narrow implications of the CJEU's rulings can be significant, at least with respect to specific policies. On several occasions, such as on the EU's agreement with the US about providing the names of transatlantic airline passengers (see Chapter 15), the CJEU has ruled, usually at the request of the EP, that an EU rule was adopted using an improper procedure and that a different decision-rule should apply. The CJEU's ruling against the Council for failing to adopt a common transport policy raised the spectre of court-imposed deregulation of road haulage, which raised the cost of no agreement for those opposed to liberalization and strengthened the hands of those who wanted more far-reaching liberalization (A. R. Young 1995). CJEU rulings have also had significant implications for member states' social and employment policies (see Chapters 11 and 12). Conversely, the CJEU has had an important impact on EU regulatory politics as a result of upholding the legality of national environmental and consumer regulations (Vogel 1995; Joerges and Neyer 1997*b*; A. R. Young and Wallace 2000; and see Chapter 5). Thus, even though the EU's legal system formally only adjudicates on how the EU's treaties and rules are applied (implemented), its rulings can have significant implications for other phases of the policy cycle by pushing issues up the agenda, generating new concepts, or changing bargaining dynamics by foreclosing options, particularly that of not acting.

Policy feedback: completing and shaping the policy cycle

The process of implementing policies, therefore, generates outcomes that feed back into the policy process, 'completing' the policy cycle. There are three distinct, but not unrelated, ways through which policy implementation feeds back into the policy cycle: evaluations of effectiveness, political feedback loops, and spill-over.

The most basic feedback loop involves evaluation of a policy's effectiveness. If the implemented policy does not address the problem that it was intended to, there might well be pressure to take additional action. The ECB's use of quantitative easing in response to the failure of interest-rate changes to stimulate the economy is an example (see Chapter 7). It is worth noting that a policy's effectiveness is not directly related to the quality of its implementation (Raustiala and Slaughter 2002): a perfectly implemented policy may be ineffective if it was insufficiently ambitious or if an inappropriate approach was chosen. Conversely, the aims of the policy may be realized in the absence of implementation as the result of other unrelated changes.

Evaluation of policy effectiveness is arguably particularly problematic within the EU. Because the EU is a multi-level polity in which policy initiation resides primarily with the Commission and policy implementation resides primarily with the bureaucracies of the member states, there is significant 'distance' between those who put policy into practice and those responsible for initiating it, which stretches the feedback loop (Falkner *et al.* 2005: 33–5; Hartlapp 2007). A key aim of the Commission's initiatives to build transnational networks of regulators is to shrink this distance. Policy feedback within the EU, however, is also complicated by the weakness of the mechanisms, which are embedded in national polities, for linking society and government—political participation, political parties, and interest groups—which is commonly known as the EU's 'democratic deficit' (see Chapter 2). This means that, unlike democratic national governments, the Commission does not have access to sources of feedback on what is wanted and what is working.

Beyond the effectiveness of a policy there are also more political feedback loops that can be either 'positive', reinforcing the policy, or 'negative', undermining it. 'Positive feedback' occurs because actors that have adjusted their expectations and behaviours to a policy or that benefit from it will mobilize to defend it (Pierson 1993: 596, 2000: 251). These actors enjoy a political advantage in that, unless the policy has a built-in expiration date, the policy represents the default position (Pierson 2000: 262). The significant number of veto players in the EU, therefore, reinforces the resilience of a policy. Such 'path-dependence' makes policies difficult to change.

Thus, path-dependence has several important implications for the analysis of policy-making (Pierson 2000: 263). First, it stresses the significance of the timing and sequencing of decisions: decisions taken earlier will constrain those taken later. Secondly, even apparently small events, if they occur at a crucial moment ('critical junctures'), can have significant, enduring effects (Pierson 2000: 251). Thirdly, policies may become sub-optimal over time: they may perform a function that is no longer valued or at a cost that is no longer acceptable (Pierson 2000: 264; Streeck and Thelen 2005: 28). Fourthly, path-dependence may be sufficiently strong to lead to non-decisions, in which previously viable alternatives are not considered (Pierson 1993: 609). Path-dependence suggests that policy change occurs as the product of 'punctuated equilibrium': long periods of policy stability disrupted by abrupt change when the mismatch between the policy and its objectives becomes unsustainable or when there is an external shock.

The 'stickiness' of policies should not, however, be overstated (Streeck and Thelen 2005; Hall and Thelen 2009).[8] As noted in the discussion of implementation, there is significant scope for policies to change during their translation into practice. Moreover, policies are continuously being contested by those who did not get their way when the policy was adopted, by new actors or by established actors whose interests the policy no longer serves (Streeck and Thelen 2005; Hall and Thelen 2009). As a consequence of these dynamics, policies may gradually atrophy, be redirected to new purposes, or even collapse (Streeck and Thelen 2005). Thus, while there is positive feedback supporting policy stability, there is also negative feedback creating pressure for change. The result, as is arguably the case with respect to the common agricultural policy (see Chapter 8), is a *politics* of institutional stability' (Hall and Thelen 2009: 6), in which the suitability of existing policies is continuously assessed against existing or plausible alternatives.

The third feedback process in the EU involves 'functional spill-over', which is central to the neo-functionalist account of integration (see Chapter 2). Spill-over does not involve feedback into the same policy process, but creates incentives for additional policy development. For example, a successful policy might cause a new set of problems, either unintended or unanticipated, such as the elimination of border controls within the EU creating incentives for intensified cooperation with respect to immigration and policing (see Chapter 15). Alternatively, further policy development might be seen as enhancing the results of an existing policy, such as the development of a single currency augmenting the creation of the single European market (see Chapter 7). Crucially, actors must make the connection between these policy problems or opportunities and push them onto the policy agenda. Functional spill-over, therefore, is not automatic. It requires agency.

Conclusion

This chapter has used the heuristic of the policy cycle to structure the discussion of how theories of policy-making drawn from both comparative politics and IR can be fruitfully applied to the analysis of policy-making in the EU. The implication is that theories rooted in the different sub-disciplines explain different phases of the policy cycle better than others. The convergence in comparative-politics and IR approaches to explaining agenda-setting and policy formation means that there is a common set of debates, if not a single analytical approach. Comparative-politics approaches are better suited to explaining EU-level executive decision-making and the politics of the EP, but insights from IR, albeit accommodating the highly institutionalized nature of the EU, are more useful when trying to understand decision-making in the Council. The first stage of policy implementation within the EU (transposition) is better illuminated by IR approaches, although how the policies are actually translated into practice is the purview of comparative politics, even if the existing literature is rather underdeveloped, with the notable exception of judicial politics. Comparative politics also provides the most extensive discussion of the dynamics of policy feedback. Thus, which sub-discipline is more appropriate depends on what one is trying to explain. Crucially, moreover, there are lively debates within each sub-discipline—primarily between rationalism and constructivism—about how policies are made.

Despite the need to tailor analytical tools to subjects of inquiry, several general implications can be drawn from the preceding discussion. First, every aspect of policy-making is contestable, from whether a condition is a problem that needs to be addressed, to how it might be addressed, to how it will be addressed, to how that decision will be carried out, and to whether that choice should be revisited. Secondly, therefore, attention to actors is essential: agency is central to policy-making. Thirdly, ideas matter: what actors want is shaped by ideas, at the very least in the sense of ends–means understandings, and actors use ideas to pursue their objectives by trying to persuade others. Fourthly, institutional settings at the very least have implications for which actors are most likely to prevail and arguably shape what those actors want. Consequently, this chapter helps to explain why policy-making in the EU varies across issue areas.

NOTES

1   I would like to thank Mark Pollack and Helen Wallace for comments on earlier versions of this chapter.

2   Drawing on both comparative politics and international relations approaches to explain policy-making is a strong, if largely implicit, theme of Moran *et al.* (2006).

3   In his 1972 article, Lowi includes a fourth type of policy 'constituent', which includes setting up new agencies (propaganda) but this is less commonly used.

4   Sabatier and Jenkins-Smith (1993: 17) use the term 'policy subsystem' to capture the same political phenomenon.

5   This inference, however, is based on the analysis of only roll-call votes, which are used only about one-third of the time, and on inferring MEPs' ideological preferences from specific votes, which might be strategic or contingent (McElroy 2007: 180).

6   For a fuller discussion of the literature, see Hayes-Renshaw and Wallace (2006: 314–17).

7   In the context of external policies, implementation often means getting others to accept the EU's preferences (as in multilateral trade or environmental agreements) or change their behaviour in line with the EU's preferences (as with regard to human rights). The EU's ability to influence others, which Laatikainen and Smith (2006) have dubbed its 'external effective-ness', has received relatively little scholarly attention (Jørgensen 2007), except with regard to its 'near abroad' (see Chapter 17).

8   Although these authors are formally discussing 'institutions', their definitions cover most policies except one-off decisions (Streeck and Thelen 2005: 10; Hall and Thelen 2009: 3).

FURTHER READING

Moran *et al.* (2006) provide an extensive overview of the analysis of public policy-making in general. With respect to agenda-setting in the EU, see Peters (1994). For a sympathetic discussion of the policy network literature in the EU, see Peterson (2004). Zito (2001) provides a nice case study of an epistemic community's impact on EU policy-making. For an overview of lobbying in the EU, see Coen and Richardson (2009). On voting behaviour in the EP, see Hix *et al.* (2007) and McElroy (2007); and on decision-making in the Council, see Hayes-Renshaw and Wallace (2006) and Golub (2012). For a review of the literature on implementation in the EU, see Treib (2008) and Sedelmeier (2012). On judicial politics in the EU, see Conant (2007). On political feedback loops in general, see Hall and Thelen (2009) and Streeck and Thelen (2005).

Coen, D., and Richardson, J. (2009) (eds.), *Lobbying the European Union: Institutions, Actors, and Issues* (Oxford: Oxford University Press).

Conant, L. (2007), 'Review Article: The Politics of Legal Integration', *Journal of Common Market Studies*, 45/1: 45–66.

Golub, J. (2012), 'How the European Union Does Not Work: National Bargaining Success in the Council of Ministers', *Journal of European Public Policy*, 19/9: 1294–1315.

Hall, P. A., and Thelen, K. (2009), 'Institutional Change in Varieties of Capitalism', *Socio-Economic Review*, 7/1: 7–34.

Hayes-Renshaw, F., and Wallace, H. (2006), *The Council of Ministers*, 2nd edn. (Basingstoke: Palgrave Macmillan).

Hix, S., Noury, A., and Roland, G. (2007), *Democratic Politics in the European Parliament* (Cambridge: Cambridge University Press).

McElroy, G. (2007), 'Legislative Politics', in K. E. Jørgensen, M. A. Pollack, and
   B. Rosamond (eds.), *The Handbook of European Union Politics* (London: Sage), 175–94.

Moran, M., Rein, M., and Goodin, R. E. (2006) (eds.), *The Oxford Handbook of Public
   Policy* (Oxford: Oxford University Press).

Peters, B. G. (1994), 'Agenda-Setting in the European Community', *Journal of European
   Public Policy*, 1/1: 9–26.

Peterson, J. (2004), 'Policy Networks', in A. Wiener and T. Diez (eds.), *European
   Integration Theory* (Oxford: Oxford University Press), 117–35.

Sedelmeier, U. (2012), 'Europeanization', in E. Jones, A. Menon, and S. Weatherill (eds.),
   The Oxford Handbook of the European Union (Oxford: Oxford University Press),
   825–39.

Streeck, W., and Thelen, K. (2005), 'Introduction: Institutional Change in Advanced
   Political Economies', in W. Streek and K. Thelen (eds.), *Beyond Continuity: Institutional
   Change in Advanced Political Economies* (Oxford: Oxford University Press), 1–39.

Treib, O. (2008), 'Implementing and Complying with EU Governance Outputs', *Living
   Reviews in European Governance,* 3/5, available on *http://www.livingreviews.org/lreg-
   2008-5.*

Zito, A. R. (2001), 'Epistemic Communities, Collective Entrepreneurship and European
   Integration', *Journal of European Public Policy*, 8/4: 585–603.

CHAPTER 4

An Institutional Anatomy and Five Policy Modes

Helen Wallace and Christine Reh

▌ Summary

By introducing the European Union's (EU's) institutional design and by explaining how the EU's and national institutions interact in five different policy modes, this chapter sets the stage for the subsequent studies of individual policy areas. In a first step, we discuss the evolving role and internal functioning of the European Commission, Council of the EU, European Council, European Parliament (EP), and Court of Justice of the European Union (CJEU). Given their importance in the EU policy process, we also look at quasi-autonomous agencies—in particular the European Central Bank (ECB)—at institutionalized control and scrutiny, and at non-state actors. The EU is part of, and not separate from, the politics of its member states, and features of the national processes pervade EU policies and the way in which they are applied. Our discussion therefore includes the relevant national and sub-national (i.e. regional and local) institutions. EU and national institutions interact differently in different policy domains. We identify five

(continued...)

EU policy modes—the classical Community method; the EU regulatory mode; the EU distributional mode; the policy coordination mode; and intensive transgovernmental-ism—that capture these different patterns of interaction and we analyse their variation and strength across the EU's policies and history.

The institutional design of the European Union

The EU has grown out of three originally separate Communities: the European Coal and Steel Community (ECSC), the European Economic Community (EEC), and Euratom, each with its own institutions.[1] These were formally merged in 1967. The main elements originally consisted of: a collective executive of sorts—the European Commission; a collective forum for representatives of member governments—the Council of the EU (often known as the Council of Ministers); a mechanism for bind-ing arbitration and legal interpretation—the CJEU (originally the European Court of Justice); and a parliamentary chamber—the EP (originally the 'Assembly'), with members initially drawn from the political classes of the member states, and later by direct election. In addition the Economic and Social Committee (ESC) provided a forum for consulting other sectors of society; since the 1990s, the Committee of the Regions (CoR) has allowed for consultation with local and regional authorities. The powers and responsibilities of these institutions are set out in the treaties, and have been periodically revised (see Table 1.1), latterly with increasing contention.

In the 1990s, the European Community (EC) became the European Union, a term which serves two different purposes. One is to imply a stronger binding together of the member states. The other is to embrace within a single frame-work the different Communities and the other arenas of cooperation that have emerged, in particular the two 'intergovernmental pillars' of the Treaty on Euro-pean Union (TEU): the 'second pillar' for common foreign and security policy (CFSP; see Chapter 18); and the 'third pillar' for justice and home affairs (JHA; see Chapter 15). The Treaty of Lisbon (ToL), which entered into force on 1 De-cember 2009, has drawn these pillars within a more unified framework, although foreign policy in particular retains its institutional and procedural idiosyncrasies. The relative powers of and relationships among the Commission, Council, and EP have changed a good deal across the years. This is the case in particular under leg-islative co-decision (formally called the 'ordinary legislative procedure'), where Council and Parliament have to cooperate closely and need to agree in order to adopt new law. The key elements of the EU's institutional system follow—readers already familiar with these can move on to the subsequent section on the EU's five policy modes.

The European Commission

The Commission is both the EU's secretariat and proto-executive. In its earliest version, as the High Authority of the ECSC (agreed in 1951), it leaned more towards being executive in nature, with considerable autonomy. This experiment generated the term 'supranational'. When the EEC was created in 1958, some member governments had second thoughts about the consequences of creating a strong autonomous institution, thus altering the 'balance' between the Commission and the Council, and giving the Commission differing powers across policy areas. The onus was left on the Commission itself to develop credibility, expertise, and a political power base of its own.

The Commission exercises its responsibilities collectively, in that the commissioners, from 2007 one from each of the now twenty-eight member states, constitute a 'college'. Although the EU's enlargement risked producing too large and too segmented a college, and although the ToL would have allowed a reduction in size to two-thirds of the member states on a rotation system, the European Council in May 2013 decided against downsizing the college. Commission decisions and legislative proposals have to be agreed by the entire college, voting, if necessary but rarely, by simple majority, at its weekly meetings. The Commission is chaired by a president, chosen by qualified majority vote (QMV) in the European Council and subject to approval by the EP. The ToL requires the European Council to take the results of the EP elections into account when deciding on their nomination. This change involved the Parliament's political groups more closely in the contest, as demonstrated by the (online) primaries and party conventions held between November 2013 and March 2014, and by the politics leading to the appointment of Jean-Claude Juncker as Commission president.

In the 2009–14 Commission, eight other commissioners acted as vice-presidents. Commissioners, each responsible for a policy portfolio, are nominated by member governments, endorsed by the Council, and subject to approval by the EP as a body, which can lead to names being withdrawn. Those chosen are senior politicians or high officials from member states, but they swear an oath of independence on taking office for a five-year term to coincide with that of the EP. The college of commissioners is accountable to the EP, which has the power to censure the college with a two-thirds vote. In March 1999, the college, presided over by Jacques Santer, was forced into resignation by the EP on a charge of financial mismanagement (see Chapter 9).

The Commission is organized into directorates-general (DGs), named after their main areas of policy activity; new DGs have been added, not always tidily, as new member states joined and as new policy powers have been assigned to the EU. In 2011, the Commission's External Relations and Development DGs were integrated into the newly created European External Action Service (EEAS). This entailed moving some 1,600 permanent staff to the functionally autonomous 'diplomatic service', which also runs the 137 EU delegations in third countries (Dinan 2011). Specialist services—most importantly the Legal Service, and the linguistic and statistical services—provide particular expertise.[2] Table 4.1 illustrates the structure under the second Barroso Commission (2009–14).

TABLE 4.1 The organization of the European Commission, 2013

Commissioner and area of responsibility	Established staff
President	
Cabinets (CA)	500
Secretariat General (SG)	460
Bureau of European Policy Advisers (BEPA)	33
Legal Service (SJ)	381
Spokespeople's Service (see DG COMM)[a]	
Vice-President and High Representative of the Union for foreign affairs and security policy	
Supported by the European External Action Service (EEAS). This incorporated staff of DG RELEX and external delegations (permanent staff nos. c. 1,643, plus c. 1,968 other staff). Also includes a new service for foreign policy instruments (FPI).	
Vice-President: justice, fundamental rights and citizenship	
Justice DG JUST	312
Communications DG COMM and Spokespeople's Service[a]	621
Publications Office (OP)	629
Vice-President: competition	
DG COMP	721
Vice-President: transport	
Mobility and transport DG MOVE	431
Vice-President: digital agenda	
DG CNECT (previously INFSO)	810
Vice-President: enterprise and industry	
DG ENTR	760
Vice-President: inter-institutional relations and administration	
Human resources and security DG HR	598
Informatics DG DIGIT	451
Infrastructure and Logistics DG Bx (OIB)	362
Lux (OIL)	111
Office for Administration and Payment (PMO)	168
European Personnel Selection Office (EPSO)	111
Staff Committee	36
Vice-President: economic and monetary affairs and the euro	
Economic and Financial Affairs DG ECFIN	650
Statistical Office Eurostat (ESTAT)	608
Commissioner: home affairs	
DG HOME	261
Commissioner: energy	
DG ENER	492
Commissioner: climate action	
DG CLIMA	137

Continued

TABLE 4.1 (Continued)

Commissioner: agriculture and rural development DG AGRI	932
Commissioner: maritime affairs and fisheries DG MARE	290
Commissioner: internal market and services DG MARKT	489
Commissioner: taxation, customs union, statistics, audit and anti-fraud Taxation and customs union DG TAXUD European Anti-Fraud Office (OLAF) Internal Audit Service (IAS)	 422 345 99
Commissioner: research, innovation and science Research and innovation DG RTD Joint Research Centre (JRC)	 1,126 1,802
Commissioner: education, culture, multilingualism, and youth Education and culture DG EAC Translation DGT Interpretation DG SCIC	 471 2,264 758
Commissioner: environment DG ENV	450
Commissioner: health Health side of DG SANCO[b]	[738]
Commissioner: consumer policy Consumer side of DG SANCO[b]	[738]
Commissioner: financial programming and budget DG BUDG	400
Commissioner: employment, social policy and inclusion DG EMPL	686
Commissioner: regional policy DG REGIO	561
Commissioner: trade DG TRADE	537
Commissioner: enlargement and ENP DG ELARG (taking some ex-DG RELEX staff) and EuropeAid (AIDCO)[c] work on neighbourhood policy (ENP)	274
Commissioner: development DG DEVCO and draws on part of EuropeAid (AIDCO)[c]	 1,187
Commissioner: international cooperation, humanitarian aid and crisis response DG ECHO	209
Total established staff temporary staff	23,703 1,043

contractual agents	5,903
national experts	1,118
special advisers	64
local agents	1,978

Source: Compiled by the authors from Commission website pages; NB totals from different sources vary slightly.

Notes:
[a] The Commission spokespeople act under the authority of the president. The spokespeople's service is attached to DG COMM.
[b] DG SANCO, with 738 total staff, provides services for both commissioners.
[c] AIDCO provides services for both commissioners.

The staffs of the DGs form the European civil service, recruited mostly in competitions across the member states, and supplemented by seconded national experts and temporary staff. Since May 2004, the emphasis has been on recruiting from the newer member states. The powers and 'personalities' of the DGs vary a good deal, as do their relationships with 'their' commissioners, which matters for the potential of political leadership. The commissioners have their own private offices, or *cabinets*, composed of appointed officials who act as their eyes, ears, and voices, inside the 'house' and vis-à-vis other institutions, including those of the member states. One DG leads on each policy topic, as *chef de file*, but most policy issues require coordination between several DGs, sometimes masterminded by the Secretariat-General and often by the *cabinets*. Though the Commission is supposed to operate collectively, in practice there are sometimes internal disagreements.

The Commission's powers vary a good deal between policy domains. In competition policy it operates many of the rules directly (see Chapter 6). In many domains the Commission is the agenda-setter: it proposes legislation, which then has to be negotiated and approved by the Council and the EP (see e.g. Chapters 5, 8, and 13). The Commission defines, in consultation with the member governments, the ways in which spending programmes operate, and it monitors national implementation of EU rules and programmes. In external economic relations it generally negotiates on behalf of the EU (see Chapter 16). In areas of policy coordination it develops cross-EU expertise to compare and coordinate national policies (see examples in Chapters 11 and 15). In intergovernmental areas the Commission is a more passive observer of member states' cooperation (see examples in Chapters 15 and 18). Recent enlargement has increased the Commission's workload overall and made the process more anglophone.

Within the classical areas of Union cooperation the Commission has a jealously guarded power of initiative through which it seeks to set the agenda (see Chapter 3). As the agenda-setter it is a target for everyone who wants to influence the content of policy (Coen and Katsaitis 2013). However, outside these areas the Commission is less entrepreneurial, either because it is not able to exploit the opportunities available to it, or because the policy regime allows less room for the Commission to play a central role. A key question is therefore how the Commission exploits its resources: the ability to build up expertise; the potential for developing policy networks and coalitions; the scope for acquiring grateful or dependent clients; the opportunity to broker legislative compromise between Council and Parliament; and the chance to help governments to resolve their own policy predicaments. This question is the subject of debate in the theoretical literature, and is addressed throughout the case studies in this volume.

In addition, there is a broader problem of capacity. The Commission is a quite small institution, with only some 23,700 or so staff in 2013 (with 10,000 more on non-tenured contracts), not very many to develop or implement policies across twenty-eight different countries. Hence, a great deal depends on how the Commission works with national institutions, which in practice implement most Union rules and programmes. Over the years this feature of the policy process has become more explicit, as several of our case studies illustrate (see e.g. Chapters 6, 10, and 12).

Partnership between the national and the European levels of governance has become one of the marked features of EU policy-making, especially when it comes to preparing and implementing legislation. One key mechanism for this is the clumsily named system of 'comitology', a dense network of committees that provides regular channels for consultation, cooperation, and control between the Commission and relevant national officials. Most of the committees are governed by legally specified arrangements, which vary according to the policy, and which strike different balances of influence between national representatives and the Commission. Insights into the workings of these committees appear in several of our case studies (see e.g. Chapters 6 and 16). Following the EP's long-standing demand to be more closely involved in monitoring the Commission's implementing powers, the ToL introduced the new category of 'delegated acts'; here, the Commission is directly scrutinized by Council and Parliament without the involvement of comitology committees. How to control the Commission's implementing powers—often enabling it to add decisive detail to EU legislation—has thus been subject to intense procedural, legal, and political battles which are likely to continue in the future (Christiansen and Dobbels 2013).

The Commission has had several high points of political impact, especially in the early 1960s (developing the common agricultural policy) and the mid-1980s (developing the single European market), under the leadership of Walter Hallstein and Jacques Delors, respectively. It has also had low points, after the 1965–6 Luxembourg crisis (when President de Gaulle withdrew French ministers from Council meetings), in the late 1970s, and the late 1990s, when the Santer Commission was forced to resign. More recently, and responding to public criticisms, the Prodi Commission (1999–2004) embarked on an administrative reform programme, and the first Barroso Commission (2004–9) came into office pledging to improve the performance of the Commission by doing 'less but better'. Compared with its heydays, the Commission's influence is in decline, strongly contrasting with both the EP's empowerment since the early 1990s and the European Council's prominence since the onset of the euro area crisis. The Commission has also been the subject of criticism, as regards weak internal management and coordination, overstretched staff, and lacklustre leadership, not least during and since the global financial crisis. The Commission faces a challenge because it needs to compete for influence with other EU institutions and the member governments, but also due to its dual role—as secretariat on the one hand, as proto-executive and as legislative agenda-setter on the other. Tensions between these more technical and more political roles may well increase following the 2014 European elections.

The Council of the European Union

The Council is both an institution with collective functions and the creature of the member governments. In principle and in law there is only one Council, empowered to take decisions on any topic, though its structures are more complex (see Figure 4.1). Its members are usually ministers from incumbent governments in the

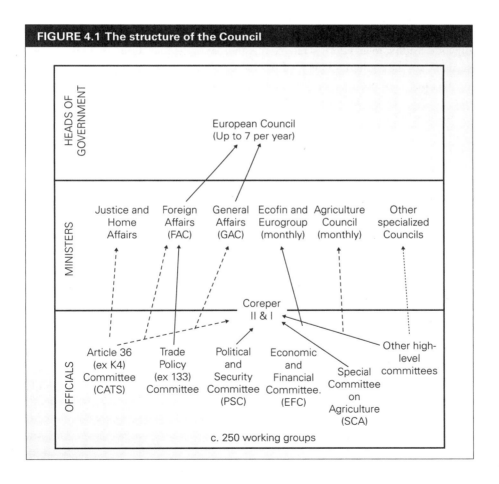

FIGURE 4.1 The structure of the Council

member states, but which ministers attend meetings depends on the subjects being discussed, and on how individual governments choose to be represented. Time and practice have sorted this out by the Council developing specialized configurations according to policy domains, each with its own culture of cooperation.

Historically foreign ministers comprised the senior configuration of the Council, reflecting their prominence as coordinators inside the member governments. However, in practice foreign ministers cannot always arbitrate, and since the onset of the euro area crisis in particular prime ministers have become much more involved at home and through the European Council. Replacing the General Affairs and External Relations Council (GAERC), post-Lisbon, the General Affairs Council (GAC) handles coordination across internal policies while the Foreign Affairs Council (FAC) deals with external policies and is usually chaired by the High Representative of the Union for Foreign Affairs and Security Policy (HR/VP). As economic and monetary union (EMU) has taken shape—and subsequently run into crisis—so the Council of Ministers for Economic and Financial Affairs (Ecofin), as well as the more informal Eurogroup, have grown in importance (see Chapter 7). With new policy areas, corresponding formations of the Council develop—JHA is a striking example (see Chapter 15). The multiplication of Council configurations has bred criticism about the fragmentation of work, leading to an effort to reduce the number of distinct configurations. Box 4.1 summarizes the configurations as of 2014 and their patterns of activity.

Meetings of ministers are prepared by national officials in committees and working groups. Traditionally the most important of these has been the Committee of Permanent Representatives (Coreper), composed of the heads (Coreper II) and deputies (Coreper I) of the member states' permanent representations in Brussels. These meet at least weekly to agree items on the Council agenda and to identify those that need to be discussed (and not merely endorsed) by ministers. In some other policy domains (trade, agriculture, EMU, JHA, CFSP) similar senior committees of national officials prepare many of the ministerial meetings; often they act as the main decision-makers.

The permanent representations collectively contain some 2,000 national officials, whose job is to follow the main subjects being negotiated in the Council, to maintain links with all the other EU institutions, and to keep in close touch with national capitals. Numerous (150 or so) working groups constitute the backbone of the Council and do the detailed negotiation of policy. Their members come from the permanent representations or national capitals—practice varies. Historically, something like 70 per cent of Council texts are said to be agreed in working groups, another 10–15 per cent in Coreper or other senior committees, leaving 10–15 per cent, the more controversial issues, to the ministers themselves. These patterns mirror the normal practice in a national government, where typically national cabinet meetings are prepared by committees of officials. Recent data suggest that decisions are shifting upwards, with around 30–40 per cent agreed in working groups, 20 per cent in senior committees, and ministers resolving the remaining issues (Naurin *et al*. forthcoming).

BOX 4.1   **Council configurations**

The Council is in law a single entity, irrespective of which ministers take part in it. It developed several specialized formations reflecting the growth of policy activities and with varying frequencies of meetings. This led to a highly segmented structure, with over twenty formations in the 1990s. From 2000 onwards efforts were made to streamline the Council into first sixteen, and then nine, configurations. However, some of these in practice meet in several parts. As of 2014, the configurations were as follows, numbers of meetings in 2012, 2008, and 2004 in brackets:

General Affairs and External Relations (GAERC), subdivided from 2012 into GAC and FAC

- general affairs, and coordination (GAC) (2012: 11, 2008: 12, 2004: 10)

- external relations/foreign affairs (FAC) (2012: 13 (inc. 2 trade and 1 development), 2008: 12, 2004: 9), plus 2 official and 2 informal meetings of defence ministers in 2012: 1 and 2 respectively in 2008

Economic and Financial Affairs (Ecofin)

- economics and finance (2012: 11, 2008: 11 (1 as heads of government), 2004: 9 (usually back-to-back with Eurogroup meetings)

- budget (2012: 1, 2008: 2, 2004: 2)

Agriculture and Fisheries (2012: 11, 2008: 12, 2004: 9)

Justice and Home Affairs (JHA) (2012: 5, 2008: 7, 2004: 9)

Competitiveness (internal market, industry, research) (2012: 4, 2008: 4, 2004: 7)

Transport, Telecommunications and Energy (TTE) (2012: 7, 2008: 7, 2004: 5)

Environment (2012: 4, 2008: 3, 2004: 3)

Employment, Social Policy, Health and Consumer Affairs (EPSCO) (2012: 4, 2008: 4, 2004: 4)

Education, Youth and Culture (EYC) (2012: 3, 2008: 3, 2004: 3)

The *European Council* met six times in 2012, five times formally in 2008 (seven times in 2004), once informally, and heads of government of Eurogroup countries met twice, also with the UK.

National governments work in parallel to the Council (Bulmer and Lequesne 2012). National officials follow each level of Council discussion and each area of Council debate, preparing ministerial positions and coordinating national policies. Ministers are involved in much of this work; how and when depends on national practices and on the degree of political salience. Much of this involvement is at the level of individual ministries, often in consultation with central, regional, or local government, public agencies, and relevant private-sector or non-governmental organizations (NGOs). Aggregating national positions is the responsibility of the coordinating units in each member government. Here again, practices vary between countries. A comprehensive view of how the Council works thus needs to recognize the continuous but varying engagement of national administrations.

What does the Council do in its various configurations? Mostly it negotiates detailed proposals for EU action, very often on the basis of a draft from the Commission. Often the Council will have indicated earlier to the Commission that it would welcome a proposal on a particular subject. On most issues the EP now co-legislates with the Council (see the section 'The European Parliament' later in the chapter). In these areas the outcome depends on the interactions among the three institutions, and on the way in which coalitions emerge within and between Council and Parliament in particular.

In the two sensitive areas of foreign and home affairs, the Council has traditionally dominated policy-making and relied heavily on its own General Secretariat to do so. Facilitator of collective decisions, institutional memory, and legal service, the Secretariat was considerably expanded after the Treaty of Amsterdam to deal with JHA and to support the newly created 'Mr/s CFSP', who originally doubled as the Council's Secretary General (see Chapter 18). Since the establishment of the European security and defence policy (ESDP) in 1999, the Council Secretariat also houses military staff seconded from the member states.

The ToL modified this arrangement in two ways. First, JHA agenda-setting and decision-making has been 'normalized', with much more prominent roles for Commission and Parliament. Secondly, foreign policy-making, previously split between the Commission's DG for external relations and the Council Secretariat, moved to the EEAS under the leadership of the High Representative who doubles as a Commission vice-president. In spite of its expertise and key role in supporting the Council presidency (see the next section), expectations that the Secretariat would become an influential policy actor in its own right have not been fulfilled.

Many of the proceedings of the Council are managed by its presidency (Tallberg 2006, 2008). This rotates among member governments every six months, although the ToL formalizes the cooperation among member-state 'trios' (Batory and Puetter 2013). The Council presidency chairs meetings at most levels of ministers and officials. A small number of important committees—such as the European Union Military Committee (EUMC) and the Economic and Financial Committee (EFC)—have elected chairs, as does the Eurogroup of finance ministers. The Foreign Affairs Council is usually chaired by the High Representative, who also now appoints a member of the EEAS as chair of the Political and Security Committee (PSC). In most areas, however, the rotating presidency prepares the agenda and conducts the meetings; it also speaks on behalf of the Council in discussions with other EU institutions and with outside partners on issues other than CFSP. Often the Council and the Commission presidencies have to work closely together, for example in external negotiations where policy powers are divided between the EU and the national levels, such as climate change policy. Under legislative co-decision, the presidency negotiates with the EP delegation to reconcile Council and parliamentary views. A recurrent question is whether individual presidencies try to impose their national preferences or whether the role pushes them towards identifying with collective EU interests (Tallberg 2006; Warntjen 2008).

The important point to bear in mind is that the Council is the EU institution that belongs to the member governments. It works the way it does, because that is the way that the governments prefer to manage their negotiations with each other. Regularity of contact and a pattern of socialization mean that the Council, and especially its specialist formations, develop a kind of insider amity. Sometimes clubs of ministers—in agriculture, in environment, and so forth—are able to use agreements in Brussels to force on their own governments commitments that might not otherwise have been accepted at the national level. Nonetheless, the ministers and officials who meet in the Council are servants of their governments, affiliated to national political parties, and accountable to national parliaments and electorates. Thus, generally their priority is to pursue whatever seems to be the preferred national policy.

The Council spends much of its time discussing the member governments' responses to Commission proposals. It does so through continuous negotiation, mostly by trying to establish a consensus (Novak 2013). Yet, the style of member-state negotiations varies, ranging from more bargaining to more deliberation (Puetter 2012). In some policy areas there are sharp disagreements and tough strategic bargaining, in particular when new regimes are at issue (see Chapters 7, 8, 9, 10, 15, 17, and 18). In other policy areas, as policy-making becomes more routine or where the issues are more technical, there is evidence of a more deliberative style, as is the case in early decision stages and, by necessity, under unanimity (see Chapters 5 and 13). The formal rules of decision-making also vary according to policy domain and over time—sometimes unanimity, mostly QMV, rarely simple majority. The decision rules are a subject of controversy and have been altered in successive treaty reforms, in particular under the Treaty of Nice (ToN) and the ToL to bring the voting weights more in line with population sizes. Broadly speaking, QMV has become the formal rule in areas where Community regimes are fairly well established, while unanimity is a requirement either in areas in which EU regimes are embryonic or in those domains where governments have tenaciously retained more control of the process. Since the ToL, an increasingly large proportion of Council decisions—as much as 96 per cent in 2010–12—is subject to the QMV rule (Naurin *et al.* forthcoming).

Yet, the formal decision rules only tell us part of the story of Council decision-making. In practice, habits of apparent consensus-seeking are deeply ingrained. This implies that explicit voting has been relatively rare, even when technically possible, because no member state contests the decision taken. The pattern that emerged from 1994 (the year voting records became publicly available) showed that only between 10 and 30 per cent of votes were explicitly contested. Yet, since 2008, and following the implementation of the ToL in particular, the level of consensus has decreased, and fell to below 60 per cent of decisions in 2012 (Naurin *et al.* forthcoming). Under QMV the knowledge that votes may be called often makes doubting governments focus on seeking amendments to meet their concerns, rather than on blocking progress altogether. Recent evidence suggests, however, that the QMV rule does not lead governments into making generous concessions to partners (Naurin *et al.* forthcoming). Formally registered 'no's' and abstentions often seem to be signals to domestic

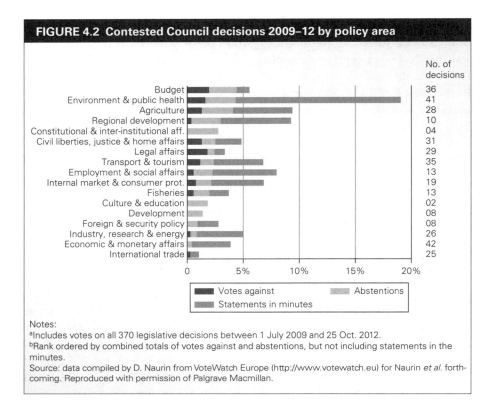

FIGURE 4.2 Contested Council decisions 2009–12 by policy area

	No. of decisions
Budget	36
Environment & public health	41
Agriculture	28
Regional development	10
Constitutional & inter-institutional aff.	04
Civil liberties, justice & home affairs	31
Legal affairs	29
Transport & tourism	35
Employment & social affairs	13
Internal market & consumer prot.	19
Fisheries	13
Culture & education	02
Development	08
Foreign & security policy	08
Industry, research & energy	26
Economic & monetary affairs	42
International trade	25

Legend: Votes against — Abstentions — Statements in minutes

Notes:
[a]Includes votes on all 370 legislative decisions between 1 July 2009 and 25 Oct. 2012.
[b]Rank ordered by combined totals of votes against and abstentions, but not including statements in the minutes.
Source: data compiled by D. Naurin from VoteWatch Europe (http://www.votewatch.eu) for Naurin *et al.* forthcoming. Reproduced with permission of Palgrave Macmillan.

constituencies, and statements recorded in the minutes also indicate reservations. Explicitly contested votes at ministerial level are concentrated in particular in policy areas with financial implications, especially in agriculture, regional development, and the budget. Among regulatory issues, environment and public health stand out as areas of contestation, followed by transport and tourism; and JHA is an increasingly contested area (see Figure 4.2). Under unanimity rules, governments have the opportunity to exercise blocking power until their views are accommodated, typically on major budgetary and spending decisions (see Chapters 9 and 10).

It is hard to track the patterns of alignments or 'coalitions' in the Council. Often governments share preferences for issue-specific reasons. There is, however, evidence of two recurrent cleavages: one between richer, more northern member governments and poorer, more southern and more eastern members; and the other between the more and the less market-minded governments (the former typically including the newer member governments). The evidence of a recurrent left/right cleavage is less clear in contrast to the strong pattern in the EP (see later in the chapter), although governments' positions do vary according to their party political affiliations. Figure 4.3 shows the pattern of contested decisions by member states.

The historic consensus culture and the absence of stable coalitions may partly explain the Council's ability to accommodate enlargement to the EU28 so well. Prior

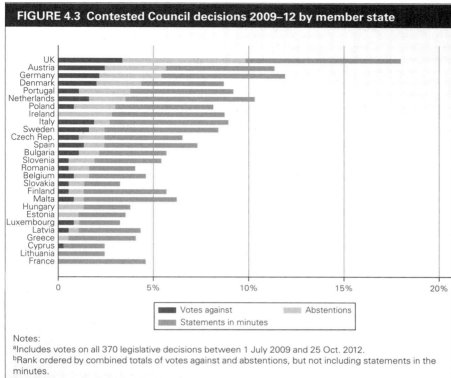

FIGURE 4.3 Contested Council decisions 2009–12 by member state

Legend:
- Votes against
- Abstentions
- Statements in minutes

Notes:
[a]Includes votes on all 370 legislative decisions between 1 July 2009 and 25 Oct. 2012.
[b]Rank ordered by combined totals of votes against and abstentions, but not including statements in the minutes.
Source: data compiled by D. Naurin from VoteWatch Europe (*http://www.votewatch.eu*) for Naurin *et al* (forthcoming). Reproduced with permission of Palgrave Macmillan.

to enlargement, concerns about an adverse impact on the Council abounded and the prognosis was gridlock. The early evidence simply did not support this—the Council worked much in the same way after enlargement as it did before (Best *et al.* 2008; H. Wallace 2007), with similar strengths and weaknesses. However, some of the case studies will show that the increased heterogeneity of preferences in the EU28 does complicate the Council's work (see Chapters 9, 13, 15, and 18). Also, as Figures 4.2 and 4.3 show, explicitly contested votes are increasing.

Two additional developments have further changed the Council's role in the EU's institutional system. First, the Council used to be the main legislator on EU policies. However, as the EP has acquired powers over legislation, the system has become more bicameral (Burns *et al.* 2013). Under the ordinary legislative procedure, still widely referred to as co-decision, the Council reaches 'common positions' which have to be reconciled with amendments to legislation proposed by members of the European Parliament (MEPs). Hence, the Council is now required to justify publicly and explicitly its collective preferences, an important change which is further strengthened by the ToL's requirement that the Council meet in public when acting in its legislative capacity.

The second development is that EMU and the euro area crisis in particular have changed the Council's policy priorities and working methods and channelled influence away from Ecofin towards the finance ministers from only euro area countries (known as the Eurogroup); the ECB, which controls the single currency; and the European Council, which is the new 'centre of political gravity' (Puetter 2012: 161). In the highly salient field of EMU, the Council thus increasingly coordinates policy rather than legislates, resorts to informal working methods, witnesses a sharper divide between euro 'ins' and euro 'outs', and is rivalled on both political agenda-setting and everyday decision-making by the European Council (see Chapter 7).

The European Council

The European Council began life in the occasional 'summit' meetings of heads of state (the Cypriot, French, Lithuanian, and Romanian presidents attend) or government (i.e. prime ministers); the Commission president is also a member and the HR/VP takes part in its work. Only the member-state representatives have a vote. Two especially important meetings, in The Hague in 1969 and Paris in 1972, were agenda-setters and package-makers for several succeeding years. From 1974 onwards, under the prompting of Valéry Giscard d'Estaing, then French president, European Councils were put on a regular footing, meeting at least three times a year. In each of 1999, 2002, 2008, 2010, and 2011, the European Council met seven times, and with the onset of the global financial crisis, formal and informal summits have become a regular and highly visible feature of EU policy-making. Successive treaty reforms have put the European Council on a more formal basis. Under the ToL the European Council has acquired a full-time President, chosen for a renewable term of two-and-a-half years. The first such President, former Belgian prime minister Herman Van Rompuy, prepared and chaired the summits and drafted conclusions; before Lisbon, these were the tasks of the rotating presidency. Donald Tusk succeeded him in 2014. Historically, one meeting of each semester was held in the country of the presidency, but under the terms of the ToN all sessions have been held in Brussels since the 2004 enlargement. By custom and practice, national delegations in the room are restricted to the president or prime minister as well as their foreign or finance ministers. Increasingly large cohorts of other ministers and officials have parallel meetings where the topics discussed depend on the preoccupations of the moment.

Conceived of initially as an informal 'fireside chat', the European Council became in the 1970s and 1980s a forum for resolving issues that departmental ministers could not agree, or that were subjects of disagreement within the member governments. By tradition it is the European Council that has been left to resolve the periodic major arguments about EU revenue and expenditure (see Chapters 9 and 10). In addition, from the negotiations over the Single European Act (SEA) in 1985 (see Chapter 5), the European Council has determined treaty reform in the closing stages of intergovernmental conferences (IGCs). More generally it is the venue for taking 'history-making decisions' (Peterson 1995), addressing the big and more strategic questions to do with the core new tasks of the EU and those that define its 'identity' as an arena for collective action. Some of our case studies, especially Chapters 5, 7, 9, 15, 17, and 18, record European Council pronouncements as the main staging posts in the development of policy. The level of activity has expanded, reflecting a sharply increasing concern on the part of the most senior national politicians to take control of the direction of the EU, including at the 'spring' summits that assess Europe's overall economic and social situation. Their offices have a direct electronic link (Primenet), and within their national settings prime ministers are strongly engaged in framing national policies on Europe.

Nowhere is this more obvious than in economic and financial governance. Here, the European Council—with the French and German voices particularly prominent—is the main crisis manager and the 'predominant player' (Puetter 2012: 168). Mirroring—and rivalling—the Eurogroup of finance ministers, the 2011 fiscal compact formalizes the 'euro summit', bringing together the euro area's heads of state and government as well as the Commission and ECB presidents under an elected chair; Herman Van Rompuy was the first to hold this post (see Chapter 7).

Overall, the European Council has thus come to exercise increasingly explicit and continuous political leadership in the EU policy process, by defining the direction of policy, by resolving controversy, and by managing the ongoing euro area crisis.

The European Parliament

Of the EU's institutions, the Parliament has changed most since the 1950s. Originally an 'Assembly' composed of national parliamentarians with few powers other than the ability to censure the Commission, the EP has been empowered to share genuinely legislative and budgetary authority with the Council, and it is an ever more audible voice in EU politics and policy-making. The EP has been directly elected since 1979 and—despite notoriously low voter turnout—it provides the Union with a source of democratic legitimacy that complements the Council's representation of member states and the Commission's guarding of the Community interest.

Since Croatia's accession in July 2013, the Seventh EP (2009–14) had 766 members, this number decreased to 751 after the 2014 elections. The EP is a multilingual parliament whose location, for reasons of member-state sensitivities, is divided among Luxembourg, Strasbourg, and Brussels. MEPs—ranging from ninety-six Germans to six Maltese—vary in their backgrounds; some have been national politicians, others bring different professional experience, and a few have made the EP their primary career. The EP is organized into political groups, each required to represent MEPs from at least one-quarter of the member states. The most important groups are the centre-right European People's Party (EPP), the centre-left Progressive Alliance of European Socialists and Democrats (S&D), and the liberal Alliance of Liberals and Democrats for Europe (ALDE). Smaller groups include coalitions of Green, far-right, far-left, and 'Eurosceptic' or nationalist MEPs. Political groups have gained in importance over time, with most MEPs voting along party rather than national lines (Hix *et al.* 2007). Much of the EP's work is carried out in its twenty specialist committees of between forty-seven (Legal Affairs) and one-hundred-forty-two (Foreign Affairs) MEPs. These committees have become increasingly adept at probing particular policy issues in detail, more so than in many national parliaments.

In the early years of integration, the EP had a marginal, merely consultative role in the policy process. During the 1970s, the EP gained important powers vis-à-vis the EU budget, and especially over some areas of expenditure (although, until the ToL, significantly not over most agricultural expenditure) (see Chapters 8 and 9). In the 1980s and 1990s, the role of the EP was transformed, as it acquired legislative powers in successive treaty reforms (see Chapter 5). These were rationalized under the ToL into: co-decision with the Council (formally the 'ordinary legislative procedure') across a wide range of policy domains, now including agriculture and JHA; consultation in those areas where member governments are wary of letting MEPs into the process, including internal market exemptions, competition law, and international agreements concluded under CFSP; and consent (formerly assent) on issues including enlargement and certain international agreements (see Box 4.2).

The EP's empowerment was, not least, won through inter-institutional battles with the Council in particular (Farrell and Héritier 2003; Hix 2002). Over time, however, relations between the two institutions have become increasingly cooperative. Co-decision is operating smoothly. Since the procedure's introduction in 1993, more than 1,200 legislative acts have been adopted, and very few of these go through the three possible readings and into 'conciliation', the mechanism for reconciling the Council's and Parliament's conflicting positions. Instead, the co-legislators make use of informal channels of cooperation and adopt most legislation at first reading (Reh *et al.* 2013). Given the increase in the number of Eurosceptic and populist MEPs following the May 2014 elections, the eighth EP will, in all likelihood, need to reply more on 'grand coalitions' between the centre-right and the centre-left in its day-to-day policy-making.

The net result of these changes is that the EP is a force to be reckoned with across a wide range of policy domains. On many areas of detailed rule-setting the EP has a real impact, as some of the case studies in this volume show, and therefore it too is the target of actors outside the institutions who seek to influence legislation (see e.g. Chapters 8, 13, and 15).

The EP's political role has increased too. Parliament acquired the right to approve the Commission as a whole in Maastricht, and to approve the Commission president in Amsterdam. In 1999, the EP gained greater political prominence as a result of provoking the resignation of the European Commission on the issue of financial mismanagement. In 2004, the EP delayed the installation of the new Commission, criticizing some proposed members. And in 2009, the EP chose to take its time endorsing the Commission president. The ToL requires the European Council to take the results of the EP elections into account when nominating the Commission president. In a characteristically expansive reading of the treaty, the Parliament and its 'Europarties' interpreted this provision as an invitation to nominate their own *Spitzenkandidaten* for the post: the Luxembourger Jean-Claude Junker (EPP);

BOX 4.2	Powers of the European Parliament

Consultation

A special legislative or non-legislative procedure under Article 289 TFEU. Commission proposals to Council are passed to EP for an opinion. EP may suggest alterations, delay passing a resolution to formalize its opinion, or refer matters back to its relevant committee(s).

Applies to: internal market exemptions, competition law, international agreements under CFSP, non-mandatory instruments.

Ordinary legislative procedure (Art. 294 TFEU)

The now standard bicameral legislative procedure in which the Council and EP adopt legislation by common agreement ('codecision'). Council and EP may both agree a proposal at first reading (close to 80 per cent in the Seventh EP). If they disagree at second reading, the EP may by an absolute majority reject the proposal, which then falls. Or the EP may amend the Council's common position by an absolute majority, in which case conciliation takes place between the Council (usually Coreper I) and the EP. The results of conciliation must be approved in third reading by both Council (QMV) and EP (majority of votes cast). Proposal falls if not agreed.

Applies since ToL to: most areas of legislation, unless otherwise specified as exempted, or falling under one of the other procedures.

Consent (formerly Assent)

A special legislative or non-legislative procedure under Article 289 TFEU. On certain issues the EP must, in a single vote, approve or reject legislation or agreements without the right to amend.

Applies to: association and trade agreements, enlargement treaties, withdrawal agreements, serious breach of fundamental rights, anti-discrimination, use of the subsidiary general legal basis under Article 352 TFEU.

Budget (Arts. 312–19 TFEU)

Parliament must give its consent, by a majority of its component members, to the multiannual financial framework (MFF). The EP may try to amend the annual budget, it must approve the budget as a whole, and it subsequently 'discharges' the accounts of the previous year's actual expenditure.

Installation of commissioners (Art. 17(7) TEU)

Since the ToA, the EP has had the right to approve nomination of the Commission president. Under the ToL, the European Council needs to take the outcome of EP elections into account when proposing a candidate. Parliament holds individual hearings with nominated commissioners and passes a vote to approve the whole college.

Censure of Commission (Art. 234 TFEU)

The EP may censure the college of commissioners by a two-thirds majority, representing a majority of its members.

the French–German duo José Bové and Ska Keller (Greens); the German Martin Schulz (S&D); the Greek Alexis Tsipras (Far Left); and the Belgian Guy Verhofstadt (ALDE). Following the 2014 elections and the emergence of the EPP as the strongest group in the incoming Parliament, this new process led to conflict between Europe's chancellors, prime ministers, and presidents, and between the European Council and the Parliament, over whether Jean-Claude Juncker as the centre-right's candidate should be 'automatically' nominated for the EU's top-executive post. The increased political standing of the EP, combined with its claims to legitimacy as the EU's only directly elected institution, has given Parliament significant influence over the policy process as a whole. This development, however, is not universally welcomed, and debates persist over whether parliamentary empowerment really is the most effective way to alleviate the EU's 'democratic deficit'.

The Court of Justice of the European Union

From the early days of integration, the rule of law has been critical in anchoring EU policy regimes. A legal system that ensures a high rate of compliance, authoritatively interprets disputed texts, and offers redress for those for whom the law was created, makes the EU process as a whole solid and predictable, and helps it to be sustained. The CJEU was established in the first treaty texts. It has played a crucial role in interpreting the incomplete contracts that are the EU's treaties, and its powers distinguish the EU from most international organizations. Through its case law, the court has undoubtedly been a motor of supranational integration, yet scholars continue to debate whether the court's power is an unintended consequence (Alter 1998), the result of judicial activism (Burley and Mattli 1993), or in line with member-state preferences (Garrett 1995).

The CJEU, sited in Luxembourg, is composed of twenty-eight judges, as well as nine advocates-general who deliver preliminary opinions on cases. The court provides an overarching framework of jurisprudence, and deals with litigation, both in cases referred via the national courts and those brought directly before it. The SEA in 1986 established a second court, the General Court (pre-Lisbon, Court of First Instance), composed now of twenty-eight judges, to help in handling the heavy flow of cases in certain specified areas, notably competition policy and intellectual property rights. There is also a European Union Civil Service Tribunal for staff cases. The courts' sanctions are mostly the force of their own rulings; they are implemented by national courts and administrations and are backed up in some instances by the court's ability to impose fines on the EU's institutions and member states or to provide a basis for the Commission or national authorities to fine those found to have broken EU law (usually companies). Moreover, as a result of its 1991 *Francovich* ruling, damages can be claimed against governments when they, national legislatures, or national courts fail to implement EU law correctly. The courts hear their cases in public, but reach their judgments in private by, if necessary, majority votes; the results of their votes are not made public, and minority opinions are not issued.

Since the early 1960s a series of key cases has established important principles of EU law. These include the direct effect of EU law in national legal orders (*Van Gend en Loos*); the supremacy of EU law over the law of the member states (*Costa v. ENEL*); requirements on EU institutions and states not to violate fundamental rights when acting within the scope of EU law (*Stauder*; *Internationale Handelsgesellschaft*); the principle of proportionality (*Fédération charbonnière de Belgique*; *Internationale Handelsgesellschaft*; *Fedesa*); mutual recognition (*Cassis de Dijon*); and non-discrimination on the basis of nationality among citizens of EU member states (*Sotgiu*). Such 'integration through law' (Cappelletti *et al.* 1986) has contributed decisively to the EU's constitutional development. The court's jurisprudence has periodically challenged member-state policies; and in some domains—notably citizenship, health, gender equality in the workplace, free movement of goods, and merger policy—court cases have been instrumental in establishing EU policy regimes (see Chapters 5, 6, and 11).

The Appendix (at the end of this volume) summarizes the pattern and volume of cases before the two courts. Collated specially for this volume, this thorough overview of cases by policy sector gives us a full picture of litigation. The caseload is impressive, with rising numbers across the years before both courts, though for our purposes the (high but decreasing) volume of EU staff cases should be discounted. There appears to be an increase in the number of cases following each enlargement of the EU. At the CJEU, agriculture is in 'gold medal' position cumulatively—not surprisingly given its preponderant volume of EU legislation—but in the 2002–11 period, agriculture has been overtaken by the areas of environment and consumers, freedom of establishment and services, and taxation. A different pattern characterizes the General Court, where agriculture takes 'silver' overall, and where the last decade has seen intellectual property, competition, and state aid dominate the new caseload. Further commentary on the roles of the courts follows in the case studies in this volume.

This strong legal dimension has a marked influence on the policy process. Policy-makers have to choose carefully between treaty articles in determining which legal base to use, to consider carefully which kind of legislation to make, and to pay great attention to the legal meaning of their texts. Policy advocates look for legal rules to achieve their objectives, because they know that these are favoured by the institutional system. Policy reformers can sometimes use cases to alter the impact of EU policies. There is also a general presumption that rules will be obeyed.

EU law comes in three main forms of legislation, as well as through the incorporation of international agreements: regulations are directly applicable within the member states once promulgated by the EU institutions; directives have to be transposed into national law, which gives member governments some flexibility; and decisions are more limited legal instruments applied to specific circumstances or specific addressees, as in competition policy (see Chapter 6). With legislative co-decision extended to most policy areas by the ToL, the Council and Parliament frequently act as joint decision-makers; yet, in clearly delimited areas, the Commission, the

Council, and the ECB each hold independent legislative powers. There has been an increase in the use of delegated acts by the Commission in areas other than agriculture, where this was long-established practice. All kinds of EU law are subject to challenge through the national and European courts.

The vigour of the European legal system is one of the most distinctive features of the EU. It has helped to reinforce the powers and reach of the EU process, although in recent years the CJEU has become a bit more cautious in its judgments. In some policy domains, however, member governments have gone to considerable lengths to limit the court's power, at least temporarily. Part of the reason for the TEU's three-pillar structure was to keep both CFSP and JHA out of the court's reach. Gradually incorporated into the supranational legal system since Amsterdam, JHA and Schengen have largely been brought within the court's jurisdiction by the ToL. Finally, the Charter of Fundamental Rights—proclaimed in 2000 and cited extensively by European and national courts since—adds an important new legal dimension. Since Lisbon, the Charter has been binding on the EU institutions and member states when acting within the scope of EU law. This draws the EU closer to the other European legal order, based on the European Convention on Human Rights attached to the Council of Europe. It is also an example of politics—and the treaties—gradually catching up with the court's much earlier jurisprudence.

The wider institutional setting

The EU institutional system includes a number of additional organizations that have an impact on, or provide instruments for, EU policies. Some provide autonomous operating arms; some provide control mechanisms; and some are consultative.

Agencies and banks

Mirroring a broader trend in national and global politics, the EU has seen a 'remarkable proliferation' of agencies since the 1990s (Rittberger and Wonka 2011b: 781). Agencies exercise specific delegated powers, to make governments' commitments more credible and to deal with complex policies more effectively. They are deliberately insulated from majoritarian politics.

The EU's oldest autonomous agency is the European Investment Bank (EIB), established in 1958. Operating like a private bank, with triple-A credit rating in money markets, the EIB generates loans for agreed investments in support of EU objectives, both within the EU and in associated third countries. Its work is coordinated with programmes directly administered by the Commission, such as the structural funds. In the 1990s, following the end of the cold war, a separate European Bank for Reconstruction and Development (EBRD) was established, with the reforming post-communist countries, other western states, and the EIB as shareholders. Responding to the Arab Spring in 2011, the shareholders extended the EBRD's mandate to the Middle East and North Africa (Hodson 2012).

More recently, the EU has contracted out regulatory and policy activities to three types of agencies. A first group of executive agencies administers one or more Commission programmes; examples include the Education, Audiovisual, and Culture Executive Agency (EACEA), and the Research Executive Agency (REA). A second group of more than thirty decentralized agencies handles regulatory functions, related in particular to policy implementation and coordination between the EU and national governments; these include the European Environment Agency (see Chapter 13), the European Food Safety Authority (EFSA) (see Chapter 8), Europol (see Chapter 15), and the European Agency for the Management of Operational Cooperation at the External Borders of the Members States of the European Union (Frontex) (see Chapter 15). A third group provides direct services for the EU institutions, such as the translation centre. There has been some discussion on whether this process could be taken even further, for example by setting up a European Competition Office clearly separate from the Commission or through networks of national regulators (see Chapters 6 and 14). The EU's 'agencification' (Pollack 2003) and the resulting fragmentation of policy-operation and programme delivery should also lead us to modify our notion of the European Commission as a centralized and centralizing policy executive.

Like the Commission itself, independent agencies face the key challenge of reconciling a technocratic mandate and political insulation with established standards of accountability and democratic legitimacy. Nowhere is this challenge more apparent than at Europe's most important autonomous operating agency: the ECB in Frankfurt (see Chapter 7). Established in 1998, the ECB defines and implements the euro area's monetary policy. Its 'primary objective' is to 'maintain price stability' (as defined by the Bank itself); 'without prejudice' to this task, it shall also 'support the general economic policies in the Community' (Art. 127 TFEU). The ECB sets the short-term interest rate for the euro area; it conducts exchange-rate policy jointly with Ecofin; and, following the global financial crisis, it has taken on a more prominent role in financial supervision, first in the European Systemic Risk Board (ESRB), established in 2010, and subsequently in the more supranational Single Supervisory Mechanism (SSM) agreed by the EP and Council in 2013 (see Box 5.3).

The ECB is organized through three decision-making bodies: (1) the Executive Board, composed of six members serving eight-year non-renewable terms of office, runs the Bank under the chairmanship of its president; (2) the Governing Council, composed of the Executive Board plus the euro area's central bank governors, formulates monetary policy; and (3) the General Council, comprising the ECB president and vice-president as well as the EU's twenty-eight central bank governors was originally designed as a transitional body but has assumed an important advisory role on financial supervision during the euro area crisis (see Chapter 7).

The ECB faces a number of well-known challenges: a 'committee-based approach' to policy-making (Hodson 2012: 211); political rows over appointments (see Chapter 7); the need to reconcile supranational and national interests when choosing the best suited monetary instruments in response to the euro area crisis; and the challenge of conducting supranational monetary policy while fiscal policy remains national. Yet, as the previous discussion demonstrates, the ECB also occupies a unique position in the EU's institutional system. It has complete control over the formulation and implementation of an entire policy; it directly and formally involves national institutions in its decision-making; it enjoys exceptional independence; and it not only accommodates the supranational and the national levels, but also brings together the 'ins' and 'outs' of the euro area. Finally, its role as a crisis manager—together with the European Council, the Commission, and the International Monetary Fund (IMF)—in the EU's most salient policy area has attracted a degree of political and media attention which is unusual for an agency.

Control and scrutiny

In the mid-1970s, concern started to be voiced that the EU policy process was subject to few external controls. At the time, the EP had limited powers, and national parliaments paid relatively little attention to EU legislation and programmes. It was the growing scale and scope of the EU budget and spending programmes that spearheaded the arguments about the inadequacy of scrutiny.

This led to the creation of the European Court of Auditors by the 1975 Budget Treaty. Since 1978 the court has, from its seat in Luxembourg, endeavoured to evaluate systematically the EU's revenue-raising and spending (see Chapter 9). Both in its annual reports and in specific reports, it has drawn attention to various weaknesses in the budgetary process, handled by the Commission and national agencies (which disburse around four-fifths of EU budgetary expenditure). Many of its criticisms fell for many years on deaf ears—member governments that were reluctant to face up to some of the issues, an EP that had other preoccupations, and a Commission which repeatedly undervalued the importance of sound financial management. In late 1998, this situation was somewhat reversed by the row over the Commission's alleged financial mismanagement.

The European Ombudsman, created in 1992 and attached to the EP, provides for another new instrument of post hoc control. The aim, borrowed from Nordic practice, is to provide a channel for dealing with cases of alleged maladministration by EU institutions. In 2012, a record 465 cases were opened. The office has been responsible for modest improvements in the operations of the policy process at the micro level.

Finally, some policy control and scrutiny depends on national institutions. Until the early 1990s, national parliaments had no official recognition in the EU institutional system. Each member state had developed its own, mostly rather limited, procedures for national parliamentary scrutiny of EU policy (Raunio 2005), and the same discontent that had led to some strengthening of European procedures started to provoke domestic debates. Both the TEU and the ToA mention the importance of encouraging national scrutiny, and the ToL allows a minimum number of at least one-third of national parliaments to hold up a 'yellow card' to Commission proposals judged to violate subsidiarity, and, as such, to impinge on national prerogatives

(Cooper 2012). Furthermore, given the heightened sensitivity to country-level pre-occupations, EU-level policy-makers, especially in the Commission, are under pressure to pay increased attention to national parliamentary discussions and appear more readily before parliamentary committees of inquiry. Indeed, national parliaments from all member states have established offices in the EP in Brussels to track EU policy. Some see more cooperation between the EP and national parliaments as promising; others argue that to date experience, for example through the Conference of Parliamentary Committees for Union Affairs of Parliaments of the European Union (COSAC), which twice a year brings together national and Euro-parliamentarians, has been disappointing.

Consultation and lobbying

The founding treaties established the Economic and Social Committee (ESC) (and the Consultative Committee for the ECSC), as a point of access to the policy process for socio-economic groups. Its creation borrowed from the corporatist traditions in some of the founder member countries, but it has not become influential. Instead socio-economic groups have found their own more direct points of access since the 1960s, through EU-level federal associations, through sector-specific trade and producer organizations, and as individual large firms (Coen and Richardson 2009). Interest-group activity intensified in the 1980s around the development of the single market. A more recent development has been the increased activity of public-interest groups and lobbies representing consumers, environmentalists, women, as well as an increasing range of advocacy groups and NGOs. Our case studies offer many illustrations of the activities of these different kinds of groups (see also Table 4.2). This growth of interest-group activity has not been uncontested. The Commission's and Parliament's joint Transparency Register, launched in 2011, is a first attempt to regulate Brussels lobbying—if falling well short of a comprehensive 'legislative footprint'.

The TEU introduced a second consultative body, the Committee of the Regions (CoR), in response to the extensive involvement of local and regional authorities in seeking to influence those EU policies that impacted on them. The CoR provides regional and local politicians from the member states with a multilateral forum, and an opportunity to enhance their local political credibility. At least as important, however, is the direct lobbying by local and regional authorities, many with their own offices in Brussels. These same sub-national authorities also engage in efforts to influence national policy positions and the implementation of Union programmes. Chapter 10 comments on this in relation to the structural funds.

National institutions

The EU and its member states form a multi-level system, and the supranational level must rely heavily on domestic institutions and political processes for its legitimacy and for policy implementation (Scharpf 2009). No account of the EU's institutional

TABLE 4.2 Representation by type of interest group

Total number of groups registered	**6,010**
Professional consultancies, law firms, and self-employed consultants	**718**
– Professional consultancies	448
– Law firms	61
– Self-employed consultants	209
In-house lobbyists and trade/professional associations	**2,998**
– Companies and groups	846
– Trade, business, and professional associations	1,841
– Trade unions	110
– Other similar organizations	201
NGOs, platforms, networks, and similar organizations	**1,563**
Think tanks, research and academic institutions	**420**
– Think tanks and research institutions	304
– Academic institutions	116
Organizations representing churches and religious communities	**34**
Organizations representing municipal authorities, public or mixed entities	**277**
– Local, regional, and municipal authorities (at sub-national level)	120
– Other public or mixed entities	157

Source: Compiled by the authors from the Transparency Register (December 2013)..

system would therefore be complete without looking at the member states' institutions. Fundamental elements in the EU institutional architecture and partners in the EU policy process, these institutions have, in turn, become 'Europeanized' through EU membership (Bulmer and Lequesne 2012). The European dimension is not just an add-on to the work of national governments; in a real and tangible sense national governments, and other national authorities and agencies, provide much of the operating life-blood of the EU. After all, in some senses what the EU system does is to extend the policy resources available to the member states. The case studies in this volume offer a variety of illustrations. Learning how to manage this extra dimension to public policy has been one of the most important challenges faced by governments in the past fifty years.

Much of that challenge has had to be faced by central governments, and the patterns of response have varied a good deal. As a broad generalization we note that the experience has been somewhat different from what many commentators had expected. The trend has been not so much a defensive adjustment to the loss of policy-making powers, but rather in most member states an increasingly nuanced approach to incorporating and encapsulating the European dimension. This has not, however, meant that central governments can operate as gatekeepers between the national and the EU levels. The points of access and opportunities for building cross-national networks and coalitions have steadily proliferated for both public agencies and private actors, and national actors—business and NGOs in particular—play important and influential roles at all stages of the EU policy process.

Yet, the EU's increasing impact on domestic institutions, politics, and policies is by no means uncontested, as the debate on Europeanization shows (see Chapter 2). Contestation is particularly high where the supranational level transforms established constitutional traditions (e.g. by introducing a hitherto unknown level of judicial review in a system of parliamentary sovereignty such as the UK's), or where EU-level policies heavily constrain the choices of elected national governments, as in the case of 'austerity politics' in countries such as Cyprus, Greece, Ireland, Italy, Portugal, and Spain (see Chapter 7). Preserving both supranational and national legitimacy in Europe's multi-level polity has therefore become one of the key challenges faced by European policy-makers today.

One Community method or several policy modes?

Central to our approach to policy-making in the EU is the view that it includes several different policy modes, which are illustrated by the empirical case studies in this volume. These policy modes—we identify five—are the product of evolution and experimentation over time in the EU, changes in national policy-making processes, and developments in economic and social behaviour. We can observe important rearrangements in the roles and behaviour of the various key actors, in the approaches to policy dilemmas, and in the instruments used to address these. There is a persistent debate about where to strike the balance between delegating policy powers to the EU and retaining those of the member states, increasingly in the shadow of globalization and challenges to the 'western' economic model. There is contestation, both as regards the 'high politics' of the EU and as regards the 'functional appropriateness' of one or other policy mode. Also of critical importance is the issue of how the EU has adapted from its original small membership of only six relatively similar countries to a large membership of twenty-eight rather more heterogeneous countries with diverse policy legacies, institutional practices, and socio-economic characteristics.

EU policy-making never takes place in a vacuum, but, on the contrary, in a context of multiple locations for addressing policy issues, ranging across levels

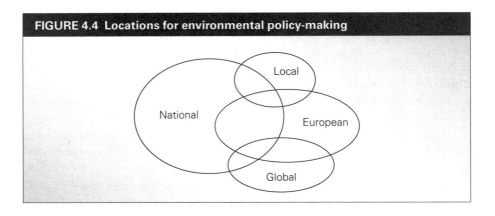

FIGURE 4.4 **Locations for environmental policy-making**

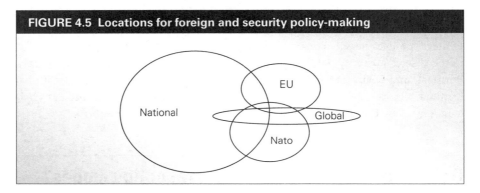

FIGURE 4.5 **Locations for foreign and security policy-making**

from the local to the global, and relying on both formal and informal processes (see Figures 4.4 and 4.5). European policy-makers have to manage the connections between these different locations, and sometimes make choices as to which they prefer for addressing a particular issue ('forum-shopping').

We set out five variants of 'day-to-day' policy-making in the EU:

- the classical Community method;
- the EU regulatory mode;
- the EU distributional mode;
- policy coordination; and
- intensive transgovernmentalism.

These modes are distinguished by their degrees of centralization, the roles of supranational, national, and societal actors, as well as the resources used. They do not include the domain of 'constitutive politics', in which member states amend the EU's core treaties. The five modes form a typology of ideal-types, devised with the deliberate objective of escaping from the either/or dichotomy between 'supranationalism' and 'intergovernmentalism'. Our central argument is that the patterns of policy-making in the EU are diverse not only because of the continuing arguments about which policy powers to transfer from the national to the European level, but also because of functional differences between policy domains and changing views about how to develop contemporary government and governance. Table 4.3 summarizes the key characteristics that delineate them. Most individual policy areas do not fall neatly within a single policy mode and there is strong variation over time, both within policy sectors and in response to events and contexts. As we shall see across the case studies in this volume, the variations persist and hybridization across types is prolific. Nevertheless, from an analytic perspective, the five policy modes serve as useful tools for classifying policy-making in specific issue areas, mapping diversity, and looking for change over time. We return to this in Chapter 19.

The classical Community method

Much of the literature on west European integration and the EU took as its starting point that a single predominant Community method of policy-making was emerging. As an early priority on the agenda of the original EEC, the common agricultural policy (CAP) set the template, defined by the late 1960s roughly as follows:

- a strong role delegated to the European Commission in policy design, policy-brokering, policy execution, and managing the interface with 'abroad';

- an empowering role for the Council of Ministers through strategic bargaining and package deals;

- a locking-in of stakeholders, in this case the agricultural interests, by their co-option into a European process which offered them better rewards than national politics;

- an engagement of national agencies as the subordinated operating arms of the agreed common regime;

- insulation from the influence of elected representatives at the national level, and only limited opportunities for the EP to intervene;

- an occasional, but defining, intrusion by the CJEU to reinforce the legal authority of the Community regime; and

- the resourcing of the policy on a collective basis, as an expression of sustained 'solidarity'.

This template was labelled as 'supranational' policy-making, in which powers were transferred from the national to the EU level. It was structured by a functionalist logic, in which those concerned with a particular policy sector could be encapsulated and build cross-national allegiances, but mediated by a form of politics in

TABLE 4.3 EU policy modes in brief

	Community method	Regulatory mode	Distributional mode	Policy coordination	Intensive transgovernmentalism
Degree of centralization	High	Varies	High, but narrow	Low to moderate	Low
Role of European Council	Rare (overcoming log jams)	Rare (overcoming log jams)	Sets parameters in major bargains	Limited	Sets direction
Role(s) of Commission	Extensive delegation—agenda-setting, implementation, and external representation	Agenda-setting and policing	Agenda-setting and implementation	Developer of networks, but more prominent role in economic and fiscal governance	Marginal
Role of Council the EU (decision rule)	Decision-making (QMV)	Co-legislator (QMV)	Decision-making (mainly unanimity)	Deliberation	Predominant in agenda-setting and decision-making
Role of EP	Limited consultative impact	Co-legislator	Limited impact originally but increasingly co-equal with Council	Limited dialogue	Excluded
Impact of CJEU	Occasional, but significant	Significant	Marginal	Excluded for 'soft' law provisions	Excluded
Member governments	Subordinated implementation of common policy	Implementation and enforcement (regulatory networks)	Paymasters and beneficiaries	Laboratories and learners	Key players

Engagement of other actors	Lock-in of stakeholders (policy community)	Policy networks and some self-regulation	Non-state actors: sub-national governments, some other agencies, international organizations	Epistemic communities, national institutions in economic governance	Excluded
Resources	Common	No budgetary costs	Focus on inter-regional transfers, sectoral support, and limited 'public goods'; more recently euro area bailouts	No budgetary costs	Increasing importance of funding for 'public goods'
Period of pre-eminence	Late 1960s–70s	Since late 1980s	Early 1970s, euro area crisis	Late 1960s, late 1990s use of OMC, euro area crisis	Early 1970s, 1990s, euro area crisis
Prime examples	CAP and trade policy pre-Lisbon; elements of CAP post-Lisbon; EMU (monetary policy); ESM (implementation of emergency lending)	Most policy-areas, traditionally including competition, single market and environment, and since Lisbon CAP, trade policy, framework conditions for economic governance and most of JHA	Budget, cohesion, ESM (establishment of criteria)	Employment, fiscal policy, economic governance and reform, aspects of JHA	CFSP/ESDP; JHA post-Maastricht; fiscal compact

which political and economic elites colluded to further their various, and often different, interests. Within the operation of the Council, a 'joint-decision trap' (Scharpf 1988) set high obstacles to the revision of common policy because of the power of veto-players.

Although this version of the Community method sets many reference points for both practitioners and commentators, how far this template ever accorded with reality, even in the case of agriculture, is a matter for debate. Chapter 8 suggests that the real story of the CAP may be different, and one in which national politics determined rather more of the outcomes. Interestingly, the fisheries regime, intended to imitate the CAP regime and delegating powers to manage quotas, never fit the template very well either (Lequesne 2005). The CAP was extensively revised in 2012 under pressure from the EP, as was the fisheries regime in 2013. The ToL now moves agriculture out of the classical Community method by involving the Parliament fully via co-decision and the budget procedure (Roederer-Rynning and Schimmelfennig 2012). Yet, while legislation on the common organization of agricultural markets as well as on the pursuit of the policy's objectives are now co-decided, measures related to fixing prices, levies, aid, and quantitative limitations continue to be adopted by the Council on the basis of a Commission proposal. What this development suggests is a split policy field, using the regulatory mode for legislation and the Community method for specific measures. As our case studies demonstrate, such a use of different modes across the same field has become a more general feature of policy-making in the EU (see Chapters 7, 8, and 15 in particular).

Aspects of EU trade policy have features of the classical Community approach, given the considerable delegation to the Commission for managing trade instruments and negotiating trade agreements. Yet, post-Lisbon, the Parliament has become extensively involved in this policy field too as it must now give its consent to trade policy generally as well as specific agreements (see Chapter 16).

It had been expected in the early years that this mode would apply in other policy sectors characterized by strong functionalist pressures. Yet, there are strikingly few examples of further common policies that were pursued according to the classical Community method, with a centralized and hierarchical institutional process, an extensive delegation of powers, limited parliamentary oversight, and the aim of 'positive integration', replacing national policies with a collective one (for more detail, see Chapter 5). The single currency is perhaps the closest-fitting example: the ECB has autonomy in designing and implementing the euro area's monetary policy, with the Ecofin Council and national central banks playing important roles but Parliament granted limited oversight. However, in this case powers are delegated to the ECB rather than the Commission, and they apply only to the monetary-policy strand of EMU and not to economic governance (see Chapter 7).

Overall, then, the classical Community method has been little replicated, and as the next sections show, where policies were 'communitarized' after an intergovernmental start, the regulatory mode—which fully involves the Parliament—has predominated.

The EU regulatory mode

As the competition regime took root (see Chapter 6) and the single market developed (see Chapter 5), so an alternative policy mode emerged. Its roots lay in the ambition of the Treaty of Rome to remove barriers between the national economies of the member states. Much of its driving force came from changes in the international economy, which began to induce new forms of regulation in some west European countries, such as the creation of independent regulatory agencies, as in the case of energy (see Chapter 14). It turned out that the EU arena was especially amenable to the further development of a regulatory mode of policy-making (Majone 1996). The strength of the European legal process, the machinery for promoting technical cooperation, and the distance from parliamentary politics were all factors that encouraged and facilitated removing national barriers to the creation of the single market (see Chapter 5). Decision-making—in and through the European Commission, the Council, and, increasingly, the EP, and anchored by the EU legal system—helped national policy-makers to escape some of the constraints of domestic politics. The EU was particularly well fitted for generating an overarching regulatory framework that could combine transnational standards yet accommodate country differences. Indeed, so successful was its implantation that this approach has informed the development of broader global regulation (see Chapters 13 and 16 for examples).

This regulatory mode provides the framework for numerous micro-level decisions and rules. It has shaped relationships with member governments and economic actors within the EU, and for those involved in relevant international regimes. It has been characterized by:

- the Commission as the architect and defender of regulatory objectives and rules, increasingly by reference to economic criteria, usually working with stakeholders and communities of experts, and often mobilizing the EU legal system;

- the Council as a forum (at both ministerial and official levels) for agreeing minimum standards and the direction of harmonization (mostly upwards towards higher standards), to be complemented by mutual recognition of national policies and controls, operated differentially in individual countries;

- the courts as the means of ensuring that the rules are applied reasonably evenly, backed by the national courts for local application, and enabling individual entrepreneurs to have access to redress in case of non-application or discrimination;

- the EP as one way to prompt the consideration of non-economic factors (environmental, regional, social, and so forth), with increasing impact as its legislative powers have grown, but with little leverage on the implementation of regulation before the ToL;

- the important role of regulatory agencies, both European and national; and

- extensive opportunities for stakeholders to be consulted about, and to influence, the shape and content of European market rules.

The EU regulatory mode has been described by some commentators as a form of 'negative integration' (Scharpf 1999), although case studies in this volume reveal regulation being used prolifically to promote 'positive integration'. This mode has shaped the development of the single market (Chapters 5 and 14), and the application of competition rules (Chapter 6). EU industrial policy has been developed in recent years mostly by using regulatory prompts and the competition regime. Insofar as the EU has a social policy (Chapter 11), it is mainly constructed through legal regulation and market-making. Employment policy also uses some regulatory instruments (Chapter 12). Much of what the EU has done in the environmental domain has relied on regulating industrial products and processes (see Chapter 13 and Pollack and Shaffer 2010). Interestingly, Chapter 8 indicates the increasing impact of the regulatory mode on the operation of the CAP as reforms are introduced. Finally, the EU's interactions with the rest of the world, including with neighbourhood and candidate countries, mirror its internal approach to regulation and industrial adjustment, as is made evident in Chapter 16 on trade policy and Chapter 17 in relation to central and eastern Europe.

During the 1990s, regulation displaced the Community method as the predominant policy paradigm for many EU policy practitioners. It had the advantage of being focused on modernization, through which the rigidities of the 'old' west European political economy would be replaced by more flexible, mainly legal, instruments of market encouragement, and through which different, and less corporatist, relationships could be forged with socio-economic actors. Interest groups, lobbyists, and corporate actors play an important role by forming networks, coalitions, and alliances in support of—or in opposition to—new regulation (Coen and Richardson 2009).

Two decades of experience in regulating the single market have led to two contrasting developments. On the one hand, regulation seems to have reached its limit. Particularly successful in dealing with product regulation, this mode is less robust in dealing with process standards, given differences either in levels of economic development or in societal preferences, sometimes within and sometimes across countries (see Chapters 13 and 17). The mode has also had rather less purchase on the regulation of services and utilities, where instead we see moves towards more decentralized, less hierarchical governance (see Chapter 14), although the global financial crisis has led to new attempts at regulating banking and financial markets in a more hierarchical way (see Chapter 5). The EU—as well as its member states, and indeed the global economy—experiments with new quasi-independent regulatory agencies, such as the EFSA (Pollack and Shaffer 2010); steered partnerships of national agencies working with the Commission, notably in competition policy (see Chapter 6); transnational consortia of national regulatory bodies, for example in the energy sector (see Chapter 14); and looser networks of self-regulation (Coen and Thatcher 2008a). These trends make it much harder to identify a single coherent EU regulatory mode.

On the other hand, the ToL makes the regulatory mode the EU's default decision procedure. as The 'ordinary legislative procedure' (or co-decision) exemplifies this mode's key procedural characteristics and now applies to most policy areas, including several that have travelled across from the Community method (CAP), from policy coordination (framework conditions for economic governance), and from intensive transgovernmentalism (JHA). This development is a direct corollary of the decline of the 'classical' Community method and of the EP's empowerment over the past two decades, and springs from the 'reflex' with which governments have complemented the introduction of QMV (which decreases indirect legitimacy via national governments) with co-decision (which adds democratic input through direct elections) (Goetze and Rittberger 2010).

The EU distributional mode

Persistently over the years the EU policy process has been caught up in distributional issues, that is, the allocation or reallocation of financial resources to different groups, sectors, regions, and countries. Thus in the EU context this mode covers both distributive and redistributive policy types (Lowi 1972; and see Chapter 3). Sometimes distributional issues were debated explicitly and intentionally; sometimes they were by-products of policies designed for other purposes. The original treaties included some elements of distribution in the EU's policy repertoire. The CAP was funded from a collective base and for a long time accounted for the lion's share of the EU budget. Farmers became both the clients of European funding and the beneficiaries of high prices, gaining transfers of resources from both taxpayers and consumers. The language of 'financial solidarity' therefore originates in the EEC's early years. From the mid-1980s 'cohesion' was added to the policy vocabulary, as EU policies were used to protect social groups or regions, marginalized in the domestic economy and rendered uncompetitive by global markets (see Chapter 10). Given fierce arguments over the distribution of the budgetary burdens and benefits of EU membership, distributional policy-making became highly politicized (see Chapters 8, 9, and 10). Enlargement added further complication.

The EU distributional mode of policy-making is characterized by:

- the Commission attempting to devise programmes, in partnership with local and regional authorities or sectoral stakeholders and agencies, and to use financial incentives to gain attention and clients;
- member governments in the Council and often the European Council, under pressure from local and regional authorities or other stakeholders, engaging in hard bargaining over a limited budget with some redistributive elements;
- additional pressure from MEPs based on territorial politics in the regions, and an increasing role for the EP by having to give consent;
- local and regional authorities benefiting from some policy empowerment as a result of engaging in the European arena, many of them with their own offices in Brussels, with, from 1993 onwards, the CoR also articulating their concerns;
- some scope for other stakeholders to be co-opted into the EU policy process; and
- recasting of the EU budget to devote more money to cohesion or to embryonic collective goods, and proportionately less to agriculture.

The opening for direct contacts between the European and the sub-national levels of government under cohesion and regional policy, as well as the politics that developed around them, led to the characterization of the EU as a system of 'multi-level governance' (Marks 1993) (see Chapter 2). Multi-level governance shifts attention away from the Brussels-centred and entrepreneur-oriented images of, respectively, the Community method and the regulatory mode, but whether it has also transformed the core characteristics of the distributional mode is debatable. Chapter 10 argues that central governments have remained in the driving seat of the bargains about EU spending and that sub-national activity should not be confused with impact. Chapter 8 suggests that it was the need to reshape the budget for an enlarged membership that has disturbed the inherited distributional mode that underpinned the CAP. The impact on public budgets of the Maastricht criteria to govern EMU as well as austerity politics in the wake of the global financial crisis added further constraints on redistribution through the EU budget (see Chapters 7 and 9). More recently, the new mechanisms through which the EU assists troubled euro area countries—the European Financial Stabilisation Mechanism (EFSM), the European Financial Stability Facility (EFSF), and the European Stability Mechanism (ESM)—display some characteristics of the distributional mode (see Chapter 7). At the same time, the bailout funds, which are outside established procedures, once again show the difficulty of neatly classifying policy regimes. On the one hand, the ESM's degree of autonomy over emergency lending recalls the Community method. On the other hand, the prominence of European Council bargains and of Commission proposals, the Council's key role in decision-making, the limited involvement of Parliament, and the close cooperation between the Commission and a multilateral, non-state actor—the IMF—in devising the programmes all echo the inherited distributional mode.

Two additional trends have recently reshaped this mode: one related to the substance, the other to the process of policy-making. The first is a shift towards funding collective goods—including innovation, research, and development; JHA measures; and CFSP actions—and away from the CAP and structural funds, which make up a still dominant but declining percentage of all EU spending (see Chapter 9). EU spending on 'sustainable growth' is nowadays highlighted as the primary objective. Meanwhile, preoccupations with internal security and the impacts of migration have generated calls for spending on collective border-control and related measures (see Chapter 15). There is also an increase in EU spending as a result of its foreign-policy activities, which (depending on how one counts) is now running at 8–10 per cent of the EU budget, in this case with limited involvement of Parliament (see Chapters 9 and 18).

The second trend is the—by now familiar—greater inclusion of the EP, which had a limited role in the original distributional mode. In budget negotiations, the Commission continues to be the agenda-setter, and member states continue to decide unanimously following hard bargaining. After Lisbon, however, the EP has to give consent to the multi-annual financial perspectives and to all forms of (compulsory and non-compulsory) expenditure in the EU's budget. It is therefore co-equal with the Council on budgetary matter (see Chapter 9). The ToL also submits the structural funds and cohesion policy—including implementing regulations—to co-decision (see Chapter 10). All in all, therefore, the distributional mode is in flux, with regard to both spending priorities and patterns of policy-making.

Policy coordination

An old contrast in the study of European collaboration has been drawn between the EU policy modes outlined earlier and what in shorthand might be described as the 'OECD technique'. The Organisation for Economic Co-operation and Development, the Paris-based club of western industrialized countries, has since the early 1960s provided a forum within which its members could appraise and compare each other's ways of developing public policies.

In its early years, the Commission used this technique to develop light forms of cooperation and coordination in fields adjacent to core EU economic competences. Such coordination was subsequently used to make the case for fully fledged delegation in the next round of treaty reform. For example, in the 1970s the Commission promoted increasingly systematic consultations among member governments on environmental issues; eventually the SEA gave the EU formal legislative powers in the field (see Chapter 13). Similar efforts were made to develop coordination of macro- and microeconomic policies, research and development, and aspects of education policy. The typical features of policy coordination are:

- the Commission developing networks of experts, or of stakeholders and/ or civil society, and accumulating technical arguments in favour of a shared approach to promote modernization and innovation;
- the involvement of 'independent' experts as promoters of ideas and techniques;
- the convening of high-level groups of national experts and sometimes ministers in the Council and occasionally the European Council, in brainstorming, problem-solving, or deliberative rather than bargaining mode;
- the development of techniques of peer pressure, 'benchmarking', and systematic policy comparisons in order to encourage policy learning;
- dialogue (sometimes) with specialist committees in the EP, as the advocates of particular approaches; and
- outputs in the form of 'soft law' and declaratory commitments rather than 'hard law' and binding commitments, oriented at gradual changes in behaviour within the member states.

In the late 1960s, policy coordination was intended as a transition mechanism from nationally rooted policy-making to a supranational regime. Latterly, however, this approach has become a policy mode in its own right, welcomed more normatively by some scholars as the emergence of a new form of postmodern or experimental governance (Scott and Trubek 2002; Sabel and Zeitlin 2010).

Three factors have driven this development. First, the choice of a form of EMU with a single monetary policy and 'coordinated' national macroeconomic policies required an effort to move on from the looser form of pre-EMU policy coordination to forms of more intense and more structured policy coordination. This led to the adoption of the Broad Economic Policy Guidelines (BEPGs) and the Stability and Growth Pact (SGP). Macroeconomic policy coordination—with an emphasis on budgetary discipline—has been intensified in response to the euro area crisis, in particular through the 'six-pack' and the fiscal compact based in an international agreement outside the EU treaties (see Chapter 7).

A second impulse came from the Lisbon Strategy adopted in March 2000, which specifically identified the 'open method of coordination' (OMC) as a distinctive policy technique. The OMC uses 'soft' policy incentives to shape behaviour, rather than 'hard', legally binding methods to require compliance (see Chapter 12). Used specifically in those fields of socio-economic (mainly microeconomic) policy-making where the EU lacked—and was unlikely to gain—strong competences, the OMC was to engage member governments, relevant stakeholders, and civil society in iterative comparison, benchmarking, and continuous coordination as ends in themselves (Sapir *et al.* 2004; Kok 2004).

A third factor was the increasing recognition of cross-country variations in policy and economic performance. In an enlarged EU of now twenty-eight member states it became harder to argue for uniform policy templates that would be applicable across the whole of the EU.

Employment policy (see Chapter 12) illustrates particularly well the debates about and features of the OMC as a technique. Comparing national, local, and sectoral experiences of labour-market adaptation, its objective is not so much to establish a single common framework, but rather to share experience and to encourage the spread of best practice.

Assessments of the OMC's effectiveness vary greatly, ranging between considerable scepticism as to the value of so 'soft' a form of joint policy-making (see Chapter 12), and great enthusiasm for its success—and further potential—in influencing those parts of the domestic-policy processes where deep obstacles to a more formal delegation of power remain. Judging between these assessments is especially hard against the backcloth of a sluggish European economy where causality and outputs are hard to pin down, and where some of the changes being sought are to social behaviour in the hope of improving economic performance. The heterogeneity of the EU28 makes indicators of socio-economic reforms particularly hard to compare and the notion of common EU-wide policy templates particularly implausible—and perhaps inappropriate. Furthermore, policy coordination diffuses and disperses political responsibilities, making it harder to define political 'ownership' and to exercise political accountability. In spite of these challenges, policy coordination is likely to persist as the mode of choice where functional pressures call for cross-border cooperation, but where national sensitivity, electoral salience, and preference heterogeneity prevent a formal delegation of competences to the supranational level.

Intensive transgovernmentalism

Throughout the EU's history some examples of policy cooperation have depended mainly on interaction between the relevant national policy-makers, with little involvement by the EU institutions. This has been especially so on policies that touch sensitive issues of state sovereignty, and which lie beyond the Union's core competences for market-making and market-shaping. Generally described as 'intergovernmentalism'—by both practitioners and commentators—this mode has widely been regarded as a weaker and much less fruitful form of policy development. In the early 1960s, General de Gaulle promoted the controversial Fouchet Plans, which aimed to shift sensitive areas of cooperation well away from the then EEC into a firmly intergovernmental framework. This was vigorously resisted by some of the more integration-minded governments. Nonetheless, in the early 1970s intergovernmental policy cooperation on exchange rates and foreign policy did develop, largely outside the EU treaties. In both domains, heads of state or government were key. Often their preferences were developed in smaller groupings, with policy development sometimes catalysed by Franco-German bilateral cooperation. In the 1980s, and more intensively in the 1990s, some EU countries chose to develop policy cooperation outside the EU framework to establish a common external border with liberalized internal borders through the Schengen Agreements, deliberately excluding some EU partners. The 2011 fiscal compact, with its establishment of a biannual euro summit, is the most recent example of such extra-treaty cooperation among most but not all EU governments, albeit mitigated by reliance on the EU's institutions (see Chapter 7).

The term 'intergovernmental' does not, however, fully capture the character of this policy mode. It resonates too much of the more limited cooperation between governments in many other international organizations. We therefore prefer the term 'transgovernmental', to connote the greater intensity and denser structuring of a mode where EU member governments—or their specific sub-units—have cumulatively committed themselves to rather extensive engagement and disciplines, but have judged full communitarization to be inappropriate, unacceptable, or premature.

Intensive transgovernmentalism is characterized by:

- the active involvement of the European Council in setting the overall direction of policy;
- the predominance of the Council (or an equivalent forum of national ministers) in consolidating cooperation;
- the limited or marginal role of the Commission;
- the exclusion of the EP and the courts;
- the engagement of a distinct circle of key national policy-makers;
- the adoption of special arrangements for managing cooperation, in particular the Council Secretariat and, more recently, the EEAS;
- the opaqueness of the process to national parliaments and citizens; but
- the capacity on occasion to deliver substantive joint policy.

Two factors challenge the assessment of intensive transgovernmentalism as simply a weak form of cooperation. First, this is the preferred policy mode in some other strong European regimes. Nato is one obvious example. The European Space Agency is another, and very different, case. Both have achieved quite extensive and sustained policy collaboration, albeit with evident limitations. Secondly, within the EU this mode has been a vehicle towards more extensive cooperation. With the exception of the (much younger) fiscal compact all the above policies have been gradually incorporated into the EU treaties. This incorporation is difficult to imagine without a prior period of cooperation.

Indeed, since the early 1960s the European Council, national finance ministers and officials, and central bankers produced such a sustained intensity of cooperation that the idea of a single currency became feasible and eventually acceptable (see Chapter 7; McNamara 2005; Hodson 2010). EMU then bifurcated between, on the one hand, strong delegation of monetary policy, with the ECB as the collective agent (Community method) and, on the other hand, mere coordination of macroeconomic and fiscal policy. Thus, a period of intensive transgovernmentalism led to two other modes.

In foreign policy, transgovernmental cooperation has intensified since the 1970s. Transgovernmentalism has proved particularly resilient, less voluntarist, and more cumulative. Yet, here too, cooperation has gradually become more institutionalized. European political cooperation was given a treaty base in the SEA. Maastricht created the CFSP—albeit as a distinct second pillar, whose procedures carry on after Lisbon. The ToL created the HR/VP and the EEAS (see Chapter 18).

In JHA (see Chapter 15), two transgovernmental processes have converged. On the one hand, informal policy consultations, both bilateral and multilateral, on issues such as counterterrorism have bred habits of increasingly intensive transgovernmental cooperation since the early 1970s. On the other hand, a wittingly separate treaty framework was constructed with ad hoc institutions under the Schengen Agreements. The former became the third pillar in Maastricht. The latter were incorporated into the ToA. Although the ToL normalized much of the policy field and largely submitted it to the regulatory mode, some features of transgovernmentalism persist on issues such as passports, family law, and operational police cooperation.

EMU, CFSP, and JHA have been among the most dynamic areas of EU policy development since the late 1990s, notwithstanding their heavy reliance on 'merely' transgovernmental arrangements. In each case, the EU framework has become more accepted, but the detailed institutional arrangements remain untypical. In EMU, the European Council plays an ever more prominent role—institutionalized beyond the crisis in the euro summit of the fiscal compact. CFSP—the creation of the EEAS and the High Representative notwithstanding—is still mainly conducted through unanimous decision-making in the Council. JHA has been substantially communitarized yet remains a fragmented policy area with complex opt-out arrangements for several member states and with the European Council involved in long-term agenda-setting.

These three policy areas also suggest that an important systemic change may be under way within the EU policy process. New areas of sensitive public policy are being delegated or pooled, but using institutional formats over which governments retain considerable control. Originally built through 'soft' institutions, such regimes are subsequently institutionalized and 'hardened', albeit to varying degrees.

In sum, the EU operates through different methods and different institutional patterns, changing over time and varying within as well as across policy areas. The five modes we identify have evolved organically, and continue to evolve in response to internal and external, procedural and functional factors. They provide a typology for exploring the shifting patterns of EU policy-making. The case studies in this volume should be read in the light of these evolutionary and experimental features of EU policy-making, providing examples of policy successes and of policy failures, of innovation, and of atrophy.

NOTES

1 The authors would like to thank Damian Chalmers, Dominik Hanf, Dermot Hodson, Mark Pollack, and Alasdair Young for their constructive comments on this chapter. We are hugely grateful to Daniel Naurin for sharing with us data, analysis, and insights on Council decision-making from his current research, which is to be published in Naurin *et al.* (forthcoming). Many thanks are also due to Alexander Katsaitis for his help with compiling Table 4.2.

2 In 2010, DG Translation of the Commission produced an output of 1.86 million pages, of which almost 77 per cent had been drafted in English (up from 60 per cent in 2003), 7 per cent from French (around 28 per cent in 2003), 23 per cent from German, and 14 per cent from other languages (Commission 2012*a*).

FURTHER READING

There is a huge literature on the institutions of the EU and their development. Peterson and Shackleton (2012) provide an overview, and Dinan (2004) sets the institutions into their historical context in a comprehensive but accessible account. Hix and Hoyland (2011) provide a theory-guided introduction to the interplay between EU institutions, politics, and policies. Scharpf (1999) offers an excellent and critical discussion of the EU's legitimacy. Among the many studies of the Commission, Kassim *et al.* (2013), Pollack (2003), and Spence (2006) provide valuable explanation and insights. On the Council and European Council, see Hayes-Renshaw and Wallace (2006), Naurin and Wallace (2008), Naurin *et al.* (forthcoming), and Westlake and Galloway (2005). Corbett *et al.* (2011) provide a comprehensive account of the EP, to which Hix *et al* (2007), Rittberger (2005), and Thomson (2011) provide nuanced complements. The courts and the EU's legal system are covered by Alter (2009), Dehousse (1998), and Stone Sweet (2000). On the national dimension, see Bulmer and Lequesne (2012), Cowles *et al.* (2001), and Ladrech (2010). These academic texts should be supplemented by primary sources, including the extensive material available on the website of the EU institutions, for which the point of access is *http://europa.eu*.

Alter, K. J. (2009), *The European Court's Political Power: Selected Essays* (Oxford: Oxford University Press).

Bulmer, S., and Lequesne, C. (2012) (eds.), *The Member States of the European Union*, 2nd edn. (Oxford: Oxford University Press).

Corbett, R., Jacobs, F., and Shackleton, M. (2011), *The European Parliament*, 8th edn. (London: John Harper).

Cowles, M. G., Caporaso, J. A., and Risse, T. (2001) (eds.), *Transforming Europe: Europeanization and Domestic Change* (Ithaca, NY: Cornell University Press).

Dehousse, R. (1998), *The European Court of Justice* (Basingstoke: Palgrave Macmillan).

Dinan, D. (2004), *Europe Recast: A History of European Union* (Basingstoke: Palgrave Macmillan).

Hayes-Renshaw, F., and Wallace, H. (2006), *The Council of Ministers*, 2nd edn. (Basingstoke: Palgrave Macmillan).

Hix, S., and Hoyland, B. (2011), *The Political System of the European Union*, 3rd edn. (Basingstoke: Palgrave Macmillan).

Hix, S., Noury, A., and Roland, G. (2007), *Democratic Politics in the European Parliament* (Cambridge: Cambridge University Press).

Kassim, H., Peterson, J., Bauer, M. W., Connolly, S., Dehousse, R., Hooghe, L., and Thompson, A. (2013), *The European Commission of the Twenty-First Century* (Oxford: Oxford University Press).

Ladrech, R. (2010), *Europeanization and National Politics* (Basingstoke: Palgrave Macmillan).

Naurin, D., and Wallace, H. (2008) (eds.), *Unveiling the Council of the European Union: Games Governments Play in Brussels* (Basingstoke: Palgrave Macmillan).

Naurin, D., Hayes-Renshaw, F., and Wallace, H. (forthcoming), *The Council of Ministers*, 3rd edn. (Basingstoke: Palgrave Macmillan).

Peterson, J., and Shackleton, M. (2012) (eds.), *The Institutions of the European Union*, 3rd edn. (Oxford: Oxford University Press).

Rittberger, B. (2005), *Building Europe's Parliament: Democratic Representation Beyond the Nation State* (Oxford: Oxford University Press).

Scharpf, F. W. (1999), *Governing in Europe: Effective and Democratic?* (Oxford: Oxford University Press).

Spence, D. (2006) (ed.), *The European Commission*, 3rd edn. (London: John Harper).

Stone Sweet, A. (2000), *Governing with Judges: Constitutional Politics in Europe* (Oxford: Oxford University Press).

Thomson, R. (2011), *Resolving Controversy in the European Union: Legislative Decision-Making before and after Enlargement* (Cambridge: Cambridge University Press).

Westlake, M., and Galloway, D. (2005) (eds.), *The Council of the European Union*, 3rd edn. (London: John Harper).

PART II

Policies

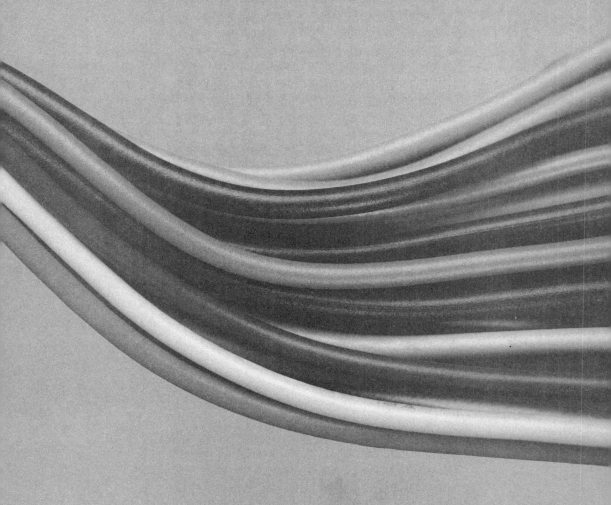

CHAPTER 5

The Single Market
From Stagnation to Renewal?

Alasdair R. Young

▌ Summary

The single European market programme marked a turning point in European integration. Although the Treaty of Rome called for the creation of a common market—with the free flow of goods, services, capital, and workers—among the member states, realizing that objective had proved difficult. Detailed harmonization of different standards had proved a frustrating approach to market integration, especially as external competition challenged European industry. New ideas about market regulation permeated the European Union (EU) policy process and, supported by Court of Justice of the European Union (CJEU) judgments and Commission entrepreneurship, facilitated legislative activism and important changes in the policy-implementing processes, culminating in the '1992 programme' to make the single market a reality. Although the task of 'completing' the single market remains unfinished, it has moved to the heart of European integration and altered the pattern of state–market relations in Europe. The 2008 financial crisis and its aftermath presented challenges to the single market. Subsequent concerns about stagnant economic growth have raised its political profile.

Introduction

The end of 2012 marked the twentieth anniversary of the 'completion' of the single market and saw renewed efforts to realize its full potential. The decision in the mid-1980s to complete the single market induced an explosion of academic interest in the EU. Before 1985, the theoretical debate on political integration had stalled, studies of EU policy-making were sparse, and few mainstream economists devoted themselves to the analysis of European economic integration. In the late 1980s all that changed, as competing political analyses proliferated and the economic consequences of the single market programme, which aimed to realize the free movement of goods, services, capital, and labour among the EU's member states by 1992, were examined. Indeed, many new theoretical approaches to the study of European integration have taken the single market as their main point of reference, just as many earlier theorists had taken agricultural policy as their stimulus. For many, the single European market (SEM) programme constitutes the critical turning point between stagnation and dynamism, between the 'old' politics of European integration and the 'new' politics of European regulation.

This chapter re-examines the renewal of the SEM as a major turning point in European policy-making. In essence, it presents the argument that many of the analyses that proliferated in response to the Single European Act (SEA) and the SEM overstated their novelty and understated some of the surrounding factors that helped to induce their 'success'. Thus, accounts in the late 1980s emphasized the newness of the SEM programme. In retrospect we can observe a significant degree of continuity with what had come before. Nonetheless, the incorporation of the SEM programme represents a very significant redefinition of the means and ends of policy. It enabled the European integration process to adapt to new constellations of ideas and interests and produced a different policy mode that has permeated many other policy areas (Majone 1994).

The SEM is also important for its impact on the European public policy model *within* the member states. Thus, market regulation at the supranational level of European governance jostles, often uneasily, with other issues on the political and economic agendas of the EU member states. Many have come to see 'more single market' as a way to foster economic growth in a time of austerity. At the same time, structural reforms introduced by some member states in order to secure international assistance with their sovereign debt crises (see Chapter 7) threaten to undermine the political legitimacy of the single market. This distrust of the markets reinforces tensions that predate the financial crisis between supranational regulation for transnational markets, which engage transnational regulators and large market operators, and encapsulated national politics, which engage those responsible for, and dependent on, the reduced domestic political space, such as smaller scale entrepreneurs, local regulators, and national or regional politicians. Thus, in the words of former Commissioner Mario Monti (2010: 6), 'The single market today is less popular than ever, while Europe needs it more than ever.'

The implications of the single market have not been confined to the EU's member states. The formal and informal impact on the Union's neighbours, partners, and competitors has been powerful. The SEM has been extended formally to neighbouring countries through the European Economic Area (EEA) and various forms of association with candidate and non-candidate countries and to many eventually by full accession (see Chapter 17). The SEM has also changed the conditions under which foreign goods and services may enter the world's largest market and prompted other states to align their rules with the EU's.

Establishing the single market

The objective of establishing a single market started with the Treaty of Rome (see Box 5.1). It set targets for creating a customs union and the progressive approximation of legislation, as well as for establishing a 'common market', complete with the free movement for goods, services, capital, and labour (the 'four freedoms'), all within a single regime of competition rules (see Chapter 6). The path was more clearly defined for the customs union than for the common market (Balassa 1975; Pelkmans 1984), reflecting the greater preoccupation of policy-makers in the 1950s with tariffs and quotas than with technical barriers to trade (TBTs) and trade in services.

In the 1960s and 1970s, however, new technologies, new products, new concerns with consumer welfare and environmental protection, and pressure from domestic firms to curb competition all contributed to the adoption of new national rules and regulations, which, whether intentionally or not, impeded trade. Thus, as tariffs among the member states were removed through the creation of the customs union, other barriers were revealed, and even reinforced. Local market preferences, as well as national policy and industrial cultures, became increasingly divisive.

BOX 5.1	The treaty base of the single market
Art. 34 TFEU (ex Art. 30 EEC)	Prohibition on quantitative restrictions on imports and all measures having equivalent effect
Art. 45 TFEU (ex Art. 48 EEC)	Free movement of workers
Art. 49 TFEU (ex Art. 52 EEC)	Right of establishment
Art. 56 TFEU (ex Art. 59 EEC)	Freedom to provide services
Art. 63 TFEU (ex Art. 67 EEC)	Free movement of capital
Art. 114 TFEU (ex Art. 100 EEC)	Approximation of laws that affect the establishment or functioning of the common market

Harmonization and its increasing frustration

In the early 1960s, the Commission began to tackle the negative impact of divergent national rules on trade. These efforts gathered pace after the complete elimination of customs duties between member states on 1 July 1968 (Dashwood 1977: 278–89). Initially the Commission tended to regard uniform or 'total' harmonization—the adoption of detailed, identical rules for all the member states—as a means of driving forward the general process of integration. After the first enlargement, however, the Commission adopted a more pragmatic approach and pursued harmonization only where it could be specifically justified.

The principal instrument of the original European Economic Community (EEC) for advancing the four freedoms was the directive, in principle setting the essential framework of policy at the European level and leaving the 'scope and method' of its implementation to the member states. In the case of TBTs, harmonization was based on Article 100 EEC (Art. 114 TFEU). Other articles provided the legal foundation for the freedom of movement for services, capital, and labour and for aligning many other national regulations (see Box 5.1).

Harmonization measures were drafted by the Commission in cooperation with sector-specific working groups, composed of experts nominated by member governments. The Commission also regularly invited comments on their drafts from European-level pressure groups (Dashwood 1977: 291–2). Beginning in 1973 with the 'Low-Voltage Directive', the Commission, where possible, incorporated the work of private standard-making bodies—primarily the Committee for European Norms (Standards) (CEN) and the Committee for European Electrical Norms (Standards) (CENELEC)—into Community measures by 'reference to standards' (Schreiber 1991: 99).

Different national approaches to regulation and the pressures on governments from domestic groups with an interest in preserving the status quo made delays and obstruction frequent (Dashwood 1977: 296). The need for unanimity in the Council of the European Union gave those most opposed to change a veto over harmonization. The Commission exacerbated this problem by overemphasizing the details and paying too little attention to the genuine attachment of people to familiar ways of doing business and buying goods (Dashwood 1977: 297). As a result, only 270 directives were adopted between 1969 and 1985 (Schreiber 1991: 98).

European harmonization could not keep pace with the proliferation of national rules as the member states increasingly adopted measures to protect their industries and to respond to new concerns about consumer and environmental protection in the late 1970s and early 1980s (Dashwood 1983; Commission 1985b). As a consequence, some of the earlier progress in integration was undone, contributing to a decline of intra-EU imports relative to total imports (Buigues and Sheehy 1994: 18) and a sharp increase in the number of CJEU cases concerning the free movement of goods.

The CJEU's jurisprudence began to bite at the heels of national policy-makers. In 1974, the *Dassonville* ruling established a legal basis for challenging the validity of national legislation that introduced new TBTs. The famous *Cassis de Dijon* judgment in 1979 insisted that under certain specified conditions member states should accept in their own markets products approved for sale by other member states (Dashwood 1983: 186; Alter and Meunier-Aitsahalia 1994: 540–1). There was cumulative frustration in the Commission and in the business community, however, at the slow pace of progress and the uncertainties of reliance on the CJEU, whose rulings apply only to the cases lodged. The high level of economic interdependence within the EU made these TBTs costly and visible (Pelkmans 1984; Cecchini *et al.* 1988).

In the early 1980s, the governments of western Europe were facing an economic crisis. The poor competitiveness of European firms relative to those of their main trading partners in the US and, particularly, Japan contributed to large trade deficits (Pelkmans and Winters 1988: 6). Transnational companies proliferated and often squeezed the profit margins and markets of firms confined to national markets. The sharp increase in oil prices following the revolution in Iran in 1979 helped to push west European economies into recession. Inflation and unemployment both soared during the early 1980s. Business confidence was low and investment, both foreign and European, began to turn away from the Community (Pelkmans and Winters 1988: 6).

The emerging reform agenda

While the crisis was clear, the response was not (see e.g. Tugendhat 1985). Large budget deficits and high inflation constrained the ability of member governments to use expansionary economic policies to bring down unemployment. Economic interdependence further reduced the efficacy of national responses to the crisis and provided an incentive for a coordinated response to the region's economic problems.

The prospects for a collective response were enhanced by changes within the member states. These are widely described in the political-integration literature as a convergence of national policy preferences during the early 1980s (Sandholtz and Zysman 1989: 111; Moravcsik 1991: 21, 1998: 369; D. Cameron 1992: 56). This convergence, it is claimed, reflected widespread acceptance of neo-liberal economic ideas, which stress that markets are better than governments at generating economic growth. Neo-liberal ideas thus advocate that governments should interfere less in economies by privatizing state-owned industries and removing regulations, particularly those governing economic competition.

Although new government policies certainly did emerge in the early 1980s, closer examination reveals that these differed substantially between countries in terms of their origins, motivations, and intensities (see Moravcsik 1998: 343–4). Political parties advocating neo-liberal economic policies came to power in the

UK, Belgium, the Netherlands, and Denmark, in part due to a rejection of the parties that had overseen the economic decline of the late 1970s (Hall 1986: 100). The rejection was less marked in Germany, where the underlying strength of its economy preserved an attachment to the established 'social market' framework. In France the 'policy learning' was explicit. Expansionary fiscal policies had led to increased inflation and unemployment, exacerbated the trade deficit, and swelled the public debt (Hall 1986: 199). By 1983, the French government had started to look for European solutions, reversing the threat it had made in autumn 1982 to obstruct the common market (Pearce and Sutton 1985: 68). The Spanish government sought to link socialist modernization at home with transnational market disciplines abroad. Convergence is thus something of a misnomer—European market liberalization served quite different purposes for different governments and different economic actors.

New ideas about markets and competition thus started to be floated in response to the problems of the European economy. The appeal of these ideas was influenced by the wave of deregulation in the US in the late 1970s and early 1980s (Hancher and Moran 1989: 133; Sandholtz and Zysman 1989: 112; Majone 1991: 81). Furthermore, the CJEU's 1979 *Cassis de Dijon* judgment provided the Commission with a lever with which to pursue greater market integration (Dashwood 1983).

From the early 1980s, European Council communiqués repeatedly expressed concern about the poor state of the single market (Armstrong and Bulmer 1998: 17) and in December 1982 it created an Internal Market Council. Throughout 1983, support for revitalizing the single market continued to grow. In April, the heads of some of Europe's leading multinational corporations formed the European Round Table of Industrialists (ERT) to advocate the completion of the single market (Cowles 1994). The Union of Industrial and Employers' Confederations of Europe (UNICE) added its voice to calls for greater market integration.

The single European market programme

Meanwhile the Commission began to look for ways to attack barriers to market access, both by systematically identifying them and by exploring ways of relaxing the constraints on policy change. It suggested the 'new approach' to regulatory harmonization, which advanced 'mutual recognition' of equivalent national rules and restricted much of harmonization to agreeing only 'essential requirements'. It thus built on the jurisprudence of the CJEU, notably the definition in *Cassis de Dijon* of essential safety requirements (Schreiber 1991) and drew on the experience of the 'low voltage' directive. It also built on UK support for deregulation and French and German efforts to coordinate the activities of their national standards bodies (H. Wallace 1984). Towards the end of 1983 the Commission privately persuaded the French, German, and UK governments to accept this new approach, which was formally adopted by the Council in May 1985 (*Bulletin of the European Communities*, 5/1985).

The 'new approach' limits legislative harmonization to minimum essential requirements and explicitly leaves scope for variations in national legislation (subject to mutual recognition). Under the 'new approach' responsibility for developing detailed technical standards is delegated to CEN and CENELEC. It is paralleled in financial services by 'home-country control', which sets minimum standards for national regulation of financial service providers, but then allows them to operate throughout the single market regulated by the government of the country in which they have their headquarters (home country). A similar approach was adopted with respect to mutual recognition of professional qualifications once common minimum standards were agreed.

In 1985, after consultations with the member governments, the new president of the Commission, Jacques Delors, decided that a drive to 'complete the single market' was perhaps the only strategic policy objective that would enjoy any sort of consensus (Moravcsik 1998: 362). In his inaugural speech to the European Parliament (EP), Delors committed himself to completing the single market by the end of 1992. The European Council in Milan in June 1985 endorsed the White Paper (Commission 1985*a*) drawn up by Lord Cockfield, the commissioner for the single market, containing 300 (later reduced to 282) measures (see Table 5.1).

During this same period, but outside the Community framework, the French and German governments in 1984 agreed the Moselle Treaty in order to mitigate the impact of border controls. In 1985 it was converted, at the insistence of the Benelux (Belgium, the Netherlands, and Luxembourg) governments, into the first Schengen Agreement (see Chapter 15).

The Single European Act

The development of the SEM programme coincided with the most significant reform of the European Community's (EC's) institutions since the Treaties of Rome. In June 1984, the meeting of the European Council in Fontainebleau cleared the way for institutional reform by resolving the question of Britain's budget rebate and the outstanding issues of the Iberian enlargement. At this meeting, the Commission tabled the 'new approach' and the UK government tabled a memorandum that called *inter alia* for the creation of a 'genuine common market' in goods and services (Thatcher 1984). The meeting established the Ad Hoc Committee on Institutional Reform (Dooge Committee) to consider reforms to the Community's decision-making procedures with the Iberian enlargement in mind. Earlier that year in its Draft Treaty on European Union, the European Parliament (1984) had sought to focus attention on institutional reform, calling *inter alia* for increased parliamentary powers and greater use of qualified majority voting (QMV) in the Council.

By December 1985, a remarkably quick and focused intergovernmental conference (IGC) had agreed the terms of institutional reform that became the SEA. In addition to its important focus on accommodating enlargement, the SEA specifically

TABLE 5.1 The White Paper on the single market: a taxonomy

Measures \ Markets	Products	Services	Persons and labour	Capital
Market access	• Abolition of intra-EC frontier controls • Approximation of: – technical regulations – VAT rates and excises • Unspecified implications for trade policy	• Mutual recognition and 'home-country control', removal of licensing restrictions (in banking and insurance) • Dismantling of quotas and freedom of cabotage (road haulage) • Access to interregional air travel markets • Multiple designation in bilaterals (air transport)	• Abolition of intra-EC frontier checks on persons • Relaxation of residence requirements for EC persons • Right of establishment for various highly educated workers	• Abolition of exchange controls • Admission of securities listed in one member state to another • Measures to facilitate industrial cooperation and migration of firms
Competitive conditions	• Promise of special paper on state aid to industry • Liberalization of public procurement • Merger control	• Introduction of competition policy in air transport • Approximation of fiscal and/or regulatory aspects in various services markets	• European 'vocational training card'	• Proposals on takeovers and holdings • Fiscal approximation of: – double taxation – security taxes – parent-subsidiary links
Market functioning	• Specific proposals on R&D in telecoms and IT • Proposals on standards, trademarks, corporate law, etc.	• Approximation of: – market and firm regulation in banking – consumer protection in insurance – EC system of permits for road haulage – EC standard for payment cards	• Approximation of: – income tax provisions for migrants – various training provisions • mutual recognition of diplomas	• European economic interest grouping • European company statute (2001) • Harmonization of industrial and commercial property laws • Common bankruptcy provisions
Sectoral policy	• CAP proposals: – abolition of frontiers – approximation and mutual recognition in veterinary and phytosanitary policies • Steel: – call to reduce subsidies	• Common crisis regime in road transport • Common air transport policy on access, capacity, and prices • Common rules on mass-risks insurance	• Largely silent on labour-market provisions	• Call to strengthen EMS

Source: Pelkmans and Winters (1988: 12).

endorsed the '1992 programme' to complete the single market and altered the main decision rule for single-market measures (with the exceptions of taxation, free movement of persons, and the rights and interests of employed persons) from unanimity to QMV. It also enhanced the powers of the EP by introducing the cooperation procedure for single-market measures. Thus, a strategic policy development and institutional reform were linked symbiotically and symbolically.

This linkage was crucial. First, it locked together institutional change and substantive policy goals. Secondly, the agreement to proceed with the single market was embedded in a broader set of agreements. This was connected with the accommodation of new members and budgetary redistribution, but a number of flanking policies—such as the environment and technology policy—were also included to assuage the concerns of some member governments about the liberalizing dynamic of the SEM programme (Armstrong and Bulmer 1998: 14).

Squaring the theoretical circle

Theoretical accounts of the SEM and SEA fall into two main approaches: one that emphasizes the role of supranational actors (neo-functionalism), the other that stresses the importance of the member governments (liberal intergovernmentalism) (see Chapter 2). Comparisons of the two approaches are complicated by the fact that some observers focus on the SEM, whilst others concentrate on the SEA.

Those analysts who concentrate on the SEM programme tend to stress the role of supranational actors. Cowles (1994) and van Apeldoorn (2001, 2002) emphasize the importance of transnational business interests in shaping the EU agenda in favour of the completion of the single market. Sandholtz and Zysman (1989) also give pride of place to supranational actors, although they cast the Commission in the leading role, with big business lending support. Garrett and Weingast (1993) contend that it was the CJEU's idea of mutual recognition that provided a focal point for agreement among member governments that favoured liberalization. Alter and Meunier-Aitsahalia (1994) recognize the importance of the idea of mutual recognition, but stress the Commission's entrepreneurial exploitation of this idea as a formula for liberalization.

There was not one unambiguous understanding of the single market programme, however (van Apeldoorn 2001, 2002; Jabko 2006). In addition to the neo-liberal vision of boosting economic efficiency by freeing trade among the member states and thus increasing competition, there was also a more competitiveness-oriented vision, in which the creation of the single market, not least through enabling European firms to take advantage of greater economies of scale, would make European firms more competitive internationally. Jabko (2006) contends that the Commission strategically exploited the ambiguity about the meaning of the market in order to advance European integration. By contrast, van Apeldoorn (2001, 2002) argues that the clash between competition and competitiveness factions within the ERT was won by the competitiveness faction, which wanted the removal of internal barriers to trade to be accompanied by higher barriers to imports from outside the EU and by a European industrial policy, but this agenda was thwarted by opposition from neo-liberal member states (see also Parsons 2008). Despite differences of emphasis, accounts of the SEM programme tend to emphasize the role of supranational actors and are thus at least compatible with neo-functionalism.

Analysts who focus on the SEA, by contrast, stress bargaining among the member governments (intergovernmentalism), although their preferences were influenced by domestic economic pressures (Cameron 1992; Moravcsik 1991, 1998). Moravcsik (1998: 374) argues that the SEA was the product of interstate bargaining, principally between the French, German, and UK governments, and that traditional tools of international statecraft, such as threats of exclusion and side-payments, explain the final composition of the '1992 programme' and the SEA. He does, however, recognize that supranational policy entrepreneurs, particularly the Commission, played a 'significant if secondary role' in packaging existing proposals, presenting them as a response to economic decline and helping to mobilize transnational interests (Moravcsik 1998: 372, 374). Both Moravcsik (1998) and Garrett (1992) argue that the member-state governments were willing to accept limits on their policy autonomy because they were engaged in an extended cooperative project and wanted to be able to ensure that their partners would comply with agreements. Parsons (2008), however, argues that proponents of the SEM, most notably the UK government, accepted institutional reform only as the price demanded by those states less enthusiastic about liberalization, but more committed to integration, not because they considered institutional reform necessary for realizing the project. Thus, while there is broad agreement that the contours of the institutional bargain were defined by bargaining among self-interested governments, precisely why they accepted the outcome they did is contested.

As the neo-functionalist and intergovernmentalist approaches seek to explain distinct, albeit related, events, both may be broadly accurate. The Commission, transnational business interests, some member governments, and to an extent the CJEU, played the lead role in shaping the SEM programme, while bargaining among the member governments primarily determined the outcome of the SEA (Armstrong and Bulmer 1998: 19). This account is consistent with different types of actors having different impacts on different types of policy (Cowles 1994; Peterson 1995). When it comes to 'history-making' decisions, such as the SEA, the member governments are the crucial actors. When dealing with policy-framing decisions, of which the SEM is a particularly weighty example, the supranational institutions, and their allies, tend to be important.

Subsequent institutional reform

The SEA set the institutional framework for the single market programme, and its broad parameters remain largely unchanged. The most significant subsequent change was the introduction of the co-decision procedure in the Maastricht Treaty on European Union (TEU). The Treaty of Amsterdam established clearer guidelines about when member governments might adopt national rules stricter than agreed common rules. The Treaty of Lisbon (ToL) made only modest changes to the single market programme by increasing the EP's role in legislation to liberalize specific services (Art. 59 TFEU) and by establishing a formal mechanism for establishing European intellectual property rights (Art. 118 TFEU). Lisbon also introduced a mechanism by which the Commission can impose financial sanctions on member states that fail to transpose EU legislation (Art. 260(3) TFEU). More strikingly, the institutional reforms—QMV and the co-decision procedure—first introduced with respect to single-market measures have been subsequently extended to other areas of policy-making, becoming the 'ordinary legislative procedure' in the ToL.

The politics of policy-making in the SEM

The SEM and SEA fundamentally changed the politics of market integration within the EC. First, the SEM revived 'negative integration', that is, the removal of national rules that impede economic exchange. This is most obvious in the mutual recognition principle, the abolition of frontier controls, and the elimination of exchange controls. Secondly, the SEA changed the institutional framework for 'positive integration'—agreeing common rules to replace national ones—by extending and activating QMV and enhancing the powers of the EP. In addition, with respect to the 'new approach' and 'home-country control', the SEM blurred the distinction between positive and negative integration by setting only minimum common requirements. These different modes of integration have profound political implications as they both affect who the key actors in the policy process are and shape their relative influence (see Table 5.2).

TABLE 5.2 Different modes of market integration		
Type of integration	**Form**	**Description**
Negative	Mutual recognition principle	Different national standards assumed to be equivalent in effect
	'New approach'	Common objectives with reference to voluntary standards
Positive	Approximation	Common detailed rules
	Common authorization	Common approval of individual products required

Source: Adapted from Holmes and Young (2001).

Negative integration

Negative integration is the elimination of national rules that impede economic exchange. It can occur as the result of political agreement among the member governments on the basis of a proposal from the Commission, as was the case with eliminating border procedures and abolishing exchange controls. In such instances, negative integration, for all intents and purposes, looks much like positive integration (see the following section). More commonly, however, negative integration occurs as the result of a national measure being found incompatible with the treaties as the result of a judicial process. In such instances, firms are usually the initiators, and the courts (ultimately the CJEU) are the decision-makers.

The principle of mutual recognition is at the heart of negative integration. It is deceptively simple. The basic idea is that all member-government regulations, whatever their differences in detail, should be assumed to be equivalent in effect. Consequently, products produced legally in one member state should be considered equally safe, environmentally friendly, etc. as those produced legally in any other member state. If one member government prohibits the sale of a product produced legally in another member state, the producing firm can challenge that prohibition under European law. If successful, the importing member government must accept the product, and negative integration has occurred.

Under EU law, however, member governments have the right, albeit within limits, to enforce strict national rules despite the principle of mutual recognition. Crucially, the principle applies only when the assumption holds that the national rules are equivalent in effect. This is not always the case, and Article 36 TFEU (ex Art. 36 EEC) permits restrictions on trade for a number of public-policy reasons, including public morality and the protection of human, animal, and plant health and safety. It is, therefore, possible that a government's more stringent regulation will be upheld by the courts if there is a legal challenge.

As a consequence, there are incentives for its trading partners to negotiate a common rule in order to eliminate the disruptive impact on trade of different rules (Vogel 1995; A. R. Young and Wallace 2000). This is one of the reasons why mutual recognition applies primarily to relatively simple products. It also means that strict-standard governments, particularly those with valuable markets, can play an important role in setting the agenda for positive integration.

Positive integration

Because different countries, for a wide variety of reasons, adopt different regulations and because those regulations serve public policy goals and usually impede trade only as a side effect, it is frequently not possible simply to eliminate national rules ('negative integration'). In such cases, in order to square the twin objectives of delivering public policy objectives and liberalizing trade it is necessary to replace different national rules with common European ones ('positive integration').

Given the relative importance of 'positive integration' in the EU's market-integration project, it is more appropriate to describe the SEM as *re*regulatory, than *de*regulatory.

The policy cycle and institutional actors

Formally the Commission is the agenda-setter for positive integration, as only it can propose new measures. The reality is somewhat more complicated. The Council and EP can request that the Commission develop proposals. In addition, as noted previously, the member states can indirectly shape the agenda by pursuing policies that disrupt the free flow of goods or services within the single market. In addition, member governments, as part of compromises on legislation, often build in 'policy ratchets' requiring that an issue be reconsidered by some specified time in the future.

As discussed earlier, the SEA introduced two important changes to the legislative process on single-market measures: QMV and the enhanced role of the EP. In the late 1990s to early 2000s, voting was the norm on single-market measures (Hayes-Renshaw *et al.* 2006), but more recently there have been fewer explicitly contested votes (see Figure 4.2). It is difficult, however, to assess how significant QMV has been to the single market programme as measures are put to a vote only when they are sure to pass. Votes against measures might, therefore, be more to appease domestic constituencies or to signal potential implementation problems than to express strong opposition (see Chapter 4).

By increasing the power of the EP, the SEA and subsequent treaties have made the adoption of single-market measures more complicated (Parsons 2008). Since the TEU strengthened the EP's ability to reject proposals, it has been a co-legislator with the Council (Hix 1999: 96). The EP's increased influence, formally in decision-making and informally in proposal-shaping, has affected policy outcomes by enhancing the representation of civic interests, such as consumer and environmental groups (Peterson and Bomberg 1999; A. R. Young and Wallace 2000).

As just under half of the SEM legislative programme, including the measures with the widest scope and significance, takes the form of directives, the member states have a central role in implementation. The transposition of directives into national law is a necessary, but not very visible, process, since in most cases it occurs through subordinate legislation that is not much debated. Criticisms of 'Brussels bureaucracy' often relate to rules that have been transposed into national law without debate and with little attention from national parliamentarians, but then 'Brussels' is always an easy scapegoat for unpopular changes.

Although the Commission formally has a role in enforcing the single market, its staff is too small and its policy remit too broad for it to engage actively in policing all of the nooks and crannies. Instead, the job of ensuring compliance is decentralized and relies heavily on firms and non-governmental organizations (NGOs) identifying issues and either bringing them to the Commission's attention or addressing them directly through the courts.

The policy players

The SEM is about regulation, and, in keeping with Theodore Lowi's (1964) characterization of regulatory politics, interest-group competition characterizes the politics of single-market measures. 'Brussels' had for a long while attracted pressure groups and lobbyists, but the SEM contributed to both a dramatic expansion of such activity and some changes in its form.

In part, the increase in the number of 'Eurogroups' was a simple reaction to the range and quantity of sectors and products affected by the SEM programme and the speed with which they were being addressed. Organizations (pressure groups, firms, local and regional governments, and NGOs) that had previously relied on occasional trips to Brussels started to establish their own offices there or to hire lobbyists on retainer. This shift to Brussels was also a response to the looming shadow of QMV, which meant that firms and interest groups could no longer count on 'their' member government being able to defend their interests. Building alliances with like-minded groups from other countries, other member governments, and within the Commission became crucial, and that meant having a presence in Brussels. The Commission, with limited staff and pressed for expertise, readily opened its doors to these actors.

Another change following the SEA and the launch of the SEM was the increase in the number of civic-interest groups, although they found it much harder to exercise effective political muscle. The consumer and the purchaser had been the intended beneficiaries of the SEM programme and the 'minimum essential requirements' of harmonizing and liberalizing directives were often to help them or their assumed interests. However, it is easier to discern consumers as objects of policy than as partners in the process, although they are often sporadic participants (A. R. Young 1997; A. R. Young and Wallace 2000).

In addition to changes in the volume and types of interest groups active in Brussels, the SEM also contributed to changes in the form of interest-group participation in policy-shaping. Individual firms and direct-member associations came to rival the previously dominant conventional peak and trade associations in the consultative processes. Another change was greater reliance on consultancy (an import from the US), which started to erode the old distinctions between public policy-making and private-interest representation. The Commission, member governments, and firms all found themselves relying increasingly on consultants to inject 'expertise'.

Although the single market programme made 'Brussels' much more important, firms and interest groups retain close contacts with their national governments as they remain important players in the SEM policy process. Rather than consistently preferring national or European policy, the SEM contributed to a rise in 'forum-shopping', with non-state actors pursuing their policy objectives at whichever level of governance they consider more likely to deliver the desired result.

In this process the Commission plays a pivotal role. Its sole right of initiative ensures that, but what really matters is how the Commission has chosen to use it. Although *re*regulatory rather than *de*regulatory, the SEM did have the effect of liberalizing markets and increasing competition among firms from different member states. In such circumstances, the costs of policy change (liberalization) are concentrated on the protected firms and the benefits tend to be disbursed thinly across a wide range of actors (consumers and users), although some particularly competitive firms are likely to benefit. In such circumstances, a policy entrepreneur is required to champion change and galvanize support—a role that the Commission has grasped with gusto.

Opening up the policy space

The reinvigoration of European policy-making also affected state–market relations in Europe. It did so in two principal ways: increasing governments' autonomy from society and opening up existing policy networks. Participation in any international negotiation privileges governments with respect to societal actors (Putnam 1988; Moravcsik 1993b). In particular, governments may be able to use an international (including European) agreement or external pressure to push through desired domestic reforms that have been blocked by powerful domestic interests.

In addition, the policy networks surrounding the SEM—both because they involve actors from multiple member states and because the participants are not directly involved in implementing policy decisions—tend to be more open than those in individual member states. As a result, a large number and wide variety of interests have access to the policy process. Furthermore, if there is to be a European regulation, producers tend to want their national rules to provide the template. As a consequence, powerful business interests often compete with each other in the European policy process, thereby undermining the typical 'privileged position' of business vis-à-vis other, less organized actors.

Hence, SEM regulations are usually contested by 'advocacy alliances', tactical, often loose groupings of diverse proponents and opponents of particular policies (A. R. Young and Wallace 2000: 3). Such 'advocacy alliances' bring together combinations of member governments, supranational European institutions, and producer and civic interests. Thus, these alliances bridge the agenda-setting, policy-formulation, and policy-decision phases of the policy cycle.

A greater focus on services

Legislative activity in the 1980s and through the 1990s concentrated primarily on the free movement of goods (Vogt 2005). With respect to the free movement of capital, there was the crucial 1988 Directive 88/361 that scrapped all remaining restrictions on capital movements between residents of the member states from 1 July 1990. There were also efforts to galvanize the free movement of labour by removing disincentives to relocating to another member state (see Chapter 11). Services, however, despite their economic importance—they account for more than 65 per cent of EU gross domestic product (GDP) and employment (Commission 2012b)—were relatively neglected until the turn of the century.

What single-market legislation there was on services focused primarily on eliminating quantitative restrictions on service providers, for example in air transport and road haulage, or on introducing competition in sectors dominated by public monopolies, such as electricity and telecommunications (see Chapters 6 and 15). A version of the 'new approach' with mutual recognition explicitly underpinned by agreement on common minimum principles for national regulation was applied to financial services, where 'home-country control' was introduced, and a number of professions in which mutual recognition on the basis of agreed common qualifications was established. The provision of services within the EU was therefore governed primarily by the right of establishment and the freedom to supply cross-border services enshrined in the Treaty of Rome. As a consequence, the provision of services within the EU was regulated primarily by national rules (Langhammer 2005).

The 2000 European Council in Lisbon identified removal of barriers to services as a key component to boosting the EU's competitiveness. The 2006 Services Directive (2006/123), which was the response to this challenge, pitted neo-liberalism against 'social Europe', saw the EP play a major role, and essentially divided the old and new member states (see Box 5.2). It thus revealed how politically fraught liberalization

---

BOX 5.2   The Services Directive

The Commission's 2004 proposal for the Services Directive was radically liberalizing in that it sought to formalize mutual recognition in services through the 'country of origin' provision, under which a service provider would be able to operate throughout the EU in accordance with the regulatory requirements of its country of origin. It was also potentially very broad in scope. The most controversial aspect of the proposal was that it might undermine enforcement of the 1996 Posted Workers Directive (96/71/EC), which specifies that host-country labour and wage laws, where they exist, apply. This issue became much more sensitive after the 2004 enlargement because of the much larger wage differentials between the new and old member states. Playing on this aspect of the proposal, its opponents, notably labour unions in the old member states, managed to frame the directive as permitting a particularly inequitable kind of social dumping, as workers working side by side would be paid different wages and foreign workers would face host-country prices while being paid home-country wages.

The EP responded to these concerns by adopting, over the votes of many MEPs from central and east European countries, a substantially modified version of the draft directive that replaced the concept of 'country of origin' with 'freedom to provide services' and exempted a number of sectors. Most of the central and east European member states, Finland, and the UK preferred the Commission's proposal, but the Commission, in the face of entrenched opposition to radical liberalization, accepted most of the Parliament's amendments. The Council adopted this version with only minor, slightly liberalizing changes, with only Belgium and Lithuania abstaining. The directive, therefore, was significantly less liberalizing than the Commission had intended.

Source: Hay 2007; Howarth 2007a; Nicolaïdis and Schmidt 2007.

within the EU can be. The directive, which covers services accounting for 45 per cent of EU GDP, was implemented in 2012 and its main economic effects are not expected to be felt for five to ten years after implementation (Commission 2012*b*: 1). As a consequence, despite 'significant progress', 'burdensome' national requirements remain and continue to restrict intra-EU services trade (WTO 2011: ix). The 2008 financial crisis prompted renewed attention to the fragmented regulation of financial services and gave a new impetus to European financial regulation (see the section 'From stagnation to opportunity?' later in the chapter).

The regulatory policy mode

The SEM policy process, therefore, combines high levels of interest-group engagement with Commission entrepreneurship, Council bargaining, and parliamentary deliberation over common rules. These rules are subsequently often enforced through the courts by private actors. As such, the SEM is the exemplar of the EU's regulatory policy mode (see Chapter 4).

It is, however, important to recognize that the regulatory mode actually contains two distinct dynamics: one that promotes market liberalization, the other, more stringent regulation. These different dynamics apply to different types of regulation and broadly mirror patterns in other polities. With regard to economic regulations—such as controls on prices or competition—the SEM has been liberalizing. With regard to social regulations, such as consumer safety or environmental product standards, the SEM has tended to increase competition among European firms, but by producing relatively stringent common rules (Sbragia 1993; Peterson 1997; Scharpf 1999; A. R. Young and Wallace 2000).

There are two keys to these different dynamics. The first concerns policy ideas. While neo-liberalism has expounded the benefits of removing restrictions on competition (Majone 1991), post-material values and more recent ideas such as the 'precautionary principle' have supported more stringent social regulations (Vogel 2012; Weale 1992). The second key concerns how the potential for negative integration affects the bargaining power of the member governments within the Council under the shadow of QMV. With regard to economic regulations, the prospect of negative integration is pronounced, putting those member governments with restrictions in a weak position to do more than slow the pace of liberalization (Holmes and McGowan 1997; Schmidt 1998; A. R. Young and Wallace 2000). With regard to social regulations, however, the Treaty establishing the European Community accepts, within limits, the right of member governments to adopt social regulations that impede trade. In addition to putting such issues on the agenda, as noted earlier, this puts the stricter standard country in a stronger bargaining position; its firms are protected and its citizens are content, while foreign goods or services are excluded. The cost of no agreement, therefore, falls more heavily on its partners. Under QMV no individual government can hold out alone for stricter standards, but there is usually an 'advocacy alliance' of civic-interest groups, stringent-standard producers, several member governments, the Parliament, and often the Commission in favour of more stringent standards. As a consequence, the SEM has tended to contribute to 'trading up' (Vogel 1995).

The regulatory policy mode still predominates in single-market legislation, but it is no longer as pre-eminent as it once was. Particularly in the 2000s, there was a proliferation of European regulatory agencies that were set up by secondary European legislation (Kelemen 2012). Some—such as the European Medicines Agency (EMA); the European Food Safety Authority (EFSA); and the European Chemicals Agency (ECHA)—conduct risk assessments that inform regulatory decisions on specific products (common approvals). In the case of medicines, the Commission takes the decision. With food safety, including biotechnology, and chemicals, the Commission is assisted by representatives of the member states through comitology (see Chapter 4). Should the member states neither approve nor reject a product, the Commission decides. Other regulatory agencies—such as the European Aviation Safety Authority (EASA)—implement and enforce EU legislation, including, in the case of aviation, providing type-certification of aircraft and components and authorizing non-EU airlines to operate in European airspace. Moreover, these regulatory decisions tend to have direct effect. This development thus represents a departure from the regulatory mode.

Outputs and assessment

The legislative output of the SEM programme has been impressive, with 1,420 directives and 1,769 regulations in force as of 1 October 2012 (Commission 2013a: 9). This legislative output is widely believed to have translated into significant economic impacts, although the 'exact economic worth' of the single market in terms of economic growth generated and jobs created is difficult to determine (see AmCham EU 2012: 9; Pelkmans 2011: 3–5). There are, however, persistent gaps in the legislative programme. There is still significant variation in national regulation of services (WTO 2011: xi) and even goods (inference from WTO 2008: Annex D). In addition, as economic activity continues to develop the single market it is arguable that the SEM will never be truly 'complete' (Commission 2002a: 4).

Even where rules are in place, the correct transposition and adequate implementation of SEM directives has been a pressing and persistent concern (Commission 2002b: 11, 2009a: 17; Grech 2010: 18). Although the member states have improved their individual transposition rates, the proportion of EU directives that have not been implemented by all member states on time has remained stuck at about 5 per cent (Commission 2013a: 16). The American Chamber of Commerce to the EU estimated that the 'lack of proper implementation and application' in tax, services, goods, and public procurement 'may be reducing the expected economic gains from core directives and regulations by as much as one-third. The cost of this "lack of enforcement loss" can be estimated to be in excess of €10 billion' (AmCham EU 2012: 17).

Beyond these problems with regulatory approximation, differences in member states' regulations disrupt the effective functioning of the single market because of problems with applying the mutual recognition principle. These problems are most pronounced with regard to technically complex products (e.g. buses, lorries, construction products, and precious metals), products that may pose a threat to safety or health (e.g. foods), and services, although the principle works quite well when applied to relatively simple products (Commission 2002b: 2). These problems stem in part from significant underlying cultural differences among the member states. Furthermore, consumers in different markets may prefer different product characteristics or may feel more comfortable doing business with established local firms (Müller 2003). Thus, cultural differences also have a bearing on whether the removal of legal and physical barriers is sufficient to create a single market.

The problems of translating legislative activism into results on the ground are reflected in European consumers' views of the single market. In a 2009 survey, one-third of respondents did not answer or could not name one thing that came to mind when they heard the phrase 'the internal market of the European Union' (Eurobarometer 2010: 8). Moreover, while most respondents viewed the single market positively—particularly in terms of increasing the variety of products available, boosting competitiveness, creating jobs, and responding to crises—most felt that the single market benefits only large companies and sizeable minorities considered that the single market had made things worse; such as by eroding consumer protection, worsening working conditions, and threatening national identity and culture (Eurobarometer 2010: 10). This thus reflects a loss of support for the neo-liberal, Anglo-Saxon regulatory model that underpinned the single market programme. The financial crisis and the austerity and restructuring measures associated with sovereign debt bailouts (see Chapter 7), have contributed to greater public and political distrust of markets in general (Grech 2010: 17; Monti 2010: 12). There is thus a widely shared sense that the single market lacks popular legitimacy (Grech 2010: 17; Monti 2010; Pelkmans 2011: 8).

From stagnation to opportunity?

As the global financial crisis began unfolding in the autumn of 2008 there were concerns that the single market might unravel (see e.g. Barroso 2009). In October, for instance, despite an agreement among France, Germany, Italy, and the UK to coordinate their responses to the crisis, Germany announced unilaterally that it would guarantee all bank deposits. This prompted other member states to follow suit. In the wake of the Icelandic government's decision not to guarantee non-Icelandic deposits, including those in internet bank Icesave, and the UK government's decision to step in to cover UK depositors, there was uncertainty about who was responsible for guaranteeing deposits held outside a bank's home country.[1] In addition, British, Greek, and Spanish politicians suggested that banks that received public funds should lend first to domestic firms and households (see Chapter 7). Despite the initial fears, former Internal Market and Competition Commissioner Mario Monti (2010: 23) concluded in May 2010 that the single market had survived the crisis 'virtually unscathed' (see also *The Economist*, 22 Oct. 2009: 58), although there are still some causes for concern (see *The Economist*, 20 Oct. 2012: 51).

The financial crisis and its aftermath, however, have had political implications for the single market. During the 2000s the single market was relatively neglected; seen as largely complete or at least not a political priority (Egan 2012: 407; Monti 2010: 12). The rapid expansion of new forms of cross-border economic activity, notably associated with the digital economy, meant that policy was falling behind practice. From about 2010 the single market has received greater political attention as it has been presented, not least by the Commission, as a means of fostering much-needed growth in a period of austerity (Barroso 2011; European Council 2011: 2). The opportunities, and the difficulties, of advancing the internal market after the 2008 financial crisis can be illustrated in two cases of policy-making: the proposed banking union (see Box 5.3) and, particularly, the Commission's 'Single Market Act' initiative, a two-part action plan of priority actions addressing particular 'levers' 'to boost growth and strengthen confidence' (Commission 2011*a*).

BOX 5.3   The struggle towards banking union

The 2008 global financial crisis exposed a number of shortcomings in European financial regulation.[2] Regulators did not foresee the crisis and the rules did not prevent excessive risk-taking by banks. When the crisis struck there was confusion about whether bank deposits were guaranteed and by whom, a particular problem in the case of cross-border banking operations. As noted earlier, there was initially an uncoordinated response to bank guarantees, with individual governments adopting ad hoc policies to cover deposits with public funds. The costs of covering extensive bank losses virtually bankrupted the Irish and Cypriot governments, and put a severe strain on Spain's finances. The Greek government's partial default on its debt in 2012 pushed Greek (and Cypriot) banks to the brink, as the government bonds they held as reserve assets lost over half their original value. The banking union is a central component of the EU's response to these problems (see also Chapter 7).

In June 2012, almost four years after the financial crisis struck, the European Council agreed to establish a banking union. A banking union would, like the US Federal Deposit Insurance Corporation, ideally involve five elements:

(1) a single bank supervisor to adopt and enforce common rules;

(2) a resolution authority able to 'resolve'—restructure or wind up—failed banks;

(3) a single resolution fund (paid for by industry) to cover costs associated with resolving failed banks;

(4) a credible euro-area wide guarantee on deposits to reassure savers that their euros are equally safe in whichever country they are saved; and

(5) a common backstop in case the resolution fund runs out of money.

Banking union is thus particularly controversial because of its potential redistributive character, not only between private creditors and debtors but also between countries. Creditor countries, most vocally Germany, are reluctant for their taxpayers to cover the mistakes of bankers and bank supervisors elsewhere.

Progress towards banking union, once started, has as a result been acrimonious. The smoothest part was establishing the European Central Bank (ECB) as the single supervisor. Under legislation adopted by the Council and the EP in October 2013, from late 2014 the ECB will directly supervise the 130 largest and most systemically important banks in the euro area and oversee national supervision of another 6,000. In December 2013, the EU's finance ministers reached agreement on the second and third elements. The resolution authority is complex, involving the ECB, the resolution board, and the Commission, as well as member states should the Commission not follow a board recommendation to wind up a bank. Due to German opposition, the single resolution fund will only gradually pool national funds over ten years. During this period, again due to German opposition, there will be no common backstop should the resolution funds prove insufficient. The single resolution mechanism is therefore not as streamlined or as robust as the Commission, supported by France and Italy, had proposed. Both the ECB and EP criticized the deal, suggesting that it will not reassure the markets about the stability of the banking system. In spring 2014 the EP secured concessions that strengthened the hand of the ECB in closing failing banks and accelerated the establishment of the common backstop before approving the single resolution mechanism, which will come into effect in 2015. The fourth element of banking union, a system of guarantees for bank depositors, has languished in the face of German objections. Thus, the politically charged issue of transfers between countries combined with European and national legal complexities have made progress towards banking union painful and incomplete.

Source: *The Economist*, 8 Sept. 2012, 13 Dec. 2012, 8 June 2013, 14 Dec. 2013; *Financial Times*, 8 May 2013; 10 July 2013; 18 Dec. 2013; 8 May 2014; *New York Times*, 12 July 2013; 18 Dec. 2013; *The Wall Street Journal*, 17 May 2013.

In this emphasis on the need for 'more single market' there are echoes of the factors contributing to the launch of the single market programme in the 1980s. There are broad similarities in the desires to promote growth and create jobs and to foster the competitiveness of European firms relative to foreign rivals (Barroso 2011; European Council 2011: 1). In addition, although the sources of constraint are different, expansionary fiscal policies are not a viable option given debt levels and monetary policy is already almost as expansionary as possible (Monti 2010: 9; European Council 2011: 1).

There are important differences in the details between the 1980s and 2010s, however: for one thing, the nature of economic competition has changed. In the 1980s, the emphasis was on economies of scale; in the 2010s, transnational production, innovation, and product differentiation are more important, as are the digital, knowledge, and service economies (Egan 2012: 407; Monti 2010: 16; Pelkmans 2011: 5).

This has implications for what the single market should be trying to achieve, with less emphasis on common rules and more emphasis on removing obstacles to innovation (Egan 2012: 407; Pelkmans 2011: 5).

It is also arguably the case that it is less clear what needs to be done to revitalize the single market than it was to create it. According to one senior diplomat quoted in the *Financial Times* (8 May 2012), 'Everybody thinks the single market is the answer but nobody knows what to do'. This lack of consensus is evident in the results of the Commission's consultation on the Single Market Act.[3] Although respondents could select up to ten of the Commission's fifty proposals as important, none were supported by a majority of the 740 submissions made through the standard online form. There was a similar lack of consensus even among the sixty-four companies and seventy-nine industrial federations that participated. Perhaps reflecting this lack of a clear steer, the Commission's Single Market Act included something for everyone (see Table 5.3). *The Economist's* (20 Oct. 2012: 51) Charlemagne columnist characterized the first batch of proposals as a 'mishmash'. The Single Market Act's proposals certainly lack the oomph of the original '1992' initiative (contrast Tables 5.1 and 5.3).

A third difference from the 1980s is that the political imperative does not seem to be as strong (Pelkmans 2011: 7). The unified patent, which will ensure uniform protection for an invention across the participating member states on the basis of a single application, was the only one of the first twelve priority items that was adopted by the, admittedly ambitious, end-of-2012 target. It was already well advanced in legislative process when the Single Market Act was presented. In addition, it was only adopted by (and thus only applicable in) twenty-five member states, and thus is an example of enhanced cooperation, because Italy and Spain refused to participate as only English, French, and German are the official languages for patent applications (*The Economist*, 15 Dec. 2012). Such intransigence on patents and the belated and faltering progress on banking union (see Box 5.2), although formally a crisis-management measure and not part of the Single Market Act, suggest that politicians are reluctant to make politically difficult compromises even when anticipated gains are considerable.

Lower key policy-making, however, is continuing. Arguing that the financial crisis reveals the costs of weak legislation and enforcement while the ensuing economic crisis has focused attention on the costs associated with regulation,[4] the Commission (2012c) is pursuing a 'smart regulation' agenda which involves assessing the economic impact of proposed legislation, particularly on small and medium-sized enterprises, and simplifying and codifying existing legislation. It also includes greater attention to implementation and enforcement. In particular, in December 2012 the Commission launched a Regulatory Fitness and Performance (REFIT) Programme to 'identify burdens, inconsistencies, gaps and ineffective measures' (Commission 2012c: 3). This initiative is thus the latest manifestation of the 'better regulation agenda', which has its roots in the Commission's 2001 White Paper on governance (see A. R. Young 2010).

TABLE 5.3 Key actions in the Single Market Act		
'Levers'	Single Market Act I COM(2011) 206 final 13 April 2011	Single Market Act II COM(2012) 573 final 3 October 2012
Access to finance for SMEs	Legislation on venture capital funds	Facilitate access to long-term investment funds
Mobility of citizens	Revise system for the recognition of professional qualifications	Develop true European placement and recruitment tool
Intellectual property rights	Legislation setting up unitary patent protection	
Consumers	Legislation on alternative dispute resolution	Revise General Product Safety Directive and adopt Regulation on Market Surveillance
Services	Revise legislation on European standardization system	Revise Payment Services Directive
Networks	Energy and transport infrastructure legislation	Fourth Railway Package, 'Blue Belt' Package for maritime transport, Accelerate implementation of Single European Sky, Action plan to improve implementation and enforcement of Third Energy Package
Digital single market	Legislation on eSignature, eIdentification, and eAuthentification	Common rules on high-speed broadband
Social entrepreneurship	Legislation to facilitate the development of social investment funds	
Taxation	Review energy tax directive	
Social cohesion	Legislation on implementation of Posting of Workers Directive and on clarifying the exercise of freedom of establishment/ services alongside fundamental social rights	Legislation to give all EU citizens access to basic payment account, ensure bank account fees are transparent and comparable, and make switching accounts easier
Business environment	Legislation simplifying Accounting Directive	Modernize EU insolvency rules
Public procurement	Revise procurement directives	Make electronic invoicing standard

Source: Commission (2012d: Annexes I and II). © European Union, 1995–2014.

Policy linkages

The elimination of legal barriers to cross-border exchange has also shifted attention to the processes and conditions under which goods are produced and services provided. Irrespective of other arguments for European policies on environmental and social issues (see Chapters 11 and 13), the preoccupation of entrepreneurs with operating on a level playing field turned attention to the relevance of such rules for costs, competitiveness, and profitability. Moreover, the Commission seems to consider addressing the social and environmental impacts of increased competition as necessary for maintaining support for the single-market project (Commission 2010a: 8–9, 22–4). In addition, renewed efforts to enhance the mobility of workers before and after retirement can have significant implications for the functioning of European welfare states (see Chapter 11).

There have also been higher profile policy spill-overs from the single market. It was invoked to build support for the two big policy initiatives that followed it: economic and monetary union (EMU) (see Chapter 7) and justice and home affairs (see Chapter 15). As we have seen, the crisis in the euro area has now fed back into the single market, creating a new impetus to 'complete' it.

The single market also has implications for the EU's external policies. Single-market rules profoundly affect the terms on which third-country goods and services enter the EU (see Chapter 16; A. R. Young and Peterson 2014). As a consequence of the stringency of many of its common rules and its more general regulatory capacity, the EU is considered 'the predominant regulator of global commerce' (Bradford 2012: 5; see also Drezner 2007: 36; Jacoby and Meunier 2010: 306). Differences between single-market rules and those of the EU's trade partners have now moved to the centre of the EU's bilateral trade relations, most prominently in the context of the negotiation of a Transatlantic Trade and Investment Partnership (see Chapter 16; A. R. Young and Peterson 2014). Single-market rules have also provided a core framework for relations with the EU's 'near abroad': the members of the EEA, current and former candidate countries, and states participating in the European neighbourhood policy (see Chapter 17; A. R. Young and Wallace 2000). Moreover, the Commission (2007a: 7) advocates 'expanding the regulatory space of the single market' by *inter alia* 'ensuring that European norms are a reference for global standards'. The external significance of the EU's rules, particularly the single market, have prompted Damro (2012) to argue that in its external relations the EU should be conceptualized as 'market power Europe'.

Conclusion

The SEM programme represents an approach to policy different both from that within the EU prior to the mid-1980s and from that found in most member states. It is an explicitly regulatory mode of policy-making. As a consequence, new relationships have been established between public and private actors at the EU level and between actors operating at the national and European levels. This has tended to open up the policy process, although business groups, especially large firms, have a 'privileged position', as they do at the national level. There is, however, more likely to be competition among such privileged actors at the European level than within member states.

The SEM has also reduced the dependence of many economic actors on national policy. The scope for national policy-makers to control economic transactions on their territories has become more limited and will remain limited as long as the transnational legal regime of the EU holds together. The resilience of the single market in the face of the financial crisis is testament to this. That is not to say, however, that the political turf has been won by EU-level policy-makers, since the new regulatory mode involves a diffusion of policy authority rather than its concentration at the European level, as the tussle over banking union starkly illustrates. This inclination is likely to be reinforced by the imperatives of regulating an enlarged, and more diverse, single market in which innovation and flexibility are prized.

Although the Commission has been heavily engaged in promoting the single market, its own net gain in authority is open to debate, not least since it has also become the butt of residual criticism about the downside effects of market liberalization. Moreover, the member governments—as participants in decision-making, the enforcers of most EU legislation, defenders of the losers from the single market, and the proponents of subsidiarity—remain key players in the regulatory process.

Because liberalization, at least in the short run, creates losers as well as winners, the single market programme has to be seen as an important element of the legitimacy test faced by the EU since the early 1990s. This has been recognized in the Single Market Act's emphasis on delivering tangible benefits to consumers and citizens. The political implications of the 2008 financial crisis has not totally undermined the idea prominent in the 2000s that less regulation is better, but it has certainly given greater impetus to reregulation rather than deregulation, most starkly in financial services.

NOTES

1 Iceland is not a member of the EU, but is a member of the EEA and so was bound by the 1994 directive on deposit guarantees giving its actions EU resonance. In January 2013, the European Free Trade Area court ruled in favour of Iceland arguing that given the systemic nature of its banking crisis it was not liable for its deposit-guarantee scheme not working properly (see S. Browers, 'Court rules against UK in £2.3bn Icesave deposit guarantees battle', *The Guardian*, 28 Jan. 2013).

2 Thanks to Dermot Hodson for constructive comments on this box. All errors are my own.

3 Available on *http://ec. europa.eu/internal_market/smact/consultation/2011/debate/index_en.htm*.

4 The spring 2013 *Eurobarometer* (Commission 2013b: 59) reported that 74 per cent of respondents thought that the EU generates 'too much red tape'.

FURTHER READING

On the original development of the 1992 programme, see Cockfield (1994) and Pelkmans and Winters (1988). For an influential assessment of the single market in the context of the financial crisis, see Monti (2010) and for a review of the literature on the single market, see Egan (2012). For discussions of the political dynamics of the SEM, see Armstrong and Bulmer (1998), Majone (1996), Scharpf (1999), and Young (2007). For a discussion of EU risk regulation in a comparative perspective, see Vogel (2012), particularly Chapters 8 and 9.

Armstrong, K., and Bulmer, S. (1998), *The Governance of the Single European Market* (Manchester: Manchester University Press).

Cockfield, Lord (1994), *The European Union: Creating the Single Market* (London: Wiley Chancery Law).

Egan, M. (2012), 'Single Market', in E. Jones, A. Menon, and S. Weatherill (eds.), *The Oxford Handbook of the European Union* (Oxford: Oxford University Press), 407–21.

Majone, G. (1996) (ed.), *Regulating Europe* (London: Routledge).

Monti, M. (2010), 'A New Strategy for the Single Market: At the Service of Europe's Economy and Society: Report to the President of the European Commission José Manuel Barroso', 9 May.

Pelkmans, J., and Winters, L. A. (1988), *Europe's Domestic Market* (London: Royal Institute of International Affairs).

Scharpf, F. W. (1999), *Governing in Europe: Effective and Democratic?* (Oxford: Oxford University Press).

Vogel, D. (2012), *The Politics of Precaution: Regulating Health, Safety, and Environmental Risks in Europe and the United States* (Princeton, NJ: Princeton University Press).

Young, A. R. (2007), 'The Politics of Regulation and the Internal Market', in K. E. Jørgensen, M. A. Pollack, and B. Rosamond (eds.), *The Handbook of European Union Politics* (London: Sage), 373–94.

CHAPTER 6

Competition Policy
Defending the Economic Constitution

Stephen Wilks

▌ Summary

European competition policy has steadily increased its effectiveness in controlling restrictive practices, abuse of dominant position, mergers, state aid, and the liberalization of utilities. Its success rests on the free-market approach now predominant in all
European Union (EU) countries including the new member states. The central dominance of the Directorate-General for Competition (ex DG IV, now DG COMP) in the Commission has been perpetuated, although it now shares enforcement with the national
competition authorities (NCAs) in the member states. The exceptionally powerful treaty
provisions and apparatus of legal enforcement mean that competition policy has become a supranational policy competence which can be regarded as an 'economic constitution' for Europe. Two recent developments have been: first, the decentralization of
antitrust enforcement to the national agencies and courts through the 'Modernization

(continued...)

Regulation' of 2003; and, secondly, a 'turn to economics' in which economic analysis has been substituted for legal tests to move towards an 'effects-based' (effect on competition) interpretation of the law. This is part of a process of Americanization in which the senior decision-makers in DG COMP have embraced US competition economics and have also adopted US-style enforcement mechanisms. This turn to economics and to US enforcement methods has been criticized as a shift to a more Anglo-Saxon, or 'neo-liberal', interpretation of competition policy, which is regarded with suspicion by supporters of a 'social market' approach in continental Europe. The 2008 financial crisis challenged both the practical enforcement of competition policy and its ideological biases. Both these challenges were successfully resisted by the Commission, which defended and therefore further consolidated, the free-market European economic constitution.

Introduction: competition policy and the European market

Competition policy is concerned with setting standards of conduct rather than with obtaining tangible goals, and is anchored in the principles of free-market capitalism. The character and role of competition policy have therefore been controversial across the EU and in individual member states. Its enforcement has a differential effect across the very varied economic systems ranging from highly liberalized markets to those where the state has played an important role in the economy, to the post-socialist states which started to embrace capitalism only in the 1990s (V. Schmidt 2002). European competition policy is broad and includes antitrust, merger control, and the control of state aid (subsidies to industry). Its overall thrust has been to press on every front for the liberalization of markets.

Competition policy draws its importance from the central role that economic factors and market principles have played in the evolution of the EU. The vision in 1958 was of a common market that would generate benefits for all participants through market integration. This was a liberal economic vision, then controversial, which rested on a faith in traditional market capitalism. The vision was the natural alternative to the centrally planned economies of central and eastern Europe, but it was also regarded sceptically by many west European business and policy elites. It became a dominant principle only as a result of the neo-liberal revolution of the 1980s and the single market programme of 1992 (see Chapter 5). This vision was consolidated by the collapse of Soviet communism and the remodelling of the economic systems of control in central and eastern Europe in alignment with the capitalist norms of the Union. Under free-market capitalism, competition is the central dynamic of entrepreneurial activity and the means of energizing the economic system to deliver welfare benefits. Those aspects of economic life that hinder competition—monopoly, oligopoly, cartels, restrictive practices, market-sharing, subsidies, and state protection—also prevent it from generating and distributing wealth efficiently. Just as the European Central Bank (ECB) guarantees a sound currency and low level of inflation (see Chapter 7), so the EU competition rules guarantee a free market and economic efficiency, providing an 'economic constitution' for Europe (see Wilks 2010).

This emphasis placed upon the market and economic integration means that competition policy has been of central importance in the EU. The Commission has expanded competition policy as one of its supranational EU competences. It has drawn on powerful treaty provisions, received support from the Court of Justice of the European Union (CJEU) (previously the European Court of Justice (ECJ)) and the General Court (previously the Court of First Instance (CFI)), and entrusted policy to DG COMP, one of the most effective DGs in the Commission, directed by a series of able commissioners. Competition policy has taken on constitutional characteristics, thus structuring other policy areas (e.g. research and development (R&D) and environmental policy), or framing specific sectoral policies (e.g. media and telecommunications). Indeed, competition policy has been used to discipline governments as well as companies, so that all economic actors must recognize the economic structure that it defines.

The salience of competition policy

Competition policy is about protecting and expanding competition as a process of rivalry between firms in order to win customers, and also as a process of creating and protecting markets. There are both political and economic rationales for competition policy. The political rationale comprises a commitment by governments to allow economic actors freedom to compete in the market, and to protect consumers from exploitation by powerful companies. The US is the home of competition policy, where it is still called 'antitrust', which reveals its origins in the late nineteenth century as a commitment to protect 'the little man' from the power of the big industrial 'trusts'. The more recent, economic rationale is becoming an orthodoxy. It is based on the standard neo-classical theories of market competition, which affirm that competition creates wealth through the generation of economic efficiency, both productive efficiency (making more goods for the same cost), and allocative efficiency (giving consumers what they want). Accordingly, Motta (2004: xvii) defines competition policy as 'the set of policies and laws which ensure that competition in the market place is not restricted in such a way as to reduce economic welfare'. There are criticisms of the 'consumer welfare' orthodoxy among economists (Budzinski 2008), and wider criticisms of a neo-liberal interpretation of the competition rules

(Buch-Hansen and Wigger 2011) but the prevailing orthodoxy is that economies where competitive pressure is intense will be more efficient than those where it is restrained. This argument was overshadowed by the more sceptical reaction to pure market economics engendered by the financial crisis and was barely mentioned in the Commission's 'Europe 2020' growth strategy, which was launched in 2010. At that time, the competition-policy community was seriously concerned that increased state intervention and the rejection of market principles would seriously inhibit the enforcement of competition policy. Those fears have not been realized and this chapter argues that competition policy continues to provide a distinctive economic constitution for Europe.

The impact of EU competition policy is evident on a day-to-day basis, as it increasingly affects how we do our jobs, how benefits are distributed, and how and what we consume, from football to cosmetics, the price of cars, and the proximity of supermarkets. This means that a policy area that was traditionally regarded as specialist and arcane makes the headlines. This applies to the big merger cases, such as the prohibition of the proposed *Ryanair/Aer Lingus* merger in 2007 (confirmed on appeal in 2010),[1] and stretches beyond intra-EU cases to those with a global or extraterritorial dimension. In the *Deutsche Börse/NYSE Euronext* case in 2012 the European Commission controversially prohibited the merger despite earlier approval by the US Department of Justice.

Equally dramatic have been abuse of dominance actions against large corporations. A long-running example is the Commission's findings that Microsoft abused its near monopoly and acted illegally in bundling its Media Player software into its Windows operating system. The Commission ruled that Microsoft must share details of its software design with competitors, and in March 2004 Mario Monti, the then Competition Commissioner, announced a fine of €497 million, the highest ever against a single company, which produced headlines such as 'Mario Monti's Broken Windows' and even 'The Full Monti' (*Financial Times*, 25 Mar. 2004). The Microsoft confrontation continued into 2009 with fines for non-compliance. By 2013, the Commission had fined Microsoft a total of €1.6 billion for abuse of dominant position. Early in 2014, Google faced a comparable challenge to its quasi-monopoly in European internet searches when Commissioner Joaquín Almunia rejected its proposals to eliminate discrimination in its search results. This raised the prospect that 'Brussels threatens a war on Google' (*Sunday Times*, 5 Jan. 2014).

Such headlines dramatize the ways in which competition policy structures the business environment for companies across Europe. EU competition policy has a 'direct effect' on companies, but until the mid-1990s most companies treated competition policy as an afterthought, not at the heart of decision-making. By contrast, today the 'competition rules' are a dominant regulatory constraint when companies formulate their corporate strategy or consider their competitive behaviour. They employ legal expertise to advise on the impact of the rules and most big firms will have an in-house 'compliance programme' to train their staff to avoid breaching the competition provisions.

This shift in corporate awareness is partly due to the steady refinement and expansion of the law and the activism of the competition authorities. For corporate executives, European law does not yet allow prosecution of individuals, which is commonplace in the US. But the UK law does include a 'criminal cartel offence', and criminal penalties, including imprisonment, have been discussed at the EU level. In practice, the most dramatic threat is the increasingly frequent 'dawn raids' when competition officials swoop in on factories, offices, and private residences across several countries to seize papers and computers in order to find evidence of secret agreements, or 'cartels', to manipulate markets. Some raids arise from the successful adaptation by the Commission of a US-style leniency programme, a system of exemptions for 'whistle-blowers' who provide information about a cartel in which their firms are involved. The intensification of action, in particular against 'hard-core' cartels, has resulted in a huge escalation of fines. In 2001, the Commission fined fifty-six companies a total of €1.83 billion, more than the cumulative total of all fines previously levied in the history of EU competition law. In the three-year period 2005–7 a massive €5.86 billion was levied against participants in twenty cartels. In 2012, a new record was reached for fines on a single cartel with fines of €1.47 billion imposed on seven companies in the cathode ray (TV) tube cartel (Commission 2013c: 11). Policies that pack this sort of punch simply cannot be ignored.

It is worth remembering that competition policy was not always regarded with such approval, and competition was once regarded as wasteful and destructive. The use of cartels was widespread in Europe and not regarded as essentially illegitimate until the late 1960s (Harding and Joshua 2003). The industrial policies of many west European countries rested upon nationalization, selective intervention, indicative planning, encouragement of concentration and economies of scale, and the support of 'national champions'. Although these industrial policies became discredited, they still attract some support among trade unions and national politicians and have re-emerged in response to the recessions following the global financial crisis. Thus, there remains a tension between competition policy and company support, as well as with policies to encourage regional economic development, science and technology, and small and medium-sized enterprises. In all these areas, competition is being distorted by governments for alternative policy goals.

The move from planning and intervention to the liberalization of markets and competition played an important part in the enlargement of the EU in 2004 and 2007. For over forty years, ten of these twelve new member states had centrally planned economies in which competition was an alien concept and capitalism was condemned. These countries have telescoped the post-war years of west European economic evolution into ten years as they have adopted the EU competition policy embodied in the *acquis communautaire*, as part of the Europe agreements (see Chapter 17). All these countries now have competition laws, competition agencies, and a commitment to competition. Competition policy thus emerges as an essential component for making enlargement work and ensuring that diverse economic systems converge with the market principles that unify the EU economy.

The substance of policy

There are five components of European competition policy, each of which relies on specific legal powers:

- a prohibition on agreements between firms that limit competition (Art. 101 TFEU; ex Art. 81 TEC; ex Art. 85 EEC);
- a prohibition on the abuse of a dominant position by one or more large firms (Art. 102 TFEU; ex Art. 82 TEC; ex Art. 86 EEC);
- the control of mergers which create a dominant position (Regulation 4064/89; revised in Regulation 139/2004);
- the control of aid given by a member state to a firm or category of firms (Arts. 107 and 108 TFEU; ex Arts. 87 and 88 TEC; ex Arts. 92 and 93 EEC); and
- the liberalization of measures by member states to favour domestic utilities, and infrastructure industries (Arts. 37 and 105; ex Arts. 31 and 86 TEC; ex Arts. 37 and 85 EEC).

The sophistication and effectiveness of these components have grown over time to create a complex agglomeration of principles and powers enshrined in practice and case law. Effective control of state aid began only in the late 1980s, control of mergers in the early 1990s, and liberalization of utilities in the late 1990s. At the heart of competition policy, however, is the prohibition on anti-competitive agreements. The first major decision taken by the Commission under Article 101 TFEU came in 1964 and Table 6.1 sets out the subsequent development of policy with the proviso that all these areas had to be defended in the face of the post-2008 financial crisis and recession. The following sections review each area.

Antitrust: restrictive practices

Policy on anti-competitive agreements, or restrictive practices, is specified in Article 101, which 'prohibits' all agreements and concerted practices between firms that affect trade between member states and 'have as their objective or effect the prevention, restriction or distortion of competition within the common market'. The article also specifies efficiency exemptions from the prohibition in cases where an agreement 'contributes to improving the production or distribution of goods or to promoting technical or economic progress' (Art. 101(3) TFEU). These provisions raise extraordinary problems of interpretation. Taken literally, virtually every agreement will 'restrict or distort' competition: that is what agreements are for, and every business spends much of its time and energy in foiling its competitors. On the other hand, some agreements foster competition, although interpretation will often depend on the theoretical biases of the economic analysis involved. In practice, implementation has allowed extensive discretion to the case officials in DG COMP;

TABLE 6.1 Stages in the development of EU competition policy

	1960s	1970s	1980s	1990s	2000s	2010s
(1)						
Antitrust: agreements	Regulation 17; cases	Develop principles	First fines	Enforcement intensified	Stress cartels; modernization	Intense action against cartels
(2)						
Antitrust: abuse of dominance	Dormant	First cases	Develop principles; first fines	Idea of collective dominance	Moderate application; modernization	Few cases but reform
(3)						
Merger control	Not in treaty	No action[a]	Regulation in 1989	Early enforcement	Intensified enforcement and reform	Negotiations, remains permissive
(4)						
State aid	Dormant	Gradual development	Becomes priority; first survey 1988	Tighter sectoral regimes	Lisbon Agenda reinforces; steady progress	Crisis brings controlled relaxation
(5)						
Liberalized utilities	Ignored[b]	Ignored	More transparency; action on telecoms	Becomes priority systematic challenge	Continued pressure; mixed progress	Sectoral focus more effective

Notes:
[a] 'No action' means that the problem was recognized but could not be acted on without legal powers;
[b] 'Ignored' means that the problem was not recognized.

their interpretations of the rules have usually been confirmed in appeals to the CJEU or more recently to the General Court.

On the basis of case law and accepted economic theory some practices are presumed to be illegal (Goyder 2003: 97). These include resale price maintenance, horizontal price fixing, export bans, and market sharing. The most damaging agreements between companies are horizontal cartels, which are conspiracies between companies at the same level in the supply chain to share markets, restrict output, increase prices, and exclude competitors. These are nowadays unambiguously illegal under virtually every competition regime and it was expected that they would gradually die out. In fact, cartels seem to be prevalent in many European and global markets and may even be increasing in number (Utton 2011).

DG COMP has made an attack on cartels one of its major priorities since the 1990s. It has become almost a crusade and has revealed astonishing illegal practices by leading companies and senior executives meeting in secret, using codes and subterfuge in attempts to outwit the authorities. The Commission has registered some spectacular successes aided by a leniency regime, introduced in 1996, that provides immunity for the first whistle-blower. Indeed, the Commission has been so successful that it risks being swamped with cartel enforcement work. In 2012, there were sixty leniency applications, but only five cartel decisions: window mountings, water management systems, switchgear, and freight forwarding, in addition to the TV tubes cartel mentioned earlier. In the five years from 2009 to 2013, the Commission imposed fines of €7 billion, which are paid into the EU budget (Commission 2013o). DG COMP has become an important source of EU revenue, to the extent that business representatives are beginning to complain that the size of fines is threatening the viability of companies and sectors.

At the other end of the spectrum, the majority of agreements will be perfectly legal. This applies to most distribution agreements, supply agreements (including discounts), and the many small agreements that affect only a small section of the market. Many agreements will also be exempt because they aid efficiency and 'economic progress'. In order to provide certainty the Commission has issued about a dozen 'block exemptions', which define acceptable agreements in areas such as R&D, maritime transport, and insurance (Goyder 2003: 114–15). Similarly, principles have evolved to define the legality of agreements relating to intellectual property (where it can be pro-competitive to cooperate), and in respect of 'vertical agreements', that is, agreements between enterprises at different stages in the supply chain, which are now generally regarded as acceptable.

Antitrust: abuse of dominance

While the control of restrictive practices is regarded as a Commission success story, the same cannot be said of the second component of competition policy: controlling the abuse of dominance. This is covered by Article 102 TFEU, which prohibits 'any abuse by one or more undertakings of a dominant position within the common market'. This prohibition is aimed at monopolies or, since full monopoly is rare, at oligopoly, where a small number of firms dominate a market. European governments are decidedly ambivalent about the control of oligopoly, the law itself has several significant flaws, and the Commission has been hesitant about exploiting this aspect of its powers. Cini and McGowan (2009: 98) call it 'the weakest link in the Commission's competition policy chain', although they note that efforts are being made to clarify enforcement through an 'effects-based' approach.

For member states, large companies have several attractive features. They enjoy economies of scale, they have financial muscle, and are representative of national industrial prowess, but most of all they can fund high technology and may operate as powerful multinationals able to compete directly with Japanese and US multinationals in global markets. These are the classic features of 'national champions', and many governments, including those of France, Germany, Italy, and the Netherlands, have been loath to see these benefits eroded by active attack from the competition authorities, particularly since Article 102 TFEU, unlike Article 101 TFEU, does not provide for an efficiency defence. This in part explains the hesitancy of the Commission.

Article 102 TFEU is, however, also unsatisfactory in that it requires that the authorities first establish dominance (usually taken as at least 40 per cent of the market as indicated in the 1978 *United Brands* judgment; Whish 2008: 177); and only then can they establish 'abuse'. The law is also weak in attacking oligopolies. The Commission has attempted to establish a principle of 'collective dominance' (several companies working together in an oligopoly), but it was not until the *Italian Flat Glass* case in 1992 that it received any encouragement from the General Court, and even now the concept remains ambiguous (Clarke 2006: 44). If successful in establishing illegal abuse, the Commission has powers to fine, to issue a 'cease and desist' order, and under the 2003 Modernization Regulation (see the section 'DG COMP in context' later in the chapter) it now has powers to break up companies by forcing divestiture. This last option is the antitrust equivalent of a nuclear strike and has never been imposed by the Commission.

A small number of high-profile cases indicate the potential to rein back huge, market-dominating companies. The 2004 action against *Microsoft*, which has led to continued monitoring of its operations, and more recent actions against Gazprom and Google in particular stand out. Proceedings against Gazprom were opened in 2012 to investigate its dominance of the gas market in central and eastern Europe. Google's dominance as an internet search engine prompted the Commission to initiate proceedings in 2010 but at the beginning of 2014 it was still unclear whether Google would be found in breach of Article 102 or whether the Commission would be content with commitments to modify its behaviour (Commission 2013o: 22–3). It is intriguing that these actions are directed at non-EU companies giving some credence to the regular US criticism that EU policy is aimed at protecting competitors (in the shape of large European companies) rather than competition.

Merger control

The third component of policy is the control of mergers and acquisitions that have the potential to generate monopolies. This is the dramatic face of competition policy which attracts huge media attention and frenzied political lobbying so that big mergers present theatrical shows of Shakespearean proportions. They affect thousands of jobs, transform household-name companies, make or break fortunes in financial markets, and establish or destroy the reputations of captains of industry. In most EU countries, unlike the UK, 'hostile' takeovers (i.e. without the agreement of the management of the target company) are unusual and provoke acute opposition. DG COMP has, for example, approved (with conditions) the agreed *Pfizer/Pharmacia* merger to create the largest pharmaceutical company in the world, and the agreed *Pechiney/Alcan* merger (again with conditions) to create the largest aluminium company in the world.

The Merger Regulation (Regulation 4064/89 replaced by Regulation 139/2004) emerged as a result of a decade of pressure from DG COMP and came into effect in September 1990. It was regarded as the crowning triumph of Sir Leon Brittan's highly successful period as Competition Commissioner and established the prestige and influence of DG COMP, prompting the conclusion that, by the early 1990s, the European competition regime had become globally pre-eminent (Wilks with McGowan 1996: 225). The Merger Regulation created a 'one-stop shop' which permitted the Commission to control the largest mergers above a high threshold (mergers below the threshold continue to be dealt with under national legislation). The current threshold is set at an aggregate turnover of €5 billion (Whish and Bailey 2012: 839), which catches about 300 mergers a year. Companies are in favour of the EU process, which is rapid, transparent, and avoids having to seek approval from every state in which they operate.

Cases can, however, be transferred between European and national authorities. Compromises reached during the passage of the regulation introduced Article 9, the 'German clause', so called because it was demanded by the German authorities, which wanted the opportunity to control large national mergers. It allows the Commission to transfer jurisdiction to a member state where the market is mainly national. On the other hand, Article 23, the 'Dutch clause', was demanded by the Dutch authorities and allows a member state to request the Commission to act on its behalf, and also (in the most recent reforms of 2004) allows the merging parties themselves to request that the Commission handle the case. The Commission has pressed for greater flexibility in case-handling and, in a spirit of subsidiarity, regularly transfers jurisdiction to NCAs.

DG COMP implements a logical two-stage process in which most mergers are cleared within one month and only the difficult cases are examined in more depth through the 'Phase 2' procedure. The objective is to block or amend mergers which threaten to create a dominant position that might then be abused. The wording of the test is of vital importance and in 2003 the Commission persuaded the Council to pass a reformed Merger Regulation which introduced an adaptation to the wording of the test (Regulation 139/2004, Arts. 59–68). This retains the dominance test, which has been extensively criticized by the US and the UK (which both now use the 'substantial lessening of competition' test; Vickers 2003: 102), but it now prefaces it by attacking 'a concentration which would significantly impede effective competition'. This change has had little impact in practice, and policy continues to be based on an economic test rather than on public-interest or non-economic considerations.

Throughout the 1990s, the Commission gained confidence, won court cases, and became gradually more interventionist. It is still very unusual for a merger to be blocked completely; only four mergers were blocked outright between 2003 and 2012 (see Table 6.2). It is, however, becoming standard practice for the Commission to accept or impose conditions (often divestiture of part of the merged entity) before approving the merger at Phase 1 or at Phase 2. On this basis, the Commission built up to a crescendo of activity in 2007 when it received 402 notifications.

Since 2000, however, merger policy has suffered some major setbacks. In 2001, the prohibition of the *GE/Honeywell* merger precipitated a torrent of criticism from the US accusing the Commission of arrogance, poor economics, outdated thinking, and incompetent analysis. This was followed by a disastrous year in 2002 when a General Court judgment overturned the Commission's prohibition of the *Airtours/ First Choice* merger, the first appeal that DG COMP had lost. The General Court was damning. It criticized the Commission processes, its use of evidence, the quality of its economic analysis, and stated that the Commission had committed 'manifest errors of assessment' (Veljanovski 2004: 184). This led US critics to renew their allegation that the Commission was defending 'competitors not competition' or, in other words, protecting big European companies and not the interests of consumers (which is now the main declared objective of US antitrust policy). The shock was compounded by two further defeats in the *Schneider Electric* and *Tetra Laval* cases later in 2002. In response, the Commission reformed the merger regime and reinforced economic analysis across the DG. This was symbolized by the creation of a new post of chief economist, held from 2013 by Massimo Motta. The Competition Commissioner for 2000–4, Mario Monti (2003: 7), also an economist (and later prime minister of Italy), noted revealingly that 'to develop an economic interpretation of EU competition rules was … one of my main objectives when I took office.' Where the balance is struck between law and economics and, indeed, what sort of economics is employed, has a marked effect on the development of policy in mergers and across the entire policy area.

State aid

With the fourth component of policy, state aid, the style and focus of policy takes on a very different form. Here the treaty powers are less clear, the processes of implementation are less powerful, and the Commission typically enjoys less cooperation from national governments, which are themselves the targets of control. In this area (as with the liberalization of utility regulation) the Commission is more than the

| | Phase 1 | | | Phase 2 | |
Year	Notifications	Approved	Approved No Conditions	Approved with Conditions	Refused
2003	212	223	2	6	0
2004	247	240	2	4	1
2005	313	308	2	3	0
2006	356	346	4	6	0
2007	402	392	5	4	1
2008	348	326	9	5	0
2009	259	238	0	3	0
2010	274	257	1	2	0
2011	309	304	4	1	1
2012	283	263	1	6	1
Total	3003	2897	30	40	4

TABLE 6.2 Merger regulation cases, 2003–12

Source: Commission, *http://ec.europa.eu/competition/mergers/statistics.pdf*.
Note: lines do not add up due to notifications withdrawn or settled the following year.

agent of the member governments; it transcends national interests and aspires to operate as a truly 'supranational' body enforcing unique powers not found in any other competition authority.

Article 107 TFEU affirms that aid to business, whether private or state-owned, that distorts competition is 'incompatible with the common market'. This applies most clearly to direct state subsidies to companies. However, the concept extends to all forms of assistance, including tax breaks, preferential purchasing, loans, and even loan guarantees. Some forms of aid, and especially large subsidies, were a major tool of industrial policy as recently as the 1980s. Periodic crises in industries such as shipbuilding, coal, aerospace, and the motor industry persuaded governments to grant massive rescue subsidies. Until 2008, these had been virtually eliminated under the tightening state aid rules, but other aspects of aid may, as Cini and McGowan (2009: 166) point out, 'be a good thing' in areas such as R&D, environmental protection, or backward regions, where it may help to overcome market failures and guarantee social benefits. All aid must be notified to the Commission, which assesses its compatibility and has developed frameworks and exemptions to clarify acceptable types and purposes of aid.

A useful technique, developed first when Peter Sutherland was Competition Commissioner in the late 1980s, has been to 'name and shame' governments and reveal the sheer scale of state aid through periodic surveys. This was reinforced after the 2000 Lisbon Agenda through the creation of a state aid register and an online 'scoreboard' in 2001. The Commission found itself frequently working with the grain as national governments, especially in the UK, made greater efforts to reduce the use of subsidies. In 1988, state aid accounted for about 10 per cent of public expenditure or 3–5 per cent of gross domestic product (GDP), in other words, a hugely distorting degree of cross-subsidy from the taxpayer to industry. By 2002, the figure had fallen to about 1.2 per cent of public spending and 0.6 per cent of GDP and by 2006 to 0.4 per cent of GDP (see the Scoreboard on the DG COMP website, *http://europa. eu/competition*).

After the successful decentralization of antitrust enforcement, the Commission moved to reform the state aid regime beginning in 2005 with the State Aid Action Plan (SAAP). The aim was to rationalize the increasingly complex regime by clarifying principles, harmonizing evaluation of schemes, increasing transparency, improving procedures, including a general block exemption, and intensifying the processes of recovering illegal aid. But this modernization was halted in its tracks by the financial crisis. The shape of things to come was indicated by the Commission's swift approval of the UK government's rescue of the collapsed bank Northern Rock in September 2007. Any hopes that the Commission could or should maintain principled opposition to subsidies was dashed by the avalanche of massive and irresistible bank bailouts that followed the collapse of Lehman Brothers in the US in September 2008. The avalanche was accompanied by calls from national leaders, including French President Sarkozy, for the state aid regime to be suspended.

The reaction of Competition Commissioner Neelie Kroes was creative and pragmatic. Rather than suspend the regime, the Commission enacted a 'temporary framework' in December 2008 which in effect allowed rescue and restructuring aid but which aimed to influence aid measures to make them conform as far as possible with eventual restoration of competitive markets. Aid measures were reviewed and made subject to conditions that would come into effect when the worst of the crisis was past. As the recession deepened and the risk of sovereign debt defaults increased in the euro area, so a second round of rescues and restructuring, especially in respect of banks, necessitated a continuation of the crisis regime. The permissive framework was repeatedly extended until it began to be wound down in 2012 with new regulations on State Aid Modernization (SAM) in a package that included a communication on banking in August 2013 that tightened up control of bank rescues by insisting on prior instead of post hoc approval of bank restructuring aid (Commission 2013*d*).

It is evident that the state aid regime failed to prevent a huge escalation in industrial subsidies across the EU. The headline figures drawn from the Commission's State Aid Scoreboard show that over the period October 2008 to December 2011 aid to banking alone totalled an extraordinary €1.6 trillion, equivalent to 13 per cent of

EU GDP. But even this vastly understates the scale of financial commitments. The amount of aid approved (much of it not actually used) during the crisis was an astonishing €5.1 trillion or 40 per cent of the EU's 2011 GDP (Commission 2012e: 31). The majority of this was represented by loan guarantees but it also involved huge amounts of direct state subsidy. So, for instance, in December 2009 the Commission approved plans by the UK government to invest up to €111 billion in the Royal Bank of Scotland. It was, said the Commission spokesman with feeling, 'the largest amount of state aid ever received in the EU's history' (Andrew Willis in euobserver. com, 14 Dec. 2009). The UK committed aid to financial institutions equivalent to 50 per cent of UK GDP but even larger commitments were entered into by Belgium, Denmark, Greece, the Netherlands, and Spain. The most extreme was Ireland, which approved aid equivalent to 365 per cent of GDP (see Lyons and Zhu 2013). Crisis aid to non-financial companies was far smaller and non-crisis aid continued at less than 0.5 per cent of EU GDP.

The vast bulk of the crisis aid was committed in 2008–9, and by 2012 the Commission felt able to return to the postponed issue of modernization with the SAM package. This package involved considered improvements to the regime with consultation and changes in all the main state aid guidelines and frameworks. The driving aims are to ease the approval of what then Competition Commissioner Almunia (2013) referred to as 'good aid', which is pro-growth, responds to market failure, or meets non-economic policy goals such as regional development or environmental protection. The parallel aim is to tighten the regime on anti-competitive 'bad aid', especially the larger cases which are becoming more widely regarded as problematic and therefore vulnerable to complaints from competitors, to legal challenge, and to potential repayment of aid.

How should we assess the state aid regime in the context of Europe's prolonged financial crisis? It was really too early in 2013 for a definitive assessment while many EU countries were still in recession and the euro area contradictions remained unresolved (but see Kassim and Lyons 2013). In addition, of course, the state aid regime was only one facet of a whole range of actions intended to deal with the industrial and financial crises. Nonetheless, we could consider a positive assessment that would be articulated by DG COMP, as against a negative assessment from those who argue that the crisis justified more radical change. On the positive side, the maintenance of the state aid regime could be seen as a mild triumph. It did not buckle under the weight of subsidies, the Commission kept its nerve, it resisted intra-European protectionism, it negotiated improvements, and it followed through with a series of conditions and divestments, which aimed to restore more competitive markets. On the negative side, the regime failed to prevent a remarkable intensification of subsidies that were pursued by national governments and allowed them to gain advantages in the market. Arguably the state aid regime also failed in a wider sense; it has returned to the status quo. It continues to pursue neo-liberal market solutions and appears to be one element reproducing the industrial structures of oligopoly and dominant banks that helped to create the financial crisis. There has, in other words, been a failure to visualize a less Americanized model of capitalism, which is perhaps symptomatic of a wider failure of imagination across the whole competition policy arena (Buch-Hansen and Wigger 2011: 142).

The liberalization of utilities

The fifth and final component of competition policy concerns competition in the public sector and the privatized utilities. As with state aid, a primary target is the national governments that own nationalized industries, grant monopoly powers to state or private utilities, or operate regulatory regimes that suppress competition. The industries in question are the key utility and infrastructure sectors, such as telecommunications, energy, water, post, transport, and airlines, although the issues of state control also extend to the financial sector, insurance, and the media. State ownership of utilities and infrastructure industries had become the norm from the 1950s onwards and the fact that they were 'network' industries was often used to justify them as 'natural monopolies', on the ground that the need for maximum efficiency through a single network (as for electricity distribution) required operation by a single company. Moreover, since these industries performed public services they were deemed to operate in the public interest, and thus to be potentially exempt from competition law (see Chapter 14). In many countries, exemptions were incorporated into national legislation. In the 1990s, this immunity was challenged by technological change, by a shift towards market solutions, and by evidence that such industries were inefficient, inflexible, and far too costly.

The case for liberalization in these sectors, in the interests of efficiency and European competitiveness, was underlined by the single market programme (see Chapter 5), and by the example of the UK where privatization also showed how much change could be achieved. Despite its powers under Article 105(3) TFEU to require member states to liberalize utilities, the Commission recognized how delicate and political such moves could be in areas of such vital importance to the quality of life, which often excited great public support and were typically heavily unionized and politically powerful. There has also been acceptance that competition policy should recognize the importance of public service obligations as part of a wider constitutional debate about European citizenship rights (Prosser 2005: 205). Nevertheless, considerable progress in liberalization has taken place in telecommunications, air transport, and energy. There have been efforts to liberalize postal services, but less activity in water and surface transport. Taking energy as an example, DG COMP and worked closely with DG ENER (energy) to employ a range of competition instruments including antitrust, mergers, and state aid to implement a legislative package passed in 2011 aimed at opening up access to energy networks and creating an EU-wide single energy market (see Chapter 14). The competition agenda has been overshadowed by issues of climate change (and support for renewable energy) and by energy security but the issues are balanced in a sectoral approach to energy rather than a narrow focus on individual competition infringements. The sectoral approach informed the three pillars of EU energy policy: competitiveness, sustainability, and security of supply so that competition tools seek to pursue sustainability and security in addition to their traditional emphasis on competitiveness.

Thus, European competition policy has gone through a process of incremental development (see Table 6.1) including a legal foundation of accumulation of jurisprudence and the creation of a cadre of career competition specialists in big international law firms. Competition policy also needs to be assessed against the economic cycle. In boom periods, merger activity increases, state aid work decreases, and on the whole DG COMP faces less opposition. In recession, companies and governments feel more vulnerable and the interventionist voices within the Commission and its other DGs begin to prevail. There has also been a cycle of economic theory, and European competition enforcement has ridden on the wave of post-Thatcher neo-liberalism. In exploiting these stages of development, the single most important element lies in the nature, leadership, and competence of the responsible agencies and their staff.

Agencies and implementation: DG COMP

The development and implementation of competition policy is centred in the Commission in a Directorate-General, formerly DG IV, now DG COMP. It is a small organization, which employs 721 staff (Oct. 2013) of whom 436 are senior administrative officials who make decisions and contribute to policy. The senior ranks were traditionally dominated by lawyers, though economists are now playing a greater role. Its political head is the Commissioner, from 1999 to 2004 Mario Monti, an Italian economist; from 2004 to 2009 Neelie Kroes, a Dutch businesswoman; and from 2009 to 2014 Joaquín Almunia, a Spanish socialist politician and previously Commissioner for Economic and Monetary Affairs. DG COMP is regarded as one of the most attractive postings both for the commissioner and for the director-general, and the relationship between them is of key importance. In 2009, the Dutchman Alexander Italianer became director-general. One feature of DG COMP is that many of its senior officials have spent their entire careers in its ranks: this brings benefits of continuity but at the same time carries the risk of insularity. The Commission does not practise the 'revolving door' exchange of lawyers between the private and government sectors, which is common in the US.

The DG was reorganized in 2004 in a surprising move which abolished the Merger Task Force and distributed merger control across five sectoral directorates. The sectoral approach is usual amongst competition agencies and is the model used by the German Bundeskartellamt (BKA) and the UK Office of Fair Trading (OFT). The current structure of nine directorates includes one dealing with state aid, one dealing with cartels, two with planning, strategy, and international links, and five organized to engage with sectors of industry (Cini and McGowan 2009: 50).

A key question when assessing DG COMP concerns its level of independence. Decisions affecting competition are made by the entire college of Commissioners, who are expected to reach agreement as a collective body. The Competition Commissioner must therefore risk opposition to controversial policies and decisions: member governments often press 'their' commissioner to influence policy and decisions can rest on political negotiation and compromise, and will—albeit rarely—go to a vote, especially in cases of state aid. Observers often therefore point to 'the perception that the European competition regime is highly politicized' (Cini and McGowan 2009: 222), and 'the lack of independence of the Community competition law enforcement mechanisms' (Laudati 1996: 230). This critique has prompted periodic calls for the creation of a more clearly independent European Cartel Office (Wilks 2005b: 128). The extent of DG COMP's vulnerability to industrial lobbying is less clear, although Buch-Hansen and Wigger (2011) contend that corporate lobbying has had a great influence on the development of merger policy and the 'turn to economics'.

On the other hand, DG COMP is relatively free from control from the Council and the Parliament, for two main reasons. First, in implementing specific treaty articles it enjoys unambiguous legal authority. Secondly, in 1962 the Council delegated to the Commission extensive procedural powers to implement the relevant articles. These delegated powers were set out in Regulation 17/62 and effectively renewed through the Modernization Regulation (1/2003). Independence is far from absolute, but can be compared with the great independent regulatory agencies of the US, such as the Federal Trade Commission (FTC) (Wilks with Bartle 2002; Wilks with McGowan 1996), and is a prized feature of competition agencies the world over. Such independence is regarded as essential to protect the absolute values of economic competition, to avoid improper influence by business, and to avoid self-interested influence by other government departments or agencies (and, in the EU, by national governments which are among the targets of implementation).

The theme of independence serves to underline the claim that DG COMP is perhaps the most powerful competition authority in the world. It is certainly the most impressive example of an administrative system in which the initiative is taken by public officials and it provides a convincing alternative to US-style antitrust where enforcement operates through the courts. There are now over 100 competition agencies worldwide and the major ones are ranked annually on a peer-reviewed basis by the *Global Competition Review*. The five 'elite' agencies, ranked at a maximum of five stars, were the US FTC, the US Department of Justice Antitrust Division, the EU's DG COMP, the BKA (raised to elite status in 2011), and the UK Competition Commission (which is small and depends on references from the OFT) (Global Competition Review 2013). DG COMP's ability to mobilize the twenty-eight European competition agencies (see the following section) enhances its globally pre-eminent position. In the US, there are two powerful authorities (the FTC and the Antitrust Division of the Department of Justice), and much of the dynamism is provided by private actions in the courts, which are still very unusual in the EU. The EU administrative model of enforcement offers a globally attractive alternative to the US prosecutorial system. It does, however, demand an effective, well-led, and well-resourced organization. With a mere 436 senior administrative officials to police a market of over 500 million consumers, DG COMP was, and remains, acutely understaffed. The only plausible explanation for under-resourcing is that the member states see resources as one of the few pragmatic ways in which to restrain the ambitions of the DG. On the other hand, as we see in the next section, the modernization reforms have allowed DG COMP to mobilize the resources of the NCAs.

There has been repeated criticism of DG COMP from both businesses and legal firms for its lack of accountability. It is said that the Commission is 'prosecutor, judge, and jury' or, to extend the metaphor, it is 'policeman, arbitrator, prosecutor, judge, jury, and prison officer'. This criticism arises essentially from the Article 101 TFEU restrictive practices procedure. A case is opened either following a complaint or as a result of an in-house investigation ('policeman'). The case is handled by one senior member of staff, the rapporteur, who investigates the abuse and often negotiates with the companies involved to change their practices ('arbitrator'). If this fails, the rapporteur constructs a case, argues it in the office, discusses it with the Legal Service, and presses for a decision ('prosecutor'). Senior staff of the DG decide ('jury'), and settle on a penalty ('judge') which is then imposed or negotiated with the companies ('prison officer'). Not all of this is done by the same person, but much rests in the hands of the rapporteur and the whole process takes place within one organization, albeit with attention to natural justice and arrangements such as access to the file and information meetings, as well as the involvement of a neutral 'hearings officer' to ensure fair play. Despite efforts to improve accountability, and despite the independent sanction of the courts, there is some truth in the accountability criticism. As DG COMP has become more powerful, so the problem has become more acute.

DG COMP in context

How DG COMP operates has also to be seen in a broader EU institutional context. No sector of industry is excluded from the competition rules, although there are some exemptions, particularly in agriculture. Thus, all the sectoral DGs such as Transport and Energy need to cooperate with DG COMP. As regards competitiveness and market integration, DG MARKT (internal market) and DG ENTR (enterprise and industry) are key partners, which have accepted the argument that strong competition enhances productivity and competitiveness. Nonetheless, there is ambiguity about what objectives should animate competition enforcement. Should economic efficiency be the sole aim or should other policy objectives come into play? Recently, DG COMP has moved to a much stricter economic definition of goals and articulated a 'consumer welfare' framework leaning heavily on US doctrine. This interpretation raises strong ideological issues and, as Townley (2009: 70) points out, is inconsistent with the TFEU, which emphasises many other goals such as environmental protection and public health. In addition, DG COMP's Article 101 decisions have historically stressed such non-economic goals and EU case law has recognized such alternative goals. Thus, Townley argues, competition enforcement should give due recognition to other policy goals and not simply emphasize the competition rules and a consumer-welfare standard.

The legal apparatus therefore imposes a constraint on DG COMP. Within the Commission, the Legal Service has to be consulted about all legally binding acts and is therefore in constant contact with the DG. The Legal Service represents the Commission before the CJEU and the General Court, and is inherently risk-averse, which at times causes serious tension. The European courts themselves are very important. The CJEU and the General Court provide the cement of European integration and are the most supranational of the European institutions. The CJEU was originally the venue for litigation and appeals in competition matters, and issued a series of key judgments, which not only supported the Commission, but defined market integration as a central goal of European competition policy (a goal unique to the European regime).

The overload of complex and detailed competition cases led to the creation of the CFI as a junior court under the 1986 Single European Act, and now renamed the General Court. The General Court has a less formal procedure and is more specialist. It hears the majority of competition cases in small panels of five judges and in some cases (e.g. mergers) can operate rapidly through an 'expedited process'. It has been less forgiving to the Commission than the CJEU, which had been accused of being too lenient to DG COMP, especially over procedural inadequacies. In contrast, the General Court has been rigorous and has reinforced the need for procedural correctness over matters such as giving a fair hearing, defining the exact case to be answered, and setting out key evidence. In more recent cases, the General Court has also challenged the substantive content of decisions, challenged the reasoning and the interpretation of the evidence, and emphasized the need for more rigorous economic analysis. Thus, we are seeing a shift to a more adversarial stance in the relationship between the Commission and the court. But the key point remains—that competition policy is being taken forward through a framework of European law within which policy developments are discussed, enacted, and resolved in a legal environment and using legal discourse.

A further contextual factor in the Commission's ability to develop competition policy lies in its relationship with the NCAs in the member states, which may include executive agencies, courts, tribunals, or government departments. In 1958, there was virtually no competition machinery in the member states, making it easier for policy to be centralized in Brussels. Some member states, such as Austria, Germany, Ireland, and the UK, had their own antitrust traditions, embodied in laws and agencies which predated their EU membership. There is thus a pattern of long-established agencies, such as the BKA and the OFT, followed by creation or reform of established agencies in the remaining member states up to the late 1990s. In each case, the legislation and the agency roles have converged on the model of European law and DG COMP (Drahos 2001; van Waarden and Drahos 2002). The members that joined subsequently were not given any choice; acceptance of the competition rules and the entire weight of European jurisprudence as part of the *acquis* were conditions of accession, as was the allocation of reasonable resources to support active competition agencies and courts.

The face of EU competition policy has been changed radically since the introduction of the Modernization Regulation (1/2003). Previously, the enforcement of the antitrust rules had been undertaken by the Commission alone. By contrast, the new system empowers the NCAs of the member states to make decisions, grant exemptions, and hear appeals. This was a once-in-a-generation reform which carried the risks of incoherence, inconsistency, and conflict in the application of Articles 101 and 102 (see Wilks 2005a, 2007). In practice, modernization has proved very successful from the point of view of the Commission, which has replaced national laws with EU law (for all cases that involve trade between member states) and has established supervision over the NCAs. It has achieved effective control by a remarkable exercise in policy innovation built on normative agreement over the merits of competition, and administrative coordination through the European Competition Network (ECN) (Wilks 2007). As a result, DG COMP now sits at the heart of a distinctive regulatory network that binds together the twenty-eight competition agencies of the member states. These range from the large, elite, well-resourced agencies of France, Germany, Italy, the Netherlands, and the UK to small and under-resourced agencies such as those of Austria, Belgium, and Estonia (Wilks 2007). The 'Big 4' agencies together employ nearly 1,000 senior staff, more competition specialists than DG COMP and substantially more than in the US (Global Competition Review 2013). These agencies share information through the ECN, allocate cases, engage in cooperative enforcement, and develop policy options. This constitutes a striking model of regulatory cooperation by more or less independent agencies whose actions converge in response to the economic and legal acceptance and enforcement of the treaty competition rules.

This picture of the effective organization of European competition enforcement partially conceals continued US intellectual and ideological influence. US competition priorities and economic theories provide the reference points and inspiration for much European competition innovation and have encouraged movement towards two further aspects of US antitrust: private actions and settlements. On private actions, the Commission issued a Green Paper in 2005 exploring ways in which private parties injured by illegal behaviour could sue in national courts without involving NCAs. This is the typical mode of enforcement in the US but is far less attractive in Europe owing, for instance, to the absence of class action suits (which allow injured parties to club together) and of treble damages (which allow successful claimants to recover three times the damage suffered). In June 2013, the Commission issued a draft directive on 'Rules governing actions for damages under national law' (Commission 2013*e*), which sidestepped the vexed question of collective re-dress (class actions) by encouraging national governments to consider permissive legislation. Nonetheless, the overall focus is on providing access to compensation for injured parties, and an additional element of deterrence will clearly come into play.

In terms of settlements, the second aspect of convergence with the US, in 2008 the Commission issued a notice allowing settlement of cartel cases through paying an agreed fine but avoiding a formal procedure or appeal. Here the similarity is with the 'consent decrees' by which the majority of US cases are settled and it was hoped that this would enable the backlog of European cases to be reduced. So far this has not been particularly successful. In these initiatives we see a procedural convergence with US antitrust to complement the internal, European convergence evident in modernization and the ECN.

For some observers, this procedural Americanization is a symptom of a deeper-seated ideological Americanization. In fact, the shift of EU competition enforcement towards US antitrust is no secret; it reflects a consensus among practitioners and is applauded by officials (Wilks 2007). More controversial are the implications of this shift. First is the proposition that Anglo-Saxon-style competition enforcement embeds neo-liberalism and threatens traditional German-style neo-corporatist or 'Rhenish' capitalism (Townley 2009: 80; Wigger 2007: 497–500). Secondly, is the suggestion that the move to US-style economic tests favours large transnational cor-porations and that this policy stance has been lobbied for by large European corpor-ations. The result is that large corporations are tolerated and even encouraged by EU policy (Freyer 2006: 303; Lowe 2006). This is an important emerging debate, which confirms European convergence in competition policy, but convergence on a model that in its principles, procedures, and effects is encouraging European industry to move towards an Anglo-Saxon liberal market economy.

Competition policy as regulatory policy

Competition policy displays significant features of two of the policy models outlined in Chapter 4—the Community method and regulatory policy—and shows virtually no similarity with the transgovernmental and distributional modes. However, recent reforms also indicate a limited move towards the policy coordination mode. It is not surprising that two of the policy modes are exemplified in competition policy. This policy area is both a leading example of the success of the Community method and provides much of the raw material that allowed Majone (1996) to develop his analy-sis of European regulation.

The main alignment of competition policy with the traditional Community method lies in the strong role for the Commission in designing and enforcing policy, especially over the period in which policy has been highly centralized and domi-nated by DG COMP. In competition policy, the Commission has enjoyed exceptional freedom from the Council and the member governments. Its key partners are the courts, and as long as its actions are legally defensible the Commission has been able to act assertively and directly. In line with the Community method, the Commission has pursued the goal of 'positive integration' with great determination. It has therefore sought to create a market without frontiers and has strongly attacked measures by firms (or governments) that segment markets, limit trade, or apply different practices in different geographical areas. Following modernization, this strong version of centralized policy has continued.

Competition policy exhibits an even closer resemblance to the regulatory mode of policy-making. This draws on the exceptionally fertile theories advanced by Majone (1996: 55, 287) about the position of the EU as a 'regulatory state', specifying behaviour in legislation and ensuring compliance through the legal system (Majone 1996: 63), where its ability to undertake regulatory policy is almost limitless. The legal process based on the treaty is enhanced by the legal apparatus of regulations and decisions, supplemented by the 'soft law' of guidelines, frameworks, opinions, and notices, and has been reinforced by supportive judgments of the CJEU which have provided the foundation of Community competence. The primacy of Community law and the supremacy of the European courts mean that, as long as the Commission can win appeals in them, its decisions become binding on companies and governments across the EU—and sometimes extraterritorially. Moreover, this process is extremely inexpensive, at least in terms of its burden on the EU budget. The administrative costs of regulation are borne by the courts, the legal systems of the member states, and the clients of law firms, whilst the substantive costs of compliance and alterations of business practices are hidden and borne by firms.

The freedom of the Commission to regulate is enhanced by the weakness of the EP, a feature shared in this field with national systems. Its legitimacy therefore rests on the acceptance of its market-economy approach and ultimately on how far it succeeds in creating greater efficiency and ensuring some degree of equitable access to benefit from the wealth created. Majone (1996: 296) has argued, subtly and provocatively, that regulation does not need to be legitimized by control through the institutions of popular democracy, but can be legitimized through debate and deliberation among experts, observing due process, and pursuing objective standards of efficiency. His analysis has stimulated a wider debate about 'non-majoritarian' agencies, and about the values of independence and expertise embodied in regulatory agencies. DG COMP provides the classic example of independent European regulation (Wilks with Bartle 2002), perhaps as an extreme case of law-driven policy-making, conducted with a legal discourse through a network of legal institutions, courts, and law firms across the EU. Indeed, the process of modernization may perhaps best be understood as the mobilization of ideas through a legal community spreading across the member states.

The modernization reforms have changed the face of European competition policy and have created a new mode of policy formulation and implementation in the form of the ECN. This invites an evaluation of whether modernization and reform of merger and state aid policy can be seen as an example of the new policy mode of 'policy coordination'. The creation of independent competition agencies in all the member states since the mid-1980s means that the future implementation of policy will depend to a far greater extent on negotiation, coordination, and networking, as the coordination model both predicts and celebrates.

Conclusion

This chapter argues that competition policy has a special place in the European policy matrix because it defends the essential mobilizing principle of the EU, the collective interest in economic efficiency secured through the creation of a common market. In its pursuit of integration, the Commission has employed a shrewd strategy of using the market and appealing to free-market principles. Its success has produced what Jabko (2006: 183) has called a 'quiet revolution' that has created a truly European political economy. The European economy has grown in parallel with institutions of European economic governance. The most salient institution is economic and monetary union (EMU), led by the ECB (see Chapter 7), but of equal importance and wider effect are the competition rules and DG COMP. In these areas 'the European Union has become a real *federal power*' (Jabko 2006: 183). We can argue therefore that, as Europe converts its treaties into a constitution, so the economic provisions of those treaties become constitutional principles underpinning the operation of the European economy; in other words, the competition rules can be analysed as an 'economic constitution' (Wilks 2010). This proposition underlines the importance and influence of the competition rules and has three further implications.

First, it emphasizes the independence of the agencies and especially DG COMP. Implementation of constitutional principles makes DG COMP doubly insulated from national political pressures. Secondly, it identifies the deepening of a process of legalization of economic regulation and an expansion of economic law which could be termed 'juridification' of the economic sphere. The economic constitution protects certain economic rights but at a cost of legal process. Thirdly, and most speculatively, the constitutional perspective suggests that certain market principles have become embedded in European institutional practice and constitutional provisions. Clearly Europe is based on market principles, but what sort of market? Jabko (2006) has argued that the Commission integrationists have employed a brilliant market rhetoric but have never defined what sort of market Europe was working towards. It is the argument of this chapter that the competition rules have moved towards a free market which is in fact more neo-liberal, more purely market-oriented, than many in Europe would be inclined to accept. This raises the political stakes and, in terms of the focus of this book on policy-making, it suggests that competition policy has transmuted into a still poorly understood mode of constitutional politics.

The financial crisis threatened this economic constitution from a number of angles. It could have undermined the competition policy instruments, especially the state aid regime. It could have led to an outbreak of protectionism, state intervention, and nationalistic discrimination against non-national companies. It could have discredited the neo-liberal or Anglo-Saxon model in favour of a more collectivist German or Rhineland model of capitalism. In 2009, a rise in state intervention and a rejection of the neo-liberal model were very widely forecast. None of these threats materialized. The Commission successfully defended the economic constitution, just as it defended the euro area. There is an increasingly optimistic sense of a 'return to normal'. Whether this is a benign outcome is a deeply normative question. Arguably EU- and US-style competition policy was an important institutional component of the system that collapsed in 2008. Should we be celebrating a return to the principles of that system? That question has been marginalized by European competition policy-makers, who have focused on the creation and successful working of their modernized, networked, continental competition regime. To end with a mildly triumphalist quote from Joaquín Almunia (2013) in a speech delivered in July 2013: 'the picture that emerges from this quick review of competition policy … is quite encouraging. The reform of 2004 that radically changed the enforcement of EU antitrust is producing results. Together the Commission and the NCAs form a much stronger team across the EU'.

NOTE

1 For complete references to these and other Commission merger and antitrust decisions, see the Tables of Cases and Legislation at the front of this volume.

FURTHER READING

The best guide to the evolution of European competition policy is the Commission's annual report which provides a review of Commission and court activities over the previous year, highlights strategic policy priorities, the Commission's own rationale, and, to some extent, the debates surrounding new initiatives. These latter aspects are also covered in the quarterly *Competition Policy Newsletter*, published by DG COMP. Both publications are available on the excellent DG COMP website (*http://ec.europa.eu/competition/*). More critical accounts of EU and member-state policy can be found in the *European Competition Law Review* and the *European Competition Journal*.

A good introduction can be found in Cini and McGowan (2009) and an excellent introduction to the broader political context is provided by Amato (1997). Wilks (2010) offers a comprehensive overview of the subject area whilst further analysis of the Commission and modernization appears in Wilks (2005*a*, 2007). Wigger and Nölke (2007) and Buch-Hansen and Wigger (2011) provide excellent critical perspectives. There is an extensive legal literature that is accessible to the general reader. Especially valuable are the opening and closing chapters of Goyder (2003), the study by Drahos (2001), and the more technical seventh edition of Whish and Bailey (2012). The best introductions to the economic basis of policy can be found in Motta (2004) and Budzinski (2008). For cartels, see Utton (2011), and for state aid the 2013 special issue of the *Journal of Industry, Competition and Trade*, 13(1) is valuable.

Amato, G. (1997), *Antitrust and the Bounds of Power* (Oxford: Hart).

Buch-Hansen H., and Wigger A. (2011), *The Politics of European Competition Regulation* (London: Routledge).

Budzinski, O. (2008), 'Monoculture versus Diversity in Competition Economics', *Cambridge Journal of Economics*, 32/2: 295–324.

Cini, M., and McGowan, L. (2009), *Competition Policy in the European Union*, 2nd edn. (Basingstoke: Palgrave Macmillan).

Drahos, M. (2001), *Convergence of Competition Laws and Policies in the European Community* (Deventer: Kluwer).

Goyder, D. (2003), *EC Competition Law*, 4th edn. (Oxford: Oxford University Press).

Motta, M. (2004), *Competition Policy: Theory and Practice* (Cambridge: Cambridge University Press).

Utton, M. (2011), *Cartels and Economic Collusion* (Cheltenham: Edward Elgar).

Whish, R., and Bailey D. (2012), *Competition Law*, 7th edn. (Oxford: Oxford University Press).

Wigger, A., and Nölke, A. (2007), 'Enhanced Roles of Private Actors in EU Business Regulation and the Erosion of Rhenish Capitalism: the Case of Antitrust Enforcement', *Journal of Common Market Studies*, 45/2: 487–513.

Wilks, S. (2005a), 'Agency Escape: Decentralization or Dominance of the European Commission in the Modernization of Competition Policy?', *Governance*, 18/3: 431–52.

Wilks, S. (2007), 'Agencies, Networks, Discourses and the Trajectory of European Competition Enforcement', *European Competition Journal*, 3/2: 437–64.

Wilks, S. (2010), 'Competition Policy', in W. Grant, D. Coen, and G. Wilson (eds.), *The Oxford Handbook of Business and Government* (Oxford: Oxford University Press), 730–56.

CHAPTER 7

Policy-Making under Economic and Monetary Union
Crisis, Change, and Continuity

Dermot Hodson

█ Summary

Economic and monetary union (EMU) provides the European Union (EU) with a major role in macroeconomic policy-making. As of 2015, nineteen members of the euro area have exchanged national currencies for the euro and delegated responsibility for

(continued...)

monetary policy and financial supervision to the European Central Bank (ECB). Member states have also agreed to coordinate their budgetary policies and structural reforms, to provide financial assistance to member states facing fiscal crises, and to speak with one voice on international issues. EMU is a high-stakes experiment in new modes of EU policy-making insofar as the governance of the euro area relies on alternatives to the traditional Community method, including policy coordination, intensive transgovernmentalism, and delegation to de novo bodies. This experiment has suffered a number of setbacks since the launch of the euro in 1999, not least following the global financial crisis of 2007–8. The crisis has served as a catalyst for comprehensive reforms to policy-making in EMU, which some see as paving the way for a more centralized approach to economic policy but which provide no evidence of a return to the Community method thus far.

Introduction

Macroeconomic policy is a province of public policy that has traditionally been closely guarded by national politicians, civil servants, and central bank officials.[1] It typically entails the setting of short-term interest rates (monetary policy) and decisions related to government expenditure and taxation (fiscal policy) and can include measures designed to influence the external value of the currency (exchange-rate policy). Macroeconomic policies are closely intertwined with structural reforms and financial market policies. Structural reforms include regulatory changes aimed at improving the functioning of product and labour markets. Financial market policies encompass the regulation and supervision of banks and other financial institutions. The goals of macroeconomic policy include the pursuit of price stability, higher economic growth, sound public finances, and the smooth functioning of both the balance of payments and the financial system. These are technical goals, to be sure, but the difference between meeting and missing them can have a profound effect on people's standards of living.

EMU entails a radical shift in macroeconomic policy-making in the EU. As of 1 January 2015, nineteen euro area countries—Austria, Belgium, Cyprus, Estonia, Finland, France, Germany, Greece, Ireland, Italy, Latvia, Lithuania, Luxembourg, Malta, the Netherlands, Portugal, Slovakia, Slovenia, and Spain—have exchanged their national currencies for the euro and delegated responsibility for monetary policy to the ECB. Member states have retained varying degrees of control over the other aspects of macroeconomic policy, although they have agreed to coordinate these policies in informal settings such as the Eurogroup and euro summit. National governments have, in addition, accepted limits on how much they can borrow under the Stability and Growth Pact (SGP) and agreed to coordinate fiscal policies and structural reforms via a patchwork of procedures. They have also, following the global financial crisis of 2007–8, created the European Stability Mechanism (ESM) to provide financial assistance to euro area members and launched a single supervisory mechanism for euro area banks as part of plans for European banking union (see Chapter 5).

EMU has a threefold significance for students of EU policy-making. First, the single currency is among the most tangible symbols of European integration for the 335 million people who live in the euro area. Secondly, the euro is a major global currency that is second only to the US dollar in terms of its international usage, making EMU central to the EU's ambitions to become a leading player on the world stage. Thirdly, and critically for the themes of this volume, EMU is a high-stakes experiment in new modes of EU policy-making. As discussed in Chapter 4, the traditional Community method involves the delegation of key responsibilities to the Commission. Under EMU, responsibility for monetary policy and financial supervision have been delegated to a new kind of supranational institution, the ECB, and the ESM has been given a key role in the management of financial crises. Other elements of economic policy—most noticeably those concerning fiscal policy and structural reform—can be seen as a pioneering attempt at policy coordination among national governments. The euro summit and the external representation of the euro area, meanwhile, are closer to intensive transgovernmentalism.

This chapter explores the origins and evolution of EMU as the euro approaches its third decade. The first section puts the creation of EMU in historical context. The second looks at the economic performance of the euro area from 1999 to EMU's sovereign debt crisis. The third section looks at the ECB and the ESM as variations on the Community method. The fourth section takes stock of EMU's experiment with policy coordination and the manifold reforms to euro area governance in the light of the global financial crisis. The fifth section views the emergence of the Eurogroup and the euro summit and EMU's fragmented system of external representation through the lens of intensive transgovernmentalism.

The origins of economic and monetary union

The 1957 Treaty of Rome (EEC) contained few references to macroeconomic policy and no reference to EMU (see Table 7.1 for a chronology). One reason why the treaty did not go further here was that the Keynesian consensus that held sway among economists at the time stressed the need for national control of macroeconomic policy instruments. Specifically, governments were expected to trade off higher inflation for lower unemployment and, in the event of an economic downturn, to stimulate aggregate demand through a combination of tax cuts, expenditure increases, and interest rate reductions. Another relevant factor was that member states chose not to challenge the Bretton Woods Agreement of 1944, which sought exchange-rate stability among industrial countries by linking the US dollar to gold and linking national currencies to the dollar (see Maes 2004).

TABLE 7.1 Chronology of EMU (Part 1)

July 1944	Bretton Woods Agreement signed
Mar. 1957	Treaty of Rome signed
Oct. 1970	Werner Group adopts its final report
Mar. 1971	Member states agree to three-stage plan for EMU
Mar. 1973	Collapse of the Bretton Woods system
Mar. 1979	Launch of the European Monetary System (EMS)
Apr. 1989	Delors Committee adopts its final report
July 1990	Stage 1 of EMU begins
Feb. 1992	Treaty on European Union signed at Maastricht
Sept. 1992	Italy and the UK exit the exchange-rate mechanism (ERM)
Aug. 1993	Reform of the ERM
Jan. 1994	Stage 2 of EMU begins
June 1997	European Council in Amsterdam adopts the SGP
Dec. 1997	European Council in Luxembourg creates the Eurogroup
May 1998	EU leaders decide that 11 member states have met the convergence criteria; ECB established
Jan. 1999	Stage 3 of EMU begins and the euro area is created

In December 1969, EEC leaders invited the Luxembourg prime minister, Pierre Werner, to work out a plan for EMU. This plan was part of European attempts to address the global macroeconomic imbalances that emerged under the Bretton Woods system (James 2012: 2). These imbalances occurred, in part, because the US could no longer maintain the dollar's link with gold amid the inflationary effects of the Vietnam War. There were also concerns at the time that flexible exchange rates would disrupt trade relations within the EEC and make the common agricultural policy more costly (Commission 1969).

The Werner Plan was adopted in 1971 but abandoned after member states' initial attempts at exchange-rate cooperation foundered following the disintegration of Bretton Woods in 1973 and the oil crisis that same year. In 1979, EEC member states made a fresh attempt at exchange-rate cooperation through the European Monetary System (EMS). The centrepiece of the EMS was the exchange-rate mechanism (ERM), which was designed to minimize fluctuations among national currencies. A weighted basket of EEC currencies, the European currency unit (ecu), was used as the denominator for this system. The EMS had its ups and downs but it helped to promote exchange-rate stability and to reduce inflation, especially in the second half of the 1980s when national governments resorted less frequently to the practice of devaluing their currencies.

McNamara (1998) links the creation of the EMS to member states' move towards monetarism from the mid-1970s onwards. Monetarism challenged Keynesianism by rejecting the existence of a long-term trade-off between growth and employment and prioritizing the pursuit of low inflation through restrictions on money-supply growth. The ERM, McNamara argues, was viewed as a commitment device for achieving monetarism's primary objective of price stability. A case in point was France, where President François Mitterrand used the ERM to reinforce his efforts to reduce inflation and restore macroeconomic credibility after abandoning Keynesianism in 1983.

In June 1988, the European Council asked the Commission president, Jacques Delors, to lead a high-level committee comprised chiefly of central bank governors to draw up a fresh plan for EMU. Using this plan as a starting point, EU leaders adopted a three-stage transition to EMU that was enshrined in the Treaty on European Union (TEU), signed at Maastricht in 1992. Stage 1 (1990–4) included the removal of the remaining barriers to the free movement of capital and the granting of political independence to central banks. Stage 2 (1994–8) required member states to demonstrate their commitment to macroeconomic discipline by meeting convergence criteria (see Table 7.2). It also saw the launch of the Broad Economic Policy Guidelines (BEPGs), a set of non-binding recommendations on the economic policies of the member states and the Community proposed by the Commission and

TABLE 7.2 Summary of the convergence criteria

What is measured?	How is it measured?	Convergence criteria
Price stability	Harmonized index of consumer prices (HICP)	Not more than 1.5 percentage points above the three best performing member states
Sound public finances	Government deficit as % of GDP	Reference value: not more than 3%
Sustainable public finances	Government debt as % of GDP	Reference value: not more than 60%; if above this reference value, government debt should have sufficiently diminished and must be approaching 60% at a satisfactory pace
Durable convergence	Long-term interest rates	Not more than 2 percentage points above the three best performing member states in terms of price stability
Exchange-rate stability	Deviation from a central rate	Participation in ERM II for two years without severe tensions

Source: Commission (2008d: 8) © European Union, 1995–2014.

endorsed by EU finance ministers. Stage 3 (1999 onwards) included the irrevocable fixing of exchange rates and the creation of the ECB. In keeping with the new classical economics, the intellectual successor to monetarism in the 1980s, the treaty tackled concerns about the ability of short-sighted governments to make the right long-term choices for the economy. The treaty did this, first, by guaranteeing the ECB's independence from political control and, secondly, through the excessive deficit procedure, which prohibits member states from running budget deficits in excess of 3 per cent of gross domestic product (GDP).

European integration scholars are divided as to the rationale for resuscitating plans for EMU at this time (see Sadeh and Verdun 2009). Neo-functionalists emphasize the importance of spill-over from prior stages of economic integration. Padoa-Schioppa (2000), for example, argues that the single European market programme (see Chapter 5) forced member states to choose between EMU and flexible exchange rates because the free movement of capital rendered the EMS unworkable. Intergovernmentalists, in contrast, explain EMU as the outcome of interstate bargaining. In a variation on this theme, Moravcsik (1998) views EMU as an attempt by national governments, motivated primarily by economic interests, to lock in the benefits of macroeconomic stability at the EU level. The benefits of this enterprise, he argues, were modest for Germany because of the privileged position of the deutschmark in the EMS. For Moravcsik, this explains why the TEU enshrined macroeconomic principles that enjoyed a high degree of support among German policy-makers, especially the overriding importance attached to price stability.

Economists have generally been more circumspect than political scientists about the *ex ante* economic rationale for EMU. Following Mundell (1961), the prevailing view in the 1980s and 1990s was that European countries would struggle to form an optimum currency area (OCA) because of the prevalence of asymmetric shocks (economic disturbances that affect different countries in different ways) and the perceived lack of flexibility in product and labour markets. Of course, the logic of OCA theory is not undisputed. Mundell himself later warned that floating exchange rates could be a cause of, rather than a cure for, macroeconomic instability as national financial markets become more integrated (De Grauwe 2006). Furthermore, the macroeconomic costs of giving up national exchange rates must be weighed against the microeconomic benefits of monetary union, which include the elimination of exchange-rate uncertainty, the transaction cost savings of doing business in one currency, and the competitive gains from increased price transparency between countries (De Grauwe 2012).

In the early 1990s, preparations for EMU hit a stumbling block when a combination of German unification and falling economic growth and rising unemployment in the rest of the Community generated significant strains within the EMS. Following intense currency speculation, Italy and the UK were forced to suspend their membership of the ERM in September 1992. A year later, the ERM was made much less binding after the remaining member states adopted extra-large margins of fluctuation between their currencies. In May 1998, EU leaders finally agreed that eleven member states—Austria, Belgium, Finland, France, Germany, Ireland, Italy,

Luxembourg, the Netherlands, Portugal, and Spain—fulfilled the convergence criteria and could proceed to Stage 3 of EMU. The inclusion of Belgium and Italy on this list was politically controversial since public debt in these countries, though it was diminishing in line with the treaty requirements, exceeded 100 per cent of GDP.

The European Council took a number of steps on the eve of the euro's launch to strengthen economic policy coordination. In June 1997, the heads of state and government signed the SGP, an agreement designed to reinforce the TEU's excessive deficit procedure. In December of the same year, the European Council agreed that the finance ministers of euro area members could meet informally with representatives of the ECB in attendance in a forum that would come to be known as the Eurogroup. In July 1998, EU finance ministers adopted the first set of country-specific recommendations under the BEPGs. Although these recommendations were non-binding, they signalled the EU's growing interest in public finances; product, labour, and capital market reforms; and other aspects of member states' economic policies.

This intensification of policy coordination can be seen as a response to the twin problems of adjustment and spill-over under EMU. The problem of adjustment follows from OCA theory insofar as the irrevocable fixing of exchange rates within a monetary union leaves its members dependent on fiscal policy and relative prices and wages to adjust to asymmetric shocks. The problem of spill-over refers to the possibility that policy decisions taken in one member of a monetary union could generate negative externalities for other members. Seen in these terms, the SGP sought to reconcile the problems of adjustment and spill-over by encouraging member states to run only modest budget deficits. The pursuit of product and labour market reforms through the BEPGs, meanwhile, can be understood as an attempt to encourage greater flexibility in price- and wage-setting in readiness for asymmetric shocks (Calmfors 2001). Taken together, these arguments for policy coordination owe a debt to the new Keynesian paradigm that emerged in the 1990s, with its emphasis on tying governments' hands through fiscal rules and its preoccupation with product and labour market reforms (see Schelkle and Hassel 2012).

From the launch of the single currency to the sovereign debt crisis

The euro became legal tender on 1 January 1999 alongside the creation of the ERM II, an exchange-rate regime in which member states aspiring to adopt the single currency agree to minimize fluctuations between their currencies and the euro (see Table 7.3 for a continued chronology of EMU). Greece joined the euro area in January 2001, twelve months before the changeover from national currencies to euro notes and coins. In January 2007, Slovenia became the first of the EU's 'new' member states to join the euro, followed by Cyprus and Malta in 2008, Slovakia in 2009, Estonia in 2011, Latvia in 2014, and Lithuania in 2015.

TABLE 7.3 Chronology of EMU (Part 2)	
Jan. 2001	Greece joins the euro area
Jan. 2002	Changeover to euro notes and coins
Mar. 2005	European Council in Brussels revises the SGP
Jan. 2007	Slovenia joins the euro area
Jan. 2008	Cyprus and Malta join the euro area
Jan. 2009	Slovakia joins the euro area as the euro marks its tenth anniversary
May 2010	EU–IMF financial support package for Greece
May 2010	European Financial Stability Mechanism (EFSM) and European Financial Stability Facility (EFSF) established
Nov. 2010	EU–IMF financial support package for Ireland
Dec. 2010	European Systemic Risk Board (ESRB) established
Jan. 2011	Estonia joins the euro area
May 2011	EU–IMF financial support package for Portugal
Oct. 2011	Euro summit established
Dec. 2011	Six-pack enters into force
Feb. 2012	ESM Treaty signed
Mar. 2012	Fiscal compact signed
June 2012	EU financial support package for Spain
Sept. 2012	ECB unveils outright monetary transactions
Oct. 2012	ESM inaugurated
Mar. 2013	EU–IMF financial support package for Cyprus
May 2013	Two-pack enters into force
Jan. 2014	Latvia joins the euro area
Jan. 2015	Lithuania joins the euro area

The first decade of the single currency was successful in terms of achieving EMU's headline goal of maintaining price stability. The annual rate of consumer price inflation between 1999 and 2008 was just 2.2 per cent (see Figure 7.1), which is low by historical standards and close to the ECB's target (see next section). Although consumer prices were stable overall, this picture masked macroeconomic imbalances elsewhere in the euro area. A case in point was Ireland, which saw property prices grow by an average rate of 10 per cent per annum in real terms between 1999 and 2007 (OECD 2013). EMU may have been partly to blame here. If Ireland had not been a member of the euro area, then the Central Bank of Ireland could have increased interest rates, which in turn would have reduced the runaway demand for mortgages. Be that as it may, Irish financial authorities could have addressed excessive risk-taking by banks and individuals but they chose not to do so (Nyberg 2011).

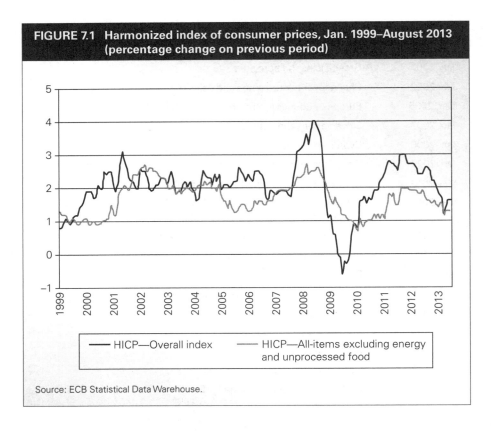

FIGURE 7.1 Harmonized index of consumer prices, Jan. 1999–August 2013 (percentage change on previous period)

HICP—Overall index
HICP—All-items excluding energy and unprocessed food

Source: ECB Statistical Data Warehouse.

The euro area's growth performance during the first decade of EMU was disappointing. GDP growth averaged 2.1 per cent between 1999 and 2008, which is lower than in previous decades and compared to the performance of other industrialized economies (Table 7.4). Also worrying were persistent differences in growth rates across euro area members during EMU's first decade. Whereas Ireland, Greece, and

TABLE 7.4 Gross domestic product at 2000 market prices (average annual percentage change)

	1961–70	1971–80	1981–90	1991–8	1999–2008	2009–13
Euro area	5.3	3.4	2.4	1.7	2.1	−0.4
UK	2.8	2.0	2.8	2.8	2.7	−0.1
US	4.2	3.3	3.2	3.7	2.5	1.0
Japan	10.2	4.5	4.6	0.9	1.1	0.4

Source: Commission 2014e.

Spain posted very high rates of GDP growth throughout, member states such as Portugal, Italy, and Germany recovered slowly from the downturn of 2001–2. That these differences did not dissipate more quickly was seen by some economists as evidence that member states were adjusting too slowly to asymmetric shocks, in keeping with the optimum currency area critique of EMU (Commission 2006a). For Hancké (2013), wage-setting proved to be particularly problematic in this regard. EMU's first decade produced serious macroeconomic imbalances, he argues, because economies in the core of the euro area (most noticeably Germany) relied on modest wage rises to boost the competitiveness of their exports, while those on the periphery (e.g. Greece) let their wages rise rapidly and lost competitiveness as a result.

EMU's first decade was also marked by a lack of fiscal discipline by euro area members. Problems began when some member states failed to reduce their government borrowing sufficiently during the economic upturn of the late 1990s in spite of periodic pleas to do so by the Commission and the Council of Ministers for Economic and Financial Affairs (Ecofin). As a consequence, France and Germany, among others, posted excessive deficits once economic conditions slowed in 2001–2. Although these member states had reduced their budget deficits to below 3 per cent of GDP by 2008 (see Figure 7.2), government debt as a percentage of GDP remained high in many cases and in triple digits in Belgium, Italy, and Greece (Commission 2013f). There was also, with the benefit of hindsight, a serious problem of statistical governance in Greece. The magnitude of this problem became clear in October 2009 when

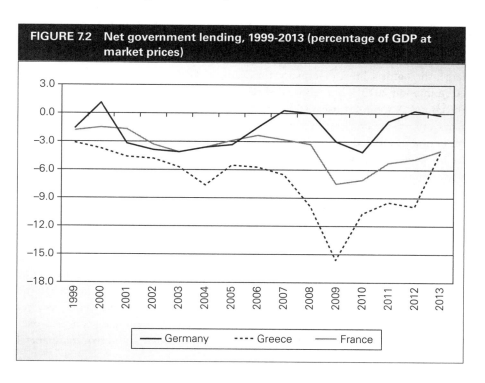

FIGURE 7.2 Net government lending, 1999-2013 (percentage of GDP at market prices)

the newly elected government of George Papandreou announced that the country's budget deficit was much higher than previously indicated (Panagiotarea 2013: 129). As a result, the Greek budget deficit was close to 10 per cent by the time that the single currency celebrated its tenth anniversary (see Figure 7.2).

The world experienced financial turmoil in 2007 and 2008 on a scale that had not been witnessed since the Wall Street Crash of 1929. The crisis has variably been attributed to global macroeconomic imbalances (see Obstfeld and Rogoff 2009) and financial innovation (Crotty 2009) among other factors. The immediate trigger, however, was the collapse of the US subprime loan market after borrowers who had been granted loans in spite of their poor credit ratings struggled to make repayments as house prices plummeted (Shiller 2008). This crisis sowed the seeds for a global credit crunch as inter-bank markets froze and loans to businesses and individuals dried up. This credit crunch was followed by a banking crisis after Lehman Brothers, a major US investment bank, filed for bankruptcy in September 2008 as a result of subprime-related losses. This crisis engulfed European banks and the failure of euro area members to rescue cross-border banks such as Fortis—and before that to prevent precarious business practices by such institutions—exposed significant short-comings in EU financial market regulation and supervision (Quaglia, Eastwood, and Holmes 2009).

In October 2008, EU member states agreed to set aside €2 trillion to rescue Europe's distressed banks alongside new rules on deposit insurance to protect savers. These measures helped to stabilize European banks in the short term but credit shortages and a sharp contraction in world trade sowed the seeds for a severe recession. No euro area member was immune from this sudden slowdown, but those that entered the financial crisis with serious macroeconomic imbalances were, by and large, the hardest hit. In Germany, for example, GDP fell by 5.1 per cent in 2009 (Commission 2013*f*), but rebounded rapidly the following year thanks, in part, to the country's room for fiscal stimulus and its impressive external competitiveness. Recovery was much slower to materialize in member states that saw housing bubbles burst or entered the crisis with high levels of government borrowing. Ireland, for instance, began the crisis with a balanced budget but saw government borrowing reach an astonishing 30.8 per cent of GDP in 2010 after house prices plummeted and the government stepped in to guarantee the country's troubled banks (Commission 2013*f*). House price falls were more modest in Greece but the country posted a budget deficit of 15.6 per cent in 2009 after its aforementioned sins of statistical omission came to light (Commission 2013*f*).

By the beginning of 2010, budget deficits in Greece, Portugal, Ireland, and Spain were close to or above 10 per cent. As a result, the global financial crisis paved the way for a euro area sovereign debt crisis as financial markets lost confidence in the ability of governments in these countries to honour their national debts. As a result, long-term interest rates on government debt soared, reinforcing concerns over sovereign default. It was clear that euro area member states would require financial assistance to break this vicious cycle.

BOX 7.1	**Economic adjustment in Greece**

The economic adjustment programme signed by Greek authorities in May 2010 identi-fied a detailed set of expenditure cuts, tax increases, and structural reforms designed to get government borrowing under control. These measures included controversial com-mitments to cut the entitlements of civil servants, increase value-added tax rates, and prepare of a plan for the sale of state-owned assets. Not all these measures were im-plemented in full, but the degree of fiscal adjustment that followed was well above the norm for programmes of this sort (IMF 2013*a*: 20). Greece's cyclically adjusted primary balance—a measure of government borrowing—improved by 15 percentage points between 2009–13 with the result that a primary budget surplus (a key condition for reduc-ing overall debt levels) was in sight (IMF 2013*b*: 4). Whether this medicine was the right one is a matter of fierce debate among economists, but even those who see such fiscal adjustment as unavoidable cannot deny its devastating impact on the Greek economy in the short term. Between 2009 and 2013, the Greek economy contracted by 21 per cent and unemployment rose from 9.5 to 27 per cent of the civilian labour force (European Commission AMECO Database).

Still, it took until May 2010 for EU leaders to agree on a package of €110 billion loans for Greece. These loans were co-financed by EU member states and the Inter-national Monetary Fund (IMF) with the disbursal of loan instalments contingent on compliance with an economic adjustment programme (see Box 7.1) overseen by officials from the 'troika' of the Commission, the ECB, and the IMF.

One reason for the delay over Greece was that the balance of payments support, originally envisaged by the EEC and now codified in Article 143 TFEU, applies only to member states that had not adopted the single currency. Thus, while the EU provided emergency loans to three euro outs, Hungary, Latvia, and Romania, in 2008–9, it could not offer similar support to Greece. Another reason was that EU policy-makers could not initially agree on involving the IMF (see Hodson 2011). Euro outs such as the UK were keen to minimize their exposure to the sovereign debt crisis and so emerged as early champions of involving the IMF. France, among others, was wary of doing so because it feared for the euro area's autonomy and prestige if it looked to a third party for financial support and economic advice. Germany had a decisive say in such debates since it stood to be the largest contributor to any loan package and Chancellor Angela Merkel eventually insisted that the EU must join forces with the IMF.

The EU and IMF package of loans allowed Greece to finance its public debt with-out resorting to financial markets, but in return Greek authorities committed to a drastic set of austerity measures designed to get government borrowing under con-trol. Within days, the heads of state and government agreed to offer similar terms to other euro area members via two ad hoc stability mechanisms. The first was the €60 billion European Financial Stability Mechanism (EFSM). The second was the €440 billion European Financial Stability Facility (EFSF). Ireland became the first member state to access these funds in November 2010 as part of an EU–IMF package worth €85 billion. Portugal was next, securing €78 billion in loans from the EU and IMF in May 2011. In October 2012, a new permanent stability mechanism, the ESM, was launched with a lending capacity of €500 billion. Spain became the first member state to benefit from this instrument after euro area finance ministers agreed to set aside €100 billion to help to cover the cost of recapitalizing the country's banks. Cyprus received €9 billion in loans from the ESM alongside €1 billion from the IMF in March 2013 after the government found itself with insufficient resources to support the country's bloated financial sector.[2]

It is too soon to evaluate the impact of emergency financial support for euro area members but an interim assessment is unavoidably ambiguous. In its *ex post* evaluation of Greece's first financial support programme—it received a second round of loans in March 2012 and could yet require a third—the IMF saw the defence of the country's membership of the euro area as a key success (IMF 2013*a*). This shows the high stakes surrounding a crisis in which the exit of one or more member states from EMU with potentially fatal consequences for the euro was not, and is still not, beyond the bounds of possibility. It also raises the question of whether continued membership of EMU was worth the pain. A national currency is not a panacea as Greece's fiscal crises in the pre-EMU period show (see Reinhart and Rogoff 2009), but the economic and fiscal adjustment undertaken by Greece in exchange for financial support was severe (see Box 7.1). No member state that sought external financial assistance during the sovereign debt crisis escaped the harsh effects of fiscal austerity but most did better than Greece in the short term. Ireland fared best—or, at any rate, least badly—by meeting its fiscal adjustment targets more or less as planned and resuming economic growth in 2011. In December 2013, the Irish government became the first in the euro area to exit an EU–IMF programme, leaving it reliant once again on financial markets to finance its debt.

Financial support for euro area members saved the single currency in the short term but it ultimately failed to convince financial markets that the sovereign debt crisis was under control. This is one reason why the ECB belatedly agreed in July 2013 to undertake an unlimited programme of government bond purchases through its outright monetary transactions (OMT) programme. This was a much more credible commitment than the provision of financial support via large but limited pots from the EU and IMF and financial markets reacted favourably.

That said, the OMT addressed neither concerns about the continued exposure of national governments to troubled financial institutions nor the root causes of the sovereign debt crisis. On the first of these points, euro area finance ministers agreed in June 2013 that the ESM could lend directly to banks, meaning that national governments would not directly bear the costs of bank bailouts; the absence of such a mechanism was a key reason why Ireland, Spain, and Cyprus found themselves on the brink of sovereign default after stepping in to support troubled financial institutions.

On the second point, EU member states agreed on a set of major reforms to EU economic governance, including the six-pack, two-pack, fiscal compact, and European semester (see Table 7.5 for an overview, and the section on EMU and

TABLE 7.5 New macroeconomic governance mechanisms after the financial crisis

Date*	Title	Description
May 2010	European Financial Stabilization Mechanism	Ad hoc stability mechanism created under Art. 122 TFEU used to provide financial support to Ireland and Portugal
May 2010	European Financial Stability Facility	Ad hoc stability mechanism created under an intergovernmental agreement used to provide financial support to Ireland, Portugal, and Greece
Jan. 2011	European semester	A revised annual timetable for EU economic surveillance designed to discuss national economic policies before they are adopted by member states
Jan. 2011	European Systemic Risk Board	An EU-level body created under Art. 127(6) TFEU with responsibility for financial stability in the Union, comprised chiefly of national supervisors and chaired by the ECB president
Dec. 2011	Six-pack	A set of five EU regulations and one directive adopted under Arts. 121, 126, and 136 TFEU and designed to reinforce the SGP and other elements of economic policy coordination
Nov. 2012	Fiscal compact (Treaty on Stability, Coordination and Governance in the Economic and Monetary Union)	An intergovernmental treaty ratified by 25 member states as of Jan. 2014 to reinforce national fiscal rules and other aspects of economic policy coordination
Oct. 2012	European Stability Mechanism	A permanent stability mechanism underpinned by Art. 136 TFEU but created under an intergovernmental agreement used to provide financial support to Spain and Cyprus
May 2013	Two-pack	A pair of EU regulations adopted under Arts. 121 and 136 TFEU and designed to reinforce the SGP other elements of economic policy coordination
Nov. 2014	Single Supervisory Mechanism	A mechanism created under Art. 127(6) TFEU that gives the ECB new powers of financial supervision in relation to euro area members and participating EU member states

* Established or in the case of the European semester, fiscal compact, six-pack, and two-pack entered into force.

policy coordination later in the chapter for more detail). These reforms were accompanied by the search for a new approach to financial supervision in the EU. This led to the creation of a new European Systemic Risk Board (ESRB) in January 2011 followed in October 2013 by a more ambitious agreement to delegate responsibility for banking supervision to the ECB (see the following section) as part of wider plans for European banking union (see Chapter 5). On balance, these reforms leave the euro area less vulnerable to future financial turmoil but their ability to tackle the after effects of the 2007–8 financial crisis remains an open question, the answer to which will determine the political fate of the euro.

Variations on the Community method

Policy-making under EMU is based not on a single style of decision-making but on new modes of EU policy-making that depart in different ways from the Community method (see Chapter 4). Monetary policy under EMU and, more recently financial supervision, chime with the traditional Community method since they involve the delegation of significant decision-making powers to a supranational institution. At the same time, the ECB is more akin to an autonomous EU agency than a traditional Community body such as the European Commission. The ESM is more unusual still, operating as it does at one remove from the Community's treaty and decision-making structure.

The ECB

Like the Commission, the ECB has a legal personality (Art. 9, Protocol 4 TFEU) and the right to formulate opinions, deliver recommendations, and make regulations on policies that fall within its sphere of competences (Art. 34, Protocol 4 TFEU). Even more so than the Commission, the ECB's political authority is closely linked to its credibility and technocratic expertise due, in part, to the intense scrutiny of monetary-policy decisions by financial markets.

In spite of such similarities, there are significant differences between the ECB and the Commission. A distinctive feature of the ECB is its comparatively decentralized decision-making structure, which allows national central bank (NCB) governors a seat on the ECB Governing Council alongside the ECB president, vice-president, and four other members of the ECB Executive Board (Art. 10, Protocol 4 TFEU). When it comes to the setting of short-term interest rates, each member of the Governing Council initially had the right to cast one vote, and decisions were based on a simple majority. After the number of euro area members exceeded eighteen, the total number of votes on the ECB Governing Council was capped at twenty-one. Executive Board members retain their voting rights permanently, with the remaining fifteen voting rights rotating among NCB governors (see Hodson 2010). Even after these reforms,

EMU remains an extreme example of what Blinder (2007) calls monetary policy by committee. Committees, he notes, can lead to better informed and less ideologically driven decision-making (Blinder 2007), although the sheer size of the ECB Governing Council raises concerns that it will act too conservatively (Gros 2003). By conservative, economists mean here that the ECB is likely to attach more weight to price stability than the pursuit of higher economic growth and that the bank will be otherwise slow to act in a crisis.

The ECB is also subject to fewer checks and balances than the Commission. Members of the ECB Executive Board are appointed for an eight-year, non-renewable term of office on the basis of a common accord by member states following consultation with the European Parliament (EP) and the ECB Governing Council (Art. 11, Protocol 4 TFEU). In practice, appointments are dominated by deals among the largest euro area members. This was evident when Germany's preferred choice as the first president of the ECB, Wim Duisenberg, was appointed in May 1998, but agreed to stand down early in 2003 to make way for France's choice, Jean Claude Trichet. The Governor of the Banca d'Italia, Mario Draghi, succeeded Trichet as ECB president in November 2011 after France and Germany failed to field a candidate, but political manoeuvring was evident once again in the decision shortly afterwards to replace ECB Executive Board member Lorenzo Bini Smaghi, an Italian, with Benoît Cœuré, a Frenchman, thus ensuring that France retained a seat on this key decision-making body. The EP can force the resignation of the college of commissioners, but it can do little more than invite the ECB president to appear before its committees (Art. 284 TFEU). In this sense, the EP's formal role in EMU is minor compared to some other areas of EU policy-making. Also important in this context is the fact that the ECB is located in Frankfurt rather than Brussels, Strasbourg, or Luxembourg, thus allowing it to operate at one remove from other EU institutions.

A final deviation from the Community method in euro area monetary policy is that the ECB epitomizes the idea of an autonomous operating agency with function-specific responsibilities rather than wide-ranging policy powers (see Chapter 4). The primary responsibility of the ECB is to define and implement euro area monetary policy (Art. 127 TFEU). It also holds and manages the official foreign reserves of the member states, promotes the smooth operation of European payment and settlement systems, and plays a central role in euro area exchange-rate policy. The ECB's overarching objective is to maintain price stability and, without prejudice to this goal, to support the general economic policies of the Community (Art. 127 TFEU). The US Federal Reserve, in contrast, is required to promote maximum employment, stable prices, and moderate long-term interest rates, a comparison which further fuels concerns over the ECB's conservatism.

The precise meaning of 'price stability' is not defined in the treaty, leaving the bank to devise and revise its own definition. In October 1998, the ECB Governing Council committed itself to pursuing a rate of inflation of below 2 per cent over the medium term. The euro area monetary authority was by no means the first central bank to adopt an inflation target but it was ahead of the curve in so doing. Whereas the Bank of England began inflation targeting proper in 1997, the Bank of Japan and the US Federal Reserve did not introduce targets until 2012. However, the ECB's definition of price stability is not as precise as that of other leading central banks, which has further fuelled concerns that the euro area monetary policy will be too conservative. The ECB Governing Council sought to address these concerns in 2004 by agreeing to pursue a rate of inflation of below *but close to* 2 per cent over the medium term, but this definition is still more open-ended than those of the Bank of England, the Bank of Japan, and the Federal Reserve, all of which target an inflation rate of precisely 2 per cent over a specific time frame. On balance, the ECB has been less conservative than economists feared—inflation, as noted earlier, was slightly above 2 per cent during EMU's first ten years—but still comparatively cautious. This can be seen, for example, in the ECB's reluctance to cut interest rates in the immediate aftermath of the global financial crisis for fear of fuelling inflationary pressures and in its reticence about introducing the OMT for similar reasons.

The ECB's preoccupation with price stability has made it wary about the pursuit of further competences for itself in the macroeconomic domain or other EU institutions more generally, but an important exception here concerns the bank's role in financial market policy (Hodson 2011). The ECB is required under the treaty to 'contribute to the smooth conduct of policies pursued by the competent authorities relating to the prudential supervision of credit institutions and the stability of the financial system' (Art. 127 TFEU). Although this formulation implies a supporting role for the ECB, this did not prevent some members of the Executive Board from making the case for a 'collective euro area supervisor' in the early days of EMU (e.g. Padoa-Schioppa 1999). For this reason, the ECB backed the creation of the ESRB in January 2011. This body, which is made up of national supervisors and other relevant policy-makers and headed by the ECB president, was given responsibility for safeguarding financial stability in the EU.

The ECB was more enthusiastic still about the launch of the single supervisory mechanism in 2014, which gives it significant new policy-making powers in relation to financial supervision. Under legal statutes adopted in October 2013, a purpose-built ECB Supervisory Board is empowered to authorize and de-authorize credit institutions in the euro area, thus greatly expanding the scope of the bank's activities (Regulation 1024/2013). That this role was not transferred to the ECB Governing Council can be seen, in part, as an attempt to keep the tasks of monetary policy and financial supervision separate, although this will be easier said than done. The creation of a new decision-making body within the ECB also allows non-euro area members, which are not represented on the ECB Governing Council, to participate in the single supervisory mechanism (Regulation 1024/2013, Art. 26).

The European Stability Mechanism

The EU's emerging approach to crisis resolution offers an intriguing puzzle for this volume. In some respects, the emergency loans offered to Greece and other member states looks like a variation on the distributive mode (see Chapter 4), involving as they did fierce battles between member states over financial benefits and burdens. While the heads of state and government took a lead role in such negotiations, operational decisions over the granting of loans to member states and enforcing the conditions attached to these loans was delegated to de novo bodies. A case in point is the EFSF. One of the more peculiar exhibits in the history of EU policy-making, this fund was created in May 2010 not under the treaties but as a public limited company registered in Luxembourg with euro area members or their representatives serving as shareholders. Managed by Klaus Regling, a former Director-General for Economic and Financial Affairs at the European Commission, and staffed by 90 officials, the EFSF is overseen by a Governing Council made up of the finance ministers of euro area members with the Eurogroup president acting as chair. Representatives of the Commission and the ECB attend its meetings as observers and are involved in monitoring compliance with the conditions attached to EFSF loans, but the final say over loan disbursement rests with the EFSF Governing Council. These governance arrangements contrast with those for the EFSM, which was created under Article 122 TFEU at the same time as the EFSF and which gives the Commission a major say over the disbursement of loans to euro area members.

The reasons for creating multiple stability mechanisms at this time were threefold. First, there were concerns over the legality of both instruments therefore it made sense not to rely on either one. The EFSM relied on a controversial reading of Article 122 TFEU—which provided for financial assistance in the event of 'natural disasters and occurrences beyond [a member state's] control'—and the EFSF had no standing in EU law. Secondly, the EFSM was limited in size to €60 billion because of the maximum margin available under the EU's own resource ceiling (see Chapter 6). Thirdly, even without these financial and legal constraints, member states were reluctant to give the Commission control over a new multi-billion euro fund. Creating the EFSF provided a short-term fix.

The inauguration in October 2012 of the ESM offered a more permanent solution. The ESM is underpinned by a revision to Article 136 TFEU, which allows for the creation of a stability mechanism for the euro area, but its statutes are set out in an intergovernmental treaty that leaves key decisions in the hands of national representatives. The ESM replaced the EFSM, which concluded its operations in 2013, and it will run in parallel with the EFSF until all loans granted through this temporary stability mechanism have been repaid.

EMU and policy coordination

Judged in terms of Chapter 4's five modes of policy-making, economic policy under EMU is an instance of policy coordination. Whereas euro area monetary policy is an exclusive competence of the Community, the treaty claims economic policy as neither an exclusive, shared, nor supporting competence of the Union (Title I TFEU). Instead, member states have agreed to coordinate their economic policies within the Union (Art. 5 TFEU). The two most important treaty instruments are the BEPGs (Art. 121 TFEU) and the excessive deficit procedure (Art. 126 TFEU). These instruments are reinforced by the SGP and, in the light of the global financial crisis, several other rules, processes, and procedures.

The Stability and Growth Pact and the Broad Economic Policy Guidelines

Policy coordination in the EU relies on decentralized forms of decision-making in which peer pressure and consensus building between member states with little or no delegation to supranational institutions is the norm (see Chapter 4). The BEPGs are emblematic of this inasmuch as they take the form of soft law statements on the economic policies of member states and the EU designed to encourage benchmarking and the exchange of best practice. Countries that breach the guidelines or otherwise jeopardize the smooth functioning of EMU face no more than non-binding recommendations. The excessive deficit procedure prohibits member states from posting budget deficits in excess of 3 per cent of GDP and government debt in excess of 60 per cent of GDP. This is a harder form of coordination than the BEPGs because member states that break these limits face the possibility of fines, but non-binding recommendations remain the standard response to non-compliance. The timetable for moving between the excessive deficit procedure's disciplinary steps is set out in the SGP, a set of Council regulations backed by an agreement between the heads of state and government. The pact also requires member states to prepare medium-term budgetary plans that target a fiscal position of close to balance or in surplus.

The Commission plays a curtailed role in relation to policy coordination under EMU. Its primary responsibilities are to monitor member states' economic policies, draw up the first draft of the BEPGs, and sound the alarm when member states violate these guidelines or the SGP. The Commission alone can propose disciplinary measures against errant member states, but the decision to issue recommendations or impose financial penalties and fines is formally taken by Ecofin. Given the soft law character of such coordination, there are, likewise, limited opportunities for the Court of Justice of the European Union (CJEU) to intervene in this policy process. The EP is informed of key decisions taken in relation to the BEPGs and the SGP but this has traditionally been a pro forma exercise.

How can we explain member states' determination to keep economic policy on a decentralized footing in EMU? For some scholars, the explanation lies in the desire of the framers of the treaty to protect the political independence of the ECB by steering clear of a *gouvernement économique* that might seek to emasculate monetary policy (Dyson 2000). Buti *et al.* (2003: 2) emphasize sovereignty concerns, arguing that

EMU reflects the limits of what can be achieved given member states' limited desire for deeper integration in this field. On a similar note, Hix (2005: 38) argues that 'if member states were serious about policy reform in a particular area, then the classic EU method would probably be the most efficient way of achieving the policy goals'.

An alternative viewpoint is that new modes of EU governance may be suited to EMU on functional and normative grounds (Hodson and Maher 2001). One reading of the theory of optimum currency areas is that a decentralized approach to policy coordination may be desirable if it gives member states greater leeway to use national budgetary policy to adjust to country-specific shocks. Likewise, allowing member states to tailor specific reform measures to the institutional specificities of national product, labour, and capital markets may be preferable to a one-size-fits-all approach. From a normative perspective, soft law may be preferable to hard law when policy goals lack precision and when the probability of revising these objectives in the future is high. Decentralized modes of decision-making may also be preferable when traditional, centralized modes of decision-making lack legitimacy. Fiscal policy and structural reform both rest uneasily with the Community method since decisions over taxation, expenditure, and the regulation of labour markets, with their significant distributional consequences and resonance for partisan politics, go right to the heart of what democratically elected governments do.

How has EMU's experiment with new modes of EU governance fared? From a bird's eye perspective, the early years of EMU coincided with a sustained improvement in euro area public finances, as budget deficits in euro area members remained below 3 per cent of GDP. In the structural domain, member states implemented a series of measures to make employment-protection legislation less stringent, to raise average retirement ages, and to introduce greater competition in some sectors, most noticeably telecommunications (see Chapters 6, 11, and 12). These reforms contributed to rising labour force participation rates, falling unemployment, and, in some sectors, falling prices before the global financial crisis struck (ECB 2008). Progress in product and labour market reforms was matched by significant progress in financial market integration.

In spite of these achievements, serious difficulties were encountered with the implementation of the SGP and the BEPGs even after reforms to both instruments in March 2005 (see Hodson 2010). The SGP was more successful than it is generally given credit for in keeping budget deficits down during the first decade of EMU, which witnessed several breaches of the 3 per cent of GDP threshold but saw most of the member states concerned make a sustained effort to restore compliance. However, the pact plainly struggled to enforce its medium-term budgetary objectives and debt criterion and evidently failed to address inaccuracies in the reporting of public finance statistics in Greece. The BEPGs, meanwhile, encouraged a regular exchange of views between economic policy-makers at the national and EU level, but failed to apply peer pressure and did too little too late on the problem of macroeconomic imbalances (Deroose, Hodson, and Kuhlmann 2008).

The six-pack and the fiscal compact

Whether any system of economic policy coordination would have survived the global financial crisis intact is doubtful. The shortcomings of the SGP and BEPG made reform inevitable, however, as did the member states' decision to provide emergency loans to Greece and other euro area members. That financial support and the reform of economic governance were linked in this way owed much to German Chancellor Angela Merkel, who saw closer economic policy coordination in general, and more stringent fiscal rules in particular, as a means to protect the interests of German taxpayers. A set of six legislative proposals—known as the 'six-pack' were duly put forward by the Commission in September 2010 and approved by Ecofin and the EP in September 2011. The involvement of the Parliament in this process flowed from a new provision in the TFEU, which extended the ordinary legislative procedure to rules governing multilateral surveillance (Art. 121(6) TFEU). Although negotiations went beyond this treaty provision, the EP insisted that all elements of the six-pack be jointly negotiated and so played its most significant role in shaping economic policy in EMU to date.

One of the more innovative elements of the six-pack is a new principle of reverse voting, which means that a recommendation by the Commission for corrective action under certain stages of the excessive deficit procedure would be carried unless a qualified majority of member states vote against it in Ecofin. This would make it considerably more difficult for finance ministers to overturn Commission recommendations for corrective action, as occurred in November 2003 (Heipertz and Verdun 2010), thus greatly increasing the EU executive's agenda-setting powers in relation to EU fiscal surveillance. That said, it remains to be seen just how important financial penalties will be under the six-pack. The scope for pecuniary sanctions is certainly plentiful; for the first time, member states face the possibility of fines for failing to meet the pact's medium-term budgetary objectives or for not taking sufficient steps to get government debt below 60 per cent of GDP and as soon as the 3 per cent reference value for government borrowing has been breached. For all this tough talk, however, fines were yet to be levied under the six-pack as of January 2014, which suggests that member states will continue to face no more than repeated non-binding recommendations providing they make sufficient effort to comply with Ecofin's policy prescriptions. In this sense, the six-pack remains rooted in policy coordination as a mode of EU decision-making.

The six-pack also provided for the creation of the macroeconomic imbalance procedure to prevent and, if necessary, correct macroeconomic developments that adversely affect 'the proper functioning of the economy of a member state or of economic and monetary union, or of the Union as a whole'. Imbalances are monitored via a scoreboard of indicators including growth and inflation differences, credit booms, housing bubbles, and other forms of imbalance. In the event that imbalances are deemed to be excessive, the Commission can recommend that Ecofin issues a recommendation to the member state concerned under Article 121(4) TFEU. Persistent offenders also face the possibility of financial penalties. Given the convoluted link between government policies and, say, current account deficits or house price rises, it remains to be seen whether the macroeconomic imbalance procedure will amount to anything other than a more focused but still soft version of the BEPGs.

In December 2011, a matter of days after the six-pack entered into force, EU member states started negotiations on a new Treaty on Stability, Coordination, and Governance in the Economic and Monetary Union. Better known as the fiscal compact, this intergovernmental agreement between all EU member states with the exceptions of Croatia, the Czech Republic, and the UK (see the section 'The euro outs' later in the chapter) seeks to reinforce the six-pack by making reverse-majority voting the norm for all steps of the excessive-deficit procedure. Also significant here is member states' commitment under the fiscal compact to transpose a balanced budget rule into national law. Viewed through the lens of Europeanization, these rules can be seen as an attempt to adapt national systems of fiscal governance so as to reinforce member states' commitment to the SGP. What impact the fiscal compact will have on EMU is difficult to predict, but, as with the six-pack, its approach appears to be largely consistent with policy coordination as a mode of decision-making. The fact that the CJEU is given new enforcement powers under the fiscal compact might suggest otherwise, but the court is allowed to intervene only in cases where national fiscal rules are inadequate and only then at the instigation of another member state. Consequently, Dehousse (2012: 4) concludes that member states' 'reluctance to accept overly strict supranational checks remains as strong today as it was in the past'.

The European semester, the two-pack, and the troika

Another innovation in EU economic policy coordination in the wake of the global financial crisis is the so-called European semester. Introduced in 2011, the European semester revises the calendar for EU economic surveillance. Under previous arrangements, Ecofin issued an opinion on member states' medium-term budgetary plans—a reporting requirement under the SGP—at a point in the year when national parliaments had typically signed off on expenditure and taxation decisions for the coming year. This made it difficult for EU policy-makers to influence national governments. Under the European semester, Ecofin has a chance to comment on member states' medium-term fiscal plans several months before national budgets have been presented to national parliaments. Critics of the European semester have expressed concern about the circumvention of democratic checks and balances over the national budgetary process (Tsoukalis 2011: 29). As with so many other aspects of EU economic policy coordination, however, recommendations issued by Ecofin under the European semester rely on peer pressure and consensus-building rather than legally binding commitments.

Building on both the European semester and the six-pack, Ecofin and the EP agreed on yet another round of reforms in March 2013. Adopted under Article 136 TFEU, which allows for closer coordination between euro area members, the so-called two-pack codifies further changes to the EU fiscal surveillance calendar and provides for enhanced surveillance of member states experiencing financial difficulties or at risk thereof. Under the regulation dealing with the first of these points, euro area members are required to submit a draft budget for the year ahead to the Commission and euro area finance ministers in October of each year with a view to adopting the final budget by December. This will require changes to national budget calendars in what can be seen as another example of the Europeanization of national fiscal policy in the light of the global financial crisis. The expectation under the European semester is that the draft budget will be consistent with each member state's obligations under the SGP and the macroeconomic imbalance procedure, but where inconsistencies are apparent the Commission can request a revised draft budget. As with the European semester, the two-pack's bark looks worse than its bite since the regulation neither specifies sanctions against member states that fail to comply with these requests nor challenges the fact that member states have first and final say over national budgets.

The second regulation in the two-pack allows the Commission to go beyond the monitoring requirements of the SGP for those member states facing, or at risk of, financial difficulties. Under this enhanced surveillance, which will be mandatory for member states in receipt of external financial assistance from the EU or elsewhere, the Commission will conduct an ongoing, intensive review of economic and financial developments. Where further action is warranted, Ecofin, acting on the basis of a Commission proposal, can recommend that the member state address financial difficulties or prepare a draft macroeconomic adjustment programme to be approved by EU finance ministers. Member states are expected to comply with this programme, but the two-pack specifies no sanctions for failing to do so other than an obligation to seek 'technical assistance' from the Commission in some cases.

For all these reforms enacted in the wake of the global financial crisis—and in spite of regular reports to the contrary—economic policy in EMU remains decentralized. Member states may have signed up to more intensive and intrusive forms of cooperation and surveillance but they retain a tight grip over the formulation and implementation of fiscal policies and structural reforms.

Whether the same can be said of member states that have turned to the EU for financial support is a matter of debate. The role of the troika in this context is especially controversial. This informal grouping of officials from the Commission, the ECB, and the IMF emerged in 2010 in response to the Greek fiscal crisis and it has since become central to the EU's crisis-management framework. Member states that seek financial support from the ESM, for example, are expected to negotiate a detailed programme of adjustment with the troika, which then visits the country on a quarterly basis to assess compliance, a positive assessment in this regard being a prerequisite for the receipt of future loan instalments.

For Scharpf (2011: 26), such arrangements are tantamount to 'a form of "receivership"' in which the EU and IMF exercise a significant degree of influence over the formulation of national economic policy. However, this interpretation overstates the troika's ability to shape national economic policies, which remain subject to the same national checks and balances albeit under economic conditions that leave limited room for manoeuvre. What a genuine EU veto would look like was suggested by German Finance Minister Wolfgang Schäuble's call in October 2012 for the creation of a 'super commissioner' with veto powers over national budgets, but this proposal enjoyed little support from other member states (Karagiannis and Guidi 2013).

That economic policy of EMU thus remains on a fundamentally decentralized footing is, in the end, not that surprising since functional and normative arguments for a more centralized approach to decision-making in the euro area remain problematic in spite of the grave crisis facing the single currency. On fiscal policy coordination, for example, the negative externalities from Greece's sovereign debt crisis may have concentrated member states' minds on the problem of fiscal spill-over, but the need for national adjustment mechanisms has not dissipated. Likewise, on structural reform the global financial crisis heightened concerns about a lack of price and wage flexibility in EMU, but differences between national product and labour markets still militate against a one-sized-fits-all approach. On normative concerns, member states are no less troubled about ceding sovereignty in a sensitive area such as macroeconomic policy. In this sense, initiatives such as the six-pack and two-pack confirm the member states' desire for the Commission to play a more assertive role in relation to peer pressure, but not in the formulation and implementation of macroeconomic policies per se.

This situation could change, of course, and the longer the euro area sovereign debt crisis drags on, the more open EU member states might become to supranational solutions. In December 2012, then European Council President Herman Van Rompuy presented a plan for a so-called 'genuine EMU' (Van Rompuy 2012). Much of this plan was taken up with the pursuit of European banking union (see Chapter 5), but a significant strengthening of EMU's fiscal dimension was also mooted. The report called for a 'temporary, targeted and flexible financial support' for structural reforms alongside 'a well-defined and limited fiscal capacity to improve the absorption of country-specific economic shocks, through an insurance system set up at the central level' (Van Rompuy 2012: 4–5). Such reforms could be a game changer for euro area governance as they would entail new distributive modes of decision-making targeted specifically at euro area members, but it remains to be seen whether Van Rompuy's plan will fly. As of January 2014, member states were mulling over ways to give financial incentives to member states for stepping up structural reforms, but they remained as wary as ever about ceding significant policy-making powers in the fiscal domain.

EMU and intensive transgovernmentalism

Intensive transgovernmentalism, as discussed in Chapter 4, describes an approach to EU policy-making premised on the active involvement of the European Council supported by the Council of the European Union with a limited role for the Commission and the EP. Aside from the external representation of the euro area (see later in this section), this mode of governance was not especially relevant for understanding EMU's first decade, although it was prevalent in earlier periods. All of this changed with the global financial crisis, which saw the heads of state and government assume a key role not only in crisis management but in questions of euro area governance more generally (Puetter 2012).

The Eurogroup

A key piece of EMU's governance jigsaw is the Eurogroup. This informal body, which was launched by the European Council in December 1997, brings euro area finance ministers together in advance of Ecofin to discuss the economic situation and shared policy challenges. One finance minister and one adviser from each euro area country attend the Eurogroup along with the president of the ECB and the commissioner for economic and monetary affairs. Meetings are confidential and, aside from the occasional communiqué, the Eurogroup produces few visible policy outputs. In the early years of EMU, the chair was filled by the president of Ecofin or the finance minister of the next euro area member in line for this post in cases where a non-euro area country held the EU Council presidency. In 2005, the Eurogroup appointed Jean-Claude Juncker for a two-year term of office, and he was reappointed in 2007, 2009, and 2011. In 2013 he was succeeded by Dutch Finance Minister Jeroen Dijsselbloem.

The Eurogroup's origins reflected a Franco-German compromise on the need for economic policy coordination under EMU (Pisani-Ferry 2006). In advance of EMU, France repeatedly made the case for a *gouvernement économique* to steer economic decision-making under EMU and provide a political counterweight to the ECB (Howarth 2007b). Germany consistently opposed such proposals for fear that they were intended as a covert attack on the independence of the bank. In a deal struck at the European Council in December 1997, member states agreed that euro area finance ministers could meet behind closed doors and without formal decision-making powers. The Eurogroup's working methods have been described by Puetter (2006) as a form of 'deliberative intergovernmentalism'. He argues that, in the absence of formal decision-making responsibilities, the Eurogroup can exchange information on shared policy challenges and reflect on national policy positions in a way that would not be possible in a busy bargaining chamber such as Ecofin.

The Eurogroup's track record as a deliberative body is mixed. On some issues, such as fiscal responses to high oil prices, euro area finance ministers have managed to pursue a relatively coherent line (Pisani-Ferry 2006). On other issues, including the external value of the euro, policy lines have been agreed but not always adhered to by euro area finance ministers (van den Noord *et al.* 2008). Furthermore, periodic public criticism of ECB monetary policy by Juncker and other euro area finance ministers during EMU's first decade shows that the Eurogroup sometimes struggled to keep discussions of the macroeconomic policy mix behind closed doors. The enlargement of the euro area may also have reduced the intimacy of the Eurogroup by adding new ministers (each with his or her own adviser) to the circle (Begg 2008).

The euro summit

The Eurogroup has emerged as both an institutional winner and loser from the global financial crisis. All euro area finance ministers have a seat on the Board of Governors of the ESM, which has overall responsibility for deciding whether to provide financial support to member states and for assessing compliance with the conditions attached to these loans. In spite of this crucial role, the Eurogroup saw its political influence curtailed during the global financial crisis due to the emergence of euro summits. These gatherings of the heads of state and government of euro area members and the president of the Commission began on an ad hoc basis. The first such summit took place in Paris in October 2008 after French President Nicolas Sarkozy invited euro area leaders to discuss the ongoing international banking crisis. A similar convocation followed in March 2010 in an effort to reassure financial markets about Greece's fiscal situation. Euro summits became commonplace thereafter as the heads of state and government sought to get to grips with the euro area's sovereign debt crises.

In recognition of this role, euro area heads of state and government agreed in October 2011—and the fiscal compact reiterated—that euro summits would take place at least twice a year to set general guidelines on economic policy, competitiveness, and convergence for the euro area. Meetings, it was agreed, would be chaired by a president of the euro summit, to be appointed at the same time as the President of the European Council. If there was any doubt about the euro summit's seniority vis-à-vis the Eurogroup, the conclusions made clear that the president of the euro summit could invite the Eurogroup to prepare meetings of euro area heads of state and government and follow up on the results of this meeting.

This shift back to intensive transgovernmentalism under EMU is partly a pragmatic development. The involvement of the heads of state and government following the global financial crisis was inevitable given the seriousness of this situation. It was also necessary to address the initial differences between member states on sensitive issues such as the involvement of the IMF in providing financial support to Greece. That said, calls for a euro summit predate the global financial crisis. In July 2007, Nicolas Sarkozy called for a euro area summit as part of his efforts to revise negotiations over *gouvernement économique*. This proposal received short shrift from German Chancellor Angela Merkel, who, like Helmut Kohl before her, feared a plot to make the ECB more politically accountable (Hodson 2011: 47). Sarkozy bided his time, however, and the confluence of a systemic banking crisis in October 2008 and France's six-month presidency of the EU provided the perfect opportunity to gather euro area heads of state and government together.

External representation of the euro area

Intensive transgovernmentalism can also be seen in the euro area's approach to external representation. On paper this looks like a domain in which the Community method might have found application since the treaty allows the Council, acting on the basis of a Commission recommendation, to establish a unified representation in 'international financial institutions and conferences' (Art. 138 TFEU). In practice, the Commission's attempts to activate this provision have been rebuffed, with member states relying instead on ad hoc and informal measures to coordinate EU involvement in the G8, G20, IMF, and World Bank.

The involvement of the Commission, the ECB, and the Eurogroup in such coordination efforts varies, leaving the EMU's external representation contingent on member states' ability to speak with one voice. Scholars such as McNamara and Meunier (2002) and Cohen (2009) are sceptical about such arrangements and others such as Bini Smaghi (2006) and Ahearne and Eichengreen (2007) have called for the euro area to be given a single seat in international financial institutions and fora.

However, whether a more centralized approach to decision-making would really help here is a moot point (see Hodson 2011). Where member states agree on international macroeconomic priorities, the benefits of a unified system of external representation are not always apparent. A case in point concerns the G20, an international forum of industrialized and developing economies of which the EU is a full member, albeit with France, Germany, Italy, and the UK also in attendance. At the landmark G20 leaders' summit on the global financial crisis in April 2009, UK Prime Minister Gordon Brown, French President Nicolas Sarkozy, and German Chancellor Angela Merkel successfully pushed a common EU line concerning tax havens without much need for the EU delegation present.

Conversely, where member states disagree, a unified system of external representation would not necessarily make much difference. One example is the IMF Executive Board, which runs the Fund on a day-to-day basis. The EU is not formally represented on this body and the representatives of individual EU member states, though they coordinate their activities through an informal body known as the EURIMF, are scattered in most cases across multi-country constituencies that include non-EU members. Although this arrangement is fragmented, there is little that a single EU constituency at the IMF could have done to expedite financial support to Greece in early 2010. EU member states were, as noted earlier, deeply divided on this issue at first and the EURIMF could present a common line within the Fund only after intensive deliberation and bargaining between EU heads of state and government. Messy though this decision-making process was, it would not have been altered by the presence of a single EU representative to the IMF.

The euro outs

Only the UK and Denmark have formal opt-outs from Stage 3 of EMU, which they secured in negotiations over the TEU. These opt-outs are likely to remain in place unless euro membership has been approved by popular referenda. This seems like a remote prospect in the UK, which hesitated about joining the euro during the premiership of Tony Blair (1997–2007), but since then has become highly sceptical about the project. Such scepticism bordered on *Schadenfreude* during the sovereign debt crisis as evidenced by UK Foreign Secretary William Hague's description of the euro as 'a burning building with no exits' (*Financial Times*, 28 Sept. 2012). Danish voters, meanwhile, roundly rejected euro membership in a referendum in September 2000. The larger Danish political parties have traditionally been supportive of EMU, but a second referendum foreseen in 2011 never materialized and public support for the single currency in Denmark has plummeted in the light of a global financial crisis, which hit the euro area much harder than the Danish economy.

The remaining EU member states are formally required under the treaty to join the euro area if and when they meet the convergence criteria. In practice, member states retain a degree of discretion over whether and when to apply for membership of the euro area. Sweden, for example, voted against euro adoption in a referendum in September 2003 and has yet to participate in ERM II, which precludes it joining the euro. As of 2015, no member state had set a target date for joining the euro area and only Denmark is a member of ERM II (see Table 7.6). For their part, euro area policy-makers have been fairly cautious about letting new members into the euro club, especially those countries making the economically and financially turbulent transition from central planning to a market economy. Lithuania's first application for euro adoption, for example, was rejected in May 2006 after it was deemed to have missed the treaty's inflation criterion by just 0.2 per cent.

TABLE 7.6 State of play for non-euro area members			
	Participating in ERM II	**Official target date for euro adoption**	**Signed the fiscal compact**
Bulgaria	No	None	Yes
Croatia	No	None	No
Czech Republic	No	None	No
Denmark	Yes	None	Yes
Hungary	No	None	Yes
Poland	No	None	Yes
Romania	No	None	Yes
Sweden	No	None	Yes
UK	No	None	No

Source: Based on ECB (2008: 84).

Note: Croatia had not yet joined the EU when the fiscal compact was signed in March 2012 but it can accede to this treaty at a future point.

If the global financial crisis has thus introduced new cleavages between euro ins and euro outs it also opened up divisions among the outs. This can be seen in relation to the fiscal compact, which all EU member states at the time except the Czech Republic and the UK signed. That Denmark was willing to do so in spite of its reticence about joining the euro area is curious. Beach (2013) argues that this puzzle is partly explained by Denmark and other euro outs not wanting to be left behind in a two-speed Europe in which a subset of countries can decide on EU economic policies. He also suggests that it reflected Germany's desire to involve member states with reputations for sound macroeconomic management in the fiscal compact since such countries are more likely to enforce the treaty.

In December 2011, UK Prime Minister David Cameron broke off negotiations over incorporating the fiscal compact into the EU treaties. A complex two-level game with unpredictable consequences is playing out in the UK (Hodson and Maher 2013). Some members of Cameron's Conservative Party are hoping that the European reforms needed in the light of the global financial crisis will provide an opportunity for renegotiation with the EU or perhaps even UK exit, moves that are opposed by their Liberal Democrat coalition partners. By the same token, the City of London could well be at a competitive disadvantage if closer cooperation between a subset of EU member states on economic matters has implications for single market matters. Having walked away from the fiscal compact, David Cameron pledged in January 2013 to renegotiate the UK's membership of the EU, if leader of a majority Conservative government, and to hold an in–out referendum on UK membership by 2017. Whether this is a ploy to extract concessions from France and Germany or rather a step closer towards UK withdrawal remains to be seen.

Conclusion

The traditional Community method has waned as EU member states have sought alternatives to centralized and hierarchical modes of policy-making. Nowhere is this more evident than in relation to EMU. Monetary policy and financial supervision rely on the delegation of key decision-making powers not to the Commission but to a new kind of Community body: the ECB. Economic policy, in contrast, relies on a combination of policy coordination for fiscal policy and structural reforms and intensive transgovernmentalism when it comes to external representation and the involvement of the heads of state and government.

EMU's first decade delivered on its promise of price stability. The member states, however, fell short in their commitment to fiscal discipline and failed to address the build-up of macroeconomic imbalances. These shortcomings amplified the effects of the global financial crisis, which sowed the seeds for banking turmoil, a steep recession, sovereign debt difficulties, and brought the single currency to the brink of collapse. EU policy-makers responded to this crisis with a wave of new procedures, rules, and processes governing economic policy and through ongoing negotiations over European banking union. Significant though these changes are, they have not relied on the Community method. EMU thus remains a high-stakes experiment in new modes of EU policy-making.

NOTES

1 Thanks to Mark Pollack, Christine Reh, Helen Wallace, and Alasdair Young for helpful comments on an earlier version of this chapter. The usual disclaimer applies.

2 For a timeline of the EU's response to the global financial crisis, see: *http://ec.europa.eu/ economy_finance/crisis/index_en.htm*.

FURTHER READING

For an introduction to the economics of EMU, see De Grauwe (2012). Dyson and Featherstone (1999), Moravcsik (1998), and McNamara (1998) explore the political dynamics underpinning EMU's creation and James (2012) offers a historical perspective on the evolution of EMU. Schelkle (2006) revisits some of the seminal contributions to the debate on euro area governance, Heipertz and Verdun (2010) provide an in-depth treatment of the SGP, and Hancké (2013) looks at the neglected issue of wage-setting under EMU. Hodson (2011) takes stock of EMU's experiment in new modes of EU policy-making from the launch of the euro to the sovereign debt crises.

De Grauwe, P. (2012), *The Economics of Monetary Union*, 9th edn. (Oxford: Oxford University Press).

Dyson, K., and Featherstone, K. (1999), *The Road to Maastricht: Negotiating Economic and Monetary Union* (Oxford: Oxford University Press).

Hancké, B. (2013), *Unions, Central Banks, and EMU* (Oxford: Oxford University Press).

Heipertz, M., and Verdun, A. (2010), *Ruling Europe: The Politics of the Stability and Growth Pact* (Cambridge: Cambridge University Press).

Hodson, D. (2011), *Governing the Euro Area in Good Times and Bad* (Oxford: Oxford University Press).

James, H. (2012), *Making the European Monetary Union* (Cambridge, MA: Harvard University Press).

McNamara, K. (1998), *The Currency of Ideas: Monetary Politics in the European Union* (Ithaca, NY: Cornell University Press).

Moravcsik, A. (1998), *The Choice for Europe: Social Purpose and State Power from Messina to Maastricht* (Ithaca, NY: Cornell University Press).

Schelkle, W. (2006), 'Economic Governance in EMU Revisited', *Journal of Common Market Studies*, 44/4: 669–864.

CHAPTER 8

The Common Agricultural Policy
The Fortress Challenged

Christilla Roederer-Rynning

▋ Summary

Today's common agricultural policy (CAP) is a policy in flux. While still absorbing a large share of the European Union (EU) budget, the CAP today bears little resemblance to the arcane and highly segmented system of market support of the 1960s. Many agricultural policy issues have become so tied up with trade, environmental, public health, energy, and budget issues that the CAP is losing its narrow sectoral character. The machinery producing CAP legislation has become more differentiated and open as competing logics of intervention increasingly drive the policy process, and the core character of farm issues and sometimes even farm players is changing. As this happens and member states have obtained increasing national flexibility, one of the main challenges for CAP policy-makers is to sustain a collective sense of purpose and prevent the fragmentation of the single agricultural market. Implementation will inevitably become a more critical and politicized phase of CAP policy-making.

Introduction

The CAP was established in a European Economic Community (EEC) of only six member states, which were recovering from severe post-war food shortages and were worried about the sustainability of food production.[1] In its classic version, which remained essentially intact until the late 1980s, the CAP was a system of market support to farmers based on guaranteed prices within the Community, and import levies and export subsidies vis-à-vis the rest of the world. This system turned the EEC into a world agricultural power. It was also expensive, created perverse economic incentives fuelling chronic production surpluses, and grew out of touch with the expectations of European taxpayers and consumers.

The five enlargements that the EU has undergone since the 1970s have further added dimensions of controversy and issues of appropriateness. The accession of the UK in 1973 enabled this long-standing critic of the CAP to advocate reform from within and set new policy priorities on the EU agenda. Since the 1995 enlargement, the UK has received support from Sweden in its quest for agricultural trade liberalization. The enlargement to Spain and Portugal in 1986 revealed the regressive bias of the CAP (which is centred on 'northern' products such as cereals or milk) and raised issues of budgetary redistribution as the structural funds doubled to meet the needs of the new members (see Chapters 9 and 10). These issues have become pressing today as the poorer member countries of central and east European (CEECs) are significant recipients of EU regional-policy subsidies.[2] The EU now has twenty-eight member states, whose agricultural structures, social make-up, and basic views on economic policy differ greatly. It is therefore not surprising that, while greeted as a bridge to bring the European peoples closer together, the CAP has been chastised in the public debate as a monument to economic irrationality and a stumbling block in the enlarged EU.

The primary objective of this chapter is to understand the processes that make up the CAP, paying special attention to how the Community method (see Chapter 4) functions in agriculture and how it upheld for decades the walls of fortress CAP. Contrary to widespread popular perceptions, the CAP is a policy in flux. Change has occurred in steps, first in the McSharry reform in 1992, then in Agenda 2000 (1999), the Mid-Term Review of the CAP (2003), the Health Check of the CAP (2008), and now with the 'CAP after 2013' reform (2013). Today's CAP bears little resemblance to the system of the 1960s, except for comparatively high tariff protection. The controversial device of price support has largely been replaced by direct payments to producers. Introduced in 1992 as a compensation for price cuts, these payments now represent the bulk of EU support in agriculture under the label of 'single farm payments'. They are *the* instrument through which the demands of the non-farm world are channelled into agricultural policy: whether to 'green the CAP', to 'decouple' farm support from production, or to 'simplify the CAP'.

The policy-making processes underpinning the CAP have changed too. The CAP has evolved into a complex policy regime driven by distinct and somewhat contradictory logics. Since 1999, efforts to embed newer forms of rural development have given birth to a separate policy regime institutionalized in 'pillar 2' for rural development side by side with traditional market concerns ('pillar 1' and market support and direct payments). This development introduced a distinct policy-making method, characterized by a more decentralized process and co-financing between the EU and member states. The Treaty of Lisbon (ToL) has further changed the rules of the game by empowering the European Parliament (EP) in CAP policy-making by applying the ordinary legislative procedure (previously known as the co-decision procedure; see Chapter 4). The Council must now share legislative power with the EP on agricultural policy and budgeting. Bringing co-decision to agriculture illustrated a more general tendency in the EU to empower the EP in areas where the Council decides by qualified majority vote, on ground of democratic accountability (Rittberger 2006). The argument that agriculture was an exceptional sector helps to explain why co-decision did not apply for so long, but this argument was ultimately insufficient to shield the CAP from broader political and institutional changes (Roederer-Rynning and Schimmelfennig 2012).

At the same time, an increasing number of linkages to other policy domains urge CAP policy-makers to respond to an ever-broadening variety of challenges. Not least today, the sovereign debt crises are reverberating in farm politics. For the first time, the level of total EU payment appropriation has fallen from the previous period; €17 billion less in 2014–20 than in 2007–13, corresponding to a decrease of 1.84 per cent. Heads of state and government in the European Council have used the negotiations on the long-term budget of the EU—the multi-annual financial framework (MFF) (see Chapter 9)—not only to recalibrate CAP expenditure, 2020-level CAP expenditure will be 15 per cent lower than 2013 levels, but also to shape policy content on a range of CAP issues. They have thus reinterpreted the ordinary legislative procedure. As the CAP today reflects a combination of heterogeneous policy-making processes, the main challenge for CAP policy-makers is to prevent the increased opportunities for national flexibility leading to fragmentation of the single market for agricultural commodities and 'greenwashing' (using public money in the name of green ideals to support activities that are actually detrimental to the environment).

Building fortress CAP: from fragmentation to compromise

The CAP was not set in stone from the beginning: it was born against a background of legal ambiguity and political fragmentation. A compromise nevertheless emerged in the 1960s in the course of protracted intergovernmental negotiations. It arose at the crossroads between ideas and power, where the modernizing ambitions of new European elites met the political and economic realities of post-war Europe. This compromise set the political parameters within which the Community method developed in agriculture, to become the foundation of fortress CAP.

Implausible origins

Observers have often noted the ambivalence and open-endedness of the parts of the 1957 Treaty of Rome (EEC) devoted to agriculture (e.g. Neville-Rolfe 1984: 194). On one point, the treaty was clear: this concerned the institutional rules to be followed in agriculture. The Commission possessed the exclusive right of initiative. The Council could request legislation, but it could not draft concrete proposals; nor could it adopt decisions without a proposal from the Commission. The Council could modify the Commission's proposal without the Commission's consent only if the member states were unanimous. Thus, it is not just 'formally', but also materially' that 'the Commission proposal is the basis of the subsequent negotiations' (Meester 1999: 2). The Council was sovereign in the decision-making phase. Competing law-makers were excluded by law, with the EP having to deliver an opinion before legislation acquired the force of law, but the Council not being obliged to take this opinion into account. National parliaments had even less to say, for CAP legislation was adopted in the form of regulations, which were directly applicable in the member states.

Beyond these procedural issues, ambiguity characterized substantive treaty provisions. The treaty envisaged a combination of negative integration ('extension of the Common Market to agriculture and trade in agricultural products', Art. 38(1) EEC), and positive integration ('establishment of a common agricultural policy among the member states', Art. 38(4) EEC). Integration was to respect principles of: market unity (single agricultural prices within the Community); community preference (common market products protected against imports); and financial solidarity (collective responsibility of member states for the financial consequences of the CAP). With regard to positive integration, the treaty specified that policy-makers must take account of 'the particular nature of agricultural activity, which results from the social structure of agriculture and from structural and natural disparities between the various agricultural regions' (Art. 39(2) EEC). Two policy tasks were thus sketched out for the CAP: first, to organize common agricultural markets (market policy measures); and, secondly, to promote modern farm structures, to support the professionalization of farmers, and to remedy regional disparities (structural policy measures). Yet, how these tasks should be accomplished remained a perplexing issue and reconciling competing objectives placed policy-makers in a situation where they had to square the circle. The future policy should: help to restructure the farm sector in order to free resources for the rest of the economy *while* stabilizing markets; and protect farm income *while* securing reasonable prices in supplies to consumers (Box 8.1).

The authors of the EEC Treaty were not careless or badly informed; the treaty simply reflected the reality of political fragmentation in late 1950s western Europe. In a country like France, the formidable farm lobbies that later became so intimately involved in European farm policy-making were embroiled in internecine conflicts (Wright 1953). Jealousies and conflicts regarding farmers' status, political ideology, commodity specialization, and specific market situations nourished

BOX 8.1	The five objectives of the CAP, Art. 39 TFEU (ex Art. 33 TEC)

- To increase agricultural production by promoting technical progress and by ensuring the rational development of agricultural production and optimum utilization of the factors of production, in particular labour;
- *thus*, to ensure a fair standard of living for the agricultural community, in particular by increasing the individual earnings of persons engaged in agriculture;
- to stabilize markets;
- to assure availability of supplies; and
- to ensure that supplies reach consumers at reasonable prices.

Note: I am indebted to Rob Peters and Robert Ackrill for pointing out to me that the second objective starts with 'thus' (my emphasis). Possibly, the treaty did not foresee objective 2 (to ensure a fair standard of living for the agricultural community) as a stand-alone objective, but as one linked to, and to be achieved through, the promotion of technical progress and the modernization of farm structures (objective 1). This point is important to remember in the light of the subsequent evolution of the CAP into a system of price support, which paid only lip-service to farm modernization.

scepticism about the organizational potential of farmers. There was no consensus either among the founding member states as to what the EEC should do in agriculture. The EC6 differed greatly in terms of their export orientations, their degrees of self-sufficiency, and the political clout of their national farm constituencies. Moreover, while all six founding members used market control, the forms, degrees, and objectives of national intervention in the farm sector varied from one country to another (Tracy 1989). Legal ambiguity reflected the absence of political consensus.

Modernization co-opted

A policy regime nonetheless emerged in the course of the 1960s.[3] In accordance with treaty requirements, a conference took place in Stresa, Italy in June 1958 to discuss policy guidelines where the EC6 broadly reasserted the dual mission of the CAP. In the following years, however, a series of intergovernmental negotiations set the CAP onto a quite different course, the essence of which is encapsulated in three main points:

- first, a policy of price support: intergovernmental deals in 1962 and 1964 guaranteed European farmers high prices for their produce while keeping world competitors away from the European markets through a system of variable import levies and export subsidies;
- secondly, a downgrading of structural policy: Commissioner Mansholt's 1968 plan to develop an ambitious policy to restructure European agriculture was watered down and structural policy remained safely anchored at the national level with the exception of a handful of relatively modest measures; and

- thirdly, a ring-fencing of CAP guarantee expenditure, as a result of the decision in 1970 to regard agriculture guarantee expenditure for market support as 'compulsory expenditure' (i.e. expenditure necessarily resulting from the treaties or from acts adopted in accordance with them) (see Chapter 9).

Far from a balanced mix of policy considerations, a single logic of market intervention based on price support prevailed in the 1960s. The protection of farm incomes had won over other considerations such as consumer concerns (insofar as prospects of 'reasonable prices for consumers' were forsaken) or the restructuring of the farm sector. European farm affairs underwent an 'agrarian turn' in the 1960s (Roederer-Rynning 2003a).

What explains this turn of events? There is evidence that Germany's influence was decisive in securing high prices on cereals—and through knock-on effects on dairy and meat products (Pinder 1991; Fennell 1997; Moravcsik 1998). It is less clear, however, why European leaders committed themselves one-sidedly to a policy of market intervention. Several explanations have emerged in the literature. 'Farm exceptionalism', a policy belief in the exceptional characteristics of agriculture, justified a high degree of state assistance in this sector (Coleman et al. 1997; Skogstad 1998; Moyer and Josling 2002). European elites wished to avoid the repetition of interwar political turbulences by reducing the gap between urban and rural incomes and thus the potential support for extremist political movements from rural areas (Majone 1995; Rieger 2005; Knudsen 2009). National politicians were happy to use EEC institutions to shield essentially clientelistic relations from public scrutiny (Vaubel 1986), without intending ever to cede core structural policy competences.

Conflicts among farmers and sword-crossing between national politicians and farm groups suggest yet an additional interpretation: the CAP of the 1960s also represented the price that modernizing European elites had to pay for securing the support of ordinary farmers and reluctant rural notables. In the 1950s, agriculture was limping behind manufacturing (Tracy 1989); post-war European elites had tended to neglect the agricultural sector in their haste to tackle more pressing economic and financial problems. European cooperation presented a unique opportunity to reduce bottleneck effects linked to a backward farm sector and to generate wealth for the economy as a whole. Yet, if the establishment of the EEC offered the proper framework and resources to carry out this agenda, the political mandate to advocate and implement the coming policy had to be forged at home, within the politics of individual member states, out of a fragmented political base where rural notables often did not see eye to eye with modernizing elites. Initially, these elites were committed to a policy of modernization featuring a European common market accompanied by a moderate price policy *and* a policy of modernization of farm structures. Eventually, they had to settle for much less to rally the support of farmers. Modernization intentions were co-opted by conservative forces in what Selznick (1984 [1949]: 260) once called 'the shadowland of informal interaction' (Roederer-Rynning 2004).

Clearly, the CAP of the 1960s resulted from complex compromises: among heterogeneous member states' preferences, but also between policy ideals and political realities. The CAP displayed an eminently *distributive logic* (see Chapter 3): divergent interests coalesced under the banner of a high-price policy and cemented two 'iron pacts' in western Europe: an agrarian pact between states and farmers now federated in formidable national lobbying groups; and an intergovernmental pact around the Franco-German axis. Views crystallized of the farming world as a special sector of the economy, necessitating special assistance from the state. Together these factors created long-term impediments to the efficient modernization of agriculture; they also raised high political and institutional obstacles in the path of advocates of change.

Before Lisbon: two variants of the Community method in agriculture

An abundant literature has documented how the Community method provided the foundation of fortress CAP. It created joint-decision-trap effects (Scharpf 1988; Roederer-Rynning 2011), entrenched agrarian worldviews (Fouilleux 2003) and closed policy networks (Daugbjerg 1999), strengthened the political clout of domestic farm interests (Roederer-Rynning 2002), and promoted rent-seeking (Vaubel 1986; Nedergaard 2006). While this literature emphasizes the independent power of institutions, it is important to highlight how the particular economic and political context specific to the agricultural sector coloured the way the Community method worked in practice. The Community method grants the Commission an important role compared with other policy modes by virtue of the axiom 'the Commission proposes; the Council disposes'. This was not an accidental construction but a deliberate choice to design decision-making by balancing intergovernmental and supranational powers. This construction required that Council and Commission be independent from each other, and that the Commission be controlled by yet another institution, the EP, using its powers of censure and consultation. It is thus in this light that the consultative powers of the EP must be understood: the consultative procedure was a means to hold the Commission accountable in the normal context of policy-making and notably to avoid Commission proposals being dictated by the interests of powerful members in the Council (Ténékidès 1970). As the case of agricultural policy shows, the role of EU institutions cannot be appreciated on the sole basis of the formal rules of the game in isolation from politics. In reality, two variants of the Community method developed within the institutional framework of the Treaty of Rome (Roederer-Rynning 2011). From the mid-1960s to the mid-1980s, 'hegemonic intergovernmentalism' characterized CAP policy-making: balanced policy-making gave way to policy-making centred on the Council. From the mid-1980s on, the CAP entered a phase of 'competitive intergovernmentalism' during which the balance between Council, Commission, and

EP was partly restored. Both variants were uncontestably intergovernmental as the Council remained the sole legislator in agriculture. The difference between the two variants of intergovernmentalism concerned the varying ability of the Commission and the EP to maintain their independent prerogatives in practice.

Hegemonic intergovernmentalism

Under this mode, which characterized the 1960s and 1970s, the member states secured extraordinary channels of influence beyond their treaty-enshrined prerogatives. This occurred first as a result of the six-month 'empty chair crisis' triggered by France on 1 July 1965 in response to a Commission proposal on the financing of the CAP. The Luxembourg compromise of 29 January 1966, which ended the crisis, led to the de facto recognition of a veto power for the members of the Council, whenever 'very important interests of one or more partners are at stake'. The text of the compromise showed how the Commission was 'neutralized' into becoming a sheer 'technical secretariat' (Cruz 2006: 275). Later, the institutionalization of the European Council secured the member states further influence by giving them collectively a right of initiative (but not of formulation) (Meester 1999). These developments weakened the Commission, not only by entrenching the norm of consensus within the Council and introducing a competing right of initiative, but also by inducing a certain degree of nationalization of the Commission itself (Averyt 1977: 88). Council–Commission relations in the age of the classic CAP were hierarchical rather than competitive, and failed to reveal the full potential of autonomy that the treaty granted the Commission.

Symptomatically, the member states also curbed the powers of the EP during these years. The 1970 decision to treat guarantee expenditure as 'compulsory' effectively removed the CAP from the scrutiny of members of the European Parliament (MEPs), paradoxically at a time when the EP began to acquire more substantive powers. Simultaneously, the Council routinely ignored the consultative powers of the EP by failing to wait for the EP's opinion before adopting CAP legislation. Thus, the Commission proposals were one-sidedly 'controlled by the legislative process, pre-empting "mistakes"' by the Commission (Cruz 2006: 275).

Farm interests were locked in within this policy tandem in both formal and informal ways. Formal segmentation within EU institutions shielded agricultural policy from the pressure of countervailing interests. A separate formation of the Council—the Council of Agriculture ministers—discussed agricultural affairs from the beginning, assisted from May 1960 by the Special Committee on Agriculture (SCA) (a sub-formation of the Council composed of senior civil servants of member states) in lieu of Coreper (Pearce 1981; Swinbank 1989). On a less formal basis, the routine consultation of farm groups to the exclusion of other interests reinforced institutional closure at all levels and phases of policy-making. At the supranational level, the *Comité des Organisations Professionnelles Agricoles* (COPA) was the main device for channelling the input of farmers, a Euro-farm lobby created at about the same time as the EEC with the active support of the agriculture commissioner, Sicco

Mansholt. Agricultural interests made themselves felt again at the implementation stage at the national level, where farm groups often received important delegated powers and seats in the myriad national agencies and commissions set up to implement the various CAP commodity regimes. In sum, the CAP displayed the characteristics of a 'policy community' discussed in Chapter 3.

Many features of this closed policy process could be attributed to characteristics of the agricultural sector. The use of a highly technical form of regulation (market management) in a fragmented policy environment consisting of millions of production units did generate distinctive features at the EU level, notably:

- a density of social interaction among the various actors involved in the policy-making process (Council, Commission, farm groups, national agencies) unmatched in other policy areas. Here, the CAP stands in clear contrast with cohesion policy—another expenditure policy—which the Council discusses only rarely, thus offering a very low degree of socialization among member governments, and between member governments and members of the Commission (see Chapter 10). The density of social interaction characterizing the CAP has provided a solid basis for building confidence among policy actors, exchanging information, and discovering common interests;

- an unparalleled asymmetric representation of interests, perhaps with the exception of fisheries policy (Lequesne 2005). Asymmetry does not just reflect the fact that counter-CAP constituencies have been notoriously difficult to organize (consumer constituencies are diffuse; most environmental groups have been present on the European scene for fewer than thirty years; their staff are small and their resources modest (see Chapter 13); finally, the food-processing industry, which otherwise might have been a driver for reform, has heterogeneous interests), but also the technical character of the CAP's market-intervention policy (Keeler 1987), which almost by nature necessitates the intervention of a farm client (Sheingate 2001);

- a particular devotion to the consensual style of policy-making. This feature is enhanced in agriculture by the unusually high level of socialization characterizing CAP policy-making as well as the segregation of producers' and consumers' concerns on an EU level; and

- a regressive form of redistribution whereby affluent farmers receive a disproportionate share of CAP payments.

On the other hand, there are limits to what can be explained with reference to the special characteristics of the farm sector. Notwithstanding descriptions of the CAP as a uniquely Europeanized regime, one must recognize the vigour of national interests and the ability of national governments to resist the pooling of competences at the supranational level. Entire areas of agricultural policy-making thus remained under the partial or exclusive competence of member states: the bulk of structural policy, of course, but also social security provisions for farmers, the regulation of the working conditions and wages of agricultural workers, and the regulation of land tenure—all representing important levers of agricultural modernization. The delegation of power to EU institutions proceeded only as long as it enabled a common financing of market policy never to encroach upon the politically sensitive area of modernization policy.

There is no doubt that the equilibrium 'discovered' at the end of the 1960s contributed to reconstructing and sustaining the power of national agrarian lobbies while postponing the 'hollowing out' of the state (Milward 1992; Grant 2005). As some have put it, 'the paradox of the CAP is that, in creating a European agricultural block, it has strengthened the place of agriculture in national politics out of proportion with the sector's economic importance' (Lowe *et al.* 2002: 14)—and the Community method during the 1960s and 1970s provided the foundation of this fortress.

Competitive intergovernmentalism

Since the mid-1980s, developments in the CAP have presented a baffling picture to the observer of European farm affairs. The global General Agreement on Tariffs and Trade (GATT)/World Trade Organization (WTO) trade negotiations (see Chapter 16), internal negotiations on the EU budget (see Chapter 9), and the serial enlargement of the EU (see Chapter 17) have exerted considerable pressures on the CAP. From the mid-1980s to the ToL, no fewer than five reforms were adopted, not counting the reforms targeting specific commodity markets like sugar (2006), wine (2008), or milk (2008) (Table 8.1). Not all reforms have proved significant. Together, however, they have brought about a significant and lasting change with the introduction of direct payments and the institutionalization of the pillared structure of the CAP. During this timespan, the balance between Council, Commission, and the EP was partly restored, starting in the late 1970s. The EP's consultative powers were reasserted in the *Isoglucose* (1979) court case, which cancelled a decision adopted by the Council without having waited for the EP's opinion. Likewise, the Commission began cultivating policy space by loosening its ties to the Council and insulating the agenda-setting phase from unwanted interference from the member states. Interestingly, the Commission's legal services played an influential role in calling off an attempt by the UK to invoke the Luxembourg Compromise during the 1983 negotiations on the agricultural price package. This development dealt a blow not only to the UK, but to all countries that had joined the EU with a 'safety valve' (e.g. Denmark, Ireland, and Greece) upon the understanding that they 'would always be able to invoke the national interest notwithstanding Treaty provisions for qualified majority-voting' (Commission official quoted in Roederer-Rynning 2011: 31).

Two main processes of change have brought about more contested policy-making: 'breaking open the policy community' and 'bypassing the policy community'. In the first path, 'breaking open the policy community', insider elites drove reform with a view to protecting the policy regime. They control the scope and pace of change often in the face of resistance from key policy-community actors. This type of change might be referred to as 'enabling change' (Peters and Pierre 1998), which

TABLE 8.1 Competitive policy-making: twenty-five years of CAP reform, 1984–2009

Reform	Main points	Context	Implication
Reform of the dairy sector (Mar. 1984)	• production quotas on dairy products	Row over the EC budget; Prime Minister Thatcher secures an automatically delivered yearly budget rebate for the UK	First binding control on production
McSharry reform (May 1992)	• *price cuts* on cereals (30% within three years) and beef and veal (15%) • *compensatory payments to producers* are coupled to production, as only farmers growing the eligible commodities may receive these payments • *accompanying measures* include: aid for the early retirement of farmers; agro-environmental schemes; support for the reforestation of agricultural land; set aside of 15% of arable land for farms beyond agreed size	Uruguay Round of the GATT focuses on agricultural goods and treats negotiations on goods as single undertaking (i.e. forming a single package)	Farm payments become chief support instrument; make CAP less market-distorting; limits on farm-payments spending place CAP expenditure effectively under control
Agenda 2000 agreement on agriculture (Mar. 1999)	Market and income support becomes *pillar 1* of the CAP: (1) *prices* are cut by 15% on cereals, 20% on beef and veal, and 15% on dairy products; (2) *cross-compliance* allows member states to make the disbursement of payments, now called direct payments, conditional on environmental criteria Rural development becomes *pillar 2* of the CAP *Modulation* enables member states to strengthen pillar 2 funds by up to 20% of the total amount of direct payments to which they are entitled	Eastern enlargement: CEECs are poorer and more rural than EU15	New rural development pillar sharpens multifunctionality of the CAP; opens up for 'greening' of CAP support

Fischler reform, also called Mid-Term Review of the CAP (MTR) (June 2003)	• *partly decouples* farm income support from production by replacing direct farm payments to producers with a *single farm payment* (SFP) • *compulsory 5% modulation* of the single farm payment with a franchise of €5,000: savings generated by compulsory modulation are to a large extent retained in the source country, where they can be used to increase rural development funds; single farm payment subject to *compulsory cross-compliance*, now extended in respect of EU rules on the protection of animal welfare, and public, animal, and plant health—besides the environmental criteria • *national envelopes* enable member states to retain up to 10% of the maximum total amount of income subsidies they receive and spend it as new pillar 1 payments to enhance environmentally friendly farming, the quality and marketing of farm products • market intervention mechanisms (for intervention, storage, and export restitutions) turned into *safety nets*	Doha Round of the WTO	Farm payments become largely decoupled
Health Check of the CAP (Nov. 2008)	• payments still coupled become *decoupled* (with some exceptions) • national envelopes (now *'article 68 measures'*) become more flexible as money no longer has to be used in the same sector as it is generated • further phasing out of *market intervention mechanisms* (pig meat, barley, sorghum) • abolition of set-aside • compulsory 10% *modulation* by 2012 with extra cut for payments above €300,000 • cross-compliance simplified	Doha Round of the WTO	Pursuit of liberalization of CAP

emerges when organizations confronted with a turbulent environment seek *to regain control* by dominating or circumventing obstacles. Under this process of change, farm elites were the protagonists of change; they used their institutional prerogatives in combination with new political realities to effect change.

A precondition for change has been the existence in the agricultural service of the European Commission of a circle of reform-minded officials willing to introduce reform proposals and able to exploit alternative policy-making venues to shield them. Given that it is farm practitioners themselves who sponsor (in the Commission) and control (in the Council) this process, change comes in the guise of CAP reforms, which, while sometimes far-reaching in their policy consequences, do not tackle the overarching institutional context of CAP policy-making.

Whereas it is open to question how enlargement has affected reform (see Box 8.2), there is no doubt that global trade talks triggered this pattern of change (Daugbjerg and Roederer-Rynning 2014). In particular, the Uruguay Round of multilateral trade negotiations provided the main levers of change for this type of process by enabling the Commission to exploit its powers of international negotiation (by virtue of Art. 207 TFEU; see Chapter 16) and fragmentation in the Council to steer a reformist course. The radical reform of the CAP in 1992 (McSharry reform 1992), the significant 'Mid-Term Review' (2003) and more modest 'Health Check' (2008) were adopted during and in the light of major rounds of multilateral trade negotiations (Table 8.1). These reforms marked milestones in the history of the CAP by phasing out the output-geared system of price support and turning farm payments into the main instrument of intervention. Change reflected the increasing political and institutional autonomy of the Commission's Directorate-General for Agriculture (DG AGRI) vis-à-vis farm ministers from the 1980s on.

Cumulatively these reforms have had considerable effects. Support has become decoupled from production and the CAP has become less market-distorting (although such support can still distort international trade (see Figure 8.1)). It has also become 'greener' as payments have been made conditional upon meeting environmental criteria. The CAP has also been modulated to finance rural-development programmes (the CAP has become more 'multifunctional'). Yet, these reforms have failed to transform the overarching objectives of the CAP and the framework of institutional segmentation.

In the second path, 'bypassing the policy community', change is sponsored and controlled by policy outsiders, in a context of crisis or quasi-crisis, and often on the basis of values different from those underpinning the policy. In an institutionalist terminology, this might be referred to as 'disruptive change' (Peters and Pierre 1998). It involves the strategic entrepreneurship of actors located *outside* agriculture. Change of this type does not lead to CAP reforms, because the actors are not CAP stakeholders, but rather to a reconfiguration of the macro-institutional and political parameters of policy-making in which the CAP is situated. Crises or quasi-crises generated by factors external to the CAP provide the main levers of this type of change. These levers are ineffectual, however, unless entrepreneurs mobilize non-farm constituencies for change and develop institutional solutions to the problems.

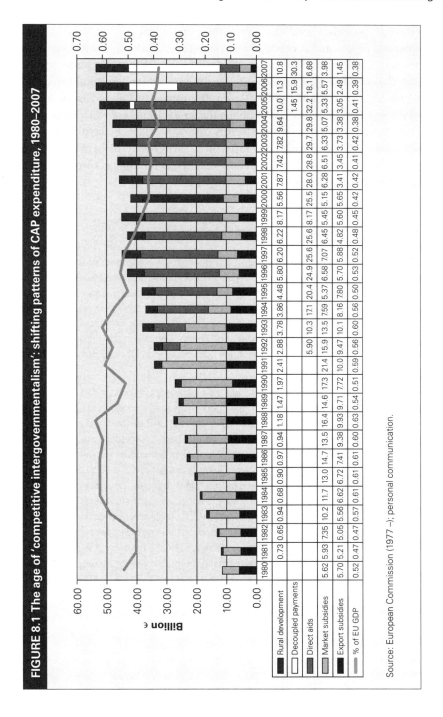

FIGURE 8.1 The age of 'competitive intergovernmentalism': shifting patterns of CAP expenditure, 1980–2007

Billion €

	1980	1981	1982	1983	1984	1985	1986	1987	1988	1989	1990	1991	1992	1993	1994	1995	1996	1997	1998	1999	2000	2001	2002	2003	2004	2005	2006	2007
Rural development		0.73	0.65	0.94	0.68	0.90	0.97	0.94	1.18	1.47	1.97	2.41	2.88	3.78	3.86	4.48	5.80	6.20	6.22	8.17	5.56	7.87	7.42	7.82	9.64	10.0	11.3	10.8
Decoupled payments																										1.45	15.9	30.3
Direct aids													5.90	10.3	17.1	20.4	24.9	25.6	25.6	8.17	25.5	28.0	28.8	29.7	29.8	32.2	18.1	6.68
Market subsidies	5.62	5.93	7.35	10.2	11.7	13.0	14.7	13.5	16.4	14.6	17.3	21.4	15.9	13.5	7.59	5.37	6.58	7.07	6.45	5.45	5.15	6.28	6.51	6.33	5.07	5.33	5.57	3.98
Export subsidies	5.70	5.21	5.05	5.56	6.62	6.72	7.41	9.38	9.93	9.71	7.72	10.0	9.47	10.1	8.16	7.80	5.70	5.88	4.82	5.60	5.65	3.41	3.45	3.73	3.38	3.05	2.49	1.45
% of EU GDP	0.52	0.47	0.47	0.57	0.61	0.61	0.60	0.60	0.63	0.54	0.51	0.59	0.56	0.60	0.56	0.50	0.53	0.52	0.48	0.45	0.42	0.42	0.41	0.42	0.38	0.41	0.39	0.38

Source: European Commission (1977 –); personal communication.

Food scares provide a good example of this path of change. The 'mad cow crisis'[4] prompted EU policy-makers to transfer competence for human and animal health away from DG AGRI to the Directorate-General for Health and Consumer Protection (DG SANCO) and from the EP's Committee on Agriculture and Rural Development (AGRI) to the (then called) Committee on Environment, Public Health, and Food Safety Policy (ENVI) and through applying the co-decision procedure to these issues (Roederer-Rynning 2003b). Change in this case was driven by actors who did not have a formal CAP policy-making competence. Farm policy-makers in the Council and in the Commission were on the defensive and had minimal control over agenda-setting and decision-making.

BOX 8.2   **Enlargement as a lever of change?**

This interpretation of change leaves open the question of the impact of the various enlargements. As a 'composite policy', enlargement cuts across all policy areas while calling for negotiated compromises between policy-makers at the sectoral and at the macro-level (see Chapter 17). Enlargement may trigger agricultural change in two main ways: (1) before accession, by tightening the grip of finance ministers on the CAP (as in the 'bypassing the policy community' path); and (2) after accession, by introducing a new range of policy preferences in the Agriculture Council (as in the 'breaking the policy community open' path).

(1) Enlargement has undoubtedly tightened the budgetary grip on the CAP. One of the outcomes of the Mediterranean enlargement was the doubling of structural funds, which constrained the resources available for CAP expenditure in a situation of scarce budgetary resources. This resulted in the establishment of an *agriculture guideline* limiting the annual growth of agriculture expenditure to 74 per cent of the annual growth rate of Union gross national product, enforced through budget stabilizers (in practice production thresholds, beyond which prices were cut automatically). Likewise, the accession of the poorer CEECs went hand in hand with the freezing of 2000–6 pillar 1 farm expenditure at the 1999 level (€40.5 billion yearly). The main impact of this new budgetary constraint was the abandonment of market intervention for rye and maize and a very gradual introduction of the direct payments in the new member states.

(2) It might be the case that majorities for CAP reform are more difficult to assemble in an enlarged EU after CEECs have been granted unhindered access to the EU market and a share in CAP subsidies (e.g. Hungary favoured liberalization before accession but defended the status quo afterwards). But the proponents of CAP reform have become more vocal with the accession of Sweden and the occasional support of Germany. Finally, enlargement, by increasing the number and heterogeneity of member-state preferences, makes it harder for the Council to override a Commission proposal as unanimity is required. In the 1990s and 2000s, this hurdle occasionally enabled a more reform-friendly Commission to trump entrenched interests in the Council (Roederer-Rynning 2011: 31).

After Lisbon: the search for a collective sense of purpose

With the entry into force of the ToL in December 2009, the EP has acquired co-equal status as regards law-making with the Council in the CAP, although the exact scope of this change has been the object of a fierce power struggle between the Council and the EP during the implementation of Lisbon.[5] Furthermore, the treaty abolished the budgetary distinction between compulsory and non-compulsory expenditure, which had excluded CAP expenditure from the EP's general budget-making competence. Thus, the Council can no longer decide alone on issues of CAP law-making and budget-making; it has to share power with the EP. These are major institutional changes.

Within this new framework, a reform of the CAP was adopted (formally by an EP vote on 20 Nov. 2013), to take effect from 1 January 2015.[6] This reform was the first major piece of CAP legislation after the implementation of the ToL and it took place in a context marked by the euro crisis. From an institutional perspective, this reform highlights the power of the purse and of informal decision-making. From a policy perspective, it brings 'national flexibility' squarely into the picture.

'The CAP after 2013': mainstreaming the 'green' agenda

Why did the EU embark on yet another round of CAP reform? What was the rationale for a new reform and how did the reform work within the overall development of the CAP policy regime? The policy narrative of previous reforms can be summed up as: (1) a progressive move towards a flatter farm payment, through the shift from price support to direct payments (McSharry reform 1992) and the progressive decoupling of farm payments from production references (Fischler reform 2003; Health Check 2008); and (2) a parallel move towards developing a new pillar of CAP support (pillar 2) for 'rural development', geared towards delivering public goods (Agenda 2000 in 1999; Fischler reform 2003).

In the 2013 reform, the agenda of the Commission was officially to mainstream greening and make the CAP simpler and fairer (Cioloş 2011). Reversing some of the previously mentioned trends, mainstreaming green objectives was to be achieved through the creation of a new 'green payment' embedded in pillar 1 (30 per cent of direct payment expenditure), and therefore fully EU-financed. The Commission also proposed using pillar 2 to fund a broader range of measures, eliminating the existing statutory obligation to spend a minimum level of 'pillar 2 rural-development' money on green measures, and thus indirectly undermining the 'green' identity of rural-development measures. One advantage of this strategy is that it allowed 'green' farming on a much larger scale; after all, rural-development expenditure remained modest as a result of a lack of political will to use it, and shifting to pillar 1 payments allowed green funds to reach a larger pool of beneficiaries. However, the Commission's greening strategy also involved the risk that mainstream green payments may not deliver effective greening. It is, indeed, more difficult to green farming by using conditionality than by using well-defined and targeted measures, which is why pillar 2 agri-environmental measures are popular with environmentalists. Furthermore, creating a new payment side by side with existing green measures involved the risk that farmers might be paid twice for providing the same service. Under these circumstances, the success of the Commission's proposal would hinge on its ability to impose a common model of targeted requirements associated with the green payment and to control the implementation of the green payment scheme.

National flexibility and the challenges of a CAP à la carte

During the negotiations, member states persistently strove to infuse 'flexibility' into the CAP reform. One aspect of this flexibility agenda concerned the very concept of 'greening'. The Commission had proposed a common model of greening resting on three much-debated criteria: crop diversification; the maintenance of permanent grasslands; and the maintenance of so-called 'ecological focus areas' (EFAs) on a minimum of 7 per cent of farmland. Member states instead wished to have the possibility to use their own model of greening instead of the criteria defined by the Commission. They won an important victory, with the agreed reform allowing *equivalent practices at the national or regional level* to replace the EU-level greening criteria under certain conditions (Box 8.3). Anticipating risks for the coherence of the single market, EU legislators have given the Commission special powers to monitor implementation (without involving the member states). Yet, it is perplexing that they provided for such a degree of decentralization of the greening requirements in the first place. If not carefully monitored, the system of equivalence will generate greenwashing, dissolve the concept of 'greening', and ultimately undermine the legitimacy of green payments.

Another important, if overlooked, aspect of the flexibility agenda concerned the *proliferation of optional tools and support schemes within pillar 1* on farm payments. 'National envelopes' provide the organizing framework of flexibility: the idea is to devolve some degree of decision-making power back to national authorities within a budgetary envelope corresponding to the amount of pillar 1 money allocated to each member state (the national envelopes). National envelopes are not new; they go back to the Fischler reform. Furthermore, the Commission itself proposed such schemes in recognition of national diversity. However, member states and sometimes MEPs have systematically sought to expand flexibility beyond the scope of Commission proposals.

During the negotiations, the member states and MEPs succeeded in increasing the percentage of the national envelopes allocated to these optional schemes and furthermore introduced a new optional scheme, the so-called 'redistributive payment',

BOX 8.3	Some elements of the 'CAP after 2013' (as adopted by the EP on 20 Nov. 2013)

Pillar 1: redesigning of direct payments

- Overall 2020 level of pillar 1 payments reduced by 13 per cent compared to 2013 level reflecting the impact of inflation on nominal values (thanks to A. Matthews for pointing this out to me);
- only *active farmers* are eligible for farm payments;
- 30 per cent of the national envelope for direct payments is devoted to a 'green payment': this payment is conditional in respect of three good environmental practices (crop diversification, maintaining grasslands, and conserving ecological focus areas) or equivalent practices at the national or regional level;
- 2 per cent of the national envelope for direct payments is devoted to a mandatory 'payment for young farmers';
- up to 50 per cent of the national envelope for direct payments may be redistributed across: a voluntary 'payment on the first hectares' (up to 30 per cent of the national envelope); a voluntary coupled support payment for farmers in sectors in difficulty (up to 15 per cent of national envelope); a voluntary payment for *less favoured areas* (up to 5 per cent of the national envelope);
- the remainder of the national envelope constitutes the 'basic payment' or 'single area payment';
- *degressivity* of payments: the 'basic payment' or 'single area payment' is reduced by 5 per cent for amounts above €150,000;
- *Sugar quotas* abolished in 2017.

Transfers between pillars: now working both ways

- Up to 15 per cent from pillar 1 to pillar 2;
- and up to 15 per cent from pillar 2 to pillar 1 (but 25 per cent for member states with lower than average per hectare direct payments).

Pillar 2

- Overall 2020 level of pillar 2 payments reduced by 18 per cent compared to 2013 level;. This is a discretionary cut;
- *30 per cent minimum spending level of rural-development programmes* on agri-environmental measures, organic projects, or environmentally friendly investment;
- *EU co-financing rate* increased to 85 per cent of rural-development projects for the less advanced EU areas;

Crisis-management tools

- including a crisis reserve and risk prevention mechanism (funded by withholding direct payments in pillar 1; not part of pillar 2).

allowing member states to redistribute up to 30 per cent of their national envelope to support smaller farms through a premium on 'the first 50 hectares of land'. This new scheme was introduced through an EP amendment sponsored by the French government. When optional schemes are added together, member states *may now redistribute half of their national envelopes as they wish* (choosing between multiple combinations of 'coupled support' for sectors in difficulty, 'natural constraints' support, and 'the redistributive payment' benefiting smaller farms). While flexibility of this sort is not new, this reform is characterized by a systematic increase in the scope of flexibility.

The consequences of this type of flexibility are hard to overestimate. On the positive side, national governments are now better able to attend to the specificity of their national agriculture and respond to domestic political priorities. In today's enlarged EU, it is impossible to develop a one-size-fits-all approach to agriculture. On the negative side, flexibility postpones the prospect of a flat payment for farmers and risks undermining the logic of the single market in agriculture. As national governments use redistribution options, the disparities in support to farmers involved in the same activity may increase significantly across national borders, not just between 'old' and 'new' member states, but also among old member states.

In the end, flexibility rather than greening may be the hallmark of this reform. While reflecting the diversity of national situations, flexibility makes the CAP a less common policy regime and resurrects internal borders, which had been painstakingly lowered through decades of integration. As the logic of flexibility unfolds, implementation will inevitably become a more critical phase of CAP policy-making.

Parliamentary power in the shadow of the multi-annual financial framework

Given that the EP is supposed to represent the common European interest, it is interesting that co-decision did not mitigate the drive towards national flexibility. An important reason lies in the eminently redistributive implications of the contemporary CAP regime. From operating along a broadly distributive logic under the classic system of price support in the 1960s and 1970s, the CAP has evolved towards a more distinctly redistributive logic under the system of farm payments. Resources are fewer (budget discipline), recipients are more (due to enlargements), and the policy instruments (direct payments) weaken the cohesion of traditional farm groups by generating internal redistributional conflict. The 'CAP after 2013' reform amplified redistributive politics. Beneath the 'greening' ambition, three grand redistributive negotiations structured the 'CAP after 2013' reform: between non-farmers and farmers regarding the rationale of farm support; between farmers in the old member states and those in the new member states regarding the distribution of direct payments (so-called 'external convergence'); and between farmers involved in different types of agricultural production (so-called 'internal convergence'). These redistributive negotiations played a defining role for the CAP reform through the cognate negotiations on the long-term budget of the CAP, the so-called multi-annual financial framework (MFF). *They empowered actors not formally granted any decision-making power in the CAP, chiefly the European Council, while often dividing MEPs along national lines.*

CAP policy-making and budgetary politics have always been intertwined since the EU's total budgetary policy-making establishes the financial envelope for CAP spending. Budgetary constraints on the CAP have increased with every round of enlargement but until recently finance ministers had little to say about the actual content of the CAP. This changed with the negotiations on the MFF 2014–20 (see Chapter 9). MFF negotiations were initiated at the same time as the negotiations on CAP reform in 2011 and resulted in an unprecedented cut in the farm budget of the EU (see Figure 8.2): a 15 per cent decrease in agriculture ('heading two') expenditure (covering both CAP pillars 1 and 2) by 2020 from 2013. Within 'heading two', the negotiators have also provided for an important reshuffling of budget flows between 'pillar 1' on direct payments and 'pillar 2' on rural development. All member states may now transfer up to 15 per cent of their annual allocation from rural development funds (pillar 2) into direct payments (pillar 1). This has been termed

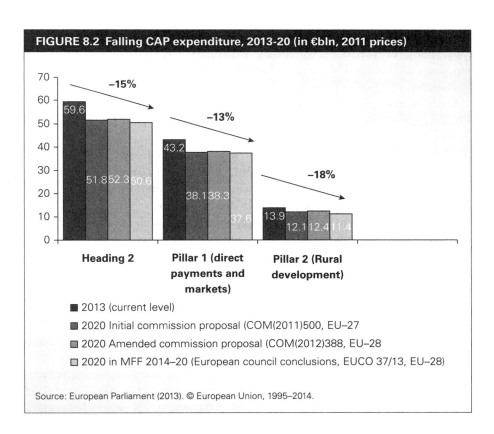

FIGURE 8.2 Falling CAP expenditure, 2013-20 (in €bln, 2011 prices)

Source: European Parliament (2013). © European Union, 1995–2014.

'reverse modulation' and it is yet another signal that the rural-development pillar of the CAP is weakening as member states prioritize pillar 1 payments.

The MFF negotiations also rapidly developed into an informal CAP decision-making forum for the member states, outside the normal perimeter of the ordinary legislative procedure. The June 2012 MFF 'negotiating box' on heading two listed various issues, besides the determination of the overall size of agricultural spending, which gave rise to a series of policy decisions by the European Council on the MFF on 8 February 2013. These concerned crucial aspects of the CAP, including: the definition of 'ecological focus areas' and of 'active farmer'; the capping of support to large farms; the convergence of support across member states; the model of internal redistribution of support among farmers; flexibility between pillar 1 on direct payments and market support and pillar 2 on rural development; the weighting of the greening component of direct payments; and criteria for the distribution of rural-development support (European Council 2013a: 26–31). The EP (2013) was very displeased about being excluded and denounced the European Council's action as an attack on its co-decision competences (see e.g. European Parliament 2013).

Faced with this demonstration of power by the member states and with the divisive redistributive implications of the issues, MEPs had a hard time sustaining a collective sense of purpose and behaved in a disorganized manner after an initially promising phase of internal coordination. When the decisive moment to amend the Commission proposals arrived, they tabled more than 7,500 amendments, many of them sponsored by national delegations, some directly sponsored by national governments, as illustrated by the introduction of the 'redistributive payment' into the legislation.

Much interest has focused on which one of the legislatures—the Council or the EP—is 'greener'; and on the whole, neither institution has shown a great interest in 'greening'. On some points, the EP has been greener. Though rather sceptical of the Commission's 'green' payment (and on the whole more interested in protecting European farmers from global competition),[7] MEPs have been more committed to green rural-development programmes than either the Council or the Commission. Not only did they strive to reintroduce a minimum level of spending on 'green' measures in pillar 2 against increasing attempts to make this pillar a catch-all category, they also (unsuccessfully) resisted the European Council's call to allow all member states to convert a significant share of pillar 2 payments into more traditional, but fully EU-financed farm payments (so-called 'reverse modulation'). Finally, after some hesitation, they also opposed the idea of a double payment for the same service and eventually brought the Council to their position. However, the EP approached the 'CAP after 2013' reform from an institutional logic of representation akin to corporatism, which privileged producer interests and was insulated from environmental concerns and actors. This outcome reflected the ability of a rather conservative EP Committee on Agriculture and Rural Development to control the legislative process at the expense of the Committee on the Environment, Public Health, and Food Safety (Roederer-Rynning 2014). At the end of the day, MEPs' own inclination for pragmatic and competitiveness-enhancing solutions and a certain resignation from the Commission cleared the path for Council-dominated compromises and national flexibility.

Conclusion

The CAP long conjured up images of medieval strongholds. Traditionally in the hands of a closed policy community, it invariably took on the guise of an impenetrable fortress built by farmers for farmers on the promontory of national sovereignty. This chapter has shown that the CAP today more fittingly summons up images of early modern European fortified cities. Society has moved inside the walls while becoming ever more connected to the outside world by a dense web of ties. This new construction must find its place in changing patterns of political consolidation at the local, regional, national, and global levels. The walls are still there—but they are lower.

Production surpluses, blatant income inequality among farmers, and repeated food scares eroded the foundations of the old regime. Budget discipline and the emergence of new policy priorities on the EU agenda depleted the resources available for the defence of traditional farm concerns. Global trade talks and successive enlargements provided venues for change. These developments contributed to shedding price supports and advancing direct payments as a pivotal instrument of support, linking farmers' concern for income support to changing public expectations regarding global trade liberalization, food safety, environmental protection, animal welfare, and balanced regional development. From operating along a predominantly distributive logic under the classic system of price support, the CAP has evolved towards a more distinctly redistributive logic under the system of farm payments.

As EU negotiations approached the CAP after 2013, proponents of change were concerned that energy pressures, the fashion for bio-fuels, and the rash of food price rises might help status quo players reverse the changes of the last decades. Some feared that the window of opportunity for change had ended with the empowerment of the EP and the accession of CEECs with large rural constituencies. MEPs have certainly taken uncertain steps towards change, tempted as they are, in a context of increased global competition, the collapse of global trade talks, and EU budget retrenchment, to sanctuarize CAP expenditure and privilege economic sustainability. But perhaps the most noteworthy aspect of 'the CAP after 2013' reform is the de facto self-empowerment of the European Council via the negotiations on the long-term budget of the EU. The CAP originated in a mix of sector-related strictures, political realities, and modernizing ambitions, and its evolution cautions us, again and again, against downplaying the role of national interests and the ability of member states to control the supranational delegation of powers. In a context of budgetary discipline, where the pie must be shared even as the size of the pie is diminishing, the challenge for CAP regulators today is not to prevent a hypothetical comeback to the price-support system or generalized market intervention but to prevent the fragmentation of the single market through a muddled implementation of greening and the consolidation of uneven regimes of support among member states.

NOTES

1   I would like to thank the persons I interviewed in 2012, 2013, and 2014. I acknowledge support from the Danish Social Science Research Council (grant # 11-104384). Thanks also go to Robert Ackrill, Carsten Daugbjerg, Wyn Grant, and Rob Peters who read an earlier version of the chapter. I am especially indebted to Alan Matthews and Rudolf Moegele, who made detailed comments on the penultimate version of the chapter, and to the editors of this volume.

2   With a population representing 30 per cent of that of the EU15, the ten CEECs generated a GNP of only 5 per cent of that of the EU at the time of their accession.

3   See also Rieger (2005: 189).

4   Bovine spongiform encephalopathy (BSE) is a fatal, brain-wasting disease, which led to the mass destruction of cattle in several member states. While the disease was identified in the late 1980s, the link between this animal disease and the human vCJD was confirmed in 1996, triggering the so-called 'mad cow crisis'.

5   Indeed, the treaty provides for all legislative acts relating to the 'common organization of agricultural markets ... and the other provisions necessary for the pursuit of the objectives of the common agricultural policy and the common fisheries policy' (Art. 43(2) TFEU), whereas for other types of acts related to 'fixing prices, levies, aid and quantitative limitations and on the fixing and allocation of fishing opportunities' (Art. 43(3) TFEU), the Council decides on a proposal from the Commission without consulting the EP.

6   These proposals were delivered in a package of four regulations on: direct payments (Commission 2011*f*); the single common market organization (Commission 2011*g*); rural development (Commission 2011*h*); and financing, management, and monitoring of the CAP (Commission 2011*i*)—or so-called 'horizontal' regulation.

7   MEPs (unlike the Council) actually favoured a model of greening involving limited penalties for not complying with greening requirements, which de facto made the green payment a voluntary top-up payment, and they (like the Council) loosened the conditionality of the greening payment by introducing a range of qualifying provisions.

FURTHER READING

For a detailed histories of the CAP, see Tracy (1989), Grant (1997), Ackrill (2000), Garzon (2006), and Cunha with Swinbank (2011). Milward (1992: Ch. 5) provides the best account of the prehistory. Fennell (1997) offers the most detailed, historically oriented policy analysis of the CAP. For a view of US agricultural politics and policies, see Orden *et al.* (1999), and for a comparison of agricultural policy reform in the EU and the US, see Moyer and Josling (2002). Greer (2005) offers a detailed account of how national governments influence the CAP at all levels of the policy cycle. Daugbjerg and Swinbank (2009) provide a detailed account of the impact of WTO trade liberalization on the CAP. For an account of the CAP as a 'welfare state of farmers', see Sheingate (2001) and Knudsen (2009). Those interested in current developments should consult *The Agricultural Situation in the European Union*, an annual publication by the Commission (Commission 1977–).

Ackrill, R. (2000), *The Common Agricultural Policy* (Sheffield: Sheffield Academic Press).

Commission (1977–), *The Agricultural Situation in the European Union*, DG AGRI (previously The Agricultural Situation in the Community).

Cunha, A., with Swinbank, A. (2011), *An Inside View of the CAP Reform Process* (Oxford: Oxford University Press).

Daugbjerg, C., and Swinbank, A. (2009), *Ideas, Institutions and Trade: The WTO and the Curious Role of EU Farm Policy in Trade Liberalization* (Oxford: Oxford University Press).

Fennell, R. (1997), *The Common Agricultural Policy: Continuity and Change* (Oxford: Clarendon Press).

Garzon, I. (2006), *Reforming the Common Agricultural Policy: History of a Paradigm Change* (Basingstoke: Palgrave Macmillan).

Grant, W. (1997), *The Common Agricultural Policy* (Basingstoke: Palgrave Macmillan).

Greer, A. (2005), *Agricultural Policy in Europe* (Manchester: Manchester University Press).

Knudsen, A.C.Lauring (2009), *Farmers on Welfare: The Making of Europe's Common Agricultural Policy* (Ithaca, NY: Cornell University Press).

Milward, A. S. (1992), *The European Rescue of the Nation-State* (London: Routledge).

Moyer, H., and Josling, T. (2002), *Agricultural Policy Reform: Politics and Processes in the EU and in the US in the 1990s* (Aldershot: Ashgate).

Orden, D., Paarlberg, R., and Roe, T. (1999), *Policy Reform in American Agriculture: Analysis and Prognosis* (Chicago, IL: University of Chicago Press).

Sheingate, A. (2001), *The Welfare State for Farmers: Institutions and Interest Group Power in the United States, France, and Japan* (Princeton, NJ: Princeton University Press).

Tracy, M. (1989), *Government and Agriculture in Western Europe* (New York, NY: Harvester Wheatsheaf).

CHAPTER 9

The Budget

Who Gets What, When, and How?

Brigid Laffan and Johannes Lindner

Summary

The budget is a focus for repeated negotiation among the European Union (EU) member states and institutions, following firmly established rules. In 1988, after several years of bruising annual negotiations, the EU moved to multi-annual 'financial perspectives', or package deals, for which the Commission makes proposals and the 'Budgetary Authority'—the Council, particularly the European Council, and the European Parliament (EP)—negotiates agreement. This has concentrated budgetary politics into periodic strategic bargains that link national costs and benefits, reforms of the common agricultural policy (CAP), regional imbalances, future-oriented policies, and enlargements. This pattern was reinforced by subsequent budget packages in 1992 (Delors-2), in 1999 (Agenda 2000), in 2006 (the Financial Perspective for 2007–13), and in 2013 (the Financial Perspective for 2014–20). Over these years, the structure of the budget changed only slightly; agricultural and regional expenditure remain the two large spending blocks. The Treaty of Lisbon (ToL) confirmed the existing practice of budgetary decision-making by giving treaty status to the system of multi-annual financial planning and by

(continued...)

abolishing the earlier distinction between compulsory and non-compulsory expenditure. The camps of net contributors and net beneficiaries are more pronounced than ever in the Union. Thus, the EU struggles to shift budgetary priorities to embrace new challenges within the Union and internationally.

Introduction

Historically, budgets have been of immense importance in the evolution of the modern state and they remain fundamental to contemporary government.[1] This chapter enters the labyrinth of EU budgetary procedures in an attempt to unravel the characteristics of budgetary politics and policy-making. Where EU money comes from, how it is spent, and the processes by which it is distributed are the subjects of intense political bargaining. Budgets matter politically, because money represents the commitment of resources to the provision of public goods and involves political choices across sectors and regions.

The politics of making and managing budgets has had considerable salience in the evolution of the EU because budgets involve both distributive and redistributive politics. The significance and challenges of budgetary politics are accentuated in difficult economic times. The euro area crisis since 2009 with its attendant policy prescription of budgetary cutbacks and fiscal consolidation has further politicized budgetary politics, including the politics of the EU budget. Budgetary issues have inevitably become entangled with debates about the nature of the EU, the competences of individual EU institutions, and the balance between the European and the national levels of governance. Budgetary flows to the member states are highly visible so that 'winners' and 'losers' can be calculated with relative ease. As a result, budgetary politics are more likely to become embroiled in national politics and national electoral competition than is rule-making. Questions about the purpose of the budget and the principles that govern the use of public finance in the Union are linked to wider questions about the nature of the EU and its evolution as a polity that go beyond the set-up of a traditional international organization. In that context, the budget is also a useful yardstick with which to measure a type of integration that differs from the creation of a single market and the harmonization of rules and regulations (see Chapters 4 and 5). The size and scope of the EU budget also have implications for the operation of a vast range of policies.[2]

The existence of the EU budget has often been justified and explained by its different functions: (1) as a means of side-payments to specific states or groups that are necessary to gain the overall consensus and political cement on further economic, particularly market, integration; (2) as the source for financing European public goods that benefit not only individual member states but European citizens at large; (3) as the basis for redistribution from richer to poorer parts of the Union which—following the value of European solidarity—fosters economic convergence towards a higher standard of living across the EU; and (4) as a means of financing Europe's role in the world.

The process of managing, rather than just formulating, budgets raises questions about the management capacity of Commission, but also about that of national authorities. All EU institutions and bodies, in particular the Court of Auditors, are paying increasing attention to the impact of fraud on the budget and searching for better ways to protect the financial interests of the EU.

A thumbnail sketch of the budget

In the early years of the Union, the budget was a financial instrument similar to those found in traditional international organizations. The budget treaties of 1970 and 1975 led to a fundamental change. These treaties established the constitutional framework for the finances of the Union in a number of important respects. They created a system of 'own resources' which gave the EU an autonomous source of revenue, consisting of three elements: customs duties; agricultural levies; and a proportion of the base used for assessing value-added tax (VAT) in the member states, up to a ceiling of 1 per cent. The 1970 agreement on own resources was subsequently altered a number of times. One basic principle was that this revenue base should apply to all member states, regardless of their size, wealth, the pattern of EU expenditure, or their ability to pay. This was to cause increasing difficulty in the years to come.[3]

The 1970 and 1975 Budgetary Treaties also altered the institutional framework for reaching decisions on the budget. The EP was granted significant budgetary powers, including the rights to increase, reduce, or redistribute expenditure in areas classified as 'non-compulsory' expenditure (essentially not agricultural spending, which was classified as 'compulsory'); to adopt or reject the budget; and to give annual discharge, through a vote of approval, to the Commission for its implementation of the budget. The 'power of the purse' gave the EP leverage in its institutional battles with the Council of Ministers and allowed it to promote its autonomous policy preferences. The 1975 Budgetary Treaty also provided for the creation of the independent Court of Auditors to enhance accountability in the budgetary process. A significant feature of EU budgets is the distinction between commitments and payments; the commitments budget is always larger than the payments budget (Box 9.1).

After 1970, the emergence of the budget as a real instrument of European public policy was constrained by a basic factor that still shapes EU finances. The EU budget was, and remains, small in relation to Union gross national income (GNI), and to the level of public expenditure in the member states. In 2012, EU spending amounted to around €147 billion which represented 1.12 per cent of EU GNI and was thus much less than domestic budgets, which collectively represent between 30 and 40 per cent of European GNI. However, although the budget has little macroeconomic

> **BOX 9.1   Appropriations**
>
> - **commitments:** legal pledges to provide finance, provided that certain conditions are fulfilled;
> - **payments:** cash or bank transfers to the beneficiaries;
> - **differentiated appropriations:** appropriations for commitments and payments often differ because multi-annual programmes and projects are usually committed in the year they are decided and are paid over the years as the implementation of the programme and project progresses. Thus, if the EU budget increases, due for example to enlargement, commitments will increase before payments do. Not all projects and programmes are concluded, and appropriations for payments are therefore lower than for commitments;
> - **non-differentiated appropriations:** apply for administrative expenditure, for agricultural market support, and direct payments. Furthermore, not all projects and programmes are concluded, and appropriations for payments are therefore lower than for commitments.
>
> Source: Commission (2013*i*). © European Union, 1995–2014.

significance for the Union as a whole, it is very important for those member states that receive extensive transfers from the structural funds. For example, net receipts from the EU budget amounted in 2011 to 4.63 per cent of GNI for Lithuania, 3.62 per cent for Latvia, and 2.22 per cent for Greece. EU spending programmes also mobilize constituencies within the member states, such as farmers (see Chapter 8) and regional groups (see Chapter 10), which have a material interest in the maintenance of their receipts. The small overall size of the budget masked impressive increases in financial resources in the Delors-1 (1988–92) and Delors-2 (1993–9) budgetary agreements. The Berlin Agreement (1999–2006) and the Brussels Agreement (2007–13) included smaller increases (see Figures 9.1 and 9.2). The agreement on the 2014–20 financial perspective represented a reduction in the EU budget for the first time in decades. This reduction reflects the impact of the euro area crisis and the politics of austerity in the member states on EU budgetary politics.

The slenderness of EU budgetary resources highlights an important feature of the emerging European polity, namely the significance of regulation as the main instrument of public power (see Chapter 5), and reflected a view that limited the role of public finance in European integration. This view was not always dominant. In the 1970s, the acquisition of sizeable financial resources for the budget was widely seen as essential to integration. In particular, it was anticipated that in the run-up to economic and monetary union (EMU) (see Chapter 7) a larger budget would be necessary to deal with external shocks and fiscal stabilization, which member governments would no longer be able to deal with through management of their own currencies.

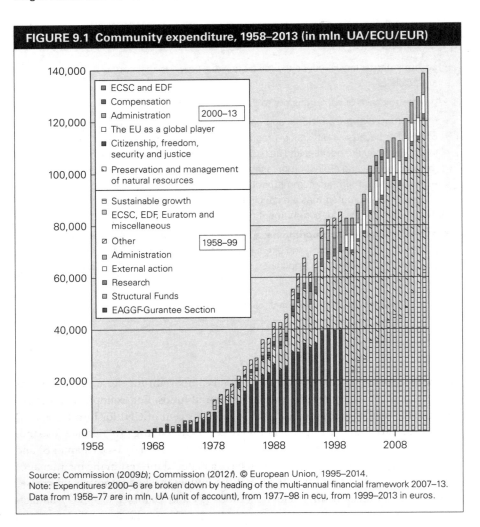

FIGURE 9.1 Community expenditure, 1958–2013 (in mln. UA/ECU/EUR)

Legend:
- ECSC and EDF
- Compensation
- Administration `2000–13`
- The EU as a global player
- Citizenship, freedom, security and justice
- Preservation and management of natural resources
- Sustainable growth
- ECSC, EDF, Euratom and miscellaneous
- Other `1958–99`
- Administration
- External action
- Research
- Structural Funds
- EAGGF-Gurantee Section

Source: Commission (2009*b*); Commission (2012*f*). © European Union, 1995–2014.
Note: Expenditures 2000–6 are broken down by heading of the multi-annual financial framework 2007–13.
Data from 1958–77 are in mln. UA (unit of account), from 1977–98 in ecu, from 1999–2013 in euros.

The euro area crisis has brought this gap in the Union's policy toolkit sharply into focus. The view that there could be strong Union government focused on liberalizing and opening-up national markets, with limited financial resources, gained ground in the 1980s, as Keynesian economic policies, which emphasized an interventionist role for the state, were discredited in favour of monetarist approaches, which stressed the efficiency of free markets and the benefits of price stability. The capture of the EU budget by agricultural interests in the 1970s made it difficult for arguments in favour of a stronger distributive role for the European centre to win political ground (see Chapter 8). The European sovereign debt crisis has placed the question of the Union's, or at least the euro area's fiscal capacity, back on the agenda.

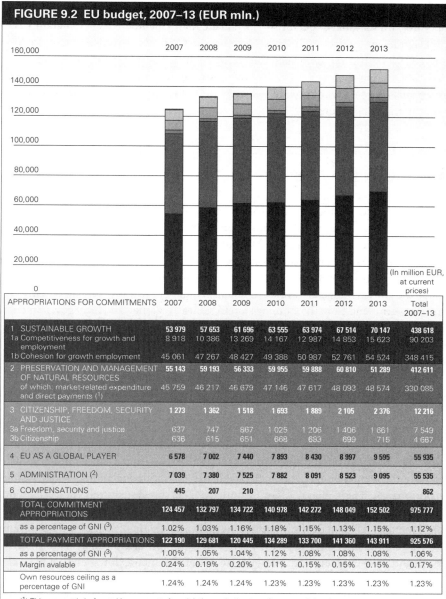

FIGURE 9.2 EU budget, 2007–13 (EUR mln.)								
APPROPRIATIONS FOR COMMITMENTS	2007	2008	2009	2010	2011	2012	2013	Total 2007–13
1 SUSTAINABLE GROWTH	53 979	57 653	61 696	63 555	63 974	67 514	70 147	438 618
1a Competitiveness for growth and employment	8 918	10 386	13 269	14 167	12 987	14 853	15 623	90 203
1b Cohesion for growth employment	45 061	47 267	48 427	49 388	50 987	52 761	54 524	348 415
2 PRESERVATION AND MANAGEMENT OF NATURAL RESOURCES	55 143	59 193	56 333	59 955	59 888	60 810	51 289	412 611
of which: market-related expenditure and direct payments (1)	45 759	46 217	46 679	47 146	47 617	48 093	48 574	330 085
3 CITIZENSHIP, FREEDOM, SECURITY AND JUSTICE	1 273	1 362	1 518	1 693	1 889	2 105	2 376	12 216
3a Freedom, security and justice	637	747	867	1 025	1 206	1 406	1 661	7 549
3b Citizenship	636	615	651	668	683	699	715	4 667
4 EU AS A GLOBAL PLAYER	6 578	7 002	7 440	7 893	8 430	8 997	9 595	55 935
5 ADMINISTRATION (2)	7 039	7 380	7 525	7 882	8 091	8 523	9 095	55 535
6 COMPENSATIONS	445	207	210					862
TOTAL COMMITMENT APPROPRIATIONS	124 457	132 797	134 722	140 978	142 272	148 049	152 502	975 777
as a percentage of GNI (3)	1.02%	1.03%	1.16%	1.18%	1.15%	1.13%	1.15%	1.12%
TOTAL PAYMENT APPROPRIATIONS	122 190	129 681	120 445	134 289	133 700	141 360	143 911	925 576
as a percentage of GNI (3)	1.00%	1.05%	1.04%	1.12%	1.08%	1.08%	1.08%	1.06%
Margin avalable	0.24%	0.19%	0.20%	0.11%	0.15%	0.15%	0.15%	0.17%
Own resources ceiling as a percentage of GNI	1.24%	1.24%	1.24%	1.23%	1.23%	1.23%	1.23%	1.23%

(1) This amount is before taking account of modulation and other transfers to rural development.
(2) The expenditure on pensions included under the ceiling for this heading is calculated net of the staff contributions to the relevant scheme, within the limit of EUR 500 million at 2004 prices for the period 2007–13.
(3) The figures are based ont the technical adjustment of the financial framework for 2013 in line with movements in GNI, adopted by the Commission on 20 April 2012 (COM(2012)184).

Source: Commission (2013h: 7). © European Union, 2013.

Since the mid-1990s, the constraints set by the fiscal framework of EMU and other pressures on national expenditure have made many member states reluctant to accept significant transfers of financial resources to the EU level. Enlargements in 2004 and 2007 have further intensified this trend. In the Union of twenty-eight, economic diversity among member states has increased significantly (see Chapter 17); yet, an expansion of the Union-wide redistribution of funds is strongly opposed by the wealthier member states.

The major players

Budgetary policy-making in the Union takes place through three types of decisions: (1) 'history-making decisions', namely the big multi-annual package deals; (2) an annual budgetary cycle; and (3) thousands of management decisions within each expenditure area (Peterson and Bomberg 1999). 'History-making decisions', taken periodically since 1988, in which the European Council is the dominant forum, shape the annual budgetary cycle. The management of the budget engages many layers of government, from the Commission to central, regional, and local governmental agencies in the member states. The Commission has responsibility for establishing the draft budget each year, and for proposals intended to shape the 'grand bargains'. The Commission has traditionally been an advocate of a bigger EU budget in order to fund policy integration, but in the 1990s it was forced to pay more attention to managing EU spending. In addition, the Commission tries to play the role of honest broker in budgetary battles, charged by the member governments with drafting reports on sensitive issues, such as 'own resources' and net flows to the member states.

Different configurations of the Council play a central role in budgetary negotiations. The Budget Council, consisting of representatives from finance ministries who approve the annual budget, has well-established operating procedures and decision-making rules. The General Affairs Council (GAC, previously the General Affairs and External Relations Council (GAERC)), the Council of Ministers for Economic and Financial Affairs (Ecofin), and the Agricultural Council each play a key role in negotiating the big budgetary deals. The GAC attempts to coordinate across different negotiating chapters and, not least, to contain demands for spending from the Agricultural Council. Ecofin, composed of national economics and finance ministers, tries to exert budgetary discipline, especially since the euro area crisis, whereas the Agricultural Council has tended to be locked into a clientelist relationship with farmers and generally favours higher agricultural spending (see Chapter 8). Other Council configurations that oversee spending programmes have to face tough negotiations about money when their programmes are reviewed and altered. However, the European Council, where heads of state and government broker the final stages of the 'history-making' bargains, still provides the most important forum for striking the big budgetary deals. The ToL added a new actor to budgetary negotiations, namely, the full-time President of the European Council, Herman Van Rompuy, who played a central role in securing agreement on the 2014–20 financial perspective at the February 2013 European Council. Agreed by unanimity, these big bargains set the frame for EU budgetary politics for a seven-year period—thus, limiting the degree of flexibility but also the scope for potential conflict in the decision-making process for the annual budgets.

Since it was granted budgetary powers in 1975, the EP has regarded EU finances as one of its key channels of influence vis-à-vis the Council. The EP has tried to influence what happens at both the macro and the micro levels. In the annual cycle of determining detailed appropriations, the EP frequently intervenes to alter the sums assigned to specific programmes and projects. Its role in the supervision of financial management has also been pronounced. As was seen in March 1999, it was an intervention by the EP, criticizing financial management, that provoked the unprecedented resignation of the whole college of commissioners. The Parliament's role in the finalization of 2020 financial perspective was pronounced following its enhanced role under the ToL.

Budgetary politics over time

Since the first enlargement in 1973 there have been two distinct phases of budgetary politics and policy-making in the EU. The first phase (1973–88) was characterized by intense conflict about the size and distribution of EU monies, and by institutional battles between the Council and the EP over the adoption of the annual EU budget. The second phase (since 1988) has been one of relative budgetary calm as member governments succeeded in negotiating the five big budgetary bargains, known as Delors-1, Delors-2, Agenda 2000, the 2007–13 framework, and the 2014–20 agreement, and the Council and the EP cooperated closely in annual budgetary decision-making. Each phase corresponds to a specific set of rules and procedures and a distinct budgetary paradigm.

Phase 1: the dominance of budgetary battles

The first enlargement disturbed the budgetary bargain established by founder-member governments. In particular, between 1979 and 1984 the member governments and EU institutions were locked into a protracted dispute about revenue and expenditure, which contributed in no small way to a wider malaise and lack of political impetus in the Union during the early 1980s. The 1970 treaty was designed to fix the rules before the UK became a member. The revenue sources suited the six founder countries, and the main spending would flow 'automatically' to support the CAP (see Chapter 8). The package was essentially a French achievement, won in return for starting accession negotiations with the UK and the other applicants. The rules of the budgetary game were fixed to the advantage of the incumbents, above all France, making confrontation with the UK more or less inevitable (see H. Wallace 1983). Moreover, with the 1970 budgetary treaty member states half-heartedly delegated budgetary powers to the EP, introducing a complex annual procedure with a number of ill-specified rules. The mismatch between the limited desire of member states to involve the EP and the high expectations of Members of the European Parliament (MEPs) due to their newly acquired political powers soon became apparent. The considerable scope for interpretation left open by the vaguely defined treaty provisions intensified this tension. In short, both the UK and the EP entered a budgetary stage that was characterized by a 'de Gaulle budget', a budget that was formed by French preferences with an almost exclusive focus on agricultural spending.

After accession, successive UK governments struggled to get the budget issue on to the agenda and slowly managed to alter the terms of the debate to ensure that distributional issues were taken seriously. Despite being one of the 'less prosperous' member states, the UK was set to become the second largest contributor after Germany. In trying to address the problem, a key concern of UK governments was the dominance of CAP expenditure (constituting 70 per cent of the budget), from which the UK with its small agriculture sector benefited very little. The European Regional Development Fund, which was set up in 1975 to stimulate economic development in the least prosperous regions (see Chapter 10), brought only little relief.

Against this background, it became clear to the UK government that the UK problem was structural rather than the result of chance. Hence in 1979, the new British prime minister, Margaret Thatcher, began to demand a rebate system, which would guarantee the UK a better balance between contributions and receipts. The Commission and the other member governments were loath to concede the UK case at the outset. The Commission had always been reluctant to engage in discussion of the net financial flows to the individual member states, lest this encourage too narrow a calculation of the benefits of Union membership, and lead states to seek *juste retour*, that is, to extract from the Union budget more or less what they put in. The key 'orthodoxy' regarding the budget at this time was that receipts flowed from EU policies and were thus automatic. The implication of this approach was that the consequences for individual member states were not regarded as an issue to be addressed. This orthodoxy was challenged by the problem of UK contributions. Although Mrs Thatcher's confrontational approach was regarded as non-*communautaire*, she finally succeeded. At the European Council in Fontainebleau in June 1984, the UK government traded its consent to an agreement for increasing the VAT ceiling from 1 to 1.4 per cent against the establishment of a 'rebate' mechanism for dealing with excessive UK contributions on a longer term basis. The mechanism was designed to deal with the UK problem and could not be generalized to other member states, even though other states became significant net contributors.

While the member governments were engaged in restructuring the budget, the EP and the Council were involved in a continuing struggle over their respective powers on budgetary matters. The EP rejected the 1980 and 1985 draft budgets, and the annual budgetary cycle was characterized by persistent struggles between the two institutions, the 'twin arms' of the budgetary authority. The EP actively exploited the broad scope for interpretation that the ill-specified treaty provisions offered. By contrast, the Council sought to limit the level of power-sharing with the EP as far as it legally could. In 1982 (case withdrawn), and again in 1986 (Case 34/86), the Council brought an action in the Court of Justice of the European Union (CJEU) to annul the budget signed by the president of the Parliament as it disagreed with the EP's interpretation of the treaty provisions on the classification of expenditure (compulsory vs. non-compulsory expenditure). Repeated attempts to solve the disputes over the interpretation of the treaty provisions through joint declarations and agreements failed.

Against a Council that displayed little willingness to take it seriously, the Parliament was determined to use the budgetary powers which it had acquired in 1975 to enhance its position in the Union's institutional landscape and to further its policy preferences. It did this in three ways. First, it attempted to use its budgetary powers to gain some leverage in the legislative field by introducing expenditure lines in policy areas where no legal bases existed. Secondly, the Parliament used its amending power to increase expenditure in order to promote Union policies of interest to it, notably regional policy, transport, social policy, and education. Thirdly, the Parliament used the annual budgetary cycle to expand the areas considered as non-compulsory expenditure, which meant it had a larger volume of expenditure to which it could apply its margin for manoeuvre because the Parliament had a greater say regarding non-compulsory rather than compulsory expenditure. In view of these priorities, the EP tended to pay more attention to authorizing expenditure than to monitoring how it was spent, a priority reflected in the importance of the EP's budget committee, and the assignment of budgetary control to a sub-committee (Lindner 2006).

Phase 2: ordered budgetary decision-making

The year 1988 marked a turning point. After the accessions of Greece, Portugal, and Spain and the adoption of the Single European Act (SEA) (see Chapter 5), it became clear that the intense annual budgetary battles and the constant shortage of revenue could not continue. Following a proposal by the president of the Commission, Jacques Delors, the EU embarked on a far-reaching political and institutional reform in the budgetary field.

On the institutional side, it introduced the multi-annual financial perspective, which balanced revenue and expenditure and constrained the ballooning CAP by dividing the budget into different headings and setting annual ceilings for spending categories across a five-to-seven-year period. Although established by member states in the European Council, the financial perspective acquired its binding nature from the inter-institutional agreement between the Council, the EP, and the Commission. The EP accepted the constraint on annual budgetary decision-making, because the new financial perspective guaranteed a significant increase in resources and established regional spending as the second-largest part of the budget, both long-standing EP priorities.

Overall, the 1988 reform changed the rules of the game by supplanting the budget treaty with a set of superior soft law arrangements among the budgetary actors. Annual decision-making lost its place in the inter-institutional spotlight and became the domain of budgetary experts, who cooperated closely and developed a routine of adopting annual budgets on time and without major tensions. Moreover, the 1988 reform transformed the CAP-centred 'de Gaulle budget' into the 'Delors budget' that, due to its strong regional policy dimension (see Chapter 10), was more redistributive and less CAP-oriented.

In subsequent renewals of the financial perspective and inter-institutional agreement, the main institutional and distributive structure established in 1988 persisted. The requirement for unanimity did not change. The Delors-1 package and subsequent budgetary deals required the agreement of all member states. The veto made it very difficult to challenge entrenched budgetary gains such as the UK budgetary rebate or the French demands on agriculture.

The introduction of the multi-annual framework did not mean that conflict and disputes disappeared. However, tensions among member states or between the EP and the Council were kept at a manageable level during the annual procedures and channelled towards the renegotiation points of the large budget packages every five to seven years. At these renegotiation points, all players were assured that the unanimity requirement would allow them to block a package that would run contrary to their fundamental interests. This had not been the case in pre-1988 times: key players, such as the UK government, had to fight long and hard until their distributive concerns were addressed, and budgetary disputes continuously prevented the orderly adoption of annual budgets.

Delors-1

The budgetary agreement reached in February 1988 was a classic EU package deal (see Table 9.1). The fact that, for the first time, all the different elements of the budget were addressed in one reform was instrumental to the agreement. Moreover, the link to the ambitious single market programme and related institutional reforms (in the form of the SEA) motivated the German Chancellor Helmut Kohl, in particular, to secure an agreement, even though it meant a significant increase in Germany's net contributions to the budget. For the poorer member states, such as Greece, Spain, and Portugal, that did not benefit so much from CAP expenditure, a significant strengthening of cohesion spending was a prerequisite for agreeing to an internal-market project that would put more challenges to their economies than to those of wealthier member states (see Chapter 10).

Delors-2

The pattern established by Delors-1 was replicated in the negotiations on Delors-2. The political link between the SEA and Delors-1 was followed by a similar link

TABLE 9.1 The main elements of the financial perspectives, 1988–2013

	Delors-1	Delors-2	Agenda 2000	FP 2007–13
Revenue ceiling	Rise to 1.2% of GNP by 1992 and an extension of the system of 'own resources' to include a new fourth resource based on the relative wealth of the member states as measured by GNP	Unchanged for 1993 and 1994, but rise to 1.27% of GNP by 1999	Unchanged at 1.27% of GNP	Unchanged at 1.24% of GNI (which is a recalculation of the 1.27% of GDP) with average actual spending level of 1.05%[4]
UK rebate and other correction mechanisms	Continuation of the complex Fontainebleau rebate system	UK rebate maintained; slight adjustments for other net contributors	UK rebate maintained; slight adjustments for other net contributors	UK rebate maintained; slight adjustments for other net contributors
CAP	Contain the growth of agricultural expenditure at not more than 74% of GNP	Implementation of 1992 CAP reform (no significant change)	Only limited changes in the size and policy structure of the CAP	Implementation of 2003 CAP reform (no significant change in level of expenditure)
Cohesion expenditure	A doubling of the financial resources available to the less prosperous regions of the Community	Significant increase in the flows to the poorer parts of the Community	Flows to cohesion countries were marginally reduced, leaving some scope for flows to the new member states after eastern enlargement	A shift of regional expenditure from old cohesion countries to recently acceded countries

between the Treaty on European Union (TEU) and the Delors-2 package. Again, poorer member states established the link between an increase in cohesion spending (i.e. the creation of a new cohesion fund) and further economic integration (i.e. the introduction of EMU).

The debate on Delors-2 was as tortuous and controversial as that on Delors-1. The member governments grappled with their desire to reach agreement, on the one hand, and with their determination that the terms of the agreement be as favourable as possible to their own viewpoint, on the other. At the 1992 European Council in Edinburgh, an agreement was reached (see Table 9.1 for main elements).

Agenda 2000

In the mid-1990s, the balance of forces in the Union on budgetary matters began to change radically. The sizeable expansion of the budget led to the emergence of a 'net contributors' club, a group of member governments concerned about the level of their financial commitments to the EU budget. At the European Council in Copenhagen in 1993, the member governments had accepted the principle of an eastward enlargement of the Union but the accession of so many comparatively poor states would generate pressure for more redistribution and a larger budget.

Against these developments it is surprising that the institutional setting and the distributive character of the budget proved so robust. The status quo was by and large confirmed but, in contrast to the significant increases recorded in 1988 and 1992, the Union's budgetary resources were consolidated, with no major increase in the size of the EU budget. The new member states were still not at the table and thus had little impact on the negotiations (see Table 9.1).

The Financial Perspective for 2007–13

The negotiations of the 2007–13 financial perspective took place against the background of three developments. First, at the European Council in Lisbon in 2000, the EU set itself the strategic goal of becoming 'the most competitive economy in the world' by the end of the decade. Heads of state and government committed to take measures that would increase the competitiveness of their economies and raise investments in research and technology. The Lisbon goal was taken up by a report of an independent group of high-level experts headed by the Belgian economist, André Sapir (Sapir *et al.* 2004). The report strongly criticized the dominance of CAP spending and suggested refocusing the budget on European public goods, most importantly research and technology. Although fiercely criticized by some in the Commission, the report clearly established a link between the Lisbon goal and the EU budget. Secondly, most member states, in particular the large euro-area members, Germany and France, were experiencing low growth rates and strong pressures on their national budgets. Their failure, in three subsequent years (2002–4), to meet the terms of the Stability and Growth Pact (SGP), which commit members of the euro area to compliance with the Maastricht criteria (see Chapter 7), further limited their willingness to accept increases in the EU budget. Thirdly, for the first time the ten new member states sat at the negotiation table with high expectations of budgetary transfers and a full veto right (see Chapter 17).

The negotiations for the financial perspective began in early 2004 with a proposal by the Commission. Romano Prodi, then president of the Commission, emphasized the need to give the EU the resources to match its political priorities. The Commission sought to transform the redistributive 'Delors budget' into a more distributive 'Lisbon budget' that would strengthen expenditure for public goods and reduce the emphasis on redistributing resources to poorer regions/member states or to farmers.

For the first time since the inception of the financial perspective in 1988, the Commission envisaged an overhaul of the expenditure headings so as to reflect the new policies and priorities of the enlarged EU.

Finding an agreement was again not easy. Essentially, three key cleavages dominated the debate. First, net contributors were unwilling to accept an increase in the spending level, while governments from beneficiary member states, such as Spain and Portugal, stressed the continued importance of pursuing the objective of 'economic and social cohesion' (see Chapter 10). Secondly, among the beneficiaries of regional expenditure, 'old' beneficiaries wanted to prevent an abrupt ending of transfers and demanded compensation, while the new member states feared that these compensation payments would be financed by cuts in transfers to them. Thirdly, the UK government strongly opposed any attempt to abolish its rebate through its replacement by a generalized mechanism, which was naturally favoured by all the other net contributors. Significantly, the Commission's ambition to strengthen expenditure for public goods found very few active supporters, except the EP. There was little space left for new spending programmes in fields such as innovation and technology given the fact that agricultural expenditure was excluded from the negotiations (under a Franco-German agreement concluded in 2002) and that regional expenditure was dominated by strong vested interests in the new and old member states. An agreement was finally reached in late 2005 which broadly retained the status quo (see Table 9.1).

A new style of budgetary politics: shifting the status quo?

Although the agreement on the financial perspective for 2007–13 did not alter the established structure of the Union's budget, three subsequent events have given rise to expectations that a new style of budgetary politics might evolve. First, the ToL incorporated significant changes to the treaty provisions on budgetary decision-making. Secondly, when adopting the new financial perspective for 2007–13, member states seemed keen to demonstrate that they were, in principle, open to considering more far-reaching reforms of the budget. Consequently, mandated by the European Council, the Commission launched a review of the budget in 2007–8. Thirdly, the euro area crisis heralded a new phase in budgetary politics, particularly in those states that were faced with acute pressures to cut back their domestic budgets. The crisis raised fundamental challenges to the euro and demanded a complex set of policy responses from the member states and EU institutions, including the development of a range of additional financial instruments such as the European Stability Mechanism (ESM) that were outside the EU budget (see Chapter 7). Moreover, the crisis transformed the environment in which the member states set out to agree the 2014–20 financial perspective.

The Treaty of Lisbon

Although the ToL included significant changes to the treaty provisions for the budgetary procedure, the main elements of the 'new' budgetary procedure reflected the existing inter-institutional agreement. Lisbon thus constitutionalized the existing modus operandi (see Figure 9.3).

Under the ToL both arms of the budgetary authority have equal decision-making power over all components of the EU budget, including CAP spending, in the annual budget procedure. Similar to the co-decision procedure in legislative politics, a Conciliation Committee features as the key forum for brokering deals between the EP and the Council before their respective final readings. These seemingly innovative features were much in line with the informal arrangements that were in place prior to the ToL. Most

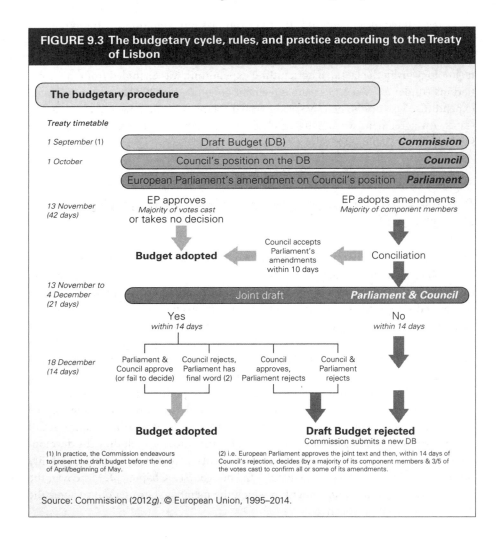

FIGURE 9.3 The budgetary cycle, rules, and practice according to the Treaty of Lisbon

Source: Commission (2012g). © European Union, 1995–2014.

of the time, the annual budget is de facto adopted in a conciliation meeting between the Council and the EP shortly before the second reading in Council. Given that negotiations at the conciliation meeting cover all areas of the budget, the distinction between compulsory and non-compulsory expenditure had become less relevant over time. The Council and EP each simply used their budgetary powers over the respective classifications of the budget as bargaining chips when striking a deal over the whole budget. Under the provisions of the ToL, the Council may prevent an agreement in the Conciliation Committee and thus trigger a new budget proposal by the Commission. Granting this de facto right of rejection to the Council upheld the existing balance.

With regard to the financial perspective, the ToL institutionalized the procedures for the multi-annual budget plan (as laid down in the inter-institutional agreement) requiring a unanimous decision in the Council and the consent of the EP. If no agreement is reached, the ceilings of the previous multi-annual budget plan remain in place. There is thus a strong lock-in effect in the rules because any significant change would require the agreement of all twenty-eight member states and the EP. The shift from soft law (inter-institutional agreements) to the hard law of the treaty also raises the stakes for the EP in the negotiations of the financial perspective. Since the EP can no longer renounce the financial perspective once it has agreed to it, there is an incentive for it to bargain hard on the terms of the seven-year budgetary deal and it did so following the February 2013 European Council (see the section 'The Financial Perspective for 2014–20').

The budget review

Although the 2007–8 review did not really lead to a wide public debate on the budget and the challenges of the Union, it did spark a number of academic and political contributions that advanced new or already known reform proposals (BEPA 2008). On the expenditure side, there were numerous calls for shifting the budget more towards the financing of public goods, such as defence, security, and research and development. Some also recognized the link between CAP and the UK rebate and hoped that reform of the former could lead to the abolition of the latter. On the revenue side, proposals for Union-wide taxes based on, for example, air traffic, CO_2 emissions, or financial transactions gained some momentum, with the former Austrian Chancellor, Wolfgang Schüssel, as well as the EP, presenting this as a way to establish a direct link between European taxpayers and the EU budget (European Parliament 2007; Le Cacheux 2007; Schüssel 2007). Many analyses criticized the strong status quo bias of the existing institutional arrangement for budgetary decision-making. The negotiations on the 2014–20 financial perspective offered an opportunity to address the status quo bias.

The Financial Perspective for 2014–20

The negotiations on the 2014–20 financial perspective took place against the backdrop of the continuing euro area crisis, the emergence of deep economic divergence within the euro area, and growing differentiation within the EU arising from the challenge of developing the institutions and policy toolkit for managing a single currency (see Chapter 7). The Commission presented its first set of proposals for the future finances of the Union entitled 'A Budget for Europe 2020' in June 2011. The emphasis in the proposals was on the value-added of spending at the EU level with a focus on an innovative budget designed to address pan-European challenges, particularly growth and employment (Molino and Zuleeg 2011). The Commission sought a commitments budget of €1,025 billion (1.05 per cent of GNI) and a payments budget of €972 billion (1.01 per cent of GNI) over seven years. The proposals looked for increases in spending on competitiveness, infrastructure, citizenship and security, and 'global Europe' and were designed to shift EU spending from agriculture and cohesion to other policy areas in ways that would test the status quo bias of budgetary politics in the Union. The negotiations took place in multiple fora, including unsuccessfully at the November 2012 European Council. The member states finally reached agreement at the European Council in February 2013, but a tense and difficult period of negotiations with the EP followed. Herman Van Rompuy, in his role as European Council President, was the major institutional player during the end-game of the negotiations, working closely with the Commission to mould an agreement.

The member states were divided into three main groupings. First, the net contributors club morphed into the Friends of Better Spending. This group consisted of Austria, Finland, Denmark, Germany, the Netherlands, and the UK (see Figure 9.4).

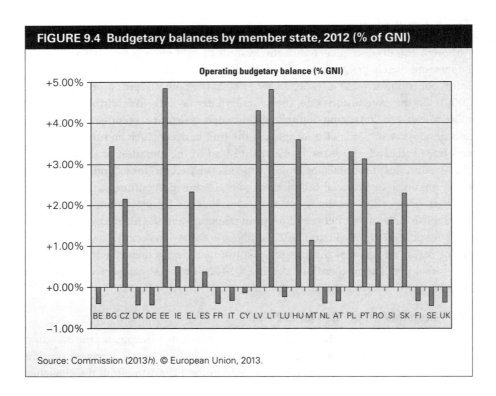

FIGURE 9.4 Budgetary balances by member state, 2012 (% of GNI)

Operating budgetary balance (% GNI)

Source: Commission (2013*h*). © European Union, 2013.

They shared a commitment to containing the size of the budget, but also had individual preferences to which they were committed, notably the perennial UK commitment to keeping its rebate off the negotiating table. The other net contributors also sought limits to their contributions. Germany was the pivotal state in this group and Chancellor Merkel was the central political actor in securing agreement. While committed to containing the size of the budget, Chancellor Merkel wanted an agreement and also wanted to avoid the isolation of the UK prime minister, David Cameron, who had made a major speech on the future of UK relations with the EU that included reference to renegotiating the terms of UK membership of the EU followed by an in–out referendum not long before the February 2013 European Council.

The second group was composed of the newer member states from central and eastern Europe led by the Polish prime minister, Donald Tusk. The new member states were primarily interested in the two traditional expenditure policies, agriculture and cohesion. Poland, in particular, was a major beneficiary of cohesion policy and also had an interest in securing increased funding under the CAP (see Chapter 17).

The third group—consisting of France, Greece Italy, Portugal, and Spain—emerged in the month before the final agreement. It was committed to a larger budget than was acceptable to the Friends of Better Spending, which would support economic growth in addition to maintaining agricultural and cohesion spending. These states wanted a status-quo-plus outcome. The Mediterranean states, in particular the old cohesion countries, wanted to ensure that they would continue to benefit under structural spending. The French president, François Hollande, was torn between promoting policies for growth and the deep-seated French commitment to the CAP. Other countries, such as Belgium and Ireland, did not fall decisively into any one of these camps but sought to get a deal they could live with by focusing on particular issues.

Agreement was reached on 7 February 2013 after two days and one night of deliberation, and thus continued the tradition of lengthy and tortuous budgetary negotiations. The European Council conclusions contained the main elements of the agreement regarding the structure of EU spending, the overall size of the budget, and detailed provisions on all spending areas. The Friends of Better Spending succeeded in ensuring that the EU budget would represent a smaller share than before of EU GNI for both commitments and payments. The UK retained its rebate and the other net contributors, including Denmark, benefited from reductions in their contribution level. It had become clear as early as the November 2012 European Council meeting that the Commission's proposals on agriculture and cohesion would not fly: the member states might agree to reductions in spending in these areas, but not to the levels contained in either the Commission's or Van Rompuy's proposals. The agreement included a reduction in spending on agriculture from €336 billion to €278 billion and on cohesion from €354 billion to €325 billion over seven years (see Chapters 8 and 10). Both policy areas represent a declining proportion of the budget and for the first time cohesion overtook agriculture as the largest item in the EU budget. Spending on competitiveness was increased from €91 billion to €125 billion in addition to a relatively minor increase in the international budget of the Union.

During the negotiations that followed the February 2013 deal, MEPs across the political spectrum adopted a tough negotiation position, even threatening to reject the deal reached between the European Council and the Commission in their struggle to reaffirm the EP's role within the EU decision-making process under the Lisbon rules. Initially, the EP put forth several conditions for the negotiations with the Council of which ensuring maximum flexibility with regard to the budget and an obligatory mid-term review were the most salient. The EP sought flexibility so that it could further influence the allocation of resources during the life of the agreement and a mid-term review so that it would not have to wait until 2020 to further its demands. On 3 July, the EP and its lead negotiator, Alain Lamassoure (a French member of the European People's Party) endorsed the outcome of its negotiations with the Council. In particular, the EP succeeded in inserting a 'revision clause' that will allow the next EP and Commission to make a legislative proposal to revise the budget beginning in 2016. Furthermore, the EP's key demand to increase its flexibility with regards to payment appropriations and commitments, which effectively enables it to move expenditures around between years and headings, will be the subject of continued negotiations that will clarify the distribution of funds within each policy area. In addition, the EP succeeded in securing a commitment from the Council to close the payments gap for the year 2013 to make sure that the new multi-annual financial framework (MFF) is not affected by any 'legacy' bills from the 2007–13 financial period. With the MFF entering into force, a High-Level Group will be established to review the own-resources system and propose changes ahead of the next budget period.

In sum, even though not all of the EP's conditions were met, escalating the conflict with the Council yielded important benefits for the EP. From an institutional perspective, the EP was able to assert itself vis-à-vis the Council and seized the opportunity to give some influence over the budget to the next EP through the 'revision clause'. Moreover, the EP highlighted its concern about the social dimension of the European project ahead of the upcoming EP election. Nevertheless, the EP continued to haggle over insulating the 2014 budget from 'legacy' bills and restoring the budget lines of the Commission's initial proposal of June in the sectoral committees. Despite the protracted negotiations, MEPs approved the MFF (2014–20) and an accompanying inter-institutional agreement in November 2013.

Notwithstanding the high politics of budgetary negotiations and the powerful forces that oppose a larger financial capacity for the Union, major developments in EU finances may come within the euro area as the member states develop further policy instruments for the single currency. The June 2012 Van Rompuy report and its subsequent follow-up reports in October and December 2012 on creating a Genuine Economic and Monetary Union made reference to a number of policy instruments with budgetary implications (Van Rompuy 2012; and see Chapter 7). Among the most salient were the creation of a single resolution mechanism as part of a banking union that would be supported by backstop, a reference to financial support for euro area member states that enter a contractual arrangement on structural reform, and post-2014 reference to the possibility of creating a 'limited fiscal capacity' in the euro area to deal with economic shocks (Van Rompuy 2012). While the overall policy direction is towards more centralized capacity in the euro area, the road map for such a Genuine Economic and Monetary Union has been more prescriptive about the next steps to 2014 than it is in relation to what should happen once a banking union is in place. Moreover, the political momentum in the European Council for advancing integration further in the domains of fiscal and economic policies has diminished since 2012. The collective issuing of sovereign bonds within the euro area is not on the formal political agenda and its prominence in public debate has declined since the height of the sovereign debt crisis. Developments in the euro area have already led to the development of a number of off-budget financial instruments which could be enhanced in the years to come—depending on how the economic and financial situation of the euro area evolves and on whether banking union creates spill-overs towards other policy fields (P. Becker 2012).

Managing a larger budget

Agreeing the overall size of the EU budget and how it should be spent is the stuff of redistributive politics and 'history-making' decisions at the highest political level. Managing the EU budget involves a different kind of politics; namely, executive politics and multi-level administration. The struggle for budgetary resources in the EU and the inter-institutional battles about budgetary power initially overshadowed questions of 'value for money' and the quality of the Commission's financial management but these considerations became an increasingly important focus of budgetary politics as the financial resources of the budget grew.

Managing a budget that involves around 400,000 individual authorizations of expenditure and payment each year is a major challenge, particularly as the management of the EU budget is characterized by a fragmentation of responsibility between the Commission and public authorities in the member states: 80 per cent of the budget is managed on behalf of the Union by the member states. There is a great diversity of public-management and public-finance cultures across Europe, and there are limits to the auditing capacity of a number of states. Press reports and investigations carried out by the European Anti-Fraud Office (OLAF) have highlighted scams involving the forging of customs documents in order to claim export refunds, avoiding anti-dumping duties, non-payment of excise duties, switching labels on foodstuffs to claim higher refunds, claiming payments for non-existent animals, and putting non-existent food into intervention storage. No one knows with any degree of certainty the level of fraud affecting the EU budget: estimates of between 7 and

10 per cent of the budget are often cited, but have never been convincingly demonstrated. There are suggestions that some member states are dilatory in pursuing cases of fraud against the EU budget, as this would, paradoxically, mean devoting additional national resources in order to obtain less money from the EU budget.

In the 1990s, attempts were made to improve financial management, but they proved insufficient to prevent financial mismanagement becoming an explosive political issue in 1999 when the Santer Commission was forced to resign. The Prodi Commission that took over in autumn 1999 was given a mandate to reform the Commission services by the European Council. Commission Vice-President Neil Kinnock, who was given responsibility for administrative reform, proposed a White Paper on the reform strategy in March 2000 (Commission 2000*b*). Not unexpectedly, reform of financial management and control systems was one of four priorities in the White Paper. The implementation of the White Paper led to a new Financial Regulation (*Official Journal*, L248, 16 Sept. 2002) and extensive management changes in the Commission services. The Commission is also adopting a stricter approach with the member states, taking the unprecedented step in July 2008 of suspending aid worth over €500 million to Bulgaria because of corruption. The Kinnock reforms have enhanced the regulatory framework and the capacity of EU institutions to practise sound financial management, but the EU budget remains highly fragmented and is dispersed across many countries and levels of government, which continues to cause problems.

Conclusion

Budgetary politics in the EU is marked by elements of both continuity and change. The capture of the EU budget in the 1960s by agricultural interests has proved relatively enduring. France, the main defender of the CAP, has been successful in preserving its interests in this policy domain. However, agricultural support has moved decisively since 1992 from market measures to compensation payments, and the funding has started to shift from consumers to taxpayers (see Chapter 8). Cohesion funding assumed a central role in budgetary politics in the late 1980s with the arrival of Spain and Portugal (see Chapter 10). Structural funds remain an entrenched part of the budgetary *acquis*. However, the outcome of the 2014–20 budgetary negotiations reduced the weight of these big budgetary items for the first time and the resources devoted to cohesion policy also outstripped agriculture for the first time.

Agreement in 1988 to the Delors-1 financial perspective represented a steep change in how EU budgets were made. Since 1988, multi-annual bargains have become the norm, and are now part of the *acquis*. Although difficult and protracted negotiations have characterized all five budgetary bargains outlined in this chapter, the political process, characterized by a set of integrated Commission proposals, intensive negotiations across a range of Councils, and high-level bargaining in the European Council, demonstrated a capacity to frame an outcome that would enjoy broad consensus. The tough negotiations between the EP and the Council following the February 2013 European Council underline the growing assertiveness of the Parliament in the wake of the ToL. That said, the Union's annual budgetary cycle was successfully locked into a medium-term financial perspective, which in turn reduced the dangers of acrimonious arguments and inter-institutional conflicts.

The system of multi-annual financial planning and big budgetary agreements has endured, notwithstanding the significant increase in the number of member states. Following accession in 2004, the new member states played a very active role in the budgetary negotiations on the 2007–13 financial perspective and again in 2013. Poland, as the largest of the new member states, was particularly engaged. Since 2004, the new members states have benefited from cohesion expenditure and funds have been shifted away from the 'old' to the 'new' cohesion states (see Chapter 10). Moreover, they have sought the benefits of the CAP though direct transfers to their farmers. The increase in the economic diversity in the Union as a consequence of enlargement suggests that there will be a strong 'cohesion club' in the Union for the foreseeable future (Seifert 2011). The net contributors' club, however, remains very resistant to endowing the Union with significantly larger financial resources. Hence, there are limits to EU solidarity and to transfers to the east.

The small size of the EU budget persists as a key characteristic of the finances of the Union. The limits of budgetary resources were brought sharply into relief during the euro area crisis when it became clear that the Union did not have a fiscal capacity to deal with a major economic shock. Paradoxically, the crisis put renewed pressure on the budget and reinforced the arguments of the net contributors club. The pressure to cut budgets at national level reinforced the determination to limit the size of the EU budget. Attempts by the Commission to refocus the EU budget towards European public goods and thus to reduce the redistributive emphasis within the existing 'EU distributional mode' have met with limited success. A strong status quo bias in EU budgetary politics, in terms of both institutional structures and the preferences of the major actors, makes significant changes in the distributive order of the Union unlikely. This creates a mismatch between the expenditure priorities of the EU budget and key policy priorities facing Europe. Moreover, the difference between an integrated monetary policy and a weak fiscal capacity at the European level has emerged as an issue in the political debate being identified as a potential additional variant of this mismatch. The 2008 financial crisis and the euro area crisis brought a renewed focus to the macroeconomic arguments in favour of a European stabilization policy and a burden-sharing arrangement for the financial and economic crisis. It will be interesting to see whether—beyond the creation of the crisis-management tools (i.e. the ESM) and the establishment of a banking union—the arguments advanced in the context of EMU will create momentum for new budgetary policies in the years to come, at least within the single currency area.

NOTES

1 This chapter draws on the EU budget chapter by Brigid Laffan and Michael Shackleton in the fourth edition. Michael Shackleton's consent is gratefully acknowledged. Valuable research assistance was received from Tobias Tesche. The views expressed in the chapter do not necessarily reflect those of the European Central Bank.

2 For the most comprehensive and detailed treatments of the development of the EU budget and the rules that govern it, see Laffan (1997) and Lindner (2006).

3 This chapter draws heavily on the analysis of Laffan (1997), Lindner (2006), and Shackleton (1990, 1993*a*, 1993*b*).

4 The figure 1.24 per cent of GNI equals 1.27 per cent of GDP. The switch from GDP to GNI reflects a new national accounting methodology that the European Commission adopted in line with the 1993 System of National Accounts.

FURTHER READING

A comprehensive volume on the EU budget is Laffan (1997). Lindner (2006) presents a thorough institutionalist analysis of EU budgetary decision-making over three decades, and for a non-academic, but detailed, account of the finances of the EU see Commission (2013*g*). For an analysis of the revenue side, see Begg (2005). For developments in EU finances in the period 2007–14 in addition to the shaping of the 2020 budgetary deal, see Enderlein *et al.* (2007), Patterson (2011), Seifert (2011), and Benedetto and Milio (2012).

Begg, I. (2005), *Funding the European Union*, Federal Trust Research Reports (London: The Federal Trust for Education and Research).

Benedetto, G., and Milio, S. (2012) (eds.), *European Union Budget Reform: Institutions, Policy and Economic Crisis* (Basingstoke: Palgrave Macmillan).

Commission (2013*g*), *Financial Report 2012* (Luxembourg: Office for Official Publications of the European Communities).

Enderlein, H., Lindner, J., Calvo-Gongalez, O., and Ritter, R. (2007), 'The EU Budget: How Much Scope for Institutional Reform?', in H. Berger and T. Moutos (eds.), *Designing the New European Union* (Oxford: Elsevier), 129–59.

Laffan, B. (1997), The *Finances of the European Union* (Basingstoke: Palgrave Macmillan).

Lindner, J. (2006), *Conflict and Change in EU Budgetary Politics* (London: Routledge).

Patterson, B. (2011), *Understanding the EU Budget* (London: Searching Finance).

Seifert, J. (2011), 'Change and Stability in the EU Budget', Working Paper No. 3 (Singapore: EU Centre in Singapore).

CHAPTER 10

Cohesion Policy

A New Direction for New Times?

Ian Bache

▌ Summary

Cohesion policy is the European Union's (EU's) main redistributive policy and is aimed primarily at reducing the social and economic differences between EU regions. Academic analysis of cohesion policy has generated insights that have framed wider debates about the nature of the EU as a whole, most notably through the concept of multi-level governance. Moreover, while cohesion policy has taken up a growing share of the EU's budget, now accounting for more than one-third of all EU spending, its purpose, effectiveness, and durability have been increasingly challenged. This chapter reflects on these issues and suggests that a more rounded concept of cohesion policy, guided by broader indicators of success, could be a route to a more sustainable policy in the longer term, not least politically.

Introduction

Cohesion is a broad and often vaguely defined concept.[†,1] How it is used in the EU context—and specifically in relation to this policy domain—is often misunderstood and generally from usages in other contexts, not least within member states. Part of the confusion is because a number of terms are employed in this policy area, sometimes interchangeably—cohesion policy, structural policy, and regional policy being the most common—although each has a precise meaning. In essence, the EU's cohesion policy refers to the governing principles of the EU structural funds and the Cohesion Fund. This policy aims mainly at reducing the social and economic differences among Europe's regions by promoting economic growth, job creation, and competitiveness. It accounts for around one-third of the total EU budget and has been described as 'the world's largest development policy based on a single legal and institutional framework' (McCann and Ortega-Argilés 2013: 428). It is also one of the most visible of EU policies due its prominent signage at project sites.

There is a reasonably familiar 'story' to be told of cohesion policy—one that weaves its narrative around the periodic reforms negotiated at EU level, their implementation within member states, and what all of this tells us about the relative power and influence of key actors. This is a policy area that has been thoroughly researched empirically, typically guided by academic debates concerned with changes in the role and power of national governments vis-à-vis the Commission and, for reasons specific to the policy area, sub-national actors. The field has generated considerable insights into inter-institutional dynamics that have framed wider debates about the nature of the EU as a whole through the concept of multi-level governance (see Chapter 2).

Yet while this is a familiar story in some respects, an important feature is the fluctuation in the power and influence of key actors on different issues, at different levels and stages of policy-making, and over time. Thus, while the contours of the debate have been largely shaped by supranational–national theorizing and, more specifically, by the debate on multi-level governance, contestation within this debate has been prominent. However, that this debate has been continued around common themes since the first policy steps in the 1970s has provided a sustained level of empirically informed theorizing that is perhaps unique among EU policies. As such, an important part of this chapter is to do justice to this contribution.

Yet the chapter also seeks to 'add value' to the existing literature in two ways. The first is to reflect briefly on how the cohesion policy process relates to the 'five modes' of policy-making set out by Wallace and Reh (see Chapter 4). The second is to reflect critically on the notion of 'cohesion policy' more than is usual in the 'familiar story'. Both issues may be of interest in taking research forward. The chapter is organized in five sections. The first section covers the history of the policy, outlining its various reforms from the 1970s to the present day, and the second looks at the main theoretical debates. The third section examines the implementation of cohesion policy in practice and the fourth section assesses cohesion policy in terms

---

[†] The chapter is dedicated to the memory of Dave Allen who did an excellent job on this topic for many years and was a great guy. We all miss him.

of Wallace and Reh's five policy modes. The chapter concludes by arguing that cohesion policy may need a new direction to demonstrate its value more effectively, but also suggests that the policy has made an important political contribution that is not always acknowledged.

History

The EU's cohesion policy has from the beginning been a moving target, with multiple funds distributing ever-larger amounts of EU funding according to an ever-more elaborate set of policy guidance. As such, it is important to understand how the policy has evolved historically to understand the nature and purpose of the policy as it currently exists. As a starting point it is useful to explain some key terms relating to the policy field that were mentioned in the introduction. *Regional policy* refers primarily to the European Regional Development Fund (ERDF) and was most prominent in the 1970s. *Structural policy* refers collectively to the ERDF and other funds, including the European Social Fund (ESF) and the guidance section of the European Agricultural Guidance and Guarantee Fund (EAGGF) that were explicitly brought together by the Structural Funds Regulation of 1988. *Cohesion policy*, which become most prominent from the 1990s, incorporates these and other funds and has the broadest meaning conceptually. All of this is explained further later in the chapter.

While economic and social disparities across and within member states were understood to be significant from the creation of the European Economic Community (EEC), it was not until the 1970s that any serious attempt was made to address them. Agreement to create the ERDF at the Paris summit of 1972 reflected the increased salience of regional disparities in the context of the impending enlargement to include the UK, Denmark, and Ireland. The UK government in particular pushed for the fund, needing something tangible to persuade a reluctant public and parliament of the benefits of EEC membership. The other influential factors in the creation of the ERDF were a push towards economic and monetary union (EMU) provided by the Werner Report of 1970 and Commission plans to curb member states' aid to industries.

Agreement on the ERDF finally came only when the Irish and Italian governments threatened to boycott the Paris summit of 1974 over the issue. The size of the initial fund (1.3 billion European units of account) disappointed the *demandeur* member states, but was nonetheless considered an important policy breakthrough. It would provide up to half of the cost of development projects in eligible regions, with the remaining cost met from domestic sources. This principle of co-financing (or 'match-funding') aimed to ensure domestic commitment to EU-funded projects and has remained a fixture of regional and cohesion policies ever since.

It was not until 1988 that the regional fund and other structural-funding instruments were integrated into a cohesion policy, within a more coherent supranational framework. Until then, national governments prevented a more effective supranational approach. They ensured that the ERDF was distributed according to national quotas thrashed out by governments, rather than by Community criteria. Moreover, each government demanded a quota, even though this meant that relatively prosperous regions in wealthier member states would receive funding at the expense of poorer regions elsewhere. This carve-up of distributions meant funding was dispersed over 40 per cent of the total EU population rather than concentrated on areas of greatest need.

At this stage, the regional policy process was reasonably characterized as a 'virtual paragon of intergovernmentalism' (McAleavey 1992: 3). Governments dominated not only the EU-level process, but also policy implementation. In particular, they were reluctant to accept the additionality requirement that 'the Fund's assistance should not lead member states to reduce their own regional development efforts but should complement these efforts' (Commission 1975). On this issue, the UK government was particularly difficult (Wallace 1977). Resistance to this early supranational principle of regional policy remained even after the Commission secured greater influence after 1988 (see the following section), and the struggle over this issue became an important barometer for measuring the relative strengths of national, supranational, and sub-national actors. Additionality apart, the only other notable supranational policy aspects before 1989 were experiments with non-quota programmes after 1979 and with multi-annual programmes after 1984 that proved to be important for later policies.

The emergence of cohesion policy

In the 1986 Single European Act (SEA), cohesion had a treaty base for the first time and the birth of cohesion policy proper followed in 1988 with a major reform of the structural funds. Tarschys (2003: 55) describes how Jacques Delors, the Commission president, and his collaborators cast around for a new label to describe the reformed policy to signal a more solidaristic approach and considered a number of options before settling on the concept of 'economic and social cohesion', which has its roots in the preamble to the Treaty of Rome (1957). Both the completion of the single market programme and enlargements to include Greece, Portugal, and Spain provided impetus for strengthening cohesion. The former raised the possibility that poorer regions would be left behind in a more open and competitive European market and the latter brought two new member states with a significant number of relatively poor regions. In this context, member states agreed that financial allocations to the funds would double by 1993. The reform brought together the ERDF with two other financial instruments, the ESF and the guidance section of the EAGGF (see Chapter 8). The aim was to coordinate their activities more effectively with each other and also with those of the European Investment Bank (EIB) and other financial instruments (Commission 1989: 11). The reform was set out in three main regulations that came into effect on 1 January 1989.

> **BOX 10.1** **Priority objectives of the 1988 reform**
>
> - **Objective 1**: promoting the development of 'less developed regions', i.e. those with per capita GDP of less than, or close to, 75 per cent of the Community average under 'special circumstances' (ERDF, ESF, and EAGGF—Guidance Section).
> - **Objective 2**: converting the regions seriously affected by industrial decline (ERDF, ESF).
> - **Objective 3**: combating long-term unemployment—assisting people aged over 25, unemployed for over a year (ESF).
> - **Objective 4**: assisting the occupational integration of young people, i.e. people below the age of 25 (ESF).
> - **Objective 5**: (a) accelerating the adjustment of agricultural structures (EAGGF—Guidance Section); (b) promoting the development of rural areas (EAGGF—Guidance Section, ESF, ERDF).

The reform contained important policy revisions. The *additionality* requirement was clarified and was accompanied by three new principles: *concentration* focused funds on areas of greatest need; *programming* required regions to develop strategic multi-annual plans to ensure coherence between projects funded; and *partnership* required that funds be administered through regional partnerships within each state, consisting of representatives of national government, regional (or local) government, and the European Commission.

Following the principle of concentration, structural-fund expenditure was focused on five objectives, three with an explicit regional dimension (see Box 10.1). The bulk of spending was focused on the most disadvantaged regions eligible under Objective 1 (approximately 65 per cent of total structural-fund allocations). In addition to the 'mainstream' funds allocated according to the five objectives, approximately 9 per cent of the ERDF budget was retained for 'non-quota' 'Community Initiative' programmes. These were programmes devised and overseen by the Commission to meet outstanding regional needs, often focusing on particular types of regions such as those suffering from the decline of a dominant industry (e.g. coal, steel, and ship-building).

The Cohesion Fund

The Cohesion Fund was agreed in the Treaty of Maastricht of 1992 and was aimed at member states with a gross domestic product (GDP) of less than 90 per cent of the Community average (Greece, Ireland, Portugal, and Spain), not at specific regions. It funded environment and transport projects and supported up to 85 per cent of the costs: a higher proportion than for any of the structural funds. The key principles

guiding the structural funds did not apply to the Cohesion Fund. There was no reference to partnership and the decisions on projects (not programmes) to be funded were
made by the Commission in agreement with the member state concerned. In terms
of additionality, the preamble to the interim regulation stipulated that member states
should not 'decrease their investment efforts in the field of environmental protection
and transport infrastructure', but the more tightly defined principle of additionality
included in the structural fund regulations did not apply. These relaxed requirements
recognized the pressures on public expenditure in the context of moves towards monetary union, which were expected to be experienced most strongly in the 'cohesion four'
countries benefiting from the fund. Moreover, that the types of projects funded were
generally large scale and few in number meant that programming had less relevance.

Reform in the 1990s

The principles agreed in 1988 were maintained in the 1993 reform, although some
adjustments were made, the most significant being to the additionality principle. The
Council amended the wording on additionality to state that the principle should take
account of 'a number of specific economic circumstances, namely privatizations,
an unusual level of public structural expenditure undertaken in the previous programming period and business cycles in the national economy' (Council Regulation
2082/93, Art. 9). This meant that member states would be able to reduce their spending on related domestic policies without contravening the additionality requirement.
Other notable developments in 1993 were the addition to the structural funds of the
new Financial Instrument for Fisheries Guidance (FIFG) and the introduction of a
new Objective 6 status for sparsely populated regions in response to the impending
enlargement to include Austria and especially Finland and Sweden.

By 1999, the focus of reform was on preparing the ground for the accession of
countries from central and eastern Europe, with an average GDP of typically around
one-third of the EU average. The challenge was twofold: securing member-state
agreement to a reduction in their structural-fund allocations to facilitate enlargement; and adopting measures to develop the institutional capacity and capability in
the accession states that would allow them to absorb large-scale structural funding
effectively. Not without the usual horse-trading between governments, agreement
was reached on the principle of large-scale transfer of structural funding away from
existing member states to the new members post-enlargement. On the second challenge, a number of instruments were created for the 2000–6 period. Building on
the earlier Poland and Hungary: Assistance for the Restructuring of the Economy
(Phare) programme, designed to strengthen economic and social cohesion and to
develop administrative and institutional capacity during the pre-accession period,
the Instrument for Structural Policies for Pre-Accession (ISPA) provided funding for
environment and transport projects as a forerunner to Cohesion Fund allocations,
while the Special Accession Programme for Agricultural and Rural Development
(SAPARD) played a similar role for rural areas (see Chapter 17).

> **BOX 10.2   Priority objectives of the 1999 reform**
>
> - **Objective 1** continued to assist the least developed regions and be more strictly enforced and included the regions that previously qualified under Objective 6, which were the sparsely populated regions of Finland and Sweden.
> - **Objective 2** merged the existing Objectives 2 and 5b and concentrated funds on no more than 18 per cent of the EU population, with the safety-net mechanism ensuring that no member state's Objective 2 population would be less than two-thirds of its coverage under the 1994–9 programme period.
> - **Objective 3** applied across the EU, except for Objective 1 regions, to assist with modernizing systems of education, training, and employment.

Additional changes in 1999 included the concentration of funds on three objectives instead of six (see Box 10.2) and a reduction in the number of Community Initiatives from thirteen to four. There were revisions to programming to give the Commission a more strategic role, delegating more day-to-day responsibility to domestic actors. One innovation to promote the principle of efficiency was the allocation of 4 per cent of funding to be allocated to member states on the basis of programme performance.

The 2006 reform

The context of this reform was shaped by the effects of the 2004 enlargement and by the Lisbon Agenda (see Chapters 7 and 12), which accorded cohesion policy an important role. The 2004 enlargement led to a doubling of socio-economic disparities in the EU and a decrease in the average per capita income in the EU of twenty-five by 12.5 per cent, emphasizing the need for significant financial transfers among member states. The Lisbon Agenda, aimed at making the EU 'the most competitive and dynamic knowledge-based economy in the world' (European Council 2000), prioritized growth and jobs, and challenged broader notions of cohesion and policies aimed at social inclusion (see below).

The Sapir Report (2004), commissioned by European Commission President Prodi to review the EU economic system in the context of the Lisbon Agenda, set out the argument in favour of focusing aid on the new member states and recommended that 'providing money only to the new member states and to their national budgets, rather than to their regions (more of a macroeconomic than a regional approach to diversity), would be more effective' (Allen 2010: 249). This Report prefigured the Commission's (2004a) proposals for cohesion policy for 2006–13 that were set out in its Third Report on Economic and Social Cohesion.

As with previous reforms, the proposals signalled the beginning of a bargaining process. A number of states, led by the UK, argued that there should be an end to any financial transfers to the richest member states. This would reduce the gross

> **BOX 10.3**   **Architecture of cohesion policy for 2007–13**
>
> - The *convergence* priority covered those regions with a per capita GDP of less than 75 per cent of the Community average (previously covered by Objective 1).
> - The *regional competitiveness and employment* priority, effectively replacing Objectives 2 and 3, acquired two strands: regional programmes to promote the attractiveness and competitiveness of industrial, urban, and rural areas; and national programmes to promote full employment, quality and productivity at work, and social inclusion.
> - The *territorial cooperation* priority was built on the experience of the Community initiative Interreg, to promote cooperation on issues at cross-border, transnational, and inter-regional levels.

contributions to the EU budget of the richer states, which could then use the savings for their own regional policy purposes: a partial renationalization of policy. This proposal was eventually resisted by the Commission with the support of southern member states. However, the Commission's concession was to repackage Objectives 2 and 3 as the 'regional competitiveness and employment' objective, which was linked to the goals of the Lisbon Agenda. Moreover, member states had to 'earmark' 75 per cent of their expenditure under this objective and 60 per cent of that under the new 'convergence' objective in pursuit of the Lisbon Agenda.[2] Alongside these two objectives in a simplified architecture was just one more, for 'European territorial cooperation' (see Box 10.3). While giving member states responsibility over the designation of specific geographical areas, the repackaging of these objectives also allowed the Commission to retain its influence over cohesion policy in the new member states (Bachtler and Mendez 2007: 545).

The Cohesion Fund became part of cohesion policy proper through being included in the convergence objective. The EAGGF and the Community Initiative Leader programme were replaced by the European Agricultural Fund for Rural Development (EAFRD) (see Chapter 8) and the FIFG became the European Fisheries Fund (EFF). Both the EAFRD and EFF were given their own legal basis and were no longer part of cohesion policy (Commission 2007c: 11). The overall cohesion policy budget for the 2007–13 period was €347 billion, 81.5 per cent of which would be spent in the 'convergence' regions.

The key principles again remained intact, with some minor amendments and a new programming instrument introduced—the National Strategic Reference Framework (NSRF)—to provide an overall vision for each member state and to tie these visions more closely to the Lisbon Agenda. The principle of *proportionality* was introduced to place limits on the amount of funding devoted to the administration and monitoring of programmes in response to criticism from longer standing member states over excessively bureaucratic Commission requirements (Allen 2010: 241).

Outside the framework of cohesion policy, a new Instrument for Pre-Accession Assistance (IPA) was introduced in January 2007. It brought together all of the existing pre-accession instruments (including ISPA, Phare, and SAPARD) into a single framework. This new instrument covered the then candidate states (Croatia, the Former Yugoslav Republic of Macedonia, and Turkey) and the potential candidate states (Albania, Bosnia and Herzegovina, Montenegro, and Serbia—including Kosovo) (see Chapter 17).

The 2013 reform

Discussions over the reform of cohesion policy for the post-2014 period took place in the context of the economic crisis and the proposals were inevitably linked to recovery. In this context, the Commission instigated a set of hearings on the future of cohesion policy, coordinated by the economist Fabrizio Barca, of the Italian ministry of economy and finance. The report that emerged criticized key aspects of cohesion policy and called for a 'comprehensive reform', including a concentration of priorities and changes to governance. It argued for a 'clear and explicit distinction' between measures aimed at increasing income and growth ('efficiency objectives') and those aimed at reducing inequalities (social inclusion) and for 'greater coherence with the place-based or territorial concept' (Barca 2009: viii). It suggested that a concentration on fewer issues that would 'attract political and public attention to the measures implemented and enable the Commission better to focus its human resources and efforts and play a more strategic role' (Barca 2009: viii). In particular, the report suggested the need for a system of incentives and sanctions through which the policy could foster the institutional reforms necessary for good development (McCann and Ortega-Argilés 2013: 431).

Influenced by the Barca Report, the Commission's proposals for the post-2014 period aimed to revive some of the core purposes of cohesion policy that had been diluted in the previous two decades, including:

- a stronger contractual relationship between the Commission and member states through 'partnership contracts';
- a greater focus on core priorities (including a 'territorialized' social agenda) involving more rigorous programming, monitoring, and evaluation; and
- the institutionalization of high-level strategic reporting on effectiveness to the Council and Parliament (Mendez 2013: 646).

These proposals stopped short of the coherent place-based approach as the Commission sought to strengthen the focus on results and the effectiveness of cohesion-policy spending by tying cohesion policy more systematically to the successor of the Lisbon Agenda, the Europe 2020 strategy (see Chapters 7 and 12). However, the proposals would bring more EU-wide accountability in exchange for greater member-state control over implementation.

> **BOX 10.4**   Cohesion policy funding 2014–20
>
> Total: up to €325.1 billion.
>
> - 'Investment for growth and jobs': €313.2 billion (€164.3 billion for less developed regions; €31.7 billion for transition regions; €49.5 billion for more developed regions; €66.4 billion for member states supported by the Cohesion Fund).
> - 'European territorial cooperation': €8.9 billion.
> - Top-up for youth employment initiative: €3 billion.

In February 2013, the European Council reached agreement on the 2014–20 multi-annual financial framework (see Chapter 9). It agreed that cohesion policy would pursue two goals: 'Investment for growth and jobs', to be supported by all funds; and 'European territorial cooperation', to be supported by the ERDF specifically. Cohesion funding overall would not exceed €325.1 billion, representing an overall reduction from 2006–13 (see the previous section), and funding for 'investment for growth and jobs' would take a huge share of funding (€313.2 billion: see Box 10.4).

As in 2006, a number of governments favoured partial renationalization but were opposed by a majority of governments and the European Parliament (EP). A key argument against partial renationalization was that it would undermine the integrity of the policy and could weaken the commitment of the wealthier member states to sustaining the policy in the longer term—a concern of newer member states in particular.

Explaining cohesion policy

While the Commission's role was important in keeping the idea of regional policy alive in difficult circumstances in the 1960s and early 1970s, there is academic consensus that the major decisions on the creation of regional policy were taken by heads of government and that the Commission's influence over financial allocations and early policy guidelines was limited (Keating and Jones 1985; Armstrong 1989; Bache 1998). The major academic debates took off over the 1988 reform when the policy became more sophisticated and financial allocations doubled.

The design of the policy framework introduced in 1989 is generally attributed to the Commission, which had long pushed for the principles of additionality, concentration, partnership, and programming, and had sought to experiment with some of these principles in ad hoc programmes before 1988. Thus, Hooghe (1996b: 100) argued that the Commission emerged 'as the pivotal actor in designing the regulations' through its 'monopoly of initiative'. However, Pollack (1995) argued that agreement to this framework could be explained by changes in the preferences of key member states—in particular net contributors such as the UK,

France, and Germany—and as a result of the accessions of Greece, Portugal, and Spain. The preferences of the net contributors changed in three ways. First, with the Iberian enlargement, the proportion of structural funds received by the 'big three' member states decreased significantly. This meant that, for these governments, 'the idea of greater Commission oversight seemed less like an intrusion into the internal affairs of one's own state, where E[U] spending was minimal, and more like a necessary oversight of the poor member states where the bulk of E[U] money was being spent' (Pollack 1995: 372). Secondly, the Iberian enlargement made France, like the UK and Germany, a net contributor to the EU budget, thus giving the 'big three' governments a common interest in the efficient use of the structural funds. Thirdly, the spiralling costs of both the common agricultural policy (CAP) and the structural funds made the level and efficiency of EU spending a 'political issue' of increasing concern to the governments of France, Germany, and the UK in the 1980s (Pollack 1995: 372; and see Chapters 8 and 9).

In terms of the budgetary envelope agreed in 1988, an intergovernmentalist interpretation found favour amongst most commentators. The more prosperous member states strongly supported the completion of the single market (see Chapter 5) and the doubling of the structural funds was accepted by the likely paymaster governments as a 'side-payment to Ireland and the Southern nations' in exchange for their political support on this (Moravcsik 1991: 62). Although not contesting this fundamental argument, Marks (1992: 198) conceptualized the side-payment argument as an illustration of forced spill-over, 'in which the prospect of a breakthrough in one arena created intense pressure for innovation in others', thereby linking it to a neo-functionalist analysis, and giving it a more supranationalist interpretation.

While the context of the 1988 reform gave the Commission considerable scope for advancing its policy preferences, the 1993 reform represented a reassertion of control by the member governments in key areas. A good example was additionality. The tenacity with which the Commission had sought the implementation of additionality after 1988 (see the section 'Additionality' later in the chapter) was met by governments effectively diluting the requirement in 1993. In addition, given the convergence criteria for monetary union agreed at Maastricht (see Chapter 7), for the Commission to pursue genuine additionality at this time would have been difficult: while additionality required member states to demonstrate additional public expenditure, the Maastricht convergence criteria limited domestic public spending. Other changes in 1993 also reflected the reassertion of government preferences. While the partnership principle was confirmed, governments remained in control of the designation of 'appropriate partners'. The creation of a Management Committee to oversee Community Initiatives curtailed Commission discretion. In summary, the 1993 reform provided a measure of how the relative influence of actors fluctuated over a short period of time.

The dominant interpretations of the creation and operation of the Cohesion Fund in 1991 were also intergovernmental (Scott 1995: 38; Morata and Muñoz 1996). In particular, they emphasized the push given by poorer member states led by Spain— which anticipated otherwise being a net contributor to the EU budget by 1993—for an additional compensatory financial instrument in the context of moves towards economic and monetary union (EMU).

In 1999, the key 'supranational' principles were again retained, but national governments continued to retain control of key levers relating to partnership and additionality. The reduction in the number of Community Initiatives, and of financial allocations to them, also limited the Commission's scope for autonomy and innovation. More generally, in the context of enlargement, the Commission's initial proposals were themselves relatively modest. Yet, while aspects of the reform suggested a partial renationalization, the Commission retained a key role in aspects of the policy process, such as over issues of eligibility, programming, allocating the performance reserve, and in the design and implementation of Community Initiatives.

If the 2006 reform saw national governments again shaping key aspects of the reform, it was those most likely to meet the costs. As Andreou (2007: 26) argued, the outcome 'bears much more resemblance to the financially restrictive approach of the net payers, than to the original Commission proposal supported by the less prosperous member states'. Bruszt (2008: 616) argued that the new regulations 'did not alter the "renationalizing" tendencies of the [Structural Funds] policies significantly. For the time being, the Commission does not seem to be interested in re-kindling its pro-regional activism of the 1990s'. Instead, the priority was on ensuring the effective absorption of the funds, which often meant the development of central capacity.

So, as suggested earlier, assessments of the role and influence of different actors have fluctuated over time and, as discussed later, at different stages of the policy process and in difference places. However, as Bachtler and Mendez (2007: 551) suggest, it is important not to see cohesion-policy negotiations purely in terms of a struggle between the Commission and the member states. While negotiations on some issues have been adversarial, on others there has been more collaboration and consensus. Related to this point, power relations between the Commission and member states should not necessarily be conceived in zero-sum terms, in which for one party to gain the other must lose. Instead, there is evidence of positive-sum outcomes, in which both parties achieve more of their goals. Moreover, Bachtler and Mendez (2007) suggested that claims over the renationalization of cohesion policy, while valid in some respects, are less convincing when applied to the development of the principles of concentration and programming, where the Commission's influence has been greater than acknowledged in much of the literature.

The Lisbon Agenda raised fears that some of the main goals and core principles of cohesion policy would be undermined. Mendez (2013: 644) argues that: 'If anything economic goals have trumped the social and territorial dimensions owing to the Lisbon agenda's emphasis on global competitiveness, encouraging a "misconceived" and "overly narrow" focus on innovation'. Lisbonization did lead to a centralized approach in some states to promote more effective expenditure (see the section 'Partnership' later in the chapter) and was seen more generally to lead to goal-congestion and confusion (Begg 2010). In this light, it has been suggested that a subtext to the 2013 reform was the aim of re-legitimizing cohesion policy, leading to the most fundamental review since 1988 (Mendez 2013).

Implementation

While much of the literature reviewed earlier focuses on the making and periodic revision of the regulations governing structural and cohesion funds, there has also been significant attention devoted to cohesion-policy implementation. There is space here to give only a flavour of the issues covered in relation to two key principles: additionality and partnership, which have been important to conceptual reflection and development. Implementation studies have generally been structured around the themes of multi-level governance and Europeanization. The notion of *multi-level governance* refers to increasingly complex vertical relations between actors organized at various territorial levels and horizontal relations between actors from public, private, and voluntary spheres. It is a process of change characterized by the emergence of 'territorially overarching policy networks' (Marks 1993: 402–3) and one that challenges the role, power, and authority of national governments. *Europeanization* is variously defined but is taken here to refer to a process of domestic change resulting from EU policies (see Chapter 2).

Additionality

Under the additionality rule, the Commission requires member states to demonstrate that EU funds are spent in addition to any planned domestic spending and are not used to substitute for this. If member states do not comply, they risk losing funding. It is thus an important indicator of the relative influence of the Commission and member governments.

The crucial test case of the implementation of the additionality principle arose from a dispute between the Commission and the UK government, when it became apparent that the latter had not changed its non-compliance with additionality despite the clearer requirement contained in the 1988 reform. The details of the dispute are complex and have been well documented (McAleavey 1992; Marks 1993; Bache 1998), but a key feature was an alliance between the Commission and UK local authorities against the UK government. This alliance led to an apparent government climbdown in the run-up to the 1992 general election. In developing the concept of multi-level governance, Marks (1993: 403) argued that:

Several aspects of the conflict—the way in which local actors were mobilized, their alliance with the Commission, and the effectiveness of their efforts in shifting the government's position—confirm the claim that structural policy has provided subnational governments and the Commission with new political resources and opportunities in an emerging multilevel policy arena.

However, a study of the implementation of the agreement reached at the end of the dispute demonstrated that little changed in terms of additional spending on regional development in the UK (Bache 1999). Instead, it appeared that while the government had climbed down largely to defuse tension on the issue in some marginal constituencies, once re-elected it continued to frustrate the additionality principle, but in a manner that was more difficult for the Commission to demonstrate. In other words, the 'gatekeeping' role of the national government extended deeply into the implementation process. Thus, while the interaction between the levels of government was indisputable, the outcomes from this interaction were less clear. This raised an important critique of multi-level governance—the distinction between distributed participation and distributed power—that continues to be a feature of debate. That is, while it may be clear that more actors appear to have a say over decisions, it is far less clear that this makes a difference to what is decided.

Partnership

The partnership principle introduced in the 1988 reform was widely seen as a key innovation and one that promised to outflank central-government gatekeepers by giving sub-national governments and other actors a formal role in the decision-making process. Like the additionality principle, it was a key to multi-level governance accounts of the policy area and a number of studies have since reflected on the extent to which EU cohesion policy has promoted multi-level governance and Europeanization. Hooghe's (1996c) study on the effects of the 1988 reform principles on 'territorial restructuring' within eight member states found that the implementation of the partnership principle varied considerably across member states. Actors at EU, national, and sub-national levels owned and mobilized different sets of resources in different contexts and this shaped their ability to influence the implementation process. In states where strong central governments sought to play a gatekeeper role, such as in the UK, they could do so with some success. As with the additionality dispute, sub-national actors were engaged in the policy process through the partnership requirement, but this did not necessarily shape outcomes. In more federalized states, by contrast, constitutionally stronger sub-national (regional) authorities were generally better placed to take advantage of the opportunities offered by partnership. Later research for the European Commission (Tavistock Institute 1999) confirmed this pattern of a highly differentiated multi-level governance beginning to emerge through cohesion policy.

As cohesion policy focused more on the countries of central and eastern Europe (CEECs), so much of the academic research followed. Conceptually, the debates on multi-level governance remained prominent, but often within the framework of a Europeanization process. Again, the role of the Commission in promoting multi-level governance through the empowerment of sub-national actors was a central feature. The academic consensus was that, although the Commission had sought to promote regionalization in CEECs in the early pre-accession period, as accession came closer it became pragmatically more concerned with ensuring the funds were absorbed within the enlargement timetable—even if this meant the greater channelling of funds through central ministries (Leonardi 2005: 164; Marcou 2002: 25). Research findings echoed those of earlier studies on the older member states. A study of the Czech Republic, Estonia, Hungary, Poland, and Slovenia identified national government 'gatekeepers' which were 'firmly in control' of sub-national actors—the latter being able to participate in policy-making but not significantly to influence outcomes (Bailey and De Propris 2002).

Again, the importance of institutional traditions in different states was found to be important in shaping the nature and extent of multi-level governance emerging (Hughes, Sasse, and Gordon 2004*a*, 2004*b*). Bruszt (2008) explained how the Commission's shift to more centralized national administration of funds pre-accession was resisted in some countries and thus features of multi-level governance emerged. In these cases, a 'layering' took place in which there were marginal changes to governance, 'implying local rule transformation within a basically unchanged institution that does not challenge the dominant characteristics of the mode of governance' (Bruszt 2008: 620). The study of Austria, Hungary, and Slovakia by Batory and Cartwright (2011: 714) emphasized the limited influence of civil-society actors, concluding that 'both the EU and national governments have some way to go to secure genuine societal involvement in and control over cohesion policy'. Baudner and Bull (2013: 218), focusing on the vertical dimension of multi-level governance, found a strengthening of national government in the Italian case and the strengthening of regional government in the German case, illustrating 'institutional heterogeneity and the competition for the gatekeeper position'.

The study by Bache (2008) considered the impact of cohesion policy on Type I and Type II multi-level governance in the EU25. Type I describes system-wide governing arrangements in which the dispersion of authority is restricted to a limited number of clearly defined, non-overlapping jurisdictions at a limited number of territorial levels, each of which has responsibility for a 'bundle' of functions. Type II describes governing arrangements in which the jurisdiction of authority is task-specific, where jurisdictions operate at numerous territorial levels and may be overlapping. The study identified a trend towards multi-level governance across Europe, although this was very uneven across and indeed within countries. Moreover, the study found that while this trend was generally not due to states' engagement with the EU, it was not possible to understand the changes taking place without reference to the EU and its cohesion policy. However, the effects of EU cohesion policy were more pronounced on Type II multi-level governance than on Type I, with ad hoc functionally specific governance arrangements emerging at various territorial levels directly through cohesion policy. For the most part, this Europeanization effect was driven by rational responses to EU financial incentives, although there was also evidence that deeper learning, characterized by the voluntary adoption of EU practices in the domestic sphere, could take place in the longer term.

Recent research has examined the impact of cohesion policy and related pre-accession instruments on governance in the candidate states of south-eastern Europe. Here too a familiar story emerges of limited governance capacities—particularly but not exclusively at sub-national level—resulting in an emphasis by the Commission on centralized administration in the first phase, with a strong EU oversight. Despite this, some nascent aspects of multi-level governance have been identified in Croatia and the Former Yugoslav Republic of Macedonia (Bache *et al.* 2011).

Policy modes

Wallace and Reh set out in Chapter 4 five variants of the modes through which the EU policy process handles day-to-day policy-making: the classical Community method; the EU regulatory mode; the EU distributional mode; policy coordination; and intensive transgovernmentalism. These modes are identified as 'a typology of ideal-types, devised with the deliberate objective of escaping from the either/or dichotomy between "supranationalism" and "intergovernmentalism"'. Moreover, no individual policy is expected to 'fall neatly' into one mode or another: 'there is strong variation over time, both within policy sectors and in response to events and contexts ... hybridization across types is prolific'.

Cohesion policy is a case where hybridization is evident and, as discussed previously, there is also significant variation at different stages of the policy process. While financial allocations and the broad regulatory framework are subject to a bargaining process involving national governments and the Commission, the implementation process engages a broader set of actors and is guided by a reasonably clear policy framework that emphasizes partnership and programming, among other principles.

Thus, there are elements of the *classical Community method* evident in cohesion policy. There is a strong role delegated to the European Commission in policy design, policy brokering, and policy execution, although the earlier discussion illustrates that the Commission has at times been reined in by national governments in terms of policy design. There is an empowering role for national governments through strategic bargaining and package deals—EU funds have often been side-payments to states for agreement in other areas (e.g. enlargement, the single market). There is a distancing from the influence of elected representatives at the national level and only limited opportunities for the EP to impinge, although the influence of the EP has arguably grown over time as its powers have increased.

However, the nature of cohesion policy affords a central place to the *distributional policy mode*. Although as this is the policy most closely connected with this mode, it is worth reflecting on Wallace and Reh's description closely. The characteristics of the distributional policy mode are set out in italics below.

The Commission attempting to devise programmes, in partnership with local and regional authorities or sectoral stakeholders and agencies, and to use financial incentives to gain attention and clients. This is a generally accurate characterization of cohesion policy, but there is significant involvement of national authorities in devising programmes, even though the Commission may have for a long time 'attempted' for this not to be the case. It has always happened to some degree and, if anything, the role of national authorities here has strengthened in recent reforms.

Member governments in the Council and often the European Council, under pressure from local and regional authorities or other stakeholders, engaging in hard bargaining over a limited budget with some redistributive elements. This cohesion-policy process neatly fits this description and overlaps with elements of the classical Community method.

Additional pressure from members of the European Parliament (MEPs) based on territorial politics in the regions, and an increasing role for the EP by having to give consent. Again, an accurate characterization, but this is not a feature that has been emphasized as particularly important in the academic literature.

Local and regional authorities benefiting from some policy empowerment as a result of engaging in the European arena, many of them with their own offices in Brussels, with, from 1993 onwards, the Committee of the Regions also articulating their concerns. This is a broad claim and one on which it is hard to come to firm conclusions based simply on an analysis of cohesion policy. There is no doubt that local and regional authorities have mobilized and engaged extensively since the major reform of structural policy in 1988 in particular, but the evidence of 'policy empowerment' resulting from this engagement is at best mixed and often disputed (see Jeffery 2000).

Some scope for other stakeholders to be co-opted into the EU policy process. This has undoubtedly been the case and it is hard to think of another EU policy area that has such structured participation from such a broad range of stakeholders at the implementation stage. Here the partnership principle is key and, as noted earlier, has over time broadened out the range of stakeholders seen as relevant (see Bache 2010).

Recasting of the EU budget to devote more money to cohesion or to embryonic collective goods, and proportionately less to agriculture. Again accurate: since leaping forward in financial terms between 1989 and 1993 the proportion of the EU budget allocated to cohesion policy has continued to grow incrementally, while that for agriculture has declined (see Table 10.1).

TABLE 10.1 Policies' share of the EU budget			
	Percentage of European budget		
Year	**Regional policy**	**Common agricultural policy**	**Size of EU Budget as % of EU GNP or GNI**
1975	6.2	70.9	0.53
1980	11.0	68.6	0.80
1985	12.8	68.4	0.92
1988	17.2	60.7	1.12
1993	32.3	53.5	1.20
2000	34.9	44.5	1.07
2007	36.7	47.1	1.04
2013	38.1	43.0	0.93

Source: House of Lords (2008: 19).

Note: in this table the term 'regional policy' is taken as being synonymous with 'cohesion policy'.

Most recent have been developments that might be most closely identified with Wallace and Reh's category of 'policy coordination' and particularly the development of 'soft' policy incentives to shape behaviour rather than 'hard' methods to secure compliance. Mendez (2011) identified 'experimentalist governance' in cohesion policy in the 2007–13 period influenced by the Lisbonization process. The relevant innovations included: the joint definition of EU goals at Council level and the adoption of national strategies to guide implementation; an 'earmarking' approach to encourage spending on Lisbon-related measures; and strategic performance and review mechanisms introduced at the EU level to stimulate policy learning.

Conclusion

This chapter began by describing cohesion in the context of EU policy as broad and vaguely defined. It has multiple dimensions—social, political, economic, and, most recently, territorial—but throughout the history of EU cohesion policy it is the economic dimension that has received most attention and this has been reinforced in recent times by the Lisbon Agenda and the effects of the 2008 financial crisis. Yet there is acknowledgement in some circles that a more effective policy would require a more balanced and more complete conception of cohesion and one that recognized the close and complex interrelationship among its various dimensions. The Barca Report made the case for a 'territorialized social agenda' as part of cohesion and spoke of a 'strategy for social inclusion … by guaranteeing socially agreed essential standards to all and by improving the well-being of the least advantaged' (Barca 2009: vii, 55). In a similar vein, the Committee of the Regions (2011) has proposed that the allocation of funds should not in the future be allocated solely on per GDP per capita, but also according to environmental and social indicators. Such arguments resonate with wider trends relating to the development of broader indicators of progress, including the EU's own 'GDP and Beyond' initiative that provides a road map of five key actions to improve the EU's indicators of progress, including greater use of environmental and social indicators and more accurate reporting on distribution and inequalities (see Bache 2013). A more rounded concept of cohesion policy guided by correspondingly broader measures of success may be a pathway to a more sustainable policy in a number of senses, not least politically. It may help in demonstrating a broader range of ways in which cohesion policy 'works' and, by promoting wider goals, help to bridge the divide between net payers and net recipients. In short, cohesion policy may need a new direction for new times.

Yet, it can be argued that the political domain of cohesion policy has proved every bit as important over the past four decades as the economic domain, and illustrates the close interconnection between different dimensions of cohesion. This is not only through the widely recognized expression of solidarity between richer and poorer parts of the EU the policy has sought to represent, but also through governing principles such as partnership, programming, and additionality. The governing principles of cohesion policy that were advanced principally to promote economic goals have had such an impact on governance and politics that the term 'multi-level governance' is now part of the lexicon of policy-makers across the world. The term informs the development policies of the United Nations and World Bank among others and shows no sign of fading. Of course, many other forces have promoted multi-level governance in a range of contexts, but amongst EU policies, cohesion has been first and foremost.

NOTES

1   I would like to thank George Andreou for his advice on sections of this chapter.
2   According to Baun and Marek (2008), the old member states exceeded their targets while the new member states achieved 59 per cent expenditure against both targets.

FURTHER READING

Key contributions to the intergovernmental–supranational debate are Marks (1992), Pollack (1995), Bache (1999), and Bachtler and Mendez (2007). Detailed studies of policy implementation and particularly their effects on multi-level governance are: Hooghe (1996); Bache (2008); Baun and Marek (2008); and Bache and Andreou (2011). Other helpful contributions are Leonardi (2005), Barca (2009), and Allen (2010).

Allen, D. (2010), 'The Structural Funds and Cohesion Policy: Extending the Bargain to Meet New Challenges', in H. Wallace, M. A. Pollack, and A. R. Young (eds.), *Policy-Making in the European Union*, 6th edn. (Oxford: Oxford University Press), 229–52.

Bache, I. (1999), 'The Extended Gatekeeper: Central Government and the Implementation of EC Regional Policy in the UK', *Journal of European Public Policy*, 6/1: 28–45.

Bache, I. (2008), *Europeanization and Multilevel Governance: Cohesion Policy in Britain and the European Union and Britain* (Lanham, MD: Rowman & Littlefield).

Bache, I. and Andreou, G. (2011) (eds.), *Cohesion Policy and Multi-Level Governance in South East Europe* (Oxford: Routledge).

Bachtler, J., and Mendez, C. (2007), 'Who Governs EU Cohesion Policy? Deconstructing the Reforms of the Structural Funds', *Journal of Common Market Studies*, 45/3: 535–64.

Barca, F. (2009), 'An Agenda for a Reformed Cohesion Policy: A Place-Based Approach to Meeting European Union Challenges and Expectations', Independent Report prepared at the request of Danuta Hübner, Commissioner for Regional Policy (Brussels: DG Regional Policy).

Baun, M., and Marek, D. (2008) (eds.), *EU Cohesion Policy After Enlargement* (Basingstoke: Palgrave Macmillan).

Hooghe, L. (1996*a*) (ed.), *Cohesion Policy and European Integration: Building Multi-Level Governance* (Oxford: Oxford University Press).

Leonardi, R. (2005), *Cohesion Policy in the European Union* (Basingstoke: Palgrave Macmillan).

Marks, G. (1993), 'Structural Policy and Multi-Level Governance in the EC', in A. Cafruny and G. Rosenthal (eds.), *The State of the European Community, Vol. 2: The Maastricht Debates and Beyond* (Boulder, CO/Harlow: Lynne Rienner/Longman), 391–409.

Pollack, M. A. (1995), 'Regional Actors in an Intergovernmental Play: The Making and Implementation of EC Structural Policy', in C. Rhodes and S. Mazey (eds.), *The State of the European Union, Vol. iii: Building a European Polity?* (Boulder, CO: Lynne Rienner), 361–90.

CHAPTER 11

Social Policy
Left to the Judges and the Markets?

Stephan Leibfried

▌ Summary

Though many assume that the European Union (EU) is minimally involved in social policy, the dynamics of market integration have spilled over substantially into the EU social arena. Resistance by national governments to loss of autonomy, and conflicting interests between rich and poor regions, or between employers and employees, present formidable obstacles to EU policies. However, in the 1980s and 1990s, the EU accumulated significant regulatory mandates in social policy, reaching out more recently to anti-discrimination politics. Yet, under the pressures from integrated markets member governments have lost more control over national welfare policies than the EU has gained in transferred authority, although this development may have stopped, affected by the EU's responses to the economic crises since 2008. The resultant multi-tiered pattern is largely law- and court-driven, marked by policy immobilism at the centre and by 'negative' market integration,

(continued...)

which significantly constrains national social policies. The increase in heterogeneity with eastern enlargement and southern indebtedness challenge *traditional* twentieth-century EU social policy and point to *new* regulatory horizons for the twenty-first.

Introduction

Accounts of European social policy typically report a minimalist EU involvement (D. Collins 1975; Falkner 1998).[1] The EU is seen as 'market-building', leaving an exclusive, citizen-focused, national welfare state, its sovereignty formally untouched, though perhaps endangered by increasing economic interdependence. 'Welfare states are national states' (Swaan 1992: 33; Offe 2003), and, at first sight, the European ones indeed look national. There are no EU laws granting individual entitlements against Brussels, no direct taxes or contributions, no real funding of a 'social budget' for such entitlements, and no significant Brussels welfare bureaucracy. Territorial sovereignty in social policy seems alive and well. However, an alternative view has become plausible: European integration has eroded both the sovereignty (legal authority) *and* the autonomy (regulatory capacity) of member states to conduct their own social policies. What began as a parallel universe turned into a single conflict arena (U. Becker 2004*a*). National welfare states remain the primary institutions of European social policy, but they are built into an increasingly constraining multi-tiered polity (Pierson and Leibfried 1995).

While there have been extensive barriers to an explicitly collective European social policy (Obinger *et al.* 2005), the dynamics of the single market have made it increasingly difficult to exclude social issues from the EU's agenda. The emerging multi-tiered structure, however, results less from the ambitions of Eurocrats to build a welfare state than from spill-overs from the single market process, which has invaded the domain of social policy (Falkner 1998). In the 1980s, the single-market initiative (see Chapter 5) on the free movement of goods, persons, services, and capital was based on a version of regulation that assumed that the single European market could be insulated from social-policy issues, which would remain the province of member states. This assumption runs directly contrary to central tenets of political economy, which stress that economic action is embedded within dense networks of social and political institutions (North 1990; Hall 1999). The neat separation between supranational 'market' and national 'social issues' appears unsustainable. To be sure, there have been 'high politics' struggles over proposals to strengthen treaty provisions on social policy and to develop social charters. Yet, it is rather the movement towards market integration that gradually erodes national welfare states' autonomy *and* sovereignty, and increasingly situates them in a complex, multi-tiered web of Europeanized public policy.

This transformation occurs via three processes (see Table 11.1). *Positive* integration results from policy initiatives taken at the 'centre' by the Commission and the Council, increasingly pushed by the European Parliament (EP), along with the often expansive

TABLE 11.1 European integration transforms national welfare states		
Pressures and processes	**Key actors**	**Examples**
Direct policy pressures of integration → *positive* initiatives to develop uniform social standards at EU level	Commission, expert committees, CJEU, and since 1992 institutionally entrusted corporate actors like UNICE, CEEP, ETUC (background actors: EP, ESC; diverse lobbies)	*Old politics*: national and gender equality; health and safety; Social Protocol 'corporatism' since 1992, generalized 1997, with expansion of competences and of QMV; 1989 EC Social Charter, 'incorporated' in ToA; extending notion of European citizenship
		New politics: expanding anti-discrimination law beyond nationality and gender to 'any ground such as' *race*, colour, *ethnic* or social *origin*, genetic features, language, *religion or belief*, political or any other opinion, membership of a national minority, property, birth, *disability, age or sexual orientation*' (items in italics already in Art. 13 TEC; others Art. 21 EU Charter of Fundamental Rights)
→ *negative* policy reform imposing market compatibility requirements at EU level	CJEU, Commission, Council (national governments), national legal institutions	Labour mobility, since the late 1980s freedom to provide and consumer services, combined with impact of the European Treaty's 'competition regime'
Indirect pressures of integration → adaptation of national welfare states	Market actors (employers, unions; sensitive sectors: private insurance, provider groups), Council, individual national governments in fields outside social policy	Further 'social dumping' accented by eastern enlargement, EMU, and Maastricht criteria; harmonization of tax systems; single market for private insurance; since the 1980s, transforming the 'public utilities state', the traditional outer mantle of the welfare state; since 2007, public debt and fiscal crises

interpretations of the Court of Justice of the European Union (CJEU), previously the European Court of Justice (ECJ). In the 1990s, the treaty mandate was strengthened, providing a Euro-corporatist anchor, drawing European trade unions and employer organizations towards that centre. Since then a softer version of policy-making has evolved via the open method of coordination (OMC) (see Chapter 12), which might amplify positive integration—as in modernizing social protection systems—or step in where the EU would otherwise have little competence, or even turn into hard law despite the many obstacles to achieving this (Heidenreich and Zeitlin 2009). *Negative* integration occurs as the CJEU imposes market-compatibility requirements via the four freedoms (Barnard 2007)—especially free movement of labour and of services—that restrict member states' social policies. Both positive and negative initiatives create direct, mostly *de jure*, pressures on national welfare states through new instruments of European social policy. Finally, European integration creates an escalating range of *indirect de facto* pressures that encourage adaptations—convergence (see Starke *et al.* 2008)—of national welfare states. These pressures strongly affect national welfare states, but they are not directly derived from EU social-policy instruments.

Positive initiatives from the centre have generally prompted major social conflicts, and have repeatedly been attempted. The 1957 Treaty of Rome, for instance, met stiff resistance in the French National Assembly in part because weak social clauses were seen to endanger the well-developed French welfare state, making French industry less competitive. Negative integration efforts were, at first, less visible, but are just as old. The coordination of rules governing labour mobility was enshrined in one of the earliest European Community (EC) legislative acts (1958), whereas similar action on services dates only from the mid-1980s, reaching a high plateau at the end of the 1990s. Indirect pressures are more recent in response to the development of economic integration. With ascendant centre-right parties the primacy of economic integration was locked firmly into the EU policy-making level from 1957 onwards. In contrast, the social democrats in their two phases of ascendance in the 1970s and late 1990s, were unable—and often unwilling—to lock in a similarly effective social integration perspective (Manow *et al.* 2004); they invented OMC instead. With eastern enlargement these trajectories seem frozen into place, though this is challenged in the course of the financial and economic crisis that began in 2007.

The limited success of activist social policy

Discussions of social policy generally focus on prominent actors like the Council, the Commission (and the responsible directorate-general (DG)), and increasingly the EP (and its committees), and the representatives of business and labour in an emerging corporatist policy community. The Commission has been a central actor in attempting to construct a 'social dimension' for its 'European social model' (Commission 1994, 2000*a*, 2003*c*, 2008*f*, 2012*h*, 2012*i*, 2013*j*)—areas of European social policy with uniform or at least minimum standards. These attempts have occurred in fits and starts during the past decades, with high aspirations and modest results, marked by plenty of cheap talk, produced in the confident knowledge that unanimous—or even qualified-majority—voting in the Council would block all ambitious blueprints (Streeck and Schmitter 1991; Lange 1992). The main point is that focusing on the efforts of Euro-federalists to foist a social dimension on a reluctant Council has been somewhat misleading. European integration did alter European social policy-making, but largely through mechanisms operating *outside* the welfare dimension proper. The obstacles to an activist role for Brussels in social-policy development are formidable, increasing, and twofold (Pierson and Leibfried 1995).

Institutional constraints

The EU process makes it much easier to block than to enact reforms. Only narrow, market-related openings for social legislation have been available (see Table 11.2) and reform requires at least a qualified majority. Member governments are jealous gatekeepers for initiatives requiring Council approval and protect their prerogatives, especially in countries like Germany with a supreme court that defends national pre-eminence in social-policy matters. Since the second world war, the scope of national sovereignty has gradually diminished. The welfare state remains one of the few key realms where national governments have usually resisted losses of policy authority, not least because of the electoral significance of most social programmes.

Until the early 1990s, legislative reform was limited to a few areas where the Treaty of Rome, or the single-market project, allowed more latitude, mainly the gender-equality provisions and health and safety in the workplace. In the 1970s, the Council unanimously agreed to a number of directives giving the equal-treatment provision some content. Over the past thirty years, the CJEU has played a crucial activist role, turning Article 119 EEC and the directives into an extensive set of requirements and prohibitions related to the treatment of female, and occasionally male, workers (Ostner and Lewis 1995; Hoskyns 1996; Mazey 1998; Walby 2005; Costello and Davies 2006). These rulings have required extensive national reforms. The Single European Act (SEA) in Article 118a allowed qualified majority voting (QMV) on health and safety and QMV on gender equality followed in the 1990s (now all gender directives are recast in Directive 2006/54/EC). Surprisingly, policy-making has produced neither stalemate nor lowest-common-denominator regulations in health and safety, but rather high standards. Furthermore, European regulators moved beyond regulating products to production processes (Eichener 1997, 2000).

The shifting balance of power among social interests

The 'social democratic' forces most interested in a strong social dimension are relatively weak and often Eurosceptical (Manow *et al.* 2004). Across most of the EU, unions and social democratic parties had become weaker since the 1980s. In the second half of the 1990s, social democracy—bent less on traditional social than on 'new' employment, on labour market 'activation' policy—grew again, although Union power did not. Meanwhile, business power grew considerably, partly fostered by European- and OECD-wide capital markets. This shifting balance of power has further hindered efforts to deal with institutional blockages, limited fiscal resources, and widely divergent and deeply institutionalized national social policies.[2]

The historical trajectory is one from noisy public-policy fights since the 1980s, with a consolidating high point in the Treaty of Amsterdam (ToA) in 1997, to a slow slide into the sounds of silence of the twenty-first century, though with new

TABLE 11.2 Assignment of social-policy mandates to the EU up to the Treaty of Lisbon

Field of mandate	European Economic Community (EEC) 1957 (1958)	Single European Act (SEA) 1986 (1987)	Treaty on European Union (TEU) 1992 (1993)	Social Protocol (SP) 1992 (1993)	Treaty of Amsterdam (ToA) 1997 (1999)	Treaty of Nice (ToN) 2000 (2003)	Treaty of Lisbon (ToL)[a] 2007 (2009)
1 Discrimination on grounds of nationality	Unan. 7	No ref.	QMV 6	No ref.	QMV 12	QMV 12	QMV 18
2 Basic principles of anti-discrimination incentives, harmonization excluded	No ref.	No ref.	No ref.	No ref.	QMV 13(2)	QMV 13(2)	QMV 19 II
3 Free labour movement	Unan. 48–50	QMV 48–50	QMV 48–50	No impact	QMV 39–40	QMV 39–40	QMV 45–46
4 Gender equality in pay[b]	Unan. 119	Unan. 119	Unan. 119	Unan. 6	QMV 141	QMV 141	QMV 157
5 Gender equality for labour force[b]	No ref.	No ref.	No ref.	QMV 2(1)v	QMV 137(1)iv	QMV 137(1)i	QMV 153(1)i
6 Working environment	No ref.	QMV 118	QMV 118a	QMV 2(1)i	QMV 137(1)i	QMV 137(1)a	QMV 153(1)a
7 Working conditions (outside former Art. 118a, line 6)	No ref.	No ref.	No ref.	QMV 2(1)ii	QMV 137(1)ii	QMV 137(1)b	QMV 153(1)b
8 Worker information and consultation	No ref.	No ref.	No ref.	QMV 2(1)iii	QMV 137(1)iii	QMV 137(1)e	QMV 153(1)e
9 Integration of persons excluded from labour market[c]	No ref.	No ref.	No ref.	QMV 2(1)iv	QMV 137(1)h	QMV 137(1)h	QMV 153(1)h

#	Policy area						
10	Combating of social exclusion	QMV 153(1)j	QMV 137(1)j	No ref.	No ref.	No ref.	No ref.
11	Modernization of social protection systems	QMV 153(1)k	QMV 137(1)k	No ref.	No ref.	No ref.	No ref.
12	Public health	QMV 168	QMV 152	QMV 152	No ref.	QMV 129	No ref.
13	Social security coordination	QMV 49	Unan. 42	Unan. 42	n.a.	Unan. 51	Unan. 51
14	Anti-discrimination measures	Unan. 19(1)	Unan. 13(1)	Unan. 13(1)	No ref.	No ref.	No ref.
15	Social security and protection of workers	Unan. 153(1)c, (3)	Unan. 137(1)c	Unan. 137(3)i	Unan. 2(3)i	No ref.	No ref.
16	Protection of workers (employment contract termination)	Unan. 153(1)d, (3). If not QMV 153(2) last para.	Unan. 137(1)d	Unan. 137(3)ii	Unan. 2(3)ii	No ref.	No ref.
18	Employment of third-country nationals	Unan. 153(1)g, (3). If not QMV 153(2) last para.	Unan. 137(1)g	Unan. 137(3)iv	Unan. 2(3)iv	No ref.	No ref.
19	Funding for employment policy[c]	No ref.	No ref.	Unan. 137(3)iv	Unan. 2(3)v	No ref.	No ref.
20	Pay	Excl. 151(5)	Excl. 137(5)	Excl. 137(6)	Excl. 2(6)	No ref. 100a (2)	No ref.
21	Right of association	Excl. 151(5)	Excl. 137(5)	Excl. 137(6)	Excl. 2(6)	No ref. 100a(2)	No ref.
22	Right to strike and to impose lock-outs	Excl. 151(5)	Excl. 137(5)	Excl. 137(6)	Excl. 2(6)	No ref. 100a(2)	No ref.

TABLE 11.2 (Continued)

Field of mandate	European Economic Community (EEC) 1957 (1958)	Single European Act (SEA) 1986 (1987)	Treaty on European Union (TEU) 1992 (1993)	Social Protocol (SP) 1992 (1993)	Treaty of Amsterdam (ToA) 1997 (1999)	Treaty of Nice (ToN) 2000 (2003)	Treaty of Lisbon (ToL)[a] 2007 (2009)
23 Mandates for the open method of coordination (OMC)[d]							
Employment					(128) 140	(128) 140	(148) 156 1st dash
Labour market and working conditions						140	156 2nd dash
Professional education and training						140	156 3rd dash
Social security						140	156 4th dash
Prevention of occupational accidents and diseases						140	156 5th dash
Protection of health at work						140	156 6th dash
Law of coalitions and collective agreements between employers and employees						140	156 7th dash

Notes: years for treaties refer to the signing and (in parentheses) the ratification of the treaty. Numbers listed in the table refer to articles in each treaty. Unan. = unanimity required; QMV = qualified majority voting; No ref. = no reference to mandate; n.a. = not applicable; Excl. = mandate explicitly excluded. Medium shading denotes weaker mandate. Heavy shading shows explicit denial of mandates, anchored in the treaties only since 1992 in these areas.

[a] As a rule the table refers to explicit powers mentioned in the treaties, in contrast to unspecified general powers, as under Arts. 100 and 235 EEC (now Arts. 95 and 308 TEC (now Arts. 114 and 352 TFEU = Treaty on the Functioning of the European Union = part of ToL), or to non-enabling norms (on an exception, see note b).

[b] Between the original Treaty of Rome and the 1992 Social Protocol, the CJEU had interpreted gender equality ever more widely. Art. 119 EEC (now Art. 141 TEC) contained no express enabling clause; respective directives were based on Art. 100 or 235 EEC, which required unanimous decisions. In the end Art. 141(3) TEC in 1997 brought the first special mandate and QMV.

[c] From 1992 to 1997 this QMV mandate excluded the one for funding, where unanimity was required according to Art. 2(3) of the Social Protocol and then Art. 137(3) TEC, thus maintaining anti-poverty spending programmes as highly veto-prone.

[d] The term 'open method of coordination' is not mentioned in any of the treaties.

Source: The table started out from Falkner (1998: 82), is more detailed, and shows subsequent treaty developments. The author owes special thanks to Josef Falke, University of Bremen, for his continuous help in updating and legal advice over several editions.

frontiers in sight. At least until the 1993 Social Protocol, which was annexed to the Maastricht Treaty on European Union (TEU), after the UK secured an opt-out, UK opposition rendered serious initiatives impossible (Kleinman and Piachaud 1992). Member governments, European officials, and interest groups were left free to make rhetorical commitments to a grand social dimension (Ross 1995*a*, 1995*b*; Streeck 1995). Disputes over initiatives to increase EU social-policy mandates regularly far exceeded the true implications of the proposals made and the results achieved. The struggle over the Social Charter in the 1980s was typical (Falkner 1998).

The 1989 Community Charter of the Fundamental Social Rights of Workers and the 1961 European Social Charter of the Council of Europe, however, were both silently incorporated into the 1997 ToA through a reference in the preamble. These rights reappeared in the Charter of Fundamental Rights of the European Union, proclaimed in Nice on 7 December 2000 (ToN) by the European Council and EP, and were finally incorporated in Article 6 of the Treaty of Lisbon (ToL).

The high point of these developments was the 1997 ToA with its Social Chapter, accepted at last by the UK as a hard 'constitutional' achievement. Two mandates— health and safety in the 'working environment' and gender equality 'in pay'—were broadened; the first to all 'working conditions' and the second to all 'labour force' issues. Both were subject to QMV, which was new for gender equality. Two additional mandates—worker information and consultation and integration of persons excluded from the labour market—were introduced, also subject to QMV, but without EU financing. Five new topics were introduced subject to unanimous decision-making: social security and worker protection; protection of workers when employment contract is terminated; collective interest representation; employment of third-country nationals; and funding to integrate the excluded. Three topics were declared off-limits: levels of pay, the right of association, and the right to strike or to impose lock-outs. Agreement was also reached on applying more widely the powers of the 'social partners' (unions and employers) to adopt quasi-legislative agreements. The ToA included a new Title VIII Employment, Arts. 125–130, based on a Swedish initiative, mainly about coordinating national employment initiatives via OMC (Johansson 1999; Tidow 2003; Zeitlin *et al.* 2005). Since then OMC has been extended to pensions, social inclusion, health, and migration, and in 2005 was 'streamlined' beyond recognition (Commission 2003*b*; Casey 2003; Daly 2008; and see Chapter 12) and is now subordinated to economic and fiscal 'semester' politics.[3]

The revised Social Chapter (Arts. 136–145 ToN) facilitated efforts to expand EU social policy. First, a country's capacity to obstruct legislation diminished. By 1992, the four cohesion states—Greece, Ireland, Portugal, and Spain—no longer commanded enough votes to block policy under QMV. Their minority status became more pronounced after the enlargement in 1995 brought in advanced industrialized economies with strong welfare states. The obstruction that had met the 1989 Social Action Programme (Falkner 1998) was made impossible. The Working

Time 93/104/EC, Young Workers 94/33/EC, European Works Council 94/95/EC, Parental Leave 96/34/EC, Part-Time Work 97/81/EC, Burden of Proof in Sex Discrimination Cases 97/80/EC, and Fixed-Term Contracts/Temporary Work 99/70/EC Directives were passed (see Falkner *et al.* 2005). They represented successes of a form of Euro-corporatism endowed with legislative powers. The social partners seemed ready to negotiate, now 'in the shadow of the [Council] vote', and based on their own experience. But no other major directives followed; instead, the social partners sidestepped this with a 2002 Framework Agreement on Teleworking. For the first time the social partners committed their own members to direct implementation, and sought no ratification through the Council of Ministers. This approach was seen as having greater political promise—but also the risk of having little effect (UNICE *et al.* 2006). But, since 2012 agreements foreshadowing directives on special groups (fishermen—implementing an International Labour Organization (ILO) convention; hairdressers; employees in harbour sector) have emerged.

All these directives belong to the *acquis communautaire* and thus have legal effect in the thirteen countries that have joined the EU since 2004. As yet little is known of how effective they are on the ground (Kvist 2004; Falkner *et al.* 2008; Maydell *et al.* 2006), though we know that large differences in wages, hours worked, and in the scale of the informal economy plus the collective bargaining situation may make implementation a problem (Vaughan-Whitehead 2007). Also, thirteen additional member states with less interest in Social Europe have made it harder to muster a qualified majority in favour of new legislation.

While most aspects of the Social Charter have moved forward, other initiatives have been modest and have largely consolidated older initiatives and not covered new ground. From the early 1990s until today, the Commission has continued to engage in intensive soul-searching on its proper social-policy role (Ross 1995*b*). Efforts to combat stubbornly high levels of European unemployment moved centre stage during the mid-1990s (Commission 1994, 2003*a*, 2003*c*), as reflected in the 1997 ToA and the 2000 ToN with efforts to 'modernize social protection systems' and to 'combat social exclusion' (Art. 137(1)(k), (j)). The Commission seemed to have accepted at least some of the UK case for the need to promote labour market 'flexibility' (Commission 1993*b*: 116ff.). This trend has intensified, with the 'slimming down' of national welfare states now a regular and prominent topic on the agenda of the Council of Ministers for Economic and Financial Affairs (Ecofin), the European Council, and the Commission—and with the Employment and Social Policy Council and the corresponding Commission DGs mostly on the defensive. Member governments seem unlikely to allow the Commission to take the lead here, thus leaving the immediate prospect as consolidation, with the completion of some current agenda items, but with few new initiatives—though the crises after 2007–8 have provoked initiatives to develop a European unemployment-insurance mechanism (A.B. Atkinson 2013; Commission 2013*j*: 11f.).

Less noted has been the *silent revolution* in the treaties to combat discrimination. While the 1992 TEU held to the old politics of prohibiting labour discrimination by nationality and gender, the 1997 ToA Article 13 prohibited discrimination based on 'racial and other origins, religion or belief, disability, age or sexual orientation', and Article 21 of the 2000 EU Charter of Fundamental Rights amplified this by prohibiting discrimination on 'any' further 'ground such as' colour, social origin, genetic features, language, political or any other opinion, membership of a national minority, property, birth, and disability. There followed the 'Article 13 Package' of two directives (anti-racism (2000/43), framework (2000/78)), and an Action Programme in 2000 (Eichenhofer 2004) and a subsequent directive on gender-equality standards (2002/73) (Costello and Davies 2006: 1567f.; Husmann 2005). The CJEU has in recent years addressed age discrimination, as in 2005 in *Mangold* (C-144/04). In a more heterogeneous and veto-prone EU the anti-discrimination-cum-court route may well become the regulatory route for social policy in the twenty-first century—though since 2009 attempts to further extend anti-discrimination legislation 'outside the labour market' have been blocked.

US experience may be relevant here. After the 1960s civil rights reforms, there was a burst of anti-discrimination regulatory politics that burdened private parties only, promising well-being whilst by-passing burdens on public budgets, and that relied mainly on court rulings (Kochan *et al.* 2001; Nivola 1998). Similarly, anti-discrimination might also develop into an apparent European panacea for a welfare-guaranteeing state, especially in a more heterogeneous EU (Heidenreich 2003; Franzius 2003). One example is the struggle to require private insurance companies to offer men and women the same premiums, which has repercussions across all types of insurance (Schwark 2003; House of Lords 2004; Boecken 2005; Rothgang 2007). As a consequence of the European Court of Human Rights ruling on 1 March 2011 in the *Test-Achats* case (C-236/09) and Commission guidelines for the industry on implementing it (European Commission, IP/11/1581, 22 Dec. 2011), EU equality regulation was extended to motor insurance, life insurance, and retirement products such as annuities at the end of 2012. Such a transformation to an anti-discrimination policy focus emphasizes employment with a 'citizenship-consumer' focus, which might accommodate the very different welfare traditions in Europe as well as echo US consumer welfare (Rieger and Leibfried 2003). A slow legal convergence and harmonization seems to emerge, following anti-discrimination leaders like the UK and the Netherlands (House of Lords 2000).

To sum up, to focus on the highly politicized and widely publicized struggles in the EU over positive, centre-imposed social policies misses the point. Devices such as the Social Charter in the 1980s and the Social Protocol in the early 1990s are probably much less pertinent than measures such as the 1992 Maternity Directive (92/85/EEC), or directives under the Social Protocol (1992) and the 'constitutionalized' Social Chapter of 1997. EU legislative activity is now at least as extensive as federal social-policy activity was on the eve of the US New Deal in the 1930s (Robertson 1989; Pierson 1995a; Leibfried and Obinger 2008)—and it is moving in great strides to match the US anti-discrimination era dating since the 1970s.

European integration and market compatibility requirements

Lost amidst the noisy fights about treaty changes and Brussels-based positive social policy has been the quiet accumulation of constraints on national social policy by market integration.[4] The last four decades have witnessed a gradual expansion of EU-generated 'regulation' in all its varieties (Table 11.3) and court decisions that have seriously eroded the sovereignty of the national welfare states and overlaid it with a new mobility- and competition-friendly regime. Rather few political scientists (Falkner 1998; Falkner *et al.* 2005; Hantrais 2007; Conant 2007*b*) paid attention to the 'low politics'—let alone the judicial politics—of what was happening, since most were entranced by the 'high politics' of treaty bargains. The topic was left to European labour and welfare lawyers and the scholars who monitored the courts (Burley and Mattli 1993; Shapiro and Stone 1994; Stone Sweet and Caporaso 1998; Weiler 1999; Chalmers 2004; Eichenhofer 2013; Barnard 2010; Bercusson 2009; Conant 2007*b*; the best overview, though in German, is U. Becker 2012)—and has been confronted with a backlash literature from political science only recently (Scharpf 2009, 2010; Höpner and Schäfer 2008; Caporaso and Tarrow 2009).

Since the 1960s the CJEU has delivered close to 1,400 decisions on social-policy topics, representing 15 per cent of all its judgments (*output*) (see Table 11.4). These decisions were distributed roughly evenly among free movement for workers and their social security (31 per cent); third-country migrants' (36 per cent), and workers' protection and equal treatment (34 per cent)—all within the scope of now Articles 151–161 TFEU. Also, the Commission brought to court member governments for violating social-policy provisions of the treaties (see Table 11.5, Referrals by the European Commission). The social-policy caseload (*input*) (see Appendix, Table A.1) in 2012 accounted for 6 per cent of all cases brought. This put it fifth—behind environmental and consumer issues, intellectual property, taxation, and justice and home affairs—out of thirty for demand of CJEU decisions. And if we added freedom of movement cases (5 per cent), which often overlap, social policy would constitute the most prominent area of CJEU activities. These statistics do not include freedom of services cases, and those of all other categories that may occasionally impact upon national welfare states.

There have been in addition many lawsuits initiated by EU staff for whom the CJEU serves as a labour and social security court (see Appendix, Tables A.1, line 20 and A.2, line 22), a huge demand on CJEU resources, which was partly the reason for the founding of the Court of First Instance (CFI) in 1989 (Emmert 1996; Forwood 2008), after 2009 renamed General Court, with the CJEU now serving only as a court of appeal. But the social status of EU civil servants does not serve as a welfare model for EU citizens—as it had in some member states, such as Germany and

TABLE 11.3 EU legislation in employment and social policy (as of 1 July 2013)

Legal acts	Institutions	Statistics	Freedom of movement for worker	General social provisions	Anti-discrimination, gender equality	Working conditions, work hours	Safety at work	Industrial relations	Employment policy	Globalization Adjustment Fund	Social security, general	Social security of migrant workers	Total
Regulations	EP and Council	4	1	1	1		2			1	3	1	14
	Council	4		4			1		3			7	19
	Commission	44		11		1	6		1		1		64
Directives	EP and Council		2		2	9	9	3					25
	Council	1	2	1	2	7	21	2	2		1		39
	Commission						4						4
Decisions	EP and Council			6	2				2	83			93
	Council	1	1	9	1		1		18			1	31
	Commission	2	6	4	3	12	10	1	4		3		45
	Committee[a]	1										100	100
Recommendations	Council		1		2	3	2	1	8		3		20
	Commission	1		3		4	4	1	6		3	1	24
	Committee[a]											9	9

(Continued)

TABLE 11.3 (Continued)

Legal acts	Institutions	Statistics	Freedom of movement for worker	General social provisions	Anti-discrimination, gender equality	Working conditions, work hours	Safety at work	Industrial relations	Employment policy	Globalization Adjustment Fund	Social security, general	Social security, security of migrant workers	Total
Resolutions	Council	4	1	8	10	2	2				2	1	55
	Council and member states[b]	1	2	3	10	2	1		9	3	1		29
Total		61	17	51	33	40	63	7	78	84	17	120	571

Notes:
[a] Administrative Committee on Social Security for Migrant Workers.
[b] Representatives of the Governments of the Member States.
Source: The data were gathered by Josef Falke, University of Bremen, from the Directory of European Union legislation in force, Chapter 5 'Freedom of movement for workers and social policy', http://eur-lex.europa.eu/legis/latest/chap05.htm. © European Union, http://eur-lex.europa.eu/, 1998–2014.

TABLE 11.4 Distribution of CJEU judgments on social policy by functional subcategories, 1975–2012

Period	Total CJEU judgments No. (= 100%)	Freedom of movement of workers		Social security of migrant workers		Workers' protection and equal treatment		Social policy (all)	
		No.	%	No.	%	No.	%	No.	%
1954–60	61	0	0	0	0	1	1.6	1	1.6
1961–5	136	0	0	8	5.9	0	0	8	5.9
1966–70	172	1	0.6	20	11.6	0	0	21	12.2
1971–5	345	13	3.8	40	11.6	1	0.3	54	15.6
1976–80	565	16	2.8	68	12.0	7	1.2	91	16.1
1981–5	859	22	2.6	47	5.5	26	3.0	95	11.1
1986–90	953	40	4.2	52	5.5	41	4.3	133	14.0
1991–5	968	63	6.5	75	7.4	75	7.7	213	22.0
1996–2000	1,340	77	5.7	75	5.6	107	8.0	259	19.3
2001–5	1,516	84	5.5	54	3.6	84	5.5	222	14.6
2005–10	1,557	77	4.9	31	2.0	82	5.3	190	12.2
2011	309	14	4.5	11	3.6	19	6.1	44	14.2
2012	316	13	4.1	7	2.2	19	6.0	39	12.3
1954–2012	**9,097**	**420**	**4.6**	**488**	**5.4**	**462**	**5.1**	**1,370**	**15.1**

Source: The data were gathered by Josef Falke using the CJEU case law search form, *http://curia.europa.eu/juris/recherche.jsf?language=en*.

France—so these cases do not affect the harmonization of national social policies. Nor do the statistics include some 100 decisions on social-policy issues (see Appendix, Table A.1, lines 8, 10, 19), which mostly address conflicts over distributive criteria in the European Social Fund (ESF).

The social-policy cases (*output*) are distributed unevenly across the member states (see Table 11.5). The most come from Germany, Belgium, the Netherlands, and the UK. France and Italy have consistently produced few cases (Stone Sweet and Brunell 1998*a*). The Netherlands and Belgium produce more than the average number of court cases per capita. Even small countries with few cases may trigger big consequences, as the 1998 *Kohll* and *Decker* cases from Luxembourg show (see the section 'Freedom of services and the European competition regime' later in the chapter). Late joiners have been involved in fewer cases, though some of them, such as Austria (66 cases) and Spain (48) show a strong profile, with small states, like Denmark (23), Sweden (19), and Greece (21) again disproportionately active. Since plaintiffs usually may not appeal to the CJEU directly, the national legal profession and its activist stance play a critical intermediary role in feeding cases to the CJEU (Conant 2007*b*). Referrals by the Commission reveal countries officially deemed culprits; here a few other countries show up: Belgium (18) and Italy (17) score highest on breaching the rules on free movement of workers, France (7) and Belgium (5) on social security for migrant workers, and Italy (with a record of 20) on workers' protection and equal treatment.

The EU's social dimension is often advocated as a corrective to market-building, but in practice seems to have been part of it, as free movement and increasing competition have prompted court cases and thus expanded the bite of European law on national social provisions. Only cases dealing with European citizenship (Bieback 2003; Besson 2007; Shaw 2007) or legitimate residency (Eichenhofer 2003) would generate a social dimension separate from market-building. We can already see signs of this as regards Union citizenship (Art. 17 ToN), as the heated exchanges over the *Grzelczyk* decision of 2001 (C-184/99) indicate (Hailbronner 2004*a*, 2004*b*; Epiney 2007), a decision that granted access to Belgian welfare benefits to a French citizen studying at the Catholic University of Louvain-la-Neuve based on Union citizenship. More broadly, the CJEU in its jurisprudence increasingly cites citizenship provisions in undoing, revising, or adjusting secondary European law (Besson and Utzinger 2007).

Freedom of movement for workers

Over a period of fifty years a complex patchwork of regulations[5] and court decisions has partially eroded national sovereignty over social policy in pursuit of European labour mobility, now Articles 39–42 EC (Slaughter *et al.* 1997; Jorens and Schulte 1998; Eichenhofer 2013; Schulte 2012; Numhauser-Henning and Rönnmar 2013). These legislative and judicial developments constrain national capacities to limit eligibility for social transfers 'by territory' (Maydell 1991: 231; Maydell *et al.* 2006)

TABLE 11.5 CJEU rulings in social policy by functional subcategories and EU member states, 1954–2012

Countries	Preliminary rulings				Referral by the European Commission			
	A	B	C	Total	A	B	C	Total
Austria	20	15	21	66	2	0	6	8
Belgium	51	138	29	218	18	5	5	28
Bulgaria	0	1	1	2	0	0	0	0
Cyprus	0	0	0	0	0	0	0	0
Czech Republic	0	1	0	1	0	0	0	0
Denmark	0	1	22	23	2	0	1	3
Estonia	0	0	0	0	1	0	0	1
Finland	2	3	6	11	0	0	0	0
France	23	50	17	90	10	7	7	24
Germany	94	112	94	300	6	2	2	10
Greece	9	4	8	21	11	2	3	16
Hungary	1	0	1	2	0	0	1	1
Ireland	2	0	8	10	3	0	1	4
Italy	23	10	24	57	17	0	20	37
Latvia	0	0	0	0	0	0	0	0
Lithuania	0	0	1	1	0	0	0	0
Luxembourg	12	6	3	21	7	1	9	17
Malta	0	0	0	0	0	0	0	0
Netherlands	31	82	34	147	5	2	2	9
Poland	0	2	0	2	0	0	0	0
Portugal	1	0	0	1	3	0	2	5
Romania	0	0	1	1	0	0	0	0
Slovakia	0	0	0	0	0	0	0	0
Slovenia	0	0	0	0	0	0	0	0
Spain	7	12	29	48	12	1	2	15
Sweden	6	3	10	19	1	0	0	1
UK	30	25	75	130	2	0	7	9
Total	306	465	384	1,155	100	20	68	188

A = Freedom of movement for workers
B = Social security of migrant workers
C = Workers' protection and equal treatment

Source: The data were gathered by Josef Falke using the ECJ case law search form, *http://curia.europa. eu/juris/recherche.jsf?language=en*.

and to shape autonomously welfare-state reform trajectories (Conant 2002). The most significant constraints are:

- A member state may no longer limit most social benefits to its citizens. As regards non-nationals from within the EU, the state of legal residence no longer has any power to determine whether they are entitled to benefits, though the UK is most actively trying to enforce 'right-to-reside tests' with CJEU infringement procedures started in 2013. Benefits must be granted to all—or withheld from all. This development is remarkable, because 'citizen-making' through social benefits—demarcating the 'outsider'—was a watershed in the history of state-building on the continent, especially in France and Germany. This restriction encourages attempts to develop innocent-looking, but devious, discrimination mechanisms at the national level, many of which reach the CJEU in due course (as did the German private-pension Riester-subsidy (C-269/07) in 2009).

- A member state may no longer insist that its rights and benefits only apply to, and can only be provided within, its territory. Here child benefits were the historical bone of contention, with France trying, unsuccessfully, to limit benefit flow to Italy. Today, states may determine the territory of benefit consumption to only a limited extent—basically when providing in-kind or universal means-tested benefits, and in unemployment insurance (see Husmann 1998), though the latter may change with the modernization and simplification of coordination regulation (with implementing Regulation EC 883/04 replacing Regulation EEC 1408/71).

- A member state is no longer entirely free to prevent other social-policy regimes from directly competing on its own territory. This is a problem for many states, and conflicts have been reported across the EU (Dølvik 2006) over posted construction workers (Directive 96/71/EC) from other EU countries, who work for extended periods at their national wage level, while covered by many of their home country's social regulations. Cases arising in 2007 from Scandinavia like *Viking* (C-438/05) and *Laval* (C-341/05), and in 2008 from Germany like *Rüffert* (C-346/06), in which national wage minimums were undercut by the free movement of enterprises, have had major political reverberations in a time where Europe's social dimension came under additional stress due to post-2008 coping with the economic crisis; the court kept to its course in *Commission v. Luxembourg* (C-319/06) in 2008 and the compensatory regulation (Commission 2012k) was blocked in the subsidiarity complaint procedure. Thus, the state has lost some of its exclusive power to determine how the people living within its borders are protected, though there have been successful attempts since the 1990s (Directive 96/71/EC) to contain such losses through obligatory minimum wages and holidays (see Streeck 1998; Eichhorst 1998, 2000; Menz 2003; Boeri and Brücker 2006).

- Member states have no exclusive right to administer claims to welfare benefits from migrants. Instead, the authorities of other states may also have a decisive say in adjudicating benefit status. This controversial arrangement seemed to facilitate benefit fraud, as has been revealed repeatedly in Germany and elsewhere, as in the *Paletta* cases of 1992 and 1996 (C-45/90, C-206/94) which stated that a doctor's certificate from the present country of abode (Italy) entitled a worker directly to sickness benefit in the country of employment (Germany).

Compared with the US, migration within the EU has been small, though emigration has been on the rise since the euro area crisis took hold in countries like Greece, Spain, and Portugal. Member states also have quite different migration profiles (see Chapter 15). Prior to the 2004 enlargement, only about five million workers in the EU, including their dependants, exercised the freedom of movement, far outnumbered by third-country migration into the EU (Angenendt 1997; Mau and Verwiebe 2009: 111ff.; Recchi and Favell 2009). Eastern enlargement has changed this situation, a factor that could generate a good deal of CJEU litigation. In 2012, there were 15.2 million foreign citizens working in the EU, which amounts to 7 per cent of total EU employment: 6.6 million (3.02 per cent) were citizens of another EU member state and 8.6 million (3.98 per cent) third-country nationals. From 2010 to 2012 the overall numbers had increased by 6.5 per cent—with Spain, Italy, Ireland, and smaller 'other EU' member states showing marked decreases in such labour force participation.[6]

For the law to bite, however, does not require a large volume of intra-EU migration. Only a few individuals as litigants and national courts that refer cases to the CJEU, as has been the pattern since 1959, is required. Similarly, third-country migrants have prompted important cases, and concerns about irregular labour migration has been one of the driving forces behind the development of justice and home affairs (see Chapter 15).

Complete national legal authority has ceased to exist in the EU. Supranational efforts to broaden access to social policy and national efforts to maintain control go hand in hand, are recalibrated from conflict to conflict, and are moving piecemeal into a new, albeit sketchy, system. Member governments have resisted this transformation. Individually, they have baulked at implementing some facets of coordination, although the CJEU has often taken them to task for this. Collectively, they sought to roll back some aspects of coordination in the early 1990s, unanimously agreeing to revisions that would allow them to restrict the portability of benefits in a somewhat broader range of cases following proper 'notification' (Schuler 2005).

Arguably the result is an incremental, rights-based homogenization of social policy. Neither supranationalization nor harmonization describes this dynamic: each implies more policy control at the centre than currently exists. The CJEU is central to this process by applying a light, but far-reaching, hand, reshaping the boundaries of national autonomy. The process structures the interfaces between twenty-eight national social-policy systems with potentially far-reaching implications for the range of national policy options available.

Freedom of services and the European competition regime

The EU's agenda on market integration has covered the freedom to provide services since 1957 (now Arts. 56 and 57 TFEU). The signatories of the Treaty of Rome were aware that an explicitly coordinated social policy would affect their national welfare states (Romero 1993), but saw no connection between this and the freedom of services, for which they had only financial services in mind. But developments since the mid-1980s under the 1986 SEA have shown that implementing this freedom could entail far-reaching consequences for national social-policy regimes. Several ECJ judgments—notably *Kohll* (C-158/96; concerning a Luxembourg citizen who obtained dental treatment in Germany without authorization), and *Decker* (C-120/95; concerning a Luxembourg citizen who bought prescription glasses in Belgium without authorization)—have found that freedom to provide services includes both the freedom of consumers 'of social policy' to shop in other EU countries and the right of service providers to deliver their services 'across the border' in another country. These rules have thus redrawn the demarcation line between the national welfare state and the EU-wide market (U. Becker 2004*b*, 2005*a*; Kingreen 2007).[7] This spill-over has generated European conflicts over social-policy—especially health—reform (Maydell 1999; U. Becker 1998, 2005*b*), with member-state ministries reclaiming their social-policy turf 'from Europe', though its precise effects are disputed (Obermaier 2008). These developments have potentially wide ramifications, not least since 5–10 per cent of the national labour forces are involved in the delivery of national social policies, a growing sector in an ageing continent.

This encompassing understanding of a free market for services has four general implications for the sovereignty of national welfare states. First, the treaty provisions set up a tension between 'economic' activity and 'solidaristic' action, which now frames all of the welfare state, but that tension is characterized by two polarized trajectories (Schulz-Weidner 1997): they protect some core components of the 'old' welfare state (redistribution, pay-as-you-go, etc., which belong to the 'social-security provider monopoly'); but, as redistribution measures contract, the welfare state (in whole or in part) moves over the borderline into the sphere of 'economic activity', thus becoming subject to the freedom of services and establishment (see Chapter 5) and the competition regime (see Chapter 6). Thus, slowly a single European 'social security' *market* is emerging, with a level playing field for private actors (Giesen 2005). For example, several member states already allow for private competitive provision in accident insurance. There is no general exemption from the treaties' market freedoms for welfare-state activity per se (U. Becker 1998, 2007*a*). The continuous redrawing of the fine line between 'economic' and 'solidaristic' action is what much of the legal conflict (e.g. *Sodemare* 1997 (C-70/95)) is about. That is, whether the state may allow non-profit-making private operators to participate in running its social-welfare system by concluding contracts which entitle only them to be reimbursed by public authorities for the costs of their health-care services. Only at the end of a long process will we know the real contours of this interface between European law and national welfare states (Graser 2004).

The second implication is that consumer and provider rights have come to the fore since the mid-1990s, challenging the closed shops of the welfare state. Member governments may no longer exclusively decide who provides social services or benefits. They may no longer exclusively organize social-service occupations, since the mutual recognition of degrees and licences from other member states intervenes. And their capacity to protect national service organizations from the competitive inroads of service organizations in other member states has shrunk radically.

Thirdly, European law has transformed the procurement side of the welfare state. The old 'purveyor to the court' system has given way to controlled bidding processes under the oversight of European subsidy and procurement law (Directive 2004/18/EC).

Fourthly, health care has become a crucial, EU-wide testing ground for the turf battle between national welfare states and the EU-cum-national-market, as represented by private insurance, service providers, producers of medical equipment and drugs, etc. (Mossialos and McKee 2002; Commission 2004c: section 4.4; Mossialos *et al.* 2002; Thomson and Mossialos 2007; Permanand *et al.* 2010; Greer and Kurzer 2013). Compared with pensions, health insurance has more 'market traces' in most national systems, is more fragmented by provider groups already operating in markets (medical instruments, pharmaceuticals), or quasi-markets (doctors in private practice), and has been traditionally exposed to substantial private provision in most countries. Some producers are more likely to take the European route than others, especially private international-service organizations involved in hospitals, medical drug markets, and the provision of medical equipment (Bieback 1993: 171). They are likely to become strong actors at the EU level, vis-à-vis the Commission or in the courts. National reforms have pointed increasingly to 'market cures', opening themselves to particular single markets, like a single drug market (Schwarze 1998; Kotzian 2002, 2003; Hancher 2010; Chatwin 2011; Timur *et al.* 2011). As health is a general concern for Europeans, a European Health Insurance Card was introduced in 2006 and is already seen by some as the health-policy equivalent of the euro. It covers about 190 million Europeans.

The single market for private insurance provides a telling example of the Europe-wide transformation of the social-policy sphere that reaches far beyond health care. Since 1994, national private insurance has been drawn into the European single market, as the Commission has actively sought to establish a single occupational-pensions market, among others with a Pension Funds Directive (2003/41/EC), also supported by the CJEU (see decisions *Danner* (C-136/00) and *Skandia* (C-422/01); Schulz-Weidner 2003). These funds were successfully defended against the Solvency II Directive (2009/128/EC) in 2013, which sought to treat them like banks. The proliferation of cross-border mergers and acquisitions is creating a heavily inter-locked insurance sector operating Europe-wide (Vauhkonen and Pylkkönen 2004: 105–10; Klumpes *et al.* 2007). Integrated European insurance markets allow for a greater differentiation of policy-holders by risk groups, and thus for cheaper policies with lower operational costs. This integrated private sector confronts twenty-eight national, internally segmented, public-insurance domains, often themselves caught up in spirals of deregulation, and thus already exposed to challenges from private markets. Insurance providers with the option of relocating to more lenient member states will gain influence over national social regulation. The clash between particu-lar national regulatory styles and the different traditions of competing insurers from other member states is likely to intensify.

For some time there has been considerable evidence from studies of national wel-fare states that the reform of private-sector markets may dramatically affect the pro-vision of public services (Rein and Rainwater 1986). Public and private insurance compete mainly in occupational pensions (Pochet 2003; Pedersen 2004), life insur-ance, and supplemental health insurance (Thomson and Mossialos 2007). Permanent turf battles seem likely concerning where 'basic' (public) coverage should end and 'additional' (private) insurance begin. Private or competing 'out-of-state' public actors may arm themselves with the 'economic action' approach. The welfare state, which has traditionally been important for demarcating the lines between public and private, is bound to be affected by such a redrawing of boundaries (Hagen 1998).

The balance between a market and institutionally autonomous national welfare states, both embedded in the EU treaties, is not static but has become dynamic, with national reforms—heading for privatization-cum-deregulation—and the single-market regime both feeding into each other in a race towards 'marketization' (Bieback 2003). Brussels finds a wide-open terrain here, with a large potential for restruc-turing welfare-state delivery regimes. The Commission's *White Paper on Services of General Interest* (Commission 2004c) and the December 2006 Services (Bolkestein) Directive (2006/123/EC), 'the legislative hot potato of the early twenty-first century' (Barnard 2008a: 323; Commission 2004b; Neergard *et al.* 2008; Hendrickx 2008; Koeck and Karollus 2008), and street demonstrations in 2005 may foreshadow a much more prominent role for the Commission here than in the coordination arena, despite the fact that the directive currently excludes social and health services, which may become the subject of a special directive like the Patient Rights Directive (2011/24/EU). The Commission took the initiative with a 2007 Commission White Paper, *Together for Health: A Strategic Approach for the EU 2008–2013* (Commission 2007f), but two months later the stalled progress on a framework directive for cross-border health care (Commission 2008e) already showed the rough road lying ahead.

So, even if we focus exclusively on issues of freedom of movement for workers and to provide services, we see a wide range of market-compatibility requirements, through which either EU regulations or CJEU decisions impact on the design and the reform of national social policies. Examples of other welfare-state effects of single-market measures could easily be multiplied—for example, restrictions of subsidies for economic activities in regional policy (Schulz-Weidner 2004) or to state aid for services (U. Becker 2007*b*). The broader point is clear: a whole range of social-policy designs that would be available to sovereign welfare states—and belong to the traditional policy toolkit—are prohibited, or made more costly, to member states within the EU's multi-tiered polity.

European integration and indirect pressures on national welfare states

In addition to the direct ways the EU intervenes in the social policies of member states outlined earlier, European integration *indirectly* significantly affects national policies. Indirect effects are hard to measure; nonetheless they exert supranational influence on the design of national social policy. Two particularly prominent indirect pressures are concerns that due to optimized EU freedoms states will have to compete more to attract business by curtailing expensive welfare programmes (social dumping) and that the constraints on fiscal policy imposed by economic and monetary union (EMU), particularly in the light of the post-2008 economic crises (see Chapter 7), will limit welfare provision. While the former generates greater fears that current evidence warrants, the opposite held true for the latter until 2008.

Social dumping refers to the prospect that firms operating where 'social wages' are low may undercut the prices of competitors, forcing higher-cost firms out of business, or to relocate to low-social-wage areas, or pressure their governments to reduce the social wage. The surge of Polish plumbers into France, alleged to have happened just before the 2005 French referendum on the EU Constitutional Treaty, epitomizes this expectation; in 2013 Belgium complained about central and east European meat-packers in Germany. In extreme scenarios, still being relied on in countries bordering on the eastern enlargement, the corresponding actions fuel a downward spiral in social provision, eventually producing rudimentary, lowest-common-denominator welfare states. These kinds of pressures may have restricted social expenditure in the US, where labour—and capital—mobility is traditionally far greater than in the EU (P. E. Peterson and Rom 1990). The evidence that European integration will fuel such a process remains limited (Majone 2005). The 'social wage' is only one factor in investment decisions, and firms will not invest in low-social-wage countries unless worker productivity justifies it. Even in eastern enlargement, a huge wage disparity leads to only a relatively small productivity disparity benefiting the east (Vaughan-Whitehead 2003; Guillén and Palier 2004). Neo-classical trade theory suggests that high-social-wage countries should be able to continue their policies as long as overall conditions allow profitable investment. A sign of the ambiguous consequences of integration is that northern Europe's concerns about 'sunbelt effects' are mirrored by southern, and now eastern, Europe's heightened concerns about 'agglomeration effects' in which investment flows towards the superior infrastructures and high-skilled workforces of Europe's most developed regions.

EMU, with its tough requirements for budgetary discipline may also encourage downward adjustments in welfare provision (see Chapter 7), although the economic crisis has led to a (temporary?) relaxation of these tough requirements. To participate in EMU, for example, Italy had to reduce its budget deficit from 10 to about 3 per cent of GDP by the end of the 1990s (Ferrera and Gualmini 2004; della Sala 2004). This legitimated efforts by successive governments to make cuts in old-age pensions and other benefits in 1994–5. Although not all would-be euro members have faced such radical adjustments, the Maastricht convergence criteria present formidable problems for most of them and have increased reform pressures (Martin and Ross 2004: 316–21; Townsend 2007: 270–3). These constraints are of particular weight in the context of the current economic recession and bear heavily on the economies of central and eastern Europe, described by some as a 'bill that could break up Europe' (*Economist*, 2 Feb. 2009: 13). Governments would have faced austerity pressure anyway (see Pierson 2001) and this simply became more acute. The euro area crisis has added massively to these pressures for cutting back the welfare state in Cyprus, Greece, Ireland, Portugal, and Spain.[8] The convergence criteria do not require budget reductions, as tax increases could also reduce overall budget deficits—but they strengthened the hand of those seeking cuts. A backlash against the Maastricht criteria, however, has built up since 2002, and this can be read under the heading 'national welfare states strike back'. EMU could prod the EU into a more active role in combating unemployment (see Chapter 12), maybe even European unemployment insurance (Atkinson 2013; Commission 2013j: 11f.). Historically, the prospects for EMU were seen as coupled with the need for social policies to address emerging regional imbalances (Ross 1995b; Leibfried 2013; Marjolin Report 1975). EMU would strip national governments of macroeconomic policy levers, and a passive EU-wide macroeconomic stance would create significant regional unemployment. Flexible exchange rates allowed national adaptations to economic conditions. Once these instruments were dismantled, combating pockets of regional unemployment at the national level became more difficult (Eichengreen 1992). The euro area crisis has also created an integrated, top-down social-policy perspective or short circuit—creating pressures for convergence—with national leaders like Angela Merkel. This is shown by a remark of hers on 18 May 2011, even if the facts at issue may not be correct: 'It's also about not getting a pension earlier than in Germany in countries like Greece, Spain, and Portugal. All of us have to show a similar level of work input'.[9]

The single market is also encouraging a movement towards narrowing differences in national value-added tax (VAT) rates (Uhl 2008), which may prompt downward harmonization thus putting further pressure on welfare spending. In March 2009, for example, labour-intensive services were exempted from the standard minimum rate of 15 per cent, with member states permitted to set the rate as low as 5 per cent, a step which encourages the downward movement in harmonization. In theory, governments whose VAT revenues are lowered can increase other taxes. Because it is politically easier to sustain indirect taxes, however, this movement may create growing constraints on member-state budgets, with clear implications for some national social policies (Hibbs and Madsen 1981). This is a problem for countries like Denmark, which relies on high indirect, rather than payroll, taxes to finance its generous welfare state (Petersen 1991, 2000; Hagen *et al.* 1998) and resists 'upper limits' for VAT. The Commission (2011*b*) has also sought to expand VAT generally to public services thus increasing overall welfare-state costs.

A further indirect pressure on national welfare states stems from the consequences of dismantling the 'public service state', which happened partly for EU reasons, but partly for purely national, endogenous rationales. Trains, mail, air transport, electricity, gas, and other utilities, together with local services, used to be public enterprises, financed by tariffs that ensured equal service across the nation, urban and rural, often cross-subsidizing poor with rich services. Since the mid-1980s, branch after branch of these public structures has been privatized (V. Schneider *et al.* 2005; Tenbücken 2006). Supranational prodding via EU regulation based on competition law (S. K. Schmidt 2004*a*, 2004*b*; and see Chapter 14) and privatization in the UK and deregulation in the US were exacerbated by domestic cuts in state spending and the levelling of the playing field for different kinds of enterprises, and resulted in radically increased competitive pressure in newly internationalized markets. Private, multinational companies became active in branches of public service that had been national or regional. The welfare state, in a sense, is the last domino of the public-service state that has not fallen, but since most other dominoes did, the burden of proof for its legitimacy has now shifted to the last fully standing one. We have seen a transnationalization of the public-service state and a national lock-in of welfare-state change (Leibfried and Zürn 2005)—and thus the loss of the welfare state's protective outer skin (Leibfried 2001). The principles established here may well be applied to the welfare state proper.

What are the consequences of these indirect pressures for welfare states? Many of the potential problem areas lie in the future, and some of the others are difficult to measure. One has to weigh the reform pressures against the welfare state's powers of resilience (Pierson 2001). The picture that emerges is of national governments with diminished control over many of the policies that traditionally supported national welfare states—the currency, macroeconomic policies, public finance, tax policies, the public services, and also industrial-relations systems (Hurrelmann *et al.* 2008).

Europe's multi-tiered social policy

Attention has focused on the Commission's efforts to establish a European social dimension (Numhauser-Henning and Rönnmar 2013). These efforts have modified national social policies in relatively few areas, such as labour law (see e.g. Burley and

Mattli 1993; Stone Sweet and Caporaso 1998; Weiler 1999; Bercusson 2009). But the expansion of EU competence and QMV indicate that an 'activist' threshold may have been reached. Important, but less visible, have been the policy effects of the single market's development itself: some of these occurred directly, as the Commission, national courts, and the CJEU have reconciled national policy autonomy with the creation of a unified economic space, and others indirectly, through contextual pressures on national welfare states.

We are living through an epoch of transformation in the relations between states and an increasingly global market system (Leibfried and Zürn 2005; Hurrelmann *et al.* 2008; Leibfried and Mau 2008; Castles *et al.* 2010; Leibfried *et al.* 2015), and that transformation is hastened in unforeseen ways by the global economic crisis (Kahler and Lake 2013), strengthening the nation states' hands at least initially. In the EU, both member-state sovereignty and autonomy have diminished (Leibfried 1994; Pierson 1996). Eastern enlargement greatly enhanced territorial inequality, probably lastingly so (Heidenreich 2003). The economic crisis has exacerbated territorial differences: the process is subtle and incremental, but member governments find their revenue bases attacked, welfare-reform options circumscribed, delivery regimes threatened by competition, and administrators obliged to share control of implementation. What is emerging is a distinctive multi-tiered social-policy system, with four distinctive characteristics: a propensity towards joint-decision traps and immobility; a prominent role for courts in policy development; a tight coupling to market-making; and a propensity to harmonize social policies within diversity.

The EU level is inclined towards joint-decision traps and immobility, because European policy-makers are hemmed in by the Council's scepticism, dense social-policy commitments within countries, and limited fiscal or administrative capacities. Compared with other multi-tiered systems, the EU's social policy-making apparatus is bottom-heavy (Pierson and Leibfried 1995; Obinger *et al.* 2005). The centre's capacity for positive social policy is limited; policy evolves rather through mutual adjustment and accommodation. The centre generates various constraints on social-policy development, and no clear mandates for positive action. But member states' capacity to design their own welfare states has weakened considerably (Pierson 1995*b*), and authority, albeit of a largely negative kind, has gravitated towards the EU level. Loss of autonomy and sovereignty occurred without member governments paying much attention. Sometimes—as when Italy pushed for labour mobility in the Treaty of Rome—they actively sought erosion of sovereignty. Resistance to some of the single market's implications jostles with fears of jeopardizing benefits from integration. Resistance is further checked by a ratchet effect. Within the EU, a member state is bound by all CJEU rulings, and can pursue reforms only subject to complicated EU procedures. Diminished member-state authority combined with continued weakness at the EU level restricts the room for innovative policy. Member governments still choose, but from an increasingly restricted menu. As control over social policy increasingly means announcing unpopular cuts, governments are sometimes happy to be constrained in their options. Moving towards a multi-tiered system opens up new avenues for a politics of 'blame avoidance' (Weaver 1986). This dynamic may strengthen national executives against domestic opponents (Milward 1992; Moravcsik 1998). Yet, in escaping from domestic constraints, executives have created new ones. Decision-makers at both levels face serious restrictions of their regulatory capacity, since they have 'locked themselves in' through previous steps towards integration.

As a consequence of these constraints on central policy, many of the requirements that do emanate from the centre are court-driven.[10] A series of CJEU rulings foster activism. Responding to the cases brought before it, the CJEU cannot avoid making what are essentially policy decisions: the court relies on secret simple-majority votes, sheltering it from political immobility, a common feature of the EU legislative process. Only a unanimous vote of the Council can generally undo CJEU decisions on European primary law. The EU system therefore places the CJEU centre stage. Attempts at corporatist policy-making generated much drama surrounding Europe's social dimension, but until recently (Falkner 1998) businesses and unions had little direct involvement in making legally binding requirements for member states' policies. Today, the CJEU's backsliding on balanced corporatism (in *Laval*, etc.) delegitimizes that whole policy-making effort. Generally, legal strategies have the advantage of leaving taxing, spending, and administrative powers at the national level—even more so, as they are regulatory in nature. But a court-led process of social-policy development has its own logic. Legal decisions reflect demands for doctrinal coherence more than substantive debates about policy outcomes. The capacity of reforms built around a judicial logic to achieve substantive goals is limited. Furthermore, courts heed political constraints in prescribing solutions less and may exceed the tolerance of important political actors within the system. In this sense, the scope for a more explicit form of EU policy-making was made difficult because CJEU activism may generate resentment. This is one aspect of the disquiet over the EU's 'democratic deficit' (see Scharpf 2009, 2010).

The EU system of social policy is tightly connected to market-building since social policies intersect in various ways with market systems. In the past, social policy had generally been seen as a spontaneous 'protective reaction' against market expansion (Polanyi 1994), as an outcome of politics *against* markets. In the EU case, however, even in areas such as gender where the EU has been activist, policies have been directly connected to labour-market participation. As the centrality of decisions on labour mobility and free service markets reveals, EU social policy has been an *integral part of* market-building itself. Never before in the world has the construction of markets so visibly and intensively shaped the trajectory of social policies.

From a bird's eye view, the social policies of member states have converged and, especially, all have been exposed to similar reform approaches (stressing pension equivalence to contributions, privatization of some pension elements, and increase of pension age; labour market activation; more prevention in health, better access to health services, etc.). A very different pattern of international learning has evolved, one that has a vertical spin, is characterized by supranationalization through a common moderator, and has a pattern that is more self-enclosed, learning more from other member states than from third countries (U. Becker 2012: 91). Thus, the EU has a propensity to harmonize social policies within diversity.

The overall scope of EU influence has been crucial: national welfare states are now part of a larger, multi-tiered system of social policy. Member governments influence this structure, but no longer fully control it. Such governance occurs at multiple levels. Although the EU's process differs from those found in classical federal states—it is characterized by a weak policy-making centre, court-driven regulation, and strong links with market-making—it is radically different from any national European welfare state (Streeck 2000). One stalemate increasingly needs breaking: 'the policy-making capacities of the union have not been strengthened nearly as much as capabilities at the level of member states have declined' (Scharpf 1994: 219; Offe 2003). While the latter process is a permanent feature of globalization and Europeanization, the former is an optional one, one which can be shaped politically. Perhaps the current euro area crisis will be a catalyst for a reconfiguration of this constellation, since it forces at least the euro area states to step forward or slide backwards (Leibfried 2013). They certainly cannot stand still.

NOTES

1 This chapter is based on, but substantially revised and updated, Leibfried and Pierson (2000) and the more elaborate Leibfried (2005). I am indebted to the editors and to Eberhard Eichenhofer, Bernd Schulte, Dieter Wolf, and especially to Josef Falke, for their help.

2 Recommendations 92/441 (Common Criteria Concerning Sufficient Resources and Social Assistance in Social Protection Systems, 24 June 1992) and 92/442 (Objectives and Policies of Social Security Systems, 27 July 1992) reflect these difficulties and point to social-policy convergence (Maydell 1999). In contrast, in the 1970s harmonization was still the major focus (see Fuchs 2003).

3 Semester politics secure the hegemony of economic and fiscal policy over all other policy areas at the EU level: 'The European Semester represents a yearly cycle of EU economic policy guidance and country-specific surveillance. Each year, the European Commission undertakes a detailed analysis of EU Member States' programmes of economic and structural reforms and provides them with recommendations for the next 12–18 months'. (*http://ec.europa.eu/ economy_finance/economic_governance/the_european_semester/index_en.htm*).

4 U. Becker (2012: 87, under point 2) takes an interesting bird's eye view on European social-policy effects on nation-states relying on Georg Jellinek's (1914) three dimensions of statehood: territorial ties and closure; the personal-citizenship ligaments; and internal organizational control. In this chapter we capture the same dimensions in the prism outlined in Table 11.1.

5 The first regulations were EEC 3/58 and 4/58; later EEC 1408/71 and 574/72. These were extended to third-country nationals in Regulation EC 859/03. After 29 April 2004, all coordination regulation was modernized under Regulation EC 883/04.

6 Eurostat data available on: *http://epp.eurostat.ec.europa.eu/statistics_explained/index.php/ Labour_market_and_labour_force_statistics*. Also see there Table 8: Employed persons aged 15+ taking up residence within the EU other than their country of citizenship or from outside the EU within the last two years, by nationality [and by member state], 2010 and 2012. See also the current issues of *EUREPORT social* on reports on such statistics.

7 Much welfare-state activity falls under 'services' in the terms of the treaty, not only 'social services'. Private insurance is a matter of financial services. So is the (monetary) 'transfer state', when considered as 'economic' activity rather than 'true welfare-state activity', as, for example, when public pensions are shorn of all their redistributive elements in welfare-state reform.

8 Systematic studies on the retrenchment of the welfare state going on in these countries are slow to emerge: on Greece, see Matsaganis (2011) and Papadopoulos and Roumpakis (2012, 2013); on Spain, see Ramos Diaz and Varela (2012); on Ireland, see Considine and Dukelow (2012) and Dukelow (2011); for a general overview see Jónsson and Stefánsson (2013).

9 See tagesschau.de-Archiv, 18 May 2011, *http://tsarchive.wordpress.com/2011/05/18/rentenalter102/*.

10 Falkner (personal communication 2004) pointed us to a budget-driven factor which shapes national thinking on some social problems and policies, insofar as national agencies tailor their projects to specific EU programmes as a way of obtaining complementary EU funding.

FURTHER READING

For the main contours of the subject, see Leibfried and Pierson (1995); the first and last chapters provide a guide to theoretical explanations, and the second chapter details the core contours of social policy. For more recent analyses, see Castles *et al.* (2010), Hantrais (2007), Eigenmüller (2013), Eigenmüller and Börner (2014), and Offe (2003). For an outspoken UK view, see Kleinman (2001). For a broad 'continental' view, see Scharpf (1999: Ch. 4). On eastern enlargement expectations, see Kvist (2004). For an overview of the legal dimension on labour law, see Bercusson (2009) and, on welfare law, see the comprehensive and updated German contributions by Eichenhofer (2013), Schulte (2012), and Fuchs (2013) for which here are no English-language equivalents. On health law, see Mossialos and McKee (2002); on health policy, see Mossialos et al. (2002); and on the European vis-à-vis the basic health-policy types at the national level, Rothgang *et al.* (2010). On the withering away of the services (public utilities) mantle of the welfare state due to EU competition law, see Leibfried and Starke (2008). On the patterns of international policy learning, see Obinger *et al.* (2013). Recent CJEU cases may be consulted on *http://www.curia.eu.int/*. For a comprehensive analysis of the new corporatist perspectives, see Falkner (1998). Both the *Journal of European Social Policy* (1991–), and the *Journal of European Public Policy* (1994–) contain useful articles. Since 1993, regular policy news is reported monthly in the German bulletin, *EUREPORT social* (until Feb. 1995 entitled *EUREPORT*), published by the European representation of the German social insurance (*http://dsv@esip.org*) in Brussels, which is a member of the network European Social Insurance Partners (ESIP; *http://www.esip.org*). No equivalent English source exists.

Bercusson, B. (2009), *European Labour Law*, 2nd edn. (Cambridge: Cambridge University Press).

Castles, F. G., Leibfried, S., Lewis, J., Obinger, H., and Pierson, C. (2010), *The Oxford Handbook of the Welfare State* (Oxford: Oxford University Press).

Eichenhofer, E. (2013), *Sozialrecht der Europäischen Union*, 5th rev. edn. (Berlin: Erich Schmidt).

Eigenmüller, M. (2013), 'Europeanization From Below: The Influence of Individual Actors on the EU Integration of Social Policies', *Journal of European Social Policy*, 23/4: 363–75.

Eigenmüller, M., and Börner, S. (forthcoming 2014), 'Social Security in Europe between Territorialisation, Legitimacy and Identity Formation. Towards a Diachronic Perspective for Analysing Social Policy Rescaling', *European Journal of Social Theory*.

Falkner, G. (1998), *EU Social Policy in the 1990s: Towards a Corporatist Policy Community* (London: Routledge).

Fuchs, M. (2013) (ed.), *Europäisches Sozialrecht*, 6th edn. (Baden-Baden: Nomos).

Hantrais, L. (2007), *Social Policy in the European Union*, 3rd edn. (Basingstoke: Palgrave Macmillan).

Kleinman, M. (2002), *A European Welfare State? European Union Social Policy in Context* (Basingstoke: Palgrave Macmillan).

Kvist, J. (2004), 'Does EU Enlargement Start a Race to the Bottom? Strategic Interaction among EU Member States in Social Policy', *Journal of European Social Policy*, 14/3: 301–18.

Leibfried, S., and Pierson, P. (1995) (eds.), *European Social Policy: Between Fragmentation and Integration* (Washington, DC: The Brookings Institution Press).

Leibfried, S., and Starke, P. (2008), 'Transforming the "Cordon Sanitaire": The Liberalization of Public Services and the Restructuring of European Welfare States', *Socio-Economic Review*, 6/1: 175–82.

Mossialos, E., and McKee, M. (2002), *EU Law and the Social Character of Health Care* (Brussels: PIE-Peter Lang).

Mossialos, E., Dixon, A., Figueras, J., and Kutzin, J. (2002) (eds.), *Funding Health Care: Options for Europe* (Buckingham: Open University Press).

Obinger, H., Schmitt, C., and Starke, P. (2013), 'Policy Diffusion and Policy Transfer in Social Policy in Comparative Social Policy Research,' *Social Policy & Administration* 47/1: 111–29.

Offe, C. (2003), 'The European Model of "Social" Capitalism: Can It Survive European Integration?', *Journal of Political Philosophy*, 11/4: 437–69.

Rothgang, H., Cacace, M., Frisina, L., Grimmeisen, S., Schmid, A., and Wendt, C. (2010), *The State and Health Care: Comparing OECD Countries* (Basingstoke: Palgrave Macmillan).

Scharpf, F. W. (1999), *Governing in Europe: Effective and Democratic?* (Oxford: Oxford University Press).

Schulte, B. (2012), 'Supranationales Recht', in B. Baron von Maydell and F. Ruland (eds.), *Sozialrechtshandbuch (SRH)*, 5th edn. (Baden-Baden: Nomos), 1434–500.

CHAPTER 12

Employment Policy
Between Efficacy and Experimentation

Martin Rhodes

▌Summary

Attempts to put in place an employment policy for the European Union (EU) have been bedevilled by a complex and long-standing regulatory conundrum: how to accommodate member-state diversity in employment regulation and industrial-relations practices while also resolving conflict between member states over both the direction of labour-market reform and the assignment of policy powers to the EU. That conflict has been exacerbated by the post-2008 financial and economic crisis. Nevertheless, by the 2000s the EU had acquired an extensive regulatory system for employment based on three different modes of policy-making and governance: EU legislation and Court of Justice of the European Union (CJEU) hard law that promote employment rights; 'law

(continued...)

via collective agreement' between the EU-level social partners; and the adoption from the late 1990s of a 'soft law' process, the European Employment Strategy (EES). All three have seen ongoing contestation of the form, substance, and level of regulation, as well as persistent power games between member states and the supranational institutions. Only the first two modes, with strong legal bases, have survived this contestation intact, while the EES as an independent process may well be in terminal decline.

Introduction

In recent years, employment policy has moved close to the centre of EU policy preoccupations, after several decades of policy initiatives, institutional and treaty innovations, and experimentation with negotiated and 'new' modes of governance. Employment policy is currently formulated and implemented via several parallel modes of policy-making, including the standard Community method of legislating, including the case law of the CJEU; the post-Maastricht method of 'making law via collective agreement' between European representatives of European workers and employers; and a softer mode of policy-making and innovation via the EES. Their coexistence reveals the frequent renovation of the EU's employment policy architecture, triggered by the 'essentially contested' nature of employment regulation.

These modes of policy-making are similar to those found in other policy domains (see Chapter 4), but in some respects are quite distinct. The classical Community method has been used as much as possible in employment policy as it has the strongest institutional legitimacy and the legislation it produces can be backed up by the CJEU. The latter also plays a critical role in reconciling employment rights with other important EU rights deriving from the freedom of movement (of goods, capital, services, and people)—a role that resides within the 'regulatory mode' discussed in Chapter 4 and that has moved to centre stage in employment-policy conflict and debate in recent years. 'Making of law by collective agreement', which resulted from the merger of the Community method with industrial-relations practices found across the EU, is unique to employment policy, and acquires additional legitimacy from social-partner involvement. The EES has emerged at the interface of the 'regulatory', 'distributional', and 'policy coordination' modes presented in Chapter 4. It seeks coordination among member-state policies but also, importantly, it has sought to by-pass traditional member-state vetoes on supranational influence over national regulatory systems.

Innovation and contestation in this policy system come from four directions. First, the European employment policy-making agenda has shifted over time, following the end of full employment after the 1970s, the challenge of 'welfare without work' in the 1990s, the problems of post-industrial, service-sector employment crea-tion, and the impact of the financial and economic crisis on labour markets. As many countries have discovered, if service-sector employment is to be generated in the private sector, then labour-market regulations may have to be more flexible than hitherto. This has complicated policy-making, producing new national strategies that seek—though not always successfully—to rebalance flexibility for firms and security for employees (Hemerijck *et al.* 2006). It has also provided a major impetus for the EES and the EU's 'flexicurity' agenda. That agenda seeks to facilitate more 'flexible' (fixed-term, part-time, or agency) jobs, by loosening employment regula-tion and using tax and social policies to mitigate any consequent income insecurity.

Secondly, the diversity of European industrial-relations and labour-market regula-tion complicates attempts to tackle both employment protection and promotion at the EU level. Employment regimes are coupled closely with national social security, pen-sions, and unemployment benefit arrangements (see Chapter 11), and employment regulation and industrial relations differ considerably across countries. They range from those in which the state plays a central role through comprehensive labour-market legislation (e.g. in Belgium, France, Germany, Greece, the Netherlands, Luxembourg, Italy, and Spain); to those where the state has traditionally abstained from interven-tion in labour markets (the UK and Ireland); to those where many rules are still set by corporatist-type agreements between employers and unions (Denmark and Sweden). Enlargement to the east has further complicated the mix by adding a fourth model, one in which state intervention is combined with weak levels of unionization and firm-level representation. Such diversity makes EU attempts to intervene in issues regarding the information, consultation, and participation of workers in firms especially problematic.

These four models, it should be noted, do not coincide with other (related) ty-pologies regarding the implementation of EU employment laws (see Falkner *et al.* 2005; Falkner and Treib 2008). Implementation is influenced by factors beyond industrial-relations and labour-market systems, and may be affected by the ways in which the 'double cleavage' manifests in national political systems (see below).

Thirdly, EU employment policy-making in the Commission, the Council, and the European Parliament (EP) has always been riven by a two-way conflict, or double cleavage: that between supporters and opponents of an EU 'social dimension', which would elevate social and employment policy-making to the European level; and that between competing conceptions of how labour markets and social systems should be organized (M. Rhodes 1992). Actors (politicians, trade unionists, and public officials, both national and European) can be found in various locations across this space of political contestation (see Figure 12.1). Although often considered a 'tech-nocratic' part of the EU system, the CJEU has also been subject to the same political currents and pressures, as it has attempted to deal with the often competing claims and priorities of EU economic rights (e.g. the freedom of movement of enterprises) and member-state social and employment protection. The centrality of the CJEU in arbitrating between market freedom and employment rights merits a separate section on the topic later in the chapter.

FIGURE 12.1 The 'double cleavage' in EU employment policy

		Level of policy-making	
		National	European
Nature of regulation	Less/ flexible	Market liberals UK government employers' organizations	Advocates of the EES/ OMC
	More/ rigid	Most national unions	European unions Socialists/social democrats

And fourthly, the financial and economic crisis, which has led to very high rates of unemployment in many European countries, has only added to the controversies surrounding the orientation of EU employment policy and the decisions of the CJEU. Although not originating with the crisis, economic dislocation and higher unemployment have bolstered claims (from national and European trade unions, labour lawyers, and academic critics) that European employment policy has failed and contributes, moreover, to 'negative integration', 'competitive deregulation', the decline of European 'solidarity', and the dominance of a 'neo-liberal' agenda in EU policy-making. Although such claims are often exaggerated, they do signal the appearance of more acute fault lines in the two-way conflict referred to earlier.

The three modes of policy-making and governance

Three modes of policy-making and governance in European employment policy have been developed since the 1960s (Figure 12.2 provides a summary). The first is that of legislated 'rights', based on the classical Community method, and used in fits and starts for employment issues since the 1960s. This mode of policy-making has been based on both unanimity and (after the Single European Act (SEA)) qualified majority voting (QMV) in the Council and implemented via directives. The CJEU acts both as an arbiter of legal controversy over European employment law and a critical actor in its own right in reconciling employment rights with the four freedoms established under the Treaty of Rome regarding the movement of goods, services, capital, and people. The second mode of 'law via collective agreement' has its roots in the social dialogue promoted by the Commission from the 1980s

FIGURE 12.2 Policy instruments and modes of governance

Legal instrument

		Binding	Non-binding
Implementation	Rigid	I. Coercion (Mode one)	III. Targeting (Mode two)
	Flexible	II. Framework regulation (Mode two)	IV. Voluntarism (Mode three)

Source: derived from Treib *et al.* (2007: 14).

between European-level employer and trade union confederations. It was backed by Article 118b EEC (now Art. 154 TFEU), and formally institutionalized in the social-policy agreement (Art. 4; now Art. 155 TFEU) of the Maastricht Treaty on European Union (TEU). This allows the social partners to request a Council decision on an employment-policy agreement, or alternatively the implementation of directives via collective bargaining and 'national practice'. The third mode is the more recent and more experimental EES—a 'new' mode of governance, using the 'open method of coordination' (OMC) and dependent for implementation on persuasion via benchmarking and peer review.

The first mode—legislated rights—employs binding legal instruments (directives) and a rather rigid form of implementation via labour law, backed by the courts (both national and European). This is the most coercive form of governance in this domain of policy. However, treaty requirements insist that employment legislation respects variations in industrial-relations and labour-law systems. Employment directives therefore typically avoid harmonizing objectives and aspire instead to 'partial harmonization' or 'diversity built on common standards' (Kenner 2003: 30–1). Legislation sets *minimum* and not lowest-common-denominator standards, and there is nothing to prevent member states from implementing more stringent rules.

The second mode—'law via collective agreement'—produces binding but flexible instruments (e.g. framework legislation), as well as non-binding but rigid instruments, such as targeted recommendations that contain explicit rules of conduct for workers and employers. This is a flexible form of governance, but one still potentially conducive to effective implementation. Although the impact of directives produced in this pillar has been rather weak, owing to political opposition to upward harmonization and the institutional fragility of this form of law-making, it has nonetheless been responsible for some major legislative advances, as in parental leave and fixed-term and part-time work regulation.

The third mode—the EES and the OMC—uses non-binding and flexible instruments. This is a 'voluntarist' form of 'network' governance with uncertain links between policy inputs and outputs. Open-ended experimentation, in both the form and substance of policy-making, takes priority over the search for efficacy (Citi and Rhodes 2007).

Over time, the second and third modes of policy-making and governance have been added to the first, due largely to the efforts of the European Commission and pro-integration elites to work around member-state vetoes and to neutralize the double cleavage. However, 'new' and experimental modes of governance have not even begun to replace the old. Following from a process of experimental 'venue-shopping' (Baumgartner and Jones 1993) by an EU employment policy advocacy coalition, searching for the best institutional forum, with the least powerful vetoes, all three modes remain important, though with fluctuating fortunes, in promoting and implementing European employment initiatives.

Employment policy-making before Amsterdam

Mode one: the 'Community method' and the EU regulatory model

The history of EU employment legislation has been a tortured one, and despite many failures, the successes have been remarkable. It makes little sense to expect (as many critics do) that EU employment policy should transform the nature of European labour-market regulation in a more thoroughly social democratic direction, or to create, alongside social policies, a supranational tier of entirely upwardly harmonizing labour relations, rules, and regulations to replace national systems. The appropriate comparison is with other federal systems, such as the US or Canada, where social policy has been developed with different degrees of internal variation, across their constituent units (states and provinces), not with Europe's historically most highly-regulated, highest-spending welfare states.

Against all the odds, the Commission has acted as a tireless promoter of new regulatory objectives and rules, often in the face of intense political opposition; the Council has forged agreements on a host of minimum standards, to be implemented differentially in individual member states; and the CJEU has provided frequent strong backing for those standards, even if it has also refrained from overzealous judgments where the treaty basis is unclear. Use of the Community method proper has been restricted to those areas where there has been a sound treaty basis for legislation (e.g. some aspects of health and safety, and gender equality at work), or where the original legal base for directives has been replaced by a stronger treaty alternative.

The Treaty of Rome (EEC) made only ambiguous provision for EU social or employment policy. Articles 117–122 EEC (social provisions) conferred few real powers on the EU institutions. Under Article 117 EEC working conditions and standards were intended to flow from the functioning of the common market, as well as from law, regulation, or administrative action, thus triggering the ensuing conflict between pro-integration forces which relied on the second of these assumptions, and their opponents who invoked the first. Article 118 EEC simply required the Commission to promote cooperation between the member states through studies, opinions, and consultations. Given the market-oriented nature of the Treaty of Rome, social and employment policies were to be used for correcting obvious market failures, not for creating a supranational welfare state (see Chapter 11). National welfare states, it was assumed by the founding philosophy of the European Community, would 'embed' the new economic area in systems of social protection that would remain distinct from one another.

But there was early conflict among member governments over whether and to what extent European rule-making could be used to defend national systems from regulatory competition—still a source of much debate today. Whereas the French believed that social-security harmonization would prevent their high social charges from creating competitive disadvantage, and that their gender-equality provisions should be transferred to the treaty, the Germans were opposed to any legal competence for the supranational authorities in this domain (M. Rhodes 1999). The only substantial concession made to the French was Article 119 EEC on the principle of equal pay for men and women.

As a result, many employment-policy advances from the 1960s on were based on alternative articles. In the early 1970s, the Council of Ministers made extensive use of Articles 100 EEC, the single market provision, and 235 EEC, the 'flexible clause' that allowed the Council to adopt by unanimity any provisions directly related to the 'aims of the Community'. These empowered the Council to issue directives and regulations for the 'approximation' of national regulatory systems, including laws, insofar as they directly affected the establishment and functioning of the common market, and led to directives on dismissals (in 1974) and workers' rights in the event of mergers (1975).

Subsequent treaty revisions sought to strengthen the basis for employment policy, but only meagre steps could be taken, and each time only after major clashes and compromises between member states. In the SEA, Community competences were bolstered, but only for health and safety issues where regulation could be justified as preventing market distortions. Article 118a EEC thus granted the Commission the right of initiative in health and safety legislation after consultation with the Economic and Social Committee, gave the EP a second reading of proposals through the new cooperation procedure, and allowed the Council to act under QMV—with the proviso that small and medium-sized firms were protected from excessive regulatory burdens. Elsewhere in the SEA, although Article 100a EEC introduced QMV for measures essential for the construction of the single market, UK and German opposition ensured that those relating to the free movement of persons and the rights and interests of workers were excluded (M. Rhodes 1992; Majone 1993).

By the time of the TEU, and as the single market deepened and the prospect of currency union came closer, a broader coalition of member states supported European employment rules to prevent a regulatory 'race to the bottom'. Yet opposition from the UK government placed a major constraint on any new supranational transfer of powers, as did the TEU's reinforced subsidiarity principle. The ambition, especially of northern member states (apart from the UK), was to resolve procedural disputes by bringing most areas of labour-market policy under QMV, and to extend Community competence to contractual rights as well as workers' representation and consultation. In the final agreement, adopted as a 'Social Protocol' to the treaty by eleven member states (the UK opted out), only health and safety, work conditions, and equality at work fell under QMV.

Only with the Treaty of Amsterdam (ToA) in 1997—when the New Labour government also revoked the UK's opt-out—was QMV extended to worker information and consultation and the integration of persons excluded from the labour market. But most areas of employment policy remained under the unanimity rule, while pay, the right of association, the right to strike, and the right to impose lock-outs were excluded from Community competence altogether (Art. 137(6) TEC; now Art. 153(5) TFEU).

Given these constraints, the Commission set out to exploit the fragile treaty bases to the maximum, sometimes backed up by CJEU case law, sometimes by undertaking 'soft law' initiatives. Thus, it put forward recommendations and codes of practice to strengthen the application of existing laws, and also issued 'solemn declarations', such as the 1989 Social Charter, or 'social action programmes', designed to further its coalition-building efforts and set the agenda for new EU initiatives. In this way, in the mid-1970s, the Commission's Social Action Programme, adopted by a Council resolution, provided the 'soft law' basis for negotiation and coalition-building around a new series of employment-policy directives (see Kenner 2003: Ch. 2)—a practice that continues to this day.

The Commission also proposed a series of employment initiatives by playing the 'treaty-base game'. This tactic sought to stretch as far as possible the interpretation of 'health and safety' to include directives affecting the workplace, thereby allowing the use of QMV to minimize member-state (especially UK) opposition (M. Rhodes 1995). This broad definition was backed by the CJEU when the UK challenged the Commission's strategy in 1996 (Barnard and Deakin 2002: 405–8). Thus, although the 1989 Social Charter on the basic rights of workers was vague and non-binding, and 'harder' instruments, including a framework directive on rights and a binding workers' statute, were defeated, the Commission's policy activism succeeded in promoting a raft of legislative proposals and gave powerful impetus to social-policy advances subsequently achieved at Maastricht and Amsterdam (M. Rhodes 1991).

None of this produced a more solid legal basis for EU legislation, and a considerable difference in the nature and quality of regulation emerged between those areas of policy where there were firm legal foundations and those where the Commission resorted to 'creative regulation'.

The firm treaty-based measures emerged from the Social Action Programme of the 1970s. Making use of Article 100 EEC (now Art. 115 TFEU), designed for single-market-related laws, and Article 235 EEC (now Art. 352 TFEU), which provided for law-making in areas not covered specifically in the treaty, the Council produced Directive 75/129 on procedural rights under collective redundancies, Directive 77/187 (revised in 2001/23/EC) on rights of employees under changes of ownership of undertakings, and Directive 80/987 (revised in 2002/74/EC) which guaranteed state compensation to employees of insolvent companies. All were deemed appropriate in an era of extensive industrial restructuring, and received CJEU support. Spurred on by the CJEU, which had linked direct effect with the supremacy of Community over national law in key judgments (*Van Gend en Loos*, 1963; *Costa*, 1964; *Van Duyn*, 1974), a half-dozen directives on equal pay and equal treatment in the 1970s and 1980s were based on the more solid Article 119 EEC (now Art. 157 TFEU), which requires unanimity in the Council. CJEU jurisprudence on equal pay and equal treatment also helped to ensure the implementation of these directives (Barnard and Deakin 2002: 402–3). Using Article 118a EEC (now part of Art. 153 TFEU), the first framework directive (80/1107) on health and safety at work produced a series of 'daughter directives' on specific hazards, plus the 'soft law' Council recommendation on a forty-hour week and four weeks' annual paid holiday (a forerunner of the Working Time Directive). A second framework directive on health and safety (89/391) laid down general objectives and obligations on employers and workers, while leaving scope for varied application at the national level, and ultimately produced fourteen daughter directives and a series of action programmes.

Legislation produced in the late 1980s and early 1990s via the 'treaty-base game' was less successful. The effort to define workers' rights as a health and safety issue to avoid a UK veto severely weakened the directives. Thus, the Pregnancy and Maternity Directive (92/85) has ensured health protection, but has been less effective with regard to employment discrimination. The Working Time Directive (93/104)—which provided minimum daily and weekly rest periods, a maximum forty-eight-hour working week, and a minimum of four weeks' annual leave—was innovative in allowing some elements to be implemented through collective agreements. But it excluded a number of sectors, and allowed important derogations for certain member states (e.g. the opt-out for individual workers, currently used by some 16 countries) (Barysch 2013). Subsequent attempts to fill those gaps, with Directive 2003/88/EC and a failed attempt to use 'law via collective agreement' (see the following section) have all been embroiled in controversy. The Young Workers Directive (94/33) created rights for workers under the age of 18, and banned work under the age of 15, but contained many derogations (such as the UK's special entitlement to delay implementation) (Kenner 2003).

Those directives revealed the limits to hard law harmonization across an increasingly diverse set of member states after enlargement to the UK, Ireland, and

Denmark in 1973 and subsequently in the 1980s to Greece, Portugal, and Spain. Labour-market diversity, coupled with the complexity of expanding service-sector employment delayed agreement on an agency work directive, begun in the 1980s, until 2008 (Directive 2008/104/EC). But EU legislation in the 1980s and 1990s did succeed in placing a floor of minimum standards under national systems to prevent a process of competitive deregulation.

Mode two: the social dialogue and law via collective agreement

A key innovation of the Maastricht TEU was its creation of an alternative mode of law-making—an 'inter-professional social dialogue'—involving European employers and trade unions. Several forces converged behind this reform. For the European labour movement, especially the powerful German unions, this new procedure would strengthen the weak European Trade Union Confederation (ETUC), and bolster its influence after the defeat of the unions in the dilution of the 1989 Social Charter. For the European Commission and a number of member states, it would help to counteract obdurate UK opposition to EU employment legislation. And for defenders of national sovereignty, a shift to directives produced at EU level, but implemented via negotiation in the member states, would better accommodate the diversity of European industrial relations.

Europe's employers, acting through the Union of Industrial and Employers' Confederations of Europe (UNICE; since 2007 BusinessEurope: The Confederation of European Business) and the European Association of Craft, Small and Medium-Sized Enterprises (UEAPME) had tried to keep the social dialogue in check, and consistently opposed both EU-level collective bargaining and any enhancement of workers' participation rights in transnational companies. Commission entrepreneurship was therefore critical in gaining this concession. Article 118b EEC (now Art. 154 TFEU) obliged the Commission to promote dialogue between management and labour, and it worked hard to promote discussions between UNICE/UEAPME, the public employers' association—the European Centre of Enterprises with Public Participation and of Enterprises of General Economic Interest (CEEP)—and the ETUC through joint union–employer working parties on the economy, employment, social dialogue, and new technologies.

Originally launched in the Val Duchesse talks in 1985, after 1989 this process became more focused, prioritizing education and training, and producing four joint opinions on the promotion of labour mobility, education, vocational guidance, and management–labour partnerships. They, in turn, provided the groundwork for two key agreements: the September 1990 framework agreement, signed by CEEP and the ETUC, on improving vocational training and health and safety via social dialogue; and, most importantly, a joint submission to the intergovernmental conferences, which in 1991 negotiated the TEU, proposing a new role for the social partners in making and implementing EC policy (M. Rhodes 1995; Falkner 1998).

This submission was inserted almost verbatim into the Social Protocol of the TEU (later integrated into the ToA and TFEU), and allowed for the pursuit of law via collective agreement. All directives, whether adopted by QMV or by unanimity, could henceforth be entrusted to 'management and labour' at their joint request for implementation via collective agreement; the Commission was obliged, before submitting social-policy proposals to the Council, to consult management and labour on the possible consequences of Community action, to which the social partners could respond with an 'opinion' or a 'recommendation'; and, most importantly, the social partners could now negotiate directly the content of Commission proposals, proceeding, given consensus, to a collective agreement. Such agreements could then be implemented by further negotiation in the member states in accordance with their own procedures and practices, or via a Council decision on a proposal from the Commission (see Art. 155(2) TFEU).

The process has had some high-profile failures as well as successes. In numerous instances, it has proven easier to get legislation through the Community method than under this second mode.

The procedure was first used in 1993, when the Commission—engaged in active venue-shopping—presented a proposal on the creation of European works councils (EWCs) that had failed by the normal legislative route. In the event, the social-dialogue channel also failed, and the directive—under which management must institute forums for informing and consulting employees in all companies with more than 1,000 employees and more than 150 employees in at least two member states—was finally passed under the Social Protocol, using the standard legislative process, in 1994 (Directive 94/45/EC). A revision of that directive, submitted to the social partners in 2004, also failed to secure their joint agreement and was approved instead (with strengthened consultation procedures and representation rules) via the standard legislative path in Directive 2009/38/EC—though social-partner consultation was important for revising the final Commission text of the law (Laulom 2010).

An attempt by the Commission to steer a temporary agency work directive through this new channel also failed: consigned to the social partners after legislative failure in the early 1990s, it was transferred back to the legislative route in 2001. It eventually emerged as Directive 2008/104/EC in a form that, according to its critics, has done little to protect agency workers from exploitation (e.g. Contouris and Horton 2009), while others (e.g. Schlachter 2012) take a more positive view. But like the EWC Directive, social-partner support was crucially important: the employers in the sector (Eurociett) and the union (Uni-Europa) produced a joint declaration in May 2008 that helped to facilitate the political deal. In 2011–12, social-partner discussions on a revision of the Working Time Directive (2003/88/EC) in line with CJEU jurisprudence (which had strengthened the law in a decade's worth of jurisprudence, including *Simap, Jaeger, Gerhard Schultz-Hoff*, and *Singer and Others*) collapsed in disagreement over ending derogations and opt-outs, and counting 'on-call work' towards working time—none of which the employers would sanction.

But other proposals were successfully translated into social-framework agreements, also after failing under the legislative route. Indeed, nine collective agreements have been turned into directives since 1995, including four intersectoral agreements, and five agreements stemming from the EU-level sectoral social dialogue. Intersectoral agreements led to Directives 96/34/EC on parental leave, 97/81/EC on part-time work, and 99/70/EC on fixed-term work. In June 2009, the social partners began discussions to revise the Parental Leave Directive that they had agreed to in 1996, presenting a series of proposals that were inserted into a new directive and passed virtually unchanged by the Council (2010/18/EU). Not only was the upgrade significant—parental leave was extended from three to four months; one of those months should be non-transferable to encourage both parents to take leave; and all contract types are affected, including fixed-term and part-time work—but this was also something of a milestone as the first successful joint revision, by union and employer representatives, of a social-partner agreement.

As for the sectoral social dialogue, since 1988 a total of forty dialogue committees have been created covering 145 million workers, producing some 500 texts in the form of joint opinions, autonomous agreements, and the five agreements that have been given legal force via directives: 1999/63 on the working time of seafarers (modified in 2009/13); 2000/79/EC on the working time of workers in civil aviation; 2005/47 on the working conditions of mobile workers in cross-border services (railways); 2009/13 which amended the 1996 directive on the working time of seafarers; and 2010/32/EU on the prevention of injuries from sharps (needles, scalpels, blades, disposable scissors, suture equipment, broken test tubes, and glass) in hospitals and the health-care sector (Broughton 2010).

This legislation does provide real regulatory added value, but its critics argue that its minimal standards and flexibility have limited its impact to the least well-regulated countries. The 1996 directive on parental leave has been criticized as a lowest-common-denominator agreement (though its revised version makes significant improvements); the directive on part-time work has been regarded as weak, consisting of a series of non-obligatory provisions unlikely to remove discrimination against this category of workers; and the directive on fixed-term work has been called a 'missed opportunity' to regulate one of the most insecure forms of agency work: in most member states little or no change was required to existing law (Kenner 2003: 290). Cross-sectoral accords or 'joint opinions'—such as those agreed to by the social partners in March 2005 on a 'framework of actions' in four priority areas of gender equality in the workplace, or in October 2007 on 'guidelines for defining 'flexicurity'—are really statements of good intent and therefore obviously even weaker.

A more optimistic interpretation argues that this mode of governance can act as 'a catalyst for mutual learning' (Deakin 2007: 18ff.), a favourable view usually reserved for the OMC (see the following section). Deakin points out that the part-time and fixed-term work directives have stimulated policy innovations that have strengthened contract requirements in the UK, and loosened them in more highly regulated

Germany; while in both countries, the Parental Leave Directive has created the parameters for a new debate on the subject, and the definition of a new consensus—as revealed in the relatively problem-free passage of the revised Parental Leave Directive in 2010.

Such legislation also provides the opportunity for subsequent 'hardening' by CJEU case law as, for example, in the July 2006 judgment in *Adeneler* (C-212/04) and the April 2008 ruling in *Impact* (C-268-06), both of which bolstered the implementation of Council Directive 99/70 on fixed-term work (following the social partners' framework agreement), regarding the definition of successive fixed-term employment contracts, coverage of both public- and private-sector workers and the importance of national law in preventing the abuse of such contracts. CJEU case law between 2000 and 2004 (in *Bofrost*, *Kühne & Nagel*, and *ADS Anker*) was also important for upgrading the European Works Council Directive (94/45) in 2010 (2009/38) by clarifying, for example, employers' obligations to obtain and transmit information to workers' representatives. Although the social partners did not succeed in passing this law themselves, their influence over its content, and the interaction with CJEU jurisprudence, makes this another example of successful policy-making hybridity.

Nevertheless, and regardless of a commitment by the social partners at the European Council in Laeken in 2001 to a new and more autonomous bipartite social dialogue (backed by a Commission communication on the future of the social dialogue in 2002, reiterated in the presentation of the social partners' work programme for 2003–5, and reaffirmed in 2005 at the twentieth-anniversary social dialogue summit), progress in this mode of policy-making is still heavily dependent on the Commission acting as an entrepreneurial prime mover, typically by threatening (and taking) recourse to hard law in the absence of social-partner agreement (Keller 2008; Smismans 2008).

Employment policy innovations post-Amsterdam

Mode three: the EES and the OMC

The launch in 1997 of the EES marked a radical departure from the existing two policy modes, adding employment creation to European policy ambitions and seeking to extend EU influence to jealously guarded areas of national sovereignty.

In part, the EES was a political response by pro-social-dimension elites and interest groups to economic and monetary union (EMU), which limited the use by individual countries of expansionary monetary and fiscal policies to boost employment (see Chapters 7 and 11). But it was also a response by the same employment-policy coalition to failures and blockages in the two existing policy modes, the creation of a new venue for channelling issues that has been opposed in other fora, and a further attempt, therefore, to overcome the enduring 'double cleavage' in the politics of EU social and employment policy.

The EES began to take form following the Delors Commission's White Paper on *Growth, Competitiveness, and Employment* in 1993 (Commission 1993*b*). Attempting to blend the priorities of European social democrats, Christian democrats, and liberals, the tactical aim was to strike a new political balance between notions of solidarity and competitiveness behind the EU's 'social dimension'. But due to counter-pressures from several member states, including Germany and the UK, there was little real progress at the time (Goetschy 2003; Mosher and Trubek 2003). The Commission spurred progress along by striking alliances with key European political groups (most importantly the Party of European Socialists) and by organizing peer pressure on the most reluctant member states.

An agreement to create an EES was reached at the European Council in Amsterdam in 1997. The goals and procedures of the EES were set out in Title VIII (later XI) of the ToA (Arts. 125–30 TEC; now Arts. 145–50 TFEU) on employment. The main objective was a high level of employment, to be achieved by promoting a 'skilled, trained and adaptable workforce and labour markets responsive to economic change'. The guidelines were never binding—an essential feature for the compromise that eventually brought all member states on board. But by its inclusion in the ToA and then TFEU, the EES became part of the processes in which member states are obliged to participate.

The process of policy deliberation was put into effect at the European Council in Luxembourg in November 1997, since when it has changed considerably. The first set of (nineteen) European Employment Guidelines (EEGs) adopted that year were based on four 'pillars': employability, entrepreneurship, adaptability, and equal opportunities, each containing between three and seven guidelines. The 2000 European Council in Lisbon confirmed its support for the EES and committed the member states to striving for 'full employment', coupled with new quantitative objectives: a 70 per cent overall employment rate and a 60 per cent female employment rate by 2010. Successive Council presidencies, held by social-democratic governments, acted closely in alliance with the Commission and the EP to sustain the coalition and propel the EES forward, adding new targets over the next several years, including older workers (a 50 per cent employment rate) and childcare (to cover 33 per cent of children under 3 and 90 per cent between the age of 3 and mandatory school age).

The OMC was also extended to other areas of policy such as pensions and social exclusion, giving this new form of policy formulation greater scope, and in principle greater legitimacy (van Riel and van der Meer 2002). Nevertheless, the EES remained highly contested terrain, both ideologically and in power games between the Council and the Commission, and was subjected to a series of ongoing and destabilizing reforms which, by 2013, had severely reduced its role and visibility as an independent policy process. In the view of one recent appraisal (Peña-Casas 2013), 'the EES has faded into the background, to such an extent that we could ask if it still exists'.

The rise and demise of the EES as a 'new mode of governance'

The purported key characteristics of the EES—the heterarchical participation of actors; a 'new' problem-solving logic based on deliberation and 'policy learning'; and the use of benchmarking and reference to 'best practice'—have all been considered advantages over traditional modes of policy-making by its advocates (Scott and Trubeck 2002; Cohen and Sabel 2003; Borrás and Jacobsson 2004). But regardless of these theoretical advantages, ultimately the EES was a political strategy and its success or failure determined by hard political realities. Those include subjection to the same political conflicts over sovereignty and the state–market balance that have characterized the two other policy modes. But given its lack of strong institutionalization, the 'soft law' EES has been much more vulnerable than hard-law processes with stronger constitutional—and therefore institutional—strength (Rhodes and Visser 2011).

Formally, the roles of the EES actors and relations between them can be set out in terms of the EES 'policy coordination' cycle, which has been reformed substantially several times since its initial inauguration—reflecting a high level of institutional instability and vulnerability to shifts in member-state influence, the left–right balance in the European Council, and the 'ideology' of the Commission. It was reformed first at the European Council in Brussels in June 2003, not only to 'mainstream' the EES within the Lisbon Agenda, but also in response to complaints from the member states over the complexity of EES guidelines, the overlap between the EES and other processes, and the duplication of work for national officials (see Jacobsson 2004). The cycle was reformed again with the relaunch of the Lisbon strategy—renamed the Growth and Employment Strategy (GES)—by the Barroso Commission in 2005, and again following the adoption of the Europe 2020 Strategy in 2010.

In each of these iterations, the process has been structured around jointly agreed guidelines. The Commission draws up the guidelines, which are then endorsed by the Council via QMV, and policy objectives are then decided. Before 2002, they took the form of 20 or so guidelines, organized around the four pillars of employability, entrepreneurship, adaptability, and equal opportunities, but were reduced thereafter to ten 'results-oriented' priorities structured around three objectives: full employment, quality and productivity at work, and social cohesion and inclusion. In 2005, those objectives were further reformed under member-state pressure via the 'European Employment Taskforce' (EET), chaired by Wim Kok, to focus more closely on 'jobs and growth' and the Commission's new 'flexicurity' agenda (in 2007, eight common principles of flexicurity were adopted by the Council). Also in 2005, those revised EES objectives were integrated alongside broader macroeconomic goals into the Broad Economic Policy Guidelines (BEPGs; see Chapter 7).

In the most recent reform of the EES guidelines, in conjunction with the adoption of the Europe 2020 Strategy (Commission 2010*b*), two core 'Headline Targets' were adopted for employment and the labour market (75 per cent of people aged

20–64 in work, and 40 per cent of 30 to 34-year-olds having completed tertiary-level education, including vocational training), supported by three guidelines (focusing on labour-market participation and skills acquisition), and flanked by two flagship initiatives—*Youth on the Move* and *Agenda for New Skills and Jobs*. These flagship initiatives are supported by several support measures: an 'Employment Package', a 'Social Investment Package', and the 'Youth Guarantee'.

In its original pre-2005 formulation, the Commission made individual recommendations based on these guidelines, endorsed by the Council, to each member state. The recommendation tool, as defined in the ToA, has been a key element of influence distinguishing the EES from other OMCs. Member governments then prepared their national action programmes (NAPs) in response to the recommendations. These were then 'peer reviewed' in the so-called 'Cambridge process'— a closed two-day meeting of the Employment Committee (EMCO), which has two delegates from each member state and two members from the Commission, followed by bilateral meetings on the NAPs between the latter and government representatives.

But after 2005, reflecting the inherent instability and vulnerability of this 'soft law' process, the annual NAPs were effectively merged with the new three-year National Reform Programmes (NRPs), which combined macro- and micro-economic goals recommendations with those of employment policy. The Europe 2020 Strategy altered the policy architecture yet again. Since 2010, with the creation of the 'European Semester' (which coordinates macroeconomic, budgetary, and structural reform) (see Chapter 7), the NRPs are submitted annually by member states along with their medium-term budgetary strategies in response to strategic objectives provided by the Council, informed by the Commission's Annual Growth Survey (AGS) (Weishaupt and Lack 2011).

This sequence of reforms has integrated employment policy more closely with the core economic objectives of the Commission and those of the member states. But it has also reduced the visibility of employment issues, the detail in member state reporting on outcomes, and the capacity of the Commission to monitor them, as well as the respective roles of EMCO, the Commission's Directorate-General for Employment, Social Affairs and Inclusion (DG EMPL), and the Employment, Social Policy, Health and Consumer Affairs Council (EPSCO) vis-à-vis the Directorate-General for Economic and Financial Affairs (DG ECFIN) and the Council of Economic and Finance Ministers (Ecofin) (Zeitlin 2008). That process of rationalization has been compounded by the new system of economic governance in the EU that has emerged during the economic and financial crisis, with its much stronger focus than in the past on budgetary discipline, as enshrined in a series of EU budgetary pacts.

As shown by Peña-Casas (2013: 1348), as a consequence of this decade-long process of reform, the EES has disappeared—first from European rhetoric and second as a set of distinctive OMC-like procedures. The key principles of the EES—activation, employability, adaptability, and flexicurity—survive within the Europe 2020 Strategy, but only in the form of 'quasi-concepts' (Peña-Casa 2013: 136) whose utility for soft-governance processes derives precisely from their ambiguity, malleability, and susceptibility to multiple and even competing interpretations in the EU's multi-level policy-making process. The experimental processes of consensus-seeking deliberation so strongly hyped by its founders have thus been marginalized.

It is tempting to attribute this fading into insignificance (as many do) to the economic crisis and its empowerment of a neo-liberal coalition between key European institutions and powerful member states. However, it also stems in large part from the nature of this soft-governance policy instrument as such. The EES was always ineffective, even when its policy centrality seemed more secure. As for its supposedly 'heterarchic' character, the participation of the social partners and even the EP was always limited and its policy cycle rather closed, elitist, and arguably much less democratic and accountable than the standard Community method (Syrpis 2002, 2008). As a means of shaping reform, the NAP procedures were insufficiently integrated into national decision-making structures and budget allocations to make them matter, and national politicians were highly resistant to interference with their own policy priorities (Begg *et al.* 2010). Within member states, left–right partisan ideology clearly prevailed over the EU policy orientations imparted by the EES/OMC (Delfani 2013). Less a deliberative process of policy-learning or best-practice diffusion, the EES could best be described as a 'double standards game' in which governments endorsed European guidelines, but frequently failed to take responsibility for their implementation at home (Jacobsson and Vifell 2003, 2007).

The problems afflicting this form of governance are therefore twofold. The first is the institutional weakness that stems from the legal and institutional ambiguities and uncertainties surrounding forms of 'soft' law and governance as such (the fate of the other social OMCs is similarly unclear). The second is that there has never been any real political support from a coalition of member-state governments (even social democratic ones) for a hardening or upgrading of the rules for employment-policy coordination. This has been revealed frequently, as in intergovernmental conflict within EMCO over strengthening the 'naming-and-shaming' ambitions of the Commission regarding member-state employment-policy performance (see Jobelius 2003), and regarding the deployment of financial resources to help meet EES objectives. In sum, far from neutralizing the 'double cleavage' generating political conflict in European employment policy, the EES has clearly fallen victim to it.

A new source of contestation: social and employment versus economic rights in EU law

As noted at numerous points previously, the CJEU has been a central actor in EU employment policy as a critical component of the standard Community method (see also Chapter 11). It has played an important role in extending the influence of employment-related legislation by building up a powerful body of jurisprudence and by striking down numerous challenges to the Commission's broad interpretation of sometimes ambiguous treaty foundations. More generally, the CJEU's case law has largely reinforced the view of social and employment policy that stems from the Treaty of Rome: that a floor of minimum EU policy provisions, rather than an extended upward harmonization of welfare states, is the proper objective, and that the free movement of goods, persons, services, and capital should not undermine national systems of social protection.

Nevertheless, the CJEU's position regarding the 'fair balance' between those systems and the four freedoms has shifted over time, as it has sought to respond to political pressures from other Community institutions and the member states in interpreting the treaty and refining its earlier jurisprudence (see also Chapter 11). It is the recent shift in a more 'market-friendly' direction that has raised enormous controversy about the compatibility of recent CJEU case law and fundamental social and employment rights, notably the right to strike.

As the single market has been consolidated, and as many barriers to the freedom of movement have been struck down, national employment laws, implementing fundamental rights (e.g. the right to assembly and strike), have also been targeted as constituting such barriers, and the CJEU has not been unsympathetic to such claims. This is not the first time that such controversy has been engendered by CJEU intervention. Thus, in a neo-liberal phase that followed the landmark free-trade-promoting judgments in *Dassonville* (1974) and *Cassis de Dijon* (1979) (see Chapter 5), the court struck down a series of national laws that it deemed to impede free trade, including (in *Macrotron*, 1990) the German Federal Employment Office's monopoly of job placement (Eliasoph 2007–8).

Yet the court's deregulatory enthusiasm was dampened by the prospects of a major political clash over state sovereignty that threatened to undermine its legitimacy. In 1991, in both *Keck* (1993), regarding a French law prohibiting the resale of commercial goods for lower than their purchase price, and *Poucet and Pistre* (also 1993), in which a French insurance fund for the self-employed was claimed to contravene Community competition law, the CJEU sided with national regulators, and applied the principle of 'solidarity' to protect social-welfare schemes from competition rules. In 1999, in *Albany*, the court took a cue from the new social provisions in the ToA to exclude from Article 81(1) (now Art. 101 TFEU)—which prohibits agreements that restrict or distort competition—a supplementary pension scheme negotiated by Dutch social partners in the textile industry. In all of these cases, the protection of national social regulations was privileged above competing claims on behalf of market freedoms (Eliasoph 2007–8; Barnard 2008b).

However, CJEU case law did not side with national employment regulation in all cases. In 1990, in *Rush Portuguesa*, the court ruled against a requirement imposed by the French state on a Portuguese service provider that it obtain work permits for its Portuguese employees. But at the same time it reassuringly stated that EU law does not prevent member states from extending their legislation or collective labour agreements to any person employed—even temporarily—within their territory, no matter where the employer is established. This seemed more consistent with *Keck* and *Poucet and Pistre* (and their accommodation of national regulations) than with the free-trade judgments made in *Cassis* and *Dassonville* (Syrpis 2007).

But in 1991 in *Säger*—the source of current controversy (see later in this section)—the court ruled that only an 'imperative' reason relating to 'the public interest', could justify a 'proportionate' discrimination or restriction against a provider of services based in another member state. This judgment extended the market-access priority applied by the CJEU to cross-border services to the sphere of employment. The implication was that a business wishing to set up in another member state could justifiably claim that complying with that state's employment laws would restrict its freedom of movement (Barnard 2008*b*).

Much recent EU legislation has in practice sought to protect national systems of employment regulation from deregulatory pressures stemming from greater freedom of movement, partly in response to earlier CJEU rulings that might endanger such regulations. Thus, in an effort to clarify *Rush*, the Posted Workers Directive (96/71/EC) set out to ensure that workers posted to another member state are guaranteed the working conditions and pay in effect in that state, including collectively agreed provisions and arbitration. Ten years later, the Services Directive (2006/123/EC) (see Chapter 5) exempted all matters coming under the Posted Workers Directive. The final version explicitly stated that the Services Directive does not affect national labour law, social-security legislation, or the exercise of fundamental rights (Syrpis 2007; Barnard 2008*b*).

And yet, between 2005 and 2010, four highly controversial CJEU judgments resurrected the market-access priority and the principle established in *Säger* that only an 'imperative' reason relating to 'the public interest', could justify a 'proportionate' discrimination or restriction against a provider of services based in another member state. In *Viking* (2007) a strike by the Finnish Seaman's Union against a Finnish company that flagged a ferry operating out of Helsinki as Estonian was judged to be an interference with the company's rights under Article 43 TEC (Art. 49 TFEU) preventing restrictions on the freedom of establishment. In *Laval* (2007) Swedish union action against a Latvian company building a school in Sweden, using Latvian workers who were paid 40 per cent less per hour than locally bargained wage rates for Swedish workers, was judged unlawful under Article 49 TEC (Art. 56 TFEU) on the freedom to provide services. And in *Rüffert* (2008) a decision by the state of Lower Saxony to terminate a contract with a German firm employing Polish workers at wages 46 per cent lower than the locally applicable collectively bargained wage was similarly judged to violate Article 49.

In both *Laval* and *Rüffert*, the CJEU argued that the Posted Workers Directive sets out *maximum* rather than *minimum* protection of workers, and that in all three cases the regulations being defended by national actors were 'disproportionate' and 'unjustified' (Davies 2008; Kilpatrick 2009). Further, in *Commission v. Federal Republic of*

Germany (2010) German local authorities were judged to have contravened the EU's public procurement directives (92/50/EEC and 2004/18/EC) by awarding a services contract for occupational old-age pensions above a certain size to bodies referred to in a collective agreement, rather than by a call for tenders at the EU level (Syrpis 2011).

All four judgments raise important questions about the robustness of numerous social and employment rights in the EU, including the right to strike and the right to establish national standards by collective bargaining if and when subject to a strict application of the court's proportionality test.

Interestingly enough, neither the ratification of the ToL nor its attribution of legally binding status to the EU Charter of Fundamental Rights (2000), which defends but does not guarantee the right to collective bargaining and action (including the right to strike), is likely to have any impact on the CJEU's decisions, or on EU employment policy-making as such, for those rights are already acknowledged by the court—it is simply their 'proportionate use' that is at stake. Much more important in protecting national employment regulations against incursions based on the freedom of movement will be political pressure from member states and from national and EU-level organized labour and the new threat to CJEU legitimacy that such pressure will create—including challenges to the applicability and supremacy of EU legislation (Bücker and Warneck 2010).

The controversy surrounding the passage of the so-called 'Monti II Regulation' (based on a report by former European Competition Commissioner, Mario Monti) reveals the emergence of such pressure—and the problems of containing it. In 2010, the Commission's proposal No. 30 of its document on 'relaunching the internal market' (Commission 2010c) announced legislation to resolve the dilemmas created by *Viking et al.* But the proposed regulation (Commission 2012k) contained no clarification of CJEU jurisprudence regarding the protection of workers' fundamental rights: it simply repeated the need to use the 'proportionality principle' in reconciling the freedom to provide services and the right to strike. It provoked strong protest from the ETUC (which called for a new constitutionalization of fundamental social rights in the EU treaties) and national unions, and twelve national parliaments adopted 'reasoned opinions' expressing concerns related to the added value of the draft regulation, the choice of legal basis, and EU competence to regulate this matter. The proposal was withdrawn in September 2012 in the face of member-state opposition (Ashiagbor 2013).

European labour lawyers (e.g. Syrpis 2008 and Ewing 2012) argue that accession to the European Convention for the Protection of Human Rights and Fundamental Freedoms (ECHR), provided for in Article 6(2) TEU (Art. 281 TFEU), may provide a solution under Articles 10 and 11 regarding freedom of expression and assembly and association. For, unlike the CJEU which takes the economic goal of free movement as its starting point and then assesses the proportionality of any restrictions placed on it, the European Court of Human Rights (ECtHR) does the reverse: it begins with convention rights and assesses the proportionality of restrictions on those rights. ECtHR case law (e.g. *Demir and Baykara*, 12 Nov. 2008 and *Enerji Yapi-Yol Sen*,

21 Apr. 2009) confirms the right of workers to engage in collective bargaining and collective action. In the event of EU accession to the ECHR, there is bound to be a clash between CJEU and ECtHR jurisprudence.

Assessment: EU employment policy—a multi-tiered opportunity structure?

This chapter began by noting that employment policy poses some of the most difficult regulatory problems in the EU, precisely because both the assumption of Community competences and the nature of regulation itself in this domain have been so fiercely contested. But, over time, an EU employment advocacy coalition, spanning the member states, the EP, the Commission, the CJEU, and the European labour movement (and, one should add, European labour lawyers) has kept the issue alive. Opposition has been evaded or diffused by shifting the parameters of the regulatory system and, via a process of 'venue-shopping',—seeking alternative institutional channels conducive to the integrationist project in employment policy. That process has included a creative interpretation of the treaty base, the transfer of legislation to the 'inter-professional dialogue', and, finally, an attempt to shift emphasis to the soft-law-based EES.

The success of that process has been variable, and each of the three policy modes has had fluctuating fortunes, with the third mode—the EES—now in terminal decline as an independent policy forum and viable alternative to the other two. Together, these modes created, at their recent apogee, what could be considered either a barely legitimate layering of institutional innovations (Wendler 2004) or a multi-tiered opportunity structure, holding out the possibility of a complementary or integrated use of policy instruments and governance modes. Now the choice of options appears to be restricted to the standard legislative route or law via collective bargaining.

In contrast to the soft-law, voluntarist EES/OMC, and the many claims made in the past on its behalf, the Community method of legislation has remained highly active and is the most successful in launching and securing political support for new initiatives (Arnold *et al.* 2004). EU employment legislation since 2000 includes a substantial list of measures:

- the Employment Equality Framework Directive (2000/78/EC) to combat employment discrimination on the grounds of religion, disability, age, or sexual orientation;

- the Council Regulation governing the creation of a European Company Statute (2157/2001) and an accompanying directive on worker involvement (2001/86/EC);

- a directive regulating the transfer of undertakings (2001/23/EC) and protecting workers' rights (especially against dismissal) if a workplace is transferred from one employer to another;
- a controversial framework directive on national information and consultation rules (2002/14/EC), under which firms over a certain size (the threshold is twenty or fifty depending on the member state) must put in place mechanisms for informing and consulting employees;
- agreement on a directive implementing the principle of equal treatment between men and women in the access to and supply of goods and services (2004/113/EC);
- a directive (merging earlier directives on employment equality) on the principle of equal opportunities and equal treatment of men and women in matters of employment and occupation (2006/54/EC);
- a directive regulating temporary agency work (2008/104/EC); and
- and a directive (2008/94/EC) ensuring payment of employees' outstanding claims to salary and pensions contributions in the event of employer insolvency (member states to set up an institution to guarantee the payments).

Some of these directives have stronger effects than others, but together they amount to an extraordinary corpus of EU law with extensive impact across the EU of twenty-eight member states, as well as non-EU members of the European Economic Area.

Several proposals for new directives have entered the legislative process since 2008, although with uncertain fortunes. This has been attributed (rather simplistically) by some to the 'neo-liberal' orientation of the Barroso Commission. It is more accurately explained by heightened political friction surrounding employment policy during the post-2008 economic crisis and the sovereignty issues raised by recent CJEU case law. These proposals include the Common Position in the Council (EC No. 23/2008) to amend and strengthen the Working Time Directive (which failed both the standard Community-method and law-via-bargaining routes by 2012); the 2012 proposal for a regulation on the exercise of the right to take collective action within the context of the economic freedoms of the single market (the so-called 'Monti II Regulation'), which was rejected by member-state parliaments; and a proposal for a directive concerning the enforcement of the provision applicable to the posting of workers in the framework of the provision of services which aims to increase protection for posted workers, and like 'Monti II', to clarify the conflict between the primacy of freedom to provide services and collective employment rights (for an overview, see Ashiagbor 2013; on 'Monti II', see Commission 2012j).

Beyond the controversy over the exercise of collective rights, however, the CJEU continues to play a critical role, both in driving the expansion of employment rights (as in the case of the 2006 Employment Equality Directive, which responded to

CJEU case law in *Barber*, *Bestuur van het Algemeen Burgerlijk Pensioenfonds*, and *Pirkko Niemi*) and in enforcing directives underpinning those rights, as in December 2004 when five member states—Austria, Finland, Germany, Greece, and Luxembourg—were referred by the Commission to the CJEU for failing to transpose the 2000 Framework Equality Directive. The CJEU continues to clarify and strengthen the implementation of the Working Time Directive (as in C-78/11 *ANGED*) on annual leave entitlements, even as its revision in the light of previous jurisprudence continues to fail in the legislative process. The CJEU's consistent support of *individual* employment rights and their reinforcement across the member states contrasts with the ambiguity that now prevails (as a result of *Viking et al.*) in its defence of *collective* rights to take industrial action or to bargain on behalf national social-policy entitlements.

The second mode—the more experimental social dialogue—appears to have weakened over time. With the exception of the more limited sectoral dialogues and related directives, such as the 2008 agreement and directive to improve working conditions in the maritime industry, the transfer of draft directives from the first legislative mode dried up in the 2000s. The focus of the social dialogue has apparently shifted to 'new generation' framework agreements. The latter include agreements on 'teleworking' (2002), 'work-related stress' (2004), 'harassment and violence at work' (2007), and 'achieving an inclusive labour market (2010). These agreements are well intentioned but, very much in line with Europe's employers' associations' preferences, do not have the force of a directive, are not subject to threats by the Commission to proceed with directives, and their implementation is heavily shaped by ongoing national power games between social partners and the state (Larsen and Andersen 2007; Keller 2008). Nevertheless, the 2010 Parental Leave Directive was successfully negotiated by the European social partners, made significant advances on its 1996 predecessors, and was adopted with little ado by the Council. There appears to be life in the second mode yet.

Moreover, the Commission has not become any less entrepreneurial in promoting this and related fora for exerting influence in employment policy, especially in using unions and employers as a sounding board for future legislative proposals, to help to set its agenda for future policy initiatives, and to police the implementation of existing legislation. Examples include the Commission's 2005 call on social partners to begin negotiations on promoting and monitoring best-practice guidelines for industrial restructuring and the operation of EWCs, which helped in the adoption of a recast Works Councils Directive in December 2008 (2009/38/EC); the Commission's regular consultation of the social partners with a view to developing new employment legislation (e.g. on the issue of the cross-border transfer of undertakings in 2007, on transnational company agreements in 2012, and on undeclared work in 2013); its use of unions to report on the implementation of employment guidelines in member states; and the mobilization of social partners across Europe behind the new integrated Commission programme for employment and social solidarity, *Progress*. *Progress* replaced previously separate action programmes in 2006 on anti-discrimination, gender equality, the fight against social exclusion, and employment measures, and promotes network creation, projects, and partnerships between governments, non-governmental organizations (NGOs), and employers' and workers' organizations to help to bring national policy reforms into line with European guidelines. Such initiatives that foster the creation of national advocacy coalitions continue to provide the Commission with a degree of access to, and (soft) influence over, member-state policy-making that it would not otherwise enjoy.

The third mode, the EES, which has tried over many years to formalize and institutionalize this kind of 'soft power' in changing member-state employment policies and priorities, had three principal aims: cooperation among actors, the coordination of national employment policies, and convergence in outcomes (Jacobsson and Vifell 2003). But there was never any clear consensus or institutional commitment to these goals across the EU member states, or to developing further more effective means for achieving them. Opposition to its marginalization has come from the European labour movement and some parts of the EP, but there have been no high-visibility attempts to resurrect the EES/OMC by key member states. Some (e.g. Vanhercke 2013) hold out the prospect of it being redeveloped 'under the radar' by key actors in DG EMPL, EMCO and its social-policy equivalent, the Social Protection Committee (SPC), but its future is highly uncertain, to say the least. One should note in this context the narrowing of employment objectives to 'flexicurity' in recent Commission documents—such as the 'Strategic Report on a Renewed Lisbon Strategy for Growth and Jobs' (Commission 2007b) that was presented to the 2008 spring European Council—a trend that mirrors the parallel narrowing of priorities in the EES noted earlier. Both the ETUC and the EP have lobbied against such developments, though without much success, seeking a more 'balanced' approach that would strengthen the 'social dimension' of EU employment guidelines within the Lisbon strategy.

What, then, is the future of EU employment policy (and EU social policy more generally) given the 'regulatory conundrum' that has always bedevilled it and the trifurcation of policy formulation that has emerged in response? A potential solution (e.g. Scharpf 2002) to the trade-off between efficacy and experimentation in favour of the former in both the weaker social dialogue and the EES has always been to strengthen the links between these 'softer' modes and the still vigorous first mode of policy-making. That aim could be achieved, it has been argued, by using instruments of soft law (e.g. peer review and benchmarks) to facilitate the implementation of hard law, or by using hard law to ensure the implementation of soft-law initiatives. Examples of such combinations have been referred to earlier, and point to the potential for deploying the Community method, European social agreements, and the coordination mechanisms of the EES together in pushing the employment-policy agenda forward. In theory, this could give the necessary hierarchy, or 'legal backbone' required by soft-law policy-making (Rhodes and Visser 2011) and create scope for regulatory innovation across employment-policy modes of governance.

But there are clear limits to such institutional and regulatory creativity. Even if the EES had remained a strong and independent alternative for exercising policy influence, its combination with other venues was restricted by its lack of democratic and constitutional legitimacy, and by the absence of clarity in relations between the EES/OMC and the standard Community method (Senden 2010). Furthermore, the account of EU employment policy presented previously suggests that the more standard processes, as well as the substance of employment measures, will remain politically highly contested—even in the absence of such high-risk initiatives—and their operation far from smooth. Indeed, the battle has only just begun regarding the challenges posed by recent CJEU cases to the fragile balance that has been struck until now between advancing the 'four freedoms' and the protection of core elements of national social compacts and sovereignty.

 FURTHER READING

Employment policy is a constantly moving target. For ongoing developments, the European Industrial Relations Observatory (EIRO) online is an indispensable resource. For a legal perspective, which is really the only way that employment policy is thoroughly analysed in the literature, see the authoritative contributions of Kenner (2003), Barnard (2012), and Davies (2012). Syrpis (2007) provides a rare conceptual analysis of EU intervention in national labour law. Ronnmar (2008) examines the multi-level interplay between EU- and national-level industrial relations. As for political science approaches, Falkner *et al.* (2005) provide the best analysis of EU employment regulation and compliance. For in-depth analyses of the EES (which has absorbed more attention than any other aspect of EU employment policy by non-lawyers), see Zeitlin and Pochet with Magnusson (2005), Heidenreich and Zeitlin (2009) and Begg, Erhel, and Mortensen (2010). Borrás and Greve (2004) and Heidenreich and Bischoff (2008) provide a more general analysis of the OMC. On new modes of governance more generally, see Linsenmann *et al.* (2007) and Héritier and Rhodes (2011).

Barnard, C. (2012), *EU Employment Law* (Oxford: Oxford University Press).

Begg, I., Erhel, C., and Mortensen, J. (2010), 'Medium-Term Employment Challenges', CEPS Special Report (Brussels: Centre for European Policy Studies).

Borrás, S., and Greve, B. (2004) (eds.), 'The Open Method of Coordination in the European Union', special issue, *Journal of European Public Policy*, 11/2: 181–336.

Davies, A. C. L. (2012), *EU Labour Law* (Cheltenham: Edward Elgar).

Falkner, G., Treib, O., Hartlapp, M., and Leiber, S. (2005), *Complying with Europe: EU Harmonisation and Soft Law in the Member States* (Cambridge: Cambridge University Press).

Heidenreich, M., and Bischoff, G. (2008), 'The Open Method of Coordination: A Way to the Europeanization of Social and Employment Policies?', *Journal of Common Market Studies*, 46/3: 497–532.

Heidenreich, M., and Zeitlin, J. (2009) (eds.), *Changing European Employment and Welfare Regimes: The Influence of the Open Method of Coordination on National Reforms* (London/New York: Routledge).

Héritier, A., and Rhodes M. (2011), *New Modes of Governance in Europe: Governing in the Shadow of Hierarchy* (Basingstoke: Palgrave Macmillan).

Kenner, J. (2003), *EU Employment Law: From Rome to Amsterdam and Beyond* (Oxford: Hart).

Linsenmann, I., Meyer, C., and Wessels, W. (2007) (eds.), *Economic Government of the EU: A Balance Sheet of New Modes of Policy Coordination* (Basingstoke: Palgrave Macmillan).

Ronnmar, M. (2008), *EU Industrial Relations versus National Industrial Relations* (The Hague: Kluwer Law International).

Syrpis, P. (2007), *EU Intervention in Domestic Labour Law* (Oxford: Oxford University Press).

Zeitlin, J., and Pochet, P. with Magnusson, L. (2005) (eds.), *The Open Method of Coordination in Action: The European Employment and Social Inclusion Strategies* (Brussels: PIE-Peter Lang).

CHAPTER 13

Environmental Policy
Contending Dynamics of Policy Change

Andrea Lenschow

▌ Summary

Environmental policy has become a well-established field of European Union (EU) engagement over the years. Its development was characterized by institutional deepening and the enormous expansion of environmental issues covered by EU decisions and regulations. From its typical regulatory policy mode follow some challenges for policy-makers, including the choice of appropriate instruments, improvement of implementation performance, and better policy coordination at all levels of policy-making. This chapter points to the continuing adaptations that have been made in these areas. It also highlights some more recent challenges. First, recent enlargements brought a number of countries into the Union that were expected to resist further intensification of environmental policy efforts due to the financial implications this might have for them. But, in fact, we witness no retrenchment of environmental policy and new member states seem to have

(continued...)

accommodated well. Secondly, however, the economic crisis following the global financial crisis has dampened member-state ambitions to advance the level of environmental protection. Thirdly, the global dimension has become a major aspect of EU environmental policy causing a great deal of mobilization internally and externally. Yet, even the field of climate policy, declared the next 'big idea' of the EU a few years ago, has lost momentum due to the crisis. Nonetheless, EU environmental policy has gained an undeniable profile over the years, not least due to ambitions of international leadership in this field.

Introduction

Since the adoption of the first Environmental Action Programme (EAP) in 1972 environmental policy-making in the EU has become solidly institutionalized.[1] Over the years, EU environmental policy itself has evolved into one of the most active areas of EU policy-making.

This chapter begins by briefly tracing the history of this institutional 'success story'. It continues by providing a deeper understanding of the role of the primary policy actors in the EU, highlighting their role in the environmental policy process and in the expansion of the policy over time. The chapter then illuminates some challenges that have emerged with the rise of the EU's regulatory agenda, on the one hand, and with the development of an international role for the EU in environmental policy, on the other. With the growth of the regulatory output, questions about the effectiveness of the policy gained in saliency. The EU has responded to this challenge by increasing attention to the implementation process, addressing the issue of better policy coordination (both horizontally across policy fields and vertically across levels of governance), and diversifying its portfolio of policy instruments. Over the years, the EU has become an important actor in international environmental policy. After a period of establishing the EU as a formal participant in international organizations and environmental regimes, the EU is now claiming a leadership role for itself. The challenge of giving credibility to the EU's ambition to be a leader in global environmental politics and new dynamics that follow from it for regulatory policy-making inside the EU will be discussed by focusing on the issue of climate change.

History

The evolution of environmental policy in the EU can be characterized by steady deepening in institutional terms as well as expansion in substantive responsibilities. Many authors (e.g. Zito 1999; Knill and Liefferink 2007) distinguish three phases in order to point to some characteristic institutional and political features in this evolution. The first phase (1972–87) followed some earlier incidental policy-making in the environmental field (Hildebrand 1993: 17) and established the institutional and normative core for a fast-growing new policy area in the European Economic Community (EEC) and its member states. Environmental policy during this period followed primarily trade-related motivations and was legally based on the single-market provisions in the treaties (see Chapter 5). Common environmental standards for products and the regulation of production processes in order to protect air, water, and soil or ensure the safe treatment of hazardous waste during industrial activity were decided in order to level the playing field for economic actors and to remove non-tariff barriers to trade emerging from different regulatory practices at the national level.

Generally, in the 1970s the time for environmental policy seemed ripe at the national, European, and international levels, and pioneering states (Andersen and Liefferink 1997) pushed for a growing range of measures at a high level of environmental protection. These leading states, supported by a proactive Commission, began establishing a new policy field at Community level, building linkages to the market-building task of the Community and pointing to transboundary effects of environmental pollution. Despite the need for unanimity, states lagging in environmental protection policy agreed to common European standards in order to secure market access—and to maintain legitimacy in a 'greening' European and international discourse.

The Single European Act (SEA) initiated the second phase, lasting from 1987 to 1992, codifying Community competence in this policy area and laying down the objectives, principles, and decision-making procedures that formally framed the regulatory mode of policy-making that had characterized this field from the start (see Chapter 4). More specifically, the SEA provided an explicit legal basis for environmental regulation, introduced qualified majority voting (QMV) in the Council for some areas of environmental policy, and increased the powers of the European Parliament (EP) in decision-making. During the following years, the EU witnessed a steep rise in activities in this field. Its third EAP laid out the general objectives and strategies of European environmental policy for this period, declared 'high levels of protection' a principle of EU policy, and emphasized the role of prevention as well as the need to integrate the objective of environmental protection in other policy areas. This period also witnessed a trend to more specific and emission-oriented regulation aiming at controlling environmental pollution at the source (Johnson and Corcelle 1989).

The third phase of EU environmental policy began with the Maastricht Treaty on European Union (TEU) coming into force in 1993, which strengthened EU competence still further. Knill and Liefferink (2007: 20–4) identify two opposite trends as characteristic of this phase. On the one hand, the legal and institutional basis for environmental policy-making was consolidated and improved with the EP gaining co-decision powers and QMV being introduced for almost all aspects of environmental policy in the Council. The 2009 Treaty of Lisbon (ToL) further streamlined decision-making and made EU competencies in energy and climate change issues explicit (Benson and

Adelle 2013). On the other hand, the momentum in policy expansion slowed and attention shifted to reform of the European regulatory agenda in this field. The fifth EAP, covering the period 1993 to 2000, announced the 'new governance' approach to environmental policy, emphasizing: (1) the need for greater public participation in decision-making and implementation and (2) the advantages of more flexible and context-sensitive policy instruments. The sixth EAP (2002–12) continued calling for improved regulatory policy and deeper collaboration with industry and EU citizens. The seventh EAP (Decision No. 1386/2013/EU), adopted in November 2013, largely refrains from setting new impulses and focuses on consolidation and implementation: 'The proposal recognises that most of the elements needed to achieve the priority objectives are already in place, but that additional efforts are needed to improve implementation, the evidence base for policy, the investment framework and integration into other policies and sectors …' (Commission 2012*k*: 3).

Despite the increasingly cautious tone with regard to further expanding the coverage of EU environmental policy, the 2000s also witnessed the formulation of a number of significant environmental policies designed to tackle critical problems—such as water pollution, chemicals control, and climate change—and employing new regulatory approaches (see the section 'Regulatory policy-making at the crossroads' later in the chapter). The enlargements of the EU in 2004 and 2007 did not, as anticipated by some, result in a retrenchment of the policy and the new member states were absorbed into policy-making without significant disruption. The economic crisis following the global financial crisis, however, is reflected in increasing resistance to introducing stricter environmental standards and targets; such as was the case with automobile emissions and emissions trading (see the section 'The European Commission: a fragmented entrepreneur' later in the chapter). But we also witness the ability of EU policy-makers to adjust programmatically—even reframe—European environmental policy to changing circumstances, such as by emphasizing the competitive potential of resource-efficient, low-carbon 'road maps' towards 'smart, sustainable and inclusive growth' (Commission 2010*b*, 2011*c*, 2011*d*).

Box 13.1 provides an overview of the development of the legal basis for environmental policy over time and corresponding procedural and substantive characteristics of the policy.

Key players

This section introduces the main actors in EU environmental policy-making, namely the four main EU institutions, Commission, Council of the European Union, EP, and Court of Justice of the European Union (CJEU), and outside the institutional set-up of the EU, environmental interest groups. It highlights intra-institutional relations—including the conflicts between proponents and opponents of more or stricter environmental standards within each institution—and procedures. It also

BOX 13.1	Key treaty changes and associated characteristics of environmental policy

Treaty base	*Characteristics of environmental policy*
1957: Treaty of Rome (EEC Treaty)	
• Article 100 (EEC) on the single market (new Art. 115 TFEU)	• *Decision rules*: unanimity, EP consultation
• Catch-all Article 235 (EEC) on general functioning of the Community (new Art. 352 TFEU)	• *Substantive implication*: environmental policy needed to be linked to the completion of the single market and the general economic mission of the Community
• Article 2 (EEC) on living and working conditions in the Community	
1987: Single European Act (SEA)	• Environmental policy established as an official task of the Community
• Article 100a (EEC) (new Art. 114 TFEU) on the single market cites environmental regulation explicitly	• *Decision rules*: (1) Article 130(r)–(t) calls for unanimous voting in the Council; (2) Article 100a follows new 'cooperation procedure', allowing for QMV and extending the EP's participation rights
• Article 130(r)–(t) (EEC) (new Art. 191(3) TFEU) on environmental policy	• *Substance*: objectives and principles of environmental policy are defined, building the basis for policy expansion and fairly high standards of protection
1993: Treaty of Maastricht (TEU), amending the EC Treaty (TEC)	
• Modification of Articles 100a (new Art. 114 TFEU) and 130s (new Art. 192 TFEU)	• *Decision rules*: (1) QMV is extended to most areas of environmental policy; (2) Article 100a introduces co-decision with the EP
• Article 2 (TEU) introduces the concept of 'sustainable growth respecting the environment'	• *Substance*: formal commitment to a high level of protection and the integration of environmental policy objectives into other policy areas
1999: Treaty of Amsterdam (ToA)	
• Article 2 (TEU and TEC) and Art. 6 (TEC) establish concept of sustainable development and strengthened commitment to integration principle	• *Decision rules*: co-decision (Art. 175 TEC) for measures adopted under Article 174 TEC (ex Art. 130r TEC)
2003: Treaty of Nice (ToN)	• *Decision rules*: adjustments to QMV raise the threshold for reaching qualified majority
2009: Treaty of Lisbon (ToL)	• *Decision rules*: revision of the system of QMV (replacing weighed voting in the Council) and establishing the ordinary legislative procedure as a rule for environmental policy (with few exceptions)

> **BOX 13.1**   **(Continued)**
>
> - Article 3 (TEU) on sustainable development internally and externally
>
> - Article 11 (TFEU) (ex Art. 6 TEC) on integration principle
>
> - Article 191(3) (TFEU) maintains environment title (ex Art. 174(6) TEC)
>
> - *Substance*: introduction of an Energy Title XXI and Title XXIII on Civil Protection (both prospectively strengthening climate policy); broadened emphasis of sustainable development 'of the Earth' (Art. 3)

places specific emphasis on the inter-institutional relations that are characteristic of this policy field.

The European Commission: a fragmented entrepreneur

The general structure and functions of the Commission correspond to those in other policy areas following the regulatory mode of EU policy-making (see Chapter 4). The following discussion will therefore highlight some of the specific challenges characterizing environmental policy-making, namely the challenge of horizontal policy coordination and the balancing act of establishing a European profile for a policy field that emerged as a flanking policy to the core economic functions of the EU, on the one hand, and responding to member-state preferences (i.e. acting as their agent), on the other.

First, part and parcel of the development of a European environmental policy was its institutionalization as a more or less discrete sector, with its own legal basis (after the SEA), a dedicated directorate-general (DG) within the Commission, a specialized 'Environment Council' within the Council, and so on. Yet, environmental policy is also a 'horizontal' policy, affecting economic sectors ranging from agriculture to transportation and requiring coordination among a diverse set of DGs within the Commission. The often conflictual relationship among DGs poses problems for co-ordinated and coherent policy formulation. These conflicts became widely acknowledged with the adoption of the fifth EAP in 1993, which introduced a new consensual rhetoric pointing to win-win solutions and joint responsibility for environmental and economic objectives. Newly established coordination arrangements making operational the principle of environmental policy integration laid down in the treaty, however, were soon found to go against a tradition of respecting 'turf' boundaries in the Commission (Jordan *et al.* 2008: 166). These coordination arrangements had far-reaching organizational implications but lacked high-level political support (cf. Jordan and Schout 2006). Especially in the presence of potent economic interests inside the Commission or among the policy addressees, they proved rather ineffective.

The regulation of automobile emissions is a classic example, where cross-DG turf battles and even conflict within the college of commissioners hinder coordinated and effective environmental policy. In the 1990s, the Directorate-General for Environment (DG ENV), the Directorate-General for Energy (then DG TREN, later to become DG ENER), and the Directorate-General for Enterprise and Industry (DG ENTR) were frequently pitched against each other. The so-called Auto-Oil Programme in the 1990s invited the automobile and oil industries to think jointly about the most cost-effective solutions for tackling air pollution from cars and thus to overcome conflicts within the Commission. The attempt to delegate coordination functions to industry, however, proved to be of limited success, not least due to coordination problems between the industries, each of which understandably hoped to shift the adaptive burden to the other (Friedrich *et al.* 2002). Similarly, the CARS21 process launched in 2005 (and relaunched in 2010; Commission 2010*f*) to engage industry in developing recommendations for a suitable regulatory framework to support a competitive automobile industry did not overcome conflicts between DG ENV and DG ENTR or prevent a fight between Commissioners Stavros Dimas (Environment) and Günther Verheugen (Industry) over a planned regulation aiming at reducing CO_2 emissions from automobiles becoming public in 2007 (*European Voice*, 6 Dec. 2007).

A special case for environmental policy coordination is the establishment of the Directorate-General for Climate Action (DG CLIMA) in February 2010. Previously, climate policy had been within the remit of the DG ENV. Spinning off the new DG gave climate policy a significantly higher profile in organizational terms, but at the same time complicated intra-Commission coordination in climate policy by adding a new actor that first needed to ascend from its earlier position as 'junior partner'. The 2011 conflicts between the Commissioners for Climate Action, Connie Hedegaard, and Energy, Günther Öttinger, about the coordination of climate and energy policy may be read in that light. The Energy Efficiency Directive (2012/27/EU) had been developed by DG ENER with the announced (side-)effect of climate change mitigation, but critics argued that it may undermine the effectiveness of the EU's Emissions Trading Scheme, the 'baby' of DG ENV and now Climate Action (Jaureguy-Naudin 2011). The corresponding open public conflict between the commissioners may be unusual, but it revealed the challenge of complying with the principle of environmental policy integration even inside the Commission. Ongoing conflicts over the regulatory treatment of diesel cars show that one cannot even be sure of the smooth cooperation between DG ENV, supporting the end of preferential tax treatment for diesel cars, and DG CLIMA, pointing to the crucial role of diesel cars in the overall CO_2-reduction strategy.

The second challenge confronting the Commission is the need to balance its ambition as the 'motor of integration' with the need to be responsive to the member states, and hence raise the chances of successful decision-making and effective policy implementation. Especially during the 1970s and 1980s, when the institutional and normative position of environmental policy was still weak at the EU level, the Commission used the policy-formulation stage to advance its role as a supranational actor and to promote tough environmental rules exceeding the status quo in the member states. From an inter-institutional perspective, this role put the Commission in almost natural opposition to many member states and hence to the Council. While developing a profile in environmental policy, it invited long-winded negotiations and poor implementation due to national resistance. But even during the early phases of EU environmental policy-making, this description risks being a caricature. During the 1970s, several member states began to develop an interest in environmental protection policy and—partly in order to reduce the risk of competitive disadvantages—sought to 'upload' national regulation to the EU level. Hence, the Commission regularly responded to national demands for European policy in developing its proposals. With a small staff of about 500 policy officials, the Commission was dependent on national expertise and regularly sought the opinion of the national ministries in order to ensure the feasibility of its proposals and anticipate the conflicts that might otherwise hamper decision-making.

This attentiveness to the member states' points of view has increased further since the early 1990s due to a reordering of the Commission's priorities. Deficient implementation moved the Commission to improve its relations with the implementers 'on the ground', namely the relevant agencies in the member states, during the policy-design stage. Beginning with the fifth EAP, the Commission began to speak of the member states as partners; formal and informal dialogue networks were created to put this cooperative approach into practice (Commission 1993a: 113–16). Supranational entrepreneurship seemed more promising in such cooperative settings than within a confrontational modus operandi.

The Commission's policy-shaping activities, however, are starkly evident in climate policy. Both in organizational terms and substantively it has framed climate change as an integrative project of the Union—relevant for jobs and competitiveness and environmental protection as well as its credibility as a 'world partner' (see also Chapter 14). Environmental measures related to the climate-change issue are presented with much verve and with demanding standards. But arguably, traditional environmental policy became sidelined by this dominant topic; and the principle of environmental policy integration has been effectively reduced to 'climate policy integration' (Kurze and Lenschow forthcoming).

The Council of the European Union: cross-cutting cleavages

The Council, like the Commission, is characterized by segmentation. There is little coordination between the Environment Council and the various other Council formations. Similarly, the Secretariat General of the Council and the pyramid of Council committees by and large follow a sector-specific approach. Coordination is expected to occur 'at home' in the preparation of the national positions—an expectation that is frequently disappointed by some member states, however (e.g. Germany).[2]

At first sight, a single cleavage, separating environmental leaders from laggards, appears to run through the Council. Simply put, the leaders—such as Germany, the Netherlands, Sweden, and Denmark—are the richer, northern states, whereas the laggards are the poorer, southern states—such as Greece, Portugal, and Spain—and the newer member states, which have other investment priorities and do not face electorates pushing for tougher environmental standards. The UK, given its insular location, which protects it from some transboundary effects, and the legacy of its heavy-industry sector, was long considered the 'dirty man' of Europe, although this changed in the 1990s (Jordan 2002). The existence of this north–south, rich–poor cleavage was visible in previous rounds of enlargement. To fight off potential demands for an easing of environmental standards, the southern enlargements in 1981 and 1986 were accompanied by a substantial increase and refocusing of the Community's financial-support schemes for environmental investments. In 1993 the Cohesion Fund, spending about 50 per cent of its monies on environmental projects, was launched (see Chapter 10). The 'northern' countries, which joined in 1995, in turn, negotiated provisions that allow them to exceed EU environmental standards under certain conditions. As Liefferink and Andersen (1998) pointed out, the influence of these 'green' states was felt at the EU level although countries pursued different strategies—ranging from 'opting out' and seeking national exceptions to direct 'pushing' for EU environmental measures. The impact of enlargement has emerged starkly with the addition of twelve mostly central and east European countries (CEECs) in 2004 and 2007. Unlike previous accession countries, these new members have had to adopt the entire environmental *acquis* with very few exceptions and without comparable side-payments.[3] Nevertheless, a distinct CEEC 'bloc' of opposition to strict environmental policy cannot generally be identified (Skjærseth and Wettestad 2007), although there are issues where the new member states have allied to fight against financial burdens imposed on them. A prime example was the negotiation of the climate change package in 2008–9 where special treatment of the new member states was successfully fought for in the context of internal EU 'effort-sharing' arrangements as well as within the emissions trading scheme.

Despite a notable line of conflict between the rich, northern leaders and the poor, southern/eastern laggards discussed earlier, the cleavage structure in the Council has never been one-dimensional. Three reasons account for this greater complexity. In the first place, member states face different environmental problems and suffer from distinct economic vulnerabilities. The richer, more highly industrialized countries are likely to be more concerned with air quality, waste treatment, and noise pollution, while at the same time being protective of core industries (e.g. chemicals, automobiles), whereas poorer countries with a larger rural sector and dependence on tourism place greater value on the quality of soil, nature protection, and sufficient quantities of water. Secondly, countries differ in their regulatory philosophies and styles (Richardson 1982; Vogel 1986; Wurzel 2008). Hence, their governments argue not only about the level of standards, but also about the type of policy instrument, the amount of administrative flexibility or regional variation, and the degree of scientific certainty required before agreeing to EU measures. Thirdly, member states' positions change over time, if economic and environmental conditions change or a new government with different policy priorities comes to power. In sum, despite a strong political rhetoric emphasizing the socio-economic divide, alliance-building in the Council is shaped by more complex, cross-cutting cleavage patterns and is hard to predict in the field of EU environmental policy.

The European Parliament: still the environmental champion?

As indicated earlier, the EP has gained decision-making power over the years. Today the ordinary legislative procedure—giving equal 'co-decision' powers to Parliament and Council—applies to most aspects of environmental policy. But even earlier the EP had left its mark.

Traditionally, the EP has been the 'greenest' of the three main environmental policy-making bodies. Already in the early 1970s, the EP was instrumental in the emerging EU-level nature-protection policy—that is, a sub-field of environmental policy that was hard to link to the internal-market agenda and thus dependent on broad societal support. The 1979 Wild Birds Directive (79/409/EEC) is a prime example: it can be traced back to 1971 when the EP requested the Commission to take up this issue (Haigh 2004: 9.2). In the 1980s, the EP played a well-documented role (e.g. Arp 1992) in the difficult negotiations about stricter mandatory emission limits for automobiles with the Directive 91/441/EEC finally establishing the first EURO norm. In the 1990s, the EP brought the issue of implementation in environmental policy to the fore and pushed the Commission to engage more systematically with societal and administrative actors on the ground (Collins and Earnshaw 1992; European Parliament 1996). Most recently, the EP used its budgetary powers in times of financial restraint in the member states to push for a 43 per cent higher budget for the now €3.46 billion LIFE Programme for Environment and Climate Action in the period 2014–20 (Regulation 614/2007), which includes a new €864 million sub-programme for climate action. The latter amounts to a tripling of the climate-action budget compared to the 'LIFE+' programme in 2007–13.[4] Also, the EP contributes to policy implementation by handling citizens' petitions (under Art. 227 TFEU) and through correspondence of individual members of the European Parliament (MEPs) with the Commission.

The continuous engagement of the EP for extending European environmental policy notwithstanding, the implications of co-decision for the EP's contribution to 'greening' EU policy are hard to generalize. Without doubt, the relative empowerment of the EP has resulted in tripling its workload since the mid-1990s (Burns 2013: 146) and thus more influence over EU environmental policy. But has greater influence translated into tighter environmental standards? Burns and Carter (2010) show that the amendments submitted by the EP since 1999 have moderated, and that by striving for agreement in first reading the EP has become more pragmatic.

There are several reasons for this more moderate approach. First, the 'green' position inside the Parliament has become weaker—not least because Green parties find little support among voters from the new member states. According to preliminary results of the June 2014 EP elections, the size of the Green/EFA group shrank to fifty members (out of 751) from seventeen countries (for the first time including East European Greens) and fell to sixth position among the European party groups represented in the Parliament. In addition, it also stood against a clear centre-right majority elected in 2004 and 2009, and will most likely operate in the shadow of an informal grand coalition of Socialists and Christian Democrats following the 2014 elections. Secondly, the ordinary legislative procedure has facilitated a turn towards informal negotiations with the Council aiming at early agreement. After some initial resistance inside the EP, the so-called trialogue meetings are now widely used, leading to earlier de-politicization in order credibly to reach backroom compromises. Nonetheless, compared to national parliaments, the EP is still considered 'environmental' in its overall orientation, although this inclination does not apply across the board and is issue-dependent.[5]

Here, it certainly matters that the MEPs in the European multi-level governance system are some steps removed from the operational level (and demands of accountability) and hence prone to articulate more general programmatic ideas. Debates over policy design and setting hardly become known to the wider public and individual MEPs will rarely be held accountable for their policy initiatives, but will instead be judged on their European visions at large. As long as environmental policy is widely considered a field with self-evident EU responsibility (as Eurobarometer data (still) suggest), the EP has an institutional interest to point out its contribution to the (European) public good in general terms without necessarily risking lost battles due to contentious substantive details.

The third reason for the EP's periodic more moderate approach has to do with personalities[6] and more generally with relations among EP committees. The driver of environmental considerations inside the EP has historically been its Environment, Public Health and Food Safety Committee (ENVI).[7] A proactive and often uncompromising attitude in the operation of this committee in the 1980s and 1990s under the chairmanship of the Scottish Labour MEP Ken Collins (1979–99)[8] is legendary (Sbragia 2000). His conservative successors Carolyn Jackson (1999–2004) and Karl Heinz Florenz (2004–7) were regarded as environmental advocates in their party groups and moved environmental issues from the margin to the political centre. The outright environmental sceptic Miroslav Ouský of the Czech Republic (2007–9) led this large committee in a professional manner, but did not care for its environmental credentials.[9] After the 2009 EP elections, chairmanship of the committee passed to the German Social Democrats. Under Jo Leinen (2009–12), a former regional environment minister in Saarland and previously chair of the EP constitutional committee, and Matthias Groote (since 2012), previously visible as rapporteur on the tricky car-emission dossier, the Committee returned to a more proactive role in environmental matters.

Relations among committees within the EP have become a significant determinant of the EP's positions on environmental policies—most notably in complex matters such as the so-called climate package in 2008–9. Here non-environmental committees—such as the Industry, Research and Energy (ITRE) or Internal Market and Consumer Protection (IMCO) committees—share responsibility in preparing the EP position in procedures that also aim at rationalizing policy-making by pre-negotiating and reducing the number of amendments presented to the plenary. Thus, policy conflict tends to be handled at the level of committees with the rapporteurs and shadow rapporteurs playing critical roles—actors who at the same time engage in informal negotiations with the Council. Once more, processes of pragmatic intra- and inter-institutional consensus-seeking or deal-making go hand in hand with general notions of environmental advocacy that can still be identified as characteristic for the EP.

The Court of Justice of the European Union: from policy-enabling to enforcement

In the history of EU environmental policy, the case law of the CJEU has played a crucial role in establishing the legitimacy of environmental measures at the EU level and in insisting on participatory procedures. In the *Danish Bottle* case it ruled that the principle of free movement of goods can be overridden if the policy in question serves to achieve common environmental objectives. The ruling upheld a Danish recycling law that limited the range of containers that could be used to bottle beverages. In the *Titanium Dioxide* case, the court eased the way towards delineating the decision-making procedures in the environmental field and supported further empowerment of the Parliament. Here the court found that the objectives of the directive to harmonize and eventually eliminate waste from the titanium dioxide industry were compatible both with single-market and environment provisions of the treaties and ruled that under such conditions the legal base should be chosen that best reflects the fundamental democratic principle that the peoples should take part in the exercise of power through the intermediary of a representative assembly. It thereby legitimated the choice of the single-market legal basis for solely procedural reasons as it provided for with a greater role for the EP. In the medium term, this ruling induced the unifying of procedures in environmental policy-making.

The main responsibilities of the court in the later, legally consolidated, phase of environmental policy relate to implementation and enforcement. First, in infringement proceedings usually initiated by the Commission against member states (Art. 258 TFEU), the court ensures compliance with EU law. Under the Article 260 TFEU procedure it may impose pecuniary sanctions in cases of prolonged non-compliance or poor compliance. The ToL introduced some changes to accelerate the infringement procedures—such as enabling the Commission in urgent cases to request that the court order interim measures before the final ruling (under Art.

279), and that penalties are included in the first ruling under Article 258 if member states fail to adopt implementing legislation of a new directive by the deadline. In March 2013, the Commission referred Poland and Cyprus to the court for failing to transpose the Renewable Energy Directive by the 5 December 2010 deadline and proposed daily penalties of €133,229 (Poland) and €11,405 (Cyprus) (Commission 2013*k*). Nevertheless, both Commission and member states generally work towards reaching compliance in the pre-judicial phase or before a court ruling.

Under Article 267 TFEU, if an individual argues before a national court that a national law or policy conflicts with EU law, the national court may seek guidance from the CJEU by seeking a preliminary ruling. This procedure operates analogously to an enforcement mechanism, as individuals or groups are able to bring legal action against national authorities that have failed to transpose or comply with EU law.[10] In 2012, preliminary rulings accounted for 50 per cent of all new environmental cases brought to the court, a ratio that lies below the average in other policy fields, however (Court of Justice of the European Union 2013). Whether this suggests a comparatively reserved attitude of the national judiciaries towards the EU level or rather the exceptionally high ratio of Commission infringement cases in environmental policy is yet to be analysed. In summary, however, we note that the court no longer plays the same enabling role as in the early years of EU environmental policy but carries a heavy load of legal enforcement tasks.

Environmental interest groups: more than just a lobby

Environmental policy is influenced by a wide range of interest groups representing environmental, consumer, or industrial interests. Among the environmental groups, the European Environmental Bureau (EEB) has the longest history in Brussels. It was set up in 1974 with the help of the European Commission, which had an interest in garnering societal support for expanding European competencies to the environmental field and in establishing a counterweight to the strong industrial associations. In 2013, the EEB is a federation of 143 organizations from thirty-one European countries. Together with the Friends of the Earth (FoE), Greenpeace International, and the World Wide Fund for Nature (WWF), which established their Brussels offices in the late 1980s, the EEB founded the 'Gang of Four' in 1990, an informal coalition of leading environmental non-governmental organizations (ENGOs) active at the European level. This coalition subsequently expanded to ten, being joined by Climate Action Network Europe, the European Federation for Transport and Environment (T&E), BirdLife International, Health and Environmental Alliance, International Friends of Nature, and, as the latest addition in 2005, Bankwatch. Both enlargement and the adoption of new policy priorities by the EU have led to new arrivals. For instance, Bankwatch, which was founded in 1995, is a network of central and east European ENGOs concerned about unsustainable practices sponsored by international finance institutions. Thus, the

Brussels alliance of ENGOs has extended not only geographically but also in its thematic portfolio.

Given the volatile nature of membership and public campaigning contributions, nine of the 'Green Ten' also rely on Commission funding for their regular operations.[11] Based on Regulation (EC) No. 614/2007 of the European Parliament and of the Council of 23 May 2007 concerning the Financial Instrument for the Environment (Life+), 'operational activities of NGOs that are primarily active in protecting and enhancing the environment at the European level and involved in the development and implementation of Community policy and legislation' are eligible for funding. For 2014, €9 million has been allocated to this purpose—maintaining the allocation from previous years. A 2013 analysis of the data in the EU transparency register shows that Brussels-based NGOs representing a European interest rely heavily on grants from EU institutions for their funding (on average getting 43 per cent of their funding from these sources (Greenwood and Dreger, 2013)). There is, however, considerable variation among ENGOs, with Greenpeace not accepting any EU funding. In addition, the difference in overall resources available to business organizations compared to ENGOs is smaller than expected. The overall financial situation of EU-level ENGOs may thus be considered solid, though partly at the price of losing independence and becoming service providers for the Commission.

ENGOs also pursue different lobbying strategies, reflecting differing ties to the EU Commission (Adelle and Anderson 2013: 158f.). Generally, the Brussels-based staffs concentrate on the policy-formulation phase. Yet, some emphasize their role as pressure groups while others operate also as advisers, offering expertise and information to the Commission. With the exception of Greenpeace, the Green Ten seek to be consulted during the policy-formation phase. During the decision-making phase all ENGOs resort to the classic tools of the environmental movement and use public campaigns to create awareness and seek direct contacts with member governments and MEPs to ensure the desired majorities. The range of activities is reflected in today's professional operations and the increasingly diversified environmental policy expertise present in Brussels. How these actors interact in the policy process is neatly illustrated by the 2006 REACH Directive (see Box 13.2). The REACH legislation set procedural rules controlling the market entry of potentially hazardous chemicals and established the European Chemicals Agency (ECHA) for implementation. It is widely considered the most significant piece of EU environmental legislation adopted in the 2000s.

Compared to national industrial federations or firms, which may also get involved in the policy-formulation and decision-making stages, national ENGOs (which may also be members of the Brussels-based groups) are crucial during the implementation and enforcement phases of policy-making. In addition to national legal action, environmental groups can use the complaints procedure to inform the Commission of any gap in implementation that are found in the member states.[12] This mechanism can offer valuable information to the Commission given the absence of an EU inspectorate in the member states.

| BOX 13.2 | The making of the REACH chemicals package |

The REACH (Registration, Evaluation, Authorization and Restriction of Chemicals) package[13] resulted in a consolidation and renewal of the EU chemicals policy, which has a history going back to the late 1960s and covered over 100 pieces of EU legislation. The initial critics of REACH disapproved of: (1) its complexity; (2) its insufficient protection of the environment and human health from hazardous chemicals (especially from the vast amount of already existing chemicals); and (3) the lack of guidelines or incentives for the substitution for hazardous chemicals with less harmful substances.

Policy initiation was dominated by 'green states' (Austria, Denmark, Germany, the Netherlands, Sweden, and the UK), hoping to export their ambitious national goals to the European level (Selin 2007: 78) and leading the Environment Council in 1999 to request the Commission to develop a new chemicals policy. These green states were joined by DG ENV in the Commission (and the then new Swedish Commissioner Margot Wallström), which presented a White Paper on *Strategy for a Future Chemicals Policy* in February 2001, as well as the majority of the Environment Committee in the EP and many ENGOs. Opposition to the initiative was led by CEFIC (European Chemical Industry Council), representing 27,000 chemical companies across Europe, which mobilized support in DG ENTR as well as the EP committees ITRE and IMCO.

The policy-formulation and decision-making stages were characterized by heavy consultation of stakeholders and policy experts aiming to raise awareness of insufficient regulation (spectacular in this context was the DetoX campaign led by the WWF) and improve acceptance of regulation among industrial actors (e.g. Long and Lorinczi 2009). Furthermore, decision-making was exemplified by a high degree of institutional 'depillarization' (Hey *et al.* 2008: 439f.). This involved: (1) joint responsibility assigned to DG ENV and DG ENTR in the Commission; (2) the Council negotiations taking place in the horizontal Competitiveness Council where both economic and environmental ministers (and experts at the working-group level) met; and (3) close cooperation among the leading ENVI committee and the IMCO and ITRE committees in the EP to produce the committee report.

Both the participatory and the institutional strategies had the effect of strengthening the influence of industry in the policy process by extending access beyond the initial small 'green' alliance. Not surprisingly, therefore, the Commission proposal presented in October 2003 envisaged, compared to its earlier White Paper, weaker registration, information, and substitution requirements, as well as some exemptions. Also, the Council common position agreed in December 2005 under the UK presidency departed from the earlier position formulated in the Environment Council by acknowledging the need to protect the competitiveness of the European chemical industry.

Interestingly, while depillarization in the Commission and Council was introduced with the dual aims of renewing the regulatory framework for chemicals and fostering a more cooperative climate, the situation in the EP was characterized by open antagonism. Industrial and environmental lobbies had successfully polarized the debate; in particular, industry opponents of REACH kept delaying the process hoping for more favourable majorities in the EP and in the Council after European Parliament (2004) and German (2005)

> **BOX 13.2**   **(Continued)**
>
> elections. In the end, the ENVI committee, in order to avoid the collapse of the negotiations, had to compromise with the industrial coalition by agreeing to relaxed information and testing requirements for chemicals produced in small volumes and relaxed conditions for substitution (Pesendorfer 2006; M. P. Smith 2008).
>
> The REACH package was passed in second reading in December 2006. It introduced a mix of instruments, with obligatory procedural standards limited to hazardous substances, self-regulatory information, and risk management of industry being the core of the new system, accompanied by new rules of transparency to allow for bottom-up pressure. The new ECHA, which was inaugurated in June 2008, shares with national regulatory agencies responsibility for implementing REACH, in particular by ensuring uniform practices. In short, the final decision reflects a compromise both in substance and in the choice of governance mechanisms. In sum, this case study prominently shows the strong and yet highly contingent impact of intra- and inter-institutional arrangements, rendering unviable a simple assessment of who are the losers and who the winners of the negotiations.

Regulatory policy-making at the crossroads

By the turn of the century, years of EU environmental activism had not significantly improved the state of the environment in Europe (European Environment Agency 1999). Some critics condemned the cost of environmental regulation and the EU's tendency towards ad hoc and 'wild' regulatory expansion with European industry suffering disadvantages vis-à-vis global competitors due to comparatively high and ever rising standards. Others deplored the apparent lack of coordination between environmental and other EU policy areas, such as transport, energy, agriculture, or the single market, and wished to see better integration of environmental objectives into general policy-making in the EU. The evolution of car-emission policy has served as ammunition for both sides. On the one hand, the move from the EURO I to the EURO V and VI norms for automobile emissions illustrates rolling demands on the European automobile sector to invest in environmental improvements. On the other hand, environmental critics argue that these standards are still too low and indicate the insufficient contribution of the transport sector to tackling the environmental costs of climate change. Furthermore, despite some justified concerns about the quality and comparability of the Commission's own data (Börzel 2001), EU environmental policy continues to suffer from an implementation deficit exceeding that of other policy areas, including the single market, industry, and consumer affairs (see Figure 13.1). At the level of infringement proceedings as well as court referrals (see Figure 13.2) and court rulings (Krämer

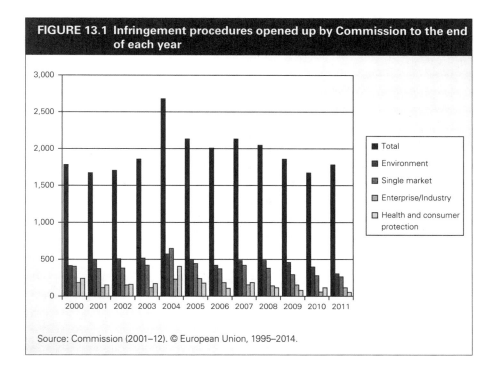

FIGURE 13.1 Infringement procedures opened up by Commission to the end of each year

Source: Commission (2001–12). © European Union, 1995–2014.

2008: 3–5), environmental cases amount to the largest policy grouping although the proportion is decreasing.

EU policy-makers responded to these challenges in several ways. First, the Commission started several initiatives to improve implementation and enforcement. The European Network for the Implementation and Enforcement of Environmental Law (IMPEL), made up of Commission officials and representatives of relevant national (or local) authorities, has become an important forum for considering the feasibility of EU proposals early in the policy process, as well as for improving the capacity and willingness of local implementers through exchange of experiences. In order to tackle structural problems in some outstanding areas, such as waste, water, air, nature protection, and impact assessment, DG ENV formed implementation task forces, and the Commission generally became more proactive by offering guidelines, interpretive documents, and training initiatives to increase implementation capacities on the ground. Following its 2008 communication, 'A Europe of Results—Applying Community Law', the Commission introduced the IT-based 'EU Pilot' as a tool to communicate with member states about questions concerning the correct application of EU law or the conformity of national law with EU law at an early stage (i.e. before an infringement procedure is launched under Art. 258 TFEU). The files submitted via EU Pilot include a description and questions on particular aspects of implementation. One-third of all files handled by the Commission and

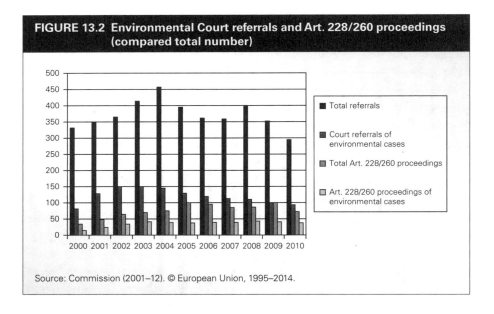

FIGURE 13.2 Environmental Court referrals and Art. 228/260 proceedings (compared total number)

Source: Commission (2001–12). © European Union, 1995–2014.

the member states under the procedure concern violations of environmental law. According to the Second Evaluation Report (Commission 2011e), the EU Pilot has helped to reduce the number of infringement proceedings compared to the previous informal practice of sending administrative letters to the member states.

Overall, the past reforms in the handling of implementation and non-compliance reflected the appreciation of the management approach to implementation (Tallberg 2002), focusing on building states' capacity and expertise to implement policies, rather than punishing lack of implementation. The ToL revisions of the infringement articles, however, re-emphasized the sanctioning approach and the seventh EAP (Decision 1386/2013/EU) points to a need for extended requirements on inspections and surveillance in response to continuing high number of non-compliance cases in environmental policy.

The second response to the apparent lack of effectiveness of EU environmental policy has been to modify the choice of policy instruments. Arguably, EU environmental policy remains dominated by a regulatory mode of governance (see Chapter 4) and the corresponding reliance on regulatory instruments (Holzinger et al. 2008). Since the turn of the century, however, innovation has been evident. The EU has adopted a number of *environmental framework* directives that aim both to avoid overregulation and to generate greater coherence of EU legislation. The 2000 Water Framework Directive (2000/60/EC), for instance, consolidates previous regulatory output by replacing seven earlier water directives. By requiring all member states to cooperate in the management of river basins, the EU brought the hitherto neglected cross-boundary and cross-media effects of water pollution into focus (Grant et al. 2000: 167–75). The Waste Framework Directive

(2008/98/EC) lays down basic principles of waste management, establishes new recycling and recovery targets, and incorporates provisions on waste oils and hazardous waste from now repealed earlier directives. The 2008 Air Quality Directive (2008/50/EC) merged four existing directives and one Council decision on air quality and followed a new approach by combining strictly binding environmental targets with considerable leeway for the selection of air-quality measures and for the concrete allocation of competences between different levels of government. It also set out detailed planning and transparency requirements (Becker *et al.* forthcoming). These framework directives represent both an attempt at consolidating a patchwork of previous legislation and the hybridization of hard and soft regulatory instruments.

Though not presented as a framework directive, the climate and energy 'package' proposed in January 2008 by the Commission also aimed to achieve an overarching goal, namely to cut CO_2 emissions in the EU by 20 per cent by the year 2020. The climate package is also characterized by an innovative *instrument mix* with regulatory, market-based, and investment tools. Box 13.3 highlights the complex intra- and inter-institutional coordination and successful framing efforts required to build the compromise.

The diversification of policy instruments, with an emphasis on more context-oriented and flexible approaches, represents a change in regulatory philosophy first announced in the fifth EAP. Information-based instruments aim to raise awareness and trigger learning effects. Economic instruments attach a price (in the form of fees, taxes, or withheld subsidies) to environmentally harmful activities or create a market for permits or allowances. Voluntary agreements with private actors complement this toolbox of 'new' instruments. Compared to the total legislative output of the EU in environmental policy, these new policy instruments are still limited (Héritier 2002) though growing in number (Holzinger *et al.* 2008). As a result, the repertoire of EU environmental policy tools has become surprisingly varied.

The third response to the apparent limited impact of EU environmental legislation has been greater attention to better policy integration. Policy integration has been pursued in two senses. In one sense, several measures pay attention to the combined effects of pollution on different environmental media (air, water, and soil), and the interdependency between these media. The sixth and seventh EAPs have pursued this perspective by following thematic strategies, such as the focus on climate change, resource-efficient low-carbon growth, and the connection between environment and health. The directives on environmental impact assessment (2011/92/EU), on strategic impact assessment (extending the impact perspective from individual projects to policy programmes, effective since 2004, 2001/42/EC), and on integrated pollution prevention and control (2008/1/EC) facilitate pollution control beyond the initial medium affected by a discharge.

Policy integration in a second sense applies to policy coordination. In June 1998, the European Council in Cardiff appeared to represent a breakthrough for the policy integration principle. Most configurations of the Council, ranging from

BOX 13.3	The internalization of external pressure: the EU climate change package

In January 2008 the European Commission responded to the European Council decision establishing the so-called 20-20-20 target with a package of four proposals on climate and energy. The proposed measures included:

- an *improved emissions trading system (ETS)* covering more emissions and allowing firms in one EU country to buy allowances in any other country;
- an *emissions reduction target for industries not covered by the ETS* (e.g. buildings, transport, waste);
- *legally enforceable targets for increasing the share of renewables* in the energy mix—taking into account each country's individual needs and potential, but amounting to an overall increase of 20 per cent; and
- new rules on *carbon capture and storage (CCS)* and on *environmental subsidies.*

Negotiations in the EP were conducted under enormous time pressure, as it was the declared aim to reach an agreement within the EU before the EP elections in June 2009 and far in advance of the United Nations Climate Change Conference in Copenhagen at the end of that year. Relations between the involved committees (most notably ENVI and ITRE) were shaped by the perceived need to reach a compromise. This tamed the free exchange of views and restrained open conflict otherwise typical for the first reading stage (Lenschow 2009).

Similar time pressure was felt at Council level. In October 2008, in the midst of the financial crisis, the European Council declared its commitment to stick to the ambitious climate and energy targets agreed in 2007 and 2008 (European Council 2008). The financial crisis induced some heavy attacks (see Chapter 15) on the ETS dossier in particular by east European countries, with other countries adding their demands for special treatment. Also, energy-intensive industry fought for leniency during economically tough times, and argued, for instance, against emission permits being allocated by auction. Yet, the French presidency negotiated a compromise which was agreed at the European Council in December 2008, on schedule for the Copenhagen agenda. The compromise considerably watered down the initial Commission proposal, but the 20-20-20 target was maintained. On 17 December 2008, the package was endorsed in the EP and by April 2009 all related EU legislation was formally adopted in the Council. Further discussions took place at the European Council of October 2009.

Hence, despite softening the environmental measures and corresponding heavy criticisms by the ENGO community, the EU was set to appear on the international scene as a leader sticking to its core commitments even in tough economic times. Turning the perspective inward, the enormous dynamic triggered by the EU in international negotiations has been remarkable. The issue of climate change was effectively utilized by environmental policy-makers to push internal decisions on difficult issues such as energy consumption and industrial and car emissions. At a more general level, 'climate change' was used to give the Union a more visible profile internally and to enhance its public image.

agriculture to the Council of Ministers for Economic and Financial Affairs (Ecofin), were called on to develop an environmental integration strategy, and member governments were supposed to exchange 'best practice' models (Lenschow 2003). But the commitment of the EU's political leadership to environmental integration has been volatile, especially following the economic downturn. While the economic and financial crisis has not led to a retrenchment of EU environmental policy, it certainly has dampened hopes of 'mainstreaming' environmental objectives in all EU policies. Even climate, energy, and resource-efficiency policies, which initially appeared high on the environmental integration agenda (Pallemaerts 2013), were reframed as growth strategies (Kurze and Lenschow forthcoming) and are encountering increasing member-state resistance (Egenhofer and Alessi 2013; Dröge 2013).

The EU as an international actor

So far EU environmental policy has been presented as being largely internally motivated, either to facilitate the internal market or to deal with European transboundary effects. A significant number of EU environmental measures, however, can be traced back to international agreements related to water, the atmosphere, waste, wildlife, etc. (Baker 2003: 25). The EU is a party to about sixty multilateral environmental agreements (MEAs)[14] and uses both bilateral relations and its neighbourhood policy to bolster environmental standards at international, regional, and national levels. As a so-called 'Regional Economic Integration Organization', the EU has acquired the legal status to act at the international level either as a full party to MEAs and related Conferences or Meetings of the Parties (COPs or MOPs) or—in the UN context—as an observer.

Historically, the question of whether the EU would be a party to an international environmental agreement was controversial both internally and externally (Sbragia 1998). Today, the TFEU (Art. 191) mentions the external environmental competencies of the EU as 'implied powers' of the internal scope of environmental policy. The EU shares these competencies with the member states (Art. 4 TFEU), which means that MEAs are negotiated with a Union negotiator (the Commission) and member-state negotiator(s) (either jointly represented through the presidency of the Council or by individual member-state negotiators) present and signed as 'mixed agreements'. Although EU member governments have become increasingly willing to coordinate their positions and act collectively, the dual representation of the EU has produced some controversies even recently. Since the failure of the EU to play a leadership role at the 2009 United Nations Climate Change Conference in Copenhagen was attributed partly to a lack of internal coherence, the Commission has argued for receiving a full negotiation mandate in subsequent international negotiations producing some inter-institutional battles (Delreux 2011). Especially in ongoing international negotiations, however, these formal issues of representation have become secondary to more pragmatic considerations of effective representation—calling for both continuity and expertise. Thus, in the climate negotiations the EU established a structure of 'issue leaders' in Council working parties and expert groups support-ing 'lead negotiators' coming from a chosen member state or the Commission in the COPs, who speak on behalf of the rotating presidency. This evolution and attempt at professionalization of EU external representation in environmental negotiations reflects its objective to build on global environmental leadership for its profile as an international 'normative power' (Manners 2002; Lenschow and Sprungk 2010). This was particularly evident in climate policy. In the case of the 1997 Kyoto Protocol, the intra-EU burden-sharing agreement allocating different commitments for the reduction of greenhouse gases to the member states strengthened the EU's negotia-tion position as it was able to commit itself to the toughest (collective) target of an 8 per cent reduction in greenhouse gas emissions from 1990 levels by 2008–12.[15] This target (together with the burden-sharing agreement) became binding when the Pro-tocol came into force on 16 February 2005. With the Kyoto targets expiring in 2012, difficult negotiations took place under the United Nations Framework Convention on Climate Change (UNFCCC) with the goal of reaching a global agreement govern-ing action beyond that date. The EU had hoped to lead by example with strong and credible internal commitment. Thus, in March 2007 it pledged to reduce by 2020 the greenhouse gas emissions of the EU by 20 per cent from the 1990 baseline and promised a 30 per cent cut if other countries joined in. Furthermore, the EU adopted concrete policies aiming to achieve the ambitious targets of reducing greenhouse gas emissions. The prospect of losing credibility among the international partners spurred the internal policy developments related to climate change and at the end of the French presidency in December 2008 it underpinned the deal among the mem-ber states and the endorsement of Parliament (see Box 13.3).

Yet, the Copenhagen Conference turned out as a defeat of the EU ambitions not least as the EU had underestimated the influence of Brazil, Russia, India, and China (the BRICs) and the need to form alliances with small island and developing coun-tries. In subsequent meetings in Cancun (2010), Durban (2011), and Doha (2012), the international negotiators slowly moved towards a post-Kyoto agreement. On 8 December 2012, the parties to the Kyoto Protocol adopted the 'Doha Amendment to the Kyoto Protocol'. In Annex 1 of the agreement (industrialized countries), the par-ties committed to reducing their overall greenhouse gas emissions by at least 18 per cent below 1990 levels in the eight-year period from 2013 to 2020.[16] As part of the agreement the EU committed to a reduction of 20 per cent by 2020 and 'reiterate[d] its conditional offer to move to a 30 per cent reduction by 2020 compared to 1990 levels, provided that other developed countries commit themselves to comparable emission reductions and developing countries contribute adequately according to their responsibilities and respective capabilities' (Doha Amendment to the Kyoto Pro-tocol, Art. 1.A).[17] Other big players have not improved their previous commitment laid down in the Kyoto Protocol. Although encountering some resistance of member states on interim (2030) and specific targets, EU leaders have endorsed the objective of reducing Europe's greenhouse gas emissions by 80–95 per cent by 2050 compared to 1990 levels, thus keeping up its claim to international leadership also prior to the 2015 climate conference in Paris.

In sum, the EU undoubtedly has become an important actor in international environmental policy and is able to set the agenda through ambitious internal policies. Yet, it was forced to realize that international leadership cannot be founded on progressive internal policies alone, but requires high capacity in international diplomacy.

Conclusion

What—in a nutshell—are the key features of EU environmental policy-making? Empirically, it is a story of policy expansion, deepening, and institutionalization, which has been traced back to pragmatic and adaptive policy-makers in the Commission, a competitive dynamic between the member states, and the facilitating role of the court, the EP, and societal interests. Processes of gradual institutionalization moved environmental policy principles from the status of programmatic statements into the formal *acquis* and finally into prominent treaty provisions. This prevents a rolling back, even in times of little political enthusiasm for new initiatives and rising criticism about high degrees of interventionism, excessive costs, and poor records of implementation especially during periods of economic recession. In this field, which is dominated by a regulatory policy mode, not contraction but adaptation and some experimentation with new or softer regulatory formats appear as the pattern of change, with the critics of yesterday becoming the reformers of tomorrow.

While the early 2000s were not characterized by great enthusiasm inside the EU for environmental protection in general, the climate-change issue appeared to mobilize forces not only in environmental policy, but also in areas such as energy, transport, agriculture, industry, international development, and the neighbourhood policy. In the issue area of climate change, EU environmental policy has become embedded in a larger project of policy coordination, which otherwise continues to be an unresolved problem in environmental policy. 'Climate policy integration' was helped by the presence of overarching policy targets and the political will to pursue some of the many dimensions of the climate issue—be it implications for the environment, energy security, industrial modernization, or the EU's international profile. The economic and financial crisis, however, has seen increasing resistance from the member states to ambitious climate-change targets, and the policy's focus has narrowed to a 'low-carbon' economic growth agenda. It remains to be seen whether this will be sufficient to maintain global leadership and, conversely, whether the Union's international reputational interest will continue to feed back into internal environmental policy-making.

NOTES

1 I gratefully acknowledge the research assistance of Jenna Juliane Schulte in the process of completing this chapter.

2 Interviews conducted in Brussels (June 2013).

3 The new member states have received between three (Czech Republic) and ten (Poland) transitional arrangements; the transition periods vary between countries and environmental sectors (the longest periods apply to industrial pollution). Complete data can be accessed at the Commission website: *http://europa.eu.int/comm/enlargement/ negotiations/*.

4 See the European Commission's web page on the Life Programme: *http://ec.europa.eu/ clima/policies/finance/budget/life/index_en.htm*.

5 Author interview, EP, May 2008.

6 Besides the committee chairmen, the rapporteurs assigned to individual policy proposals also play an important role in shaping the discussions within and between committees.

7 Its earlier name was Committee on the Environment, Public Health and Consumer Protection. Consumer protection has now moved to the Internal Market and Consumer Protection Committee (IMCO).

8 Ken Collins was chairman from 1979–84 and 1989–99, and vice-chairman from 1984–9.

9 Author interview, EP, May 2008.

10 For both individuals and environmental NGOs, this is effectively the only way to take legal action against the breach of EU law unless they are directly affected by the breach. This issue of access to the CJEU, which depends on the *locus standi* of the plaintiff, has created some public and legal controversy over the years, but it continues to be handled restrictively.

11 The Commission relies on the expertise of national as well as interest-group representatives in developing its policy proposals. In order to counterbalance the well-resourced industry influence, it has actively contributed to the presence of environmental or consumer-protection groups at the European level.

12 The process of implementation can be described as: (1) the formal transposition of the EU legislation (in the case of a directive); (2) notification of transposition; and (3) the actual application of the law 'on the ground'.

13 The regulatory framework for the management of chemicals and the establishment of the European Chemicals Agency consists of: (1) Regulation (EC) No. 1907/2006 of the European Parliament and of the Council of 18 December 2006 concerning the Registration, Evaluation, Authorisation and Restriction of Chemicals (REACH), establishing a European Chemicals Agency, amending Directive 1999/45/EC and repealing Council Regulation (EEC) No. 793/93, and Commission Regulation (EC) No. 1488/94, as well as Council Directive 76/769/EEC and Commission Directives 91/155/EEC, 93/67/EEC, 93/105/EC, and 2000/21/EC; and (2) Directive 2006/121/EC of the European Parliament and of the Council of 18 December 2006 amending Council Directive 67/548/EEC on the approximation of laws, regulations and administrative provisions relating to the classification, packaging and labelling of dangerous substances in order to adapt it to Regulation (EC) No. 1907/2006 of the European Parliament and of the Council concerning the Registration, Evaluation, Authorisation and Restriction of Chemicals (REACH) and establishing a European Chemicals Agency.

14 A complete list (dated Feb. 2012) can be found on the Commission homepage: *http://ec.europa. eu/environment/international_issues/pdf/agreements_en.pdf*.

15 Compared to 7 per cent for the US (albeit still hypothetical in the absence of a US signature) and 6 per cent for Japan.

16 See the United Nations Framework Convention on Climate Change web page on the Kyoto Protocol, at: *http://unfccc.int/kyoto_protocol/items/2830.php*.

17 Doha Amendment to the Kyoto Protocol at: *http://unfccc.int/files/kyoto_protocol/application/ pdf/kp_doha_amendment_english.pdf*.

FURTHER READING

The regularly updated manual of EU environmental policy (Farmer 2011) provides a brief overview of all EU environmental legislation and its political development. Knill and Liefferink (2007) provide a good, book-length overview of EU environmental governance and Jordan and Adelle (2013) put together core articles on this topic. Jordan (2002), Knill (2001), as well as Liefferink and Jordan (2004) look at the interplay between (selected) member states and EU policy-making—a topic only alluded to in this chapter. A useful overview of the EU's international role in environmental policy can be found in Delreux (2011); for climate policy, see Oberthür and Pallemaerts (2010) and Wurzel and Connelly (2011). On new policy instruments in the EU and in the member states, see Wurzel *et al.* (2013) and for implementation, Knill and Lenschow (2000). For an overview of the contributions all this research has made to our understanding of European integration, policy-making, and governance, see Lenschow (2007).

Delreux, T. (2011), *The EU as International Environmental Negotiator* (Farnham: Ashgate).

Farmer, A. (2011, continuously updated) (ed.), *Manual of Environmental Policy* (London: Taylor & Francis).

Jordan, A. (2002), *The Europeanization of British Environmental Policy: A Departmental Perspective* (Basingstoke: Palgrave Macmillan).

Jordan, A., and Adelle, C. (2013) (eds.), *Environmental Policy in the European Union: Actors, Institutions and Processes*, 3nd edn. (London: Earthscan).

Knill, C. (2001), *The Europeanisation of National Administrations: Patterns of Institutional Change and Persistence* (Cambridge: Cambridge University Press).

Knill, C., and Lenschow, A. (2000) (eds.), *Implementing EU Environmental Policy: New Directions and Old Problems* (Manchester: Manchester University Press).

Knill, C., and Liefferink, D. (2007) (eds.), *Environmental Politics in the European Union: Policy-making, Implementation and Patterns of Multi-Level Governance* (Manchester: Manchester University Press).

Lenschow, A. (2007), 'Environmental Policy in the European Union: Bridging Policy, Politics and Polity Dimensions', in K. E. Jørgensen, M. A. Pollack, and B. Rosamond (eds.), *Handbook of European Union Politics* (London: Sage), 413–32.

Liefferink, D., and Jordan, A. (2004) (eds.), *Environmental Policy in Europe: The Europeanisation of National Environmental Policy* (London: Routledge).

Oberthür, S., and Pallemaerts, M. (2010), *The New Climate Policies of the European Union: Internal Legislation and Climate Diplomacy* (Brussels: Brussels University Press).

Wurzel, R. K. W., and Connelly, J. (2011) (eds.), *The European Union as a Leader in International Climate Change Politics* (London: Routledge).

Wurzel, R. K. W., Zito, A. R., and Jordan, A. J. (2013), *Environmental Governance in Europe. A Comparative Analysis of New Environmental Policy Instruments* (Cheltenham: Edward Elgar).

CHAPTER 14

Energy Policy

Sharp Challenges and Rising Ambitions

David Buchan

▋ Summary

Energy policy has rapidly gained in importance for the European Union (EU), as it faces the challenges of creating an internal energy market, increasing energy security, and playing an active role in combating climate change. Reform of the energy market has been a constant activity since the late 1980s. Reform has been based on liberalizing cross-border competition, but this risks being increasingly undermined by member-state intervention and subsidy to promote renewable energy and to ensure adequate back-up power. Energy security has been an area of EU energy policy of little added value for member states, but this is changing with measures to improve infrastructure, to increase resilience against external shocks, such as interruptions of Russian gas, and to diversify supplies. Finally, efforts to curb energy use and to develop low-carbon energy are at the heart of Europe's new programmes and targets to combat climate change. These three strands of policy involve different policy-making communities and illustrate a range of different policy modes.

Introduction

Worries about dependence on energy imports, see-sawing oil prices, and energy-driven climate change have brought energy policy to the top of the EU's agenda in recent years. At the same time, energy-market liberalization, which has remained a constant on the EU agenda for the past twenty-five years, has been pushed harder than ever by the Commission. This chapter focuses on the EU's three main energy-related preoccupations: the internal energy market, energy security, and efforts to develop a low-carbon economy.

Each of these strands of energy policy has different characteristics and dynamics, involving different circles of policy-makers and stakeholders. These strands also have varied connections to other EU policy domains: energy-market liberalization is part of the single-market programme (see Chapter 5) and has been heavily affected by competition policy (see Chapter 6); energy security connects to EU foreign and security policy (see Chapter 18), while climate change brings together energy and environmental concerns (see Chapter 13).

As regards the internal energy market, the Commission in particular has, over the past several decades, sought adoption and implementation of several 'packages' of liberalizing legislation, with a controversial third package winning approval by the European Parliament (EP) in April 2009 and by the Council in June 2009. In 2007, dissatisfaction with the lack of competition and frequency of discrimination in the energy market had led the European Commission to make another push to open access to Europe's gas and electricity grids, where the first and second packages were judged to have largely failed in their aims (see the section 'Issues and interests' later in the chapter). The Commission proposed in its third package that energy supply companies should be forced to sell or 'unbundle' the ownership of any networks they owned. In the course of 2008, the Commission compromised in the face of solid opposition from the French and German governments, and agreed to let the member states opt for reinforced independent management of their networks. Nonetheless, the Commission managed to use antitrust pressure to get some significant ownership-unbundling in Germany.

Energy security, defined as having adequate access to energy at reasonable prices, has acquired far greater salience for the Union, especially because of new member states' concerns about over-reliance on Russia. Nowhere have the Union's 2004 and 2007 enlargements to central and eastern Europe had more impact than on relations with Russia, given the region's energy dependence on, but political animosity towards, Russia. Yet the twenty-eight member states still seem unsure about how far to go towards having a collective EU energy policy towards Russia, as distinct from national policies and bilateral deals with Moscow. But repeated interruptions in the flow of Russian energy along the traditional transit routes of Ukraine and Belarus have encouraged the EU to do more to diversify away from Russian energy altogether. In 2011, for the first time ever, member states gave the Commission a mandate to negotiate a legal framework for the import of energy, in this case gas from the Caspian. A further effort to reduce dependence on Russian energy followed Russia's annexation of the Crimean region of Ukraine in March 2014.

Europe's ambitious climate-change goals aim to transform almost every aspect of its energy system, given that energy use accounts for around two-thirds of global greenhouse gas emissions. When the European Council and the EP agreed in December 2008 on the new climate and renewable-energy package, it seemed that the perceived urgency of climate action might have the potential to develop an integrationist dynamic comparable to that created by the '1992' single-market programme (see Chapter 5). This has not proved to be the case. Economic recession, starting with the 2008 financial crisis and prolonged by the debt woes of the euro area, and the rest of the world's failure so far to match EU climate action, have dampened enthusiasm for what many see as an expensive go-it-alone European climate policy.

Scope and history of EU energy policy

The goals of energy policy—ensuring that energy is as cheap, secure, and clean as possible—are the same at the EU level as at the national level. But the remit for EU policy is narrower, addressing the internal energy market and environmental aspects of energy.

In the early years of European integration, coal and nuclear power did figure prominently, in the form of the 1951 Treaty of Paris (European Coal and Steel Community, ECSC) and in the 1957 Treaty of Rome (European Atomic Energy Community, or Euratom). The ECSC was essentially a political scheme to put coal, which had been an economic engine of war-making, under international constraints. That done, the ECSC continued for fifty years as a social instrument to assist, with money and re-training, the run-down of west European coal mining (and steel production). When that task was largely completed, the ECSC Treaty was allowed to expire in 2002. Euratom, which is still in force, had some of the same political rationale, namely to create international supervision over something that could be used as a weapon, although it was also thought that civil nuclear energy could be developed effectively on a collective European basis. In practice, Euratom has since functioned more as a technical agency, while EU governments have kept nuclear-policy decisions very much in their own hands. The ECSC and Euratom, therefore, were not devised, and have not served in practice, as parts of a common energy policy.

Both coal and nuclear power declined in importance relative to oil, the use of which expanded greatly in the 1950s and 1960s. The first oil crisis in 1973–4 was dealt with largely by the founding in 1974, on a US initiative, of the International Energy Agency (IEA) to organize the holding and sharing of emergency oil stocks among its members (Black 1977). The EU also has legislation on oil stocks, but for the nineteen EU states that belong to the IEA (which also includes Australia,

Canada, Japan, New Zealand, and the US) it is essentially secondary to their IEA obligations. So there was far less to the foundation of EU energy policy than initially meets the eye.

While the treaties contained no separate and specific article on energy policy, over the years policy-makers borrowed legal competence from the economic and environmental parts of the treaties to justify proposing and passing energy measures. Energy's economic importance gained recognition in the 1986 Single European Act (SEA) and the subsequent single-market programme (see Chapter 5). Leaning on the treaties' market-opening and antitrust principles (see Chapter 6), the Commission in 1989 set about the task of liberalizing the electricity and gas markets, a task in which it is still engaged today. EU policy thus far has such a narrow focus because it concentrates on those energy sources that are especially dependent on fixed, cross-border networks and which require regulation to prevent market abuse by dominant suppliers. By contrast, oil and coal have a more flexible transport system that is inherently less susceptible to market abuse. Therefore the EU policy focus on oil relates to security of supply and the level of stocks, and even then the EU plays a secondary role to the IEA.

The 1992 Maastricht Treaty on European Union (TEU) gave the EU competence to improve cross-border energy infrastructure in a programme known as Trans-European Networks (TENs) and increased the EU's ability to act on the environment (see Chapter 13 and Matlary 1996). It is on this legal foundation that the EU's ambitious climate-change programme has been erected.

More recently, two factors have combined to push up the agenda the idea of a more ambitious energy policy. On the one hand, the growing concern about climate change has focused attention on the need to reduce the use of carbon and to control emissions more effectively. On the other hand, eastern enlargement has drawn more attention to the issue of security of energy supplies. Hence, the Treaty of Lisbon (ToL) has given the EU a bigger role in energy. It states in Article 176A that:

In the context of the establishment and functioning of the internal market and with regard for the need to preserve and improve the environment, Union policy on Energy shall aim, in a spirit of solidarity between Member States, to:

- ensure the functioning of the energy market;
- ensure security of energy supply in the Union;
- promote energy efficiency and energy saving and the development of new and renewable forms of energy; and
- promote the interconnection of energy networks.

But the same article of the ToL goes on to reaffirm that 'such measures shall not affect a member state's right to determine the conditions for exploiting its energy resources, its choice between different energy sources and the general structure of its energy supply'. Thus the ToL does not reduce the autonomy that the member states currently enjoy. France is perfectly free to use nuclear reactors to generate most of its electricity, just as Poland does with its deep coal seams. Likewise, the UK has been free to go full steam ahead in extracting its oil and gas, just as the Netherlands has been free to husband its gas reserves carefully. Therefore the EU role in energy policy is weaker than the role of central governments in more developed federations. In the latter, even where fossil-fuel reserves are the property of states or provinces or (in the case of the US) private landowners, the federal authorities levy royalties, impose retail taxes, and own all offshore reserves and some onshore reserves. In the EU, national governments decide how to exploit their energy resources, how they tax energy, and what mix of energy sources they choose to rely on (with the exception of renewable energy for which national targets are agreed at an EU level).

Energy security has been the weakest side of the EU energy-policy triangle. Enlargement has increased the case for strengthening it. New central and east European states are keen for an EU energy-security policy to help them to avoid over-reliance on Russia, while older and bigger member states in western Europe still prefer to settle energy ties with Russia bilaterally. In the past, EU authorities have had little legal right to involve themselves in securing energy supply. Only with the ToL did they get formal competence 'to ensure security of energy supply'. One result of this has been that the Commission has been authorized to negotiate, on the EU's behalf, a legal framework for the import of Caspian gas as an alternative to Russian gas.

Internal energy market

The construction of the internal energy market has been the longest standing of the three strands of the EU's energy policy. It is situated at the intersection of two robust EU policies—the single European market (see Chapter 5) and competition policy (see Chapter 6). Progress to date has been hard-fought, but in 2011 the European Council formally set 2014 as the date for completion of the internal energy market.

Issues and interests

The Commission has been the champion of liberalization in the European energy market. Knowing the resistance from some governments, it was understandably slow in the 1990s to start its liberalization drive. Yet, once launched in this direction, the Commission has doggedly persisted, even after energy security and climate change began to eclipse liberalization as an issue. Its main goal is to curb the natural monopolies of the gas and power networks by ensuring open, non-discriminatory access for all third parties to these grids. It started with a first package of directives in 1996 (Electricity Directive 96/92/EC) and in 1998 (Gas Directive 98/30//EC), but soon decided these measures were too weak. So it proposed a second package of legislation (Electricity Directive 2003/54/EC and Gas Directive 2003/55/EC) that required the 'legal unbundling' of supply networks from energy generation, causing energy companies to put network grids at arm's length by placing them in separate subsidiaries. Again, the Commission soon decided that these measures did not go far enough to liberalize the market. So in 2007 it proposed its third package of measures, incorporating the concept of ownership unbundling (OU), forcing energy companies either to sell their networks outright or to put these networks under entirely independent management. These proposals provoked strong opposition from France and Germany as well as a number of small member states.

Behind the Commission's persistence is its conviction that a competitive and fully interconnected energy market would also help to tackle energy security (by making emergency stocks easily transferable around the EU) and climate change (by maximizing efficient use of energy and minimizing emissions). Another reason is that the Directorate-General for Competition (DG COMP) became heavily involved, when, in response to consumer complaints about rising gas and electricity prices, it started in mid-2005 an in-depth investigation into EU energy markets. This investigation uncovered, according to DG COMP, 'serious shortcomings' (Commission 2007d), particularly with regard to attempts by companies to keep rivals off their grids. As well as paving the way for some antitrust suits (see the following section), this sector-wide investigation led DG COMP to conclude that grids and networks had to be made stand-alone operations, and the way to do this was new ownership-unbundling legislation. In this, the DG then responsible for energy and transport (DG TREN) concurred. In 2010, DG TREN was divided into DG ENER responsible solely for energy policy and DG MOVE (mobility and transport).

A large number of member states backed the Commission's proposals on OU. This was not surprising as nearly half the EU members—thirteen to be precise—had already by 2007 taken their own national decisions to introduce a form of OU in electricity. Seven of these countries had also done so in gas. One factor was the UK's hardening of support for OU within the EU. Despite having led the unbundling revolution in the 1980s with the break-up of British Gas, the UK had for a long time paid little attention to the unreconstructed nature of the continental energy industry. But from 2000, as the UK turned from gas exporter to importer, it began to realize that it needed to ensure that the terms on which it imported gas from continental Europe were as competitive as possible.

Arrayed against OU were France, Germany, and six smaller states. In France, where the energy sector has been dominated by state-owned Electricité de France and Gaz de France, many politicians anathematized OU as forced privatization. In Germany, with its privately owned energy sector and constitutionally guaranteed property rights, many in industry as well as in politics lambasted OU as expropriation. Some smaller member states argued that their energy companies were too small to be unbundled.

Internal energy-market legislation is a matter for co-decision by the EP and the Council. While there was a clear majority in the EP for OU in electricity, many

members of the European Parliament (MEPs) shared the reluctance of some governments in the Council to interfere with the structure of a gas industry stretching far
beyond the EU. Most MEPs followed the line set by their political groups, rather
than their national governments. Particularly vociferous in speaking against their
governments' opposition to OU were Green MEPs from Germany and Luxembourg,
who claimed that the big utilities had deliberately kept renewable energy off their
grids, and urged that they should be broken up.

Significantly, the EU-level body of national regulators, European Regulators
Group for Electricity and Gas (ERGEG), endorsed the Commission's OU proposals. Whatever the line taken by their governments, almost every one of the
national regulators (twenty-seven at the time) supported the concept of stand-
alone networks because they were clearer and simpler to regulate. Lobbying over
energy-market reform takes place at several levels—at the member-state level
especially in the case of big state-owned producers, in special consultative fora
created by the Commission (see the following section), and through EU-wide associations. Among the latter, it has naturally been energy users who have lobbied
for a more competitive energy industry, including OU if necessary. Prominent
among these user groups is the European branch of the International Federation of Industrial Energy Consumers, together with its powerful German national affiliate, the Verband der Industriellen Energie und Kraftwirtschaft. The
Commission has been receptive to energy users' complaints about over-pricing
and anti-competitive practices. Such complaints spurred the Commission into
launching its 2005 competition inquiry into the energy sector and its third legislative package in 2007.

On the producers' side, the electricity industry, as represented by its main trade association, Eurelectric, generally responded more constructively to the Commission's
third package proposal than did the gas industry, represented by Eurogas whose
opposition to OU was more rigid. Electricity companies have felt less need to hang
on to their networks at all costs, in terms either of ownership or of management,
because networks are a relatively small part of their business, which is dominated
by power generation. Belatedly, the Commission realized that its campaign to force
energy-supply companies out of owning transmission infrastructure carried the risk
of discouraging much-needed new investment in transmission wires and pipes. In
2013, it issued guidance to the effect that it would be happy to see financial investors
put their money into Europe's energy infrastructure because such investors had no
energy-supply interests that could cause a conflict of interest.

In this strand of energy policy, the pattern of issues and interests is familiar from
many other sectors caught up in the drive to develop the single European market,
with persistent arguments between the enthusiasts and the doubters as regards the
pace of liberalization. The bias within the EU has been towards a faster pace, although in some member states powerful coalitions of governments and industries
have been able to apply the brakes now and then (see Chapter 5). The energy sector
has much in common with experience in other industries.

Third time lucky for liberalization?

In developing the internal energy market, the EU has been acting in classic regulatory or re-regulatory mode—and with considerable success, if the ambition of the task is taken into account. The Commission has been trying to open up to cross-border competition a sector that was historically organized around 'national champion' companies, backed, if not owned, by national governments, as well as to break up vertical integration in a sector where that structure has been the standard business model. By way of comparison with another federal system, the twenty-eight member states now have more of a standard electricity-market design than the fifty US states.

In terms of agenda-setting, a typical role of the Commission, there has been little surprise. The Commission has essentially been trying for years to push through the same agenda or to achieve the same goal—open access on energy networks. The greater power for national regulators that the Commission sought as part of its third package, and the proposal to separate ownership and operation of networks from other parts of the energy business, was to ensure that owners and operators of networks do not abuse their monopolies (see Table 14.1). In terms of the policy cycle (see Chapter 3), this raises a question about the implementation and enforcement of earlier directives. The Commission has pursued most member states for their failure to implement the third package, which should have been transposed into national law by 2011. The most widespread infringement of internal energy-market rules relates to the failure of many governments to limit the regulation of retail end-user electricity and gas prices to just the poor and vulnerable sections of their populations as is permitted by EU rules.

What has been new in recent years is the close cooperation between the Commission's energy and competition Directorates-General, and how competition

TABLE 14.1 Re-regulating energy				
	Unbundling of networks	**Access to networks**	**Market opening**	**National regulation**
First legislative package 1996–8	Separate management and accounts	Negotiated or regulated terms of access	Power: 35% open by 2003.Gas: 33% open by 2018	Mechanism for regulation
Second legislative package 2003	Separate subsidiary	Regulated terms of access	Power and gas markets 100% open by July 2007	Specific regulator for energy
Third legislative package 2009	Separate ownership or operator	Regulated terms of access	No change from second package	Upgraded and harmonized powers for national energy regulators

policy has been brought in to bolster liberalization. It was not like this at the outset. When in 1991 Leon Brittan, the Competition Commissioner, announced his intention to apply competition policy to energy, DG TREN was nervous that this would be 'a very costly political strategy' (Matlary 1996: 272) and might backfire. There was also a view, particularly promoted by France, that energy was special, and that it should be exempted from competition policy because it was a 'service of general economic interest'. The Commission produced a Green Paper (Commission 2003*d*) and then a White Paper (Commission 2004*c*) on services of general interest, but did not find evidence that energy liberalization had failed to serve the general interest.

DG COMP has used the in-depth knowledge it gained as a result of its 2005–6 energy-sector investigation in support of liberalization. In May 2006, it launched surprise inspections—or 'dawn raids' as the press like to call them—on a number of gas-company premises across western Europe. In December 2006, it did so with several electricity companies. In addition, during the following two years it launched formal antitrust investigations against several companies for allegedly shutting competitors out of their markets or manipulating prices. DG COMP subsequently turned its attention to the energy market in the newer member states. In 2012, it launched an antitrust inquiry into allegations that Gazprom had abused its dominant market position in eight central and east European member states to make them pay more for Russian gas than the prices it charges west European member states with access to alternative supply sources (European Commission press release, IP/12/937). In December 2013, Gazprom said it would seek a negotiated settlement of the allegations with the Commission.

Antitrust pressure provided an interesting interaction with the legislative reform process. The Commission maintained that the scale and nature of the conflict of interest inherent in vertically integrated energy companies required the sort of structural remedy that could be achieved only by legislation requiring 'stand-alone' networks, not through isolated antitrust actions imposing behavioural remedies (usually fines) on individual companies. 'This requires comprehensive structural reform [because] even the most diligent competition enforcement cannot solve all the problems in these markets'. noted Neelie Kroes (2007), then Competition Commissioner, launching the Commission's third package.

In parallel with the legislative measures over the past decade to equalize network access has been the trend towards more European-wide regulation. The big difference, however, between the two developments is that while there is an agreed goal of creating a single energy market, there is little desire—among governments or even in the Commission—to create a single European regulator. The Commission plays a central role, but often does so through its creation of, and influence over, various European regulatory and industry groups. Each package of liberalizing legislation has been accompanied by some development in regulation. The first package of 1996–8 was followed by the creation of industry fora. The Florence Forum was set up in 1998 as a twice-yearly meeting of all the stakeholders in the electricity industry—producers, transmission system operators (TSOs), consumers, traders—with national regulators, government officials, and the Commission. In 1999, the Madrid Forum was set up to do the same for the gas industry. The fora have provided a useful process of consultation between the regulators and the regulated. But, lacking any law-making or mandatory enforcement powers, they have been little more than regulation by cooperation. During this period, however, network operators were encouraged, particularly by the Commission, to form themselves into EU-wide associations—the European Network of Transmission System Operators for Electricity (ENTSOE) and the European Network of Transmission System Operators for Gas (ENTSOG)—to make consultation easier. As Cameron (2007: 104) points out, this constituted a form of unbundling at the European level by separating the TSOs out, irrespective of what was happening at the national level.

Moreover, the changing structure and ownership of national industries have required more explicit regulation, leading to the considerable expansion of the roles of national energy regulators. Their role began to acquire a European dimension under the first package of open-access directives of 1996 and 1998, which allowed the option of 'regulated' third-party access to networks on the basis of tariffs approved by national regulators. The second package of directives of 2003 required every member state to have a national energy regulator; by that stage all member states had one except for Germany, which finally set up a network regulator in 2005. National regulators were given a minimum set of powers and an instruction to coordinate with each other and liaise with the Commission. The Commission decided to make a kind of carbon copy of the Council of European Energy Regulators (CEER) (which the regulators had set up in 2000 as their own informal club), to call it the European Regulators' Group for Electricity and Gas (ERGEG), and to give it the formal duties of advising the Commission and consulting with industry on regulation. Despite these developments, the competences and independence of national regulators varied considerably, and they lacked any European mandate to take a broader view.

The Commission's third package (Electricity Directive 2009/72/EC and Gas Directive 2009/73/EC) promised a step-change in the national regulators' European role. It harmonized up the powers of national regulators. More importantly, it upgraded ERGEG into the Agency for the Cooperation of Energy Regulators (ACER) (Regulation 713/2009), which has, for the first time, the power to take and enforce binding decisions. This will enable national regulators to exercise some European powers. The Commission argued that such changes were necessary to ensure that whatever is decided on unbundling would be implemented and enforced. But as far as ACER is concerned, the Commission has not wanted this particular acorn to develop into an oak. In particular, it has been reluctant to give ACER power over the European associations of TSOs.

The Commission has used ENTSOE and ENTSOG to spearhead the completion of the internal energy market by 2014, in particular by drafting vital network codes for the EU grids following framework guidelines set by ACER, itself under Commission supervision. It was unusual to ask one part of an industry to draft rules for the rest of that industry. TSOs, though unbundled to varying degrees, are still commercial organizations, and their semi-legislative role has been queried by some other energy companies. However, they have been judged to be the only bodies with the expertise to carry out this technical task.

The Commission's stated reason for pulling its punches on ACER's powers was constitutional. The Court of Justice of the European Union (CJEU) in its 1958 *Meroni* ruling and other case law, has held that an authority to which power is delegated (like the Commission) cannot confer on another body (like ACER) powers different from those possessed by the delegated authority under the treaty, and that there should be no delegation of powers involving a wide margin of political discretion between different objectives and tasks that would escape democratic control. The Commission's Legal Service maintained that the *Meroni* doctrine must limit ACER's powers, while other Commission officials said they were nervous about ACER being used as the thin end of the wedge in a long-standing campaign by some to remove competition powers entirely from the Commission and give them to an independent agency (see Chapter 6). However, the Parliament rapporteur claimed (European Parliament 2008) that his proposals for ACER would respect *Meroni*, because, while the agency would have a prime role on codes of a technical nature, responsibility for network codes on politically sensitive competition and market issues would stay with the Commission. Some MEPs felt the Commission was inhibited less by a fifty-year-old ruling than by a desire to dominate a weak agency.

To sum up, carrying through the third package of energy-market reform has been the result of unusually close cooperation between the Commission's DG COMP and DG ENER, with antitrust action used as the spearhead for legislative reform. It may prove the high-water mark of energy-market liberalization, which has become somewhat eclipsed, even compromised, by issues of energy security and climate change that increasingly require non-market rules and mechanisms (see Box 14.1).

BOX 14.1   **Limiting state intervention in a liberalized market**

This has become a major preoccupation for the Commission. The issue also relates to energy security and climate policies discussed later in this chapter, but is addressed here because of its significant influence on the internal energy market. In its March 2013 Green Paper on the 2030 framework for energy and climate policy (Commission 2013*l*), the Commission admitted that it had overestimated the speed of energy infrastructure and market integration, and underestimated the impact of national renewable schemes, so far the most successful part of EU climate policy, and the knock-on effect of these subsidy schemes on the electricity market. In particular, intermittent, weather-dependent renewables have increasingly been pushing off the grid the very conventional fuels—gas, and to a lesser extent coal and nuclear—that these renewables need for occasional back-up security of supply. The problem is that progress on *integrationist* policies to link national markets with cross-border infrastructure and common trading arrangements is lagging behind the *disintegrationist* development of national renewable and back-up subsidy schemes. The Commission reluctantly accepted, in the 2009 energy and climate package, member states' insistence on running their national renewable subsidy schemes, and now, to the Commission's dismay, most governments are now planning to subsidise loss-making conventional power plants, especially gas-fired generation, that the utility companies say that they would otherwise have to close. The common feature of these capacity schemes is that they all have an autarkic, security-begins-at-home feature, favouring domestic over imported electricity. The Commission would like member states to rely more on each other for emergency power, but this presupposes cross-border interconnectors that are often not yet built or cross-border trading arrangements not yet agreed. To try to regain control of these *disintegrationist* tendencies, the Commission (2013*m*) issued guidelines in autumn 2013 that seek to persuade member states to Europeanize, or at least regionalize, their renewable and capacity schemes. If such persuasion does not work, the Commission is threatening to use the new set of state-aid rules that it is preparing for the energy and environment sector in order to enforce the guidelines, as indeed the big European utilities are begging the Commission to do.

Energy security

Energy security has traditionally been the weakest of the EU's three energy policy strands. The 2004 and 2007 enlargements have increased the case for strengthening it. The central and east European member states are keen for an EU energy-security policy to help them to avoid over-reliance on Russia, while bigger and more established member states generally prefer to deal with Russia bilaterally on energy issues. In the past, EU authorities have had little authority to involve themselves in securing energy supply. Only with the ToL did they get formal competence 'to ensure security of energy supply'. For the EU itself, energy security has habitually been more about gas, especially pipeline gas that locks customers into dependency on suppliers, rather than about oil, the supply of which can be more easily drawn from the global oil market. Instability within Middle East oil suppliers raises concerns for oil consumers in Europe, as elsewhere, but as mentioned in the Introduction these concerns are primarily dealt with in the wider forum of the IEA. The dependency concern about piped gas has created considerable interest, and some division, among EU member states about the possibility of Europe reviving its indigenous gas industry through replicating the US revolution in hydraulic fracturing, or fracking (see Box 14.2).

Issues and interests

The issue of energy security has gone up and down the ladder of salience within the EU depending on how easy it has been for Europeans to gain reliable access to energy supplies and on the variations in energy, especially oil, prices. In the 1970s, there were two moments of 'crisis' related to the actions of Middle East oil producers.

BOX 14.2   **Shale gas in Europe: a role for the EU?**

Until recently, the EU institutions have stayed largely on the sidelines in the shale gas debate, as have the US federal authorities, and for the same reasons—EU member states, like individual US states, play the main regulatory role and are divided on the 'fracking' issue. France and Bulgaria have passed legal bans on hydraulic fracturing, so far the only known commercial way of extracting shale gas or oil, while Poland has forged ahead and accounts for almost all of the fracking that has taken place in the EU. Several other governments, notably that of the UK, profess strong interest in exploiting their shale potential, but local opposition has constrained drilling. Reticence to act at the EU level also stems from the fact that the ToL clearly leaves it to member states to decide their energy mix. But the EU has been drawn in because the shale gas issue has become part of a wider debate about the perceived conflict between Europe's competitiveness and its unilateral climate policy. In this debate, the contrast is made between an economically depressed Europe and a US that has both embraced shale gas and avoided saddling itself with a burdensome climate policy. The particular fear is that Europe's energy-intensive industries will migrate to the US in search of cheaper energy input for manufacturing.

In 2012–13, the EP passed several resolutions which broadly affirm the right of member states to exploit shale gas, but call on them to do so under strict regulation that might require amending or extending existing EU environmental legislation. With existing directives on mining waste, water protection, water depletion, air pollution, and bio-diversity, the EU has environmental legislation covering almost all possible side effects of fracking for shale gas (Buchan 2013). However, in order to ensure consistency in the implementation of this legislation and a level playing field in fracking operations, in January 2014 the Commission (2014c) laid out, in the form of a formal recommendation, a list of measures that it expected member states to take to address health and environmental risks. It said it would review the application of the recommendation after eighteen months, and if the recommendation was ignored, new legislation might be proposed.

In subsequent years European consumers relaxed as new sources of oil and gas were discovered, including in Norway and the UK, and supplies seemed to be more reliably available. In recent years, however, concerns about energy security have re-emerged as, on the one hand, reserves in the EU have been depleted and, on the other hand, the doubts about the reliability of foreign suppliers, especially Russia, have increased.

The Commission has historically been a *demandeur* in energy security, seeking a role that has not been granted by the member states, particularly regarding negotiating with any specific supplier country. Its approach has been general: to police the level of emergency oil stocks; to hold energy dialogues with countries or groups of countries (e.g. the Organization of Petroleum Exporting Countries (OPEC)); and to try to export EU energy rules and policy to neighbouring countries through such mechanisms as the Energy Charter Treaty and the Energy Community (see the following section).

The weakness of EU energy-security policy is commonly put down to the fact that among the older member states, the bigger ones prefer to conduct their own foreign energy policies. In relation to Russia, it should be pointed out that energy is only part of the bilateral foreign policies that countries such as Germany, France, and Italy conduct with Moscow. Moreover, the energy element of these foreign policies—though backed by governments—is carried out largely by leading national champion companies, such as Germany's Eon, Gaz de France, and Italy's Eni, which have long-term contracts with Russia's Gazprom, because both sides see this as being in their interest. So the weakness of EU energy-security policy vis-à-vis Russia stems in part from a wider weakness in Europe's common foreign and security policy (see Chapter 18).

It is an open question whether having a major oil or energy company really contributes to a country's feeling of energy security. But the fact is that, while not all large EU states have an oil major, none of the smaller states do. Smaller states are therefore more interested in the EU having a common external-energy-security policy and speaking with one voice. Where the central and east European member states differ from other smaller states is that they want this voice, when directed at Moscow, to be a tough one. The central and east European member states still carry a strong anti-Russian animus from their days as forced members of Soviet institutions and alliances. Among this group the three Baltic states are in a unique position, because they are still linked to the Russian electricity grid, and not yet connected to the main EU grid. The European Council of February 2011 committed the EU to ending this energy isolation of the Baltic states by 2015.

Energy security is not a universal concern for European energy providers. The electricity sector is more concerned about network reliability and stability in the growing influx of intermittent renewable energy sources such as wind power (discussed in the next section on climate policy). The gas sector, which depends overwhelmingly on foreign gas and is tied to inflexible supply lines from abroad, by contrast, is very sensitive about energy security. This concern persists even though shipments by sea of liquefied natural gas (LNG) to Europe are increasing. Concerns about energy security contributed to the gas industry's hostility to the Commission's OU proposals, which threatened to make the companies sell their gas-transport and logistics facilities. Not only have the gas companies wanted to hold on to their pipelines, but many of them have also sought to raise the proportion of their gas sales that they can cover with gas from their own upstream assets, as insurance against gas shortages or price spikes. This has tended to incline Europe's gas companies against supporting a collective EU energy-security policy, if that were to make it harder for them to compete with each other for the lease of upstream assets from gas-producing states around Europe, such as Algeria and Russia, and, in the past and probably in the future, Egypt and Libya.

Overall, therefore, the discussion of energy security is marked by an untidy patchwork of different concerns and conflicting interests. These do not easily coalesce around collective and consistent European interests or yield a clear priority list of issues to be pursued.

Driven by events

In energy security, there is a gap between potential (what EU states could do together) and performance (what they actually do together). It is also difficult to characterize in terms of the EU's usual policy modes. The EU has taken some energy-security decisions—for instance, the 2004 Gas Security Directive (2004/67/EC), the 2005 Electricity Security Directive (2005/89/EC), the 2010 Gas Security of Supply Regulation (994/2010), and the establishment in 2011 of the Gas Coordination Group (representing government and Commission officials, regulators, and gas industry representatives)—in its traditional regulatory mode.

In terms of its grand design, however, EU energy-security policy is harder to categorize. It hardly falls into the category of policy coordination, because few member states have formal policies to coordinate. Most, if not all, member states would subscribe to the general desirability of having a diversity of energy types and energy sources. This is particularly the wish of Bulgaria, Estonia, Finland, Latvia, Lithuania, Romania, and Slovakia, which are entirely dependent on Russia for their gas imports. But only Spain has had a formal limit (60 per cent) on the maximum amount of gas that it can import from any one country, which was set in 2000 and corresponded to the level of Spain's imports from Algeria at the time (these have since proportionally declined). National energy-security policies tend to be just the random result of the accretion over time of decisions on energy mix and sourcing.

Nor can EU decision-making in energy security be remotely described as intensive transgovernmentalism in or outside EU institutions. Until recently, member states barely talked to each other about energy security. Nineteen member states can discuss energy-security issues in the IEA, but their decisions there on security of supply relate only to emergency oil stocks.

Events have tended to be the driver in energy security. The first measure to address oil security, the 1968 Oil Stocks Directive (68/414/EEC), which required the holding of minimum reserves, was taken well before the build-up to the first oil shock of 1973–4. That price-and-shortage shock prompted further legislation in the 1970s, but this was really to implement the regime for oil crisis management instituted by the IEA. This regime helped the EU to weather the second oil shock of 1979–80, which from the mid-1980s was followed by a long period of relative calm, even price decline, in energy markets that lasted until the long run-up in oil prices started from 2000.

The Soviet Union's collapse in 1991 jolted the EU into creating the Energy Charter Treaty (ECT). It was designed to create a legal framework for cross-border investment and trade in the energy sectors of the countries of the former Soviet Union, though it was dressed up as a wider international agreement and has more than fifty signatories. The ECT was an interesting attempt to export EU policy to countries from which the EU imports energy. It has, however, been only a limited success, not least because the most important target country, Russia, has not ratified the treaty or a subsequent protocol on gas transit. Gazprom objected to the transit provisions of the ECT, which it felt threatened its effective monopoly control over the flow of gas in Russia and the flow of gas from central Asia across Russia.

The EU has since exported its energy policy successfully in another direction. In 2005 it set up the Energy Community for south-eastern Europe to include the west Balkan countries of the former Yugoslavia, as well as Albania and, until they joined the EU, Bulgaria and Romania. The original aim of this Community—which obliges its members to accept EU energy-market principles and decisions—was to provide a framework for EU financial aid in repairing the shattered grid of the former Yugoslavia and to prepare states for eventual EU membership. Subsequently, it has come to be seen by Commission officials in Brussels as a valuable potential bridgehead for exporting EU energy-market policy and practice further east, to Turkey and beyond. The Commission has been keen to attract energy transit countries to the Energy Community, and of two countries that are key to the transport of pipeline gas to Europe, Ukraine joined in 2011, but not yet Turkey.

The 2004 and 2007 enlargements were thus a catalyst for policy on energy security. Central and east European states brought with them serious concerns about energy dependence on Russia and high expectations of the EU easing these concerns. These expectations were initially disappointed. When the Commission brought out its second Strategic Energy Review in November 2008 (Commission 2008*b*), it was a far more modest affair than the first strategic review in 2006 (Commission 2006*b*), which led to the new EU energy and climate programme. The energy-security aspect of this second review proposed revision of the 2004 Gas Security Directive, updating of oil-stocks policy to approximate to IEA practice, and greater EU involvement in planning and supporting energy infrastructure, including new pipelines to bring Caspian-region gas to Europe as an alternative to Russian supply. But to turn these proposals into action, it took the serious disruption of Russian gas supplies to much of south-eastern and central Europe in January 2009, as well as the impact of the ToL, with its first-time mentions of ensuring 'security of energy supply' in the EU 'in a spirit of solidarity'. The result was passage of the 2010 Gas Security of Supply Regulation (994/2010) which imposed requirements for larger gas storage and more gas pipe interconnections between member states, and the formal setting up in 2011 of the permanent Gas Coordination Group to deal with any gas security issues or crises. The acute political crisis in EU–Russian relations caused by Russia's behaviour in Ukraine in 2014, and the consequent threat to the supply of Russian gas to Europe through Ukraine, has also spurred further efforts to improve the Union's resilience to external energy shocks over Ukraine, and to diversify sources of energy imports away from Russia. Following Germany's decision, in the wake of Japan's 2011 Fukushima nuclear disaster, to accelerate its exit from nuclear power without consulting any of its EU neighbours, an Electricity Coordination Group was also set up, primarily to discuss any national energy-mix decisions that might impact EU partners.

To sum up in one sentence, the EU was ill-prepared for the implications of enlargement for its energy security, but events finally forced energy security on to the top of the EU agenda and into the ToL.

Climate change

The third strand of EU energy policy, climate change, is arguably the one in which the EU has shown the greatest ambition. EU policy-makers see themselves as pioneers in developing both international and domestic measures to mitigate climate change, especially through the part they played in negotiating the Kyoto Protocol and its implementing provisions and the role it has tried to play in the negotiation of a follow-on international climate agreement (Sbragia 2000; Lenschow 2005). Ambition to lead internationally (see Chapter 13) has translated into an effort to lead by example and thus to ambitious internal targets for reducing greenhouse gas emissions. Because of energy production's significant contribution to greenhouse gas emissions, this has had major implications for internal energy policy. However, the EU has found it very difficult to adjust its key climate-policy instrument, the Emissions Trading System (ETS), to the reality of Europe's prolonged economic downturn, and the price of carbon traded on the ETS has fallen too low to change the behaviour of either electricity generators or users. In January 2014, the Commission (2014*b*) proposed new emission targets for 2030 and a reform of the ETS.

Issues and interests

The Commission has been particularly entrepreneurial with regard to climate change. Internally, it managed to reverse some initial European scepticism about using a cap-and-trade system to control carbon emissions, which involves putting a reduced (and gradually declining) cap on emissions, issuing permits for emissions up to that overall cap, and allowing trading of these permits. In 2003, the EU created the ETS (Directive 2003/87/EC 'establishing a scheme for greenhouse gas emission allowance trading within the Community') and turned it into the central instrument for implementing the EU's Kyoto obligations.

Externally, the Commission exploited the US rejection in 2001 of the 1997 Kyoto Protocol by effectively taking over leadership of international efforts to combat climate change (see Chapter 13). Most member states shared the Commission's desire for EU leadership in the United Nations climate negotiations. Consequently, the member states' governments have by and large acquiesced in the Commission's redesign of climate-change policies, challenging its detail more than its principles. The publication of the Stern Review (2006), which focused on the economics of climate action and showed the pay-off of early action to combat global warming, may have constituted a critical juncture at which there was a paradigm shift to put climate change ahead of other concerns. Indeed, in some member states governmental portfolios were rearranged by collocating the relevant energy and environmental ministries under the same minister, as France did in 2007 and the UK in 2008, in order to improve policy-making coherence. The EP, where Greens are well represented, is also strongly committed to combating climate change.

That said, climate-change policies evoke different reactions within governments. Energy or industry ministers tend to want to temper the climate-change enthusiasm of their environment ministerial colleagues with realism about the competitive effects of making European industry pay for stringent carbon controls. The newer member states have tended to be less enthusiastic about taking radical measures to address climate change, worried about the cost implications for their relatively poor and energy-intensive economies. Moreover, some of them are heavily dependent on coal for electricity generation; coal generates 95 per cent of Polish power, for instance.

Energy-intensive industries—particularly aluminium, cement, and steel—concerned about foreign competition, particularly amid the economic downturn from 2008, are very concerned about the implications of the increased energy costs associated with addressing climate change because their competitors outside Europe would not face the same costs.

There were two particular drivers to the development of the EU's climate-change-related energy policy in 2008. One was the desire for leadership in the negotiation of a successor agreement to Kyoto, which, it was hoped, would set binding emissions targets from 2012. The other was to prevent 'gaming' of the allocation system by national governments for the benefit of their own industries. In January 2008, the Commission (2008a) proposed a set of binding targets for reductions in emissions, increased use of renewables, greater energy efficiency, and a more centralized allocation of permits under the ETS.

External ambition and internal compromise

The major feature of the negotiations leading up to the EU's December 2008 climate and renewable energy agreement was the revolt of new member states over its cost for their relatively poor economies. In its January 2008 blueprint, the Commission had tried to head off this revolt by proposing that central and east European member states should get: (1) less demanding targets for increases in renewables with several concessions; (2) permission to increase emissions in sectors outside the ETS (mainly transport, building, agriculture, and services), in contrast to emissions cuts for richer, older member states; and (3) a slightly larger share of ETS allowances to auction than their share of economic output would warrant.

But the central and east European member states made clear during the course of 2008 that they wanted more. They organized within the Council and negotiated as a bloc with the French presidency. Eventually they settled after getting two more concessions—a further increase in ETS auction revenue and transitional free allowances for their power sectors. However, central and east European states still face adjustment problems to the new climate and green-energy policies that accelerate the adaptation these countries have already had to make from the energy wastefulness of their communist past.

In the December 2008 agreement, the Commission did succeed in securing greater centralization of the allocation of carbon permits under the ETS. Under the agreement, allocation moved in 2013 from national governments to a mixture of market auctioning and allocation by the Commission.

However, the Commission largely failed in its attempt to design a parallel pan-EU system for trading renewable electricity. This was not totally surprising. While the Commission had a fairly clear field in designing the ETS—only the UK and Denmark had prior national emission schemes—it had, in the trading of renewables, to steer around twenty-seven national support schemes, often dear to their governments' hearts. The EP largely strongly supported the Commission's proposals, but they too disliked the Commission proposal for free cross-border trade in renewable electricity because of its probable effect in disrupting generous green-power subsidies. The opposition of the EP, supported by several key governments in the Council, meant that restrictions on trade in renewables were retained. Nonetheless, the initiative also sets differentiated renewable-energy targets for all twenty-seven member states, despite ToL language letting countries keep control of their energy mix. The agreement also sets a common bio-fuels target for all (see Box 14.3), despite MEPs' criticism that this would aggravate food shortages and price surges by encouraging crop-based fuels. MEPs did secure changes to encourage renewable road fuels not based on food crops.

The economic downturn during 2008 also affected the strength of support amongst the old member states, although primarily in the form of seeking special treatment of selected sectors. It caused Chancellor Angela Merkel's German government—with very separate environment and economics departments under ministers from different parties—to insist that major exporting industries, such as Germany's, should continue to have free carbon permits as long as they remained in danger of losing market share to foreign rivals with no carbon constraints. The downturn also fuelled similar demands from poorer central and east European states for free allocations, especially if, like Poland, they were heavily dependent on dirty coal for power generation.

BOX 14.3	The EU energy and climate change goals for 2020, agreed in December 2008

- 20 per cent reduction in greenhouse gas emissions by 2020 compared to 1990; up to 30 per cent in the case of a matching international agreement;

- 20 per cent renewable share in total energy consumption by 2020, based on binding targets for individual member states;

- 10 per cent minimum share for renewable energy in all forms of transport. Second-generation bio-fuels, made from wood and waste and that do not compete with food, and electricity to power cars count extra towards this target;

- 20 per cent improvement in energy efficiency by 2020 compared to business-as-usual projections. This is not a binding target nor will it mean a cut in overall energy use.

Citing the problems of recession and foreign competition, European industry has lobbied effectively for a gradual phasing-in of paid carbon allowances, under a system whereby companies would have to buy their carbon allowances at auction, instead of being given them free, in the reform of the ETS. The electricity industry in the old member states accepted early on that it would have to pay for its permits in the future. Not being exposed to competition from outside the EU, the power sector can pass on the cost of permits to its EU customers without fear of losing market share. This, of course, raises costs for its customers, especially electricity-intensive industries that are exposed to extra-EU competition, and therefore, if they pass on all of their higher energy bills to customers, they risk losing market share or jobs to non-EU competitors. So in the reform of the ETS they lobbied for, and won, the promise that they would continue to receive free allocations of emissions permits. Thus, while most of the broad intent of the Commission's proposal survived in the December 2008 agreement, a number of compromises were made to diminish the economic impact on some actors, be they member states or industries.

However, all the pressures that had made the 2008 reform of the post-2012 ETS a considerable feat of negotiation had magnified by 2014. By then the problem on the ETS was not free allowances, but simply far too many. Within one year, 2012, the surplus of allowances hanging over the trading system had doubled from 1 billion to 2 billion allowances, for a variety of reasons. Demand for allowances was down due to recession, while supply was inflated by an influx of international credits, by companies carrying over unused allowances from previous ETS phases, and by the Commission selling some reserve allowances in order to fund other energy objectives such as carbon capture and storage.

Persuading member states to make an extra effort, and to pay an extra price, would have been far easier if the EU still had a sense of leadership in international climate negotiations. But this sense largely evaporated at the 2009 climate summit in Copenhagen (see Chapter 13). The EU arrived there with a firm legal commitment to cut its own emissions, which it hoped would form the keystone of a new binding international treaty. However, it found itself completely bypassed by the US and leading developing countries, which rejected any binding commitments in favour of allowing countries to offer voluntary emissions reductions as they saw fit. At the 2011 Durban climate summit, the EU regained some ground in helping to broker an agreement aimed at producing in 2015 an emission-reduction deal of some unspecified legal force, but which would not take effect until 2020. Yet, at subsequent climate summits in Doha in 2012 and Warsaw in 2013 the EU had little to show for its efforts to accelerate progress towards a 2015 deal.

For several years after Copenhagen, therefore, the Commission found little enthusiasm for an extra climate effort on Europe's part. Eventually, the Commission came up with a short-term solution known as backloading, for which it won hard-fought approval from the Parliament in 2013. This backloading will not reduce the number of allowances on the ETS, but merely delays auctioning 900 million of them until near 2020.

Struggling to keep its own carbon-trading system patched together, the EU has scaled down its aspirations for international climate leadership. For instance, the EU had boldly decided to require, from the start of 2012, all international airlines to obtain ETS carbon allowances for all and any of their flights ending in or originating from European airports. It has since suspended this requirement following an outcry from third countries such as the US and China, pending the outcome of international aviation talks on emissions. Structural reform of the ETS is clearly vital, if the EU is to have real credibility in the next major round of world climate talks in 2015.

In an effort to bolster the long-term credibility of the ETS, the Commission (2014d) proposed in January 2014 the creation of, from 2021 on, 'a market stability reserve' to regulate automatically carbon-allowance liquidity in the ETS; allowances would be put into the reserve in times of excess liquidity, and returned to the market at time of tighter liquidity. This reform came as part of the Commission's (2014b) proposed energy and climate targets for 2030, designed to provide policy certainty to investors in low-carbon energy and to set out Europe's contribution to the global climate negotiations in 2015.

The main proposed targets are for a 40 per cent reduction in emissions by 2030 compared to 1990, and for a EU-wide binding target for a 27 per cent renewable share in total energy consumption. The Commission claimed that the 40 per cent emission target was compatible with the long-term goal of the EU, along with other developed economies, to cut emissions by 80–95 per cent by 2050, but was criticized for its lack of ambition by environmental groups. The latter, however, reserved their main criticism for the Commission proposal to replace, post-2020, national renewable targets with a relatively low, single EU-wide target that posed evident problems of enforcement. The Commission said the switch was to give member states more flexibility in reducing emissions, and it proposed a new 'governance framework' based on Commission supervision of national energy plans. The idea is explicitly borrowed from the European Semester process of Commission supervision of national fiscal and economic policies. In policing policy in this area, the Commission has, effectively, an external ally in the capital markets which quickly penalize governments showing fiscal laxity. Whether the same system can be translated to energy and climate policy, where there is no instant danger for governments letting their national policies stray from the EU or Commission line, is doubtful.

To sum up with regard to climate change, the EU is acting in what might be called a 'revolutionary regulatory mode'—seeking to change the way Europeans live, produce their energy, make their products, heat their houses, and take their holidays, and by taking the lead in climate-change negotiations seeking to some extent to change the rest of the world's lifestyle. As it has turned out, many Europeans were not ready for the revolution, and the EU's international partners have been similarly wary of accepting the EU's global climate leadership.

The EU showed some capacity to learn from the mistakes in the early phases of the ETS when it came to designing later stages. But climate-change policy depends on a tricky trade-off between economic and environmental factors, requiring complex brokering of competing interests within both EU institutions and national governments, a process which is susceptible to economic cycles. The difficulty of adapting the ETS to new realities is a reminder that EU legislation is as hard to modify as it was to pass in the first place.

Conclusion

EU energy policy has developed unevenly because it is part economic policy, part environmental policy, and part security policy. Market-making came first, but it took several decades before environmental policy took off, and the EU is still stumbling over security policy. Future energy policy will also develop unevenly, with different policy strands moving at different paces and also becoming more intertwined. An increasing threat to the goal of a geographically unified energy market achieved through liberalization is the existence of twenty-eight national renewable-energy subsidy schemes and the emergence of national-capacity subsidy schemes to guarantee back-up for these renewables. These schemes are a challenge to market unity because they favour national energy providers, and to liberalization because they are state interventionist in nature. However, they may be inevitable if Europe is to meet its climate goals and deal with a potentially wider risk of the lights going off than was posed by the occasional cut-off of Russian gas in the past. One solution is for the EU to redouble its traditional focus on improving cross-border energy infrastructure so that member states could trade more renewable energy among themselves and rely more on neighbouring states in times of energy shortage. This would make it easier to regionalize, and eventually Europeanize, these subsidy schemes that may become a lasting feature of the low-carbon economy.

As for climate change, the EU is unlikely to recover that first-flush enthusiasm that came from inventing and implementing the first international emissions trading system, until it finds that its leadership has some serious followers in the international community. Therefore a revival of EU climate policy requires not only some structural reform of its ETS that leads to a permanently tighter adjustment downwards of the supply of allowances to achieve real reductions in emissions. It also depends on the EU recovering its nerve about economic competitiveness, which may require either a shale gas revolution in Europe or a waning of the shale gas revolution in the US. Most of all, it will depend on the world's two largest emitters, the US and China, submitting themselves to some form of carbon restraint.

FURTHER READING

Black (1977) and Matlary (1996) provide useful background to the development of classic EU energy policy, and Helm (2007) sets the scene for the broadening of energy policy to tackle climate change. On the three main strands of energy policy, Cameron (2007) is comprehensive on the internal energy market, while Barysch (2008) and Skjaerseth and Wettestad (2008) are informative on key aspects of energy security and climate change, and Stern (2006) addresses the economic and policy dimensions of climate change. Buchan (2009) discusses all of these issues in more depth. However, EU energy and climate policy has recently come in for increasing criticism, much of which is summed up in Helm (2013). On the shale gas revolution and its implications for the EU, see Buchan (2013). For news, a good website for tracking EU energy policy is *http://www.euractiv.com* and for analysis, go to *http://www.energypolicyblog.com/*.

Barysch, K. (2008) (ed.), *Pipelines, Politics and Power: The Future of EU–Russia Relations* (London: Centre for European Reform).

Black, R. E. (1977), 'Plus Ça Change, Plus C'est la Même Chose: Nine Governments in Search of a Common Energy Policy', in H. Wallace, W. Wallace, and C. Webb (eds.), *Policy-Making in the European Communities* (Chichester: John Wiley), 165–96.

Buchan, D. (2009), *Energy and Climate Change: Europe at the Crossroads* (Oxford: Oxford University Press).

Buchan, D. (2013), *Can Shale Gas Transform Europe's Energy Landscape?* (London: Centre for European Reform).

Cameron, P. (2007), *Competition in Energy Markets: Law and Regulation in the European Union*, 2nd edn. (Oxford: Oxford University Press).

Helm, D. (2007), 'European Energy Policy: Securing Supplies and Meeting the Challenge of Climate Change', in D. Helm (ed.), *The New Energy Paradigm* (Oxford: Oxford University Press), 440–51.

Helm, D. (2013), *The Carbon Crunch: How We're Getting Climate Change Wrong—and How to Fix It* (New Haven, CT: Yale University Press).

Matlary, J. H. (1996), *'Energy Policy: From a National to a European Framework?'* in H. Wallace and W. Wallace (eds.), *Policy-Making in the European Union*, 3rd edn. (Oxford: Oxford University Press), 257–77.

Skjaerseth, J. B., and Wettestad, J. (2008), *EU Emissions Trading: Initiation, Decision-Making and Implementation* (Farnham: Ashgate).

Stern, N. (2006), *The Economics of Climate Change: The Stern Review* (London: HM Treasury).

CHAPTER 15

Justice and Home Affairs
Institutional Change and Policy Continuity

Sandra Lavenex

▌ Summary

The control of entry to, and residence within, national territory, citizenship, civil liberties, law, justice, and order lie very close to the core of the state. Nevertheless, the permeability of borders within the European Union (EU) has prompted cooperation among governments, and in fewer than twenty years, justice and home affairs (JHA) have moved from a peripheral aspect to a focal point of European integration. Given the judicial and legal implications of rising cross-border movement, cooperation among national agencies concerned with combating crime, fighting terrorism, and managing borders, immigration and asylum has thus gradually moved from loose
(continued...)

intergovernmental cooperation to more supranational governance within the EU. The Treaty of Lisbon (ToL) constitutes a milestone in the communitarization process, introducing the ordinary legislative procedure to the whole of JHA. However, member governments remain reluctant to transfer sovereignty in these areas, and some issues, like immigration, have become increasingly politicized. Agreement on common policies has thus often been tedious and implementation of agreed commitments is patchy.

Introduction

The ambition involved in creating an 'area of freedom, security, and justice' (AFSJ) within the EU may be compared with that which propelled the single market (see Chapter 5). The ToL lists the establishment of an AFSJ second in the general aims of the EU (Art. 3 TFEU), right after the promotion of peace and well-being and before the functioning of the single market. In contrast to economic integration, however, which has been at the core of the European integration project since its inception, JHA touches on many issues that are deeply entrenched in national political and judicial systems and have strong affinities to questions of state sovereignty; since the seventeenth century, the state has drawn legitimacy from its capacity to provide security for its inhabitants (Mitsilegas *et al.* 2003: 7). Cooperation in JHA also has direct implications for democratic values and for the balance between liberty and security in the Union and its member states. The intergovernmental decision-making procedures that prevailed until recently in this area have privileged security considerations over those relating to 'freedom' or 'justice'.

A second characteristic of JHA cooperation has been member-state reluctance to engage in 'hard' supranational legislation. The sensitivity of issues such as immigration and organized crime in national political debates and electoral campaigns and the diversity of legal traditions and problem constellations in the member states have sustained reservations about transfers of responsibilities to the EU. As a consequence, transgovernmental governance is the dominant mode of integration in JHA. Transgovernmentalism combines elements of the traditional 'Community method' with more intergovernmental ones: it is characterized by the relative weakness of legal harmonization and a focus on more operational aspects of coordination between national authorities, usually under the auspices of an independent regulatory agency such as Europol for police cooperation, the European Agency for the management of Operational Cooperation at the External Borders of the Member States of the European Union (Frontex) for external border controls, or the European Asylum Support Office (EASO) for asylum.

The ToL strengthened EU competence in JHA; extended the ordinary legislative procedure, as well as the judicial power of the Court of Justice of the European

Union (CJEU), to all sub-fields that were formerly intergovernmental; and upgraded the Charter of Fundamental Rights to a legally binding instrument. This may constitute a watershed in the evolution of the AFSJ. These institutional reforms emphasize the human-rights dimension of JHA and provide the basis for stronger supranational legislation. Whether the member states will make use of this altered institutional framework to promote true communitarization, however, will depend in large part on their political readiness to go down this road.

This chapter starts with a short review of the emergence and institutionalization of JHA cooperation in the EU treaties; it then presents its key actors and institutional set-up and discusses the main policy developments in related fields and their implementation in the member states.

The institutionalization of justice and home affairs cooperation

The dynamics of this new area of European integration reside both within and outside the EU and its member states. One important internal motor has been the spill-over from the achievement of freedom of movement in the single market (see Chapter 5). The decision in the 1985 Schengen Agreement to apply the elimination of internal border controls that had been in place among the Benelux countries since 1948 to five contracting member states—Belgium, France, Germany, Luxembourg, and the Netherlands—spurred concern about safeguarding internal security and prompted closer cooperation on questions relating to cross-border phenomena such as immigration, organized crime, and drug trafficking. The surge of asylum-seekers from outside western Europe in the 1980s which followed the closure of legal channels for economic immigration, the phenomena of organized crime and terrorism, and the end of the cold war, which opened the EU's previously closed eastern border to hopeful immigrants and criminal networks, generated external pressures for closer cooperation.

This intensified coordination could draw on informal cooperation among security services and law-enforcement agencies that had developed since the 1970s. These included the Pompidou Group on drugs, set up in 1972 within the wider Council of Europe, and the Trevi Group created at the December 1975 European Council in Rome to coordinate cooperation against organized crime and terrorism.

In 1990 two important international treaties set the guidelines for future European cooperation. The Schengen Implementing Convention (SIC) devised 'compensatory measures' for the removal of frontier controls, covering asylum, a common visa regime, illegal immigration, cross-border police competences, and a common computerized system for the exchange of personal data (Schengen Information System (SIS)). The Dublin Convention on Asylum, concluded among all EU member states, incorporated the asylum rules also included in the SIC and established the responsibility of the state in which an asylum-seeker first enters for the examination of an asylum claim.

Thus, prior to the 1992 (Maastricht) Treaty on European Union (TEU) there was already an extensive network of cooperation that operated both outside and under the overall authority of the European Council. Cooperation took place on several political and executive levels, ranging from ministers through directors-general of the relevant ministries to middle-ranking civil servants, and representatives of police forces and other agencies. Cooperation among the initially five Schengen states was to turn into a motor for and 'laboratory' of integration and had an influential impact on the subsequent communitarization of cooperation (Monar 2001).

From Maastricht's intergovernmental 'third pillar' to Amsterdam's partial communitarization

JHA were included in the EU treaties for the first time in Maastricht's 'third pillar'. Contrary to an earlier proposal by the Dutch Council presidency, which suggested bringing both the common foreign and security policy (CFSP) and JHA into a single integrated structure, JHA cooperation was introduced, like the CFSP, on a purely intergovernmental basis in a separate 'pillar' (on CFSP, see Chapter 18). The 'third pillar' included asylum policy, rules and controls on external border-crossing, immigration policy, and police and judicial cooperation in civil and criminal matters as 'matters of common interest'. In this way, the existing network of committees was formalized without transforming the framework of authority and accountability (see Lavenex and Wallace 2005).

Despite this loose intergovernmental structure, a transformation of the working practices of interior ministries and of police forces occurred, which had remained among the least internationally minded within national governments, leading to the emergence of an intensive transgovernmental network (see Chapter 4). By the mid-1990s, Europol was taking shape as a coordinating agency for cooperation among national police forces, even though the Europol Convention had not yet been ratified by all member states. Four common databases were being set in place: the SIS was already up and running; the Customs Information System was being computerized; and the Europol Information System and Eurodac, the fingerprint database for asylum-seekers, were being developed. Ministries of justice, however, were not yet embedded in a similar European network.

Despite these achievements, the intergovernmental procedures bore three principal weaknesses that ultimately lay behind the Amsterdam reforms:

- ambiguity about the legal and constitutional framework, evident in the frequency with which institutional issues were entangled with policy proposals;

- lack of democratic accountability and political visibility of this essentially bureaucratic framework for policy, which allowed the practice of cooperation to develop far beyond what was reported to the European and the national parliaments or to national publics; and

- the absence of mechanisms for ensuring national ratification or implementation.

The prospect of eastern enlargement added to the political salience of the policy fields covered by JHA cooperation and exacerbated the limits of decision-making structures based on unanimity.

The Treaty of Amsterdam (ToA) contained substantial changes to the framework for JHA. A new Title IV transferred migration and other related policies to the first pillar, specifying a number of measures to be adopted within five years (by May 2004, ex Art. 62(3) TEC). A transition clause according to which supranational decision-making procedures would apply only after adoption of these measures (including co-decision with the EP and qualified majority voting (QMV)) and limitations on the powers of the CJEU symbolized member states' hesitation towards communitarization. Police cooperation and judicial cooperation in criminal matters remained in a revised and lengthened 'third pillar', replacing the opaque legal instruments of the TEU by well-established, legally binding instruments (with the exception of framework decisions), and the Schengen *acquis* was integrated into the treaties. It is important to note that the ToA did not provide for comprehensive competences in the sense of creating 'classic' EU 'common policies', even in the case of the 'common visa policy' or the 'common asylum system', which come closest to this idea. While the Treaty of Nice (ToN) dealt primarily with the question of how to accommodate the entry of new member states, JHA remained largely unchanged until the ToL.

Towards a supranational AFSJ? The Treaty of Lisbon

JHA occupied a central stage in the convention leading to the (failed) Constitutional Treaty and, subsequently, the ToL. The justification for the Lisbon reforms draws heavily on public concerns about internal security and citizens' expectations that the EU should 'do something' about it (e.g. Eurobarometer 2008). The phraseology of an 'area of freedom, security, and justice', first introduced with the ToA, was a precursor of this attempt at 'making Europe more relevant for its citizens' (see Monar 1997; McDonagh 1998). A second reason for the Lisbon changes was dissatisfaction with the weak implementation of agreed commitments. The main innovations of the ToL are summarized in Box 15.1.

Flexible geometry in the AFSJ

National sensitivities about sovereignty have prompted a series of important opt-outs from the AFSJ, most of which date from the Amsterdam period. Denmark, for

---

BOX 15.1   **Changes to JHA in the Treaty of Lisbon**

- Article 3 TFEU lists the goal of establishing the AFSJ second in the hierarchy of goals pursued by the EU, right after the promotion of peace and economic well-being.
- The abolition of the pillar structure extends the ordinary legislative procedure to most former 'third pillar' matters and lifts most of the existing limitations on judicial control by the CJEU.
- Article 77 TFEU formalizes the goal of integrated border management.
- Article 78 and 79 TFEU postulate 'common policies' on asylum and immigration; but the 'right of member States to determine volumes of admission', for example for economic migration is, however, 'not affected' (Art. 79(5)), and legislation regarding immigrant integration in the member states is excluded (Art. 79(4)).
- In the field of criminal law, Article 82(1) TFEU codifies the principle of mutual recognition. Article 82(2) introduces an explicit competence for legislation in the field of criminal procedure, while Article 83 strengthens the basis for common measures regarding substantive criminal law.
- Article 86 TFEU opens the possibility for establishing a European public prosecutor, subject to a unanimous vote in the Council.
- An annex introduces national parliaments as guardians of the principles of proportionality and subsidiarity and as participants in the evaluation of the work of JHA bodies and agencies.
- A general safeguard according to which the Union has to 'respect essential state functions including ... maintaining law and order and safeguarding national security' (Art. 4(2)) was introduced.

---

example, is a Schengen member and participates in the free movement area, but is free to adopt relevant European provisions as international law rather than EU law (thereby avoiding its direct effect and CJEU jurisdiction). Ireland and the UK maintain their opt-out from Schengen and retain internal frontier controls, but adhere, on a selective basis, and subject to unanimous agreement by 'insiders', to the flanking measures of the JHA *acquis* such as asylum, police, and judicial cooperation in criminal matters, and the SIS.

Apart from these voluntary exemptions from the JHA *acquis*, the conditionality of the Schengen accession mechanisms adds a more compulsory form of flexibility. Notwithstanding their obligation to adopt the JHA *acquis* including the Schengen provisions in full, new member states have first to prove their capacity to effectively implement these tight border-management provisions before being recognized as having achieved what is often referred to as 'Schengen maturity' by the old members. By the end of 2013, full Schengen members included all old EU member states with the exception of Ireland and the UK plus three non-EU members (see later in this section). Bulgaria, Croatia, Cyprus, and Romania were still in the process of qualifying for 'Schengen maturity'.

Existing opt-out provisions and extended opportunities for enhanced cooperation under the treaties have not prevented individual member states from engaging in selective forms of intergovernmental cooperation outside the provisions of the treaties. The most prominent example is the Prüm Treaty concluded on a German initiative with Austria, Belgium, France, Luxembourg, the Netherlands, and Spain in 2005. Facilitating and widening the conditions for the exchange of data included in the various JHA databases (see the section 'The proliferation of semi-autonomous agencies and databases' later in the chapter) and intensifying operational cooperation between police, law-enforcement, and immigration offices, this treaty is also sometimes referred to as 'Schengen III', a laboratory for deeper police cooperation among a vanguard of a few member states. As with the integration of Schengen into the ToA, the German Council presidency in 2007 recognized the case for extending these intensified forms of cooperation to the rest of the member states by steering the incorporation of the Prüm provisions into EU legislation. The ToL now provides that pioneer groups of at least nine member states can engage in enhanced cooperation on certain criminal justice and police cooperation matters within EU treaty structures.

That non-EU member states participate in JHA cooperation exacerbates the variable geometry of the 'area of freedom, security, and justice'. Norway and Iceland, as members of the pre-existing Nordic common travel area, have been included within the Schengen area, and are fully associated with the Schengen and Dublin conventions by way of an international agreement. So are Switzerland and Liechtenstein, two countries entirely surrounded by Schengen members, but not (like Norway and Iceland) members of the wider European Economic Area.

Key actors

The fragmentation of cooperation in JHA is also reflected in the multiplication of actors dealing with its development, both inside and outside formal EU structures. While supranational organs have steadily widened their powers, intergovernmental cooperation between national law-enforcement authorities has equally deepened, leading to a complex patchwork of actors.

Organization and capacities of EU institutions

With the new powers attributed to it by the ToL, the Commission gradually expanded its organizational basis in JHA. It gained the exclusive right to propose legislation in matters formerly under the 'third pillar'. However, the treaty also introduced the possibility of an initiative from one-quarter of the EU member states in three areas:

judicial cooperation in criminal matters, police cooperation, and administrative co-operation (Art. 76 TFEU). The organizational set-up of JHA in the Commission has changed over time. Under the second Barroso Commission, the Directorate-General for Justice, Liberty, and Security (DG JLS) was split into home affairs (DG HOME) and justice (DG JUST). This development followed a steady increase in the size of the relevant units. The original JHA Task Force established within the Secretariat of the Commission under the TEU counted, in 1998, only forty-six full-time employees. In 2008, the size of DG JLS was already comparable to that of DG TRADE or DG MARKT with 440 employees. By 2012, DG HOME had 352 and DG JUST 268 employees, as well as some sixty external collaborators and over 100 staff in the Shared Resource Directorate. JHA expenditure also saw a steep increase. According to DG HOME's 2012 Activity Report, its budget more than tripled from 2007 to 2012, reaching €1.25 billion in commitment appropriations, representing 0.83 per cent of the EU budget, and €799 million in payment appropriations (Commission 2012m). Of this expenditure, more than 40 per cent has gone to the securing of the EU's external border and the return of irregular migrants. In 2012, DG JUST had a budget of €181 million. This evolution mirrors the growing political priority attributed to JHA in the EU.

The expansion of Commission resources has mitigated the original dominance of the Council Secretariat, which had been more generously staffed than the Commission during the 1990s. Its position was further strengthened under the ToA when the, previously separate, Schengen Secretariat was integrated into its structures and permanent representations of the member states in Brussels were drawn in, adding legal advisers and officials seconded from interior ministries to their staffs.

The JHA Council inherited from Trevi and from the TEU's third pillar a heavily hierarchical structure of policy-making. It is one of the few areas in the Council that has four decision-making layers. Agendas for JHA councils are prepared by the Committee of Permanent Representatives (Coreper) II, which meets weekly at ambassadorial level. Between Coreper and the working groups, the JHA structure has an additional intermediary level composed of special coordinating committees, which bring together in Brussels senior officials from national ministries, normally meeting once a month. The JHA Council currently has four such coordinating committees: Coordinating Committee for Police and Judicial Cooperation in Criminal Matters (CATS); Strategic Committee on Immigration, Frontiers, and Asylum (SCIFA); Standing Committee on Internal Security (COSI) set up after the entry into force of the ToL; and the Working Party on Civil Law Matters. Set up initially for a five-year transitional period, these committees of senior national officials, which constitute an anomaly in communitarized (formally 'first pillar') issues, have turned into permanent structures, reflecting the intergovernmental legacy of JHA cooperation. The lowest level is composed of working groups of specialists from national ministries and operational bodies.

Although not foreseen by the treaties, the European Council has occupied a growing importance in JHA through multi-annual strategic programming. The ground was laid with the first European Council focused specifically on JHA held under the Finnish Council presidency in Tampere in 1999, which set out far-reaching objectives and fixed deadlines for their adoption. The 2004 European Council in The Hague followed with a new, ambitious JHA multi-annual programme, which was in turn succeeded by the so-called Stockholm Programme, adopted under the Swedish Council presidency in 2009. These strategic planning documents were devised to counter incrementalism in developing cooperation and to ensure greater efficiency in implementing agreed commitments.

The uneven flow of policies, however, shows that the unsettled institutional procedures that preceded the ToL and the domestic sensitivity of the field led to a gap between ambitions and implementation that has persisted (see the section 'The flow of policy' later in the chapter). Although the new Article 68 TFEU confers power on the European Council to 'define the strategic guidelines for legislative operational planning' in the AFSJ, the supranational decision-making procedures and above all the Commission's right of initiative are likely to circumscribe its influence. A flavour of the Commission's assertiveness was given by its Action Plan implementing the Stockholm Programme (Commission 2010*d*), which was subsequently criticized by the Council for going far beyond the wording of the Programme.

The most remarkable change in the formal decision-making structure has been the strengthening of the role of the European Parliament (EP) with the introduction of the ordinary legislative procedure for most aspects of JHA. Until 2005, when the transitional period of the ToA expired, the EP had not been granted any powers to amend or block legislation by the Council and the Council had only to 'consult' the EP prior to adopting a measure—a requirement that was repeatedly violated (Lavenex 2006*a*). In its June 2006 resolution on the AFSJ, the EP explicitly complained that it often did not get all of the preparatory documents necessary to participate in the decision-making process. The Council's failure to comply with the consultation requirements had been a topic of contention during several legislative procedures and had led the EP to file legal complaints before the CJEU, including concerning the 2003 Family Reunification Directive and the 2005 Asylum Procedures Directive. Under the ToL, only four fields are excluded from the ordinary legislative procedure involving both co-decision by the EP and QMV in the Council: passports and identity cards (Art. 77); family law (Art. 81); operational police cooperation (Art. 81); and the potential decision to create a European public prosecutor's office (Art. 86 TFEU). In addition to the EP, the role of national parliaments has also been strengthened (see Box 15.1). The possibility for national parliaments to block legislation when it is seen to violate the subsidiarity principle might, however, turn into a future limit to the newly acquired supranational powers.

The continuity of intergovernmentalism

Faced with the increasingly assertive role of the EP, but also with the expansion of member states participating in JHA Council meetings 'in a large, windowless conference hall of the Council building in Brussels' accommodating 'some 150 representatives of the Presidency, the European Commission, the Council Secretariat and national delegations' and speaking in twenty-three different official languages (Oel and Rapp-Lücke 2008: 23), several member states, under German lead, have resorted to intergovernmental forms of cooperation outside EU structures. The Prüm Treaty, mentioned previously, is but one manifestation of this trend. In May 2003, the interior ministers of the five biggest member states—France, Germany, Italy, Spain, and the UK—created the so-called G5 in order to try to speed up the move towards operational goals and to circumvent the lengthy decision-making processes of the Council. In 2006, Poland joined the group, making it the G6. The G6 meets twice a year at the ministerial level and has a rotating presidency.

A second intergovernmental forum of EU home affairs ministers is the Salzburg Forum on police cooperation founded in 2000 on the initiative of Austria. It also involves the Czech Republic, Hungary, Poland, Slovakia, and Slovenia and, since 2006, Bulgaria and Romania with Croatia as an observer. Like the G6, this group meets twice a year at ministerial level and has a rotating presidency.

Both groups see their roles as elaborating and testing, in a smaller context of like-minded states or contiguous neighbours, measures that can subsequently be exported to all member states. Despite widespread criticism of such circumventing of the official institutions of the EU and of their lack of transparency and accountability, both groups have continued operating since the ToL came into force. These intergovernmental structures are reminiscent of the 'Schengen laboratory' that drove JHA cooperation from 1995 to 1999 and have obviously gained acceptance in the interest of efficiency in an increasingly complex decision-making context.

The proliferation of semi-autonomous agencies and databases

A further distinctive characteristic of the governance of the JHA is the proliferation of semi-autonomous special agencies and databases (see Box 15.2). The multiplication of actors and the widening of their competences since 2005 have been impressive. As it stands, the JHA agencies are mainly concerned with information exchange and coordination among national law-enforcement authorities, often supported by the establishment of databases. Due to their research and in particular risk-analysis activities, they have also developed into important information sources for policy-makers in the Commission and elsewhere. This model of governance illustrates the preference for promoting European integration through the better coordination of national law-enforcement systems rather than by replacing them with new supranational structures.

The earliest agencies were established on the basis of first-pillar secondary legislation: the European Monitoring Centre for Drugs and Drug Addiction (EMCDDA) set up in 1993 in Lisbon; and the European Monitoring Centre on Racism and Xenophobia (EUMC) established in 1997 in Vienna, which in 2007 was replaced by the European Fundamental Rights Agency (FRA). Most subsequent developments, however, took place in the framework of the third pillar. Here the earliest agency was the *Unité de coordination de la lutte anti-fraude* (UCLAF), the predecessor of OLAF,

> **BOX 15.2   JHA agencies and bodies**
>
> - European Monitoring Centre for Drugs and Drug Addiction (EMCDDA), set up in 1993 in Lisbon to provide factual information on the European drug problems, *http://www.emcdda.europa.eu.*
> - European Police Office (Europol), set up in 1999 in The Hague to share and pool intelligence to prevent and combat serious international organized crime, *http://www.europol.europa.eu.*
> - European Police College (CEPOL), set up in 2000 in Bramshill, UK and then moved to Budapest to approximate national police-training systems, *http://www.cepol.net.*
> - European Police Chiefs' Task Force (PCTF), set up in 2000 to promote exchange, in cooperation with Europol, of best practices and information on cross-border crime and to contribute to the planning of operative actions, without headquarters and web page.
> - Eurojust, set up in 2002 in The Hague to coordinate cross-border prosecutions, *http://www.eurojust.europa.eu.*
> - Frontex, set up in 2005 in Warsaw to coordinate operational cooperation at the external border, *http://www.frontex.europa.eu.*
> - European Fundamental Rights Agency (FRA), set up in 2007 in Vienna as the successor to the European Monitoring Centre on Racism and Xenophobia (EUMC) to provide the Community and its member states when implementing Community law with assistance and expertise relating to fundamental rights, *http://fra.europa.eu/.*
> - European Asylum Support Office (EASO), established in 2011 in Valletta, Malta to promote the approximation of national asylum-recognition practices, *www.easo.europa.*
> - European Agency for Large-Scale IT Systems, set up in 2011 in Tallinn, Estonia to manage common databases in JHA (no website yet).

the now communitarized European Anti-Fraud Office (see Chapter 4). The Europol Convention had been adopted in 1995, but it was not until 1998 that it entered into force, after lengthy national ratification procedures, and Europol became operational a year later. In 1998, the European Judicial Network was launched, as a predecessor to Eurojust, the 'college' of senior magistrates, prosecutors, and judges which became operational in 2002, to coordinate cross-border prosecutions. The European Council in Tampere in 1999 proposed the creation of two new bodies: the European Police College (CEPOL), based in the UK, to develop cooperation between the national training institutes for senior police officers in the member states; and the European Police Chiefs' Task Force (PCTF) to develop personal and informal links among the heads of the various law-enforcement agencies across the EU and to promote information exchange. In 2009, the European Asylum Support Office (EASO) was created to gather and exchange information on countries of origin and asylum proceedings in the member states. The hope is thereby not only to assist countries in implementing EU asylum directives but also to promote the approximation of recognition practices.

The most dynamic and contested agency is the Agency for the Management of Operational Cooperation at the External Borders (Frontex), which was established in Warsaw in 2005. While primarily tasked with coordination and risk analysis, its mandate was extended considerably in 2007 through the creation of Rapid Border Intervention Teams (RABITs) as a means of providing swift operational assistance for a limited period to a requesting member state facing a situation of 'urgent and exceptional pressure' at external borders. The creation of RABITs was a reaction to the difficulties encountered in mobilizing the necessary personnel and equipment from the member states for joint operations at sea or land borders. Frontex's operational burden-sharing dimension has been further enhanced through the European Patrol Network (EPN) for Mediterranean and Atlantic coastal waters. This organizational expansion has been backed by a steep rise in the agency's budget from €19 million in 2006 to €85 million in 2012, thus indicating the enduring political salience of border management in Europe. The upheavals in the EU's Arab neighbours and the difficulties faced by the EU's southern member states with the immigrant influx, in particular Greece (see the section 'Asylum and immigration policy' later in the chapter), Italy, and Malta, have nourished the sense of urgency attributed to the management of the EU's external borders.

The fact that Frontex approaches border management from a pre-eminently security-oriented perspective raised concerns early on. Gradually, the agency has endorsed a fundamental rights strategy and a code of conduct. Furthermore, the EU institutions agreed to amend the Frontex Regulation so as to include the requirement to protect fundamental rights. Changes were also introduced to nominate a fundamental rights officer and create a consultative forum on fundamental rights. The amended rules added obligations to provide training on fundamental rights; to respect the principle of *non-refoulement*, which prohibits the return of refugees to places where their life or physical well-being would be threatened; and to terminate or suspend joint operations or pilot projects in the event of serious or persistent breaches of fundamental rights or international protection obligations. Yet, by 2013, these reforms were deemed insufficient by both the Council of Europe, which issued a critical report on Frontex's human-rights record, and the European Ombudsman, who, reminding Frontex of its new obligations under the Charter of Fundamental Rights, issued several recommendations in a resolution (Council of Europe 2013; European Ombudsman 2013).

With these new common bodies, the number of common databases has also proliferated. Databases constitute the core coordination instrument between domestic law-enforcement and immigration authorities and are meant to boost their surveillance capacities over mobile undesired individuals in the common territory. Over time, a sophisticated surveillance system has been devised for the control of the external border. The Visa Information System (VIS), storing personal information (including biometrics) on every visa application and the SIS or its successor SIS II, containing information on persons who may have been involved in a serious crime or stay irregularly in the EU, will soon be supplemented by the entry/exit system registering all movements into and out of the Schengen area, including fingerprinting, and the Registered Traveller Programme, which facilitates the movement of frequent (business) travellers and thereby establishes a complex system of pre- and post-border-screening procedures targeting all foreign visitors to the EU. In December 2012, a new regulatory agency was created with the task of managing this increasing array of data-bases, the EU Agency for Large-Scale IT Systems in Tallinn, Estonia. Finally, the most ambitious surveillance system is the European Border Surveillance System (Eurosur), which will introduce new tools for Frontex and the member states for countering cross-border crime and undesired immigration by establishing a protected communi-cation network through national coordination centres for border surveillance.

As in most other areas of JHA cooperation, security prerogatives in developing the databases have been granted more attention than the concurrent civil-liberties or human-rights aspects. Member states took more than three years to agree the Framework Decision 2008/977/JHA on the protection of personal data processed in the framework of police and judicial cooperation in criminal matters, adopted on 27 November 2008. This instrument is widely seen as crucial for ensuring adequate personal data protection under these information systems. Yet, in its Decision, the Council took account of neither the three very critical reports issued by the EP nor the criticism of the European Data Protection Supervisor. It has been generally expected that the ToL will redress the balance towards the protection of individual rights for three reasons:

- the inclusion of an individual right to data protection in Article 16 TFEU;
- the empowering of the EP with the introduction of co-decision; and
- the new judicial powers conferred to the CJEU, in particular also through the binding nature of the Charter of Fundamental Rights and an eventual EU accession to the European Convention on Human Rights (ECHR).

The contents of cooperation in JHA are elucidated in more detail in the following section.

The flow of policy

JHA integration has long been characterized by a very hesitant approach to common supranational legislation on the one hand—manifest in delays in the decision-making process, extensive discretion in adopted texts, and gaps in implementation—and more dynamic operational and practical integration, as well as cooperation with third countries on the other hand. In substantive terms, the predominance of interior ministries in the institutional set-up and the framing of cooperation as compensatory to the safeguarding of internal security in an area without internal borders have privileged security concerns vis-à-vis human-rights considerations. As a consequence, policy output has remained fragmented and change incremental.

With the entry into force of the ToL, the general introduction of the ordinary legislative procedure, and the strengthening of the human-rights basis of JHA cooperation, the formal decision-making setting has changed, suggesting a move towards more supranational and comprehensive integration. Yet, the first years after entry into force of the ToL document the persistence of entrenched practices and the enduring reluctance about full communitarization in these sensitive policy fields.

Asylum and immigration policy

A few years after the entry into force of the ToL, the coincidence of the economic crisis and the fears of large-scale immigration in the wake of the Arab uprisings set the context for the (partial) suspension of two cornerstones of the EU's asylum and migration system. First, the French and Danish governments decided to reintroduce checks at their internal borders in 2011, effectively violating the Schengen rules. Later the same year, the CJEU prohibited the transfers of asylum-seekers to Greece, suspending the core of the 'common European asylum system' (CEAS), the Dublin Regulation (see Box 15.3 and Cases C-411/10 and C-493/10).

Policy-making for asylum and immigration issues has developed in stages. From the outset of cooperation in the mid-1980s, the emphasis has been on the fight against illegal immigration rather than on which legal immigrants to accept or how to cooperate on asylum (Lavenex and Wallace 2005). The first phase of the CEAS was to be concluded according to the measures devised in the ToA and should be completed prior to the introduction of the supranational decision-making procedures. Faced with the limitations of this generally vague legislation, The Hague and Stockholm programmes called for its thorough recasting. Under the ordinary legislative procedure, however, agreement has remained difficult to reach on revised and stronger common asylum (see Box 15.3) or immigration policies.

Agreement on which forms of immigration to classify as legal has proved particularly controversial. The main achievements were the adoption of two directives: Council Directive 2003/109/EC on the status of third-country nationals who are long-term residents in a member state of the EU, and Council Directive 2003/86/EC on the right to family reunification, both adopted on 22 September 2003. The Council's failure to consult the EP and the possibility that children over the age of 12 could be excluded from the right to family reunification led the EP to file a complaint with the CJEU, which was rejected (*European Parliament v. Council of the European Union*, Case C-540/03, 2006). In a 2008 report (Commission 2008c), the Commission attested that the directive, given its open wording, had had very little impact on member states' policies.

Despite the Stockholm Programme's claim to recast the directive, no legislative action had been taken as of late 2013. A 2001 Commission proposal on the admission

BOX 15.3	Common European asylum system

- The cornerstone of EU asylum policy is the system of exclusive responsibility for the examination of asylum claims based on the Dublin Regulation (343/2003) of 18 February 2003, establishing the criteria and mechanisms for determining the member state responsible for examining an asylum application. This instrument replaced the Dublin Convention and its implementation is linked to the Eurodac database.

- The mutual recognition of asylum determination outcomes implied by the system of responsibility allocation necessitated minimum standards on reception conditions, the definition of the term refugee, and asylum procedures. These 'Phase I' directives were adopted only after significant delays, and are riddled with delicate compromises and open questions.

- A Commission Green Paper on the future common European asylum system (CEAS) of 2007 (Commission 2007e) gave a critical assessment of progress achieved so far and identified the need for fuller harmonization of substantive and procedural asylum law in order to realize a CEAS by 2010. This deadline, later shifted to 2012 by the Stockholm Programme, has repeatedly elapsed.

- In 2011, the Dublin system collapsed when the European Court of Human Rights and the CJEU, considering the overburdening of Greece as a country of first entry and its failure to comply with refugee law obligations, declared transfer under the Dublin Regulation from other member states to Greece in breach of fundamental human rights.

- Despite pressure by the Commission and the courts to reform the system, member states have stuck to the Dublin Regulation and have made only minimal progress in the recasting of Phase I legislative instruments. Interestingly, the EP, now enjoying co-decision powers on the revised directives, has moved away from its formerly more humanitarian stance and closer to the Council's positions.

- The reluctance to accept supranational rules in this sensitive field of domestic policy has shifted asylum cooperation to more operational aspects, for example through the creation of a European Asylum Support Office (EASO).

- Burden-sharing remains a challenge. The European Refugee Fund to support reception, integration, and voluntary-return measures in the member states has increased from €216 million (2000–4) to just under €700 million (2007–13). More significant sums of money have been allocated for border controls in the border fund (€1,820 million for the same period), as well as to Frontex activities.

- Particular attention is now paid to cooperation with countries of transit and origin of asylum-seekers. Mainly geared towards enhancing migration control in those countries, this cooperation has focused on the conclusion of readmission agreements as well as, more hesitantly, the promotion of asylum procedures and reception capacities.

of immigrants for the purpose of work and self-employment, like the two before it, also found little support in the Council (Commission 2001*b*). Instead, the Commission has embarked on a sectoral approach, advancing more limited directives targeting specific, less controversial groups of economic migrants, such as highly skilled professionals, researchers and scientists, seasonal workers, and intra-corporate transfers. The 2009 Blue Card Directive confirms the reluctance of the member states to tie their hands with European immigration rules. Alluding to the US 'Green Card', the Blue Card was originally designed as a means to attract highly skilled migrants from third countries to Europe. In the end, however, the major benefit this instrument would have brought to potentially interested candidates, the automatic extension of free movement rights, was not retained. As a consequence, very few persons have made use of this new legal instrument to enter the EU, and national immigration schemes prevail.

In the absence of a common policy, cooperation regarding the integration of third-country nationals is dealt with by a 'soft' mode of coordination between the member states. These deliberations flow into an EU *Handbook on Integration for Policy-Makers and Practitioners* published every few years by the Commission. In 2011, the Commission took a slightly more proactive stance proposing a European agenda for the integration of non-EU migrants, focusing on action to increase economic, social, cultural, and political participation by migrants and putting the emphasis on local action.

In the light of enduring immigration pressure and of the internal resistance to stronger legislative integration, the emphasis of cooperation has moved outwards to an attempt to engage countries of transit and origin in the management of migration flows (Lavenex 2006*b*). EU policy was initially focused on coercive measures and the conclusion of readmission agreements, but the failure to ensure compliance by third countries has led to the emergence of a more comprehensive vision of external migration cooperation and the launch of the so-called 'Global Approach' in December 2005 and renewed in the light of the Arab Spring in 2011.

Consequently, immigration has become a main focus of the European neighbourhood policy (ENP; see Chapter 17), and consultations have also intensified with African countries. Yet, given the lack of EU competence over economic migration, the EU has little to offer to these countries in return for their cooperation in securing the EU's borders. The visa-facilitation agreements offered to eastern neighbours, in exchange for their agreement to readmit their own as well as foreign nationals who stay irregularly in the EU, remain limited.

The newest device in implementing the 'global approach' has been the conclusion of 'mobility partnerships' in which opportunities for 'circular'—that is temporary—labour migration into the EU and development cooperation are linked, as well as cooperation on readmission and the fight against irregular migration. Mobility partnerships were first concluded with Cap Verde and Moldova in 2008, followed by Georgia, Armenia, and, in 2013, Morocco. First assessments of these new tools have been rather sceptical, as the competence to grant access to economic migrants remains a prerogative of the member states (Lavenex and Stucky 2011). In the light of the economic crisis, very few legal opportunities for economic mobility have been opened. Instead, these partnerships have perpetuated the focus on the fight against irregular migration. Eventually, having a partnership with a more vocal 'pro-mobility' country given advanced status under the ENP, such as Morocco, will alter this situation.

Police and judicial cooperation in criminal matters

The dominance of non-binding instruments and the focus on operational cooperation have been traditionally strong in the fields constituting the former third pillar. Yet stronger communitarization is also making its way into these core aspects of state sovereignty. The driving forces have been internal dynamics and external pressures, such as the 9/11 terrorist attacks on the US in 2001, which prompted the European Council to adopt the EU Action Plan on Combating Terrorism, and the bombings in Madrid (March 2004) and London (July 2005), which led to the establishment of a special EU Counter-Terrorism Coordinator (European Council 2005a).

Police and judicial cooperation in criminal matters cuts across different policy areas that fall into the responsibility of law and order authorities. The same is true for the fight against terrorism, which, in addition to police cooperation, also touches on financial issues, intelligence cooperation, and external relations. While some have characterized EU endeavours to fight terrorism as 'flawed' and a 'paper tiger' (Bossong 2008; Bures 2006), the fact is that member states' policies are increasingly coordinated at the EU level. This is particularly true for the international agreements concluded with third countries, such as the Passenger Name Record (PNR) and the Society for Worldwide Interbank Financial Telecommunication (SWIFT) agreements concluded with the US and other countries (see later in this section).

Terrorist attacks have, however, also been a motor behind police and judicial cooperation more generally, for instance for the directives putting the principle of mutual recognition into place. Under the impact of 9/11, the Council devised a comprehensive system of mutual recognition encompassing the pre-trial (recognition of arrest warrants, evidence warrants, freezing orders, decisions on bail) and the post-trial stages (recognition of confiscation orders, financial penalties, probation orders, and transfer of sentenced persons). The principle of mutual recognition, adopted at the 1999 European Council in Tampere and later codified in the TFEU, was seen as an alternative to integration through supranational law. Yet, implementation of these mechanisms soon spurred the need for substantive and procedural harmonization. The ToA abolished the use of conventions dominant under the TEU and provided for the adoption of legally weak framework decisions instead. Cooperation post-Lisbon has concentrated on replacing the existing framework decisions with directives and advancing integration in procedural law, with a stronger focus on human rights and, in particular, legal-defence rights. Article 83(1) TFEU for the first time confers to the

EU powers to establish minimum rules concerning the definition of criminal offences and sanctions.

The emphasis on human-rights aspects is also visible in the field of human trafficking, which qualifies as a form of organized crime. The 2011 directive on human trafficking in human beings (2011/36/EU) and the subsequent EU strategy to eradicate human trafficking seek to approximate member states' criminal laws focusing on prevention, prosecution of criminals, and protection of victims. Integration in these areas is also promoted at the operational level through the various JHA agencies. Europol is essentially a criminal intelligence agency while Eurojust promotes co-operation among the member states concerning investigations and prosecutions. Integration in police matters has also focused on networking and the development of common operational practices such as through the PCTF and CEPOL. These networks are designed to address the main impediment to more effective cooperation among national police forces, which is the need for mutual understanding and trust between highly diverse domestic systems of law enforcement (Occhipinti 2003). With enlargement, both issues—the need for trust and problems associated with diversity—have clearly increased, prompting concern about how to invigorate the operational aspects of police cooperation. The lack of trust and the diversity of member states' legal systems have remained the main obstacles to integration in criminal-law matters, as documented in the case of the European arrest warrant (EAW) (see Box 15.4; and see Lavenex 2007; Sievers and Schmidt 2014).

BOX 15.4   European arrest warrant

- The European Council in Tampere adopted four basic principles for establishing a common European judicial space: mutual recognition of judicial decisions; approximation of national substantive and procedural laws; the creation of Eurojust; and the development of the external dimension of criminal law.

- The 9/11 terrorist attacks in the US spurred the adoption of the framework decision on the EAW in 2002.

- The EAW is a judicial decision issued by a member state with a view to the arrest and surrender by another member state of a person being sought for a criminal prosecution or a custodial sentence. It eliminates the use of extradition and is based on the principle of mutual recognition of decisions in criminal matters.

- In the absence of EU harmonization of criminal law and of mutual trust among judicial systems, the implementation of the EAW has encountered difficulties (Lavenex 2007).

- In sum, as in the case of migration, restrictive measures, such as the EAW, have been easier to adopt than those harmonizing the rights of individuals. While the ToL provides a stronger basis for both supranational measures and the protection of human rights, this impact is not yet visible in policy developments.

The external dimension of police and judicial cooperation has also expanded. Europol, Eurojust, and Frontex have all concluded cooperation agreements with a series of European and non-European countries, and at the end of 2005 the JHA Council adopted a strategy on the external aspects of JHA (European Council 2005*b*). Cooperation with the US has been particularly close and has spurred major controversies both between EU institutions and between the EU and civil-rights activists, especially in the area of data protection. These controversies are particularly telling for the nature of inter-institutional relations in JHA, the balance between security and human-rights considerations, and the role of the EP before and after being granted co-decision power in the legislative process. The 2004 US–EU PNR agreement, which requires European airlines flying to the US to provide US authorities with information on their passengers, was annulled by the CJEU in 2006 because the EP had not been adequately consulted (*European Parliament v. Council of the European Union* and *European Parliament v. Commission of the European Communities*, Joined Cases C-317/04 and C-318/04). The successor agreement, which remained the same in substance, was adopted under treaty provisions that do not require the EP's opinion. PNR has raised grave concerns among the EP, the European Data Protection Supervisor, and civil-liberties groups for failing to comply with European data protection rules (Suda 2013: 778f.). After the entry into force of the ToL, the EP, exercising its newly acquired powers, asked for an overhaul of all existing PNR agreements. However, the revised PNR agreements with Australia and the US, which were approved by the EP in 2011 and 2012 respectively, hardly differ from their predecessors in substance (Suda 2013). In sum, the dynamic external dimension of judicial and police cooperation underlines the blurring of distinctions between notions of internal and external security. As with efforts to combat immigration, they move JHA cooperation closer and closer to traditional domains of the CFSP (see Chapter 18).

The challenge of implementation

Notwithstanding the generally weak legal character of most policy instruments, which, adopted under intergovernmental decision-making procedures, rarely exceeded the lowest common denominator between the member states, implementation has remained a challenge in JHA. Limits on the jurisprudence of the CJEU have compounded this deficit.

As a response, the Commission decided to introduce half-yearly 'scoreboards'—reports monitoring progress in implementing the treaty and programme provisions under the ToA. Under the Hague Programme, 'Scoreboard Plus' was introduced which, being published openly on the Commission's website, contained detailed information on implementation deficits by individual member states, and thus tried to induce compliance by 'naming and shaming'. This practice was, however, abandoned under the Stockholm Programme without justification. A look at the problems encountered with the implementation of asylum directives, as in the case of Greece (see Box 15.3); the high number of infringement procedures for late transposition launched under virtually every adopted directive;[1] or some member states' decisions to suspend the Schengen *acquis* by reintroducing checks at their internal borders in the wake of the Arab Spring in 2011 are salient examples of member states' reticence to abide fully by agreed commitments. It is likely that JHA cases will therefore account for a large share of the CJEU's future jurisprudence under its newly acquired powers.

Conclusion

Initially justified in limited terms as compensatory measures to the abolition of internal border controls, cooperation in JHA, now framed as the creation of an 'area of freedom, security, and justice', has been elevated to a central objective of the EU. It is in this field that the ToL has introduced the most significant reforms. It lists JHA second after the overall commitment to peace promotion, and before the internal market, environmental, or social policies. It changes the balance of power between EU institutions by extending the ordinary legislative procedure. Finally, by empowering the CJEU and giving the Charter of Fundamental Rights a legally binding character, the ToL strengthens the constitutional basis of human-rights considerations vis-à-vis security objectives.

The real extent of these changes and their influence on the substance of JHA policies remains to be seen. As of late 2013, many ambitious reforms are on hold or have failed to meet expectations and the recasting of the asylum *acquis* has failed to provide significant improvements to legislation adopted under the intergovernmental procedures. In migration, the lack of EU competence to develop a genuine policy on economic migration seriously limits the scope for internal harmonization and external policy action. In police and judicial cooperation, post-Lisbon legislation has mainly focused on procedural law, with a stronger emphasis on human rights and, in particular, legal-defence rights. In sum, whereas the field of JHA has seen considerable institutional changes over recent years, in terms of policy substance, continuity prevails.

NOTE

1 See Commission Annual Implementation Reports at: *http://ec.europa.eu/eu_law/ infringements/infringements_annual_report_en.htm*.

FURTHER READING

For a fairly comprehensive overview of the JHA *acquis*, see Peers (2012). On the development of asylum and immigration policy, see Boswell and Geddes (2010), and on the effects of EU policies on the member states, see Ette and Faist (2007). Mitsilegas (2009) gives an excellent introduction to EU criminal-law cooperation, and Guild and Geyer (2008) on judicial and police cooperation. Trauner and Ripoll Servent (2015) offer an up-to date analysis of evolution in the main fields of JHA.

Boswell, C. and Geddes, A. (2010), *Migration and Mobility in the European Union* (Basingstoke: Palgrave Macmillan).

Ette, A., and Faist, T. (2007) (eds.), *The Europeanization of National Policies and Politics of Immigration* (Basingstoke: Palgrave Macmillan).

Guild, E., and Geyer, F. (2008) (eds.), *Security versus Justice? Police and Judicial Cooperation in the European Union* (Farnham: Ashgate).

Mitsilegas, V. (2009), *EU Criminal Law* (Oxford: Hart).

Peers, S. (2012), *EU Justice and Home Affairs Law* (Oxford: Oxford University Press).

Trauner, F., and Ripoll Servent, A. (2015) (eds.), *Policy Change in the Area of Freedom, Security and Justice: How EU Institutions Matter* (London: Routledge).

CHAPTER 16

Trade Policy
Policy-Making after the Treaty of Lisbon

Stephen Woolcock

▌ Summary

This chapter describes the decision-making process in European Union (EU) trade and investment policy following the changes brought about by the Treaty of Lisbon (ToL). It shows how EU policy competence has been extended progressively over many years thanks to internal institutional developments, but also in response to demands made upon the EU by external drivers. The chapter discusses the respective roles of the EU institutions and argues that effective policy-making requires above all that all of the major actors have faith in the decision-making regime. Such a regime involving the Commission and Council was developed by the EU over many years. The challenge for
(continued...)

decision-making is for the European Parliament (EP) to be integrated into this regime. In terms of policy substance, the chapter discusses how the EU has shifted to a policy that includes the active pursuit of free-trade agreements (FTAs) in parallel with efforts to promote a comprehensive multilateral trade agenda.

Introduction

This chapter focuses principally on the process of policy-making in EU trade and investment policy. Central to the discussion is therefore the question of competence. The chapter shows how the formal, *de jure* competence of the EU in this policy area has evolved over successive intergovernmental conferences (IGCs) and treaty changes and how this has lagged behind the establishment of *de facto* competence resulting from pragmatic decisions of the member states opting to cede the role of negotiating agreements to the EU. There has therefore been a steady extension and consolidation of the Community method to cover more aspects of external trade, and more recently investment policy. The chapter argues that the effectiveness of the EU in trade has depended significantly on a decision-making regime based on mutual trust between the Commission, the agent in trade negotiations, and the Council whether in the form of specialist working groups such as the Trade Policy Committee or in the Council of the European Union. This regime must now integrate the EP, especially following the enhanced role of the EP following the adoption of the ToL.

Brussels has progressively become the focal point for all trade, and increasingly investment-policy debate. When EU competence was limited to tariffs or a relatively narrow subset of external-trade issues, the member states developed trade policies and then sought to reconcile these at the EU level. But the deepening of the EU single market has meant that issues such as subsidies, technical barriers to trade, or regulations that affect trade in services and investment have become common EU policies (see Chapter 5). This, combined with the increase in competence, means that trade and now investment policy has 'spilled over' from national capitals and is now conducted more or less entirely in Brussels. As a consequence, key actors—such as sector interest groups, consumers, non-governmental organizations (NGOs), and think tanks—are also particularly active in Brussels. This shift has been further enhanced by the greater role of the EP, which over the period 2010–14 has begun to emerge as an important forum for open discussion of EU trade and investment policy.

EU external trade and investment policy is of course not only shaped by the interaction between the various EU institutions and interests. Developments in EU 'domestic' policy, such as the evolution of the *acquis communautaire*, clearly shape policy, just as is the case in trade policy elsewhere. Changes in the international trading system and external drivers, such as demands for the EU to negotiate about new aspects of trade or investment, have also influenced EU policy.

The following section describes the treaty basis for EU external trade and investment policy and especially the impact of the ToL, before showing how domestic and external factors have also led to an increase in exclusive EU competence or otherwise shaped the policy process. The chapter then analyses three central aspects of EU policy-making: how the EU negotiates trade and investment agreements; the revised legislative procedures for trade and investment; and the use of commercial instruments, such as anti-dumping duties and safeguard measures. The chapter concludes with a brief discussion of the recent reorientation of EU trade policy towards a greater emphasis on comprehensive FTAs.

Towards a comprehensive EU policy

Trade policy is an area in which the EU, as opposed to the member states, has considerable influence on the international scene due to the EU's exclusive competence for trade[1] and the size and depth of the single European market (see Chapter 5). But it has taken many years to establish a comprehensive EU competence.

The treaty provisions

The Treaty of Rome, as amended most recently by the ToL provides for exclusive EU competence for the 'common commercial policy' (Art.207 TFEU; ex Art. 133 TEC) and sets out the decision-making process.[2] In summary form, the process begins with a Commission proposal on the agenda and negotiating aims that are discussed in the Trade Policy Committee (TPC; formerly the 133 Committee) consisting of senior member-state trade officials and if necessary the Foreign Affairs Council (FAC). The Commission must also report regularly to the EP in the form of the International Trade Committee, INTA (Art. 207(3) TFEU). The Council authorizes the Commission to negotiate 'with the assistance' of the member states, which means in effect the TPC (Art. 218(2) TFEU). The EU mandate is not time-limited and can be adjusted by the Council as negotiations proceed. The results of the negotiation are adopted by the Council by qualified majority vote (QMV) and must obtain the consent of the EP. The ToL extended EU exclusive competence to all core trade and investment policies, so ratification is essentially by the EU (the Council and the EP). Ratification by member-state parliaments is still required for minor aspects of agreements, for example criminal enforcement of intellectual property-right provisions.

EU competence for trade has grown over time. The Treaty of Rome did not provide an exhaustive definition of 'common commercial policy', so the allocation of competence between the EU and the member states was at issue whenever new topics were placed on the international trade agenda (mostly by the US). The creation of a customs union required the original member states jointly to set tariffs and to develop a collective trade policy, as they did in the Kennedy Round of the General Agreement on Tariffs and Trade (GATT) negotiations (1964–7). As the trade agenda expanded, the EU was called upon to negotiate on an ever wider range of topics, such as technical barriers to trade (TBTs), subsidies and countervailing duties, and public procurement during the Tokyo Round (1973–9); and services, investment, and intellectual property in the Uruguay Round (1986–94) (Woolcock and Hodges 1996). Member-state governments pragmatically accepted that the Commission should act as the negotiator for the EU as a whole on these topics and were willing to leave aside the issue of legal competence until the ratification stage of negotiations.

Trade competence has featured in all recent intergovernmental conferences (IGCs). In the Maastricht IGC, the Commission pressed for increased EU competence to include services, investment, and intellectual property rights on the ground that these were part of the package of issues being negotiated in the Uruguay Round, but this was resisted by member states concerned about the loss of sovereignty. The member states also went out of their way to keep trade policy within the control of the technocratic policy elite of senior national and Commission trade officials and to keep the EP at arm's length. In the Amsterdam IGC, renewed Commission pressure for increased competence led to a modest compromise; a provision (Art. 133(5) TEC) that would have enabled the Council, acting unanimously, to extend EU competence without a formal treaty change, but it was never used. The 2001 Treaty of Nice (ToN) added some service activities to EU competence, but excluded sensitive services sectors, such as social (welfare) services and audio-visual services. As noted previously, finally the TFEU makes effectively all trade and investment policy exclusive EU competence.[3] The ToL does not define foreign direct investment (FDI), but, given the prevailing definitions, EU exclusive competence is likely to cover investment that implies control but not portfolio investment.

The formal treaty provisions governing EU trade policy have therefore evolved over half a century and have been mostly concerned with competence issues rather than how trade policy is made. The ToL, however, introduced two major changes to trade policy-making: it enhanced the powers of the EP (see the section 'The Council still authorizes negotiations' later in the chapter); and it placed external trade and investment policy in the single pillar of common European external action, at least on paper (Woolcock 2010). These treaty changes were not simply the result of intergovernmental negotiations, but were also a consequence of developments in 'domestic' EU policies.

The impact of the *acquis communautaire* on EU trade policy

Apart from a common external tariff (CET) and common agricultural policy (CAP) (see Chapter 8), there were in the 1960s and 1970s large areas of trade and trade-related policies on which there was no common EU policy. It was not until the late 1960s that the EU introduced common commercial instruments, such as anti-dumping and safeguard provisions. With the rise of new protectionism in the early 1970s, the individual member states used Article 115 EEC to maintain national import quotas for textiles and clothing from low-cost developing countries and national 'voluntary' export restraint agreements (VERs) to limit imports of products such as cars, consumer electronics, and machine tools from Japan and the newly industrializing countries.

Throughout the 1970s, the member states also sought to bolster the competitiveness of national companies ('champions') through the use of subsidies, the awarding of government procurement contracts, the setting of technical regulations and standards, and the (non-)application of competition policy. As a result, during the Tokyo Round the Commission was obliged to defend the 'policy space' of the member states in the face of US pressure to impose multilateral discipline on such policies.

During the 1980s, the picture changed considerably due to the achievement of a genuine single European market (SEM) (see Chapter 5). SEM reforms facilitated the emergence of a more comprehensive, rules-based and liberal EU trade policy. For example, the elimination of frontier controls within the SEM made the continuation of national quotas and VERs impossible and sufficiently loosened the grip of defensive interests to facilitate a ban of such measures (Hanson 1998). Stricter enforcement of the existing EU rules on national subsidies provided the model for a revised Agreement on Subsidies and Countervailing Duties during the Uruguay Round. In the field of government procurement, where the EU had previously blocked US attempts to open the EU energy and telecommunications markets, the adoption of a full panoply of EU directives brought virtually all public procurement under EU rules and facilitated a more positive EU position in the plurilateral negotiations on a revised Government Purchasing Agreement (GPA) in the World Trade Organization (WTO) (Woolcock 2008). The SEM also liberalized some crucial service sectors, including telecommunications and financial services, which again facilitated a more proactive EU stance in the Uruguay Round.

Generally speaking, moves towards a more liberal, rules-based regime in the Uruguay Round came as a result of US and EU cooperation. Where the support of either was lacking, there was less progress, such as in agriculture due to limited EU support, or technical barriers to trade due to US antipathy to rules that followed the EU model and went beyond the basic GATT principles of non-discrimination and national treatment. The EU overtook the US as the main driver of liberalization of services, with the US holding back the conclusion of an agreement because it sought more commitments from emerging markets (Hoekman and Sauvé 1994).

The SEM and the development of the *acquis* had a threefold effect on the EU policy process in trade. The SEM was negotiated in parallel with external liberalization and thus gave the Commission negotiators more flexibility to seek ambitious reciprocal trade agreements. At the same time, the deepening and widening[4] of the EU market enhanced the EU's influence. In negotiations on market access and to a lesser extent over rules, the ability to withhold market access largely determines how much leverage a party can apply, so the larger the EU's market, the more influence it had. Finally, the adoption of common policies in the shape of the *acquis* gave EU negotiators an agreed basis for negotiating international rules and norms in the WTO or bilaterally.

To the norms codified in the *acquis*, one must add a number of more general EU normative values shaping its trade policy. First, the *acquis* codifies an approach in which liberalization takes place within a framework of agreed rules that protect competition, the environment, and other legitimate social-policy objectives. This also shaped the EU's desire for a comprehensive multilateral agenda to include trade-related topics for reasons of trade governance as well as to enhance market access (Baldwin 2006; Lamy 2004a). The aim here was to ensure that the international rules were compatible with EU rules. A lack of compatibility would mean costs for EU exporters and importers; for example, higher EU regulatory standards could make EU producers less competitive. Another reason that the EU seeks comprehensive rules in trade is the belief, based on the European experience, that market integration cannot stop at national treatment (non-discrimination) and the removal of border measures, but requires positive integration or at least agreement on essential regulatory standards in order to facilitate genuine market access and competition. There is also a belief, again based on the EU experience, that regional economic integration has considerable economic and political benefits, which explains why the EU has been seen as the 'patron saint of inter-regionalism in international relations' (Aggarwal and Fogarty 2005).

External drivers of EU policy

External factors have also driven EU trade policy towards being more comprehensive. As discussed previously, EU member states responded pragmatically to the challenge posed by the expanding trade agenda and agreed that negotiating with one voice through the Commission was in the EU's best interest. The Commission was thus given the role of negotiating on a range on topics, but without prejudice to the formal *de jure* competence question. Once agreements had been negotiated, implementation required a resolution of the legal competence question, which was achieved through a political agreement on a joint signature after the Tokyo Round (Bourgeois 1982) or through a decision of the Court of Justice of the European Union (CJEU) as in Opinion 1/94 on the results of the Uruguay Round (Devuyst 1995).

The fact that the Commission was given the job of negotiating a variety of complex trade agreements meant that it built up negotiating capacity and expertise, as well as institutional memory that helped it progressively to establish de facto competence for the wider, comprehensive trade agenda. Other countries thus came to recognize the Commission, and the EU as a whole, as the key trade interlocutor.

Negotiating trade and investment agreements

The EU's responses to changes in the international trading system depend on process, or how decisions are made, as well as substantive policy issues and the interests at stake within the EU and internationally. The Commission has established itself as the agent for the EU in international trade negotiations and the member-state governments have served as the main principals (on principals and agents, see Chapter 3), but what is the nature of the relationship between them and what are the implications of the changes introduced by the ToL after December 2009?

The Council still authorizes negotiations

In trade—and now investment—negotiations, the Commission produces a draft mandate, drawing on the positions of the member governments and the views of business, civil society, and after consultations with the EP. The Commission rarely works from a blank sheet. In addition to the domestic *acquis*, trade negotiations are almost always an iterative process, such that positions adopted or agreements reached in previous negotiations inform current EU positions. Continuity is ensured by a strong institutional memory stored within the Commission and national trade administrations. The Commission's draft mandate is discussed in the TPC. The formal mandate is then adopted by the FAC (see Figure 16.1). The Commission reports regularly to the EP via the INTA Committee. During the past two Parliaments and particularly since the adoption of the ToL, the INTA Committee has become far more active and sought to shape opinion and thus the Commission's mandate.

However, Article 218(2) TFEU clearly states that the Council retains the right to authorize negotiations and to determine the mandate. The EP has no formal power over the mandate. In this context, it is worth making a comparison with the role of the US Congress. In many respects the enhanced role of the EP brings it closer to that of the US Congress, but Congress must authorize negotiations and grant a time-limited mandate to the US executive through Trade Promotion Authority (TPA). This gives it considerable power because if the executive fails to meet its aims, Congress can reject the agreement. As the EP does not have formal powers to determine the EU's negotiating objectives, it has a weaker veto power. As noted earlier, the EU mandate is also not time-limited and the Council can and does change the negotiating aims as negotiations proceed. The EP can then be presented with a fait accompli after the Commission, the EU's negotiating partners, as well as the member states in the Council have all agreed to an outcome. The EP can compensate for this lack of formal mandating power by seeking political commitments from the Commission or Council on negotiating aims during the course of consultations or public hearings. It can be expected to do this more in the future.

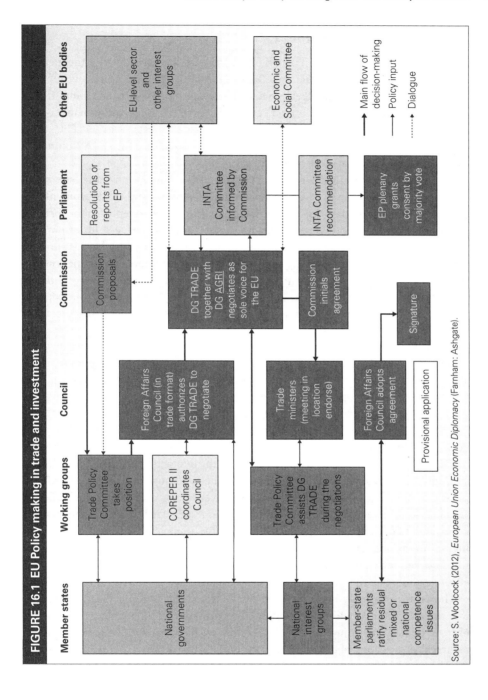

FIGURE 16.1 EU Policy making in trade and investment

Source: S. Woolcock (2012), *European Union Economic Diplomacy* (Farnham: Ashgate).

The Commission negotiates

The Commission negotiates on behalf of the EU with the 'assistance' of the member states mostly through the regular meetings of the TPC. The TPC at the level of 'titulaire' (i.e. chief trade official level) is a senior-level body. Whilst the Committee of Permanent Representatives (Coreper) can consider trade issues, most member-state ambassadors prefer to leave trade issues to their trade colleagues in the TPC. With the adoption of the ToL the Commission must now also inform the INTA Committee of the Parliament on the same basis as the TPC.

In negotiations with the EU's trading partners, the Commission is the only member of the EU delegation to speak, although officials from member governments are present in formal negotiations. The Commission is expected to report to the member states on important informal contacts with the EU's trading partners, for example to exchange information. There is a grey area here in the sense that there is no clear dividing line between exchanging information and negotiations. If negotiations are in Geneva, where the WTO has its headquarters, member states are represented by officials drawn from the national delegations to the WTO or experts from national capitals. At key junctures in negotiations or at WTO ministerial meetings, member governments are represented at ministerial level.

The Council can direct the Commission on any issue during negotiations, but in most cases new initiatives or changes result from Commission proposals, which are then discussed in the TPC. If the position proposed by the Commission does not have sufficient support, the chair will refer the matter back to the Commission. Although QMV is provided for in the treaty, the TPC hardly ever takes a formal vote but favours consensus. The prospect of a vote means, however, that member states go to considerable lengths to avoid being so isolated that they would be outvoted.

The central dynamic of EU trade policy lies in the interaction between the Commission and the member states in the TPC and Council and now with the EP. The principal–agent model, in which the member-state governments are the principals and the Commission the agent, captures what happens in the EU fairly well. But the member governments not only set the objectives and ratify the results, but also take a close interest in the progress of negotiations The EU system works well when communication between the Commission, the member governments, and now possibly the EP is effective and when the Commission is seen as a credible, trusted negotiator by them.

The degree of agency slack, however, varies from topic to topic. Generally speaking, the Commission will be granted flexibility on much of the technical substance of trade policy. The Commission will therefore wish to deal with issues by means of technical discussions of detail in the TPC and defuse sensitive political issues that might attract undue attention. More political issues are those that have a high political salience in one or more member states, such as the liberalization of a sensitive sector. Any member state(s) not happy with how the Commission is dealing with an issue in the TPC can seek to 'politicize' it and threaten to initiate a discussion of it in the Council. The normal practice is for most trade issues to be approved by the

Council without discussion. The politically sensitive issues for the EP tend to be those on which political parties have strong normative or ideological positions, such as human rights, labour standards, and sustainable development.

The balance of member-state positions

The underlying positions of the member states are an important factor in the EU decision-making process. But caution is called for when categorizing member governments as liberal or protectionist. Positions are also significantly shaped by sectoral interests; domestic political factors, such as which government is in power; not to mention economic and electoral cycles. For example, Ireland is liberal on trade in manufacturing, investment, and services, but protectionist on agriculture. France is protectionist on agriculture, but liberal on services, except audio-visual services. Germany is generally liberal on trade in goods, but less so on the liberalization of agriculture or services. Generally speaking, Sweden has tended to occupy the liberal end of the spectrum with France at the protectionist end. Denmark, Finland, Germany, the Netherlands, and the UK tend to adopt liberal positions, whereas Italy, Portugal, and Spain are more protectionist, with the other member states in swing positions. At issue is more often than not how broadly or narrowly to define reciprocity in negotiations. A broad definition would be liberal and similar to the concept of 'global reciprocity' in the GATT/WTO system; in other words, a broad balance of benefits across a spectrum of sectors and actors. A narrower definition of reciprocity is more mercantilist in that any market opening is carefully matched against opening by the trading partner in the same or a related sector. The more 'liberal' member states such as Sweden, the UK, and the Netherlands tend to view reciprocity more broadly while the more mercantilist member states tend to seek a narrower definition.

Successive enlargements of the EU have influenced this pattern. UK and Danish accession brought in two countries with deep-seated liberal trade traditions. Greek, Portuguese, and Spanish accessions tipped the balance a little towards protectionism, especially in sectors such as steel and textiles. The enlargement of 1994, which included Finland and Sweden, shifted the centre of gravity back towards a more liberal position. The 2004, 2007, and 2013 enlargements to include central and east European countries, as well as Cyprus and Malta, appear, on balance, to have been relatively neutral. Whilst Poland and Slovakia have sectors they would wish to protect, there are liberal countervailing forces in the Czech Republic, Estonia, Hungary, and Slovenia.

There is not much evidence that the recent enlargements have made decision-making harder. The TPC (and Council) has become much larger, which has made dialogue harder. At the same time, a larger TPC appears to have strengthened the hand of the Commission as initiator of policy positions (Elsig 2008). As the smaller and newer member states do not have strong views on many issues, they tend to support the Commission proposals. This helps to preserve the limited political capital they have for those things that are really of central national importance which they then expect the Commission to support.

No formal channels for NGO stakeholders

EU trade policy, like all trade policy, is shaped by sectoral or interest groups, but there is no formal channel for representation on a par with, for example, the Trade Advisory Committees in the US. The EU Economic and Social Committee (and Committee of the Regions) are consulted, but, rightly or wrongly, are not taken very seriously by policy-makers or other stakeholders.

The Commission is happy to hear the views of business. Indeed, the need for private-sector input in order to define the EU's offensive and defensive objectives has, on occasion, led the Commission to encourage the creation of new EU-level business representation where it did not previously exist. The Commission, for example, sponsored the creation of the European Services Forum (ESF) in the late 1980s. The Commission favours EU-level representation and can relatively easily fend off lobbying from sectoral interests in one or only a couple of member states on the ground that they are not representative of the EU-wide interest. The need for representation to take place at the EU level necessitates common positions among various national sectoral interests and thus makes for a more institutionalized lobbying through EU-level sectoral bodies. This, in turn, generally requires compromise and thus dilutes preferences. This may be one of the reasons why European business lobbying on trade policy is relatively less assertive than that in the US (Woll 2009). This does not, of course, preclude independent lobbying by major firms, which may in any case have a presence across the EU.

An increased sensitivity to civil-society NGOs after the 1999 Seattle WTO ministerial, among other things, led to the establishment of a semi-formal consultative forum with NGOs, including business-sector organizations as well as a wide range of civil-society NGOs. The forum has enhanced transparency, but the existence of very diverse views leaves trade officials in the Commission and TPC with scope to interpret the outcome of consultations as they wish. The enhanced role of the EP does, however, offer a further channel for civil-society and business representation. Debates and hearings organized by the INTA Committee offer arguably the most transparent forum on trade policy involving decision-makers and stakeholders. Therefore, the scope for civil-society NGOs to influence EU policy by lobbying the EP could well induce moves by the Commission to establish more effective dialogue with non-state actors.

The Council and Parliament adopt the results

The Commission negotiators initial the agreed text at the conclusion of a negotiation (see Figure 16.1). National ministers are normally present at key stages of a major negotiation to endorse last-minute agreements and compromises. Formal adoption then follows in the Council (FAC) under QMV, although in practice the Council operates by consensus (see Chapter 4). With the extension of EU exclusive competence, the scope to use the requirement of unanimity to block or shape EU trade and investment policy has been largely removed.[5]

Under the ToL, the EP must now grant its 'consent' to all trade and investment agreements covered by EU competence. Previously the EP had limited effective veto power even though its assent was required for many trade agreements. The reason for this weakness was that the EP could consider the final agreement only once it had been adopted by all the parties concerned and all EU member states. Rejection at such a late stage constituted a 'nuclear option' that was never used. The ToL, by giving the EP an earlier say, seems likely to enhance the likelihood that the EP would exercise its power to veto trade and investment agreements.

The initial years since Lisbon came into effect suggest that the EP will seek co-operation rather than confrontation with the Commission. All but one of the agreements concluded during the 2010–14 Parliament were adopted by clear majorities. Thus major agreements such as the EU–Korea FTA and FTAs with Colombia, Peru, and Central America were adopted by the EP. But a lack of trust or confidence can result in agreements not being ratified. The Anti-Counterfeiting Trade Agreement (ACTA) is one illustration of this. The ACTA was a plurilateral agreement negotiated by the EU with a number of developed countries, notably the US, with the aim of enhancing compliance with rules prohibiting trade in counterfeit goods. The agreement was controversial in the EP because some members of the European Parliament (MEPs) believed that the enforcement measures were too intrusive and restricted individual rights, such as by granting too much access to electronic data. Under intense lobbying from some NGOs, the EP had sought and obtained an assurance from the Commission that the final agreement would not go beyond the existing EU *acquis* protecting copyrights. The ACTA, however, was negotiated without much transparency because the negotiators, and in particular the US negotiators, wished to avoid a public debate that could undermine the process before a final deal had been struck. This lack of transparency fuelled suspicion on the part of MEPs and NGOs, which undermined support in the EP and it ultimately refused to grant its consent. This was the first major trade agreement rejected by the EP and it illustrates the tension between the negotiators' desire to retain flexibility and thus confidentiality during sensitive negotiations and the EP's desire for transparency and accountability.

The ToL's extension of exclusive EU competence means a reduction in the formal role of national parliaments. As was the case before Lisbon, agreements that fall entirely within EU exclusive competence are ratified by the Council and the EP. The Lisbon Treaty extended exclusive competence, but the comprehensive nature of trade and investment agreements today means that there are often a few provisions that fall outside EU exclusive competence, such as criminal sanctions in cases of non-compliance with agreements protecting intellectual property rights. Such agreements still require member-state ratification in addition to EU ratification. In order to avoid delays while waiting for all twenty-eight member states to ratify an agreement, the practice is for agreements to be provisionally implemented.

Trade legislation

The ToL introduced three major changes to the role of the EP in external trade and investment policy. The first two concern the EP's greater role in scrutinizing EU policy and confirmation of the power to grant its consent to all trade and investment agreements. The third major change is that the ToL grants the EP co-decision powers with the Council on measures defining the framework for implementing trade (and investment) agreements under co-decision (see Chapter 4). Before the ToL, the consultation procedure had been used, which meant that the Council and Commission had only to take the EP position into account. With the application of the ToL all legislation such as revisions of commercial instruments, the definitions of EU rules of origin, or autonomous (i.e. unilateral) trade measures, such as granting preferences to least developed or developing countries, will now be adopted using co-decision.

The first parliamentary term after the adoption of the ToL did not see any major changes to EU trade legislation. The most important was the revision of the generalized system of preferences (GSP), which grants preferential access to the EU's market for goods from developing countries. In 2013, however, the Commission began a reform of EU commercial instruments, notably anti-dumping policy.

Commercial instruments

Most of the discussion thus far has been on how the EU negotiates trade and investment agreements, but the application of commercial instruments such as anti-dumping, safeguards, and countervailing duties represents a further important dimension of EU trade policy. The use of such trade-defence instruments has the potential to create major disputes with the EU's trading partners, as was the case with the EU's imposition of anti-dumping duties on Chinese solar panels in 2013, and major rows within the EU between the more liberal and more protectionist interests.[6] As anti-dumping has been by far the most important commercial instrument used by the EU, it is the focus of this section.

The use of commercial instruments is disciplined by international trade rules. The GATT (1994) Article VI lays down rules that are implemented in EU regulations.[7] As noted previously, any changes to these regulations, such as measures to enhance the transparency of the process or scope for *ex officio* investigations by the Commission (rather than the Commission responding to requests), will have to be adopted under co-decision. The imposition of anti-dumping duties is currently triggered by a claim from EU producers that imports have been 'dumped'—sold below a fair market price—and have caused—or threaten to cause—'serious injury' to the industry in question. The anti-dumping unit in the Commission's Directorate-General for Trade (DG TRADE) considers the validity of the complaint. At this stage there may well be informal communications between the industry, or lawyers representing the industry, and the Commission on the strength of the case. If the Commission is persuaded that there is sufficient evidence, it seeks approval from the Anti-Dumping Committee, which is chaired by the Commission and consists of representatives from the member states, to begin an investigation. Approval to investigate requires only a simple majority of the member states voting.

The Commission has considerable discretion in an investigation. It is fully responsible for establishing whether dumping has occurred, whether there is serious injury as a result, and whether the application of duties is on balance in the 'Union interest'. In addition, the Commission can impose provisional duties. The use of this discretionary power has been criticized by trade liberals as providing scope to use anti-dumping duties as a form of contingent protection, but also by EU industry for not defending EU industry sufficiently against unfair competition.

Unlike most other trade-policy decisions, the decision to impose definitive anti-dumping duties is typically taken by vote. Successive changes in the procedures have made it easier to adopt measures, and thereby effectively given the Commission more control over the use of anti-dumping policy. In 1994, the threshold for adopting definitive duties was lowered from QMV to a simple majority of member states (Council Regulation 522/94). When the 2004 enlargement promised to make it harder to get a simple majority in favour of action, as abstentions would count as votes against and there were concerns that smaller new member states would tend to abstain unless directly affected (Molyneux 1999), a further change was made to the effect that a Commission proposal for a definitive duty was adopted unless there was a simple majority of member states *against* it (Council Regulation 461/2004). The new comitology procedures, implementing changes made in the ToL, mean that there must be a qualified majority *against* the proposal to block it. If the Commission's proposal is rejected, it can redraft it or go to an appeal committee (essentially the Council). If the issue is blocked in the appeal committee or a simple majority opposes the act, the Commission must consult with the member states. In other words, the expectation is that a compromise will be worked out so that the appeal committee can adopt the act by QMV.

EU trade strategy since the Uruguay Round

This section considers the more substantive question of how the EU has responded to the lack of progress in the multilateral Doha Development Agenda (DDA; launched in 2001) by re-emphasizing bilateral and (at least rhetorically) region-to-region agreements. In 1999, the EU adopted a de facto moratorium on new FTAs in order not to undermine the credibility of its push for a comprehensive multilateral round (Lamy 2004*b*). The EU pursued its aim of a comprehensive multilateral agenda, and WTO working groups on competition, investment, public procurement, and trade facilitation were established at the 1996 Singapore ministerial. In 1998, the US agreed, rather reluctantly, to support the EU-led proposal for a millennium round, but the attempt to launch one in Seattle in December 1999 failed due to developing-country and civil-society NGO opposition, but most importantly a lack of agreement between the EU and US on the negotiating aims. At the WTO ministerial in Doha in 2001 a new round was launched thanks to the use of the time-honoured GATT device of constructive ambiguity in the agenda, a more supportive US position in the immediate wake of the 9/11 terrorist attacks, and EU efforts on the Doha Declaration to clarify developing countries' rights to issue compulsory licences for essential medicines under the Trade-Related Intellectual Property Rights (TRIPs) Agreement, adoption of which was a key condition for developing country support for a new round.

Over the course of the round, the EU gave considerable ground on agriculture, particularly compared to the 1980s. This movement was reflected in a joint EU–US paper on agriculture agreed in the run-up to the 2003 Cancun WTO ministerial meeting (Lamy 2004*b*). This joint paper, however, provoked developing countries, led by India and Brazil, to form the G20 coalition of developing and emerging market economies in order to counter what they saw as an attempt to extend the US–EU duopoly of the trading system. With India and other G20 members opposing a comprehensive round and seeking more on agriculture than either the EU or US was ready to offer, the Cancun ministerial collapsed even though the EU had taken its key 'Singapore' issues—namely competition policy, investment, and government procurement—off the agenda as part of an effort to save the negotiations. This was a major setback for the EU.

Although the EU continues to prefer multilateralism, the stagnation of Doha led to greater attention to new preferential agreements, not least because the EU's major trading partners/competitors were engaging in active FTA strategies. This position solidified after the Hong Kong WTO ministerial meeting in December 2005 left Brussels with the perception that the EU was the only major WTO member ready to make the concessions necessary for progress in the DDA. By 2006, this perception translated into a broad consensus in favour of a more active FTA policy (Elsig 2008). The formal EU policy statement favouring FTAs with countries or regions with good potential growth prospects formed part of the Global Europe strategy paper of October 2006 (Commission 2006*c*) and was confirmed in the Trade, Growth and World Affairs statement in 2010 (Commission 2010*e*).

The EU continued to promote the DDA while launching this more active FTA policy. Within the scope provided by the internal reforms in the CAP, such as decoupling support from output, the EU made concessions on agricultural subsidies and market access. Despite the general progress made in the DDA in 2008, which some observers argued brought the round near to a conclusion, differences between the US and emerging-market WTO members, in particular India on special safeguard measures for poor farmers in India, resulted in failure to conclude the round. A further effort to conclude negotiations in 2011 also failed. In these negotiations, the

EU was, arguably for the first time since it first engaged in GATT/WTO negotiations, not one of the parties holding up agreement. In December 2013, after twelve years of trying, the ninth WTO ministerial conference in Bali finally agreed on a small package of measures including trade facilitation, food security, and some provisions on special and differential treatment for developing countries. The experience with the DDA illustrated how the trading system was changing in a way that affected the EU's role. This is not the place to describe these changes in detail (WTO 2013), but they represent a significant challenge to which EU trade and investment policy must respond.

An early major adjustment by the EU has been its shift towards negotiating preferential agreements, first with the emerging markets in order to ensure that the EU maintains its trade and investment with these growing markets and subsequently with its 'strategic' partners, including Japan and the US. There were three main reasons for this shift in policy. First, was the lack of progress in the DDA, in both comprehensiveness and ambition on topics of particular concern to the EU such as non-agricultural market access (NAMA)—that is, tariffs on manufactured goods and services. Secondly, there was the move by other major WTO members to negotiate FTAs. In 2000, China approached the Association of South East Asian Nations (ASEAN) with a view to negotiating an FTA. There were also the 'ASEAN+3' talks including China, Japan, and South Korea.[8] In addition, Japan began negotiating new-era economic partnership agreements. Perhaps most important, the US pursued an active 'competitive liberalization' policy once the Bush administration obtained TPA in 2001. The US was soon negotiating FTAs with Central America, Thailand, Korea, the Southern Africa Customs Union (SACU), as well as seeking (in vain) to conclude the Free Trade Area of the Americas (FTAA) (Evenett and Meier 2007). These FTAs offered better access to some major markets for the EU's competitors and therefore led to pressure from European industry, and particularly the service sector, for the EU to negotiate equivalent access via FTAs if the DDA was not going to deliver. Many FTAs, in particular those negotiated by the US, also included trade-related topics such as comprehensive investment provisions, government procurement, a wide range of service sectors, plus intellectual property rights as well as elements of labour and environmental policy.

The third, related reason for the shift was that many EU preferential agreements were motivated more by foreign-policy or development objectives than commercial interests. For example, the stability and adjustment agreements (SAAs) with the Balkan states were primarily motivated by a desire to promote economic and political stability in the region (see Chapter 17). Similarly the EuroMed association agreements with the littoral Mediterranean countries were aimed at promoting economic growth to counter the political instability and rise of fundamentalism in that region. The economic partnership agreements (EPAs) with the former colonies of the member states—known collectively as the African, Caribbean, and Pacific (ACP) states—which together accounted for only 4 per cent of EU exports, were motivated, for the most part, by development aims. Only the FTAs with Mexico and

Chile, both of which were negotiated to counter the trade diversionary effects of US FTAs, and perhaps the Trade Development and Cooperation Agreement with South Africa, could be said to have been with emerging markets. The result of these shifts in EU policy is that the EU, like other major WTO members, is actively engaged in a 'multi-dimensional' trade and investment policy. It retains the aim of furthering the multilateral agenda through the WTO, but is engaged in an active policy of negotiating comprehensive trade and investment agreements with what are seen as the potential growth markets.

From 2012, EU trade policy has also favoured preferential agreements with some of the EU's strategic partners. The most ambitious of these efforts is the Transatlantic Trade and Investment Partnership (TTIP) agreement, which the EU began to negotiate with the US in 2013. The negotiations strive to shape the rules that govern international trade as much as liberalize trade between the parties. Faced with a multi-polar trading system in which multilateral agreement on the rules is much more difficult, both the US and the EU are seeking to shape trade rules through 'mega regional' agreements or plurilateral agreements that cover substantial shares of trade and investment.

While the EU's strategic partners and the major emerging markets are important, the EU also has trade relations with many developing and least developed countries; indeed, the EU is the most important market for many developing countries. EU trade policy must therefore differentiate between countries such as China and the smaller or less developed ACP states with which it trades and with which it is negotiating EPAs. In 2012, the Commission proposed and the Council endorsed a communication on trade and development based on the principle of such differentiation, but how this is applied remains to be seen (Commission 2012*l*; Woolcock 2014).

Conclusion

Until well into the mid-1990s, EU trade-policy decision-making could be with confidence characterized as technocratic and rather opaque, with Commission and member-state trade officials doing much of the work and ministers making key political decisions and providing democratic legitimacy. This facilitated efficiency by keeping trade policy at arm's length from political and protectionist forces. National and EU policy interests were based on largely informal contacts with private-sector interests.

Over time, the EU's trade-policy stance shifted from a largely defensive response to a US-led trade agenda to a more proactive and liberal policy that embraced the rules-based multilateral system. This shift came about largely as a result of 'domestic' changes within the EU in the form of the creation of the single European market.

Since the mid-2000s, a lack of satisfactory progress in the Doha Round has resulted in the EU reverting to an active FTA strategy. Globalization has led to a broader, more intrusive agenda that has provoked more public debate on trade agenda, which has in turn led to pressure for more transparent and accountable decision-making. EU policy must reconcile the offensive and defensive sectoral interests and seek to ensure that the EU *acquis* is consistent with international rules governing trade and investment. Systemic challenges in the shape of new emerging markets and global environmental and developmental challenges also represent a challenge for the EU. On the one hand, it must seek to ensure access to emerging markets, but on the other hand accommodate the interests of developing countries. These challenges make the achievement of policy coherence very difficult.

In terms of EU decision-making, the response to these challenges has been a consolidation of the 'Brussels-based' decision-making process. This has occurred over time as a result of a deepening of market integration in the EU, external challenges on the EU to negotiate on more issues, and the steady gain of de facto competence by the Commission. This shift has now been codified by the ToL, which has sought to streamline competence and thus enhance the efficiency of EU external representation, whilst at the same time enhancing the powers of the EP. The first few years since the implementation of the ToL suggest more continuity than radical change, but highlight that maintaining a balance between the various conflicting aims of external trade and investment policy, effective communication, and trust remains essential and must be established between the Commission, Council, and EP in the future.

NOTES

1 The treaties actually refer to common commercial policy, which is a rather more fitting title than trade given that 'trade' today includes a range of trade-related topics such as investment, but 'trade' is used here because this is the more common usage.

2 The reference here is to formal or *de jure* competence according to which Union competence means that the provisions governing the respective roles of the member states and the European Commission and other EU institutions come into play. Union competence does not mean the Commission decides, but in practice the Commission has acquired more and more *de facto* competence in negotiating trade agreements.

3 Member states concerned about sensitive sectors, such as audio visual, health, and educational services, inserted safeguards in Art. 207(4) TFEU according to which unanimity would be required should trade negotiations 'threaten cultural and linguistic diversity or the effective provision of national health, education and social policies'.

4 Although the Eftan enlargement to include Sweden and Finland came after the Uruguay Round, states seeking accession to the EU were more or less obliged to bring their trade policies in line with EU policies before accession.

5 Art. 207(4) includes special provisions on public health, education, and social services as well as audio-visual services. In these sectors, unanimity applies when agreements risk 'seriously disturbing the national organisation of such services and prejudicing the responsibility of member states to deliver them', or risk 'prejudicing the Union's linguistic and cultural diversity'. Whether and how these will be applied remains to be seen, but for some years the EU has opposed inclusion of such services in negotiations on services trade.

6 The use of trade-defence measures by the EU has fluctuated, but there appears to be a downward trend, in line with other developed market economies. Between 1995 and 2000 the EU initiated 216 anti-dumping actions, and thirty-two countervailing duty actions. During 2007 to 2012 it initiated eighty-seven anti-dumping actions and twenty-one countervailing actions, along with just one multilateral safeguard action. See WTO statistics for each accessible at: *http://www.wto.org.*

7 The EU is bound by its obligations under the GATT, but has some flexibility in how it implements the GATT rules.

8 It has been argued that this was indeed more talk than substance, but Japan and even India began to conclude comprehensive economic-cooperation agreements that went beyond tariffs (Heydon and Woolcock 2009).

FURTHER READING

For further reading on developments in EU trade policy, see Peterson and Young (2007). A more legal approach to the question of EU competence in external trade (and other policy areas) can be found in Eeckhout (2011). The general debate on the impact of the ToL on decision-making is well covered by Devuyst (2013), and Bungenberg (2011) covers investment—the most important new area of exclusive EU competence.

Bungenberg, M. (2011), 'The Division of Competences Between the EU and Its Member States in the Area of Investment Politics', in M. Bungenberg, J. Griebel, and S. Hindelang (eds.), *European Yearbook International Economic Law*, vol. 29 (Heidelberg: Springer).

Devuyst, Y. (2013), 'European Union Law and Practice in the Negotiation and Conclusion of International Trade Agreements', *Journal of International Business and Law*, 12/2: 259–316.

Eeckhout, P. (2011), *EU External Relations Law*, 2nd edn. (Oxford: Oxford University Press).

Peterson, J., and Young, A. R. (2007) (eds.), *The European Union and the New Trade Politics* (London: Routledge).

CHAPTER 17

Enlargement
Constituent Policy and Tool for External Governance

Ulrich Sedelmeier

█ Summary

The founding treaties of the European Union (EU) already contained rules for the accession of new members, but only the end of the cold war forced the EU to devise an enlargement policy to manage relations with would-be members in post-communist Europe that it did not yet judge ready for membership. Despite initial strong reluctance both within the European Commission and among the member states, the EU achieved three rounds of eastern enlargement between 2004 and 2013; extended the

(continued...)

membership perspective to the countries of south-eastern Europe; opened accession negotiations with Turkey; and created an 'Eastern Partnership' for six successor states of the Soviet Union. The Commission has played a key role in the development of the EU's enlargement policy and in setting the agenda for candidates to progress towards membership via association agreements, legislative alignment, and accession negotiations. The EU has made every step in the enlargement process conditional not only on successful legislative alignment but also on compliance with certain political criteria. This use of conditionality has become a key instrument in EU foreign policy; it has given the EU unprecedented influence on domestic politics in its neighbourhood, even if this influence varies considerably over time, across issues, and among countries.

Introduction

Few of the policies covered in this volume have seen their importance increase as spectacularly over the past decades as enlargement. Enlargement has always been an important event for the EU, but for much of its history, enlargement was restricted to intermittent episodes. Since the end of the cold war, enlargement has become a constant item on the EU's agenda. One institutional expression of its continual importance was the creation in 1999 of a separate Directorate-General for Enlargement (DG ELARG) in the Commission, while for most of the Commission's history, enlargement had been one of many tasks of the Directorate-General for External Relations (DG RELEX) and ad hoc task forces. The higher salience is not simply due to the dramatically increased number of new, and potential, members (see Table 17.1). The main reason is that enlargement is no longer restricted to decisions about accession and the conduct of accession negotiations. It now involves the management of relations with would-be members to assist and assess their preparedness for membership, starting a long time before accession negotiations.

According to Lowi's (1972) typology (see Chapter 3), enlargement can be viewed as a major 'constituent policy' in which the focus is on the rules and institutional framework of policy-making. Enlargement has triggered changes in the EU's institutional structure, as 'widening' of membership has usually been accompanied by a 'deepening' of integration. Treaty changes have amended decision rules and institutional competences to compensate for the detrimental impact of larger numbers and increased diversity on the effectiveness of collective decision-making, the fairness of representation in the institutions, and the scope for further integration. Enlargement also has elements of a redistributive policy, especially in policy areas that receive most funding from the EU budget (see Chapters 8, 9, and 10). These constitutive and redistributive characteristics have made each enlargement controversial. For example, the French vetoes of the UK's first two applications resulted partly from the UK's opposition to budgetary rules and to the common agricultural policy (CAP) (see Chapter 9),

TABLE 17.1 History of EU enlargement: overview				
	Association agreement (signed)	**Membership application**	**Commission opinion**	**Accession negotiations (start/end)**	**Accession**
UK		Aug. 1961	*(unpublished)*	*French veto Jan. 1963*	
		May 1967	Sept. 1967	*de facto French veto Nov. 1967*	
		Oct. 1969		June 1970– Jan. 1972	Jan. 1973
Ireland		July 1961	*Suspended after French veto of UK Jan. 1963*		
		May 1967	Sept. 1967	June 1970– Jan. 1972	Jan. 1973
Denmark		Aug. 1961	*Suspended after French veto of UK Jan. 1963*		
		May 1967	Sept. 1967	June 1970– Jan. 1972	Jan. 1973
Greece	July 1961	June 1975	Jan. 1976	July 1967– May 1979	Jan. 1981
Portugal		Mar. 1977	May 1978	Oct. 1978– June 1985	Jan. 1986
Spain		July 1977	Nov. 1978	Feb. 1979– June 1985	Jan. 1986
Austria	[EEA 1992]	July 1989	July 1991	Feb. 1993– Mar. 1994	Jan. 1995
Sweden	[EEA 1992]	July 1991	July 1992	Feb. 1993– Mar. 1994	Jan. 1995
Finland	[EEA 1992]	Mar. 1992	Nov. 1992	Feb. 1993– Mar. 1994	Jan. 1995
Cyprus	Dec. 1972	July 1990	June 1993	Mar. 1998– Dec. 2002	May 2004
Hungary	Dec. 1991	April 1994	July 1997	Mar. 1998– Dec. 2002	May 2004
Poland	Dec. 1991	April 1994	July 1997	Mar. 1998– Dec. 2002	May 2004
Czech Republic	Oct. 1993[a]	Jan. 1996	July 1997	Mar. 1998– Dec. 2002	May 2004
Estonia	June 1995	Nov. 1995	July 1997	Mar. 1998– Dec. 2002	May 2004
Slovenia	June 1996	June 1996	July 1997	Mar. 1998– Dec. 2002	May 2004
Malta	Dec. 1970	July 1990[b]	June 1993; updated Feb. 1999	Feb. 2000– Dec. 2002	May 2004

TABLE 17.1 (Continued)

	Association agreement (signed)	Membership application	Commission opinion	Accession negotiations (start/end)	Accession
Slovakia	Oct. 1993[a]	June 1995	July 1997	Feb. 2000–Dec. 2002	May 2004
Latvia	June 1995	Oct. 1995	July 1997	Feb. 2000–Dec. 2002	May 2004
Lithuania	June 1995	Dec. 1995	July 1997	Feb. 2000–Dec. 2002	May 2004
Romania	Feb. 1993	June 1995	July 1997	Feb. 2000–Dec. 2004	Jan. 2007
Bulgaria	March 1993	Dec. 1995	July 1997	Feb. 2000–Dec. 2004	Jan. 2007
Croatia	Oct. 2001	Feb. 2003	Apr. 2004	Oct. 2005–Dec. 2011	July 2013
Turkey	Sept. 1963	Apr. 1987	Dec. 1989	Oct. 2005–	
Montenegro	Oct. 2007	Dec. 2008	Nov. 2010	June 2012–	
Serbia	May 2008	Dec. 2009	Oct. 2011	Jan. 2014–	
FYROM	Apr. 2001	Mar. 2004	Nov. 2005[c]		
Albania	June 2006	Apr. 2009	Nov. 2010[d]		
Bosnia-Herzegovina	June 2008				
Kosovo[e]	Initialed Aug. 2014				
Norway	[EEA 1992]	Apr. 1962	*Suspended after French veto of UK Jan. 1963*		
		July 1967	Sept. 1967	June 1970–Jan. 1972	*Negative referendum Sept. 1972*
		Nov. 1992	April 1993	Apr. 1993–June 1994	*Negative referendum Nov. 1994*
Iceland	[EEA 1992]	July 2009	Feb. 2010	July 2010[f]	
Switzerland	[EEA 1992]	May 1992	*Application suspended after negative referendum on EEA, Dec. 1992*		

Notes:

[a] Agreement with Czechoslovakia: Dec. 1991.
[b] Temporary suspension in Oct. 1996.
[c] Commission has recommended opening accession negotiations since 2009, but Greece has blocked.
[d] The European Council granted 'candidate status' in June 2014.
[e] Independence not recognized by Cyprus, Greece, Romania, Slovakia, and Spain.
[f] Negotiations suspended in Sept. 2013 by the Icelandic centre-right government elected in May 2013.

as well as its lukewarm commitment to European integration. The lengthy accession negotiations with Spain and Portugal reflected the concerns of French farmers about competition with regard to Mediterranean agricultural products.

Of course, enlargement also presents clear benefits for the EU. Additional members create a larger single European market (see Chapter 5) and can increase the effectiveness of common policies. Moreover, after the cold war, practitioners and commentators alike have hailed enlargement as the EU's most powerful foreign-policy tool (see also Chapter 18) and a distinctive instrument that helps to establish the EU as a global superpower through the use of soft power (Moravcsik 2010).

This chapter first reviews the main phases of the enlargement policy process—association, pre-accession, and accession—and clarifies for each of these stages the key decisions involved, how they are made, and how policy practice has evolved over time. The chapter then focuses on the use of enlargement as a foreign-policy tool and the development of the EU's accession conditionality. It concludes with a consideration of 'enlargement fatigue' after the 2007 enlargement and of the limits of the success of accession conditionality, both temporal (with regard to the sustainability of compliance after countries have become EU members) and geographical (with regard to the countries of south-east Europe, including Turkey, and the European successor states of the Soviet Union that might lay claim to EU membership).

Rules, procedures, and policy

From its inception, the EU had rules for the accession of new members (see Box 17.1). Article 49 TEU sets out the procedures for the EU to decide on accession—essentially requiring the agreement of all member states and (since the 1987 Single European

| BOX 17.1 | **Evolving rules for enlargement in the treaties** |

Article ~~237~~ *O 49*

Any European State *which respects the* ~~principles~~ *values set out in Article* ~~F(1)~~ *6(1) 2 and is committed to promoting them* may apply to become a member of the ~~Community~~ *Union. The European Parliament and national Parliaments shall be notified of this application.* ~~It~~ *The applicant State shall* address its application to the Council, which shall act unanimously after ~~obtaining the opinion of~~ *consulting* the Commission *and after receiving the* ~~assent~~ *consent of the European Parliament, which shall act by an absolute majority of its component members. The conditions of eligibility agreed upon by the European Council shall be taken into account.*

The conditions of admission and the adjustments to the *Treat~~y~~ies on which the Union is founded,* ~~necessitated thereby~~ *which such admission entails*, shall be the subject of an agreement between the Member States and the applicant State. This agreement shall be submitted for ratification by all the Contracting States in accordance with their respective constitutional requirements.

> **BOX 17.1**   **(Continued)**
>
> **Article F(1) 6(1) 2**
>
> The Union is founded on the ~~principles~~ *values* of ~~liberty,~~ *respect for human dignity, free-dom*, democracy, *equality, the rule of law and* respect for human rights ~~and fundamental freedoms, and the rule of law,~~ *including the rights of persons belonging to minorities. These values* ~~principles which~~ are common to the Member States *in a society in which pluralism, non-discrimination, tolerance, justice, solidarity and equality between women and men prevail.*
>
> Note: Amendments to Art. 49 since the Treaty of Rome (and to Art. 2 since the Treaty of Amsterdam) are in italics.

Act) of the European Parliament (EP). In addition, it made explicit the political conditions that a country has to meet in order to be considered a candidate for membership. This aspect of the rules has changed most in successive treaty changes (see Box 17.1). The Treaty of Rome mentioned only the requirement for applicant states to be 'European'. The Treaty of Amsterdam made the first reference to general liberal democratic values (contained in Art. 2 TEU) and the Treaty of Nice codified previous practice that the European Council could set further and specific conditions.

Yet the treaty does not elaborate much on the procedures to be followed for a state to get from the intention of joining to starting accession negotiations, apart from the need for the Commission to give its opinion at some point. The reason is that until the 1990s there appeared to be no need for such procedures. Although the preamble to the Treaty of Rome expressed the founders' desire to create 'an ever closer union among the peoples of Europe' and called 'upon the other peoples of Europe who share their ideal to join in their efforts', demand for accession was limited. The Iron Curtain precluded one-half of Europe from contemplating EU membership. The remainder of western Europe was either sceptical about deeper integration (and instead created the European Free Trade Association (EFTA)—namely Austria, Denmark, Norway, Portugal, Sweden, Switzerland, and the UK, later joined by Finland) or under right-wing authoritarian regimes (Greece, Portugal, Spain, and Turkey). Enlargement was therefore restricted to fairly discrete episodes when circumstances in the candidate countries changed, and took the form of ad hoc bargaining about the terms of accession.

The end of the cold war and the fall of communism in the countries of central and eastern Europe (CEECs) confronted the EU with the challenge of formulating an enlargement policy that went beyond the procedures for accepting new members. Apart from the EFTA members that submitted membership applications, and Cyprus and Malta, the new applicants were post-communist countries at various stages of a transition towards market economies and liberal democracies. A key challenge for the EU was therefore how to manage relations with countries that desired to join, but were not yet able to comply with the body of EU legislation—the *acquis communautaire*.

A more general element of EU policy towards post-cold-war Europe was to provide support for economic and democratic transitions. The more specifically enlargement-related challenge was to assess and to help would-be members' efforts to meet the conditions for membership. Closely related was the question of how to use the prospect of enlargement to promote and shape domestic changes in candidate countries in line with the EU's values and its broader foreign-policy objective of fostering stability in its European neighbourhood. The challenges that the EU's post-cold-war enlargement policy has thus had to confront go far beyond reaching ad hoc agreements between the member states about whether a specific candidate country can join and on what terms.

Since 1989, the EU has incrementally developed a policy framework for enlargement; which goes far beyond the procedures specified in Article 49 TEU, as the enlargement policy comes into play long before a country officially applies for membership and accession negotiations are only the final stage of a much longer process. In broad terms, we can distinguish three phases in the enlargement process. The first phase is an associate status. Association agreements provide the legal framework for pre-accession relations with potential candidate countries until accession. The second phase starts with a country being recognized as a (potential) candidate for accession; it consists of a policy framework for accession preparations through an alignment with EU legislation and meeting political conditions. The final phase is accession negotiations. After an accession treaty is signed, a candidate has the status of an acceding country. Each phase includes separate decisions by EU actors and specific policy instruments. Conditionality permeates all of these phases: the EU links progress from one phase to the next, and to intermediate steps within each phase, to the fulfilment of certain conditions (see the section 'The EU's conditionality practice and (the limits of) effective external governance' later in the chapter).

Association agreements

For much of the EU's history, a country's application for membership usually marked the start of the enlargement process—just as Article 49 TEU seems to suggest—but this is no longer the case. The reason is that the candidates up to the EFTA enlargement of 1995 were mostly already in a position to apply and to enforce the *acquis* (although doubts were expressed about this in the cases of Greece and Portugal). However, latterly (with the exception of the EFTA members) formal membership applications have been submitted at a much later stage of the actual process. Although the post-communist countries decided to pursue the goal of membership soon after the regime changes of 1989–90, they were not yet in a position to apply the *acquis* at this early stage in their transition processes. Even the front runners waited at least five years until they formally applied, as the Commission seeks to dissuade applicants for which it is unlikely to recommend opening accession negotiations in the medium term.

As a consequence, the first step in the accession process is now usually the declaration of a country's desire to join, not the formal membership application. Such dissuasion does not always work. Montenegro applied in December 2008 and Albania in April 2009, despite the Commission telling them that 'the time was not yet ripe' and that political circumstances in the EU made an agreement to open accession negotiations unlikely (*Agence Europe*, 30 Oct. 2008). In an unprecedented move, several member states, led by Germany and the Netherlands, subsequently blocked the Council's request for the Commission's opinions on these applications (which had hitherto been considered an automatic, technical act) for several months (*Agence Europe*, 18 Feb. 2009). While Montenegro started accession negotiations in 2012, the Commission had not recommended this step for Albania as of June 2014.

In the EU's evolving enlargement practice, the first stage in establishing closer relations is an association agreement. Association agreements are a long-standing instrument for the EU's external relations (see also Chapter 16), and are not limited to countries aspiring to membership. In the early 1960s, the EU concluded association agreements with Greece and with Turkey (see Table 17.1) that contained references to eventual membership. The member states came to regret their rash commitment that has since caused them much embarrassment in relations with Turkey. Another indication that the EU saw association as an expression of close relations was its unwillingness to conclude more than a more limited 'trade and cooperation' agreement with Franco's authoritarian Spain in 1970 (see also Thomas 2006). The association agreements with Cyprus and Malta foreshadowed customs unions but not membership. On a separate track, in 1972 the EU signed free trade area agreements with the EFTA states.

Over recent years, the EU has explicitly made association agreements—and a good record of implementing them—a necessary step on the path to membership. For example, in the previously mentioned negative reaction to Montenegro's plans to apply for membership, the Commission commented that the very recent signing of the association agreement made it premature to assess its correct implementation. Likewise, in 2008 the Commission stressed that Serbia could expect a positive evaluation of a future membership application only after it had demonstrated the correct application of its interim association agreement (*Agence Europe*, 6 Nov. 2008).

The EU has devised different types of association agreements for different groups of would-be members. Although they follow a similar template, there are important nuances as the following sections discuss. In addition, the European Economic Area (EEA) agreement provides an alternative legal framework for closer relations with the EU.

European Economic Area agreement

The EEA agreement (signed in 1992 and in force since 1994) is to date the closest form of economic relations between the EU and non-member states. It enables the non-members to participate (with some voice but no votes) in the EU's internal market—with the exception of agriculture—through their unilateral legal alignment with EU policies, and includes payments from the EEA's EFTA members into the EU budget, as well as a parallel legal-compliance mechanism through the EFTA Surveillance Authority.

When Commission President Jacques Delors floated the idea of an EEA in 1989, it was intended as an alternative to accession. The Commission was concerned that the membership applications by the EFTA countries Austria, Finland, Norway, Sweden, and Switzerland were motivated by the economic benefits of membership, and that the neutrality of most of them and their scepticism about political integration might present obstacles to further integration, especially in foreign and security policy. By offering them participation in the internal market Delors hoped that the EEA would ease the pressure for enlargement. Yet for some EFTA countries it served instead as a stepping-stone to membership (Phinnemore 1999).

Most of the EFTA countries considered the EEA from the start only as a transitional regime on the way to full membership (E. Smith 1999). The notion of the EEA as a stable long-term framework for relations between equals was further undermined through the Court of Justice of the European Union (CJEU) Opinion 1/1991. Initially, the EEA had envisaged an EEA Court, consisting of CJEU judges and EFTA judges, but the CJEU held that such a participation of EFTA judges was incompatible with EU law. This opinion prevented a more symmetrical relationship between the EU and EFTA in the EEA, which reduced its appeal as an alternative to membership. With the accessions of Austria, Finland, and Sweden in 1995 the EEA became a residual arrangement for Iceland, Liechtenstein, and—owing to a negative referendum on accession—Norway. Switzerland did not ratify the EEA following a negative referendum, which also led the Swiss government to suspend its membership application and to negotiate instead a number of far-reaching bilateral sectoral agreements as an alternative to ensure Switzerland's close integration into the internal market.

The Commission has also mentioned the EEA as a possibility for closer relations with some countries included in the European neighbourhood policy (ENP) (see the section 'Association agreements and the Eastern Partnership' later in the chapter). However, since participation in the EEA presumes sophisticated regulatory and administrative capacities to apply and enforce the *acquis*, it is unlikely that it will become a practicable framework for relations with further would-be members that are not advanced industrialized countries. Instead, the main template for association agreements with countries desiring membership became the 'Europe agreements' that the EU first devised for the CEECs in the early 1990s.

Europe agreements

After the fall of the communist regimes in eastern Europe in 1989, the EU moved quickly under the leadership of the Commission to conclude bilateral trade and cooperation agreements (TCAs) and to support economic reform through the Phare (*Pologne, Hongrie: aide à la restructuration des économies*) programme (Pelkmans and

Murphy 1991; Sedelmeier and Wallace 1996: 357–62; Mayhew 1998: 138–50). As the TCA merely provided for a normalization of relations, a consensus emerged around association agreements as the appropriate framework for relations with the CEECs (Kramer 1993). In December 1989, the European Council in Strasbourg agreed to devise 'an appropriate form of association' and DG RELEX quickly sketched a broad framework. The European Council in Dublin in April 1990 agreed to create 'Europe agreements' (EAs), a 'new type of association agreement as a part of the new pattern of relationships in Europe', to be offered to the leading reformers, Hungary, Poland, and Czechoslovakia.

The EAs consisted mainly of the gradual establishment of a free trade area for industrial products, in which the EU liberalized faster than the CEECs, supplemented by a 'political dialogue' on foreign policy, and backed by technical and financial assistance (through Phare) and economic and cultural cooperation. The Commission conducted the negotiations with the CEECs, based on negotiation directives that the Council had to approve unanimously. The Council working group on eastern Europe (rather than the Art. 133 Committee (now the Trade Policy Committee) of national trade officials that usually oversees trade negotiations, see Chapter 16) monitored the negotiations. The Council had to approve the final agreement unanimously and the EP had to give its assent. The inclusion of provisions for political dialogue made the EAs 'mixed agreements' involving both Union and member states' competence and required ratification by all members. The trade component, subject only to Union competence, could enter into force earlier through interim agreements.

One main controversy in the EA negotiations concerned the link between the agreements and eventual EU membership. Given that association agreements are now considered the first step towards membership, it is surprising that the CEECs' key criticism was that the EAs did not establish a clear link to future membership of the EU. Although the label 'Europe' agreements played to the symbolism of a 'return to Europe' through closer relations with the EU, most member states and most commissioners opposed raising the question of membership at this early stage.

The other key area of contestation concerned the extent of trade liberalization. While the EU offered to open its market to industrial products much more quickly than the CEECs over a period of five years, special protocols and annexes covering 'sensitive' sectors—notably agriculture, textiles, coal, and steel—offered slower and more limited liberalization. These sectors accounted for the bulk of CEEC exports and reflected their medium-term comparative advantages. Furthermore, provisions for contingent protection (anti-dumping, safeguards, and anti-subsidy measures— see Chapter 16) provided EU producers with instruments to limit competition.

The dissatisfaction of the CEECs led to two periods of deadlock in the negotiations that the Commission was able to overcome by persuading the Council to take better account of CEEC demands (Sedelmeier and Wallace 1996: 370–2). As a consequence, the EU accepted greater market access than it had initially proposed, and the preamble to the EAs recognized membership as the CEECs' final objective and that the agreement would help to achieve it. This latter concession, in particular, fell short of the firm commitment that the CEECs had hoped for, and they were far from enthusiastic about the final outcome of the negotiations.

Stabilization and association agreements

The EU drew on a very similar template for relations with the countries of the 'western Balkans', namely Albania and most of the successor states of Yugoslavia (Slovenia concluded an EA, see Table 17.1). Following the violent break-up of Yugoslavia and the US-brokered Dayton agreement that stopped the fighting in Bosnia (see Chapter 18), the EU agreed a 'regional approach' towards the countries of south-eastern Europe in February 1996. In the aftermath of the North Atlantic Treaty Organization's (Nato) military intervention in Kosovo, the European Council in Cologne in June 1999 endorsed an initiative by the German presidency for a stability pact for south-eastern Europe (Friis and Murphy 2000). The Commission elaborated proposals for a 'stabilization and association process' (SAP) that included not only the aim of supporting economic and democratic transition but also regional cooperation, as well as explicit preparation for eventual accession.

The key element of the SAP was a specific type of association agreement— 'stabilization and association agreements' (SAAs)—as well as financial assistance through CARDS (Community Assistance for Reconstruction, Development and Stabilization). The SAAs were largely modelled on the EAs as regards substance, but included much more detailed political conditionality (to be discussed later) (Phinnemore 2003). In contrast to the EU's reluctance to establish a link between the EAs and eventual membership, the European Council in Feira in June 2000 affirmed the status of the south-east European countries as 'potential candidates' even before the first SAAs were signed.

Association agreements and the 'Eastern Partnership'

The EU initially offered less preferential partnership and cooperation agreements (PCAs) to the European successor states of the Soviet Union (apart from the Baltics, see Table 17.1). Latterly policy has shifted with the decision to negotiate an association agreement with Ukraine and subsequently to make association agreements the core of the 'Eastern Partnership' (EaP). In March 2003, the prospect of eastern enlargement prompted the Commission to propose a European neighbourhood policy (ENP) as a new framework for relations with the EU's eastern and southern neighbours (Commission 2003e).

The EU developed relations with the east European countries of the ENP in the framework of the EaP. The EaP was a Polish–Swedish initiative to strengthen relations with Armenia, Azerbaijan, Belarus, Georgia, Moldova, and Ukraine in response to French President Sarkozy's proposal that led in July 2008 to the launch of the 'Union for the Mediterranean' with the southern neighbours of the ENP (and the remaining Mediterranean non-members). The European Council in June 2008 asked the Commission to prepare a proposal and in September 2008 urged it to accelerate its work after the fighting between Russia and Georgia in August 2008 prompted new attention to the region, amidst a broader debate about what kind of relationship to develop with Russia (see Chapter 18). The cornerstones of the EaP that was formally launched in May 2009 were association agreements that entailed the creation of a 'deep and comprehensive' free trade area and gradual visa liberalization. It is not obvious what is genuinely novel in the EaP. The move towards negotiating association agreements had already been under way with Ukraine. Visa liberalization is a new element—and much valued by the EU's neighbours—but it is also part of 'mobility partnerships' that the EU has not only concluded with the EaP countries Georgia, Moldova, Armenia, and Azerbaijan, but also with southern partners in the ENP (Morocco, Tunisia), as well as with Cape Verde. An Eastern Partnership cooperation programme (EaPIC), launched in 2012, provides additional financial assistance as a reward for reforms for 'deep democracy and respect for human rights' (€152 in 2012/13 for Moldova, Georgia, and Armenia, *Agence Europe,* 13 Dec. 2013), yet it is not a distinctive element of the EaP, but rather part of a more general trend for greater emphasis on the ENP's normative dimension after the Arab Spring. Despite the lack of a distinctive value, added over the ENP or developments in bilateral relations, the EaP nonetheless provides a focal point and common framework for relations with eastern neighbours for whom membership is a long-term goal, even if the EU had refused to acknowledge this possibility as of the end of 2013.

The decision to negotiate association agreements with EaP countries provoked the same debate about the link between association and membership as had the EA negotiations. Ukrainian pressure to confirm its membership prospects in the agreement's preamble was supported by the Czech Republic, Poland, Sweden, and the UK. Other member states—particularly Belgium and the Netherlands, as well as Austria, Luxembourg, Portugal, and Spain—strongly opposed such a move. In their view, the EU should not even acknowledge explicitly that Ukraine was a European country, which could apply for membership under Article 49 TEU. Instead, the agreement should clearly stipulate that it did not in any way 'prejudge the future of EU/Ukrainian relations' (*Agence Europe,* 5 Sept. 2008). The joint declaration of the EU–Ukraine summit in September 2008, reflecting a French presidency proposal, 'recognized that Ukraine as a European country shares a common history and common values with the countries of the European Union', and that the future association agreement 'leaves open the way for further progressive developments in EU–Ukraine relations'. Although the EU did not offer the prospect of membership, it 'acknowledge[d] the European aspirations of Ukraine and welcome[d] its European choice' (*Agence Europe,* 10 Sept. 2008).

The EU had envisaged the EaP Vilnius summit in November 2013 as the occasion to sign the association agreement with Ukraine and to initial the agreements with

Armenia, Georgia, and Moldova. However, the summit ended in disappointment as only the agreements with the latter two countries were initialled. In September, Armenia abandoned the association agreement despite completing the negotiations in order to join Russia's customs union with Belarus and Kazakhstan, which is incompatible with the trade provisions of the association agreement (*Agence Europe* 5 Sept. 2013). Days before the summit, Ukrainian President Viktor Yanukovych unexpectedly announced that he would not sign the association agreement (*Agence Europe*, 22 Nov. 2013). The decision resulted partly from the government's unwillingness to meet the EU's conditions (most prominently concerning selective justice and the imprisonment of former Prime Minister Yulia Tymoshenko), partly from Russian threats (of trade retaliation from the customs union, *Agence Europe*, 22 Aug. 2013) and inducements (after the decision, Russia offered an €11 billion bailout and a reduction of gas prices, *Agence Europe*, 20 Dec. 2013).

The decision sparked waves of protests, civil unrest, and riots that reflected the country's deep division over European integration. The government's violent response cumulated in the parliament's deposition of Yanukovych in February 2014. The collapse of the Yanukovych government triggered separatist violence in eastern Ukraine, and the annexation of the Crimean peninsula by Russia. The EU's response consisted of macro-financial support for Ukraine amounting to a total of €1.6 billion (*Agence Europe*, 20 May 2014) and an acceleration of the process of signing association agreements with Moldova and Georgia (*Agence Europe*, 22 Mar. 2014), which were eventually signed at the same time as the agreement with Ukraine, on 27 June 2014.

Pre-accession alignment and (potential) candidate status

Association agreements provide the legal framework for relations with would-be members until accession, even after they achieve the next step towards accession: potential candidate status and pre-accession alignment. The pre-accession policy runs in parallel with association, rather than replacing it. The point at which a would-be member enters the second main stage of the accession process is not clear-cut. Generally, it starts once the EU recognizes a country as a potential candidate country. EU practice about such an acknowledgement has changed. For the ten CEECs that joined in 2004–7, this acknowledgement happened only at the European Council in Copenhagen in 1993, after sustained lobbying from the candidates and from within the EU (Sedelmeier 2005). By contrast, the European Council in Feira in 2000 acknowledged that the south-east European countries were 'potential candidates' at a rather early stage in the process. Pre-accession alignment thus now starts even before the conclusion of association agreements, in line with the more extensive and detailed conditionality.

Origins of the EU's pre-accession policy

The need for pre-accession alignment as an element of enlargement policy reflects the specific characteristics of most candidate countries after the cold war, namely that they were not ready to comply with the EU's single-market legislation when they applied for membership. The EU's response to the challenge of how to support candidates' efforts to meet this membership condition was a pre-accession strategy focused on regulatory alignment. The first time the Commission had suggested such a strategy was the accession of Greece, which it did not consider ready for full membership. It proposed a pre-membership programme of structural adjustment and economic convergence (Preston 1997: 51–2) but, at the time, the Council rejected the Commission's suggestion and decided unanimously to open accession negotiations.

In the context of eastern enlargement, the pre-accession strategy resulted from an initiative of DG RELEX and the cabinet of Sir Leon Brittan, the Commissioner for External Economic Relations (see also A. R. Young and Wallace 2000: 118–19; Sedelmeier 2005: 141–7). Following the general endorsement of the possibility of enlargement at the European Council in Copenhagen in June 1993, these policy advocates in the DG and the Brittan cabinet were keen to use the momentum for a follow-up initiative that placed accession preparations on a concrete working footing that would keep enlargement firmly on the EU's agenda. The cornerstone of their strategy to prepare the relevant CEECs for accession was a regulatory alignment with the *acquis communautaire*. Progress with alignment would dispel fears that the CEECs were insufficiently prepared for membership and make it difficult for the EU to justify dragging its feet. Moreover, as long as the CEECs remained sufficiently flexible to set their own priorities, alignment could also be beneficial to them within the broader process of economic restructuring and in reducing the scope for the EU to use trade-defence measures. Despite initial reluctance both inside the Commission and among the member states, this particular strategy also appealed to those reluctant about enlargement; an explicit programme of legislative alignment could provide a checklist of necessary preparations that would make it easier to argue against premature accession until all the measures were in place.

The core element of the pre-accession strategy announced at the European Council in Essen in December 1994 was a White Paper (Commission 1995) that set out key elements of the internal-market *acquis* that the CEECs had to adopt and the necessary legal and institutional framework for applying them. In addition, the Commission established a Technical Assistance Information Exchange Office (TAIEX) to facilitate regulatory alignment. One of its main tasks became to organize a 'twinning' of seconded experts from the member states with their counterparts in CEEC national administrations to assist with the implementation of specific measures of the *acquis*. The pre-accession strategy would involve the CEECs establishing national programmes for the adoption of the *acquis* (NPAAs), which set out priorities and specific timetables for alignment. The Commission published annual reports to monitor progress.

Accession partnerships and European partnerships

In July 1997, the Commission advanced a 'reinforced pre-accession strategy' that envisaged bilateral 'accession partnerships' (APs) as the main instrument for the management of legislative alignment. In the APs, the candidate countries committed themselves to clear programmes for alignment by setting 'short term' and 'medium term' priorities for measures to be adopted. The CEECs then set out clearly the timetables in NPAAs. Pre-accession aid was targeted more directly at investment necessary to adopt the *acquis* through a revamping of Phare into two new financial support instruments: ISPA (Instrument for Structural Policies for Pre-accession, along the lines of the Cohesion Fund) and SAPARD (Special Accession Programme for Agriculture and Rural Development). Although the speed of alignment was in principle left to the candidates, the EU tied alignment both to financial assistance and to progress in the accession process, which created pressures for rapid and far-reaching adjustments and prompted considerable criticism that the language of partnership disguised rather thinly the imposition of EU priorities (see also Grabbe 2006: 14–18).

The EU essentially maintained this framework for pre-accession alignment for the countries of south-eastern Europe. The European Council in Thessaloniki in June 2003 agreed to a Commission proposal that introduced new instruments within the broader framework of the SAP. It adjusted financial support by replacing the CARDS programme with the Instrument for Pre-Accession Assistance (IPA). The main instruments for pre-accession alignment were new 'European partnerships', which essentially copy the APs. They identify each country's priorities in their preparations for further integration, and progress is monitored through the Commission's 'regular reports'. Once a country moves from the status of 'potential' candidate country to 'candidate country', its European partnership is replaced by an AP.

The EU's procedures for granting 'candidate' status are not very explicit. Initially, the term was only used for countries involved in accession negotiations. The EU started to acknowledge a country formally as a 'candidate state' in order to reward it for the progress that it had made, even if it did not yet consider this progress sufficient for opening accession negotiations. The European Council in Helsinki in 1999 did so for the first time with regard to Turkey. The Commission proposed this step in its opinions on the application of the former Yugoslav Republic of Macedonia (FYROM) in 2005 and on Serbia in 2011, despite otherwise recommending at the time that accession negotiations should not yet be opened. The Commission did not recommend candidate status for Albania in its November 2010 opinion, but did so in October 2013, while still not recommending the start of accession negotiations. Due to the opposition of several members, the European Council only agreed on granting candidate status in June 2014 (*Agence Europe*, 18 Dec. 2013; 28 June 2014).

The Commission obtained considerable influence on the pace of the accession process and the selection of candidates through its role in the evaluation of the candidates' progress on alignment. Its monitoring activity involved it in the domestic politics of applicant countries far more than in previous enlargement rounds, as well as more than in its monitoring of existing member states' compliance with the *acquis*.

Accession

Commission opinions

The Commission's opinion remains a key element in proceeding to the accession stage. The college of commissioners adopts the opinion with a majority vote, but in practice this was only necessary in particularly controversial cases, such as the (negative) opinion on Greece in 1976 (Preston 1997: 50). Voting aside, another indicator of controversy is if it takes the Commission a long time to prepare its opinion after a country's formal application. For example, it took two years or more for the opinions on Turkey, Cyprus, Malta, the CEECs, and Austria (the first post-cold-war EFTA applicant) (see Table 17.1).

The Commission's opinion is not binding on the Council, which decides unanimously on whether to open accession negotiations with an applicant. The opinion has an important agenda-setting function as the Council tends to follow the Commission's recommendation (see also Friis 1998). The exceptions are the cases of Greece, when the Council overruled its negative opinion, and FYROM, with Greece blocking agreement on the Commission's recommendation to open accession negotiations since 2009.

A key novelty in the opinions on the CEECs was that the Commission did not assess their preparedness at the time (except for the political conditions), but explicitly assessed their *prospective* readiness, since none of the candidates met all the conditions when the opinions were published. Moreover, the Commission's opinion has lost some of its distinctive character as the main document containing the Commission's assessment and recommendation. The Commission now publishes regular monitoring reports after the official opinion to update its assessment, as well as even prior to an official application of potential candidate countries as in recent policy practice vis-à-vis south-eastern Europe. These regular reports, usually published in October/November each year, assess in a fairly standardized manner the progress made with regard to political and economic conditions, and with legislative alignment in the various policy areas, and they can include a recommendation to start accession negotiations. For example, the 1999 regular reports proposed starting accession negotiations with Bulgaria, Latvia, Lithuania, Malta, Romania, and Slovakia, and the 2004 regular report with Turkey.

Accession negotiations

The EU established the procedures for the conduct of accession negotiations in the first enlargement negotiations with Denmark, Ireland, Norway, and the UK in the 1970s (Preston 1997; Nugent 2004). In contrast to external trade negotiations (see Chapter 16), they are not conducted by the Commission, but by the Council presidency on behalf of the member states. Although the Commission does not have a formal role in the negotiations, it has often been able to broker compromises and identify solutions (Avery 2004). Negotiations occur through bilateral 'accession conferences' that can run in parallel with more than one candidate. Prior to opening official negotiations, the Commission conducts a 'screening process' with the applicant countries. In multilateral and bilateral sessions, the Commission assesses whether an applicant is able to apply the *acquis*, and identifies possible challenges for the negotiations. After the screening, the candidates submit their negotiating positions. The Commission drafts a common EU position that requires unanimous agreement by the Council.

The Council then decides unanimously to open, and subsequently to close provisionally, negotiations on over thirty 'chapters' of the *acquis* (relating to specific policy areas, plus issues such as budgetary provisions, institutions, and 'judiciary and fundamental rights'). In the 2004 enlargement round, the procedure led to a 'chapterology' among commentators assessing relative progress towards membership in terms of chapters opened and closed.

The guiding principle of accession negotiations—that the *acquis* is not negotiable—was established in the first enlargement round. Many aspects of the *acquis*, such as the financing of the CAP, created problems for the UK. Although Article 49 TEU does not preclude a renegotiation of the founding treaties, this was precisely what the incumbents wanted to avoid. The Commission's (unpublished) opinion on the UK's first application stated the key guiding principle for accession negotiation that has since been repeatedly reaffirmed (Preston 1997: 28): the EU expects candidates to adjust unilaterally to existing EU law, even if established policies and practices do not fit their specific situation. What is negotiable is rather limited: a timetable for adopting the *acquis*, rather than permanent derogations. The best that candidates can hope for are transition periods after accession during which they do not have to apply specific elements of the *acquis*. Conversely, the member states usually seek to reduce their own adjustment costs through transition periods during which new members will not enjoy the full benefits of membership, for example with regard to market access, CAP payments, and structural funds.

In the history of enlargement, EU concessions have been rather limited. Such exceptional cases include the EFTA enlargement in 1995, when the EU allowed the new members to maintain certain higher standards of environmental protection, even though they could impede trade (A. R. Young and Wallace 2000), and the long transition periods of ten years or more that the CEECs obtained for certain investment-intensive environmental regulations that did not affect product standards. More typically, accession treaties impose harsh terms on the new members. For the UK, this was particularly the case with regard to budget contributions that remained contested until Prime Minister Margaret Thatcher negotiated the UK rebate in 1984 (see Chapter 9). Spain and Portugal had to wait ten years after accession before certain Mediterranean agricultural products enjoyed full market access in other members, as well as to accept restrictions on free labour movement for their citizens.

The accession agreements with the CEECs are also striking examples of discrimination against new members in key areas of membership. The incumbents could restrict the movement of workers from the new members for up to seven years after accession. Direct payments from the CAP were to increase only gradually from a quarter of the level paid to farmers in the old member states, to equality only after ten years. In addition, receipts from structural funds were capped at 4 per cent of the recipient's GDP (Avery 2004). Since—even under such disadvantageous conditions—the gains from membership for the new member states remained sufficiently large, the incumbents could shift the adjustment costs heavily to new members (see also Moravcsik and Vachudova 2003). Yet the cases of the UK and Spain show that adverse terms of accession can create disgruntled new members that attempt to redress these bargains once on the inside.

Once the member states and the candidate have reached an agreement, and the EP has given its assent, the accession treaty is signed by all governments and the candidate becomes an 'accession country'. The accession country and all the member states have to ratify the treaty. Ratification referendums have failed twice in Norway in 1972 and 1994. France is the only incumbent so far to hold a referendum to ratify an accession treaty, which succeeded in the case of the UK. Following constitutional amendments in 2005 and 2008 the French president must submit enlargement to a referendum unless an accession treaty is approved by three-fifths of the two houses of parliament convened in Congress (*Agence Europe*, 25 July 2008).

In sum, although the treaty rules for enlargement identify the member states as central actors, in practice the Commission has played a very significant role in each of the main phases of the enlargement process—association, alignment, and accession negotiation—and in facilitating candidates' progress from one phase to the next. The Commission has set the agenda for eastern enlargement by forging incremental agreements on the path to enlargement, managing pre-accession relations with candidates, and monitoring their adjustment efforts. It has shaped the outcome of accession negotiations by brokering compromises. Moreover, through its role in the application of accession conditionality, the Commission has enhanced its role in EU foreign policy. At the same time, enlargement policy also provides evidence that the Commission is not a unitary actor. Debates over enlargement policy often reveal transgovernmental cleavages that cut across member states and the Commission.

Enlargement as a tool of foreign policy and external governance

It has become increasingly common for academic commentators and EU officials alike to refer to enlargement as the EU's 'most powerful foreign policy tool' (see Commission 2003*e*: 5; K. Smith 2003: 66). There are two distinct ways in which enlargement can be understood as a foreign-policy tool. The first relates to anchoring fragile democracies that have emerged from authoritarian rule within a prosperous and democratic international community. This notion not only surfaced in the context of post-communist transition, but was already highly salient in the Mediterranean enlargements of the 1980s after Greece, Portugal, and Spain emerged from dictatorships.

The second way in which enlargement is a foreign-policy tool is the EU's strategic use of the incentive of membership in order to induce or preserve specific policy changes in non-member states. Accession conditionality—tying the ultimate reward of membership to certain conditions—can change the incentive structure for candidate countries in such a way as to trigger domestic changes that the existing member states desire (Kelley 2004; Kubicek 2003; Pridham 2005; Schimmelfennig and Sedelmeier 2005*a*; Vachudova 2005; Grabbe 2006; Schimmelfennig *et al.* 2006). In the context of eastern enlargement, accession conditionality has developed dramatically from 'Europeanness' as the only criterion specified by the Treaty of Rome. It now underpins every step of pre-accession relations virtually up to the day of accession (and even beyond in the cases of Bulgaria and Romania).

Evolution of accession conditionality

The EU made the first reference to political membership conditions beyond what was specified in Article 237 of the Treaty of Rome (see Box 17.1) in the context of the Mediterranean enlargements. The 'Declaration on Democracy' at the European Council in Copenhagen in April 1978 stated that 'respect for and maintenance of representative democracy and human rights in each Member State are essential elements of membership'. Although the declaration related formally to the first direct elections to the EP, it was also 'intended to strengthen the Community's leverage against any future member which might slip towards authoritarian rule' (W. Wallace 1996: 16)—which was not inconceivable in view of the attempted putsch in Spain in 1981.

The EU's use of conditionality with regard to human rights and democracy increased significantly in the context of eastern enlargement. Phare aid was provided only once countries had achieved progress in democratic transition. The EU has suspended such aid on several occasions:

- to Romania (along with trade negotiations) in 1990 after the government organized the violent repression of post-election demonstrations;

- to Yugoslavia in 1991 after the breakout of war following the secession of Slovenia and Croatia; and

- to Croatia in 1995 after the military offensive to establish government control over the Serb-held Krajina region.

The start of EA negotiations also reflected differences in democratization (see Table 17.1). In the context of negotiations with Romania, EU concerns about its fragile democracy led the Council to agree in May 1992 on a suspension clause in all association agreements that would be triggered in the event of violations of democracy and human rights. The first direct statement of accession conditions stems from the European Council in Copenhagen in June 1993.

At this meeting, the European Council declared for the first time that the CEECs that so desired might eventually become members. Many member states had been reluctant about this step, and a key debate in the run-up to the declaration concerned the criteria that potential members had to fulfil. Some opponents as well as proponents of early enlargement argued for quantitative criteria, such as a specific level of gross domestic product (GDP) per capita, in order to reduce the scope for politically motivated decisions for or against enlargement. However, the Council accepted the Commission's proposal for qualitative conditions that included not only the ability to apply the *acquis* after accession, but also political and economic criteria (see Box 17.2). In this way, although these Copenhagen criteria were primarily intended as a defensive instrument to guard against premature accessions, the EU almost accidentally invented an extremely powerful foreign-policy instrument (see also Menon and Sedelmeier 2010). A further condition related to the EU's ability to absorb new members, which resurfaced after the 2007 enlargement (see the section on 'Enlargement fatigue' later in the chapter).

The subsequent application of political conditionality by the Commission and the European Council was considerably broader than that set out at Copenhagen

---

BOX 17.2   Accession conditionality

'Copenhagen criteria' (European Council, Copenhagen, 1993):

- stable institutions guaranteeing democracy, the rule of law, human rights, and respect for and protection of minorities;

- a functioning market economy, as well as the capacity to cope with competitive pressure and market forces within the Union;

- ability to take on the obligations of membership, including adherence to the aims of political, economic, and monetary union;

- the EU's capacity to absorb new members, while maintaining the momentum of European integration.

BOX 17.3	Expanding political criteria: an illustration

Commission 'benchmarks' for opening accession negotiations with FYROM (March/June 2008):

- implementation of the SAA;
- improved dialogue with political parties;
- police reform;
- reform of the legal sector;
- reform of public administration;
- fight against corruption;
- employment policy and improving the investment environment;
- electoral law reform.

(see Box 17.3). A reference of the European Council in Madrid in 1995 to the CEECs' administrative structures has since been widely interpreted as the basis of assessing administrative capacities, judicial reform, and the fight against corruption and organized crime. The EU's emphasis on such issues became particularly pronounced in the accessions of Romania and Bulgaria. In the EU's relations with the western Balkans, the political conditions expanded further to include issues related to the ethnic conflict and the violent break-up of Yugoslavia, and touching on highly sensitive questions of statehood, such as cooperation with the International Criminal Tribunal for the former Yugoslavia (ICTY), the return of refugees, setting a threshold of 55 per cent for approval of the independence referendum in Montenegro, the establishment of good relations between Serbia and Kosovo, or constitutional and police reform in Bosnia.

By setting political conditions that are not covered by the *acquis* (despite the inclusion of Art. 2 TEU), the EU has entered new territory. Accusations of double standards in the treatment of candidate and full members strengthened calls for the development of EU competences in these areas. Political conditionality also provides scope for actors other than member-state governments to exert influence. The Commission plays a key role by setting conditions and assessing compliance, even if the ultimate decision on whether a country has met the conditions is the Council's. The conditions also reflect lobbying by actors such as the EP. For example, following the persistent advocacy by Emma Nicholson, the EP's rapporteur on Romania, the EU insisted on improvements in the standards of state-run orphanages and changes to practices for international adoptions.

Other international organizations also acquire a role in the EU policy process. Since the EU lacks rules in most areas of political conditionality, it demanded compliance with the rules of organizations such as the Council of Europe, the Organization for Security and Cooperation in Europe (OSCE), or the ICTY.

The EU's conditionality practice and (the limits of) effective external governance

Most studies of eastern enlargement agree that conditionality has provided the EU with a highly effective means to influence policy change in applicant countries. The effectiveness of conditionality depends on specific conditions—primarily that the EU's incentives are sufficiently large and credible to outweigh domestic adjustment costs (Schimmelfennig and Sedelmeier 2005a). Since these conditions were generally favourable in the CEECs, conditionality was particularly powerful in bringing about adjustment to the *acquis* in these countries. Nonetheless, such adjustment was not uniform across issues and countries; it depended, for example, on the nature of the *acquis* in an issue area and the constellation of domestic actors (Jacoby 2004). Compliance with the EU's political conditions, such as democracy and human rights, threatened prohibitively high domestic-adjustment costs for the ruling elites in countries with strongly nationalist and/or undemocratic governments. Political conditionality has therefore been ineffective in Belarus and was in Slovakia under Vladimir Mečiar and Croatia under Franjo Tudjman. However, in the latter two cases it helped to lock in democratic change once nationalist and authoritarian parties lost elections to coalitions of liberal democratic parties (Vachudova 2005; Schimmelfennig *et al.* 2006). The EU did not cause their electoral victories, but once the new governments carried out political reforms that brought the country closer to accession, the returns to power of the previous governing parties did not lead to a reversal of the reforms.

If governments did not perceive adjustment costs as prohibitively high, as was generally the case with regard to the *acquis*, then the EU's influence depended on the credibility of conditionality. Such credibility was undermined if EU actors sent out contradictory signals about the requirements for accession (Hughes *et al.* 2004a, 2004b; Sissenich 2005), or if a candidate country had reasons to doubt that the member states would agree to accession, even if it met all the conditions. In the context of its eastern enlargement, the EU's main instrument for making the prospect of membership credible was the opening of accession negotiations (Schimmelfennig and Sedelmeier 2005a).

The effectiveness of conditionality as an instrument of external governance rested on generally favourable conditions—a credible membership incentive and domestic adjustment costs that did not threaten governments' hold of office—with regard to the countries in the 2004–7 enlargement rounds. However, these conditions are less favourable with regard to remaining candidates and would-be candidates, and once a country has joined the EU. These more difficult cases indicate the limits of external governance through conditionality (Epstein and Sedelmeier 2009), although the EU has partly reacted with adjustments to its enlargement practice.

In the case of Turkey, conditionality has lost much of its credibility despite the opening of negotiations in 2005. Suggestions in Austria, France, and Germany that negotiations might not necessarily lead to accession but to a vague 'privileged partnership'—a clear break with previous policy—and the possibility of a refer-endum in France (or elsewhere) to ratify its accession have made it less credible that the EU would grant accession even if Turkey meets the conditions. The pros-pects for Turkish accession became even more uncertain after the negotiations were frozen, due to Turkey's failure to implement the customs union (owing to its refusal to recognize the Republic of Cyprus), as well as the violent repression of anti-government protests in 2013. At the same time, the diminished credibility of accession has not brought compliance with EU conditionality to a halt. The social-conservative, moderately Islamist Justice and Development Party (AKP) government continued complying with certain aspects of the EU's political con-ditionality that could strengthen its position towards the secularist establishment and the military (Masraff 2011; Saatcioglu 2010; Yilmaz 2012). Recognizing some of the progress made and the need to provide incentives for further reforms, the EU agreed in October 2013 to start again negotiations on some chapters after three years of paralysis.

Conditionality also faced unfavourable conditions in the countries of the western Balkans (see also Elbasani 2013; Noutcheva 2012). The political conditions touched on highly sensitive questions of statehood and national identity (see e.g. Freyburg and Richter 2010) and/or state capacity (see e.g. Börzel 2011), and economic de-velopment lagged behind the CEECs. The EU made some changes to its application of conditionality in order to overcome the problem that accession might be a too distant prospect for governments to incur the high costs of compliance. These ad-justments include the specification of additional intermediate steps on the path to accession as rewards for compliance (e.g. formally granting the symbolic 'candidate' status). The EU also identified additional incentives, such as lifting visa require-ments, which, however, presumed that additional criteria would be met, such as the signing of a readmission agreement for asylum-seekers (see Chapter 15). The Commission also initiated a shift in the strategy of demanding strict compliance with conditions prior to awarding the promised benefits, towards making these ben-efits more tangible before full compliance is achieved. For example, in May 2006 the EU suspended negotiations of an SAA with Serbia over the government's failure to cooperate fully with the ICTY on the arrest of the Bosnian Serbs Ratko Mladić and Radovan Karadžić. Yet, in 2008 although no progress had occurred, the EU signed the agreement just prior to the parliamentary elections in order to bolster support for the pro-EU party of President Boris Tadić, but made ratification of the agreement (and implementation of the interim agreement) still conditional on further cooper-ation with the ICTY. Likewise, the EU initialled the SAA with Bosnia in December 2007 in return for the mere promise of constitutional and police reform in the hope that making the benefits of the SAA more tangible would reduce domestic opposi-tion to reforms.

This strategy may have had some success in the case of Serbia: Tadić's party won the elections and Karadžić was arrested and extradited, although the interim SAA remained blocked by the Netherlands until Mladić was also arrested. Since then, marked improvements in relations between Serbia and Kosovo (the independence of which has not been recognized by five member states) under Tadić's nationalist successor Tomislav Nikolić, facilitated by the High Representative and Vice-President, Catherine Ashton, led the European Council to agree to open accession negotiations in January 2014 (*Agence Europe*, 29 June 2013). There has been much less to show for the EU's inducements in Bosnia. A police reform bill was passed in April 2008 prior to the signing of the SAA in June, but did not envisage the unification of police forces demanded by the EU, and constitutional reform has not yet begun. This failure to deliver on promised constitutional reforms led the Commission to open a procedure to reduce funding for Bosnia from the IPA in October 2013 (*Agence Europe*, 11 Oct. 2013). Such failures notwithstanding, EU external governance has enabled slow but steady domestic reforms in the western Balkan, despite the unfavourable starting conditions.

In turn, the impact of conditionality has led to (albeit uneven) progress towards membership across the region (see also Table 17.1). Croatia joined in July 2013; Montenegro and Serbia have started accession negotiations; FYROM has obtained candidate status (only Greece is blocking the opening of accession negotiations while the dispute over the country's name remains unresolved, but this has not diminished the credibility of the membership incentive sufficiently to stall reforms), as has Albania; and Kosovo concluded SAA negotiations in May 2014.

The EU's application of conditionality also faces unfavourable conditions with regard to Ukraine or other European successor states of the Soviet Union in the EaP. The perceived success of accession conditionality and the Commission's desire to expand its role in EU foreign policy led it to adapt the key tenets of its conditionality policy to relations with neighbours that it does not currently consider potential candidates (see also Kelley 2006). Bilateral relations in the EaP are organized around 'action plans' that are very similar to APs, and regular reports that assess a country's alignment. One obvious flaw in the framework is that the EU does not offer what most eastern neighbours value most—eventual membership—but only the rather vague incentive of 'closer relations' and association agreements. Given the high domestic adjustment costs of most of its political conditions in the EaP countries, in the absence of an unambiguous commitment to the possibility of membership, the EaP appears better equipped to achieving issue-specific objectives—such as combating illegal immigration, organized crime, human trafficking, or money laundering—through targeted aid and issue-specific rewards, such as abolishing visa requirements, than to broader foreign-policy objectives, such as fostering democratic reforms (see also Bennett 2012; Börzel and Langbein 2013; Lavenex and Schimmelfennig 2011; Sedelmeier 2007; Weber *et al.* 2007). Moreover, the decision by Ukraine's then president Viktor Yanukovych to abandon the signing of an association agreement in November 2013 rather than meeting the EU's conditions reflects the limitations of this incentive, especially when set against the positive and negative inducements provided by Russia.

Post-accession compliance

Another concern about the limits of conditionality in sustaining domestic reforms is temporal: membership loses its incentivizing role after an accession treaty is signed and a date for accession is agreed (Böhmelt and Freyburg 2013). The EU has therefore made some moves towards extending conditionality both beyond the signing of accession treaties, and even after accession itself. First, after the signing of accession treaties with Bulgaria and Romania, the Council asked the Commission to continue its monitoring and to recommend a postponement of the accession date if necessary. Moreover, in the 2004 enlargement, Article 38 of the accession treaties allows the Commission to take 'appropriate measures' even after accession, if a new member causes within the first three years of membership 'a serious breach of the functioning of the internal market' or if there is an 'imminent risk of such breach' (subsequent accession treaties added a similar specific 'justice and home affairs safeguard'). As of mid-2014, the internal-market safeguard had not been used. What is more, even well after the safeguard clause had expired, data on infringements of EU law show that new members generally comply better with EU law than the old members (Sedelmeier 2008, 2012b; Toshkov 2012). Falkner and Treib (2008) caution that this apparently positive record might mask more serious, but harder to detect, problems with the actual application of EU law.

The accession treaties with Bulgaria and Romania went a step further towards post-accession conditionality. They include a 'cooperation and verification mechanism' (CVM) without a fixed expiry date that authorizes the Commission to monitor reforms of their judicial systems and measures against corruption and organized crime. However, the two countries' progress with meeting the CVM benchmarks remains limited (Gateva 2013; Spendzharova and Vachudova 2012). The main sanction of the CVM is the stigma attached to continued monitoring; otherwise it envisages only the non-recognition of the decisions by Bulgarian and Romanian courts in other member states. The Commission's decisions in July and November 2008 to freeze a total of €520 million in aid for Bulgaria were for suspected fraud, rather than a sanction through CMV. At the same time, some member states—initially Finland and the Netherlands and more recently France and Germany—have made a link between progress with CMV and their agreement to Bulgaria and Romania's membership in the Schengen Agreement on free travel (see Chapter 15). These countries have indicated that they would veto a decision to let Bulgaria and Romania join Schengen if it were put to a vote, despite the Commission, the Council's Schengen working group, and the EP having confirmed that both countries have met the necessary conditions since 2011 (*Agence Europe*, 5 May 2011, 14 Oct. 2011, 5 Mar. 2013).

The Commission decided against proposing CMV in the subsequent accession negotiations with Croatia. However, this decision was arguably less to do with the lack of problems in these areas in Croatia, than with concerns that doing so would be perceived by the member states as an indication that the country's accession was premature. At the same time, the EU used the 'justice and home affairs safeguard' of the accession treaty for the first time against Croatia over its failure to implement the European arrest warrant (EAW) (*Agence Europe*, 18 Sept. 2013). Only three days prior to accession, the Croatian parliament limited the EAW's application to crimes committed after August 2002; seemingly to avoid surrendering Josip Perković, a Communist-era secret service chief, implicated in the 1983 assassination of a Croatian émigré in Germany. Threatened with the withdrawal of €80 million in funds to prepare for Schengen membership and closer monitoring in the area of justice and home affairs (similar to the CVM), the Croatian government subsequently agreed to bring its legislation in line (*Agence Europe*, 26 Sept. 2013).

Another concern, which also resonated in the debates preceding the Mediterranean enlargements of the 1980s, is the limited ability of EU institutions to sanction democratic backsliding once states have joined the EU. In anticipation of eastern enlargement, in the Treaty of Amsterdam the member states adopted Article 7 TEU, which allows them to sanction 'serious and persistent breaches' of the liberal democratic values in Article 2 TEU (see Box 17.1) by suspending certain treaty rights of the offending member state, including its voting rights. However, the determination of such a breach requires extremely demanding majorities in the European Council and the EP. The limits of the EU's influence against democratic backsliding in member states were amply demonstrated when the Hungarian government used its parliamentary supermajority after the 2010 elections to adopt numerous constitutional changes that cumulatively seriously undermined the spirit of liberal democratic competition without formally breaking the rule of law (Bánkuti *et al.* 2012). Despite concerns among the member states and in the EP, there was no agreement on using Article 7. The EU's intervention was therefore limited to the Commission's use of infringement procedures on the very few issues that had a separate basis in EU law: the reduction of the retirement age of judges, and measures to reduce the independence of the Hungarian Central Bank and of the data-protection authority (Sedelmeier 2014).

Acknowledging the limits of sanctioning after the fact, the EU has focused on trying to enhance the prospects that political reforms will become deeply rooted prior to accession. In December 2011, the Council endorsed the Commission's proposal for a new approach to accession negotiations. Chapters 23 and 24—on the power of the judiciary and fundamental rights and justice, freedom, and security—now have to be tackled at the very beginning of the negotiations.

Enlargement fatigue

Evidence of 'enlargement fatigue' after the 2007 enlargement is another factor that undermines the EU's ability to use accession conditionality for foreign-policy objectives. Perceived post-accession problems in Bulgaria and Romania made some member states consider their accessions to have been premature, feeding reluctance to envisage additional candidates in the medium term. Moreover, the uncertainty surrounding ratification of the Treaty of Lisbon after the failure of the Constitutional

Treaty that was partly attributed to hostility to enlargement in public opinion, combined with the economic and financial crises from 2008, made the member states and the Commission more reluctant to accelerate the ongoing enlargement processes.

The opponents of further enlargement put renewed emphasis on the EU's 'absorption capacity', which had been the fourth criterion for enlargement declared by the European Council in Copenhagen in 1993. The Commission's 2006 Enlargement Strategy Paper (Commission 2006d) suggested that absorption capacity—subtly renamed as the more positive-sounding 'integration capacity'—concerned the impact of enlargement on the EU's budget and its ability to implement common policies, and on effective and accountable decision-making. At the same time, it stressed that the term was 'first and foremost a functional concept' in order to depoliticize the debate and to reassure the candidate countries that it was not establishing new criteria. So far, there is no evidence that the EU has used concerns over its integration capacity to set tougher thresholds for current candidates than in the 2004 enlargement (Schimmelfennig 2008).

In sum, beyond the CEECs, the conditions for the EU's use of enlargement as a foreign-policy tool in its European neighbourhood have become less favourable. The member states are more divided over using membership as an incentive. The domestic adjustment costs of the EU's expanding political conditionality are generally higher than in the previous accession rounds. Nonetheless, EU external governance through conditionality continues to enjoy some qualified success, albeit more incremental and more selective than in the cases of the CEECs.

Conclusion

The EU's enlargement policy has developed considerably since the end of the cold war. It is no longer synonymous with accession negotiations, but sets the longer term framework for relations with countries desiring membership and specifies how they can proceed towards accession. This framework includes three overlapping stages—association agreements, pre-accession preparations, and accession negotiations. Each stage is underpinned by extensive and demanding conditionality that has become a powerful tool for foreign policy and external governance. Enlargement policy illustrates several policy modes (Chapter 4), in that policy within each of these three stages follows diverse procedures and dynamics.

The association framework exhibits many elements of the Community method, largely following a template forged in the early 1990s in the negotiations of the first generation of 'Europe agreements' with the CEECs. These negotiations were characterized both by intergovernmental disagreement about the link between association and potential membership, and by bargaining along transgovernmental lines about the trade component between sectoral policy-makers across the member states and the Commission, on the one hand, and foreign policy-makers, on the other.

The pre-accession alignment phase also displays characteristics of the Community method. The Commission plays a key role in formulating conditions, monitoring and assessing compliance, and making recommendations for further steps towards accession on the basis of its assessment. The European Council still has the final say, and political considerations about the desirability of closer relations and enlargement play a prominent role, but so far the Commission has largely been able to set the agenda through its role in applying conditionality.

Accession negotiations, however, are mainly the domain of 'intensive transgovernmentalism'. The member states play a key role in determining the EU's negotiation position and the shape of accession treaties, often mindful of national economic or regional interests. The Commission's informal role in identifying compromises can carry the negotiations forward and make unfavourable deals more acceptable to new members.

Moreover, its monitoring of candidates' progress in complying with the EU's enlargement conditionality has allowed the Commission to play a far more important role in the EU's external governance than it usually enjoys in other areas of EU foreign policy, the traditional realm of 'intensive transgovernmentalism' (Chapter 18). In sum, although the treaty rules for enlargement identify the member states as central actors, the Commission has achieved a very significant role in each of the main phases and has often successfully set the agenda for candidates to progress from one phase to the next.

 FURTHER READING

For overviews of the EU's enlargement rounds, see Preston (1997) and Nugent (2004). For accounts of the evolution of eastern enlargement, see Baun (2000) and Sedelmeier (2005) and, for theoretical approaches to enlargement, see the contributions in Schimmelfennig and Sedelmeier (2005b). For a key text analysing the EU's impact on candidate countries and the effectiveness of conditionality in the context of eastern enlargement, see Schimmelfennig and Sedelmeier (2005a), and Sedelmeier (2011) for a review of this literature. For the EU's impact on domestic change in the western Balkans, see Elbasani (2013) and Noutcheva (2012), and in its eastern neighbourhood, see Börzel and Langbein (2013), Lavenex and Schimmelfennig (2011), and Weber et al. (2007). For a stock-taking of whether eastern enlargement has helped to overcome the east–west divide in Europe, see Epstein and Jacoby (2014a).

Baun, M. (2000), *A Wider Europe: The Process and Politics of EU Enlargement* (Lanham, MD: Rowman & Littlefield).

Börzel, T. A., and Langbein, J. (2013), 'Convergence without Accession? Explaining Policy Change in the EU's Eastern Neighbourhood', *Europe-Asia Studies*, 65/4 (special issue).

Elbasani, A. (2013) (ed.) *European Integration and Transformation in the Western Balkans: Europeanization or Business as Usual?* (London: Routledge).

Epstein, R., and Jacoby, W. (2014*a*), 'Eastern Enlargement Ten Years On: Transcending the East–West Divide?', *Journal of Common Market Studies*, 52/1 (special issue).

Lavenex, S., and Schimmelfennig, F. (2011), 'Democracy Promotion in the EU's Neighbourhood: from Leverage to Governance?', *Democratization*, 18/4 (special issue).

Noutcheva, G. (2012), *European Foreign Policy and the Challenges of Balkan Accession: Conditionality, Legitimacy and Compliance* (London: Routledge).

Nugent, N. (2004) (ed.), *European Union Enlargement* (Basingstoke: Palgrave Macmillan).

Preston, C. (1997), *Enlargement and Integration in the European Union* (London: Routledge).

Schimmelfennig, F., and Sedelmeier, U. (2005*a*) (eds.), *The Europeanization of Central and Eastern Europe* (Ithaca, NY: Cornell University Press).

Schimmelfennig, F., and Sedelmeier, U. (2005*b*) (eds.), *The Politics of EU Enlargement: Theoretical Approaches* (London: Routledge).

Sedelmeier, U. (2005), *Constructing the Path to Eastern Enlargement: The Uneven Policy Impact of EU Identity* (Manchester: Manchester University Press).

Sedelmeier, U. (2011), 'Europeanisation in New Member and Candidate States', *Living Reviews in European Governance*, 6/1: 1–52.

Weber, K., Smith, M. E., and Baun, M. (2007) (eds.), *Governing Europe's Neighborhood: Partners or Periphery?* (Manchester: Manchester University Press).

CHAPTER 18

Foreign and Security Policy

Civilian Power Europe and American Leadership

Bastian Giegerich

▌ Summary

Diplomacy and defence are part of the core of state sovereignty, around which the practitioners of functional integration tiptoed in the formative years of the European Union (EU). The EU developed as a self-consciously 'civilian' power, with European security provided through the North Atlantic Treaty Organization (Nato) under US leadership. Policy cooperation has therefore developed under contradictory pressures. France and intermittently the UK have sought to use the EU to reinforce their international

(continued...)

strategies; the Commission has worked to expand its limited competences in external policy; other national governments have welcomed the additional international standing that EU cooperation provides, while resisting providing the resources needed for the projection of power. There is little agreement on what a common foreign policy should be about; national political cultures differ widely on appropriate international roles and national interests are only partially aligned. Intensive transgovernmentalism therefore remains the dominant mode of policy-making, with institutional development and capability-building emerging painfully from responses to external crises. The Treaty of Lisbon (ToL) has rearranged and upgraded the institutional structures for the common foreign and security policy (CFSP). While the impact of these changes on the mode of policy-making is not yet clear, they further underline a trend towards increasing coordination at the EU level.

Introduction

States have foreign policies; international organizations coordinate national positions.[1] National defence, and the mobilization of national resources for defence, require centralized command and control; concepts of national security and national interest justify strong state authority. It is hardly surprising therefore, that even the most federalist proponents of European integration have found foreign and security policy peculiarly difficult. Cooperation in this policy field has evolved gradually, often spurred by external events which exposed inadequacies. The structures and underlying assumptions of policy-making in this field today are marked by past struggles over the balance between national sovereignty and effective capabilities. National political cultures differ significantly in assumptions about appropriate roles in international politics, about the projection of power beyond national boundaries, and about the use of force (Biehl, Giegerich, and Jonas 2013). Such political cultures change slowly. While a Brussels-based set of institutions and procedures has emerged, intergovernmentalism remains the norm in the sense that the predominant actors are the member governments. This in part explains why performance in common foreign and security policy falls so far short of aspirations. Nonetheless, the increasing intensity of policy development in this field and its increased importance in the treaties suggest elements of the policy mode of 'intensive transgovernmentalism' (see Chapter 4).

West European integration began under US sponsorship, with the European Economic Community (EEC), as it was then, 'nested' within the broader framework of the North Atlantic Treaty. Consultations on foreign and security policy therefore took place within Nato, which provided the integrated structure for the defence of western Europe against the Soviet-led Warsaw Pact. The Treaty of Rome gave the

EEC limited competences for external trade relations (see Chapter 16) and assisting development in former colonial territories. French Gaullists insisted on a clear distinction between 'high' and 'low' politics: the EEC was to be confined to the low politics of commercial diplomacy, leaving the high politics of foreign policy and defence to sovereign states.

Issues of national security and foreign policy were, of course, fundamental to the development of west European integration. The French government had launched the Schuman Plan for a European Coal and Steel Community (ECSC) in 1950 in response to intense US pressure and to contain the reconstruction of West German industry within a supranational framework. The outbreak of the Korean War then led Washington to press for West German rearmament; the Pleven Plan for a European Defence Community (EDC), into which German units might be integrated, was the reluctant French response. The European Defence Treaty, signed in Paris in May 1952, committed its signatories to design the 'political superstructure' needed to give the EDC direction and legitimacy. The resulting draft treaty for a European political community would have transformed the six founding member states into a form of federation, with a European executive accountable to a directly elected European Parliament (EP). The Korean armistice and the death of Stalin in 1953, however, made so direct an attack on the core of national sovereignty less compelling, and the French National Assembly rejected the treaty. An intergovernmental compromise, promoted by the British, brought West Germany and Italy, with France and the Benelux states (Belgium, the Netherlands, and Luxembourg) into the Western European Union (WEU), a body which at first served mainly to monitor German rearmament.

Five years later, President de Gaulle chose foreign-policy cooperation as the ground on which to make his double challenge to US hegemony and to the supranational ambitions of the infant EEC. A 'conference of heads of state and government and foreign ministers' of the Six met, at French invitation, in Paris in February 1961 'to discover suitable means of organizing closer political co-operation' as a basis for 'a progressively developing union' (European Parliament 1964). This 'Fouchet Plan' (named after the French diplomat Christian Fouchet) was vigorously opposed by the Dutch, and found little support even within the German government. With the UK applying to join the EEC, and the Kennedy administration calling for a new 'Atlantic partnership', this was an evident challenge to US leadership and to Nato as such. De Gaulle's 1963 veto on UK accession negotiations sank the initiative, and the French later left Nato's integrated structures (Cleveland 1966; Grosser 1980). This chapter captures the gradual development of foreign and security policy cooperation among member states by analysing the hesitant moves from European political cooperation (EPC) to a common foreign and security policy (CFSP), and the emergence of a common security and defence policy (CSDP) as part of CFSP. Secondly, the underlying theme of national sovereignty combined with EU-level capacity is explored through a range of examples.

From European political cooperation to common foreign policy

Foreign-policy consultations among EU members—separate from those within Nato—were agreed as a concession to the French in 1969, after de Gaulle's departure. The resulting 'European political cooperation' was an entirely intergovernmental process, outside the treaties, steered by foreign ministers and managed by diplomats. The evolution of cooperation in foreign policy since then has moved in cycles: at first hesitant steps to strengthen the framework, followed by periods of increasing frustration at the meagre results achieved, culminating in further reluctant reinforcement of the rules and procedures in the face of external events.

Western Europe's self-image as a 'civilian power' in the 1970s and 1980s partly reflected the exclusion of security and defence issues, reinforced by the unresolved Gaullist challenge to US security leadership. The concept also implied a claim to normative authority, portraying western Europe as a model of peaceful diplomacy, operating through economic instruments—a self-image with a particular appeal within Germany, whose recent history had led to a rejection of 'power politics' in its domestic culture (Bull 1982; Sjursen 2007). It also appealed to the Commission, which had international capacities in the civilian dimensions of trade and development, but was excluded from the 'harder' instruments of foreign policy. Foreign ministries developed extensive networks for consultation on such harder issues through EPC, but with little policy output and almost no national or European accountability.

The revolutions in central and eastern Europe in the course of 1989, and the rapid moves towards German unification which followed in 1990, nevertheless forced foreign and security policy up the EU's agenda. The end of the cold war brought Germany back to the centre of a potentially reunited continent, and reopened underlying questions about the delicate balance between France and Germany and about US security leadership through Nato. West European governments adjusted slowly and hesitantly to this radical transformation of their strategic environment.

The end of the cold war and the launch of CFSP

The French and German governments jointly proposed, in April 1990, that the planned intergovernmental conference (IGC) should formulate a CFSP as a central feature of the EU, alongside economic and monetary union (EMU; see Chapter 7). The two governments, however, had widely different concepts of CFSP, with the French government focused on capabilities and the German on institution-building. Lengthy negotiations followed, with three cross-cutting cleavages dividing the member states:

- defenders of US leadership through Nato (the UK, the Netherlands, Portugal, and to some extent Germany) and supporters of greater European autonomy (Belgium, France, Italy, and to some extent Spain);

- defenders of national sovereignty (the UK, Denmark, and France) and proponents of transfer of foreign policy into the Community framework (Belgium, Germany, Italy, and Luxembourg);

- states with the capacity and domestic support for active foreign and defence policies—above all, the UK and France—and those like Germany for which international strategy, above all military deployment beyond national borders, was surrounded by political inhibitions (Gnesotto 1990).

External developments distracted the negotiators from their institutional designs. New regimes to the EU's east were pressing for the promise of membership (see Chapter 17). Iraq invaded Kuwait in August 1990, and the UK and France contributed significant ground forces to the US-led coalition, with some dozen or so European countries in supporting roles. The break-up of Yugoslavia began in the summer of 1991, and the Luxembourg president of the Council unwisely declared—as civilian EU monitors were deployed in Bosnia—that 'this is the hour of Europe' (*New York Times*, 29 June 1991). There was also an attempted putsch in Moscow in August 1990. The subsequent disintegration of the Soviet Union into fifteen separate states accompanied the final stages of the IGC.

The confident opening statement of Article J of the Maastricht Treaty on European Union (TEU)—'A common foreign and security policy is hereby established'—therefore papered over unresolved differences. CFSP and justice and home affairs (JHA; see Chapter 15) were to remain as the second and third 'pillars' of the EU outside the integrated, Commission-led first pillar. Policy initiative, representation, and implementation were explicitly reserved to the Council presidency, 'assisted if need be by the previous and next member states to hold the Presidency' in what became known as the 'troika'. The Commission was to be 'fully associated' with discussions in this intergovernmental pillar, and 'the views of the European Parliament ... duly taken into consideration'. Ambiguous language allowed for 'joint actions' in pursuit of agreed common aims, and referred to 'the eventual framing of a common defence policy, which might in time lead to a common defence'.

Much of the CFSP negotiation during the IGC leading to the TEU amounted to shadow-boxing behind the security umbrella which the US provided, while monetary union and social policy preoccupied heads of government. There was little discussion of the strategic implications of the transformation of European order, or of the balance between civilian and military instruments required for an effective common policy in this new context (Niblett and Wallace 2001). It was only after the IGC was concluded that the WEU secretariat, after negotiations with Nato, persuaded European governments to agree, in the 'Petersberg Declaration' (Box 18.1), to define a range of shared tasks in peacekeeping and peacemaking operations. Most unresolved issues, such as the extent of qualified majority voting in CFSP and how to define the overall institutional link between the WEU and the EU, however, were put off to a further IGC, to be convened in 1996.

BOX 18.1   The Petersberg tasks

Petersberg Declaration, June 1992, Section II, *On Strengthening WEU's Operational Role*, para. 4:

Apart from contributing to the common defence in accordance with Article 5 of the Washington Treaty and Article V of the modified Brussels Treaty respectively, military units of WEU member states, acting under the authority of WEU, could be employed for:

- humanitarian and rescue tasks;
- peacekeeping tasks;
- tasks of combat forces in crisis management, including peacemaking.

(Western European Union Council of Ministers, Bonn, 19 June 1992, available at: *http:// www.weu.int*).

The Treaty of Amsterdam's substantial revisions of the TEU's provisions in Title V on CFSP incorporated this list, as Article 17(2) CTEU. The European Security Strategy (ESS) expanded this task spectrum and the ToL, which entered into force in December 2009 following ratification by all member states, offered a further revised definition of what the CSDP was to cover.

External events nevertheless drove European governments to cooperate more closely during the course of the 1990s. The United Nations Protection Force (Unprofor), the initial peacekeeping force in Bosnia, was under French command. The French and the British provided the largest numbers on the ground; the Spanish and Dutch also contributed substantial contingents. Other European countries with troops in Bosnia or Croatia in early 1995 included Belgium, the Czech Republic, Poland, Slovakia, and Ukraine, as well as the Danes, Finns, and Swedes with Norwegians in a joint Nordic battalion. French attitudes both to Nato and to the UK shifted further under the experience of cooperation with British forces in the field, and closer appreciation of the utility of Nato military assets. Another field of closer cooperation arose from pressure exerted by the EU's southern members for Mediterranean programmes, oriented particularly towards the Maghreb, to parallel the eastern-oriented Phare programme (*Pologne, Hongrie: assistance à la restructuration des économies*) and Technical Aid to the Commonwealth of Independent States programme (TACIS), and with a comparable share of the EU budget. The Spanish presidency convened a Euro-Mediterranean Conference in Barcelona in November 1995, which committed the EU in principle to a generous long-term programme (Barbé 1998).

Nevertheless, the US continued to dominate Nato and overshadowed some of the effects of European governments working more closely together. For example, the US, which had insisted in 1991 that Yugoslavia was now a European responsibility, nevertheless intervened to supply and train Croatian forces, and dominated the negotiations which led to the Dayton Agreement in December 1995 (Neville-Jones

1997). Similarly, the US through Nato continued to define east–west political strategy, although west European governments collectively and individually provided by far the largest proportion of economic assistance to the former socialist states, including Russia. American officials promoted a parallel Nato dialogue with the Maghrebi states. At the Nato summit in Brussels in January 1994, the Clinton administration proposed to enlarge the alliance to Poland, Hungary, and the Czech Republic, ahead of their projected accession to the EU. The accession to the EU in 1995 of three more non-aligned states (Austria, Finland, and Sweden), to join neutral Ireland, further complicated the relationship between the EU and Nato.

The UK, France, and Germany were the key players in moves towards a more effective CFSP. Painful reassessment of post-cold-war German responsibilities was leading to a gradual 'normalization' of German foreign and defence policy. Attitudes in the British and French governments were converging. The French government had explicitly modelled its post-Gulf-War defence review on the British armed forces, ending conscription to focus on a smaller, better equipped, and more deployable military force. Cooperation on the ground in Bosnia built mutual respect between the French and British militaries. At the political level, the British and French shared similar frustrations over the reassertion of US leadership in the Balkans and the imposition of the Dayton Agreement. All this contributed to a convergence of attitudes between London and Paris, though the strength of Euroscepticism within the British Conservative Party and within the British press meant that its implications did not become evident until well after the election of a Labour government in May 1997.

From CFSP to CSDP: the UK and France as leaders

Given the reluctance of most member governments to clarify the strategic objectives that CFSP should serve, innovations in this field have come more from responses to external crises than from IGCs. The crisis in Kosovo, a Serbian province with an Albanian majority, in 1998 sent another surge of refugees through neighbouring countries into EU member states. The US administration led a bombing campaign against Serbian targets; the British and French were willing in addition to deploy substantial ground forces. Tony Blair, the new British prime minister, was shocked to discover how few troops other European governments could deploy beyond their borders.

Partly in response to Kosovo and partly to demonstrate the new government's commitment to closer European cooperation, the British now moved from laggard to leader in promoting European defence integration. In the defence realm, the UK and France stand apart from the other EU member states. In 2012, between them, they accounted for 44 per cent of defence expenditure in the EU, and 54 per cent of spending on defence equipment. Germany and Italy accounted for a further 17 per cent and 11 per cent of defence spending and 16 per cent and 5 per cent of equipment expenditure respectively (all figures: European Defence Agency 2014).

At a bilateral Franco-British summit in December 1998, Blair and Chirac issued the St. Malo Declaration, robustly stating that 'the Union must have the capacity for autonomous action, backed up by credible military forces', with member governments operating 'within the institutional framework of the European Union', including 'meetings of defence ministers'.

Initial reactions in Washington were mixed. The North Atlantic Council which met in Washington in April 1999 to celebrate the fiftieth anniversary of the Atlantic Alliance and to welcome three new members—the Czech Republic, Hungary, and Poland—declared in its carefully balanced communiqué that 'we reaffirm our commitment to preserve the transatlantic link', but also 'welcome the new impetus given to the strengthening of a common European policy in security and defence' (Nato 1999).

The Franco-British partnership, with the support of the German Council presidency in the first six months of 1999, pushed through some significant innovations. The strategy was to focus on EU military capabilities more than institutional change. They challenged their European partners to reshape their armed forces in order to enable European states to manage peacekeeping operations outside their region without depending on the US for crucial equipment and reinforcement. Their intention, outlined in the 1999 Cologne communiqué, was to gain stronger commitments from their partners to build deployable European forces, and then to merge the WEU into the EU in the next IGC planned in 2000. They achieved the first of these aims at the December 1999 European Council, which adopted the 'Helsinki headline goals', pledging EU governments collectively to constitute a European Rapid Reaction Force of up to fifteen brigades (60,000 troops), 'militarily self-sustaining with the necessary command, control and intelligence capabilities, logistics, other combat support services and additionally, as appropriate, air and naval elements on operations beyond their borders'—and to achieve this aim 'by 2003' (European Council 1999).

A follow-up Capabilities Commitment Conference, in November 2000, identified the major shortcomings in weapons and transport systems, and drew up a list of pledges and priorities. The working method was similar to that of the Lisbon economic-reform process, intended to spread 'best practice' from the most advanced to the laggards, and to shame the most deficient governments into improving their performances. As so often before, the US was sponsoring a parallel process through Nato, the Defence Capabilities Initiative. Neither process, however, made much impact on most governments, let alone on parliaments or public opinion. In south-eastern Europe, however, the succession of crises had left behind a very real requirement for substantial European political and military engagement. As the Pentagon withdrew US troops from deployments in Bosnia and Kosovo, the number of contributing European countries rose.

CFSP in the context of eastern enlargement

The implications of the EU's impending eastern enlargement for the European region preoccupied European governments much more directly. If enlargement is seen as a part of the EU's foreign policy (see Chapter 17), the extension of security, prosperity, and democracy within a strong international framework across eastern Europe must be counted as a major achievement. The European Council in Helsinki in December 1999 also saw reluctant heads of state and government accept Turkey as a formal candidate, under intense US pressure due to Turkey's strategic importance to western interests across the Middle East. Negotiations with Russia, with which the EU now shared a common border—jointly managed in unwieldy fashion by representatives of the Commission, the High Representative, and the rotating Council presidency—ranged from relations with Belarus to energy security (see Chapter 14) to the future of Kaliningrad (the Russian region surrounded by EU member states) to cross-border criminal networks. Nato enlargement, which passed another milestone with the Prague summit of 2002, was relatively straightforward in institutional terms. EU enlargement necessitated delicate adjustments of common policies, financial flows, institutional representation, and voting weights.

Postponement of decision on these issues in the Treaty of Amsterdam (ToA) required a further IGC, ending with President Chirac's mismanaged late-night compromises at Nice in December 2000. This failure, in turn, sparked the proposal for a broader Convention on the Future of Europe, which met from mid-2002 to July 2003, with representatives of thirteen candidate states (including Bulgaria, Romania, and Turkey) as participating observers. Meanwhile, the European Commission was attempting to focus the attention of member governments on the implications of enlargement for the wider European periphery, east and south. In early 2003, it floated proposals for a broader European neighbourhood policy (ENP), aimed at providing a framework for economic cooperation and political consultation for the states around the EU's eastern and southern borders: common foreign policy in effect, but defined and managed through civilian instruments (see Chapter 17).

Coordination in Brussels, but decisions in national capitals

CFSP remains largely in the hands of the member governments, although it is now supplemented by a cluster of Brussels-based institutions. Intensive transgovernmentalism has thus become the dominant policy mode (see Chapter 4), and its character is changing, in particular as a result of the structures created in the wake of the decision to launch CSDP. Heads of state and government remain ultimately responsible for CFSP and its overall direction through the European Council. Over the past decade, however, efforts have been made to rearrange and to upgrade the institutional arrangements for CFSP, notably under the provisions of the ToL, in force since December 2009. These are set out in the next section.

In the period before the ToL, the General Affairs and External Relations Council (GAERC, up to 2002 called the General Affairs Council), which brought together member states' foreign ministers in monthly meetings, was the main decision-making body in practice. To manage better the ever-growing agenda, GAERC was divided into two sessions. The first, prepared by the Committee of Permanent Representatives (Coreper), dealt with internal policy coordination among governments. The second, prepared by the Political and Security Committee (PSC, also known after its French acronym COPS) in coordination with Coreper, addressed the external dimension. The 2009 ToL split the GAERC into two distinct formations: the General Affairs Council (GAC) and the Foreign Affairs Council (FAC).

While there is still no formal Council of Defence Ministers, they have met in informal sessions under GAERC to discuss military-capability questions since 2002. The FAC can, depending on the agenda items to be discussed, also bring together defence ministers, development ministers, and trade ministers. Furthermore, EU member-state defence ministers serve as the steering board of the European Defence Agency (EDA), which was created in 2004. The European Council and the GAERC were supported by the Council Secretariat, which acquired a substantial number of foreign-affairs officials as well as a military staff.

The Council is formally empowered to appoint 'special representatives' for particular policy issues—generalizing the experiment adopted (with Lord Carrington, David Owen, and Carl Bildt) for the Yugoslav wars. In early 2014, the European External Action Service listed twelve special representatives (EUSRs) in different regions of the world and responsible for different issues: Afghanistan, African Union, Horn of Africa, Kosovo, Human Rights, Middle East Peace Process, Bosnia and Herzegovina, Central Asia, South Caucasus and the crisis in Georgia, the Southern Mediterranean region, Sudan, and the Sahel. They promote EU policies and seek to contribute to their overall coherence and effectiveness by acting as the 'face' of the Union. In 2012, the combined staff of political advisers and support staff for the EUSRs numbered 200.

The PSC, created on an interim basis in 2000, was formalized in 2001 and is the successor to the Political Committee of EPC. Unlike its predecessor, its members are all based in Brussels. They are permanent national representatives with ambassadorial rank who meet at least twice a week. The PSC is tasked with monitoring international affairs, drafting policy options for the Council, and overseeing the implementation of adopted policies, thus located at the centre of CFSP/CSDP's day-to-day business.

The creation of the PSC in its current form clearly reflects recognition on the part of member-state governments that coordination at the centre had to be strengthened. However, it is also a good example of the efforts governments undertake to maintain tight control of the Brussels-based institutions that they created in the field of foreign and security policy. Governments had rather diverging views on how senior their representatives in the PSC should be, with some reasoning that more junior ambassadors would be easier to control from capitals. More substantively, the divergent views relating to the 2003 invasion of Iraq illustrate that national governments will not be shy to put the brakes on cooperation if the stakes are perceived to be high. Several PSC ambassadors were issued rigid and unequivocal instructions from their respective ministries of foreign affairs to resist discussion in the EU on the issue of Iraq (Howorth 2007).

An important institutional innovation under the ToA was the creation of the post of High Representative for CFSP which was merged with the post of Secretary General of the Council (HR/SG). The job description for the High Representative was imprecise, beyond 'assisting' the Council. However, the first High Representative, former Nato Secretary General Javier Solana, made himself the external face of CFSP, tirelessly travelling in and out of Belgrade, Moscow, Washington, and across the Middle East, while carefully avoiding too open a challenge to member-state authority. As in the debate about the seniority of PSC representatives, member governments did not see eye to eye when discussing the desirability of having a political and diplomatic heavyweight like Solana in the HR/SG position. The UK in particular favoured a more junior appointment whereas more integrationist-minded governments and the Commission had argued that the post should be located inside the Commission rather than the Council, an issue that was revisited in the Constitutional Convention and the negotiations leading to the ToL.

The limited roles played by the European Commission, the EP, and the Court of Justice of the European Union (CJEU) further underline the dominance of the member governments through intergovernmental structures. The Commission has only a non-exclusive right of initiative for CFSP and it is in a difficult position to exert influence. However, given the multi-faceted nature of most foreign- and security-policy issues, the Commission, in its role of running external economic relations, is sometimes able to exploit cross-pillar linkages to make its voice heard. In response to the creation of CFSP and CSDP, it has further adapted its structures, for example through the creation of a Conflict Prevention and Crisis Management Unit (CPCMU) and a further increase of the number of units within directorates-general responsible for aspects of external relations. The EP remains limited to providing running commentary on CFSP. The treaty rules stipulate that the EP's views on all CFSP matters have to be taken into account, but in practice much depends on the Council providing a steady flow of information and on members of the European Parliament (MEPs), especially in relevant specialized committees, developing the necessary expertise to strengthen the Parliament's voice. The CJEU remains excluded from CFSP.

CSDP triggered a further raft of institutional engineering in Brussels. The EU Military Committee (EUMC), the Union's highest military body, was created in 2001 (*ad interim* from 2000) and brings together member states' chiefs of defence (CHODs). Its chair is selected for a three-year term. The EUMC usually meets in the form of the CHODs' military representatives, who are often 'double-hatted' with their nation's representatives at Nato. The EUMC provides unanimous advice and recommendations on military matters of CSDP to the Council, channelled through the PSC. For example, it evaluates different options for CSDP missions, oversees the development of an operations plan, and monitors the conduct of CSDP operations.

The EU Military Staff, some 200 strong, was set up at the same time. It works under the political direction of the European Council through the PSC and under the military direction of the EUMC. It constitutes the permanent Brussels-based military expertise that the EU can draw on for early-warning purposes, situation assessment (and intelligence cooperation), and strategic-planning tasks. It is organized like a directorate-general within the Council Secretariat. It houses a civil–military planning cell and, since January 2007, the nucleus of an operations centre which can, if reinforced through national secondments, run autonomous CSDP missions of up to about 2,000 personnel.

Mirroring these military bodies on the civilian side are the Committee for Civilian Aspects of Crisis Management (CIVCOM) and the Civilian Planning and Conduct Capability (CPCC). CIVCOM advises and drafts recommendations for the PSC on civilian aspects of crisis management. The CPCC has a mandate to plan and conduct civilian ESDP operations and in general assist the Council with regard to civilian missions. The CPCC Director serves as EU Civilian Operations Commander. In 2009, the Crisis Management and Planning Department (CMPD) was created to improve civil–military coordination of CSDP missions and operations.

Finally, several agencies play important enabling roles. The EDA is working on defence-capabilities development, armaments cooperation, the European defence technological and industrial base and defence-equipment market, and research and technology. The work of the EDA does not seek to replace national defence-planning or capabilities-development processes with a European-level equivalent but rather operates as a facilitator and to some degree coordinator of such processes. The EU's pooling and sharing agenda on defence capabilities is a prime example of this role (see Box 18.2). The EDA suffers from divergent British and French views of its primary objective: whether to focus on raising the effectiveness of national forces and their equipment, or to promote defence procurement from European manufacturers. The agency collects comprehensive data on defence programmes underway and defence-spending trends across member states, although some governments at first resisted publication of their data (Witney 2008). Its steering board consists of national defence ministers, chaired by the HR/SG. It thus remains firmly in the hands of the member governments. Furthermore, the EU incorporated the WEU's Institute for Security Studies in 2001 and the satellite centre in Torrejon, Spain, which produces and analyses space-based imagery in support of CFSP. To provide training in the field of ESDP, the Council set up the European Security and Defence College (ESDC) in July 2005. The ESDC is a virtual institution organized as a network between national institutes, colleges, and academies.

The Treaty of Lisbon as a turning point?

The ToL, which entered into force in December 2009, contains several provisions that explicitly aim to make the EU a more effective and coherent actor in the security field. These are set out in Box 18.3. The new EU High Representative (HR/VP), taking over the functions of presidency, High Representative, and Commissioner for External Relations and appointed by the European Council and Parliament for up

BOX 18.2   Pooling and sharing

The capability agenda is complicated by the effects of the economic crisis developing in 2008 and the sovereign debt crisis that developed in Europe it its wake. With governments in EU member states struggling to consolidate budgets, defence spending began to stagnate or shrink significantly. Between 2006 and 2012, according to the EDA, collective defence spending of EU member states dropped from a total of €201 billion to €190 billion, which amounted to 1.5 per cent of their combined GDP. The global balance of defence spending is thus shifting; for instance, spending in Asia has caught up quickly to that of EU member states. While in the long run such global spending trends, should they solidify and continue, are likely to limit the influence European countries can hope to field in global security matters, an immediate concern is the combined effect of shrinking European budgets and ever-increasing costs of defence equipment. At the same time, the instability in Europe's neighbourhood, particularly in North Africa and the Middle East, and the US strategic reorientation to the Asia-Pacific region underline the need for improved European instruments to deal with challenges posed by a changing security environment.

These adaptation pressures led leaders to consider an agenda for closer cooperation in security and defence matters under the label of pooling and sharing. At an informal meeting of EU defence ministers on 23–24 September 2010, Baroness Catherine Ashton, High Representative for Foreign Affairs and Security Policy, argued that EU member governments should cooperate more in order to deliver defence capability. The then German Defence Minister Karl Theodor zu Guttenberg suggested that member states should evaluate three core questions: Which capabilities would have to remain outside pooling and sharing arrangements for national security reasons? For which capability areas could member states envisage pooling arrangements? And, finally, where would member governments be willing to consider task- and role-sharing with other EU partners? Following the meeting, member governments, among themselves, identified more than 300 possible areas for pooling and sharing. Many of the areas for closer cooperation fall into the fields of education, training, logistical support, and maintenance because those areas are seen as less intrusive in terms of their impact on national autonomy. On 30 November 2011, the EDA steering board endorsed a list of eleven projects to be taken forward from 2012.

Pooling and sharing is not a new idea as such for European defence establishments. It has been discussed on and off over the years against the background of declining resources, both financially and in manpower, and growing operational demand for crisis-management deployments. But now the budget pressure that most EU member states feel in the defence realm has created a window of opportunity that should, in theory, propel governments towards closer European cooperation in defence. Progress is slow and uneven because of concerns about national sovereignty, different national strategic cultures, and possible defence industrial implications. However, the arguments for and against closer defence cooperation have been made—increasingly the focus is shifting towards implementation.

BOX 18.3	**Treaty of Lisbon provisions for CFSP**

EU High Representative (HR/VP):

- combines the functions of High Representative and Commissioner for External Relations and becomes president of the FAC;
- appointed by the European Council and Parliament for up to two five-year terms and responsible to the Council for the leadership, management, and implementation of the EU's foreign and security policy;
- vice-president of the Commission, responsible for the Commission's activities in the external-relations field, either directly, or in a coordinating role where other commissioners have the lead (e.g. enlargement, development, trade, energy, climate change);
- supported by a new European External Action Service (EEAS), drawing together officials from the Council Secretariat and Commission and diplomats seconded from the diplomatic services of the member states.

Full-time president of the European Council:

- two-and-a-half year mandate, renewable once;
- expected to 'ensure the external representation of the union on issues concerning its common foreign and security policy'.

Solidarity clause (Art. 222 TFEU) and a mutual assistance clause (Art. 42(7) TEU):

- the solidarity clause commits EU member states to support each other in the event of terrorist attacks or natural and man-made disasters. While the clause refers to military assets, it will be left to member states to decide what kind of assistance they would provide;
- the assistance clause calls on EU member states to aid each other in the case of 'armed aggression' on a member's territory and to do so with 'all means in their power'.

Redefined Petersberg tasks:

- joint disarmament operations, humanitarian and rescue tasks, military advice and assistance tasks, conflict prevention and peacekeeping tasks, tasks of combat forces in crisis management, including peacemaking and post-conflict stabilization. All these tasks may contribute to the fight against terrorism, including by supporting third countries in combating terrorism in their territories.

Permanent structured cooperation (Art. 42(6) TEU and Protocol on Permanent Structured Cooperation):

- member states 'whose military capabilities fulfil higher criteria and which have made more binding commitments to one another in this area with a view to the most demanding operations' can set up a leadership group seeking closer cooperation but within the overall framework of the EU.

to two five-year terms, is responsible to the European Council for the leadership, management, and implementation of the EU's foreign and security policy. The HR/VP also chairs meetings of the FAC, which is now the main forum for discussing CFSP (leaving other aspects of policy coordination to the now separate GAC), with its deliberations prepared by the PSC, nowadays with its chair appointed by the HR/VP. The HR/VP is at the same time Vice-President of the Commission, responsible for the overall shape of all of the Commission's activities in the external relations field, either directly, or in a coordinating role where other commissioners have the lead.

A full-time president of the European Council, with a two-and-a-half-year mandate, renewable once, is to 'ensure the external representation of the union on issues concerning its common foreign and security policy'. The expectation was that these institutional innovations would rid the EU of the inconsistencies and inefficiencies created by, on the one hand, the fragmentation of responsibilities between the Council and the Commission and, on the other hand, the previous model of the six-monthly rotating presidency. The president is tasked with generating consensus in the European Council and represents the union on matters of foreign and security policy. The former Belgian prime minister, Herman Van Rompuy, who had gained a reputation as an effective deal maker, was appointed president of the European Council and Baroness Catherine Ashton, previously the EU trade commissioner, was appointed as HR/VP in 2009. Combining what before have been separate jobs performed by several people is compelling from a policy coherence point of view. In practice, however, the resulting workload of the HR/VP is punishing for one individual, even to the extent that it undermines the ability of the HR/VP to achieve the very strategic coherence that the concentration of responsibilities was meant to achieve.

Both Ashton's and Van Rompuy's appointments followed intense periods of horse-trading where several candidates for either post fell foul of the many criteria that ultimately decide these matters in the EU (e.g. the balance between large and small member states and party-political affiliations). A similar process of intergovernmental horse-trading led to the selection in 2014 of Polish Prime Minister Donald Tusk as the new President of the European Council, and Italian Foreign Minister Federica Mogherini as the HR-VP.

The HR/VP is assisted for the purpose of external representation by the EEAS, drawing together officials from the Council Secretariat and Commission engaged in external affairs and diplomats seconded from the diplomatic services of the member states. Setting up the arrangements for the new EEAS proved to be a difficult task and took a long time, as arguments over process got in the way of the discussion of substance. As of 2013, the EEAS had a staff of some 3,400, of which approximately 2,000 served in the 139 delegations around the globe. A review of the EEAS, produced under Ashton's guidance and published in July 2013 found a misalignment of structures and responsibilities that hampers the effectiveness of the EEAS and the HR/VP (European External Action Service 2013). The review listed thirty-five recommendations covering organizational, functional, and staff-related issues. For example, some Council working groups continue to be chaired by the rotating presidency instead of having permanent chairpersons appointed by the HR/VP and the first recommendation of the review is to get rid of this inconsistency. To help to deal with the overload of the HR/VP, another recommendation proposes to create a clear system of political deputies who can stand in for the HR/VP with the full necessary representation rights.

The ToL furthermore introduces a solidarity clause (Art. 222 TFEU) and a mutual assistance clause (Art. 42(7) TEU). The assistance clause calls on EU member states to aid each other in the case of 'armed aggression' on a member's territory and to do so with 'all means in their power'. The solidarity clause commits EU member states to support each other in the event of terrorist attacks or natural and man-made disasters. While the clause refers to military assets, it will be left to member states to decide what kind of assistance they would provide.

The Petersberg tasks have been redefined. Lisbon lists these as:

joint disarmament operations, humanitarian and rescue tasks, military advice and assistance tasks, conflict prevention and peace-keeping tasks, tasks of combat forces in crisis management, including peace-making and post-conflict stabilization. ... [A]ll these tasks may contribute to the fight against terrorism, including by supporting third countries in combating terrorism in their territories.

ToL provisions regarding permanent structured cooperation (Art. 42(6) TEU and Protocol on Permanent Structured Cooperation) which allows those member states 'whose military capabilities fulfil higher criteria and which have made more binding commitments to one another in this area with a view to the most demanding operations' to set up a leadership group seeking closer cooperation but within the overall framework of the EU. As regards permanent structured cooperation, there have been disagreements among the member states regarding the feasibility of such a grouping and how the process should be organized in practice. The provisions had yet to be activated by fall 2014.

Thus, Lisbon brought wide-ranging innovations to the field of CFSP and high hopes were initially placed on the advantages to be gained from all of these innovations. However, things turned out to be rather more complicated and less clear-cut; Lisbon did not generate the push forward that was expected by many observers in academia and in the policy community. The jury is still out on how far these were teething problems or rather structural features of the new arrangements.

Nonetheless, over time the institutional set-up that has emerged clearly shows a growing trend towards more coordination at the EU level in CFSP and CSDP and thus represents a marginal shift from the original and wholly intergovernmental model of EPC towards closer association with the established Brussels institutions and thus with intensive transgovernmentalism (see Chapter 4). The result is a remarkably complex machinery which is intended to make the EU a more effective actor in the security realm through coordination of national policies. However, it is clear that governments are careful not to relinquish control.

From Iraq to the European Security Strategy

The policies pursued by President George W. Bush provided an external shock to the EU's loosely coordinated structures for foreign policy. Following the terrorist attacks of 9/11, European governments expressed their solidarity with the US by invoking for the first time ever Nato's collective defence clause, Article 5. In gathering support for its planned intervention in Afghanistan the US nevertheless ignored both Nato and the EU as consultative fora, working bilaterally with the major European states. In moving rapidly on from Afghanistan to Iraq, US policy-makers made even less effort to carry their European allies with them. The flimsy structures of CFSP, weakened further by the deterioration in personal relations between British and French leaders, namely Tony Blair and Jacques Chirac, and by the domestic politics of a German election campaign, buckled under the strain. The British offered full public support to the Bush administration, in the hope of influencing the direction of US policy, and British troops entered Iraq with the US. The French refused support for an invasion without US concessions, and resisted the British–US efforts to gain authorization from the UN Security Council for military action. The Franco-German claim to represent 'European' opposition to the invasion provoked competing statements by other groups of governments. In April 2003, the Belgian government worsened divisions by convening a summit to discuss an independent European defence headquarters, which only the French, German, and Luxembourg heads of government attended. Washington policy-makers celebrated the division between 'old Europe' and 'new Europe', as Donald Rumsfeld, then US secretary of defence, dubbed it, playing on transatlantic loyalties of the ten east European countries about to join the EU. Disintegration of a common European foreign policy over the invasion of Iraq, in the winter of 2002–3, revealed the wide gap between a 'common' policy, created out of political negotiations among heads of government and foreign ministries, and a 'single' policy built on integrated institutions and expenditure and on a Europe-wide public debate.

The intervention in Iraq constituted the sharpest crisis in transatlantic relations since the early 1970s. The underlying issue for CFSP remained how far European governments should converge towards an autonomous international role, as opposed to one rooted within the Atlantic framework and under US leadership. Bitter words among Europe's political leaders, and across the Atlantic, did not, however, prevent a rapid return to cooperation among EU governments. Here, as after previous crises, the European response to failure was to re-establish collaboration, on a firmer base where possible, following the path set by established institutions.

In June 2003, Solana's Secretariat produced a draft European Security Strategy, *A Secure Europe in a Better World*, partly as a response to the Bush administration's 2002 National Security Strategy, but also as a means of stimulating an EU-wide debate. A revised version was adopted by heads of government at the December 2003 European Council (European Council 2003). Tellingly, the 2003 ESS received scarcely any mention in national media, and little or no attention in national parliaments.

National governments, in spite of approving the document, had not wanted to encourage an open debate. Its prominent place in the Brussels-based discourse on security affairs thus served to widen the gap between Brussels and national capitals, where prior assumptions and commitments continued to drive defence policy.

The British and French governments were pushing the CSDP agenda forward together only months after the invasion of Iraq (Menon 2004). Frustrated at the failure of other governments to achieve the Helsinki capability goals, they declared in February 2004 that they would advance in defence through 'enhanced cooperation'. They announced that they would provide 'battlegroups' in response to international crises, and invited those other members (or groups of members) that could demonstrate a comparable capability to join them. The German government announced its commitment to join them the following day. The battlegroups concept was adopted at EU level in May 2004 within the framework of the military Headline Goal 2010 (see Box 18.4).

BOX 18.4   EU battlegroups

The Council of Ministers declared in May 2004 that the 'ability for the EU to deploy force packages at high readiness as a response to a crisis either as a stand-alone force or as part of a larger operation enabling follow-on phases, is a key element of the 2010 Headline Goal. These minimum force packages must be military effective, credible and coherent and should be broadly based on the battlegroups concept' (press release, 2,582nd Council Meeting, General Affairs and External Relations, 17 May 2004). Battlegroups can be provided by individual member states or as a multinational force package. High readiness is rotated on six-monthly schedules. Since the EU aims to have the capability to conduct two rapid-response operations at once, four slots need to be filled each year. An EU battlegroup, a particular military rapid-reaction element, has the following characteristics:

- its generic composition is capable of stand-alone operations across all crisis management tasks included in CSDP's remit;

- it is based on a combined-arms battalion-sized force reinforced with combat support and combat-service support units leading to a generic strength of about 1,500 troops;

- it can be initially sustained in theatre for thirty days, a period that can be extended to 120 if the battlegroup is resupplied appropriately; and

- it is deployable within five to ten days of a decision to launch an operation.

At a military commitments conference in November 2004, EU member states agreed to set up the first thirteen battlegroups, with initial operational capability from January 2005 and full operational capability from January 2007. Since 2007, the EU has had a minimum of two battlegroups on standby call at all times. Although the target strength of a battlegroup is set at 1,500 troops, the total involved can exceed 3,000 when all support and enabling capabilities are taken into account. As of fall 2014, the battlegroups had never been deployed, a fact that raised doubt about their overall utility leading some EU member governments to call for greater flexibility regarding their composition and potential use.

Operations and missions: CSDP enters the real world

CSDP became operational in 2003, when the EU formally took over command of the modest civil and military operations in the former Yugoslav Republic of Macedonia (FYROM). It took over military responsibility from Nato for the much larger mission in Bosnia in December 2004. By the end of 2013, no fewer than twenty-nine missions, almost all small, most of them civilian in nature, and more than half of them in Africa, had been launched (Table 18.1). The overall deployment of European troops on operations outside the boundaries of the EU and Nato rose from 40–50,000 in the late 1990s, peaked at over 70,000 in 2003, then gradually declined to around 50,000 by 2010. The percentage of these actually deployed through the EU nevertheless remained low. Most were committed to Nato operations, or were part of UN peace-keeping missions (Giegerich and Wallace 2004; IISS 2008; Giegerich and Nicoll 2012). EU operations were limited to the lower end of the spectrum of military tasks; even then, they relied on Nato assets for logistical support and were deficient in command-and-control and operational-planning capabilities and in tactical airlift.

The EU's decisions to deploy a military mission to the Democratic Republic of Congo (DRC) in 2003 and 2006 under the CSDP heading and the failure to do so at the end of 2008 serve as good illustrations that the EU is in some cases able to deliver substantially, in particular if there is strong leadership from a major player, while differences among capitals continue to throw up obstacles. On 11 May 2003, France indicated that it was willing to deploy a force to Bunia in the DRC following a request from the UN Secretary-General for a stopgap measure to reinforce the UN mission already in the country in the face of a deteriorating security situation. Having secured assurances for a UN Chapter VII mandate, with agreement from the relevant regional players including on the limited nature of the operation in terms of time and scope, the French government officially announced its readiness to conduct the operation. French planning for what was then dubbed 'Operation Mamba' was already well underway when then President Chirac recognized this as an opportunity to showcase CSDP 'on operations'. It was only then that Operation Artemis, the CSDP mission, was born—in essence a Europeanized French operation built on the French desire to demonstrate that CSDP could operate autonomously in Africa, which enabled the Council's decision of 12 June 2003 to launch the operation.

When in 2006 the EU was again asked to reinforce temporarily the UN's presence in the DRC to help to ensure security around the presidential elections scheduled for 30 July, the absence of such determined leadership proved problematic. France made clear that it would not lead again and was looking to Germany to fill this role. Pressure on Germany rose further after the UK indicated that it would not participate in any significant way owing to overstretch in its armed forces, then heavily engaged in Afghanistan and Iraq. Germany, however,

TABLE 18.1 CSDP missions and operations

Mission	Location	Duration	No. of personnel
Africa			
Operation Artemis	DRC	2003	1,800
EUSEC RD Congo	DRC	2005–	31
EUPOL Kinshasa	DRC	2005–7	30
Mission to support AMIS II (African Union mission)	Sudan	2005–6	50
EUFOR RD Congo	DRC	2006	2,400
EUPOL RD Congo	DRC	2007–	41
EUFOR Chad/CAR	Chad and Central African Republic	2008–9	3,700
EU SSR	Guinea-Bissau	2008–10	39
EU NAVFOR (Atalanta)	Somali coast	2008 (Dec.)–	1,200
EUTM Somalia	Uganda	2010–	80
EUAVSEC	South Sudan	2012–14	44
EUCAP NESTOR	Horn of Africa	2012–	67
EUCAP Sahel	Niger	2012–	49
EUBAM Liby*a*	Libya	2013–	110
EUTM Mali	Mali	2013–	550
Asia			
AMM	Aceh/Indonesia	2005–6	225
EUPOL	Afghanistan	2007–	350
Balkans			
EUPM	Bosnia-Herzegovina	2003–12	182
Concordia	FYROM	2003	400
EUPOL PROXIMA	FYROM	2004–5	200
EUFOR Althea	Bosnia-Herzegovina	2004–	600 (initially 7,000)
EUPAT	FYROM	2006	30
EUBAM	Ukraine/Moldova	2006–	100
EULEX Kosovo	Kosovo	2008–	2,250 (incl. local staff)
Caucasus			
EUJUST THEMIS	Georgia	2004–5	10
EUMM Georgia	Georgia	2008 (Oct.)–	262

TABLE 18.1 (Continued)			
Middle East			
EU BAM Rafah	Palestine	2005–	4
EUJUST LEX	Iraq/Brussels	2005–13	44
EUPOL COPPS	Palestine	2006–	71

Source: Updated from Giegerich (2008: 9); European External Action Service, *http://eeas.europa.eu/ csdp/missions-and-operations/index_en.htm;* CSDP Map Mission Analysis Partnership, *http://www. csdpmap.eu/.* Italic entries are military operations.

found it difficult to form a coherent position. A lack of available funding, the absence of Africa experience of the Bundeswehr (indirectly emphasizing the responsibilities of former colonial powers and those with remaining security and defence obligations in Africa), and overstretch were advanced as obstacles ultimately reflecting the fragile domestic consensus that enables the deployment of German forces abroad in general. Military intervention as a legitimate external crisis-management tool was still viewed with deep scepticism by large parts of the German population unless it could be linked to a humanitarian narrative (Junk and Daase 2013: 146–7). However, in the wake of growing EU pressure, Germany shifted its stance, at first setting out conditions similar to those France secured in 2003, while adding that, if Germany were to lead a CSDP operation, it would need to be truly multinational.

While EUFOR RD Congo, as the German-led CSDP operation became known, was eventually conducted successfully, the episode nonetheless points to national capitals' efforts to control carefully how much they might want to invest. As a result, it took the EU several months to organize a relatively limited deployment of forces. Furthermore, the successes which the EU claimed in 2003 and 2006 did not have a strategic effect on the crisis in the DRC.

However, when the security situation in eastern DRC deteriorated rapidly in autumn 2008, even a limited deployment proved to be unattainable. While the then French foreign minister, Bernard Kouchner, insisted that the EU 'has to act', including through the provision of troops, his British counterpart, David Miliband, pointed out that responsibility lay with the UN (Xinhua News Agency, 4 Nov. 2008). In December, the UN Secretary-General explicitly called on the EU to send troops as a stopgap measure so that a UN reinforcement could be arranged and deployed, not unlike in 2003. The European Council conclusions from its meeting a few days later in December 2008 were notable for their unwillingness to commit the EU. Concerns that had been looming in the minds of national policy-makers harked back to military overstretch and the thought that it would be easier to reinforce the UN mission, Monuc (United Nations Mission in the Democratic

Republic of the Congo) than to set up a new CSDP mission. In the event, the UN Security Council authorized an increase of some 3,000 troops for Monuc and extended the mandate of the mission by one year until the end of 2009. Deployment of one of the EU battlegroups was rejected by EU member governments, with some arguing that it would not represent the appropriate force package to fulfil the task at hand, a logic which further undermined the rationale for having battlegroups in the first place.

The dithering over eastern Congo in 2008 contrasts with EU member governments' closely coordinated response to the war between Israel and Hezbollah in Lebanon in summer 2006. Although proposals for a CSDP mission were rejected, the European action in response to the crisis amounts to a fairly successful example of power projection. During and immediately after the hostilities—a UN-sponsored ceasefire ended two months of fighting on 14 August—EU member states could have launched one of several possible CSDP missions: an evacuation mission for European nationals, a humanitarian assistance mission, or a peacekeeping operation. None of these options gathered wide support among member states. In part, this has to do with the fact that the UN has had a mission in place for twenty-five years and clearly enjoyed greater legitimacy as an organizational framework for action.

Thus, several EU member states, with France, Italy, and Spain in the lead, chose to contribute troops through national channels to the reinforced UN mission UNIFIL II (United Nations Interim Force in Lebanon). France, initially tapped to play a leadership role in the UN mission, remained hesitant for several weeks as the government tried to negotiate a more robust mandate and rules of engagement. While France was partially successful in this endeavour, Italy had in the meantime stepped up to fill the vacant leadership role. Between them EU governments provided some 7,000 troops (almost half of UNIFIL II) and heavy equipment, including main battle tanks, an aircraft carrier, and several other warships. The decision to commit forces was taken in Brussels in the presence of the UN Secretary-General, who had all but begged EU governments to provide the backbone of the UN operation.

In return for doing so, EU governments insisted on an interesting and unprecedented mechanism for control. They pushed through the creation of a special strategic cell at the UN headquarters in New York to direct the operation. While this cell ultimately reports to the UN Secretary-General, nineteen of the twenty-seven officers in the cell were initially seconded from EU member states, thus giving significant direct control to contributing EU governments (Gowan 2007).

It is further interesting to note that, aside from acting outside the CSDP framework, member governments also rejected the opportunity to make the EU formally the clearing house for national contributions to UNIFIL II, even though such a role is foreseen in declarations on EU–UN cooperation. Some, including France, also wanted the HR/SG, Javier Solana, to be empowered to speak on behalf of the EU and its member states during the crisis. However, this proved unacceptable to others, reflecting divisions about the desirable levels of EU and national involvement and also about the tricky question of whether to assign blame to Israel for the escalation of hostilities.

European support for UNIFIL II is nonetheless a positive story. It underpins the observation that intensive transgovernmentalism can indeed deliver substantive outcomes. Not only did EU member states rapidly deploy a sizeable force to a major crisis, they also did so in a spirit that strengthened the UN. The role played by the Directorate-General for External Relations (DG RELEX) and the European Humanitarian Aid Office (ECHO) proved vital in managing important civilian aspects of the response to this crisis, in particular refugee return and humanitarian aid, and has to be recognized alongside the military contributions by EU member states. This mixed operational track record continues to bedevil CSDP. The EU's engagement in Africa provides examples of failure whereas, simultaneously, other missions are confirming the value of CSDP.

The institutional reforms adopted in the ToL are not, by themselves, enough to overcome these difficulties, as the EU's inability to act in the 2011 Libyan crisis illustrates. The EU's response in the first half of 2011 was characterized by indecisiveness and contradiction. Ashton appeared unwilling or unable to seize the initiative and resisted military action in Libya right to the day on which the UN officially sanctioned it. A few days before she had publicly clashed with the British prime minister, David Cameron, and the French president, Nicolas Sarkozy, who had strongly argued in favour of a no-fly zone over Libya. Part of the blame for the EU's inadequate response, however, rests with member governments, which could not resist the temptation to pursue their own uncoordinated policies vis-à-vis the region instead of helping to form a united European position. The attempt to provide military options to generate a veneer of coordination turned into a prime example of the EU's lack of direction: member governments scrambled to authorize planning for Operation EUFOR Libya, offered in April 2011 to the UN but then stood down after it was clear that the UN was not interested and member governments themselves stopped pursuing it in earnest (Engberg 2014: 160–2). Two years later, in 2013, however, the EU did launch a border assistance mission (EUBAM Libya), designed to build capacity for border management in Libya, and thus very different from what was on the table in 2011. The mission will include border surveillance, airport and harbour security, and coastguard training.

Mali provided another sobering lesson for EU ambitions. While the EU had been discussing engagement in Mali for some time, the deteriorating situation on the ground in 2012 and early 2013, which triggered a French-led military intervention, meant that those discussions were overtaken by events (Engberg 2014: 172–3). The EU decided to launch its military training mission on the back of the French-led intervention. The core objective of EUTM Mali is to train and advise the Malian armed forces (under the control of legitimate civilian authorities) with a particular focus on unit capabilities, command and control, logistics, and human resources. Training will also include instruction on international humanitarian law and the protection of civilians and human rights.

More hopeful signs pointing to the value-added of the EU as a security actor also emerged from operational activity, however. For example, EUCAP NESTOR, a regional maritime-capacity-building mission in the Horn of Africa and western Indian Ocean, coordinated with the EU counter-piracy operation, EU NAVFOR Atalanta, and the EU training mission for Somali security forces (EUTM Somalia) in Uganda. EUCAP NESTOR is a civilian mission augmented by military expertise. Key objectives are to improve the capacity of governments in the region to control their territorial waters with a view to fighting piracy. In the context of the planning for NESTOR, the EU for the first time activated its operations centre in March 2012 to coordinate the activities of the three EU operations in the area (Atalanta, EUTM Somalia, NESTOR).

EUCAP Sahel Niger, another operation, kicked off in August 2012 in the Sahel region to help local police forces to improve their interoperability and strengthen their capacity to counter terrorist activities and organized crime. Through these activities the EU hopes to improve local authorities' control of their territory, which in turn would facilitate the execution of development projects. At the invitation of the government of South Sudan, the EU will try to strengthen airport security at Juba international airport through the EUAVSEC South Sudan mission. The overall goal is to create conditions where the airport can contribute to economic development and its use by criminal and terrorist networks is prevented.

The EU is keen to point out that these new missions are further building blocks in a comprehensive approach to security and are thus embedded in a larger framework which includes development, economic, and diplomatic instruments. Indeed, vis-à-vis the Sahel and the Horn of Africa, the EU is beginning to make its presence felt in many dimensions that are of relevance to security. As the EU embarks on the second decade of operational experience, Africa has emerged as the focus for much of CSDP's activity. In particular, the Horn of Africa has provided a glimpse of the coordinated approach, involving civilian and military instruments, which the EU could potentially bring to bear on crisis situations and thereby underlined the theoretical value-added of the EU as an international security actor. Nevertheless, the operational track record remains highly uneven and neither the visible geographic nor the functional focus fulfils the overall ambitions on which CSDP was originally based. CSDP has gradually been limited to civilian missions at the soft end of security and its military ambitions are now decidedly unclear.

The operational experience of CSDP captures only one—albeit crucial—dimension of the EU's presence as an international security actor. Among the key challenges of the last decade, the international community's attempts to rein in Iran's nuclear programme and address Syria's descent into civil war stand out for their magnitude and relevance to European security. On Iran, the EU—initially through the efforts of the foreign ministries of France, Germany, and the UK (the so-called E3)—has played an active role since 2003. With a dual approach of a willingness to back sanctions against Iran and the prospect of further negotiations should Iran suspend nuclear activities, the E3 and the EU scored initial successes, such as the 2003 Tehran Agreement and the 2004 Brussels and Paris Agreements. Throughout the ebb and flow of drawn-out negotiations, presentation of the European position gradually shifted towards the post that is today the HR/VP (Rhode 2010: 171–4). When the international community and Iran reached an interim agreement in November 2013 to curb the latter's nuclear activities, Ashton was negotiating with Iranian foreign minister Javad Zarif on behalf of the E3 and with approval from the US, China, and Russia. Undoubtedly, the interim agreement mostly bought time and did not in itself solve the crisis over Iran's nuclear programme. Likewise, national foreign ministers kept making backroom deals out of sight of the HR/VP. Nonetheless, Ashton was widely credited for conducting the negotiations with great care, determination, and persistence and earned praise from national capitals for facilitating and brokering the agreement (Mayer 2013).

On Syria, the EU can claim to have made its economic leverage and its potential for humanitarian-aid provision felt. European efforts have also helped to shape the debate on Syria in the UN (Gowan 2012). Ultimately, however, at the end of 2013, progress on Syria seemed to depend more than anything else on traditional great-power bargaining between the US and Russia. As Ashton noted in a speech to the EP in September 2013, referring to meetings between US Secretary of State Kerry and Russian Foreign Minister Lavrov, 'We put the EU at the disposal of the work that is on-going in order to see how we can contribute' (Ashton 2013: 3). The position of member-state governments has vacillated between countries (e.g. France and the UK indicating that they would favour more direct assistance to the rebellion, and those which have not)—a continuation of divisions that have hampered an effective European policy towards Syria for some time (Hokayem 2013: 152, 187). While the Iran issue gives credence to the utility of an EU-level approach to high politics, the Syrian crisis has seen the EU taking a backseat compared to other actors, such as the US and Russia, and other venues, such as the UN.

The EU's unity and effectiveness in foreign policy was again severely tested in late 2013 and 2014 by events in Ukraine. Mass protests, following then President Viktor Yanukovych's decision to step away from an association agreement with the EU, led to the fall of Yanukovych's regime after violent government crackdowns and confrontations with protesters. In the ensuing situation Russia annexed Crimea, part of Ukraine, in March 2014 in a clear breach of international law and began to support pro-Russian separatist militias in eastern Ukraine causing further instability and violence. EU member governments struggled to develop a united response aiming to stop Russia from meddling and support Ukrainian territorial integrity and the new government in Kiev swept in by the protests. The EU, slowly ratcheting up pressure on Moscow and support for Kiev, managed to agree limited sanctions against Russia and signed an association agreement with Ukraine in June.

The ultimate outcome of the crisis in eastern Ukraine was unclear at the time of writing, but what was clear was that the crisis and Russia's actions in it—annexing the territory of a sovereign state and lending at the very least indirect military support to separatist groups—had in the space of a few months brought about a fundamental challenge to the regional order the EU represents. The European security landscape had been altered with the Russia–Ukraine crisis demonstrating to many observers that Europe as a whole had not yet overcome the risk of conventional military conflict.

Conclusion

The communiqué of The Hague summit in December 1969, which had agreed to start EEC member governments on the road towards coordinated foreign policy, spoke of 'paving the way for a united Europe capable of assuming its responsibilities in the world . . . and of making a contribution commensurate with its traditions and mission' (European Communities 1969). Thirty-three years later, the ESS stated in more disillusioned terms that 'the European Union is inevitably a global player . . . Europe should be ready to share in the responsibility for global security and in building a better world' (European Council 2003). A heavy institutional structure now existed, occupying large numbers of ministers, officials, and military and police officers, yet the output did not measure up to the input of constant activity.

The fundamental weaknesses of this framework remain the lack of obligation to implement agreements made and the failure of member states to unite around common policies. All too often, member governments have signed up to policies in Brussels that they have neither reported back to their parliaments nor implemented. CFSP has remained a field in which national ministers and officials control the agenda, though assisted by increasing numbers of staff within the Commission and the Council Secretariat. National approaches to foreign policy, filtered through each government's interpretation of its European commitments to parliament and public, remain diverse. The ToL aims to strengthen the institutional structure further, but so far has done little to overcome persistent national defection from the principle of solidarity.

From 1969 onwards, French governments have driven CFSP forward. Their Belgian, German, and Italian counterparts have supported institution-building, though preferring a more supranational framework; they have not, however, shared French strategic objectives or France's willingness to invest in military instruments to fulfil them. In terms of defence, the UK and France constitute the dominant players; agreement between them launched CSDP. The cooling of the British Labour government and then the coalition government towards the project, and the major commitments of British forces to Iraq and Afghanistan, have contributed to the slow pace of progress since St. Malo. The greatest obstacle has, however, been the reluctance of other governments to invest in the equipment needed, or to reshape their armed forces to be able to operate effectively outside the EU—to the shared frustration of the British and French governments. CSDP has created the as yet unfulfilled promise of comprehensive (civil and military) crisis management, which adds a crucial building block to CFSP. While CSDP operations so far have been moderately successful within the limits defined by their parameters on the ground, they are in the end yet another reminder of the difficulties EU member governments face as they try to align their commonly agreed aspirations with actual policy output.

West European integration was built on a revulsion against *Machtpolitik*. Extension of the EU across southern, central, and eastern Europe has created what the head of Solana's CFSP Secretariat called a 'postmodern' state system, from which force has been excluded and across which human rights and civil liberties are enforced (Cooper 2003). Many intellectuals and politicians within European countries would like to extend this 'civilizing process' to the rest of the world, through civilian instruments and moral example—thus justifying the low level of military spending by many west European governments (Linklater 2005; Manners 2008). The EU is now a civilian power in a limited number of fields, which is making some progress towards shared civil–military capabilities.

Still, the EU punches below its weight in international diplomacy—including in the international institutions through which civilian power might best be exercised. Dependence on the US for hard security and for leadership in managing extra-European security threats betrays idealist claims to distinctively civilian power. The absence of a European public space—of a shared public debate, communicating through shared media, think tanks, political parties, responding to and criticizing authoritative policy-makers—leaves issues of global strategy and external threats to small groups of professionals.

The December 2013 European Council was supposed to help member states to make a step forward—it was explicitly billed as a Council on security and defence, the first time heads of state had focused on the security agenda within the EU framework since 2008. The closer the event, the more crowded the agenda became, until security and defence lost some of the high-profile visibility originally intended. In the event, the conclusions on CSDP of the 19–20 December 2013 European Council start with bold language: 'Defence matters' (European Council 2013b). While the meeting provided some hopeful signals on multinational capability development, pooled procurement, and strategy development, it was no breakthrough and has not significantly altered the trajectory of foreign and security cooperation (Biscop and Coelmont 2013).

European cooperation in foreign policy has gone beyond the framework of sovereign-state diplomacy, but still remains far short of an integrated single policy, with integrated diplomatic, financial, and military instruments. The dominant mode of policy-making (see Chapter 4) is predominantly intensive transgovernmentalism. There remain evident tensions between national autonomy and common policy, and (particularly for the smaller member states) between national passivity and the acceptance of the 'global. ... [R]esponsibilities' which the ESS spelled out. Acceptance of shared responsibilities and institutions since 1970 had been driven as much by a succession of external demands and crises as by competing Gaullist and federalist grand designs. It seemed likely that further development would similarly be driven by external pressures, but with the significant path-dependence of established structures and procedures through which to respond.

NOTES

1 This chapter draws extensively on the version in the sixth edition of this volume, which was co-authored by William Wallace.

 FURTHER READING

There is a substantial and growing literature on the various aspects of European foreign and defence policy as well as on the broader field of EU external relations. For a thorough introduction to the field, see Hill and Smith (2011). K. E. Smith (2008) and M. E. Smith (2004) examine the gradual development of foreign policy cooperation. Howorth (2007), Jones (2007), and Biscop and Coelmont (2012) trace the development of CSDP and European strategy. Journals such as *Survival* and the *European Foreign Affairs Review* are useful on recent developments. The *Yearbook of European Security* (2013) published by the EU Institute for Security Studies draws together core documents and key facts and figures.

Biscop, S., and Coelmont, J. (2012), *Europe, Strategy and Armed Forces: The Making of a Distinctive Power* (Abingdon: Routledge).

European Union Institute for Security Studies (2013), *EUISS Yearbook of European Security* (Paris: European Union Institute for Security Studies).

Hill, C., and Smith, M. (2011) (eds.), *International Relations and the European Union*, 2nd edn. (Oxford: Oxford University Press).

Howorth, J. (2007), *Security and Defence Policy in the European Union* (Basingstoke: Palgrave Macmillan).

Jones, S. G. (2007), *The Rise of European Security Cooperation* (Cambridge: Cambridge University Press).

Smith, K. E. (2008), *European Union Foreign Policy in a Changing World*, 2nd edn. (Cambridge: Polity).

Smith, M. E. (2004), *Europe's Foreign and Security Policy: The Institutionalization of Cooperation* (Cambridge: Cambridge University Press).

PART III

Conclusions

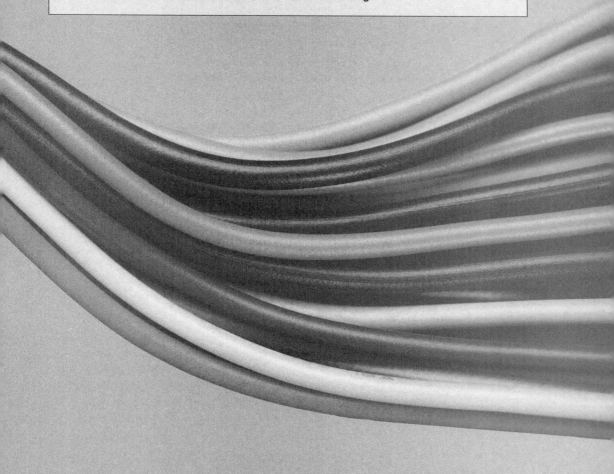

CHAPTER 19

Policy-Making in a Time of Crisis

Trends and Challenges

Mark A. Pollack, Helen Wallace, and Alasdair R. Young

▊ Summary

Policy-making in the European Union (EU) continues to develop in response to both functional demands and systemic pressures. There has been a sustained trend towards greater diversification of policy methods and modes within the EU system itself, and also at the interfaces with the national processes of the member states and the global system. Implementation of the Treaty of Lisbon (ToL) has not disrupted these trends nor radically transformed EU policy-making, although it has had non-trivial impacts on a number of policy areas, primarily by increasing the role of the European Parliament (EP). Against this backdrop enlargement from fifteen to twenty-eight member states seems to have been less dislocating than many had feared, but it has made policy-making more difficult on distributive, social, and environmental issues, as well as heightened the salience of a number of other issues, most notably immigration and relations with Russia. The impact of the financial crisis and its aftermath on EU

(continued...)

policy-making has been much more profound. In some areas, notably associated with economic and monetary union (EMU), it has spurred policy innovation and greater cooperation, but in others, ranging from the environment to defence, it is has impeded policy development. Moreover, the economic slump that followed the crisis and the emphasis on fiscal austerity, in which the EU is implicated, have undermined support for integration and called the legitimacy of the European project into question.

Introduction

The first decade-plus of the twenty-first century has been a testing time for the EU. Its membership has almost doubled from fifteen to twenty-eight member states, which is a great success story, but has complicated internal decision-making and increased the salience of some issues. After a protracted constitutional crisis, the ToL went into effect in 2009, and the policy implications have only slowly unfurled. The 2008 global financial crisis presented new problems to be addressed, as well as draining resources, sapping political will, and undermining the legitimacy of the EU. In response to these challenges the EU has continued to innovate. EU policy-making has become more diverse. Relationships between the Union and the member states have become both more politically complex and more functionally intertwined. At the same time, the interdependence between EU policy-making and global developments has also become more pronounced.

In the first section of this chapter we identify the main trends in EU policy-making that emerge from our policy case studies. Three trends particularly stand out: experimentation with new modes of policy-making, often in conjunction with more established modes, leading to hybridization; renegotiation of the role of the member states (and their domestic institutions) in the EU policy process; and erosion of traditional boundaries between internal and external policies. As a result, EU policy-making—always complex and varied—has become even more diverse as the Union faces new challenges.

How the EU has responded to the challenges of coping with a near doubling of membership, digesting the reforms adopted at Lisbon, and responding to the economic dislocation associated with the global financial crisis is the focus of the second section of the chapter. We, like other scholars, find that EU policy-making has demonstrated significant continuity in the face of enlargement, with member states again demonstrating significant pragmatism and adaptability in day-to-day policy-making. The ToL, like enlargement, represents an advance for the Union and put an end to a protracted constitutional stalemate, yet the entry into force of the treaty in December 2009 posed the challenges of creating new institutions and adjusting to new rules and new inter-institutional relationships. Our cases highlight that the extension of the EP's powers in the ToL has indeed complicated policy-making, although changes in the ordinary legislative procedure have allowed the legislative process to function, continuing, as in the past, to manage the trade-off between efficiency and democratic legitimacy. The financial crisis has proved a harder challenge to surmount. There has been significant, even remarkable, policy innovation in some areas in response to the crisis, but in other policy areas the subsequent economic crisis has undercut support for policy development, constrained resources for established policies, and eroded the legitimacy of the European project.

Trends in EU policy-making

The policy-making system of the EU has never been static (H. Wallace 2001). Typically there have been periods of gradual evolution and experimentation, interspersed with moments of explicit institutional change through reforms to the treaties. The early years of the twenty-first century have seen both. Three overarching trends stand out. First, our case studies reveal that the many changes that have occurred in policy-making methods have not pushed the Union towards a single, overarching policy mode, but instead to greater diversification within the EU system. Secondly, European policy-making has both become more contested in the domestic politics of the member states, not least because of the financial crisis and its aftermath, and involved an ever-growing collection of domestic institutions and actors through policy-coordination processes and networks. Thirdly, the distinction between 'internal' and 'external' policies has become even more blurred and artificial. Thus, it has become harder rather than easier to provide a shorthand summary of the key features of EU policy-making.

Experimentation and hybridization of policy modes

From the first edition of this volume (Wallace 1977), the editors have resisted the temptation to identify a single European Community (EC) or EU policy style, noting instead the diversity of EU policy-making across issue areas. Against that background, the policy modes identified in Chapter 4 were always intended as a series of ideal-types, which laid out the main variants in the EU system, rather than as a literally accurate description of EU policy-making in any particular issue area. Nevertheless, as ideal-types, our classification of policy modes provides a useful starting point for our analysis and for the identification of trends over time. We identify three such trends:

- the continuing diversity of policy modes;
- the use of multiple modes within individual issue areas; and
- the proliferation of hybrid and experimental modes.

All three trends are clearly visible and have, our contributors' findings suggest, accelerated over the past decade.

First, the chapters in this volume demonstrate the continued diversity of policy modes in EU policy-making, with no evidence of convergence towards a single policy mode over time. Nevertheless, we do detect some trends in the frequency or prevalence of particular policy modes. The Community method—which was traditionally associated with strongly 'communitarized' policies such as the common agricultural policy (CAP), competition policy, and trade policy—has been altered in fundamental ways by the gradual empowerment of the EP and the creation of new policy networks, and is arguably in decline. The CAP, for example, arguably functions according to the Community method in its day-to-day operations, but the empowerment of the EP in the ToL adds a strong element of regulatory policy-making (Chapter 8). The same is true of trade policy, where the power of the EP was again augmented by the ToL (Chapter 16). Competition policy, by contrast, continues to sideline the Parliament, but has always featured an important role for the EU courts as per the regulatory mode, and is increasingly incorporating networks of national regulators reminiscent of the policy-coordination mode (Chapter 6). Hence, while it may be premature to announce the death of the traditional Community method (Dehousse 2011), it is clear that the Community method has become less common, and more composite with elements of other modes, over time.

By contrast, the regulatory policy mode, the ascendance of which is associated with the completion of the single European market, remains the dominant mode for many issue areas, and arguably the predominant mode for the Union as a whole, particularly with the extension of the ordinary legislative procedure in the ToL. However, as Helen Wallace and Christine Reh note in Chapter 4, the regulatory mode has also encountered limits in particularly sensitive areas, such as public utilities and welfare provision.

Perhaps reflecting these limits, one of the most striking developments of the past decade has been the development and spread of the 'policy coordination' mode, elements of which have spread beyond the European Employment Strategy (EES) and other formal open methods of coordination (OMCs) to a growing number of issue areas where networking, benchmarking, and loose coordination are increasingly commonplace. The efficacy of such policy coordination in areas such as fiscal policy (Chapter 7) and employment policy (Chapter 12), however, remains very much in doubt.

The distributive and intensive transgovernmentalist modes retain their importance in specific, core issue areas. The distributive mode is clearly evident in the making of the EU budget, and the budgetary envelopes for cohesion policy and the CAP, albeit with a greater and now institutionalized role for the Parliament. The intensive transgovernmental mode continues to dominate in the fields of common foreign and security policy (CFSP) and to some extent justice and home affairs (JHA). It has also become increasingly important in EMU in the response to the euro area crisis. The dominance of transgovernmentalism must be qualified, however, insofar as the partial communitarization of JHA in the ToL means that the transgovernmental mode now coexists with elements of a regulatory mode as well as policy coordination through networks such as Europol and Eurojust (Chapter 15).

These observations, in turn, point to a second trend, which is the increasing use of multiple modes of governance *within individual issue areas*. Indeed, one of the most striking features of the chapters in this volume is the presence and practice of multiple policy modes and policy instruments in nearly every issue area explored. In Chapter 11, for example, Stephan Leibfried points to several distinct tracks or policy modes operating within the social-policy realm, with a regulatory programme of positive integration existing alongside a somewhat encapsulated social dialogue, which, in turn, exists alongside a strong negative-integration dynamic dominated by national courts and the Court of Justice of the European Union (CJEU). In Chapter 12, Martin Rhodes is at pains to point out that EU employment policy is *not* synonymous with the policy-coordination mode of the EES, but is also characterized by extensive and ongoing EU regulation as well as a growing series of landmark court cases that are reshaping European and national employment law in an enlarged EU. EMU, covered by Dermot Hodson in Chapter 7, is perhaps the most extreme example of multiple, proliferating policy modes within a single issue area, characterized by a strong European Central Bank (ECB)-centred Community method for monetary policy; increasingly strict and elaborate procedures for coordination of national fiscal policies; a variant on the regulatory mode being adopted for banking regulation; yet another variant on the distributive mode in the operation of the European Stability Mechanism (ESM); and a strong element of intensive transgovernmentalism with the rise of the Eurogroup and euro summits as the key decision-making forum for managing the euro area crisis. In sum, we are seeing plural policy modes operating within what EU scholars have traditionally considered coherent issue areas. The diversity of EU policy-making has thus increased within as well as across issue areas.

A third trend we observe is related to this diversification, but goes a step further, comprising a rise in 'innovative' (Tömmel and Verdun 2008), 'experimental' (Sabel and Zeitlin 2008), or 'hybrid' policy modes that combine, adapt, and adjust new and traditional policy modes and instruments in highly flexible and innovative ways in order to adjust to the ever-changing demands of the policy environment as well as the continuing sensitivities of EU member governments. Indeed, in a provocative article, Sabel and Zeitlin (2008: 278) argue that the EU is witnessing nothing less than a 'Cambrian explosion' of new and hybrid institutional forms. They contend that legislation adopted under the Community method or regulatory policy mode increasingly incorporates not only traditional command-and-control regulations but also the full range of so-called new-governance instruments, including policy-coordination efforts such as the OMC, as well as the creation of European networks of regulators that seek to coordinate national regulations in an informal, non-binding fashion (Coen and Thatcher 2008b). In Chapter 13, for example, Andrea Lenschow illustrates the use of a broad mix of policy instruments in environmental policy, where 'command and control' rules are employed alongside voluntary codes, self-regulation, and co-regulation, among other 'new instruments'. Similarly, the Commission's approach to the single market—the traditional ideal type of regulatory policy-making—aims to make use of a 'smarter mix' of policy instruments in the pursuit of market liberalization, including competition policy, self-regulation, and 'soft law' (see Chapter 5). Hence, while we are agnostic as to the deliberative possibilities of Sabel and Zeitlin's experimentalist governance, it is clear that EU member states and institutions *are* experimenting, drawing on ever-more-complex mixes and hybrid combinations of policy modes and instruments in response to both the functional demands and the political sensitivities of EU governments.

'Brussels' and national governance

The national governments of the member states have always been deeply implicated in EU policy-making, both as negotiators in the Council and as those responsible for implementing and enforcing policies on the ground. The national courts are also intertwined in the EU legal order. Nevertheless, there is increasing complexity in the interactions between 'Brussels' and national governance, and there is evidence of increasing contention and contestation around the ways that the boundaries are drawn between these two layers of governance. What is more, we see contrasting trends in different policy areas.

The shift towards centralization has been most pronounced in those policy areas most directly affected by the financial crisis (see the section on the financial crisis later in the chapter). The most extreme examples of centralization have been the requirements—fiscal consolidation and labour-market reforms—attached to the bailouts of the member states that faced astronomical borrowing costs due to financial-market doubts about their abilities to repay their debts (see Chapter 7). There was further centralization with the creation of the banking union and establishing the ECB as the supervisor of the euro area's largest banks (see Chapters 5 and 7). Disciplines on member states' deficit spending were also strengthened (see Chapter 7). In these areas there has been a marked shift towards 'more Europe'.

In other policy areas, however, there has been an emphasis on greater member-state authority. The renationalization of policy is particularly evident in the CAP, the traditional archetype of the Community method (see Chapter 8). The 2013 reform of the CAP increased the discretion that member states enjoy in allocating their 'national envelopes', a flexibility mechanism first introduced in earlier reforms, so that they may now redistribute half of their national envelopes as they wish among a suite of support options. In both competition policy (since the mid-1980s) and in energy regulation (since the mid-2000s), there have been common requirements for member states to establish independent national regulators, who play a pivotal role in implementing common EU rules (see Chapters 6 and 14). The (partial) renationalization of some EU policies began before the financial crisis and has continued since.

There has been a third trend at the intersection of centralization and decentralization; domestic governments and/or independent regulatory authorities are increasingly drawn (or co-opted) into transgovernmental networks. The modernization of EU competition policy, discussed in Chapter 6, combines centralized EU policy-making by the Commission with policy coordination and power-sharing among an ever more cohesive network of national competition regulators (the European Competition Network). In the words of Stephen Wilks, this arrangement 'constitutes a striking model of regulatory cooperation by more or less independent agencies whose actions converge in response to the economic and legal acceptance and enforcement of the treaty competition rules'. Even the single market programme, long the exemplar of the EU regulatory mode, similarly relies increasingly on cooperation among national utilities regulators, most prominently in the Agency for the Cooperation of Energy Regulators (ACER), both to devise and to implement common EU policies (Chapter 14). The development of networks of national officials has also been pronounced in JHA, where semi-autonomous special agencies and bodies have proliferated to facilitate information exchange and coordination between national law-enforcement authorities, often supported by the establishment of new EU-wide databases (see Chapter 15). In environmental policy, the Commission has created the European Network for the Implementation and Enforcement of Environmental Law (IMPEL), involving Commission officials and representatives of national or local authorities as a means of improving the capacity and willingness of local implementers. This trend illustrates that increased cooperation can occur largely horizontally among domestic policy-makers and not just vertically between Brussels and the member states. It also illustrates that intensive transgovernmentalism can serve as a complement, particularly in terms of implementation, to other modes of governance. There is thus not a singular trend towards greater centralization in EU policy-making.

In fact, there is increasing evidence of national politicians and policy-makers becoming more reluctant, more risk-averse and more prudent as regards agreeing to EU policy initiatives. Cooperation thus remains limited in a number of policy areas, such as with regard to energy security (see Chapter 14), although heightened tensions with Russia over Ukraine may shift the debate, and police and judicial cooperation (see Chapter 15). The development of cooperation in employment policy remains highly contested. Member-state opposition has required advocates to deploy creative interpretations of the treaty base, transferring legislation to the 'inter-professional dialogue', and an emphasis to the soft-law European employment strategy (see Chapter 12). Member states' reluctance to transfer authority for social policy to the EU means that integration has occurred through negative rather than positive integration; limits on national autonomy have expanded while common compensatory mechanisms remain absent (see Chapter 11). Member states' caution about further integration is even evident within the context of the single market, as the politics leading to the Services Directive and limitations to banking union illustrate (see Chapter 5). Moreover, member governments remain vigilant about their contributions to and receipts from the EU's budget, as the hard bargaining over the 2014–20 financial framework demonstrated (see Chapters 9 and 10).

There is thus a continuing argument about where 'Brussels' reigns and where national responsibilities prevail. National policy-makers have long exploited this tension and ambiguity. Participation in the EU policy process enables national politicians and policy-makers to exploit the Brussels arena in order to take forward policies that would be more difficult to implement in a narrowly national context (see Chapters 5 and 13). It is certainly the case that domestic politicians prefer to claim the credit for popular EU policies and to shift the blame to 'Brussels' for decisions that may be necessary rather than popular.

Generally speaking, the boundary between national and European authority has not become less contested with the passage of time (Szczerbiak and Taggart 2008). In fact, it has arguably become more acute in the wake of the travails of the Constitutional Treaty and of the financial crisis. Popular trust in the EU has collapsed since the financial crisis (see Figure 19.1), although on average it remains more trusted than the governments of the member states (Eurobarometer 2014: QA7.2). Perhaps unsurprisingly, therefore, there is little popular enthusiasm for the transfer of more decisions to the EU level (Eurobarometer 2014: QA13.4; Pew Research Center 2013: 24). There has concomitantly been an increase in European political parties, both radical and less so, openly expressing Euroscepticism (Henley 2014; Mudde 2014: 102). The strong showings of Eurosceptic parties in a number of member states, most notably (but not only) in France, Denmark, and the UK, in

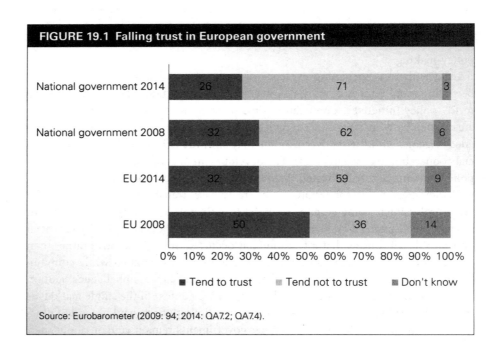

FIGURE 19.1 Falling trust in European government

National government 2014: Tend to trust 26, Tend not to trust 71, Don't know 3

National government 2008: Tend to trust 32, Tend not to trust 62, Don't know 6

EU 2014: Tend to trust 32, Tend not to trust 59, Don't know 9

EU 2008: Tend to trust 50, Tend not to trust 36, Don't know 14

■ Tend to trust   ■ Tend not to trust   ■ Don't know

Source: Eurobarometer (2009: 94; 2014: QA7.2; QA7.4).

the 2014 European Parliament elections could be a reflection of disaffection with the European project, but the campaigns were to a significant extent referenda on national governments' handling of the protracted economic crisis (Mudde 2014: 103), and Eurosceptic parties did not secure representation in a number of the countries hardest hit by the euro area crisis, including Ireland, Portugal, and Spain (*The Economist*, 26 May 2014). The relationship between 'Brussels' and the member states, therefore, remains highly controversial and is increasingly politicized.

Interacting European and global governance

Recently there has been growing scholarly attention to how the EU interacts with the world around it. Some aspects of the EU's external relations—most notably trade policy and enlargement—have long received attention. Particularly since the (Maastricht) Treaty on European Union (TEU) came into effect, there has been extensive scholarship on the EU's common foreign and security policy. More recently, however, greater attention has been paid to the intentional and unintentional external impacts of a wider range of EU policies. Taken together these dimensions have led to consideration of the EU as a 'global actor' (for a review see Peterson 2012). There has also recently been attention, albeit considerably more limited, to how external factors affect EU policies (see e.g. Falkner and Müller 2013; Young 2012).

The EU's 'external policies'—trade, foreign and security policy, and enlargement—have continued to develop in institutional and substantive terms. EU trade policy, as Stephen Woolcock demonstrates in Chapter 16, has been institutionalized and strengthened over the years, with increasing thematic coverage (most recently to include foreign direct investment) and greater centralization of power in Brussels. The rise of Brazil, India, and China, however, has made it increasingly difficult for the EU (or its traditional partner/rival, the US) to shape the form and substance of the global trade regime (A. R. Young 2011).

By contrast, the EU's common foreign and security policy (CFSP) remains largely transgovernmental (Chapter 18), with at best a secondary and supporting role for the Commission and other EU institutions. The ToL has rearranged and upgraded the institutional structures for the CFSP, further underlining a trend towards increasing coordination at the EU level, with an ever-growing set of transgovernmental committees and an increasingly prominent defence component alongside the EU's traditional 'civilian power' instruments. Recent high-profile events do not yield a clear picture of the EU's foreign-policy effectiveness. In 2011, the EU was unable to agree a common position on a no-fly zone over Libya, with some member states subsequently participating in the Nato mission. On Iran's suspected nuclear-weapons programme, by contrast, the EU has played a pivotal role, banning the import of Iranian oil in 2012 and with HR/VP Catherine Ashton leading the negotiations on behalf of the so-called E3 (Britain, France, and Germany). With respect to the Syrian civil war from 2011, the EU has sought to exercise influence through sanctions and appears to have helped to shape the debate in the UN. The response to the civil war, however, has been dominated by the stalemate between the US and Russia. While the EU's offer of an association agreement with Ukraine was the ostensible trigger for the protests that ended up toppling the government, which in turn precipitated Russia's annexation of Crimea, the EU's initial imposition of sanctions on Russia was less vigorous than some member states and the US would have liked, although it subsequently augmented them as the conflict worsened. The EU, in sum, speaks with increasing unity and authority in foreign affairs, yet a common EU position on the most important issues of the day cannot be taken for granted, and the Union still appears to play (a distant) second fiddle to the US.

Enlargement, however, is a policy tool for which the US has no analogue. As Ulrich Sedelmeier demonstrates in Chapter 17, EU enlargement policy has developed from a largely reactive process of accepting and negotiating membership applications from candidate countries, to a distinctive regional foreign policy aiming to shape EU relations with its immediate neighbours and exert substantial influence over their internal politics and institutions. The EU's political conditionality criteria include requiring stable institutions that guarantee democracy, the rule of law, human rights, and respect for and protection of minorities, as well as reforms of the public administration, police, and the judiciary, in addition to efforts to combat corruption. The effectiveness of the EU's conditionality requirements, however, depends on whether the incentive of membership is sufficiently valuable and credible to outweigh domestic adjustment costs. The higher the adjustment costs are or the less credible membership is, the less effective is conditionality. Thus, while the prospect of accession is a critical and unique power resource for the EU, it is not universally effective.

The EU's impact on the wider world, however, extends far beyond its explicitly external policies. The growing number and density of EU policies has led the EU's members to act, to negotiate, and to litigate together on the broader international stage, 'externalizing' internal policies at the global level. The concept of 'externalization' of internal policies is not new. The EU has long recognized the imperative to negotiate collectively with the rest of the world in areas where the Union has adopted common or harmonized policies, and previous editions have demonstrated the empirical significance of this phenomenon (see e.g. Sbragia 2000). The EU's efforts to externalize its energy policy, for example, have been mixed; it has created an Energy Community for south-eastern Europe, but Russia has refused to ratify the Energy Charter Treaty (see Chapter 14). The EU's claims to leadership in global climate-change negotiations rest heavily on the ambitions of its own internal climate-change commitments, but it has struggled to get other major economies to follow its lead (see Chapter 13).

Some of the most powerful external effects of the EU's internal policies are inadvertent. Single-market and European environmental regulations have internal objectives, but set requirements for products entering the EU. In a number of cases, firms choose to apply EU standards to all of their products wherever in the world they are sold, the so-called 'Brussels effect' (Bradford 2012). Moreover, some European rules—such as those governing data protection and some aspects of financial services—have extraterritorial provisions that subject foreign firms to EU rules unless the EU is persuaded that their home jurisdiction provides comparable supervision. This creates incentives for foreign firms to lobby for domestic policy changes along EU lines (Bach and Newman 2007: 836–8; Posner 2009: 673, 687). As a consequence, the *New York Times* (19 Oct. 2013: A1) has dubbed the EU a 'regulatory superpower'. The adverse impact of EU rules on foreign firms and foreign rules on EU firms creates a strong incentive for regulatory cooperation with major trading partners, although this rarely takes the form of the EU externalizing its rules, concentrating instead on establishing the equivalence of European and foreign rules, requirements, and certifications (A. R. Young 2014). Externalization has also been evident in the area of competition policy, where the EU has increasingly asserted extraterritorial jurisdiction over mergers and anti-competitive practices of foreign firms that have an impact within the EU (see Chapter 6). The ECB sets its monetary policy according to domestic objectives, but those decisions have significant implications for other countries by influencing exchange rates (see Chapter 7). The intensification of cooperation on immigration and asylum also has implications for those seeking to enter the EU to live or work (see Chapter 15). Because of the EU's economic size, all of these 'domestic' decisions can have profound ramifications for firms and people in other countries.

There are, however, also external pressures on internal policies. The Commission (2001*a*: 6) has estimated that 30 per cent of all of its legislative proposals arise from the EU's international obligations, including in environmental policy (see Chapter 13). The increased coverage and legalization of the multilateral trading system with the creation of the World Trade Organization (WTO) in 1995, in particular, has placed external disciplines on EU policy-making (Young and Peterson 2014: 144–8). Our cases also illustrate a dynamic interaction between internal policies and external negotiations, which is most evident with regard to agriculture and the environment. Reforms of the CAP have been facilitated by the potential cross-sectoral trade-offs made possible by multilateral trade negotiations and the desire for the EU to play a leadership role. Moreover, those reforms have made progress in trade negotiations possible (see Chapter 8; Woolcock and Hodges 1996; Young and Peterson 2014: 88–91). The EU's desire to play a leadership role in the development of the climate-change regime has created an impetus for the EU to demonstrate its capacity to meet its Kyoto commitments and to present concrete proposals on how to achieve ambitious targets for further reducing greenhouse gas emissions and boosting renewable-energy production (see Chapters 13 and 14). Most of our cases, as with most of the policy-making literature (see Young 2008), however, do not explicitly discuss how international obligations shape EU policy-making, which remains a promising subject for future research.

Challenges to EU policy-making

All of these trends in policy-making have taken place against a backdrop of major challenges to policy-making in the EU. The EU's membership almost doubled between 2004 and 2013 and brought in members of very different levels of economic and political development. While this was a remarkable achievement, it also posed challenges to existing patterns of policy-making. Even leaving aside the prospect of needing to accommodate different policy preferences and administrative capacities, such an expansion greatly increases the transaction costs of decision-making. The ToL, intended in part to address this challenge, posed challenges of its own, not least the need to accommodate new actors, sometimes through newly created institutions (as in CFSP) and sometimes through established institutions with broader powers (notably the EP), in existing policy processes. The global financial crisis, unlike the other two challenges, was not the product of an explicit choice by the EU and has profoundly affected the full spectrum of EU policy-making. Of the three challenges, this is the one the EU has managed least well. It poses significant challenges in the short term to the EU policy process and in the long term to the Union's legitimacy and future prospects.

The impacts of enlargement

In the past, enlargements have been something of a shock to the EU system, generating a vigorous debate about whether 'widening' the EU to new members came at the expense of 'deepening' European integration. This debate was particularly pointed with respect to the enlargement of the EU to ten east and south European states in 2004, followed by the addition of Bulgaria and Romania in 2007 and Croatia in 2013. These new members, moreover, came to the EU with very different backgrounds and concerns from those of the old 'west' European membership.

The Union's 'big bang' enlargement to the east and south was therefore accompanied by apprehension as well as hope. Many feared that the combination of greater numbers and greater diversity would make EU institutions unmanageable, leading to gridlock and policy paralysis. Optimists, on the other hand, suggested that gridlock was far from inevitable, for two reasons. First, increased numbers of member states could potentially be accommodated by some mix of formal and informal reforms to make the Union run more efficiently. Secondly, the effect of new members was likely to depend on the issue-specific interests of those members vis-à-vis the existing members; to the extent that the new members mirrored the existing members in their preferences, or were more 'pro-integration', their addition could potentially facilitate rather than paralyse EU policy-making (Kelemen, Menon, and Slapin 2014).

A decade and more on from the 2004 enlargement, we enjoy in this edition a longer perspective on these questions, and the ability to take stock of the impact of recent enlargements on EU policy-making, both overall and with respect to the various individual policies examined in this volume. The results are broadly encouraging. Notwithstanding the widespread fears, it appears that EU institutions in general have responded well to enlargement, adopting a mix of formal and informal reforms that have allowed the enlarged institutions to continue something like a 'business as usual' level of policy productivity. At the same time, however, the precise impact of enlargement clearly varies from one issue area to another, as a function of the specific constellation of preferences that the new members have brought to the Union. In some cases, the policy impacts have been minimal, as the new member states and their representatives in Brussels have taken up places within the existing distribution of preferences, while in other cases the new member states have indeed brought with them a greater diversity of preferences or more 'laggard' preferences, making agreement more difficult.

With respect to the overall functioning of the institutions and the policy process, existing studies are virtually unanimous that enlargement has not led to paralysis in Brussels (Dehousse *et al.* 2007; H. Wallace 2007; Best *et al.* 2008; Thomson 2011; Reh *et al.* 2013). Early studies revealed that the Commission after 2004 continued to produce policy proposals at similar rates to before enlargement. Legislative decisions that come through the bicameral processes of the Council and the EP are also similar in number, with the key change being that an increasing number of new laws are adopted in the first reading of the ordinary legislative procedure—thus speeding up, rather than slowing down, the legislative process (Reh *et al.* 2013). Within the Parliament, members from the new member states joined existing members in voting overwhelmingly with their political groups rather than by nationality, leading to substantial continuity in the workings of the EP before and after enlargement (Hix and Noury 2009; Thomson 2011). Even in the Council, ministers and their representatives continued to reach a large majority of their decisions by consensus, even when taking decisions under the qualified majority voting (QMV) rule (Naurin and Wallace 2008; Thomson 2011). The CJEU, for its part, has made some real progress in cutting its backlog of cases, and in reducing the time taken for judgments to be issued (Naômé 2010). Thus, in a nutshell, we find no evidence of post-enlargement gridlock in the EU policy process.

This is not to say, of course, that enlargement has brought with it no growing pains or downsides. The increasing size of all EU bodies from the Commission through the Council and the EP has led to fears that the deliberative quality of decision-making is being lost in favour of a more straightforward voting approach, and the increasing use of informal, secluded, and non-transparent procedures, such as first-reading agreements of new legislation, has led to concerns about decreased democratic accountability (Reh 2014). Furthermore, the initial optimism about new member states' compliance with EU laws and democratic norms (see e.g. Sedelmeier 2008; Levitz and Pop-Eleches 2010) has been tempered in recent years by findings that limited administrative and judicial capacities impede effective policy implementation (Falkner and Treib 2008), as well as by concerns that constitutional reforms and government practices have undermined democratic norms and accountability in some new member states, most notably Hungary and Romania (Bánkuti, Halmai, and Scheppele 2012; Epstein and Jacoby 2014*b*; Sedelmeier 2014).

Independent of these overall trends, our case studies find considerable variation in the impact of enlargement on sectoral policy-making. In some areas, new members' preferences have broadly mirrored those of the pre-2004 members, resulting in little change of policies or policy-making, while in other areas the addition of new members has brought distinctive concerns to the table, resulting alternately in stagnation of policy (where the new members have included policy 'laggards' and made agreement more difficult) or in the development of new directions for existing policies (where the new members raise policy concerns that had gone unaddressed by the original, 'western' members).

Broadly stated, in the core areas of economic regulation constituted by the single market, competition, monetary, and trade policy, the patterns of policy-making and the outcomes remain much in line with those evident before 2004, with the exception of the controversial issue of the free movement of labour within the EU (see Chapters 5, 6, 7 and 16). In the areas of environmental and social regulation, by contrast, the new member states are more hesitant about accepting strong EU disciplines (Chapters 11, 12, 13), impeding EU policy development. With respect to distributional spending policies, the arrival of a cohort of poorer, net-recipient countries has influenced budgetary bargaining, pitting the new members against the erstwhile south European net-recipients, as well as against the ranks of net contributors (Chapters 8, 9, 10). In other areas, the eastward geographical extension of the EU has radically altered the nature of the policy issues to be addressed and introduced quite different policy concerns into the discussion, as in the cases of energy security, JHA, and the CFSP (Chapters 14, 15, and 18).

As regards economic regulation, competition, and external trade, the new member states have largely taken on the obligations and accepted the implications of long-standing EU policies and legislation (Chapters 5, 6, and 16). There is little evidence of a distinctive grouping of new members with respect to the internal market: some are more liberal, and some a little less so, than older members. Nevertheless, the issue of free movement of labour in the enlarged EU has created considerable friction, generating a backlash within some of the 'old' member states, complicating the adoption of the 2006 Services Directive (Chapter 5) and contributing to the strong showing of right-wing and Eurosceptic parties in the May 2014 EP elections. EMU was to some extent insulated from the impacts of enlargement, given the high thresholds for entry into the euro area, yet even here it is notable that seven of the new member countries (Cyprus, Estonia, Latvia, Lithuania, Malta, Slovakia, and Slovenia) have adopted the currency, and all but two new members (the Czech c and Croatia) joined the March 2012 fiscal compact (Chapter 7).

As regards regulation that bites into social and environmental matters, however, the picture is less straightforward (Chapters 11, 12, 13, 14). The long-standing debate in the old EU between the 'leaders' and the 'laggards' finds expression in the post-2004 EU. Poorer countries tend understandably to be less enthusiastic in rushing towards higher social or environmental standards than wealthier countries, even without the added constraints of the financial crisis. High process standards can imply significant extra costs and could undermine what would otherwise be cost-competitiveness for central and east European countries. Moreover, physical legacies, such as the continued importance of coal for some new members, influence their policy preferences. In the area of environmental policy, Andrea Lenschow finds no simple or stark east–west divide on environmental issues. Nevertheless, some eastern members have resisted the imposition of costly new environmental regulations, most notably in the area of climate change where Poland has led a bloc of members seeking exceptions to the Union's ambitious emissions reductions (Chapter 13). In relation to the social and employment agendas, the new members come to the EU without the constraints of generous welfare states to protect (Chapters 11 and 12), and also with less vocal non-governmental groups clamouring for higher standards of social protection. In these areas, enlargement has both changed the politics and limited the prospects of future regulation.

It is on the explicitly distributional issues that the new member states form the most distinct grouping and make the most explicit difference to the line-up of positions to be accommodated in the development of collective EU policies. The prospect of eastward enlargement, for example, was one of the driving forces prompting reform of the CAP. The costs of extending the old CAP eastwards served to increase the incentives for acceptance of a shift from product and market support towards the new forms of farm payments, bringing an end to ever-rising EU agricultural budgets. Since enlargement, however, a number of new member states, notably Hungary and, particularly, Poland, have joined the defenders of the CAP, increasing the difficulty of undertaking substantial further reforms, as illustrated by the difficult negotiations on the reform of the CAP after 2013 (Chapter 8). At least as clear is the impact of enlargement on the development of cohesion policy (Chapter 10). On the one hand, based on objective criteria for distributing funding, the new member states should have pride of place as recipients, given the evident need to improve their economic infrastructures both regionally and nationally. On the other hand, old beneficiaries of the structural funds have been at pains not to let go of all of their benefits of incumbency. Accommodating both sets of demands requires more resources, but such an increase has met fierce resistance from the net contributors to the EU budget. Given the need for consensus on long-term budgetary decisions, enlargement has made negotiations on these issues even more difficult than they were previously (Chapter 9).

The new EU geography is a powerful factor in driving debates about EU policy developments, and especially so in a period in which forms of instability permeate the EU neighbourhood. Several of our case studies shed light on this. Self-evidently the attempt to elaborate the CFSP provokes difficult discussions about how to address the several and different groups of neighbours, including most importantly Russia, particularly since the Russian annexation of Crimea in early 2014 (see Chapter 18).

Efforts to improve energy security have been plagued by differences among EU members as regards their degrees of dependence on Russian-sourced energy supplies, although the combination of a new Lisbon-based legal competence, together with concerns about an increasingly assertive Russia, have prompted the Union finally to take its first steps towards a common energy-security policy (see Chapter 14). EU member states are also torn in different directions about when and whether to admit this or that neighbouring country as an actual or potential candidate for EU membership—or whether and if so how to develop alternatives to an EU membership track for some neighbours (see Chapter 17). The development of JHA has taken on many features that derive from the specificities of the new EU geography, which has altered the definition of where the relevant boundaries lie for 'controlling' the licit and the illicit movements of people and objects (see Chapter 15).

The impact of enlargement has thus varied significantly across policy areas. It has had little impact on the politics underpinning many decisions, but has greatly complicated redistributive politics and policies associated with social regulation. It has also affected the salience of some policy issues, from labour mobility to energy security. Even in the areas where the impact of enlargement has been greatest, it has heightened contestation without necessarily producing gridlock, with the possible exception of social policy.

The Treaty of Lisbon

The ToL entered into force in December 2009, capping off nearly a decade of constitutional deliberation, negotiation, and crisis. The process began with the negotiation of a Constitutional Treaty in 2002–3, only to receive a jolt with the rejection of the treaty in referenda in France and the Netherlands in 2005. After a nearly two-year delay, EU leaders agreed to revive most of the substance, but not the constitutional trappings, of the Constitutional Treaty in the more modest ToL in 2007, only to see that treaty founder due to a negative referendum in Ireland in 2008, before a second referendum saved the treaty and allowed it to go into effect in December 2009.

The ToL is a complex but, for the most part, modest document. It introduced some general institutional changes (including creating new offices, such as the standing European Council presidency and strengthening the powers of the EP); made a few minor changes to the EU's specific policy competences; and instituted more far-reaching changes in the previously intergovernmental pillars of JHA and CFSP. In mid-2014, after nearly five years of practice under the new treaty, we are in a position to assess its impact on policy-making across our various issue areas. A core finding of this volume is that the impact of the ToL has varied considerably across issue areas, but has generally been quite modest. In part, this is a function of the limits of the reforms agreed, but it also reflects the inherent difficulties of EU policy-making, which institutional changes cannot and have not fully dispelled.

In most areas of regulatory policy-making, the ToL introduced only minor changes, and our authors identify at best minor impacts on EU policy processes or outcomes. The EU's core areas of economic regulation—the internal market, competition, and EMU—were already well developed before Lisbon, and the new treaty has changed decision-making rules in these areas only at the margins. The internal market, for example, was already subject to the co-decision procedure even before the ToL formally re-dubbed it as the 'ordinary legislative procedure', and the new treaty introduced only a few marginal changes, such as increasing the power of the EP in the liberalization of some services and streamlining the Commission's ability to impose fines on member states that fail to transpose EU internal-market regulation (Chapter 5). Competition and EMU were similarly largely untouched by the ToL (Chapters 6 and 7).

EU social and environmental policies were at most modestly affected. With respect to social policy, for example, the ToL did little to change the emphasis on unanimous decision-making, with a partial switch to QMV under only a few, little-used legal bases (Chapter 11, Table 11.1), and did not unpick prohibitions on EU harmonization of national rules in sensitive areas, such as trade unions' right to organize and to strike. EU employment policy rules were similarly unchanged, and Martin Rhodes argues that even the European Charter of Fundamental Rights, now legally binding on the EU institutions, is unlikely to make a significant difference in that area, since most of the rights in question had already been acknowledged by the CJEU in practice (Chapter 12). EU environmental policy too was influenced only at the margins, particularly with respect to the Commission's increased ability to issue fines to member states for non-compliance (Chapter 13). EU competences in energy policy, David Buchan notes in Chapter 14, are still hedged with protections for the member states to act independently when it comes to decisions about the mix of energy sources such as coal, oil, natural gas, and renewables, but the ToL did introduce an explicit competence for the EU to 'ensure security of energy supply in the Union' (Art. 176A), which allowed the EU to take its first steps in coordinating the security of natural-gas supplies. With respect to trade policy, the ToL introduced two significant reforms: it extended exclusive EU competence to investment and it granted the EP the right of consent (and hence, veto power) over the range of trade policy (Chapter 16). The implications of the EP's increased influence were revealed when the EP overwhelmingly rejected the Anti-Counterfeiting Trade Agreement (ACTA), which would have strengthened criminal penalties against private citizens for copyright infringement (*The Guardian*, 4 July 2012). The nature and magnitude of the shift in the inter-institutional balance will be further defined in practice as the EU negotiates and ratifies (or fails to ratify) future trade and investment agreements.

The EU's distributive or spending policies have seen somewhat more substantial changes in treaty provisions and in policy processes and outcomes, but again nothing revolutionary. The ToL changes to the annual budget process, for example, may initially seem substantial, for instance by eliminating the previous distinction between compulsory and non-compulsory expenditure and increasing the powers of the EP with respect to the latter; yet Brigid Laffan and Johannes Lindner (Chapter 9) note that most of these provisions simply codify existing practices under the inter-institutional agreements that had governed the annual budget process over the previous several decades. Potentially more influential in the longer term are new rules on the adoption of the multi-annual financial frameworks (MFF). Again, the treaty largely codified existing practice, but it also provided that in the absence of agreement, the budget ceilings in the previous MFF will remain in place, further reinforcing the strong status quo bias in the budgetary process, and increasing the obstacles to any serious budgetary reforms. Thus the 2014–20 financial framework represented an incremental change over the previous period, with the net-contributing 'Friends of Better Spending' succeeding in imposing modest cuts in agricultural and cohesion spending, while the EP secured a stronger role in the potential mid-term revision of the budget after 2016. Moving from the overall budget process to specific spending policies, the rules governing the structural funds have emerged largely unchanged from Lisbon (Chapter 10), but the CAP has been influenced by the general move to the ordinary legislative procedure, which grants the EP new and co-equal powers with the Council over many areas of agricultural policy-making. These new powers prompted a 'fierce power struggle' between the Council and the EP after the entry into force of the ToL, according to Christilla Roederer-Rynning, and helped to shape the November 2013 reform of the CAP (reviewed in Chapter 8).

Without doubt, the most striking institutional changes introduced by the ToL can be found in foreign policy and JHA. With respect to JHA, the ToL introduced a raft of new provisions related to the Union's 'area of freedom, security, and justice', including most notably the move to the ordinary legislative procedure and the empowerment of the EP for all but the most sensitive legislation; the concomitant strengthening of the CJEU's oversight powers; and the strengthening of human-rights guarantees through the Charter of Fundamental Rights and the newly created treaty right to data protection (Chapter 15). The JHA case also demonstrates the limits of institutional reform, however, as the fundamental sensitivities of issues like immigration and police cooperation have continued to stymie any strong drive towards centralized policies, such that, 'in terms of policy substance, continuity prevails'.

Much the same could be said of the ToL changes to the CFSP (Chapter 18). The treaty changes in this area are perhaps the most far-reaching, with the creation of two new offices—the strengthened High Representative (HR/VP, taking over the previously parcelled out functions of the High Representative, the rotating Council presidency, and the Commissioner for External Affairs) and the newly created President of the European Council—designed to promote unified representation of the Union in foreign affairs; the establishment of a new European External Action Service (EEAS); new mutual assistance and solidarity clauses; and new provisions allowing for 'permanent structured cooperation' among a subset of vanguard member states. The new offices of HR/VP and European Council President were indeed created and the new EEAS instituted, but Bastian Giegerich identifies weaknesses in the roll-out of these new institutions, with HR/VP and the European Council President serving as 'managers rather than leaders', and the EEAS getting off to a rocky start. Neither the mutual assistance and solidarity clauses nor the permanent structured-cooperation provisions had yet been activated as of 2014. Perhaps most importantly, Giegerich finds, the institutional changes introduced by the ToL have failed to produce successful policies in the face of persistent differences among the member states, as illustrated by the EU's failure to take early, unified positions on the crises in Libya in 2011 and in Mali in 2012, and its rather slow and modest response to the crisis in Ukraine in 2014. Here again, institutional reforms, whatever their ultimate promise, have not altered the fundamental obstacles to progress in these sensitive areas of policy.

The financial crisis and its policy aftermath

The financial crisis, which began as a banking crisis that went global following the collapse of Lehman Brothers in the autumn of 2008, subsequently morphed into a sovereign debt crisis in some EU member states and contributed to a deep recession in much of Europe and around the world. As Dermot Hodson recounts in Chapter 7, the multiple challenges of the financial crisis, the ensuing 'Great Recession', the sovereign debt crisis, and years of fiscal austerity, particularly for the EU's highly indebted southern members, have combined to generate a profound and even existential state of crisis in the EU. Indeed, for many European citizens the EU today represents not the limitless opportunities of the internal market and the four freedoms, but instead the imposition of bitter austerity and economic hardship (Pew Research Center 2013).

Years of economic hardship and decreasing public support for the EU, in turn, have led to increasing speculation about the possible abandonment of the euro and even the disintegration of the Union and the possible exit of current member states including Greece or the UK. Others, seeing an opportunity in the midst of crisis, have called for deeper European integration as the most promising response to the ongoing crisis (see e.g. 'The Choice', *The Economist*, 26 May 2012).

For our purposes here, we bracket these existential and necessarily speculative debates on the future of Europe, focusing more narrowly and immediately on the impact, five years on, of the euro area crisis on the day-to-day making of policy in the EU. The economic shock and the policy responses to it, our authors find, have significantly impacted policy-making across the spectrum of EU policies. Rather than a single impact, however, the crisis and the responses to it have had differential implications for EU policies that have varied in their severity and their direction. The crisis has prompted new integration and initiatives in some policy areas while draining resources and impetus from others. The policy responses have tested some existing policies and contributed to an erosion of support for further integration.

The initial response to the crisis was by individual member-state governments, which bailed out failing banks and sought to protect depositors. These national-bank bailouts challenged EU competition-policy rules on state aids, but the Commission responded pragmatically, adopting a 'temporary framework' in December 2008 that allowed rescue and restructuring aid but which aimed to influence aid measures to make them conform as far as possible with eventual restoration of competitive markets. This framework began to be wound down in 2012 (see Chapter 6). In some countries, most notably Ireland, these bailouts put severe strains on government finances. The member states' response to the banking crisis was initially uncoordinated, which raised concerns about the implications for the single European market, but there was no extensive backsliding on single-market obligations (see Chapter 5).

The crisis also prompted some significant, if belated, policy innovation and institutional development at the European level. In a series of major decisions, the EU's member governments agreed new disciplines on their fiscal policies and adopted the ESM to provide financial support to governments in need (see Chapter 7). The crisis also gave new impetus to integration of the banking system, with the banking union establishing the ECB as the single supervisor for the euro area's largest banks but stopping short of centralized funds to recapitalize failed banks (see Chapters 5 and 7). The ECB, for its part, has interpreted its mandate to allow the virtually unlimited purchase of government debt on the secondary market, which has arguably saved the euro but has also prompted a major constitutional challenge in Germany (Jones and Kelemen 2014). The Commission also invoked the need for economic growth in a time of fiscal constraint as a justification for renewed efforts to complete the single market, but these efforts have been far less effective than those that led to the launch of the single market in the 1980s (see Chapter 5).

Other impacts of the crisis and its aftermath have been far less positive for European policy development. The austerity and restructuring measures associated with sovereign debt bailouts have created massive pressure for scaling back the welfare state in the recipient countries (see Chapter 11). The financial crisis and subsequent economic recession have led to very high rates of unemployment, particularly youth unemployment in many European countries (see Chapter 12). This heightened economic dislocation has contributed to criticisms that the European employment policy contributes to declining labour standards, which has made the policy area more politically contested (see Chapter 12). The financial crisis and the economic pain associated with austerity and restructuring measures have contributed to greater public and political distrust of markets in general and undermined support for the single European market (see Chapter 5). They also contributed to the (partial) suspension of two cornerstones of the EU's asylum and migration system: in 2011, France and Denmark reintroduced checks at their internal borders, effectively violating the Schengen rules; and the CJEU prohibited the transfers of asylum-seekers to Greece, suspending the core of the 'common European asylum system' (see Chapter 15). In competition policy, proposals to reform the state-aid regime were put on hold during the crisis (see Chapter 6). In environmental policy there has been increased resistance to more stringent standards, including on climate change, although the EU has largely maintained its commitment to environmental protection (see Chapters 13 and 14). Protecting the environment, however, is increasingly being framed in terms of its growth potential by emphasizing energy and resource efficiencies (see Chapter 13). The crises have also made the Commission and member states more reluctant to accelerate the ongoing enlargement processes (see Chapter 17). Thus support for European policy development has generally been eroded by the financial crisis and subsequent economic recession.

Strained national finances have also had concrete impacts on European policies. Cash-strapped member states were not willing to boost European spending, and the 2014–20 financial perspective led to the first reduction in the EU's budget in decades (see Chapter 9). This reduction included cuts in spending on agriculture (see Chapter 8) and cohesion (see Chapter 10). Moreover, most cohesion spending was to be devoted to 'investment in growth and jobs'. Efforts to develop the EU's military capability have been hit hard as member-state governments have cut defence spending in response to the twin constraints of reduced overall spending and higher social spending (see Chapter 18). Thus fewer government resources have contributed to reduced European cooperation.

Strikingly, the policy area that appears to have been least affected by the financial and economic crises has been trade policy. There has been no significant increase in protectionism. Moreover, partially in response to the crisis and partially in response to stagnation in the Doha Round of multilateral trade talks, the EU has embarked on a series of bilateral trade negotiations with some of its most important trading partners, including Canada, Japan, and the US (Young and Peterson 2014: 63–4). Trade policy, however, is very much the exception. While the acute crisis may have passed, underlying problems remain unresolved and the shockwaves continue to be felt across the European policy spectrum.

Conclusions

A common denominator across the contributions to this volume is the adaptability of the EU's policy processes. Great flexibility, formal and informal, is evident in the EU's day-to-day policy-making. Even more striking has been the institutional innovation in response to major challenges, most evident in how the EU has accommodated a dramatic increase in membership and sought to respond to the economic fallout of the global financial crisis. As a result, the diversity of forms of EU policy-making has increased within, as well as between, issue areas.

Some of the challenges to the EU's policy process—enlargement and the reforms associated with the ToL—were the product of choices by the EU. They were, therefore, prices thought to be worth paying for realizing other goals (as in the case of enlargement) or the adjustment costs necessary to realize desired ends (as in the case of the ToL). The EU has responded to both of these challenges well. In both cases policy-making has become more complicated, but less than expected in the case of enlargement, and in the case of Lisbon increased complication is the price for greater democratic legitimacy by giving the EP a greater say in the policy process. The ToL, beyond enhancing the role of the EP, did not radically transform EU policy-making, even where it created new institutions, as in the CFSP. With respect to enlargement, a variety of informal decision-making mechanisms helped to mitigate the transaction costs associated with an expanded membership, albeit not without costs in terms of other values such as deliberation and transparency.

By far the biggest challenge the EU has faced thus far in the twenty-first century has been the global financial crisis and the sovereign debt crises that followed in its wake. Some novel forms of cooperation have been adopted to respond to this crisis and its aftermath, including a raft of emergency lending measures, new fiscal-policy rules for the member states, and a nascent banking union. However, at the time of writing in the Fall of 2014, the success of these efforts remains in doubt as the euro area as a whole teeters on the brink of deflation. Moreover, the financial crisis and its economic repercussions have acted as a brake on many areas of EU policy-making. The economic crisis, rightly or wrongly, has also fuelled hostility to European integration, now associated in the minds of many European citizens not with prosperity and opportunity but with bitter austerity, and this hostility was manifest in the strong showing of Eurosceptic parties in the 2014 European Parliament elections. Day-to-day EU policy-making, in short, has generally adapted well in the face of crisis, but the long-term future and legitimacy of governance beyond the nation-state remains uncertain in the face of Europe's ongoing challenges.

APPENDIX: Caseloads of EU Courts

TABLE A.1 New cases of the European Court of Justice by subject matter, 1953–2012, in absolute numbers (#) and in per cent (%)

Subject matter*	Until 1971		1972–81		1982–91		1992–2001		2002–11		2012		Total	
	#	%	#	%	#	%	#	%	#	%	#	%	#	%
	1	2	3	4	5	6	7	8	9	10	11	12	12	14
1 Accession of new Member States							32	0.7	11	0.2	0		43	0.3
2 Agriculture and Fisheries	135	15.1	509	17.1	801	22.6	856	18.8	479	8.6	21	3.4	2,804	16.3
3 Approximation of laws							230	5.0	384	6.9	36	5.8	650	3.8
4 Brussels Convention							48	1.1	33	0.6	0		81	0.5
5 Commercial policy							63	1.4	31	0.6	7	1.1	101	0.6
6 Competition	44	4.9	162	5.4	311	8.8	211	4.6	277	5.0	30	4.9	1,035	6.0
7 Energy							7	0.2	43	0.8	3	0.5	53	0.3
8 Environment and consumers							299	6.6	724	13.1	62	10.1	1,085	6.3
9 External relations							90	2.0	98	1.8	3	0.5	191	1.1
10 Free movement of persons	48	5.4	174	5.8	363	10.2	449	9.9	251	4.5	30	4.9	1,315	7.7
11 Freedom of establishment and to provide services	1	0.1	36	1.2	133	3.7	197	4.3	604	10.9	20	3.2	991	5.8
12 Free movement of capital							25	0.5	100	1.8	11	1.8	136	0.8
13 Free movement of goods and customs	56	6.3	246	8.3	519	14.6	346	7.6	289	5.2	16	2.6	1,472	8.6
14 Industrial policy							21	0.5	132	2.4	16	2.6	169	1.0
15 Intellectual property							8	0.2	297	5.4	59	9.6	364	2.1

16 Law governing the institutions	27	3.0	53	1.8	230	6.5	94	2.1	210	3.8	21	3.4	325	1.9
17 Principles of Community/Union law	3	0.3	13	0.4	63	1.8	69	1.5	50	0.9	21	3.4	140	0.8
18 Social policy	8	0.9	92	3.1	428	12.0	265	5.8	435	7.6	38	6.2	738	4.3
19 State aid							118	2.6	235	4.2	28	4.5	381	2.2
20 Taxation							321	7.0	529	9.5	60	9.7	1,220	7.1
21 Transport							137	3.0	161	2.9	21	3.4	398	2.3
22 Rest (EC)							32	0.7	152	2.7	23	3.7	735	4.3
23 Justice and home affairs							3	0.1	215	3.9	57	9.3	275	1.6
24 Common foreign and security policy									38	0.7	6	1.0	44	0.3
25 Economic and monetary policy									10	0.2	3	0.5	13	0.1
26 European citizenship							4	0.1	47	0.8	11	1.8	62	0.4
27 Regional policy							12	0.3	30	0.5	5	0.8	47	0.3
28 Other (ECSC, EAEC)	282	31.5	64	2.1	212	6.0	69	1.5	31	0.6	0		660	3.8
29 Staff of EU institutions	291	32.5	1,630	54.7	492	13.9	122	2.7	73	1.3	5	0.8	2,613	15.2
30 Appeals							458	10.1	856	15.5	139	22.6	1,453	8.5
31 Total (100.00 %)	**895**		**2,987**		**3,552**		**4,557**		**5,540**		**616**		**17,147**	

Source: *Annual Reports of the Court of Justice and of the General Court*. Compiled by Josef Falke, Centre for European Law and Politics (ZERP) and Research Centre TranState (Transformations of the State), and by Stephan Leibfried, Research Centre TranState and Center for Social Policy Research (CeS), and tabulated by Monika Sniegs of TranState.
* Over time, in particular since 1992, the court statistics have had to become more differentiated because increasing caseload required some categories to be subdivided,
e.g. 'approximation of laws', and because new competencies were created or old ones decisively extended, such that separate reporting was deemed necessary.

TABLE A.2 New cases of the General Court by subject matter, 1992–2012, in absolute numbers (#) and in per cent (%)

Subject matter	1992–6		1997–2001		2002–6		2007–11		2012		Total	
	#	%	#	%	#	%	#	%	#	%	#	%
	1	2	3	4	5	6	7	8	9	10	11	12
1 Agriculture	715	43.5	174	9.0	84	3.9	125	4.6	11	2.0	1,109	12.3
2 Commercial policy	37	2.3	44	2.3	46	2.1	47	1.7	20	3.7	193	2.1
3 Competition	225	13.7	154	8.0	261	12.0	293	13.5	34	6.3	967	10.8
4 Customs	8	0.5	19	1.0	23	1.1	25	0.9	6	1.1	81	0.9
5 Environment and consumer policy	8	0.5	25	1.3	90	4.1	61	2.2	3	0.6	187	2.1
6 External relations			55	2.9	31	1.4	151	5.6	61	11.3	298	17.5
7 Fisheries	17	1.0	8	0.4	36	1.7	51	5.6	0		112	1.2
8 Free movement of persons and social policy	28	1.7	54	2.8	38	1.8	7	0.3	0		127	1.4
9 Free movement of goods	3	0.2	36	1.9	1	0.0	3	0.1	0		43	0.5
10 Freedom of establishment and to provide services	6	3.7	20	1.0	37	1.7	9	0.3	1	0.2	73	0.5
11 Intellectual property			90	4.7	537	24.8	999	36.8	238	44.2	1,864	20.7
12 Law governing the institutions	21	1.3	376	19.5	120	5.5	135	5.9	40	7.4	692	7.7
13 State aid	63	3.8	266	13.8	175	8.1	247	9.1	36	6.7	787	8.8
14 Taxation	3	0.2	0		7	0.3	4	0.1	1	0.2	15	0.2
15 Transport	2	0.1	8	0.4	6	0.3	7	0.3	0		23	0.3

		#	%	#	%	#	%	#	%	#	%	#	%
16	Justice and home affairs	1	0.1	1	0.1	2	0.1	9	0.3	0	0	12	0.1
17	Common foreign and security policy	4	0.2	4	0.2	17	0.8	1	0.0	0	0	22	0.2
18	Economic and monetary policy					3	0.1	8	0.3	3	0.6	14	0.2
19	Regional policy	1	0.1	6	0.3	51	2.4	56	1.2	4	0.7	118	1.3
20	Rest (EC)	37	2.3	16	0.8	44	2.0	278	10.3	60	11.1	435	4.8
21	Other (ECSC, EAEC)	36	2.2	31	1.6	16	0.7	2	0.1	0	0	85	0.9
22	Staff of EU institutions	434	26.4	537	27.9	544	25.1	172	6.3	12	2.2	1,699	18.9
23	**Total (100.00 %)**	**1,643**		**1,924**		**2,166**		**2,712**		**539**		**8,984**	

Source: *Annual Reports of the Court of Justice and of the General Court*. Compiled by Josef Falke, Centre for European Law and Politics (ZERP) and Research Centre TranState (Transformations of the State), and by Stephan Leibfried, Research Centre TranState and Center for Social Policy Research (CeS), and tabulated by Monika Sniegs of TranState.

■ REFERENCES

In addition to the substantial body of scholarly research cited below, students of the European Union can find extensive and up-to-date information about the EU's institutions and policies online. The EU's 'gateway' website provides profiles (in all of the Union's official languages) of the EU's various policies or 'activities' at: *http://europa.eu*. In addition, each of the individual institutions maintains a dedicated website, including those for the Commission (*http://ec.europa.eu*), the Council of the European Union (*http://www.consilium.europa.eu*), the Court of Justice of the European Union (*http://curia.europa.eu/jcms/jcms/j_6/home*), and the European Parliament (*http://www.europarl.europa.eu*). The EU also maintains several useful databases related to EU policies and policy-making, including most notably EUR-Lex (*http://eur-lex.europa.eu*), a keyword-searchable directory of EU treaties and legislation, and Pre-Lex (*http://ec.europa.eu/prelex/apcnet.cfm?CL=en*), which provides access to documents from all stages and from the various institutions of the EU legislative process for thousands of individual pieces of legislation. In addition to these official websites, there are a growing number of publications (such as *Agence Europe, European Report*, and *European Voice*) and websites (such as *EUobserver.com*) that provide dedicated press coverage of EU institutions and policies.

Ackrill, R. (2000), *The Common Agricultural Policy* (Sheffield: Sheffield Academic Press).

Adelle, C., and Anderson, J. (2013), 'Lobby Groups', in A. Jordan and C. Adelle (eds.), *Environmental Policy in the EU: Actors, Institutions and Processes*, 3rd edn. (London: Earthscan), 152–69.

Agence Europe, various issues.

Aggarwal, V. K., and Foggerty, E. A. (2005), 'The Limits of Interregionalism: The EU and North America', *European Integration*, 27/3: 327–46.

Ahearne, A., and Eichengreen, B. (2007), 'External Monetary and Financial Policy: A Review and a Proposal', in A. Sapir (ed.), *Fragmented Power: Europe and the Global Economy* (Brussels: Bruegel), 135–62.

Allen, D. (2010), 'The Structural Funds and Cohesion Policy: Extending the Bargain to Meet New Challenges', in H. Wallace, M. A. Pollack, and A. R. Young (eds.), *Policy-Making in the European Union*, 6th edn. (Oxford: Oxford University Press), 229–52.

Allison, G. (1969), 'Conceptual Models and the Cuban Missile Crisis', *American Political Science Review*, 63/3: 689–718.

Allison, G. (1971), *Essence of Decision: Explaining the Cuban Missile Crisis* (Boston, MA: Little Brown).

Allison, G., and Zelikow, P. (1999), *Essence of Decision: Explaining the Cuban Missile Crisis*, 2nd edn. (New York, NY: Longman).

Almunia, J. (2013), 'Doing More with Less—State Aid Reform in Times of Austerity: Supporting Growth Amid Fiscal Constraints', speech delivered at King's College London, 13 Aug., available at *http://europa.eu/rapid/press-release_SPEECH-13-14_en.htm*.

Alter, K. J. (1998), 'Who are the "Masters of the Treaty"? European Governments and the European Court of Justice', *International Organization*, 52/1: 121–47.

Alter, K. J. (2001), *Establishing the Supremacy of European Law: The Making of an International Rule of Law in Europe* (Oxford: Oxford University Press).

Alter, K. J. (2009), *The European Court's Political Power: Selected Essays* (Oxford: Oxford University Press).

Alter, K. J., and Meunier-Aitsahalia, S. (1994), 'Judicial Politics in the European Community: European Integration and the Pathbreaking *Cassis de Dijon* Decision', *Comparative Political Studies*, 26/4: 535–61.

Amato, G. (1997), *Antitrust and the Bounds of Power* (Oxford: Hart).

AmCham EU (2012), *The Single EU Market: A Work in Progress*, available at *http://www.amcham.edu/Portals/0/2012/ebooks/Single-Mrket-Study/index.html*.

Andersen, M. S., and Liefferink, D. (1997) (eds.), *European Environmental Policy: The Pioneers* (Manchester: Manchester University Press).

Andreou, G. (2007), 'Second Year Annual State of the Art Report—The New EU Cohesion Policy: Enlargement, "Lisbonisation" and the Challenge of Diversity', *EU CONSENT* (Athens: Hellenic Foundation for European and Foreign Policy (ELIAMAP)).

Angenendt, S. (1997) (ed.), *Migration und Flucht: Aufgaben und Strategien für Deutschland, Europa und die internationale Gemeinschaft* (Bonn/Munich: Bundeszentrale für politische Bildung/R. Oldenbourg Wissenschaftverlag).

Apeldoorn, B. van (2001), 'The Struggle over European Order: Transnational Class Agency in the Making of "Embedded Neo-Liberalism"', in A. Bieler and A. D. Morton (eds.), *Social Forces in the Making of the New Europe: The Restructuring of European Social Relations in the Global Political Economy* (Basingstoke: Palgrave Macmillan), 70–89.

Apeldoorn, B. van (2002), *Transnational Capitalism and the Struggle over European Integration* (Abingdon: Routledge).

Armstrong, H. (1989), 'Community Regional Policy', in J. Lodge (ed.), *The European Community and the Challenge of the Future* (London: Pinter), 167–85.

Armstrong, K., and Bulmer, S. (1998), *The Governance of the Single European Market* (Manchester: Manchester University Press).

Arnold, C. U., Hosli, M. O., and Pennings, P. (2004), 'Social Policy-Making in the European Union: A New Mode of Governance?', paper presented at the Conference of Europeanists, Chicago, 11–13 Mar.

Arp, H. A. (1992), 'The European Parliament in European Community Environmental Policy', EUI European Policy Unit Report No. 1992/13 (Florence: European University Institute).

Ashiagbor, D. (2013), 'Unravelling the Embedded Liberal Bargain: Labour and Social Welfare Law in the Context of EU Market Integration', *European Law Journal*, 19/3: 303–24.

Ashton, C. (2013), 'Speech by EU High Representative Catherine Ashton to the European Parliament on the Situation in Syria', Brussels, 11 Sept., available at *http://eeas.europa.eu/statements/docs/2013/130911_03_en.pdf*.

Aspinwall, M. D., and Schneider, G. (1999), 'Same Menu, Separate Tables: The Institutionalist Turn in Political Science and the Study of European Integration', *European Journal of Political Research*, 38: 1–36.

Atkinson, A. B. (2013), 'Ensuring Social Inclusion in Changing Labour and Capital Markets', *European Economy*, Economic Paper 481.

Atkinson, M. M., and Coleman, W. D. (1989), *State, Business and Industrial Change in Canada* (Toronto: Toronto University Press).

Avery, G. (2004), 'The Enlargement Negotiations', in F. Cameron (ed.), *The Future of Europe: Integration and Enlargement* (Abingdon: Routledge), 35–62.

Averyt, W. (1977), *Agropolitics in the European Community* (New York, NY: Praeger Publishers).

Axelrod, R. (1970), *Conflict of Interest* (Chicago, IL: Markham).

Axelrod, R. (1984), *The Evolution of Cooperation* (New York, NY: Basic Books).

Bach, D. and Newman, A. L. (2007), 'The European Regulatory State and Global Public Policy: Micro-Institutions, Macro-Influence', *Journal of European Public Policy*, 14:6, 827–46.

Bache, I. (1998), *The Politics of European Union Regional Policy: Multi-Level Governance or Flexible Gatekeeping?* (Sheffield: Sheffield Academic Press).

Bache, I. (1999), 'The Extended Gatekeeper: Central Government and the Implementation of the EC Regional Policy in the UK', *Journal of European Public Policy*, 6/1: 28–45.

Bache, I. (2008), *Europeanization and Multi-Level Governance: Cohesion Policy in the European Union and Britain* (Lanham, MD: Rowman & Littlefield).

Bache, I. (2010), 'Partnership as an EU Policy Instrument: A Political History', *West European Politics*, 33/1: 58–74.

Bache, I. (2013), 'Measuring Quality of Life for Public Policy: An Idea Whose Time has Come? Agenda-Setting Dynamics in the European Union', *Journal of European Public Policy*, 20/1: 21–38.

Bache, I., and Andreou, G. (2011) (eds.), *Cohesion Policy and Multi-Level Governance in South and East Europe* (London: Routledge).

Bache, I., and Flinders, M. (2004), 'Themes and Issues in Multi-Level Governance', in I. Bache and M. Flinders (eds.), *Multi-Level Governance* (Oxford: Oxford University Press), 1–11.

Bache, I., Andreou, G., Atanasova, G., and Tomšic, D. (2011), 'Europeanization and Multi-Level Governance in South East Europe: The Domestic Impact of EU Cohesion Policy and Pre-Accession Aid', *Journal of European Public Policy*, 18/1: 122–41.

Bachtler, J., and Mendez, C. (2007), 'Who Governs EU Cohesion Policy? Deconstructing the Reforms of the Structural Funds', *Journal of Common Market Studies*, 45/3: 535–64.

Bailey, D., and De Propris, L. (2002), 'EU Structural Funds, Regional Capabilities and Enlargement: Towards Multi-Level Governance?', *Journal of European Integration*, 24: 303–24.

Baker, S. (2003), 'The Dynamics of European Union Biodiversity Policy: Interactive, Functional and Institutional Logics', *Environmental Politics*, 12/3: 23–41.

Balassa, B. (1975), *European Economic Integration* (Amsterdam: North-Holland).

Baldwin, M. (2006), 'EU Trade Politics Heaven or Hell?', *Journal of European Public Policy*, 13/6: 926–42.

Bale, T. (2013), *European Politics: A Comparative Introduction* (Basingstoke: Palgrave Macmillan).

Bánkuti, M., Halmai, G., and Scheppele, K. L. (2012), 'Disabling the Constitution', *Journal of Democracy*, 23/3: 138–46.

Barbé, E. (1998), 'Balancing Europe's Eastern and Southern Dimensions', in J. Zielonka (ed.), *Paradoxes of European Foreign Policy* (The Hague: Kluwer Law International), 117–30.

Barca, F. (2009), 'An Agenda for a Reformed Cohesion Policy: A Place-Based Approach to Meeting European Union Challenges and Expectations', Independent Report prepared at the request of Danuta Hübner, Commissioner for Regional Policy (Brussels: DG Regional Policy).

Barnard, C. (2007), *The Substantive Law of the EU: The Four Freedoms*, 2nd edn. (Oxford: Oxford University Press).

Barnard, C. (2008*a*), 'Unravelling the Services Directive', *Common Market Law Review*, 45/2: 323–94.

Barnard, C. (2008*b*), 'Employment Rights, Free Movement under the EC Treaty and the Services Directive', Mitchell Working Paper Series No. 5/2008, (Edinburgh: Europa Institute).

Barnard, C. (2010), *The Substantive Law of the EU: The Four Freedoms*, 3rd edn. (Oxford: Oxford University Press).

Barnard, C. (2012), *EU Employment Law* (Oxford: Oxford University Press).

Barnard, C., and Deakin, S. (2002), '"Negative" and "Positive" Harmonization of Labor Law in the European Union', *Columbia Journal of European Law*, 8: 389–413.

Barroso, J. M. (2009), 'Mission Letter from the President of the European Commission', Pres(2009) D/2250.

Barroso, J. M. (2011), 'Europe's Sources of Growth: Presentation of J. M. Barroso, President of the European Commission, to the European Council of 23 October 2011', available at *http://ec.europa.eu/commission_2010-2014/president/pdf/sources_of_growwth_en.pdf*.

Barysch, K. (2008) (ed.), *Pipelines, Politics and Power: The Future of EU-Russia Relations* (London: Centre for European Reform).

Barysch, K. (2013), *The Working Time Directive: What's the Fuss About?* (London: Centre for European Reform).

Batory, A., and Cartwright, A. (2011), 'Re-Visiting the Partnership Principle in Cohesion Policy: The Role of Civil Society Organisations in Structural Funds Monitoring', *Journal of Common Market Studies*, 49/4: 697–717.

Batory, A., and Puetter, U. (2013), 'Consistency and Diversity? The EU's Rotating Trio Council Presidency after the Lisbon Treaty', *Journal of European Public Policy*, 20/1: 95–112.

Baudner, J., and Bull, M. (2013), 'The Europeanisation of National Institutions Reassessed: A Comparison of Regional Policies in Germany and Italy', *Comparative European Politics*, 11/2: 201–21.

Baumgartner, F. R., and Jones, B. D. (1993), *Agendas and Instability in American Politics* (Chicago, IL: University of Chicago Press).

Baumgartner, F. R., and Leech, B. L. (1998), *Basic Interests: The Importance of Groups in Politics and Political Science* (Princeton, NJ: Princeton University Press).

Baun, M. (2000), *A Wider Europe: The Process and Politics of EU Enlargement* (Lanham, MD: Rowman & Littlefield).

Baun, M., and Marek, D. (2008) (eds.), *EU Cohesion Policy after Enlargement* (Basingstoke: Palgrave Macmillan).

Beach, D. (2013), 'The Fiscal Compact, Euro-Reforms, and the Challenge for the Opt-Outs', *Danish Foreign Policy Yearbook*, 2013: 113–33.

Becker, P. (2012), 'Lost in Stagnation: The EU's Next Multiannual Financial Framework (2014–2020) and the Power of the Status Quo', SWP Research Paper, available at *http://www.swp-berlin.org/fileadmin/contents/products/research_papers/2012_RP14_bkr.pdf*.

Becker, S. T., Lenschow, A., and Mehl, C. (forthcoming), 'Scalar Dynamics and Legitimacy Implications of Ambient Air Quality Management in the EU', *Journal of Environmental Policy and Planning*.

Becker, U. (1998), 'Brillen aus Luxemburg und Zahnbehandlung in Brüssel: die Gesetzliche Krankenversicherung im Europäischen Binnenmarkt', *Neue Zeitschrift für Sozialrecht*, 7/8: 359–64.

Becker, U. (2004a) 'Die soziale Dimension des Binnenmarktes', in J. Schwarze (ed.), *Der Verfassungsentwurf des Europäischen Konvents: Verfassungsrechtliche Grundstrukturen und wirtschaftsverfassungsrechtliches Konzept* (Baden-Baden: Nomos), 201–19.

Becker, U. (2004b) 'Grenzüberschreitende Versicherungsleistungen in der (gesetzlichen) Krankenversicherung—Die juristische Perspektive', in J. Basedow et al. (eds.), *Versicherungswissenschaftliche Studien*, 26 (Baden-Baden: Nomos), 171–88.

Becker, U. (2005a), 'Stationäre und ambulante Krankenhausleistungen im grenzüberschreitenden Dienstleistungsverkehr—von Entgrenzungen und neuen Grenzen in der EU', *Neue Zeitschrift für Sozialrecht*, 14/9: 449–56.

Becker, U. (2005b), 'Das Gemeinschaftsrecht, die deutschen Sozialleistungssysteme und die Debatte um deren Reform', in U. Becker (ed.), *Reformen des deutschen Sozial- und Arbeitsrechts im Lichte supra- und internationaler Vorgaben: Wissenschaftliches Kolloquium zum 70. Geburtstag von Bernd Baron von Maydell* (Baden-Baden: Nomos), 15–32.

Becker, U. (2007a), 'Sozialrecht in der europäischen Integration—eine Zwischenbilanz', *ZFSH/SGB*, 46/3: 134–43.

Becker, U. (2007b), 'EU-Beihilfenrecht und soziale Dienstleistungen', *Neue Zeitschrift für Sozialrecht*, 16/4: 169–76.

Becker, U. (2012), 'Die Sozialpolitik im Spannungsverhältnis von Nationalstaat und supranationalen Institutionen', *Sozialer Fortschritt*, 61/5: 86–92.

Beer, S. (1982), *Modern British Politics: Parties and Pressure Groups in the Collectivist Age* (London: Faber & Faber).

Begg, I. (2005), *Funding the European Union*, Federal Trust Research Reports (London: The Federal Trust for Education and Research).

Begg, I. (2008), 'Economic Governance in an Enlarged Euro Area', *European Economy*, Economic Papers, No. 311.

Begg, I. (2010), 'Cohesion of Confusion: A Policy Searching for Objectives', *Journal of European Integration*, 32/1: 77–96.

Begg, I., and Grimwade, N. (1998), *Paying for Europe* (Sheffield: Sheffield Academic Press).

Begg, I., Erhel, C., and Mortensen, J. (2010), 'Medium-Term Employment Challenges', CEPS Special Report (Brussels: Centre for European Policy Studies).

Benedetto, G., and Milio, S. (2012) (eds.), *European Union Budget Reform: Institutions, Policy and Economic Crisis* (London: Palgrave Macmillan).

Bennett, H. (2012), 'Leverage and Limitations of the EU's Influence in the Eastern Neighbourhood: Compliance with the EU's Justice and Home Affairs' Standards in Georgia, Moldova and Ukraine', PhD thesis, London School of Economics and Political Science.

Benson, D., and Adelle, C. (2013), 'EU Environmental Policy after the Lisbon Treaty', in A. Jordan and C. Adelle (eds.), *Environmental Policy in the EU: Actors, Institutions and Processes*, 3rd edn. (Abingdon: Routledge), 32–48.

BEPA (Bureau of Economic Policy Advisors) (2008), *Public Finances in the EU* (Luxembourg: Office for Official Publications of the European Communities).

Bercusson, B. (2009), *European Labour Law*, 2nd edn. (Cambridge: Cambridge University Press).

Besson, S. (2007) (ed.), 'EU Citizenship', *European Law Journal*, 13/5: 573–694 (special issue).

Besson, S., and Utzinger, A. (2007), 'Introduction: Future Challenges of European Citizenship—Facing a Wide-Open Pandora's Box', *European Law Journal*, 13/5: 573–690.

Best, E., Christiansen, C., and Settembri, P. (2008) (eds.), *The Institutions of the Enlarged European Union* (Cheltenham: Edward Elgar).

Beyers, J., Eising, R., and Maloney, W. (2008), 'Researching Interest Group Politics in Europe and Elsewhere: Much We Study, Little We Know?', *West European Politics*, 31/6: 1103–28.

Bieback, K.-J. (1993), 'Marktfreiheit in der EG und nationale Sozialpolitik vor und nach Maastricht', *Europarecht*, 28/2: 150–72.

Bieback, K.-J. (2003) 'Die Bedeutung der sozialen Grundrechte für die Entwicklung der EU', *Zeitschrift für Sozialhilfe und Sozialgesetzbuch (ZFSH/SGB)*, 42/10: 579–88.

Biehl, H., Geigerich, B., and Jonas, A. (2013) (eds.), *Strategic Cultures in Europe: Security and Defence Policies Across the Continent* (Wiesbaden: Springer).

Biscop, S., and Coelmont, J. (2012), *Europe, Strategy and Armed Forces: The Making of a Distinctive Power* (London: Routledge).

Biscop, S., and Coelmont, J. (2013), 'Defence: The European Council Matters', Egmont Policy Brief No. 51 (Brussels: Egmont Royal Institute for International Relations).

Black, R. E. (1977), 'Plus Ça Change, Plus C'est la Même Chose: Nine Governments in Search of a Common Energy Policy', in H. Wallace, W. Wallace, and C. Webb (eds.), *Policy-Making in the European Communities* (Chichester: John Wiley), 165–96.

Blinder, A. S. (2007), 'Monetary Policy by Committee: Why and How?', *European Journal of Political Economy*, 23/1: 106–23.

Boecken, W. (2005), 'EG-rechtlicher Zwang zu Unisex-Tarifen in der betrieblichen Altersversorgung?', in A. Söllner, W. Gitter, and R. Waltermann (eds.), *Gedächtnisschrift für Meinhard Heinze* (Munich: Beck), 57–68.

Boeri, T., and Brücker, H. (2006) (eds.), *Immigration Policy and the Welfare System: A Report for the Fondazione Rodolfo Debenedetti* (Oxford: Oxford University Press).

Bohman, J. (1998), 'Survey Article: The Coming of Age of Deliberative Democracy', *Journal of Political Philosophy*, 6/4: 400–25.

Böhmelt, T., and Freyburg, T. (2013), 'The Temporal Dimension of the Credibility of EU Conditionality and Candidate States' Compliance with the *acquis communautaire*, 1998–2009', *European Union Politics*, 14/2: 250–72.

Borrás, S., and Greve, B. (2004) (eds.), 'The Open Method of Coordination in the European Union', *Journal of European Public Policy*, 11/2: 181–336 (special issue).

Borrás, S., and Jacobsson, K. (2004), 'The Open Method of Coordination and the New Governance Patterns in the EU', *Journal of European Public Policy*, 11/2: 185–208.

Börzel, T. A. (2001), 'Non-Compliance in the European Union. Pathology or Statistical Artifact?', *Journal of European Public Policy*, 8/5: 803–24.

Börzel, T. A. (2011), 'When Europeanization Hits Limited Statehood: The Western Balkans as a Test Case for the Transformative Power of Europe', Kolleg-Forschergruppe Working Paper, No. 30 (Berlin: Freie Universität Berlin).

Börzel, T. A., and Hosli, M. (2003), 'Brussels between Bern and Berlin: Comparative Federalism Meets the European Union', *Governance*, 16/2: 179–202.

Börzel, T. A., and Knoll, M. (2012), 'Quantifying Non-Compliance in the EU: A Database on EU Infringement Proceedings', Berlin Working Paper on European Integration, No. 15 (Berlin: Freie Universität Berlin).

Börzel, T. A., and Langbein, J. (2013) (eds.), 'Convergence without Accession? Explaining Policy Change in the EU's Eastern Neighbourhood', Europe-Asia Studies, 65/4 (special issue).

Börzel, T. A., and Risse, T. (2007), 'Europeanization: The Domestic Impact of EU Politics', in K. E. Jørgensen, M. A. Pollack, and B. Rosamond (eds.), The Handbook of European Union Politics (London: Sage), 483–504.

Bossong, R. (2008), 'The Action Plan on Combating Terrorism: A Flawed Instrument of EU Security Governance', Journal of Common Market Studies, 46/1: 27–48.

Boswell, C., and Geddes, A. (2010), Migration and Mobility in the European Union (Basingstoke: Palgrave Macmillan).

Bourgeois, J. (1982), 'The Tokyo Round Agreements on Technical Barriers and Government Procurement in International and EEC Perspective', Common Market Law Review, 19/1: 5–33.

Bradford, A. (2012), 'The Brussels Effect', Northwestern University Law Review, 107/1: 1–68.

Broughton, A. (2010), 'Commission Issues Report on EU-Level Sectoral Dialogue', European Industrial Relations Observatory Online, available at http://www.eurofound.europa.eu/ eiro/2010/08/articles/eu1008011i.htm.

Bruszt, L. (2008), 'Multi-Level Governance—The Eastern Versions: Emerging Patterns of Regional Development Governance in the New Member States', Regional and Federal Studies, 18/5: 607–27.

Buch-Hansen, H., and Wigger, A. (2011), The Politics of European Competition Regulation (London: Routledge).

Buchan, D. (2009), Energy and Climate Change: Europe at the Crossroads (Oxford: Oxford University Press).

Buchan, D. (2013), Can Shale Gas Transform Europe's Energy Landscape? (London: Centre for European Reform).

Bücker, A., and Warneck, W. (2010) (eds.), 'Viking-Laval-Rüffert: Consequences and Policy Perspectives', European Trade Union Institute Report No. 111 (Brussels: European Trade Union Institute).

Budzinski, O. (2008), 'Monoculture versus Diversity in Competition Economics', Cambridge Journal of Economics, 32/2: 295–324.

Bueno de Mesquita, B., and Stokman, S. N. (1994), European Community Decision Making (New Haven, CT: Yale University Press).

Buigues, P., and Sheehy, J. (1994), 'European Integration and the Internal Market Programme', paper presented at the ESRC/COST A7 conference, University of Exeter, 8–11 Sept.

Bull, H. (1982), 'Civilian Power Europe: A Contradiction in Terms?', Journal of Common Market Studies, 21/1: 149–65.

Bulmer, S., and Lequesne, C. (2012) (eds.), The Member States of the European Union, 2nd edn. (Oxford: Oxford University Press).

Bungenberg, M. (2011), 'The Division of Competences Between the EU and Its Member States in the Area of Investment Politics', in M. Bungenberg, J. Griebel, and S. Hindelang (eds.), European Yearbook International Economic Law, vol. 29 (Heidelberg: Springer).

Bures, O. (2006), 'EU Counter-Terrorism Policy: A "Paper Tiger"?', *Terrorism and Political Violence*, 18/1: 57–78.

Burley, A.-M., and Mattli, W. (1993), 'Europe Before the Court: A Political Theory of Legal Integration', *International Organization*, 47/1: 41–76.

Burns, C. (2013), 'The European Parliament', in A. Jordan and C. Adelle (eds.), *Environmental Policy in the EU: Actors, Institutions and Processes*, 3rd edn. (Abingdon: Routledge), 132–51.

Burns, C., and Carter, N. (2010), 'Is Co-decision Good for the Environment?', *Political Studies*, 58/1: 128–42.

Burns, C., Rasmussen, A., and Reh, C. (2013), 'Legislative Codecision and its Impact on the Political System of the European Union', *Journal of European Public Policy*, 20/7: 941–52.

Busuioc, M. (2012), 'European Agencies and Their Boards: Promises and Pitfalls of Accountability beyond Design', *Journal of European Public Policy*, 19/5: 719–36.

Buti, M., Eijffinger, S., and Franco, D. (2003), 'Revisiting EMU's Stability Pact: A Pragmatic Way Forward', *Oxford Review of Economic Policy*, 19/1: 100–11.

Buzan, B., Wæver, O., and de Wilde, J. (1998), *Security: A New Framework for Analysis* (Boulder, CO: Lynne Rienner).

Calmfors, L. (2001), 'Wages and Wage-Bargaining Institutions in the EMU—A Survey of the Issues', *Empirica*, 28/4: 325–51.

Cameron, D. (1992), 'The 1992 Initiative: Causes and Consequences', in A. M. Sbragia (ed.), *Euro-Politics: Institutions and Policymaking in the 'New' European Community* (Washington, DC: Brookings Institution), 23–74.

Cameron, P. (2007), *Competition in Energy Markets: Law and Regulation in the European Union*, 2nd edn. (Oxford: Oxford University Press).

Capelletti, M., Secombe, M., and Weiler, J. H. H. (1986) (eds.), *Integration through Law: Europe and the American Federal Experience* (New York, NY: De Gruyter).

Caporaso, J. A., and Tarrow, S. G. (2009), 'Polanyi in Brussels: Supranational Institutions and the Transnational Embedding of Markets', *International Organization*, 63/4: 593–620.

Casey, B. (2003), 'Coordinating "Coordination": Beyond "Streamlining"', in Verband Deutscher Rentenversicherungsträger (VDR) (ed.), *Offene Koordinierung in der Alterssicherung in der Europäischen Union* (Frankfurt am Main: VDR), DRV Schriften 34, 89–97 (special issue, *Deutsche Rentenversicherung*).

Castles, F. G., Leibfried, S., Lewis, J., Obinger, H., and Pierson, C. (2010), *The Oxford Handbook of the Welfare State* (Oxford: Oxford University Press).

Cecchini, P., with Catinat, M., and Jacquemin, A. (1988), *The European Challenge 1992: The Benefits of a Single Market* (Aldershot: Wildwood House).

Chalmers, D. (2004), 'The Dynamics of Judicial Authority and the Constitutional Treaty', Jean Monnet Working Paper 5/04 (New York, NY: New York University School of Law, Jean Monnet Program/Woodrow Wilson School of Government, Princeton University).

Chatwin, C. (2011), *Drug Policy Harmonization and the European Union* (Basingstoke: Palgrave Macmillan).

Checkel, J. T. (2001), 'Taking Deliberation Seriously', ARENA Working Paper WP 01/14, available at *http://www.arena.uio.no/publications/*.

Checkel, J. T. (2005), 'International Institutions and Socialization in Europe: Introduction and Framework', *International Organization*, 59/4: 801–26.

Checkel, J. T., and Moravcsik, A. (2001), 'A Constructivist Research Program in EU Studies?', *European Union Politics*, 2/2: 219–49.

Christian Science Monitor, various issues.

Christiansen, C., and Dobbels, M. (2013), 'Non-Legislative Rule Making after the Lisbon Treaty: Implementing the New System of Comitology and Delegated Acts', *European Law Journal*, 19/1: 42–56.

Christiansen, T., and Piattoni, S. (2004) (eds.), *Informal Governance in the EU* (Cheltenham: Edward Elgar).

Christiansen, T., Jørgensen, K. E., and Wiener, A. (1999), 'The Social Construction of Europe', *Journal of European Public Policy*, 6/4: 528–44.

Cini, M., and McGowan, L. (2009), *Competition Policy in the European Union*, 2nd edn. (Basingstoke: Palgrave Macmillan).

Cioloş, D. (2011), 'The CAP Beyond 2013—Challenges and Opportunities for European Agriculture', speech delivered at the Oxford Farming Conference, Oxford, 6 Jan., available at *http://europa.eu/rapid/press-release_SPEECH-11-3_en.htm?locale=en*.

Citi, M., and Rhodes, M. (2007), 'New Forms of Governance in the EU', in K. E. Jørgensen, M. A. Pollack, and B. Rosamond (eds.), *The Handbook of European Union Politics* (London: Sage), 463–82.

Clark, A. M., Friedman, E. J., and Hochstetler, K. (1998), 'The Sovereign Limits of Global Civil Society: A Comparison of NGO Participation in UN World Conferences on the Environment, Human Rights and Women', *World Politics*, 51/1: 1–35.

Clarke, R. (2006), 'Dominant Firms and Monopoly Policy in the UK and EU', in R. Clarke and E. Morgan (eds.), *New Developments in UK and EU Competition Policy* (Cheltenham: Edward Elgar), 22–50.

Cleveland, H. van B. (1966) (ed.), *The Atlantic Idea and its European Rivals* (New York, NY: McGraw-Hill).

Closa, C. (2004), 'The Convention Method and the Transformation of EU Constitutional Politics', in E. O. Eriksen, J. E. Fossum, and A. J. Menéndez (eds.), *Developing a Constitution for Europe* (Abingdon: Routledge), 183–206.

Cockfield, Lord (1994), *The European Union: Creating the Single Market* (London: Wiley Chancery Law).

Coen, D. (2007), 'Empirical and Theoretical Studies in EU Lobbying', *Journal of European Public Policy*, 14/3: 333–45.

Coen, D., and Katsaitis, A. (2013), 'Cameleon Pluralism in the EU: An Empirical Study of the European Commission Interest Group Density and Diversity across Policy Domains', *Journal of European Public Policy*, 20/8: 1104–19.

Coen, D., and Richardson, J. (2009) (eds.), *Lobbying in the European Union: Institutions, Actors and Issues* (Oxford: Oxford University Press).

Coen, D., and Thatcher, M. (2005) (eds.), 'The New Governance of Markets and Non-Majoritarian Regulators', *Governance*, 18/3 (special issue): 329–503.

Coen, D., and Thatcher, M. (2008a), 'Reshaping European Regulatory Space: An Evolutionary Analysis', *West European Politics*, 31/4: 806–36.

Coen, D., and Thatcher, M. (2008b). 'Network Governance and Multi-level Delegation: European Networks of Regulatory Agencies', *Journal of Public Policy*, 28/1: 49–71.

Cohen, B. J. (2009), 'Dollar Dominance, Euro Aspirations: Recipe for Discord?', *Journal of Common Market Studies*, 47/4: 741–66.

Cohen, J., and Sabel, C. (2003), 'Sovereignty and Solidarity in the EU', in J. Zeitlin and D. Trubek (eds.), *Governing Work and Welfare in a New Economy: European and American Experiments* (Oxford: Oxford University Press), 345–75.

Cohen, M., March, J., and Olsen, J. P. (1972), 'A Garbage Can Model of Organizational Choice', *Administrative Science Quarterly*, 17: 1–25.

Coleman, W. D., Skogstad, G. D., and Atkinson, M. M. (1997), 'Paradigm Shifts and Policy Networks: Cumulative Change in Agriculture', *Journal of Public Policy*, 16/3: 273–301.

Collins, D. (1975), *The European Communities: The Social Policy of the First Phase*, 2 vols. (London: Martin Robertson).

Collins, K., and Earnshaw, D. (1992), 'The Implementation and Enforcement of European Community Environment Legislation', *Environmental Politics*, 1/4: 213–49.

Commission of the European Union [henceforward Commission] (1969), Memorandum to the Council on the Co-ordination of Economic Policies and Monetary Co-operation Within the Community, *Bulletin of the EC*, Supplement 3/69.

Commission (1977–), *The Agricultural Situation in the European Union*, DG AGRI (previously The Agricultural Situation in the Community).

Commission (1985a), *Completing the Internal Market: White Paper from the Commission to the European Council*, COM (85) 310 final.

Commission (1985b), *Internal memo from DGIII to DGXI*, photocopy.

Commission (1989), *Reform of the Structural Funds: Explanatory Memorandum* (Brussels).

Commission (1993a), *Towards Sustainability: A European Community Programme of Policy and Action in Relation to the Environment and Sustainable Development* (Luxembourg: Office for Official Publications of the European Communities).

Commission (1993b), *Growth, Competitiveness, Employment: The Challenges and Ways Forward into the 21st Century*, White Paper, Parts A and B, COM (93) 700 final/A and B.

Commission (1994), *European Social Policy: A Way Forward for the Union*, A White Paper.

Commission (1995), *Preparation of the Associated Countries of Central and Eastern Europe for Integration into the Internal Market of the Union*, White Paper, COM (95) 163 final.

Commission (2000a), *Social Policy Agenda*, COM (2000) 379 final.

Commission (2000b), *Reforming the Commission: White Paper*, Part I, COM (2000) 200 final.

Commission (2001a), *Improving and Simplifying the Regulatory Environment: Interim Report from the Commission to the Stockholm European Council*, COM (2001) 130 final.

Commission (2001b), *Proposal for a Council Directive on the Conditions of Entry and Residence of Third-Country Nationals for the Purpose of Paid Employment and Self-Employed Economic Activities*, COM (2001) 386 final.

Commission (2001–12), *Eighteenth to Twenty-Ninth Annual Reports on Monitoring the Application of Community Law*, 2001–2012, available at *http://ec.europa.eu/community_law/infringements/infringements_annual_report_en.htm*.

Commission (2002a), *The State of the Internal Market for Services*, COM (2002) 441 final.

Commission (2002b), *The Internal Market: Ten Years without Frontiers*, available at *http://ec.europa.eu/internal_market/10years/docs/workingdoc/workingdoc_en.pdf*.

Commission (2003*a*), *Commission Recommendation on the Broad Guidelines of the Economic Policies of the Member States and the Community [2003–2005]*, COM (2003) 170 final.

Commission (2003*b*), *Communication from the Commission to the Council, Strengthening the Social Dimension of the Lisbon Strategy: Streamlining Open Coordination in the Field of Social Protection [2003–2009]*, COM (2003) 261 final.

Commission (2003*c*), *Communication from the European Commission: Modernising Social Protection for More and Better Jobs—A Comprehensive Approach Contributing to Making Work Pay*, COM (2003) 842 final.

Commission (2003*d*), *Green Paper on Services of General Interest*, COM (2003) 270 final.

Commission (2003*e*), *Wider Europe—Neighbourhood: A New Framework for Relations with our Eastern and Southern Neighbours*, 11 Mar. 2003, COM (2003) 104 final.

Commission (2004*a*), 'A New Partnership for Cohesion: Convergence, Competitiveness, Cooperation', Third Report on Economic and Social Cohesion (Luxembourg: European Communities).

Commission (2004*b*), *Proposal for a Directive of the European Parliament and of the Council on Services in the Internal Market*, COM (2004) 2 final.

Commission (2004*c*), *White Paper on Services of General Interest*, COM (2004) 374 final.

Commission (2006*a*), *EU Economy Review* (Luxembourg: Office for Official Publications of the European Communities).

Commission (2006*b*), *An Energy Policy for Europe*, COM (2007) 1 final.

Commission (2006*c*), *Global Europe: Competing in the World: A Contribution to the EU's Growth and Jobs Strategy*, COM (2006) 567 final, 4 Oct.

Commission (2006*d*), *Enlargement Strategy and Main Challenges 2006–2007, ANNEX 1: Special Report on the EU's Capacity to Integrate New Members*, 8 Nov., COM (2006) 649 final.

Commission (2007*a*), *A Single Market for 21st Century Europe*, COM (2007) 724 final, 20 Nov.

Commission (2007*b*), *Strategic Report on the Renewed Lisbon Strategy for Growth and Jobs: Launching the New Cycle 2008–2010*, COM (2007) 803 final.

Commission (2007*c*), *Cohesion Policy 2007–13: Commentaries and Official Texts* (Luxembourg: Office for Official Publications of the European Communities).

Commission (2007*d*), 'Energy Sector Competition Inquiry—Final Report—Frequently Asked Questions and Graphics', Press Release MEMO/07/15, available at *http://europa.eu/rapid/press-release_MEMO-07-15_en.htm?locale=en*.

Commission (2007*e*), *Green Paper on the Future Common European Asylum System of 2007*, COM (2007) 301 final.

Commission (2007*f*), *Together for Health: A Strategic Approach for the EU 2008–2013*, White Paper, COM (2007) 630 final, 23 Nov.

Commission (2008*a*), 'Boosting Growth and Jobs by Meeting Our Climate Change Commitments', Press Release IP/08/80, 23 Jan., available at *http://europa.eu/rapid/press-release_IP-08-80_en.htm*.

Commission (2008*b*), 'Securing Your Energy Future: Commission Presents Energy Security, Solidarity and Efficiency Proposals', Press Release IP/08/1696, 13 Nov., available at *http://europa.eu/rapid/press-release_IP-08-1696_en.htm?locale=en*.

Commission (2008c), *Report to the European Parliament and the Council on the Application of Directive 2003/86/EC on the Right to Family Reunification*, COM (2008) 610 final.

Commission (2008d), *One Currency for One Europe: The Road to the Euro* (Luxembourg: Office for Official Publications of the European Communities).

Commission (2008e), *Proposal for a Directive of the European Parliament and the Council on the Application of Patients' Rights in Cross-Border Healthcare*, COM (2008) 414 final.

Commission (2008f), *Renewed Social Agenda: Opportunities, Access and Solidarity in 21st Century Europe*, COM (2008) 412 final.

Commission (2009a), *Internal Market Scoreboard*, 18.

Commission (2009b), *Financial Report 2008* (Luxembourg: Office for Official Publications of the European Communities).

Commission (2010a), *Towards a Single Market Act: For a Highly Competitive Social Market Economy*, COM (2010) 608 final.

Commission (2010b), *EUROPE 2020—A Strategy for Smart Sustainable and Inclusive Growth*, COM (2010) 2020 final.

Commission (2010c), *Communication from the Commission to the European Parliament, the Council, the Economic and Social Committee and the Committee of the Regions: Towards a Single Market Act for a Highly Competitive Social Market Economy—50 Proposals for Improving our Work, Business and Exchanges With One Another*, COM (2010) 608 final.

Commission (2010d), *Communication on Delivering an Area of Freedom, Security and Justice for Europe's Citizens—Action Plan Implementing the Stockholm Programme*, COM (2010) 171 final.

Commission (2010e), *Trade Growth and World Affairs*, COM (2010) 612 final.

Commission (2010f), 'Commission Re-launches CARS 21 High Level Group for a Competitive and Sustainable Automotive Industry', Press Release IP/10/1491, available at *http://europa.eu/rapid/press-release_IP-10-1491_en.htm?locale=en*.

Commission (2011a), *Single Market Act*, COM (2011) 206 final.

Commission (2011b), *Communication on the Future of VAT*, COM (2011) 851 final.

Commission (2011c), *Communication from the Commission to the European Parliament, the Council, the European Economic and Social Committee and the Committee of the Regions. A Roadmap for Moving to a Competitive Low Carbon Economy in 2050*, COM (2011) 112 final.

Commission (2011d), *Communication from the Commission to the European Parliament, the Council, the European Economic and Social Committee and the Committee of the Regions. Roadmap to a Resource Efficient Europe*, COM (2011) 571 final.

Commission (2011e), *Second Evaluation Report on the EU Pilot*, SEC (2011) 1629/2.

Commission (2011f), *Proposal for a Regulation of the European Parliament and of the Council Establishing Rules for Direct Payments to Farmers under Support Schemes within the Framework of the Common Agricultural Policy*, COM (2011) 625 final/2.

Commission (2011g), *Proposal for a Regulation of the European Parliament and of the Council establishing a Common Organisation of the Markets in Agricultural Products*, COM (2011) 626 final/2.

Commission (2011h), *Proposal for a Regulation of the European Parliament and of the Council on Support for Rural Development by the European Agricultural Fund for Rural Development (EAFRD)*, COM (2011) 627 final/2.

Commission (2011i), *Proposal for a Regulation of the European Parliament and of the Council on the Financing, Management and Monitoring of the Common Agricultural Policy*, COM (2011) 628 final/2.

Commission (2012a), *Translation and Multilingualism*, DG Translation (Brussels).

Commission (2012b), *Communication from the Commission to the European Parliament, the Council, the European Economic and Social Committee and the Committee of the Regions on the Implementation of the Services Directive: A Partnership for New Growth in Services, 2012–2015*, COM (2012) 261 final.

Commission (2012c), *EU Regulatory Fitness*, COM (2012) 746 final.

Commission (2012d), *Single Market Act II: Together for New Growth*, COM (2012) 573 final.

Commission (2012e), *Commission Staff Working Paper: Autumn 2012 Update*, COM (2012) 778.

Commission (2012f), *Financial Report 2011* (Luxembourg: Office for Official Publications of the European Communities).

Commission (2012g), 'How the Budget is Decided?', available at *http://ec.europa.eu/budget/explained/management/deciding/decide_en.cfm*.

Commission (2012h), *White Paper: An Agenda for Adequate, Safe and Sustainable Pensions*, COM (2012) 55 final.

Commission (2012i), *Pension Adequacy in the European Union 2010–2050. Report Prepared Jointly by the Directorate-General for Employment, Social Affairs and Inclusion of the European Commission and the Social Protection Committee*, 23 May.

Commission (2012j), *Proposal for a Council Regulation on the Exercise of the Right to Take Collective Action within the Context of the Freedom of Establishment and the Freedom to Provide Services*, COM (2012) 130 final.

Commission (2012k), 'New Environment Action Programme to 2020: Questions and Answers', Press Release Memo/12/908, available at *http://europa.eu/rapid/press-release_MEMO-12-908_en.htm*.

Commission (2012l), *Communication from the Commission to the European Parliament, the Council and the European Economic and Social Committee, Trade, Growth and Development*, COM (2012), 22 final.

Commission (2012m), *DG Home Affairs 2012 Annual Activity Report*, available at *http://ec.europa.eu/atwork/synthesis/aar/doc/home_aar_2012.pdf*.

Commission (2013a), *Internal Market Scoreboard*, 26.

Commission (2013b), *Standard Eurobarometer*, 79.

Commission (2013c), *Report on Competition Policy 2012*, Brussels, COM (2013) 257.

Commission (2013d), *Proposal for a Directive on Certain Rules Governing Actions for Damages under National Law for Infringements of the Competition Law Provisions of the Member States and the European Union*, COM (2013) 404.

Commission (2013e), *Communication from the Commission on the Application from 1 August 2013 of State Aid Rules to Support Measures in Favour of Banks in the Context of the Financial Crisis ('Banking Communication')* (*Official Journal* C 216, 30.7.2013).

Commission (2013f), 'European Economic Forecast: Spring 2013', *European Economy*, No. 2 (Luxembourg: Office for Official Publications of the European Communities).

Commission (2013g), *Financial Report 2012* (Luxembourg: Office for Official Publications of the European Communities).

Commission (2013*h*), *General Budget of the European Union for the Financial Year 2013* (Luxembourg: Office for Official Publications of the European Communities).

Commission (2013*i*), 'Glossary: Appropriations', available at *http://ec.europa.eu/budget/ explained/glossary/glossary_en.cfm#a*.

Commission (2013*j*), *Communication from the Commission to the European Parliament and the Council Strengthening the Social Dimension of the Economic and Monetary Union*, COM (2013) 690 provisoire.

Commission (2013*k*), 'Renewable Energy: Commission Refers Poland and Cyprus to Court for Failing to Transpose EU Rules', Press Release IP/13/259, available at *http://europa.eu/ rapid/press-release_IP-13-259_en.htm*.

Commission (2013*l*), *Green Paper: A 2030 Framework for Climate and Energy Policies*, COM (2013) 169 final.

Commission (2013*m*), *Delivering the Internal Electricity Market and Making the Most of Public Intervention*, COM (2013) 7243 final.

Commission (2013*n*), *Communication from the Commission to the Council and the European Parliament on Modernisation of Trade Defence Instruments*, COM (2013) 191 final.

Commission (2013*o*), *Commission Staff Working Document: Report from the Commission on Competition Policy 2012*, SWD (2013) 159 final, 11–12.

Commission (2014*a*), 'EU Economic Governance: The European Semester', available at *http://ec.europa.eu/economy_finance/economic_governance/the_european_semester/index_ en.htm*.

Commission (2014*b*), *A Policy Framework for Climate and Energy in the Period from 2020 to 2030*, COM (2014) 15 final.

Commission (2014*c*), *Recommendation on Minimum Principles for the Exploration and Production of Hydrocarbons (such as shale gas) Using High Volume Hydraulic Fracturing*, COM (2014) 267/3 final.

Commission (2014*d*), 'Questions and Answers on the Proposed Market Stability Reserve for the EU Emissions Trading System', Press Release Memo/14/39, available at *http://europa. eu/rapid/press-release_MEMO-14-39_en.htm*.

Commission (2014*e*), *AMECO—The Annual Macro-Economic Database*, available at *http:// ec.europa.eu/economy_finance/db_indicators/ameco/index_en.htm*.

Committee of the Regions (2011), 'Opinion of the Committee of the Regions on "Measuring Progress—GDP and Beyond"', *Official Journal* C 15/04, 18.1.2011.

Conant, L. (2002), *Justice Contained: Law and Politics in the European Union* (Ithaca, NY: Cornell University Press).

Conant, L. (2007*a*), 'Review Article: The Politics of Legal Integration', *Journal of Common Market Studies*, 45/s1: 45–66.

Conant, L. (2007*b*), 'Judicial Politics', in K. E. Jørgensen, M. A. Pollack, and B. Rosamond (eds.), *The Handbook of European Union Politics* (London: Sage), 213–29.

Considine, M., and Dukelow, F. (2012), 'From Financial Crisis to Welfare Retrenchment: Assessing the Challenges to the Irish Welfare State', in M. Kilkey, G. Ramia, and K. Farnsworth (eds.), *Social Policy Review 24, Analysis and Debate in Social Policy, 2012* (Bristol: Policy Press), 257–76.

Contouris, N., and Horton, K. (2009), 'The Temporary Agency Work Directive: Another Broken Promise', *Industrial Law Journal*, 38/3: 329–38.

Cooper, I. (2012), 'A "Virtual Third Chamber" for the European Union? National Parliaments after the Treaty of Lisbon', *West European Politics*, 35/3: 441–65.

Cooper, R. (2003), *The Breaking of Nations: Order and Chaos in the Twenty-First Century* (London: Atlantic Books).

Copeland, P., and ter Haar, B. (2013), 'A Toothless Bite? The Effectiveness of the European Employment Strategy as a Governance Tool', *Journal of European Social Policy*, 23/1: 21–36.

Corbett, R., Jacobs, F., and Shackleton, M. (2011), *The European Parliament*, 8th edn. (London: John Harper).

Costello, C., and Davies, G. (2006), 'The Case Law of the Court of Justice in the Field of Sex Equality since 2000', *Common Market Law Review*, 43/6: 1567–616.

Council of Europe (2013), *Parliamentary Assembly Resolution on Frontex: Human Rights Responsibilities*, Resolution 1932, available at *http://assembly.coe.int/ASP/XRef/X2H-DW-XSL.asp?fileid=19719&lang=en*.

Court of Justice of the European Union (2013), *Annual Report 2012*.

Cowles, M. G. (1994), 'The Politics of Big Business in the European Community: Setting the Agenda for a New Europe', Ph.D. dissertation, The American University, Washington, DC.

Cowles, M. G., Caporaso, J. A., and Risse, T. (2001) (eds.), *Transforming Europe: Europeanization and Domestic Change* (Ithaca, NY: Cornell University Press).

Crotty, J. (2009), 'Structural Causes of the Global Financial Crisis: A Critical Assessment of the "New Financial Architecture"', *Cambridge Journal of Economics*, 33/4: 563–80.

Cruz, J. B. (2006), 'The Luxembourg Compromise From a Legal Perspective: Constitutional Convention, Legal History, or Political Myth?', in J.-M. Palayret, H. Wallace, and P. Winand (eds.), *Visions, Votes, and Vetoes: The Empty Chair Crisis and the Luxembourg Compromise Forty Years On* (Brussels: Peter Lang International Academic Publishers).

Cunha, A., with Swinbank. A. (2011), *An Inside View of the CAP Reform Process* (Oxford: Oxford University Press).

Dahl, R. (1961), *Who Governs? Democracy and Power in an American City* (New Haven, CT: Yale University Press).

Daly, M. (2008), 'Whither EU Social Policy? An Account and Assessment of Developments in the Lisbon Social Inclusion Process', *Journal of Social Policy*, 37/1: 1–19.

Damro, C. (2012), 'Market Power Europe', *Journal of European Public Policy*, 19/5: 682–99.

Dashwood, A. (1977), 'Hastening Slowly: The Communities' Path Towards Harmonization', in H. Wallace, W. Wallace, and C. Webb (eds.), *Policy-Making in the European Communities* (Chichester: Wiley), 273–99.

Dashwood, A. (1983), 'Hastening Slowly: The Communities' Path towards Harmonization', in H. Wallace, W. Wallace, and C. Webb (eds.), *Policy-Making in the European Communities*, 2nd edn. (Chichester: Wiley), 177–208.

Daugbjerg, C. (1999), 'Reforming the CAP: Policy Networks and Broader Institutional Structures', *Journal of Common Market Studies*, 37/3: 407–28.

Daugbjerg, C., and Roederer-Rynning, C. (2014), 'The EU's Common Agricultural Policy: A Case of Defensive Policy Import', in G. Falkner and P. Müller (eds.), *EU Policies in a Global Perspective: Shaping or Taking International Regimes?* (London: Routledge).

Daugbjerg, C., and Swinbank, A. (2009), *Ideas, Institutions and Trade: The WTO and the Curious Role of EU Farm Policy in Trade Liberalization* (Oxford: Oxford University Press).

Davies, A. C. L. (2008), '"One Step Forwards, Two Steps Back?" The *Viking* and *Laval* Cases in the ECJ', *Industrial Law Journal*, 37/2: 126–48.

Davies, A. C. L. (2012), *EU Labour Law* (Cheltenham: Edward Elgar).

Daviter, F. (2007), 'Policy Framing in the European Union', *Journal of European Public Policy*, 14/4: 654–66.

Deakin, S. (2007), 'Reflexive Governance and European Company Law', Working Paper No. 346, Centre for Business Research, University of Cambridge, available at *http://www.cbr.cam.ac.uk/pdf/wp346.pdf*.

De Grauwe, P. (2006), 'What Have We Learnt about Monetary Integration since the Maastricht Treaty?', *Journal of Common Market Studies*, 44/4: 711–30.

De Grauwe, P. (2012), *The Economics of Monetary Union*, 9th edn. (Oxford: Oxford University Press).

Dehousse, R. (1998), *The European Court of Justice* (Basingstoke: Palgrave Macmillan).

Dehousse, R. (2011) (ed.), *The Community Method: Obstinate or Obsolete?* (Basingstoke: Palgrave Macmillan).

Dehousse, R. (2012), 'The "Fiscal Compact": Legal Uncertainty and Political Ambiguity', Notre Europe Policy Brief No. 33 (Paris: Notre Europe).

Dehousse, R., Deloche-Gaudez, F., and Duhamel, O. (2007), *Élargissement: Comment l'Europe s'adapte* (Paris: Les Presses Sciences Po).

De la Porte, C., and Nanz, P. (2004), 'OMC—A Deliberative-Democratic Mode of Governance? The Cases of Employment and Pensions', *Journal of European Public Policy*, 11/2: 267–88.

Delfani, N. (2013), 'Experts versus Politicians: The Role of Partisan Ideology in European Union Employment Policy', *Comparative European Politics*, 11/1: 70–92.

della Sala, V. (2004), 'Maastricht to Modernization: EMU and the Italian Social State', in A. Martin and G. Ross (eds.), *Euros and Europeans: Monetary Integration and the European Model of Society* (Cambridge: Cambridge University Press), 126–41.

Delreux, T. (2011), *The EU as International Environmental Negotiator* (Farnham: Ashgate).

Deroose, S., Hodson, D., and Kuhlmann, J. (2008), 'The Broad Economic Policy Guidelines: Before and After the Re-launch of the Lisbon Strategy', *Journal of Common Market Studies*, 46/4: 827–48.

Derthick, M., and Quirk, P. J. (1986), *The Politics of Deregulation* (Washington, DC: Brookings Institution).

Devuyst, Y. (1995), 'The EC and the Conclusion of the Uruguay Round', in C. Rhodes and S. Mazey (eds.), *The State of the European Union, vol. iii: Building a European Polity?* (Boulder, CO/Harlow: Lynne Rienner and Longman), 449–68.

Devuyst, Y. (2013), 'European Union Law and Practice in the Negotiation and Conclusion of International Trade Agreements', *Journal of International Business and Law*, 12/2: 259–316.

Dinan, D. (2004), *Europe Recast: A History of European Union* (Basingstoke: Palgrave Macmillan).

Dinan, D. (2011), 'Governance and Institutions: Implementing the Lisbon Treaty in the Shadow of the Euro Crisis', *Journal of Common Market Studies*, 49/s1: 103–21.

Dinan, D. (2012), 'Governance and Institutions: Impact of the Escalating Crisis', *Journal of Common Market Studies*, 50/s1: 85–98.

Dølvik, J. E. (2006), 'Industrial Relations Responses to Migration and Posting of Workers after EU Enlargement: Nordic Trends and Differences', *Transfer: European Review of Labour and Research*, 12/2: 213–30.

Dowding, K. (1995), 'Model or Metaphor? A Critical Review of the Policy Network Approach', *Political Studies*, 43/1: 136–58.

Downs, A. (1972), 'Up and Down with Ecology—The Issue-Attention Cycle', *Public Interest*, 28/3: 38–50.

Drahos, M. (2001), *Convergence of Competition Laws and Policies in the European Community* (Duventer: Kluwer).

Drezner, D. W. (2007), *All Politics is Global: Explaining International Regulatory Regimes* (Princeton, NJ: Princeton University Press).

Dröge, S. (2013), 'Europäische Finanz- und Schuldenkrise: Negative Folgen für die europäische Klimapolitik', in R. Kempin and M. Overhaus (eds.), *EU-Außenpolitik in Zeiten der Finanz- und Schuldenkrise* (Berlin: Stiftung Wissneschaft und Politik), 59–68.

Dukelow, F. (2011), 'Economic Crisis and Welfare Retrenchment: Comparing Irish Policy Responses in the 1970s and 1980s with the Present', *Social Policy and Administration*, 45/4: 408–29.

Dunleavy, P. (1997), 'Explaining Centralization of the European Union: A Public Choice Analysis', *Aussenwirtschaft*, 55/1–2: 183–212.

Dyson, K. (2000), *The Politics of the Euro-Zone: Stability or Breakdown?* (Oxford: Oxford University Press).

Dyson, K., and Featherstone, K. (1999), *The Road to Maastricht: Negotiating Economic and Monetary Union* (Oxford: Oxford University Press).

Eberlein, B., and Grande, E. (2005), 'Beyond Delegation: Transnational Regulatory Regimes and the EU Regulatory State', *Journal of European Public Policy*, 12/1: 89–112.

ECB (European Central Bank) (2008), *Monthly Bulletin (10th Anniversary of the ECB)*, 05/08 (Frankfurt am Main: ECB).

ECB (European Central Bank) (2013), *The Eurosystem Household Finance and Consumption Survey: Results from the First Wave*, Statistics Paper Series No. 1 (Frankfurt am Main: ECB).

Economist, various issues.

ECOTECH (2003), *Evaluation of the Added Value and Costs of the European Structural Funds in the UK, Final Report to Department of Trade and Industry (DTI) and Office of the Deputy Prime Minister (ODPM)* (London: DTI/ODPM).

Eeckhout, P. (2011), *EU External Relations Law*, 2nd edn. (Oxford: Oxford University Press).

Egan, M. (2012), 'Single Market', in E. Jones, A. Menon, and S. Weatherill (eds.), *The Oxford Handbook of the European Union* (Oxford: Oxford University Press), 407–21.

Egeberg, M. (2008), 'European Government(s): Executive Politics in Transition?', *West European Politics*, 31/1–2: 235–57.

Egenhofer, C., and Alessi, M. (2013), 'EU Policy on Climate Change Mitigation since Copenhagen and the Economic Crisis', CEPS Working Document No. 380 (Brussels: Centre for European Policy Studies).

Eichener, V. (1997), 'Effective European Problem Solving: Lessons from the Regulation of Occupational Safety and Environmental Protection', *Journal of European Public Policy*, 4/4: 591–608.

Eichener, V. (2000), *Das Entscheidungssystem der Europäischen Union: Institutionelle Analyse und demokratietheoretische Bewertung* (Opladen: Leske + Budrich).

Eichengreen, B. (1992), *Should the Maastricht Treaty be Saved?*, Princeton Studies in International Finance, No. 74 (Princeton, NJ: Princeton University Economics Department).

Eichenhofer, E. (2003), 'Unionsbürgerschaft—Sozialbürgerschaft?', *Zeitschrift für ausländisches und internationales Arbeits- und Sozialrecht*, 17/3–4: 404–17.

Eichenhofer, E. (2004), 'Diskriminierungsschutz und Privatautonomie', *Deutsches Verwaltungsblatt*, 119/17 (1 Sept.): 1078–86.

Eichenhofer, E. (2013), *Sozialrecht der Europäischen Union*, 5th edn. (Berlin: Erich Schmidt).

Eichhorst, W. (1998), *European Social Policy between National and Supranational Regulation: Posted Workers in the Framework of Liberalized Services Provisions*, MPIfG Discussion Paper 98/6 (Cologne: Max Planck Institute for the Study of Societies).

Eichhorst, W. (2000), *Europäische Sozialpolitik zwischen nationaler Autonomie und Marktfreiheit: die Entsendung von Arbeitnehmern in der EU* (Frankfurt am Main: Campus).

Eigenmüller, M. (2013), 'Europeanization From Below: The Influence of Individual Actors on the EU Integration of Social Policies', *Journal of European Social Policy*, 23/4: 363–75.

Eigenmüller, M., and Börner, S. (2014), 'Social Security in Europe between Territorialisation, Legitimacy and Identity Formation. Towards a Diachronic Perspective for Analysing Social Policy Rescaling', *European Journal of Social Theory*.

Elbasani, A. (2013) (ed.), *European Integration and Transformation in the Western Balkans: Europeanization of Business as Usual?* (London: Routledge).

Eliasoph, I. H. (2007–8), 'A "Switch in Time" for the European Community? Lochner Discourse and the Recalibration of Economic and Social Rights in Europe', *Columbia Journal of European Law*, 14/3: 467–508.

Elsig, M. (2008), 'EU Trade Policy After Enlargement: Does the Expanded Trade Power Have New Clothes?', paper for the APSA Annual Conference, Boston, 28–31 Aug.

Elster, J. (1998) (ed.), *Deliberative Democracy* (Cambridge: Cambridge University Press).

Emmert, F. (1996), *Europarecht* (Munich: C. H. Beck).

Enderlein, H., Lindner, J., Calvo-Gonzalez, O., and Ritter, R. (2007), 'The EU Budget: How Much Scope for Institutional Reform?', in H. Berger and T. Moutos (eds.), *Designing the New European Union* (Oxford: Elsevier), 129–59.

Engberg, K. (2014), *The EU and Military Operations: A Comparative Analysis* (London: Routledge).

Epiney, A. (2007), 'The Scope of Article 12 EC: Some Remarks on the Influence of European Citizenship', *European Law Journal*, 13/5: 611–22.

Epstein, D., and O'Halloran, S. (1999), *Delegating Powers: A Transaction Cost Politics Approach to Policy Making under Separate Powers* (Cambridge: Cambridge University Press).

Epstein, R. A., and Jacoby, W. (2014a) (eds.), 'Eastern Enlargement Ten Years On: Transcending the East-West Divide?', *Journal of Common Market Studies*, 52/1 (special issue): 1-174.

Epstein, R. A., and Jacoby, W. (2014b), 'Eastern Enlargement Ten Years On: Transcending the East-West Divide?', *Journal of Common Market Studies*, 52/1: 1–16.

Epstein, R. A., and Sedelmeier, U. (2008), 'Beyond Conditionality: International Institutions in Postcommunist Europe after Enlargement', *Journal of European Public Policy*, 15/6: 795–805.

Epstein, R. A., and Sedelmeier, U. (2009), *International Influence Beyond Conditionality: Postcommunist Europe after EU Enlargement* (London: Routledge).

Eriksen, E. O., and Fossum, J. E. (2000), 'Post-National Integration', in E. O. Eriksen and J. E. Fossum (eds.), *Democracy in the European Union* (London: Routledge), 1–28.

Eriksen, E. O., and Fossum, J. E. (2003), 'Closing the Legitimacy Gap?', available at *http://www.arena.uio.no/ecsa/papers/FossumEriksen.pdf*.

Ette, A., and Faist, T. (2007) (eds.), *The Europeanization of National Policies and Politics of Immigration* (Basingstoke: Palgrave Macmillan).

EUobserver.com, various issues.

Eureport, various issues.

Eureport social, various issues.

Eurobarometer (2008), 'The Role of the EU in Justice, Freedom and Security Policy Areas', *Special Eurobarometer* 290, Brussels.

Eurobarometer (2009), 'The Europeans in 2009', *Special Eurobarometer* 308.

Eurobarometer (2010), 'The Internal Market: Awareness—Perceptions—Impacts', *Flash Eurobarometer* 263, Mar.

Eurobarometer (2014), 'The Europeans in 2014', *Special Eurobarometer* 415.

European Communities (1969), 'Communiqué of the Meeting of Heads of State or Government of the Member States at The Hague, 1–2 December 1969', available at *http://www.ena.lu/*.

European Council (1999), *Presidency Conclusions*, Helsinki European Council 10–11 Dec., SN 300/1/99.

European Council (2000), *Presidency Conclusions*, Lisbon European Council, 23–24 Mar., SN 100/00.

European Council (2003), 'A Secure Europe in a Better World: European Security Strategy', *Presidency Conclusions*, Brussels, 12 Dec., available at *http://www.consilium.europa.eu/uedocs/cmsUpload/78367.pdf*.

European Council (2005a), *The European Union Counter-Terrorism Strategy*, 30 Nov., 14469/4/05.

European Council (2005b), *A Strategy on the External Dimension of JHA*, 30 Nov., 14366/3/05, REV 3.

European Council (2008), *Presidency Conclusions*, Brussels European Council, 15–16 Oct., 14368/08.

European Council (2011), *Presidency Conclusions*, Brussels European Council, 23 Oct., 52/1/11, REV 1.

European Council (2013a), *Conclusions (Multiannual Financial Framework)*, Brussels European Council, 7–8 Feb., 37/13, CO EUR 5, CONCL3.

European Council (2013b), *Presidency Conclusions*, Brussels European Council, 19–20 Dec., 217/13.

European Defence Agency (2013), 'Defence Data 2011', available at *https://www.eda.europa.eu/info-hub/defence-data-portal*.

European Defence Agency (2014), 'National Defence Data 2012 of the EDA participating Member States', Brussels, February, available at *http://www.eda.europa.eu/docs/default-source/finance-documents/national-defence-data-2012.pdf*.

European Environment Agency (1999), *Environment in the European Union at the Turn of the Century*, Environmental Assessment Report No. 2 (Copenhagen: EEA), available at *http://reports.eea.eu.int*.

European External Action Service (2013), 'EEAS Review', Brussels, 29 July, available at *http://eeas.europa.eu/library/publications/2013/3/2013_eeas_review_en.pdf*.

European Ombudsman (2013), *Special Report in Own-Initiative Inquiry, OI/5/2012/BEH-MHZ concerning Frontex*, 12 Nov., available at *http://www.ombudsman.europa.eu/en/cases/specialreport.faces/en/52465/html.bookmark#_ftn3*.

European Parliament (1964), *Towards Political Union: A Selection of Documents*, General Directorate of Parliamentary Documentation and Information, Jan. 1964, available at *http://aei.pitt.edu/944/01/towards_political_union_1.pdf*.

European Parliament (1984), *Draft Treaty Establishing the European Union* (Luxembourg: European Parliament).

European Parliament (1996), *Working Document on Implementation of Community Environmental Law*, Committee on the Environment, Public Health and Consumer Protection, PE 219. 240.

European Parliament (2007), *Report on the Future of the European Union's Own Resources*, 2006/2205(INI), Committee on Budgets.

European Parliament (2008), *Draft Report on a Regulation Establishing an Agency for the Cooperation of Energy Regulators*, 11 Feb.

European Parliament (2013), *European Council Conclusions on the Multiannual Financial Framework 2014–2020 and the CAP: Note* (Brussels: Policy Department B).

European Report, various issues.

European Union Institute for Security Studies (2013), *EUISS Yearbook of European Security* (Paris: European Union Institute for Security Studies).

European Voice, various issues.

Evans, P. B. (1993), 'Building an Integrative Approach to International and Domestic Politics: Reflections and Projections', in P. B. Evans, H. K. Jacobson, and R. D. Putnam (eds.), *Double-Edged Diplomacy: International Bargaining and Domestic Politics* (Berkeley, CA: University of California Press), 397–430.

Evenett, S., and Meier, M. (2007), 'An Interim Assessment of US Trade Policy of "Competitive Liberalization"', University of St Gallen, Economic Discussion Paper No. 18, Feb.

Ewing, K. (2012), 'The Draft Monti II Regulation: the Inadequate Response to *Viking* and *Laval*', Institution of Employment Rights Briefing Paper (London: Institute of Employment Rights).

Falkner, G. (1998), *EU Social Policy in the 1990s: Towards a Corporatist Policy Community* (London: Routledge).

Falkner, G. (2010), 'Institutional Performance and Compliance with EU Law: Czech Republic, Hungary, Slovakia and Slovenia', *Journal of Public Policy*, 30/1: 101–16.

Falkner, G., and Müller, P. (2013) (eds.), *EU Policies in a Global Perspective: Shaping or Taking International Regimes?* (London: Routledge).

Falkner, G., and Treib, O. (2008), 'Three Worlds of Compliance or Four? The EU-15 Compared to New Member States', *Journal of Common Market Studies*, 46/2: 293–313.

Falkner, G., Hartlapp, M., and Treib, O. (2007), 'Worlds of Compliance: Why Leading Approaches to European Union Implementation Are Only "Sometimes-True Theories"', *European Journal of Political Research*, 46/3, 395–416.

Falkner, G., Treib, O., Hartlapp, M., and Leiber, S. (2005), *Complying with Europe: EU Harmonisation and Soft Law in the Member States* (Cambridge: Cambridge University Press).

Falkner, G., Treib, O., and Holzleithner, E., in cooperation with Causse, E., Furtlehner, P., Schulze, M., and Wiedermann, C. (2008), *Compliance in the Enlarged European Union: Living Rights or Dead Letters?* (Aldershot: Ashgate).

Farmer, A. (2011, continuously updated) (ed.), *Manual of Environmental Policy* (London: Taylor & Francis).

Farrell, H., and Héritier, A. (2003), 'Formal and Informal Institutions under Codecision: Continuous Constitution-Building in Europe', *Governance*, 16/4: 577–600.

Felsenthal, D. S., and Machover, M. (1997), 'The Weighted Voting Rule in the Council of Ministers, 1958–95: Intentions and Outcomes', *Electoral Studies*, 16/1, 34–47.

Felsenthal, D. S., and Machover, M. (2004), 'A Priori Voting Power: What is it All About?' *Political Studies Review*, 2/1: 1–24.

Fennell, R. (1997), *The Common Agricultural Policy: Continuity and Change* (Oxford: Clarendon Press).

Ferrera, M., and Gualmini, E. (2004), *Rescued by Europe? Social and Labour Market Reforms in Italy from Maastricht to Berlusconi* (Amsterdam: Amsterdam University Press).

Financial Times, various issues.

Fioretos, O. (2011), 'Historical Institutionalism in International Relations', *International Organization*, 65/2: 367–99.

Fisher, R., and Ury, W. (1982), *Getting to Yes: How to Reach Agreement without Giving In* (London: Hutchinson).

Fligstein, N. (2009), *Euroclash: The EU, European Identity, and the Future of Europe* (New York, NY: Oxford University Press).

Forwood, N. (2008), 'The Court of First Instance, Its Development, and Future Role in the Legal Architecture of the European Union', in A. Arnull, P. Eeckhout, and T. Tridimas (eds.), *Continuity and Change in EU Law: Essays in Honour of Sir Francis Jacobs* (Oxford: Oxford University Press), 34–47.

Fouilleux, E. (2003), *La Politique Agricole Commune et ses Réformes* (Paris: L'Harmattan).

Franchino, F. (2004), 'Delegating Powers in the European Community', *British Journal of Political Science*, 34/2: 449–76.

Franchino, F. (2007), *The Powers of the Union: Delegation in the EU* (Cambridge: Cambridge University Press).

Franzius, C. (2003), 'Der "Gewährleistungsstaat": Ein neues Leitbild für den sich wandelnden Staat', *Der Staat*, 42/4: 493–517.

Freyburg, T., and Richter, S. (2010), 'National Identity Matters: The Limited Impact of EU Political Conditionality in the Western Balkans', *Journal of European Public Policy*, 17/2: 262–80.

Freyer, T. (2006), *Antitrust and Global Capitalism, 1930–2004* (Cambridge: Cambridge University Press).

Friedrich, A., Tappe, M., and Wurzel, R. (2002), 'A New Approach to EU Environmental Policy-making? The Auto-Oil I Programme', *Journal of European Public Policy*, 7/4: 593–612.

Friis, L. (1998), 'The End of the Beginning of Eastern Enlargement: Luxembourg Summit and Agenda-Setting', European Integration online Papers, 2/7, available at *http://eiop.or.at/eiop*.

Friis, L., and Murphy, A. (2000), 'Turbo-Charged Negotiations: The EU and the Stability Pact for South Eastern Europe', *Journal of European Public Policy*, 7/5: 767–86.

Fuchs, M. (2003), 'Koordinierung oder Harmonisierung des europäischen Sozialrechts?', *Zeitschrift für ausländisches und internationales Arbeits- und Sozialrecht*, 17/3–4: 379–90.

Fuchs, M. (2013) (ed.), *Europäisches* Sozialrecht, 6th edn. (Baden-Baden: Nomos).

Gabel, M., Hix, S., and Schneider, G. (2002), 'Who is Afraid of Cumulative Research? The Scarcity of EU Decision-Making Data and What Can Be Done about This', *European Union Politics*, 3/4: 481–500.

Garrett, G. (1992), 'International Cooperation and Institutional Choice: The European Community's Internal Market', *International Organization*, 46/2: 533–60.

Garrett, G. (1995), 'The Politics of Legal Integration in the EU', *International Organization*, 49/1: 171–81.

Garrett, G., and Tsebelis, G. (1996), 'An Institutional Critique of Intergovernmentalism', *International Organization*, 50/2: 269–99.

Garrett, G., and Weingast, B. (1993), 'Ideas, Interests, and Institutions: Constructing the European Community's Internal Market', in J. Goldstein and R. O. Keohane (eds.), *Ideas and Foreign Policy: Beliefs, Institutions and Political Change* (Ithaca, NY: Cornell University Press), 173–206.

Garzon, I. (2006), *Reforming the Common Agricultural Policy: History of a Paradigm Change* (Basingstoke: Palgrave Macmillan).

Gateva, E. (2013), 'Post-Accession Conditionality: Translating Benchmarks into Political Pressure?', *East European Politics*, 29/4: 420–2.

George, S. (1991), *Politics in the European Union* (Oxford: Oxford University Press).

Gheciu, A. (2005), 'Security Institutions as Agents of Socialization? NATO and the "New Europe"', *International Organization*, 59/4: 973–1012.

Giegerich, B. (2008), *European Military Crisis Management: Connecting Ambition and Reality*, Adelphi Paper No. 397 (London: Routledge for the International Institute for Strategic Studies).

Giegerich, B., and Nicoll, A. (2012), 'The Struggle for Value in European Defence', *Survival: Global Politics and Strategy*, 54/1: 53–82.

Giegerich, B., and Wallace, W. (2004), 'Not Such a Soft Power: The External Deployment of European Forces', *Survival: Global Politics and Strategy*, 46/2: 63–82.

Giesen, R. (2005), 'Nationales Sozialrecht und europäisches Wettbewerbsrecht—das Wettbewerbsziel in der Rationalitätenfalle', in U. Becker and W. Schön (eds.), *Steuer- und Sozialstaat im europäischen Systemwettbewerb* (Tübingen: Mohr-Siebeck), 141–70.

Global Competition Review (2007), 'Rating Enforcement: The Annual Ranking of the World's Top Antitrust Authorities', June.

Global Competition Review (2013), 'Rating Competition 2013', available at *http:// globalcompetitionreview.com/rating-enforcement/*.

Gnesotto, N. (1990), 'Défence européenne: pourquoi pas les douze?', *Politique Étrangère*, 55/4: 881–3.

Goetschy, J. (2003), 'The European Employment Strategy, Multi-level Governance and Policy Coordination: Past, Present and Future', in J. Zeitlin and D. Trubek (eds.), *Governing Work and Welfare in a New Economy: European and American Experiments* (Oxford: Oxford University Press), 61–88.

Goetz, K. H. (2008), 'Governance as a Path to Government', *West European Politics*, 31/1–2: 258–79.

Goetze, S., and Rittberger, B. (2010), 'A Matter of Habit? The Sociological Foundations of Empowering the European Parliament', *Comparative European Politics*, 8/1: 37–54.

Goldstein, J., and Keohane, R. O. (1993), 'Ideas and Foreign Policy: An Analytical Framework', in J. Goldstein and R. O. Keohane (eds.), *Ideas and Foreign Policy: Beliefs, Institutions and Political Change* (Ithaca, NY: Cornell University Press), 11–26.

Golub, J. (2012), 'How the European Union Does Not Work: National Bargaining Success in the Council of Ministers', *Journal of European Public Policy*, 19/9: 1294–315.

Goodin, R. E., Rein, M., and Moran, M. (2006), 'The Public and its Policies', in M. Moran et al. (eds.), *The Oxford Handbook of Public Policy* (Oxford: Oxford University Press), 3–35.

Gowan, R. (2007), *EUFOR RD Congo, UNIFIL and Future European Support to the UN*, SDA Discussion Paper (Brussels: Security and Defence Agenda).

Gowan, R. (2012), *The EU and Syria: Everything but Force?*, Opinion 26 Jan. (Paris: Institute for Security Studies).

Goyder, D. (2003), *EC Competition Law*, 4th edn. (Oxford: Oxford University Press).

Grabbe, H. (2006), *The EU's Transformative Power: Europeanization through Conditionality in Central and Eastern Europe* (Basingstoke: Palgrave Macmillan).

Grant, W. (1997), *The Common Agricultural Policy* (Basingstoke: Palgrave Macmillan).

Grant, W. (2005), 'An Insider Group under Pressure: The NFU in Britain', in D. Halpin (ed.), *Surviving Global Change?* (Aldershot: Ashgate), 31–50.

Grant, W., Matthews, D., and Newell, P. (2000), *The Effectiveness of European Union Environmental Policy* (Basingstoke: Palgrave Macmillan).

Graser, A. (2004), 'Sozialrecht ohne Staat? Politik und Recht unter Bedingungen der Globalisierung und Dezentralisierung', in A. Windhoff-Héritier, M. Stolleis, and F. W. Scharpf (eds.), *European and International Regulation after the Nation State* (Baden-Baden: Nomos), 163–84.

Grech, L. (2010), 'Report on Delivering a Single Market to Consumers and Citizens (2010/2011(INI))', A7-0132/2010 (European Parliament: Committee on the Internal Market and Consumer Protection), 3 May.

Greenwood, J., and Dreger, J. (2013), 'The Transparency Register: The European Vanguard of Strong Lobby Regulation?', *Interest Groups & Advocacy*, 2/2: 139–62.

Greenwood, J., and Young, A. R. (2005), 'EU Interest Representation or US-Style Lobbying?', in N. Jabko and C. Parsons (eds.), *The State of the European Union*, vol. vii: *With US or Against US? European Trends in American Perspective* (Oxford: Oxford University Press), 275–95.

Greer, A. (2005), *Agricultural Policy in Europe* (Manchester: Manchester University Press).

Greer, S. L., and Kurzer, P. (2013), *European Union Public Health Policy: Regional and Global Trends* (Hoboken, NJ: Taylor & Francis).

Greven, M. T. (2000), 'Can the European Union Finally Become a Democracy?', in M. T. Greven and L. Pauly (eds.), *Democracy Beyond the State? The European Dilemma and the Emerging World Order* (Lanham, MD: Rowman & Littlefield), 35–61.

Grieco, J. M. (1996), 'State Interests and Institutional Rule Trajectories: A Neorealist Reinterpretation of the Maastricht Treaty and European Economic and Monetary Union', in B. Frankel (ed.), *Realism: Restatements and Renewal* (London: Frank Cass), 262–305.

Gros, D. (2003), 'Reforming the Composition of the ECB Governing Council in View of Enlargement: An Opportunity Missed', CEPS Policy Brief No. 32 (Brussels: Centre for European Policy Studies).

Grosser, A. (1980), *The Western Alliance: European–American Relations since 1945* (London: Palgrave Macmillan).

Grossman, G. M., and Helpman, E. (2001), *Special Interest Politics* (Cambridge, MA: The MIT Press).

Guild, E., and Geyer, F. (2008) (eds.), *Security Versus Justice? Police and Judicial Cooperation in the European Union* (Aldershot: Ashgate).

Guillén, A. M., and Palier, B. (2004) (eds.), 'EU Enlargement and Social Policy', *Journal of European Public Policy*, 14/3: 203–349 (special issue).

Haas, E. B. (1961), 'International Integration: The European and Universal Process', *International Organization*, 15/3: 366–92.

Haas, E. B. (2004) [1958], *The Uniting of Europe* (Stanford, CA: Stanford University Press; reprinted in 2004 by Notre Dame University Press, South Bend, IN).

Haas, P. M. (1992), 'Introduction: Epistemic Communities and International Policy Coordination', *International Organization*, 46/1: 1–35.

Habermas, J. (1985), *The Theory of Communicative Action*, vol. ii (Boston, MA: Beacon Press).

Habermas, J. (1998), *Between Facts and Norms: Contributions to a Discourse Theory of Law and Democracy* (Cambridge, MA: The MIT Press).

Hagen, K. P. (1998), 'Towards a Europeanisation of Social Policies? A Scandinavian Perspective', in MIRE, *Comparing Social Welfare Systems in Nordic Countries and France* (Paris: MIRE), 405–22.

Hagen, K. P., Norrman, E., and Sørensen, P. B. (1998), 'Financing the Nordic Welfare States in an Integrating Europe', in P. B. Sørensen (ed.), *Tax Policy in the Nordic Countries* (Basingstoke: Palgrave Macmillan), 138–203.

Hague, R., and Harrop, M. (2007), *Comparative Government and Politics: An Introduction*, 7th edn. (Basingstoke: Palgrave Macmillan).

Haigh, N. (2004) (ed.), *Manual of Environmental Policy: The EU and Britain*, Institute of European Environmental Policy (IEEP) (Leeds: Maney Publishing).

Hailbronner, K. (2004*a*), 'Die Unionsbürgerschaft und das Ende rationaler Jurisprudenz', *Neue Juristische Wochenschrift*, 57/31: 2185–9.

Hailbronner, K. (2004*b*), 'Diskriminierungsverbot, Unionsbürgerschaft und gleicher Zugang zu Sozialleistungen', *Zeitschrift für ausländisches öffentliches Recht und Völkerrecht*, 64/3: 603–19.

Hall, P. A. (1986), *Governing the Economy: The Politics of State Intervention in Britain and France* (Oxford: Oxford University Press).

Hall, P. A. (1999), 'The Political Economy of Europe in an Era of Interdependence', in H. Kitschelt, P. Lange, G. Marks, and J. D. Stephens (eds.), *Continuity and Change in Contemporary Capitalism* (Cambridge: Cambridge University Press), 135–63.

Hall, P. A., and Taylor, R. C. R. (1996), 'Political Science and the Three New Institutionalisms', *Political Studies*, 44/5: 936–57.

Hall, P. A., and Thelen, K. (2009), 'Institutional Change in Varieties of Capitalism', *Socio-Economic Review*, 7/1: 7–34.

Halliday, F. (2001), 'The Romance of Non-State Actors', in D. Josselin and W. Wallace (eds.), *Non-State Actors in World Politics* (Basingstoke: Palgrave Macmillan), 21–37.

Hancher, L. (2010), 'The EU Pharmaceutical Market: Parameters and Pathways', in G. Permanand, R. Baeten, E. Mossialos, and T. K. Hervey (eds.), *Health Systems Governance in Europe: The Role of European Union Law and Policy* (Cambridge: Cambridge University Press), 635–82.

Hancher, L., and Moran, M. (1989), 'Introduction: Regulation and Deregulation', *European Journal of Political Research*, 17/2: 129–36.

Hancké, B. (2013), *Unions, Central Banks, and EMU* (Oxford: Oxford University Press).

Hanson, B. T. (1998), 'What Happened to Fortress Europe? External Trade Policy Liberalization in the European Union', *International Organization*, 52/1: 55–85.

Hantrais, L. (2007), *Social Policy in the European Union*, 3rd edn. (Basingstoke: Palgrave Macmillan).

Harding, C., and Joshua, J. (2003), *Regulating Cartels in Europe* (Oxford: Oxford University Press).

Hartlapp, M. (2007), 'On Enforcement, Management and Persuasion: Different Logics of Implementation Policy in the EU and the ILO', *Journal of Common Market Studies*, 45/3: 653–74.

Hartlapp, M., and Falkner, G. (2008), 'Problems of Operationalization and Data in EU Compliance Research', WZB Discussion Paper 2008-104 (Berlin: Social Science Research Centre).

Hawkins, D. (2004), 'Explaining Costly International Institutions: Persuasion and Enforceable Human Rights Norms', *International Studies Quarterly*, 48/4: 779–804.

Hay, C. (2007), 'What Doesn't Kill You Can Only Make You Stronger: The Doha Development Round, the Services Directive and the EU's Conception of Competitiveness', *Journal of Common Market Studies*, 45/s1: 25–43.

Hayes-Renshaw, F., and Wallace, H. (2006), *The Council of Ministers*, 2nd edn. (Basingstoke: Palgrave Macmillan).

Hayes-Renshaw, F., van Aken, W., and Wallace, H. (2006), 'When and Why the EU Council of Ministers Votes Explicitly', *Journal of Common Market Studies*, 44/1: 161–94.

Heidenheimer, A. J. (1985), 'Comparative Public Policy at the Crossroads', *Journal of Public Policy*, 5/4: 441–65.

Heidenreich, M. (2003), 'Regional Inequalities in the Enlarged Europe', *Journal of European Social Policy*, 13/4: 313–33.

Heidenreich, M., and Bischoff, G. (2008), 'The Open Method of Coordination: A Way to the Europeanization of Social and Employment Policies?', *Journal of Common Market Studies*, 46/3: 497–532.

Heidenreich, M., and Zeitlin, J. (2009) (eds.), *Changing European Employment and Welfare Regimes: The Influence of the Open Method of Coordination on National Reforms* (London: Routledge).

Heipertz, M. and Verdun, A. (2010), *Ruling Europe: The Politics of the Stability and Growth Pact* (Cambridge: Cambridge University Press).

Helm, D. (2007), 'European Energy Policy: Securing Supplies and Meeting the Challenge of Climate Change', in D. Helm (ed.), *The New Energy Paradigm* (Oxford: Oxford University Press), 440–51.

Helm, D. (2013), *The Carbon Crunch: How We're Getting Climate Change Wrong—and How to Fix It* (New Haven, CT: Yale University Press).

Hemerijck, A., Keune, M., and Rhodes, M. (2006), 'European Welfare States: Diversity, Challenges and Reforms', in E. Jones, P. Heywood, M. Rhodes, and U. Sedelmeier (eds.), *Development in European Politics* (Basingstoke: Palgrave Macmillan), 259–79.

Hendrickx, F. (2008), 'The Services Directive and the Alleged Issue of Social Dumping', in J. W. van de Gronden (ed.), *The EU and WTO Law on Services: Limits to the Realisation of General Interest Policies Within the Services Markets?* (Austin: Wolters Kluwer), 97–118.

Henley, J. (2014), 'The Enemy Invasion: Brussels Braced for Influx of Eurosceptics in EU Polls', *The Guardian*, 28 Apr.

Héritier, A. (2002), 'New Modes of Governance in Europe: Policy-making without Legislating?', in A. Héritier (ed.), *The Provision of Common Goods: Governance Across Multiple Arenas* (Boulder, CO: Rowman & Littlefield), 185–206.

Héritier, A., Kerwer, D., Knill, C., Lehmkuhl, D., Teutsch, M., and Douillet, A.-C. (2001), *Differential Europe: The European Union Impact on National Policymaking* (Lanham, MD: Rowman & Littlefield).

Hey, C., Jacob K., and Volkery, A. (2008), 'REACH als Beispiel für hybride Formen von Steuerung und Governance', in G. Folke Schuppert and M. Zürn (eds.), 'Governance in einer sich wandelnden Welt', *Politische Vierteljahresschrift*, Sonderheft 41: 430–51.

Heydon, K., and Woolcock, S. (2009), *The Rise of Bilateralism: Comparing American, European and Asian Approaches to Preferential Trade Agreements* (Tokyo: United Nations University Press).

Hibbs, D. A., and Madsen, H. J. (1981), 'Public Reactions in the Growth of Taxation and Government Expenditure', *World Politics*, 33/3: 413–35.

Hildebrand, P. M. (1993), 'The European Community's Environmental Policy, 1957 to 1992: From Incidental Measures to an International Regime?', in D. Judge (ed.), *A Green Dimension for the European Community: Political Issues and Processes* (London: Frank Cass), 13–44.

Hill, C. (2003), *The Changing Politics of Foreign Policy* (Basingstoke: Palgrave Macmillan).

Hill, C., and Smith, M. (2011) (eds.), *International Relations and the European Union*, 2nd edn. (Oxford: Oxford University Press).

Hix, S. (1994), 'The Study of the European Community: The Challenge to Comparative Politics', *West European Politics*, 17/1: 1–30.

Hix, S. (1998), 'The Study of the European Union II: The "New Governance" Agenda and its Rival', *Journal of European Public Policy*, 5/1: 38–65.

Hix, S. (1999), *The Political System of the European Union* (Basingstoke: Palgrave Macmillan).

Hix, S. (2001), 'Legislative Behaviour and Party Competition in European Parliament: An Application of Nominate to the EU', *Journal of Common Market Studies*, 39/4: 663–88.

Hix, S. (2002), 'Constitutional Agenda-Setting through Discretion in Rule Interpretation: Why the European Parliament Won at Amsterdam', *British Journal of Political Science*, 32/2: 259–80.

Hix, S. (2005), *The Political System of the European Union*, 2nd edn. (Basingstoke: Palgrave Macmillan).

Hix, S. (2008*a*), 'The EU as a Political System', in D. Caramani (ed.) *Comparative Politics* (Oxford: Oxford University Press), 573–601.

Hix, S. (2008b), *What's Wrong with the European Union and How to Fix It* (Cambridge: Polity).

Hix, S., and Hoyland, B. (2011), *The Political System of the European Union*, 3rd edn. (Basingstoke: Palgrave Macmillan).

Hix, S., and Hoyland, B. (2013), 'Empowerment of the European Parliament', *Annual Review of Political Science*, 16: 171–89.

Hix, S., and Noury, A. G. (2009), 'After Enlargement: Voting Patterns in the Sixth European Parliament', *Legislative Studies Quarterly*, 34/2: 159–74.

Hix, S., Noury, A., and Roland, G. (2007), *Democratic Politics in the European Parliament* (Cambridge: Cambridge University Press).

Hocking, B. (2004), 'Diplomacy', in W. Carlsnaes, H. Sjursen, and B. White (eds.), *Contemporary European Foreign Policy* (London: Sage), 91–109.

Hodson, D. (2010), 'Economic and Monetary Union: An Experiment in New Modes of EU Policy-Making', in H. Wallace, M. A. Pollack, and A. R. Young (eds.), *Policy-Making in the European Union*, 6th edn. (Oxford: Oxford University Press), 157–80.

Hodson, D. (2011), *Governing the Euro Area in Good Times and Bad* (Oxford: Oxford University Press).

Hodson, D. (2012), 'Managing the Euro: The European Central Bank', in J. Peterson and M. Shackleton (eds.), *The Institutions of the European Union*, 3rd edn. (Oxford: Oxford University Press).

Hodson, D., and Maher, I. (2001), 'The Open Method of Coordination as a New Mode of Governance: The Case of Soft Economic Policy Co-ordination', *Journal of Common Market Studies*, 39/4: 719–46.

Hodson, D., and Maher, I. (2013), 'British Brinkmanship and Gaelic Games: EU Treaty Ratification in the UK and Ireland from a Two Level Game Perspective', *British Journal of Politics & International Relations*, doi: 10.1111/1467-856X.12015.

Hoekman, B., and Sauvé, P. (1994), 'Regional and Multilateral Liberalisation of Service Markets: Complements or Substitutes?', *Journal of Common Market Studies*, 32/3: 283–318.

Hoffmann, S. (1966), 'Obstinate or Obsolete? The Fate of the Nation-State and the Case of Western Europe', *Daedalus*, 95/3: 862–915.

Hokayem, E. (2013), *Syria's Uprising and the Fracturing of the Levant* (London: Routledge).

Holmes, P., and McGowan, F. (1997), 'The Changing Dynamics of EU-Industry Relations: Lessons from the Liberalization of the European Car and Airline Markets', in H. Wallace and A. R. Young (eds.), *Participation and Policy-Making in the European Union* (Oxford: Clarendon Press), 159–84.

Holmes, P., and Young, A. R. (2001), 'European Lessons for Multilateral Economic Integration: A Cautionary Tale', in Z. Drabek (ed.), *Globalization Under Threat: The Stability of Trade Policy and International Agreements* (Cheltenham: Edward Elgar), 203–26.

Holzinger, K., Knill, C., and Lenschow, A. (2008), 'Governance in EU Environmental Policy', in I. Tömmel and A. Verdun (eds.), *Innovative Governance in the European Union: The Politics of Multilevel Policymaking* (Boulder, CO: Lynne Rienner), 45–62.

Hooghe, L. (1996a) (ed.), *Cohesion Policy and European Integration: Building Multi-level Governance* (Oxford: Oxford University Press).

Hooghe, L. (1996b), 'Building a Europe with Regions: The Changing Role of the European Commission', in L. Hooghe (ed.), *Cohesion Policy and European Integration: Building Multi-level Governance* (Oxford: Oxford University Press), 89–128.

Hooghe, L. (1996c), 'Introduction: Reconciling EU-Wide Policy and National Diversity' in L. Hooghe (ed.) *Cohesion Policy and European Integration: Building Multi-level Governance* (Oxford: Oxford University Press), 1–26.

Hooghe, L. (2005), 'Several Roads Lead to International Norms, but Few Via International Socialization: A Case Study of the European Commission', *International Organization*, 59/4: 861–98.

Hooghe, L., and Marks, G. (2001), *Multi-Level Governance and European Integration* (Lanham, MD: Rowman & Littlefield).

Hooghe, L., and Marks, G. (2008), 'A Postfunctionalist Theory of European Integration: From Permissive Consensus to Constraining Dissensus', *British Journal of Political Science*, 39/1: 1-23.

Höpner, M., and Schäfer, A. (2008), 'Polanyi in Brussels? Embeddedness and the Three Dimensions of European Economic Integration', Max Planck Institut für Gesellschaftsforschung Discussion Paper 10/8 (Cologne: Max Planck Institute for the Study of Societies).

Hoskyns, C. (1996), *Integrating Gender: Women, Law and Politics in the European Union* (London: Verso).

Hosli, M. O. (1994), *Coalitions and Power: Effects on Qualified Majority Voting in the European Union's Council of Ministers* (Maastricht: European Institute of Public Administration).

House of Lords (2000), *Report on EU Proposals to Combat Discrimination*, European Union Committee, 9th Report, HL Paper 68 (London: TSO).

House of Lords (2004), *Equality in Access to Goods and Services Report*, Sub-Committee G (Social and Consumer Affairs), HL Paper 165–I (London: TSO).

House of Lords (2008), *The Future of EU Regional Policy*, European Union Committee, 19th Report, HL paper 141 (London: TSO).

Howarth, D. (2007a), 'Internal Policies: Reinforcing the New Lisbon Message of Competitiveness and Innovation', *Journal of Common Market Studies*, 45/s1: 89–106.

Howarth, D. (2007b), 'Making and Breaking the Rules: French Policy on EU Economic Governance', *Journal of European Public Policy*, 14/7: 1–18.

Howorth, J. (2007), *Security and Defence Policy in the European Union* (Basingstoke: Palgrave Macmillan).

Huber, J. D., and Shipan, C. R. (2002), *Deliberate Discretion? The Institutional Foundations of Bureaucratic Autonomy* (Cambridge: Cambridge University Press).

Hughes, J., Sasse, G., and Gordon, C. (2004a), 'Conditionality and Compliance in the EU's Eastern Enlargement: Regional Policy and the Reform of Sub-National Government', *Journal of Common Market Studies*, 42/3: 523–51.

Hughes, J., Sasse, G., and Gordon, C. (2004b), *Europeanization and Regionalization in the EU's Enlargement to Central and Eastern Europe: The Myth of Conditionality* (Basingstoke: Palgrave Macmillan).

Hurrell, A., and Menon, A. (1996), 'Politics Like Any Other? Comparative Politics, International Relations and the Study of the EU', *West European Politics*, 19/2: 386–402.

Hurrelmann, A., Leibfried, S., Martens, K., and Mayer, P. (2008) (eds.), *Transforming the Golden Age Nation State* (Basingstoke: Palgrave Macmillan).

Husmann, M. (1998), 'Koordinierung der Leistungen bei Arbeitslosigkeit durch EG-Recht', *Die Sozialgerichtsbarkeit*, 45/6: 245–52 (pt. 1); 7: 291–8 (pt. 2).

Husmann, M. (2005), 'Die EG-Gleichbehandlungs-Richtlinien 2000/2002 und ihre Umsetzung in das deutsche, englische und französische Recht', *Zeitschrift für europäisches Sozial- und Arbeitsrecht* (ZESAR), 4/3: 107–14 (pt. I); 4/4: 167–75 (pt. II).

Hyde-Price, A. (2008), 'A "Tragic Actor"? A Realist Perspective on "Ethical Power Europe"', *International Affairs*, 84/1: 29–44.

IISS (International Institute for Strategic Studies) (2008), *European Military Capabilities* (London: International Institute for Strategic Studies).

Inside US Trade, various issues.

International Herald Tribune, various issues.

International Monetary Fund (2013*a*), 'Greece: Ex Post Evaluation of Exceptional Access Under the 2010 Stand-By Arrangement', IMF Country Report No. 13/156.

International Monetary Fund (2013*b*), 'Greece: Fourth Review Under the Extended Arrangement Under the Extended Fund Facility, and Request for Waivers of Applicability and Modifications of Performance Criterion—Staff Reports; Staff Statement; Press Release; and Statement by the Executive Director for Greece', IMF Country Report No. 13/241.

International Monetary Fund (2013*c*), 'Towards a Fiscal Union for the Euro Area', IMF Staff Discussion Note No. 13/9.

Jabko, N. (2006), *Playing the Market: A Political Strategy for Uniting Europe, 1985–2005* (Ithaca, NY: Cornell University Press).

Jachtenfuchs, M. (1995), 'Theoretical Perspectives on European Governance', *European Law Journal*, 1/2: 115–33.

Jachtenfuchs, M. (2001), 'The Governance Approach to European Integration', *Journal of Common Market Studies*, 39/2: 245–64.

Jachtenfuchs, M. (2007), 'The European Union as a Polity (II)', in K. E. Jørgensen, M. A. Pollack, and B. Rosamond (eds.), *The Handbook of European Union Politics* (London: Sage), 159–73.

Jachtenfuchs, M., and Kohler-Koch, B. (2004), 'Governance and Institutional Development', in A. Wiener, and T. Diez (eds.), *European Integration Theory* (Oxford: Oxford University Press), 97–115.

Jacobsson, K. (2004), 'The Methodology of the European Employment Strategy: Achievement and Problems', mimeo (SCORE, Stockholm University).

Jacobsson, K., and Vifell, Å. (2003), 'Integration by Deliberation: On the Role of Committees in the Open Method of Coordination', in E.O. Eriksen, C. Joerges, and J. Neyer (eds.), *European Governance, Deliberation and the Quest for Democratisation*, Arena Report 2/03 (Oslo/Florence: ARENA/EUI), 417–58.

Jacobsson, K., and Vifell, Å. (2007), 'New Governance Structures in Employment Policy Making: Loose Co-ordination in Action', in I. Linsenmann, C. Meyer, and W. Wessels (eds.), *Economic Government of the EU: A Balance Sheet of New Modes of Policy Coordination* (Basingstoke: Palgrave Macmillan), 53–71.

Jacoby, W. (2004), *The Enlargement of the European Union and NATO: Ordering from the Menu in Central Europe* (Cambridge: Cambridge University Press).

Jacoby, W., and Meunier, S. (2010), 'Europe and the Management of Globalization', *Journal of European Public Policy*, 17/3: 299–317.

James, H. (2012), *Making the European Monetary Union* (Cambridge, MA: Harvard University Press).

Jaureguy-Naudin, M. (2011), 'Energy Efficiency versus the EU ETS: Counterproductive Tribalism in the Commission', in Institut Français des Relations Internationales, Edito Energie, available at *http://ifri.org/index.php?page=detail-contribution&id=6718*.

Jeffery, C. (2000), 'Sub-national Mobilization and European Integration: Does it Make Any Difference?', *Journal of Common Market Studies*, 38/1: 1–23.

Jellinek, G. (1914), *Allgemeine Staatslehre*, 3rd edn. (Berlin: Häring).

Jobelius, S. (2003), 'Who Formulates the European Employment Guidelines? The OMC between Deliberation and Power Games', paper presented to the ESPAnet conference, 'Changing European Societies: The Role for Social Policy', Copenhagen, 13–15 Nov.

Joerges, C. (2001), '"Deliberative Supranationalism": A Defence', European Integration online Papers, 5/8; available at *http://eiop.or.at/eiop*.

Joerges, C., and Neyer, J. (1997a), 'From Intergovernmental Bargaining to Deliberative Political Process: The Constitutionalization of Comitology', *European Law Journal*, 3/3: 273–99.

Joerges, C., and Neyer, J. (1997b), 'Transforming Strategic Interaction into Deliberative Political Process: The Constitutionalization of Comitology in the Foodstuffs Sector', *Journal of European Public Policy*, 4/4: 609–25.

Johansson, K. M. (1999), 'Tracing the Employment Title in the Amsterdam Treaty: Uncovering Transnational Coalitions', *Journal of European Public Policy*, 6/1: 85–101.

John, P. (1998), *Analysing Public Policy* (London: Continuum).

Johnson, S. P., and Corcelle, G. (1989), *The Environmental Policy of the European Communities* (London: Graham and Trotman).

Jones, E., Menon, A., and Weatherill, S. (2012) (eds.), *The Oxford Handbook of the European Union* (Oxford: Oxford University Press).

Jones, S. G. (2007), *The Rise of European Security Cooperation* (Cambridge: Cambridge University Press).

Jones, E., and Kelemen, R. D. (2014), 'The Euro Goes to Court', *Survival*, 56/2: 15–23.

Jónsson, G., and Stefánsson, K. (2013), *Retrenchment or Renewal? Welfare States in Times of Economic Crisis* (Helsinki: Nordic Centre of Excellence NordWel; Series NordWel Studies in Historical Welfare State Research 6).

Jordan, A. (2002), *The Europeanization of British Environmental Policy: A Departmental Perspective* (Basingstoke: Palgrave Macmillan).

Jordan, A. (2003), 'The Europeanization of National Government and Policy: A Departmental Perspective', *British Journal of Political Science*, 33/2: 261–82.

Jordan, A., and Adelle, C. (2013) (eds.), *Environmental Policy in the EU: Actors, Institutions and Processes*, 3rd edn. (London: Routledge).

Jordan, A., and Schout, A. (2006), *The Coordination of the European Union: Exploring the Capacities of Networked Governance* (Oxford: Oxford University Press).

Jordan, A., Schout, A., and Unfried, M. (2008), 'The European Union', in A. Jordan and A. Lenschow (eds.), *Innovation in Environmental Policy? Integrating the Environment for Sustainability* (Cheltenham: Edward Elgar), 159–79.

Jordan, G. (1998), 'What Drives Associability at the European Level? The Limits of the Utilitarian Explanation', in J. Greenwood and M. Aspinwall (eds.), *Collective Action in the European Union: Interests and the New Politics of Associability* (London: Routledge), 31–62.

Jordan, G., and Maloney, W. A. (1996), 'How Bumble-bees Fly: Accounting for Public Interest Participation', *Political Studies*, 44/4: 668–85.

Jorens, Y., and Schulte, B. (1998) (eds.), *European Social Security Law and Third Country Nationals* (Bruges: die Keure).

Jørgensen, K. E. (2007), 'Overview: The European Union and the World', in K. E. Jørgensen, M. A. Pollack, and B. Rosamond (eds.), *The Handbook of European Union Politics* (London: Sage), 507–25.

Jørgensen, K. E., Pollack, M. A., and Rosamond, B. (2007) (eds.), *The Handbook of European Union Politics* (London: Sage).

Junk, J., and Daase, C. (2013), 'Germany', in H. Biehl, B. Giegerich, and A. Jonas (eds.), *Strategic Cultures in Europe: Security and Defence Policies Across the Continent* (Wiesbaden: Springer), 139–52.

Jupille, J. (2005), 'Knowing Europe: Metatheory and Methodology in EU Studies', in M. Cini and A. Bourne (eds.), *Palgrave Advances in European Union Studies* (Basingstoke: Palgrave Macmillan), 209–32.

Jupille, J., Caporaso, J. A., and Checkel, J. (2003), 'Integrating Institutions: Rationalism, Constructivism, and the Study of the European Union', *Comparative Political Studies*, 36/1–2: 7–40.

Kagan, R. (2002), 'Power and Weakness', *Policy Review*, 113: 3–28.

Kahler, M. (2002), 'The State of the State in World Politics', in I. Katznelson and H. V. Milner (eds.), *Political Science: State of the Discipline* (New York, NY: W. W. Norton), 56–83.

Kahler, M., and Lake, D. A. (2013) (eds.), *Politics in the New Hard Times: The Great Recession in Comparative Perspective* (Ithaca, NY: Cornell University Press).

Karagiannis, Y., and Guidi, M. (2013), 'Institutional Change and Continuity in the European Union: The Super-Commissioner Sage', *Acta Politica*, 49: 174–195.

Kassim, H. (1994), 'Policy Networks, Networks and European Union Policy Making: A Sceptical View', *West European Politics*, 17/4: 15–27.

Kassim, H., and Lyons, B. (2013), 'The New Political Economy of EU State Aid Policy', *Journal of Industry, Competition and Trade*, 13/1: 1–21.

Kassim, H., Peters, B. G., and Wright, V. (2000) (eds.), *The National Co-ordination of EU Policy: The Domestic Level* (Oxford: Oxford University Press).

Kassim, H., Peterson, J., Bauer, M. W., Connolly, S., Dehousse, R., Hooghe, L., and Thompson, A. (2013), *The European Commission of the Twenty-First Century* (Oxford: Oxford University Press).

Keating, M., and Jones, B. (1985) (eds.), *Regions in the European Community* (Oxford: Clarendon Press).

Keck, M., and Sikkink, K. (1998), *Activists Beyond Borders: Advocacy Networks in International Politics* (Ithaca, NY: Cornell University Press).

Keeler, J. T. S. (1987), *The Politics of Neocorporatism in France* (New York, NY: Oxford University Press).

Keeler, J. T. S. (2005), 'Mapping EU Studies: The Evolution from Boutique to Boom Field 1960–2001', *Journal of Common Market Studies*, 43/3: 551–82.

Kelemen, R. D. (2002), 'The Politics of "Eurocratic" Structures and the New European Agencies', *West European Politics*, 25/4: 93–118.

Kelemen, R. D. (2003), 'The Structure and Dynamics of EU Federalism', *Comparative Political Studies*, 36/1–2: 184–208.

Kelemen, R. D. (2004), *The Rules of Federalism: Institutions and Regulatory Politics in the EU and Beyond* (Cambridge, MA: Harvard University Press).

Keleman, R. D. (2011), *Eurolegalism: The Transformation of Law and Regulation in the European Union* (Cambridge, MA: Harvard University Press).

Kelemen, R. D. (2012), 'European Union Agencies', in E. Jones, A. Menon, and S. Weatherill (eds.), *The Oxford Handbook of the European Union* (Oxford: Oxford University Press), 392–403.

Kelemen, R. D., Menon, A., and Slapin, J. (2014), 'Wider and Deeper? Enlargement and Integration in the European Union', *Journal of European Public Policy*, 21/5: 647–63.

Keller, B. (2008), 'Social Dialogue—The Specific Case of the European Union', *The International Journal of Comparative Labour Law and Industrial Relations*, 24/2: 201–26.

Kelley, J. G. (2004), *Ethnic Politics in Europe: The Power of Norms and Incentives* (Princeton, NJ: Princeton University Press).

Kelley, J. G. (2006), 'New Wine in Old Wineskins: Promoting Political Reforms through the New European Neighbourhood Policy', *Journal of Common Market Studies*, 44/1: 29–55.

Kenner, J. (2003), *EU Employment Law: From Rome to Amsterdam and Beyond* (Oxford: Hart).

Keohane, R. O. (1986), 'Reciprocity in International Relations', *International Organization*, 40/1: 1–27.

Keohane, R. O., and Nye, J. S. (2001), *Power and Interdependence*, 3rd edn. (New York, NY: Longman).

Kiewiet, R. D., and McCubbins, M. (1991), *The Logic of Delegation: Congressional Parties and the Appropriations Process* (Chicago, IL: University of Chicago Press).

Kilpatrick, C. (2009), 'The ECJ and Labour Law: A 2008 Retrospective', *Industrial Law Journal*, 38/2: 180–208.

Kingdon, J. W. (2003), *Agendas, Alternatives and Public Policies*, 2nd edn. (New York, NY: Longman).

Kingreen, T. (2007), 'The Fundamental Rights of the European Union: Basic Rights of Equality and Social Rights', in D. Ehlers (ed.), *European Fundamental Rights and Freedoms* (Berlin: De Gruyter), 466–89.

Kleine, M. (2013), *Informal Governance in the European Union: How Governments Make International Organizations Work* (Ithaca, NY: Cornell University Press).

Kleine, M. (2014), 'Informal Governance in the European Union', *Journal of European Public Policy*, 21/2: 303–14.

Kleinman, M., and Piachaud, D. (1992), 'European Social Policy: Conceptions and Choices', *Journal of European Social Policy*, 3/1: 1–19.

Klumpes, P., Fenn, P., Diacon, S., O'Brien, C., and Yildirim, C. (2007), 'European Insurance Markets: Recent Trends and Future Regulatory Developments', in J. D. Cummins and B. Venard (eds.), *Handbook of International Insurance: Between Global Dynamics and Local Contingencies* (New York, NY: Springer), 789–848.

Knill, C. (2001), *The Europeanisation of National Administration: Patterns of Institutional Change and Persistence* (Cambridge: Cambridge University Press).

Knill, C., and Lenschow, A. (2000) (eds.), *Implementing EU Environmental Policy: New Directions and Old Problems* (Manchester: Manchester University Press).

Knill, C., and Liefferink, D. (2007) (eds.), *Environmental Politics in the European Union: Policy-Making, Implementation and Patterns of Multi-Level Governance* (Manchester: Manchester University Press).

Knudsen, A.-C. L. (2009), *Farmers on Welfare: The Making of Europe's Common Agricultural Policy* (Ithaca, NY: Cornell University Press).

Kochan, T., Locke, R., Osterman, P., and Piore, M. (2001), *Working in America: Blueprint for a New Labor Market* (Cambridge, MA: The MIT Press).

Koeck, H. F. and Karollus, M. M. (2008) (eds.), *Die neue Dienstleistungsrichtlinie der Europäischen Union: Hoffnungen und Erwartungen angesichts einer (weiteren) Vervollständigung des Binnenmarktes* (Baden-Baden: Nomos; Vienna: Facultas-WUV).

Kok, W. (2004), *Facing the Challenge, Report of Wim Kok to the European Commission* (The Kok Report) (Brussels).

Kooiman, J. (1993), 'Social-Political Governance: Introduction', in J. Kooiman (ed.), *Modern Governance* (London: Sage), 1–6.

Kotzian, P. (2002), *Stuck in the Middle: Welfare Effects of the European Pharmaceutical Markets' Incomplete Integration and a Possible Remedy*, MZES Working Paper 59 (Mannheim: Mannheimer Zentrum für Europäische Sozialforschung).

Kotzian, P. (2003), *Verhandlungen im europäischen Arzneimittelsektor: Initiierung-Institutionalisierung-Ergebnisse* (Baden-Baden: Nomos).

Kramer, H. (1993), 'The European Community's Response to the "New Eastern Europe"', *Journal of Common Market Studies*, 31/2: 231–44.

Krämer, L. (2008), 'Environmental Judgements by the Court of Justice and their Duration', Research Papers in Law, 4/2008 (Bruges: College of Europe).

Krapohl, S. (2004), 'Credible Commitments in Non-Independent Regulatory Agencies: A Comparative Analysis of the European Agencies for Pharmaceuticals and Foodstuffs', *European Law Journal*, 10/5: 518–38.

Kreppel, A. (2001), *The European Parliament and Supranational Party System: A Study in Institutional Development* (Cambridge: Cambridge University Press).

Kreppel, A. (2002), 'The Environmental Determinants of Legislative Structure: A Comparison of the US House of Representatives and the European Parliament', paper presented at the conference, 'Exporting Congress? The Influence of the US Congress on World Legislatures', Jack D. Gordon Institute for Public Policy and Citizenship Studies, Florida International University, 6–7 Dec.

Kreppel, A. (2012), 'The Normalization of the European Union', *Journal of European Public Policy*, 19/5: 635–45.

Kreppel, A., and Hix, S. (2003), 'From "Grand Coalition" to Left-Right Confrontation: Explaining the Shifting Structure of Party Competition in the European Parliament', *Comparative Political Studies*, 36/1–2: 75–96.

Kroes, N. (2007), 'Energising Europe: A Real Market with Secure Supply'. press release IP/07/1361, 19 Sept.

Kubicek, P. (2003) (ed.), *The European Union and Democratization* (London: Routledge).

Kurze, K., and Lenschow, A. (forthcoming), 'Towards a New "Principled Priority": A Discourse Analysis of the EU's Integrated Climate and Energy Policy', *Environmental Policy and Governance*.

Kvist, J. (2004), 'Does EU Enlargement Start a Race to the Bottom? Strategic Interaction among EU Member States in Social Policy', *Journal of European Social Policy*, 14/3: 301–18.

Laatikainen, K. V., and Smith, K. E. (2006), 'Introduction—The European Union at the United Nations: Leader, Partner or Failure?', in K. V. Laatikainen and K. E. Smith (eds.), *The European Union at the United Nations: Intersecting Multilateralisms* (Basingstoke: Palgrave MacMillan).

Ladrech, R. (2010), *Europeanization and National Politics* (Basingstoke: Palgrave Macmillan).

Laffan, B. (1997), *The Finances of the European Union* (Basingstoke: Palgrave Macmillan).

Lamy, P. (2004a), 'Europe and the Future of Economic Governance', *Journal of Common Market Studies*, 42/1: 5–21.

Lamy, P. (2004b), *Trade Policy in the Prodi Commission, 1999–2004*, available at *www.acp-eu-trade.org/library/library_detail.php?library_detail_id=1827&doc_language*.

Lange, P. (1992), 'The Politics of the Social Dimension', in A. M. Sbragia (ed.), *Euro-Politics: Institutions and Policy-Making in the 'New' European Community* (Washington, DC: Brookings Institution), 225–56.

Langhammer, R. L. (2005), 'The EU Offer of Services Trade Liberalization in the Doha Round: Evidence of a Not-Yet-Perfect Customs Union', *Journal of Common Market Studies*, 43/2: 311–25.

Larsen, T. P., and Andersen, S. K. (2007), 'A New Mode of European Regulation? The Implementation of the Autonomous Framework Agreement on Telework in Five Countries', *European Journal of Industrial Relations*, 13/2: 181–98.

Laudati, L. (1996), 'The European Commission as Regulator: The Uncertain Pursuit of the Competitive Market', in G. Majone (ed.), *Regulating Europe* (London: Routledge), 229–61.

Laulom, S. (2010), 'The Flawed Revision of the European Works Council Directive', *Industrial Law Journal*, 39/2: 202–8.

Lavenex, S. (2006a), 'Towards a Constitutionalization of Aliens' Rights in the European Union?', *Journal of European Public Policy*, 13/8: 1284–301.

Lavenex, S. (2006b), 'Shifting Up and Out: The Foreign Policy of European Immigration Control', *West European Politics*, 29/2: 329–50.

Lavenex, S. (2007), 'Mutual Recognition and the Monopoly of Force: Limits of the Single Market Analogy', *Journal of European Public Policy*, 14/5: 762–79.

Lavenex, S., and Schimmelfennig, F. (2011) (eds.), 'Democracy Promotion in the EU's Neighbourhood: From Leverage to Governance?', *Democratization*, 18/4 (special issue), 885–1054.

Lavenex, S., and Stucky, R. (2011), '"Partnering" for Migration in EU External Relations', in R. Kunz, S. Lavenex, and M. Panizzon (eds.), *Multilayered Migration Governance: The Promise of Partnership* (London: Routledge), 116–42.

Lavenex, S., and Wallace, W. (2005), 'Justice and Home Affairs: Towards a "European Public Order?"', in H. Wallace, W. Wallace, and M. A. Pollack (eds.), *Policy-Making in the European Union*, 5th edn. (Oxford: Oxford University Press), 457–80.

Le Cacheux, J. (2007), *Funding the EU Budget with a Genuine Own Resource: The Case for a European Tax*, Studies 57 (Paris: Notre Europe).

Legro, J., and Moravcsik, A. (1999), 'Is Anybody Still a Realist?', *International Security*, 24/2: 5–55.

Leibfried, S. (1994), 'The Social Dimension of the European Union: En Route to a Positive Joint Sovereignty?', *Journal of European Social Policy*, 4/4: 239–62.

Leibfried, S. (2001), 'Über die Hinfälligkeit des Staates der Daseinsvorsorge: Thesen zur Zerstörung des äußeren Verteidigungsringes des Sozialstaats', in Schader-Stiftung (ed.), *Die Zukunft der Daseinsvorsorge: öffentliche Unternehmen im Wettbewerb* (Darmstadt: Schader-Stiftung), 158–66.

Leibfried, S. (2005), 'Social Policy: Left to the Judges and the Markets?', in H. Wallace, W. Wallace, and M. A. Pollack (eds.), *Policy-Making in the European Union*, 5th edn. (Oxford: Oxford University Press), 243–78.

Leibfried, S. (2013), 'Europa am Scheideweg: Wege aus der Depression', *Soziale Sicherheit*, 2/2013: 76–81.

Leibfried, S., Huber, E., Lange, M., Levy, J. D., Nullmeier, F., Stephens, J. D. (2015) (eds.), *The Oxford Handbook of Transformations of the State* (Oxford: Oxford University Press).

Leibfried, S., and Mau, S. (2008) (ed.), *Welfare States: Construction, Deconstruction, Reconstructions*, 3 vols. (Cheltenham: Edward Elgar).

Leibfried, S., and Obinger, H. (2008), 'Nationale Sozialstaaten in der Europäischen Union', in M. Höpner and A. Schäfer (eds.), *Die politische Ökonomie der europäischen Integration* (Frankfurt am Main: Campus), 335–65.

Leibfried, S., and Pierson, P. (1995) (eds.), *European Social Policy: Between Fragmentation and Integration* (Washington, DC: Brookings Institution).

Leibfried, S., and Pierson, P. (2000), 'Social Policy: Left to the Courts and Markets?', in H. Wallace and W. Wallace (eds.), *Policy-Making in the European Union*, 4th edn. (Oxford: Oxford University Press), 267–92.

Leibfried, S., and Starke, P. (2008), 'Transforming the "Cordon Sanitaire": The Liberalization of Public Services and the Restructuring of European Welfare States', *Socio-Economic Review*, 6/1: 175–82.

Leibfried, S., and Zürn, M. (2005), 'Reconfiguring the National Constellation', in S. Leibfried and M. Zürn (eds.), *Transformations of the State?* (Cambridge: Cambridge University Press), 1–36.

Lenschow, A. (2003), 'New Regulatory Approaches in Greening EU Policies', *European Law Journal*, 8/1: 19–37.

Lenschow, A. (2005), 'Environmental Policy: Contending Dynamics of Policy Change', in H. Wallace, W. Wallace, and M. A. Pollack (eds.), *Policy-Making in the European Union*, 5th edn. (Oxford: Oxford University Press), 304–27.

Lenschow, A. (2007), 'Environmental Policy in the European Union: Bridging Policy, Politics and Polity Dimensions', in K. E. Jørgensen, M. A. Pollack, and B. Rosamond (eds.), *The Handbook of European Union Politics* (London: Sage), 413–32.

Lenschow, A. (2009), 'The Internalization of External Pressure: EU Climate Change Policy', *European Union Studies Association Review*, 22/3: 4–7.

Lenschow, A., and Sprungk, C. (2010), 'The Myth of a Green Europe', *Journal of Common Market Studies*, 48/1: 133–54.

Leonardi, R. (2005), *Cohesion Policy in the European Union: The Building of Europe* (Basingstoke: Palgrave Macmillan).

Lequesne, C. (2005), 'Fisheries Policy: Letting the Little Ones Go', in H. Wallace, W. Wallace, and M. A. Pollack (eds.), *Policy-Making in the European Union*, 5th edn. (Oxford: Oxford University Press), 353–76.

Levitz, P., and Pop-Eleches, G. (2010), 'Why No Backsliding? The European Union's Impact on Democracy and Governance Before and After Accession', *Comparative Political Studies*, 43/4: 457–85.

Levy, M. A., Keohane, R. O., and Haas, P. M. (1993), 'Improving the Effectiveness of International Environmental Institutions', in P. M. Haas, R. O. Keohane, and M. A. Levy (eds.), *Institutions for the Earth* (Cambridge: The MIT Press), 397–426.

Lewis, J. (2005), 'The Janus Face of Brussels: Socialization and Everyday Decision Making in the European Union', *International Organization*, 59/4: 937–71.

Lewis, J. (2012), 'Institutions: the Council of Ministers and the European Council', in E. Jones, A. Menon, and S. Weatherill (eds.), *The Oxford Handbook of the European Union* (Oxford: Oxford University Press), 321–35.

Liefferink, D., and Andersen, M. S. (1998), 'Strategies of the "Green" Member States in EU Environmental Policy-Making', *Journal of European Public Policy*, 5/2: 254–70.

Liefferink, D., and Jordan, A. (2004) (eds.), *Environmental Policy in Europe: The Europeanisation of National Environmental Policy* (London: Routledge).

Lindberg, L. N. (1963), *The Political Dynamics of European Economic Integration* (Stanford, CA: Stanford University Press).

Lindberg, L. N., and Scheingold, S. A. (1970), *Europe's Would-Be Polity* (Englewood Cliffs, NJ: Prentice-Hall).

Lindblom, C. (1977), *Politics and Markets* (New York, NY: Basic Books).

Lindner, J. (2006), *Conflict and Change in EU Budgetary Politics* (London: Routledge).

Linklater, A. (2005), 'A European Civilising Process?', in C. Hill and M. Smith (eds.), *International Relations and the European Union* (Oxford: Oxford University Press), 367–87.

Linsenmann, I., Meyer, C., and Wessels, W. (2007) (eds.), *Economic Government of the EU: A Balance Sheet of New Modes of Policy Coordination* (Basingstoke: Palgrave Macmillan).

Lowe, P. (2006), 'Preserving and Promoting Competition: A European Response', *Competition Policy Newsletter*, 2, Summer.

Lowe, P., Buller, H., and Ward, N. (2002), 'Setting the Next Agenda? British and French Approaches to the Second Pillar of the Common Agricultural Policy', *Journal of Rural Studies*, 18/1: 1–17.

Lowi, T. J. (1964), 'American Business, Public Policy, Case-Studies, and Political Theory', *World Politics*, 16/4: 677–715.

Lowi, T. J. (1972), 'Four Systems of Policy, Politics and Choice', *Public Administration Review*, 32/4: 298–310.

Lyons, B., and Zhu, M. (2013), 'Compensating Competitors or Restoring Competition? EU Regulation of State Aid for Banks During the Financial Crisis', *Journal of Industry, Competition and Trade*, 13/1: 39–66.

Maes, I. (2004), 'On the Origins of the Franco-German EMU Controversies', *European Journal of Law and Economics*, 17/1: 21–39.

Magnette, P. (2004), 'Deliberation or Bargaining? Coping with Constitutional Conflicts in the Convention on the Future of Europe', in E. O. Eriksen, J. E. Fossum, and A. J. Menéndez (eds.), *Developing a Constitution for Europe* (London: Routledge), 207–25.

Majone, G. (1991), 'Cross-National Sources of Regulatory Policymaking in Europe and the United States', *Journal of Public Policy*, 2/1: 79–106.

Majone, G. (1993), 'The European Community between Social Policy and Social Regulation', *Journal of Common Market Studies*, 31/2: 153–70.

Majone, G. (1994), 'The Rise of the Regulatory State in Europe', *West European Politics*, 17/3: 77–101.

Majone, G. (1995), 'Quelle politique sociale pour l'Europe?', in Y. Mény, P. Muller, and J.-L. Quermonne (eds.), *Politiques Publiques en Europe* (Paris: L'Harmattan), 271–86.

Majone, G. (1996) (ed.), *Regulating Europe* (London: Routledge).

Majone, G. (2000*a*), 'Two Logics of Delegation: Agency and Fiduciary Relations in EU Governance', *European Union Politics*, 2/1: 103–21.

Majone, G. (2000*b*), 'The Credibility Crisis of Community Regulation', *Journal of Common Market Studies*, 38/2: 273–302.

Majone, G. (2005), *Dilemmas of European Integration: The Ambiguities and Pitfalls of Integration by Stealth* (Oxford: Oxford University Press).

Manners, I. (2002), 'Normative Power Europe: A Contradiction in Terms?', *Journal of Common Market Studies*, 40/2: 235–58.

Manners, I. (2007), 'Another Europe is Possible: Critical Perspectives on European Union Politics', in K. E. Jørgensen, M. A. Pollack, and B. Rosamond (eds.), *The Handbook of European Union Politics* (London: Sage), 77–96.

Manners, I. (2008), 'The Normative Ethics of the European Union', *International Affairs*, 84/1: 45–60.

Manow, P., Schäfer, A., and Zorn, H. (2004), *European Social Policy and Europe's Party-Political Center of Gravity, 1957–2003*, MPifG Discussion Paper 04/6 (Cologne: Max Planck Institute for the Study of Societies), available at *http://www.mpifg.de/pu/mpifg_dp/dp046.pdf*.

March, J. G., and Olsen, J. P. (1989), *Rediscovering Institutions: The Organizational Basis of Politics* (New York, NY: Free Press).

Marcou, G. (2002) (ed.), *Regionalization for Development and Accession to the European Unions: A Comparative Perspective* (Budapest: Local Government and Public Service Reform Initiative).

Marjolin Report (1975), *Report of the Study Group 'Economic and Monetary Union 1980'*, II/675/3/74—E fin. (Brussels: European Commission).

Marks, G. (1992), 'Structural Policy in the European Community', in A. M. Sbragia (ed.), *Euro-Politics: Institutions and Policy-Making in the 'New' European Community* (Washington, DC: Brookings Institution), 191–224.

Marks, G. (1993), 'Structural Policy and Multilevel Governance in the EC', in A. W. Cafruny and G. G. Rosenthal (eds.), *The State of the European Community*, vol. ii: *The Maastricht Debates and Beyond* (Boulder, CO: Lynne Rienner), 391–409.

Martin, A., and Ross, G. (2004), *Euros and Europeans: Monetary Integration and the European Model of Society* (Cambridge: Cambridge University Press).

Masraff, N. (2011), 'Why Keep Complying? Compliance with EU Conditionality under Diminished Credibility in Turkey', PhD thesis, London School of Economics.

Matlary, J. H. (1996), 'Energy Policy: From a National to a European Framework?', in H. Wallace and W. Wallace (eds.), *Policy-Making in the European Union*, 3rd edn. (Oxford: Oxford University Press), 257–77.

Matsaganis, M. (2011), 'The Welfare State and the Crisis: The Case of Greece', *Journal of European Social Policy*, 21/5: 501–12.

Mattila, M. (2004), 'Contested Decisions—Empirical Analysis of Voting in the EU Council of Ministers', *European Journal of Political Research*, 43/1: 29–50.

Mattli, W., and Slaughter, A.-M. (1995), 'Law and Politics in the European Union: A Reply to Garrett', *International Organization*, 49/1: 183–90.

Mattli, W., and Slaughter, A.-M. (1998), 'Revisiting the European Court of Justice', *International Organization*, 52/1: 177–210.

Mau, S., and Verwiebe, R. (2009), *Die Sozialstruktur Europas* (Konstanz: UVK Verlagsgesellschaft).

Maurer, A. (2003), 'Less Bargaining—More Deliberation: The Convention Method for Enhancing EU Democracy', *Internationale Politik und Gesellschaft*, 1: 167–90.

Maydell, B. Baron von (1991), 'Einführung in die Schlussdiskussion', in B. Schulte and H. F. Zacher (eds.), *Wechselwirkungen zwischen dem europäischen Sozialrecht und dem Sozialrecht der Bundesrepublik Deutschland* (Berlin: Duncker & Humblot), 229–36.

Maydell, B. Baron von (1999), 'Auf dem Weg zu einem gemeinsamen Markt für Gesundheitsleistungen in der Europäischen Gemeinschaft', *Vierteljahresschrift für Sozialrecht*, 1: 3–19.

Maydell, B. Baron von, Borchardt, K., Henke, K.-D., Leitner, R., Muffels, R., Quante, M., Rauhala, P.-L. K., Verschraegen, G., and Zukowski, M. (2006) (eds.), *Enabling Social Europe* (Berlin: Springer).

Mayer, C. (2013), 'Meet the Woman Who Helped Negotiate the Iran Nuclear Deal', *Time Magazine*, 25 Nov.

Mayhew, A. (1998), *Recreating Europe: The European Union's Policy towards Central and Eastern Europe* (Cambridge: Cambridge University Press).

Mazey, S. (1998), 'The European Union and Women's Rights: From the Europeanization of National Agendas to the Nationalization of a European Agenda?', *Journal of European Public Policy*, 5/1: 131–52.

McAleavey, P. (1992), 'The Politics of the European Regional Development Policy: The European Commission's RECHAR Initiative and the Concept of Additionally', *Strathclyde Papers on Government and Politics*, No. 88 (Glasgow: University of Strathclyde).

McCann, P., and Ortega-Argilés, R. (2013), 'Redesigning and Reforming European Regional Policy: The Reasons, the Logic, and the Outcomes', *International Regional Science Review*, 36/3: 424–45.

McCormick, J. (2006), 'Policymaking in the European Union', in E. E. Zeff and E. B. Pirro (eds.), *The European Union and the Member States*, 2nd edn. (Boulder, CO: Lynne Rienner), 11–31.

McDonagh, B. (1998), *Original Sin in a Brave New World: The Paradox of Europe: An Account of the Negotiation of the Treaty of Amsterdam* (Dublin: Institute of European Affairs).

McElroy, G. (2007), 'Legislative Politics', in K. E. Jørgensen, M. A. Pollack, and B. Rosamond (eds.), *The Handbook of European Union Politics* (London: Sage), 175–94.

McNamara, K. R. (1998), *The Currency of Ideas: Monetary Politics in the European Union* (Ithaca, NY: Cornell University Press).

McNamara, K. R. (2005), 'Economic and Monetary Union: Innovation and Challenges for the Euro', in H. Wallace, W. Wallace, and M. A. Pollack (eds.), *Policy-Making in the European Union*, 5th edn. (Oxford: Oxford University Press), 141–60.

McNamara, K. R., and Meunier, S. (2002), 'Between National Sovereignty and International Power: What External Voice for the Euro?', *International Affairs*, 78/4: 849–68.

Mearsheimer, J. J. (1990), 'Back to the Future: Instability in Europe After the Cold War', *International Security*, 15/4: 5–56.

Mearsheimer, J. J. (1994–95), 'The False Promise of International Institutions', *International Security*, 19/3: 5–49.

Meester, G. (1999), 'European Agricultural Policy in Transformation: The CAP Decision Making Process', unpublished paper.

Mendez, C. (2011), 'The Lisbonization of EU Cohesion Policy: A Successful Case of Experimentalist Governance?' *European Planning Studies*, 19/3: 519–37.

Mendez, C. (2013), 'The Post-2013 Reform of EU Cohesion Policy and the Place-based Narrative', *Journal of European Public Policy*, 20/5: 639–59.

Menon, A. (2004), 'From Crisis to Catharsis: ESDP after Iraq', *International Affairs*, 80/4: 631–48.

Menon, A., and Sedelmeier, U. (2010), 'Instruments and Intentionality: Civilian Crisis Management and Enlargement Conditionality in EU Security Policy', *West European Politics*, 33/1: 75–92.

Menz, G. (2003), 'Re-regulating the Single Market: National Varieties of Capitalism and Their Responses to Europeanization', *Journal of European Public Policy*, 10/4: 532–55.

Milner, H. V. (1998), 'Rationalizing Politics: The Emerging Synthesis of International, American and Comparative Politics', *International Organization*, 52/4: 759–86.

Milward, A. S. (1992), *The European Rescue of the Nation-State* (London: Routledge).

Milward, A. S. (2000), *The European Rescue of the Nation-State*, 2nd edn. (London: Routledge).

Milward, A. S., and Lynch, F. M. B. (1993) (eds.), *The Frontiers of National Sovereignty: History and Theory 1945–1992* (London: Routledge).

Mitsilegas, V. (2009), *EU Criminal Law* (London: Hart).

Mitsilegas, V., Monar, J., and Rees, W. (2003), *The European Union and Internal Security: Guardian of the People?* (Basingstoke: Palgrave Macmillan).

Moe, T. (1984), 'The New Economics of Organization', *American Journal of Political Science*, 28/4: 739–77.

Molino, E., and Zuleeg, F. (2011), 'The EU Budget in an Era of Austerity: Settling the Example of Compensating for National Spending Cuts?', paper presented at the workshop 'The Post-2013 Financial Perspectives: Re-thinking EU Finances in Times of Crisis', Turin, 7–8 July.

Molyneux, C. G. (1999), 'The Trade Barriers Regulation: The European Union as a Player in the Globalization Game', *European Law Journal*, 5/4: 375–418.

Monar, J. (1997), 'European Union—Justice and Home Affairs: A Balance Sheet and an Agenda for Reform', in G. Edwards and A. Pijpers (eds.), *The Politics of European Treaty Reform: The 1996 Intergovernmental Conference and Beyond* (London: Pinter/Cassell), 326–39.

Monar, J. (2001), 'The Dynamics of Justice and Home Affairs: Laboratories, Driving Factors and Costs', *Journal of Common Market Studies*, 39/4: 747–64.

Monti, M. (2003), 'EU Competition Policy after May 2004', paper presented at the Fordham Corporate Law Institute.

Monti, M. (2010), *A New Strategy for the Single Market: At the Service of Europe's Economy and Society: Report to the President of the European Commission José Manuel Barroso*, 9 May.

Moran, M., Rein, M., and Goodin, R. E. (2006) (eds.), *The Oxford Handbook of Public Policy* (Oxford: Oxford University Press).

Morata, F., and Muñoz, X. (1996), 'Vying for European Funds: Territorial Restructuring in Spain', in L. Hooghe (ed.), *Cohesion Policy and European Integration* (Oxford: Oxford University Press), 195–214.

Moravcsik, A. (1991), 'Negotiating the Single European Act: National Interests and Conventional Statecraft in the European Community', *International Organization*, 45/1: 19–56.

Moravcsik, A. (1993a), 'Preferences and Power in the European Community: A Liberal Intergovernmentalist Approach', *Journal of Common Market Studies*, 31/4: 473–524.

Moravcsik, A. (1993b), 'Introduction: Integrating International and Domestic Theories of International Bargaining', in P. B. Evans, H. K. Jacobson, and R. D. Putnam (eds.), *Double-Edged Diplomacy: International Bargaining and Domestic Politics* (Berkeley, CA: University of California Press), 3–42.

Moravcsik, A. (1998), *The Choice for Europe: Social Purpose and State Power from Messina to Maastricht* (Ithaca, NY: Cornell University Press).

Moravcsik, A. (1999), 'Is Something Rotten in the State of Denmark? Constructivism and European Integration', *Journal of European Public Policy*, 6/4: 669–81.

Moravcsik, A. (2001), 'Federalism in the European Union: Rhetoric and Reality', in K. Nicolaïdis and R. Howse (eds.), *The Federal Vision: Legitimacy and Levels of Governance in the United States and the European Union* (Oxford: Oxford University Press), 161–87.

Moravcsik, A. (2002), 'In Defense of the Democratic Deficit: Reassessing Legitimacy in the European Union', *Journal of Common Market Studies*, 40/4: 603–24.

Moravcsik, A. (2009), 'Europe: The Quiet Superpower', *French Politics*, 7/3–4: 403–22.

Moravcsik, A. (2010), 'Europe, the Second Superpower', *Current History*, Mar.: 91–8.

Moravcsik, A. (2013), 'Did Power Politics Cause European Integration? Realist Theory Meets Qualitative Methods', *Security Studies*, 22/4: 773–90.

Moravcsik, A., and Schimmelfennig, F. (2009), 'Liberal Intergovernmentalism', in A. Wiener and T. Diez (eds.), *European Integration Theory*, 2nd edn. (Oxford: Oxford University Press), 67–87.

Moravcsik, A., and Vachudova, M. A. (2003), 'National Interests, State Power, and EU Enlargement', *East European Politics and Societies*, 17/1: 42–57.

Mosher, J. S., and Trubek, D. (2003), 'Alternative Approaches to Governance in the EU: EU Social Policy and the European Employment Strategy', *Journal of Common Market Studies*, 41/1: 63–88.

Mossialos, E., and McKee, M. (2002), *EU Law and the Social Character of Health Care* (Brussels: PLE-Peter Lang).

Mossialos, E., Dixon, A., Figueras, J., and Kutzin, J. (2002) (eds.), *Funding Health Care: Options for Europe* (Buckingham: Open University Press).

Motta, M. (2004), *Competition Policy: Theory and Practice* (Cambridge: Cambridge University Press).

Moyer, H., and Josling, T. (2002), *Agricultural Policy Reform: Politics and Processes in the EU and in the US in the 1990s* (Aldershot: Ashgate).

Mudde, C. (2014), 'The Far Right and the European Elections', *Current History*, Mar.: 98–103.

Müller, H. (2003), 'Interests or Ideas? The Regulation of Insurance Services and the European Single Market: Trade Liberalisation, Risk Regulation and Limits to Market Integration', D.Phil. thesis, University of Sussex, Falmer.

Mundell, R. A. (1961), 'A Theory of Optimum Currency Areas', *American Economic Review*, 51/4: 657–65.

Naômé, C. (2010), 'EU Enlargement and the European Court of Justice', in E. Best, T. Christiansen, and P. Settembri (eds.), *The Institutions of the Enlarged European Union* (Cheltenham: Edward Elgar), 100–19.

Nato (1999), 'Washington Summit Communiqué Issued by the Heads of State and Government participating in the meeting of the North Atlantic Council in Washington,

DC on 24th April 1999', Press Release NAC-S(99)64, available at *http://www.nato.int/docu/pr/1999/p99-064e.htm*.

Naurin, D., and Wallace, H. (2008) (eds.), *Unveiling the Council of the European Union: Games Governments Play in Brussels* (Basingstoke: Palgrave Macmillan).

Naurin, D., Hayes-Renshaw, F., and Wallace, H. (forthcoming), *The Council of Ministers*, 3rd edn. (Basingstoke: Palgrave Macmillan).

Nedergaard, P. (2006), 'Market Failures and Government Failures: A Theoretical Model of the Common Agricultural Policy', *Public Choice*, 127/3–4: 393–413.

Neergard, U., Nielsen, R., and Roseberry, L. M. (2008) (eds.), *The Services Directive: Consequences for the Welfare State and the European Social Model* (Copenhagen: DJØF Publishers).

Neville-Jones, P. (1997), 'Dayton, IFOR and Alliance Relations', *Survival*, 38/4: 45–65.

Neville-Rolfe, E. (1984), *The Politics of Agriculture in the European Community* (London: Policy Studies Institute).

New York Times, various issues.

Niblett, R., and Wallace, W. (2001) (eds.), *Rethinking European Order: West European Responses, 1989–1997* (Basingstoke: Palgrave Macmillan).

Nicolaïdis, K., and Schmidt, S. K. (2007), 'Mutual Recognition "On Trial": The Long Road to Services Liberalization', *Journal of European Public Policy*, 14/5: 717–34.

Niskanen, W. A. (1971), *Bureaucracy and Representative Government* (Chicago, IL: Aldine-Atherton).

Nivola, P. S. (1998), 'American Social Regulation Meets the Global Economy', in P. S. Nivola (ed.), *Comparative Disadvantages: Social Regulations and the Global Economy* (Washington, DC: Brookings Institution), 16–65.

Noord, P. van den, Döhring, B., Langedijk, S., Nogueira-Martins, J., Pench, L., Temprano-Arroyo, H., and Thiel, M. (2008), 'The Evolution of Economics Governance in EMU', *European Economy*, Economic Papers, No. 328.

North, D. C. (1990), *Institutions, Institutional Change and Economic Performance* (Cambridge: Cambridge University Press).

Noutcheva, G. (2012), *European Foreign Policy and the Challenges of Balkan Accession: Conditionality, Legitimacy and Compliance* (London: Routledge).

Novak, S. (2013), 'The Silence of Ministers: Consensus and Blame Avoidance in the Council of the European Union', *Journal of Common Market Studies*, 51/6: 1091–107.

Nugent, N. (2004) (ed.), *European Union Enlargement* (Basingstoke: Palgrave Macmillan).

Nugent, N. (2006), *The Government and Politics of the European Union*, 6th edn. (Basingstoke: Palgrave Macmillan).

Numhauser-Henning, A., and Rönnmar, M. (2013), *Normative Patterns and Legal Developments in the Social Dimension of the EU* (Oxford: Hart).

Nyberg, P. (2011), 'Misjudging Risk: Causes of the Systemic Banking Crisis in Ireland', Report of the Commission of Investigation into the Banking Sector in Ireland (Dublin: The Stationery Office).

Obermaier, A. J. (2008), 'Fine-Tuning the Jurisprudence: The ECJ's Judicial Activism and Self-Restraint' (Vienna: Austrian Academy of Sciences, Working Paper 02/08).

Oberthür, S., and Pallemaerts, M. (2010), *The New Climate Policies of the European Union: Internal Legislation and Climate Diplomacy* (Brussels: Brussels University Press).

Obinger, H., Leibfried, S., and Castles, F. G. (2005), 'Bypasses to a Social Europe? Lessons from Federal Experience', *Journal of European Public Policy*, 12/3: 545–71.

Obinger, H., Schmitt, C., and Starke, P. (2013), 'Policy Diffusion and Policy Transfer in Social Policy in Comparative Social Policy Research', *Social Policy and Administration*, 47/1: 111–29.

Obstfeld, M., and Rogoff, K. (2009), 'Global Imbalances and the Financial Crisis: Products of Common Causes', *Proceedings, Federal Reserve Bank of San Francisco*, 131–72.

Occhipinti, J. D. (2003), *The Politics of EU Police Cooperation: Towards a European FBI?* (Boulder, CO: Lynne Rienner).

OECD (Organization for Economic Co-operation and Development) (2013), 'House Prices', *Economics: Key Tables from OECD*, No. 17.

Oel, M., and Rapp-Lücke, J. (2008), 'Preparing Decision-Making on the Political Level in the EU-27 Plus: The Example of European Home Affairs', Working Paper Series on EU Internal Security Governance, no. 11, Securint Collection (Strasbourg: Université Robert Schuman).

Offe, C. (2000), 'The Democratic Welfare State in an Integrating Europe', in M. T. Greven and L. Pauly (eds.), *Democracy Beyond the State? The European Dilemma and the Emerging Global Order* (Lanham, MD: Rowman & Littlefield), 63–89.

Offe, C. (2003), 'The European Model of "Social" Capitalism: Can It Survive European Integration?', *Journal of Political Philosophy*, 11/4: 437–69.

Olson, M. (1965), *The Logic of Collective Action* (Cambridge, MA: Harvard University Press).

Orden, D., Paarlberg, R., and Roe, T. (1999), *Policy Reform in American Agriculture: Analysis and Prognosis* (Chicago, IL: University of Chicago Press).

Ostner, I., and Lewis, J. (1995), 'Gender and the Evolution of European Social Policy', in S. Leibfried and P. Pierson (eds.), *European Social Policy: Between Fragmentation and Integration* (Washington, DC: Brookings Institution), 159–93.

Padoa-Schioppa, T. (1999), 'EMU and Banking Supervision', lecture delivered at the London School of Economics, Financial Markets Group, 24 Feb.

Padoa-Schioppa, T. (2000), *The Road to Monetary Union in Europe: The Emperor, the Kings and the Genies* (Oxford: Oxford University Press).

Page, E. C. (2006), 'The Origins of Policy', in M. Moran, M. Rein, and R. E. Goodin (eds.), *The Oxford Handbook of Public Policy* (Oxford: Oxford University Press), 207–27.

Pagoulatos, G., and Tsoukalis, L. (2012), 'Multilevel Governance', in E. Jones, A. Menon, and S. Weatherill (eds.), *The Oxford Handbook of the European Union* (Oxford: Oxford University Press), 62–75.

Pallemaerts, M. (2013), 'Developing More Sustainably?', in A. Jordan and C. Adelle (eds.), *Environmental Policy in the EU: Actors, Institutions and Processes*, 3rd edn. (London: Earthscan), 346–66.

Panagiotarea, E. (2013), *Greece in the Euro: Economic Delinquency or System Failure?* (Colchester: ECPR Press).

Papadopoulos, T., and Roumpakis, A. (2012), 'The Greek Welfare State in the Age of Austerity: Anti-social Policy and the Politico-economic Crisis', in M. Kilkey, G. Ramia, and K. Farnsworth (eds.), *Social Policy Review 24, Analysis and Debate in Social Policy, 2012* (Bristol: Policy Press), 205–29.

Papadopoulos, T., and Roumpakis, A. (2013), 'Familistic Welfare Capitalism in Crisis: Social Reproduction and Anti-social Policy in Greece', *Journal of International and Comparative Social Policy*, 29/3: 204–24.

Parsons, C. (2003), *A Certain Idea of Europe* (Ithaca, NY: Cornell Univrsity Press).

Parsons, C. (2008), 'The SEA Story and Globalization', paper presented to the 38th UACES Annual Conference, Edinburgh, 1–3 Sept.

Parsons, C. (2012), 'Sociological Perspectives on European Integration', in E. Jones, A. Menon, and S. Weatherill (eds.), *The Oxford Handbook of the European Union* (Oxford: Oxford University Press), 48–61.

Parsons, C. (2013), 'Power, Patterns, and Process in European Union History', *Security Studies*, 22/4: 791–801.

Patterson, B. (2011), *Understanding the EU Budget* (London: Searching Finance).

Pearce, J. (1981), *The Common Agricultural Policy: Prospects for Change* (London: Routledge & Kegan Paul).

Pearce, J., and Sutton, J. (1985), *Protection and Industrial Policy in Europe* (London: Routledge).

Pedersen, A. W. (2004), 'The Privatization of Retirement Income? Variation and Trends in the Income Package of Old Age Pensioners', *Journal of European Social Policy*, 14/1: 5–2.

Peers, S. (2012), *EU Justice and Home Affairs Law* (Oxford: Oxford University Press).

Pelkmans, J. (1984), *Market Integration in the European Community* (The Hague: Martinus Nijhoff).

Pelkmans, J. (2011), 'The Case for "More Single Market"', CEPS Policy Brief No. 234 (Brussels: Centre for European Policy Studies).

Pelkmans, J., and Murphy, A. (1991), 'Catapulted into Leadership: The Community's Trade and Aid Policies vis-à-vis Eastern Europe', *Journal of European Integration*, 14/2–3: 125–51.

Pelkmans, J., and Winters, L. A. (1988), *Europe's Domestic Market* (London: Royal Institute of International Affairs).

Peña-Casas, R. (2013), 'Desperately Seeking the European Employment Strategy in the New Economic Governance of the EU', in D. Natali and B. Vanhercke (eds.), *Social Developments in the European Union 2012, 14th Annual Report* (Brussels: ETUI/OSE), 123–145.

Permanand, G., Baeten, R., Mossialos, E., and Hervey, T. K. (2010) (eds.), *Health Systems Governance in Europe: The Role of European Union Law and Policy* (Cambridge: Cambridge University Press).

Pesendorfer, D. (2006), 'EU Environmental Policy under Pressure: Chemicals Policy Change between Antagonistic Goals?', *Environmental Politics*, 15/1: 95–114.

Peters, B. G. (1992), 'Bureaucratic Politics and the Institutions of the European Community', in A. M. Sbragia (ed.), *Euro-Politics: Institutions and Policy-Making in the 'New' European Community* (Washington, DC: Brookings Institution), 75–122.

Peters, B. G. (1994), 'Agenda-Setting in the European Community', *Journal of European Public Policy*, 1/1: 9–26.

Peters, B. G. (1997), 'Escaping the Joint-Decision Trap: Repetition and Sectoral Politics in the European Union', *West European Politics*, 20/2: 22–37.

Peters, B. G. (1999), *Institutional Theory in Political Science: The 'New Institutionalism'* (London: Continuum).

Peters, B. G. (2001), *The Future of Governing*, 2nd edn. (Lawrence, KS: University of Kansas Press).

Peters, B. G. (2012), 'Coordination in the EU', in E. Jones, A. Menon, and S. Weatherill (eds.), *The Oxford Handbook of the European Union* (Oxford: Oxford University Press), 795–809.

Peters, B. G., and Pierre, J. (1998), 'Institutions and Time: Problems of Conceptualization and Explanation', *Journal of Public Administration Research and Theory*, 8/4: 565–83.

Petersen, J. H. (1991), 'Harmonization of Social Security in the EC Revisited', *Journal of Common Market Studies*, 29/5: 505–26.

Petersen, J. H. (2000), 'Financing of the Welfare State: Possibilities and Limits', in B. Baron von Maydell (ed.), *Entwicklungen der Systeme sozialer Sicherheit in Japan und Europa* (Berlin: Duncker & Humblot), 289–318.

Peterson, J. (1995), 'Decision-Making in the European Union: Towards a Framework for Analysis', *Journal of European Public Policy*, 2/1: 69–93.

Peterson, J. (1997), 'States, Societies and the European Union', *West European Politics*, 20/4: 1–24.

Peterson, J. (2004), 'Policy Networks', in A. Wiener and T. Diez (eds.), *European Integration Theory*, 1st edn. (Oxford: Oxford University Press), 117–35.

Peterson, J. (2009), 'Policy Networks', in A. Wiener and T. Diez (eds.), *European Integration Theory*, 2nd edn. (Oxford: Oxford University Press), 105–24.

Peterson, J. (2012), 'The EU as a Global Actor', in E. Bomberg, J. Peterson, and R. Corbett (eds.), *The European Union: How Does it Work?*, 3rd edn. (Oxford: Oxford University Press).

Peterson, J., and Bomberg, E. (1999), *Decision-Making in the European Union* (Basingstoke: Palgrave Macmillan).

Peterson, J., and Shackleton, M. (2012) (eds.), *The Institutions of the European Union*, 3rd edn. (Oxford: Oxford University Press).

Peterson, J. and Young, A. R. (2007) (eds.), *The European Union and the New Trade Politics* (London: Routledge).

Peterson, P. E., and Rom, M. C. (1990), *Welfare Magnets: A New Case for a National Standard* (Washington, DC: Brookings Institution).

Pew Research Center (2013), *The New Sick Man of Europe: The European Union*, available at *http://www.pewglobal.org/files/2013/05/Pew-Research-Center-Global-Attitudes-Project-European-Union-Report-FINAL-FOR-PRINT-May-13-2013.pdf*.

Phinnemore, D. (1999), *Association: Stepping-Stone or Alternative to EU Membership?* (Sheffield: Sheffield Academic Press).

Phinnemore, D. (2003), 'Stabilisation and Association Agreements: Europe Agreements for the Western Balkans?', *European Foreign Affairs Review*, 8/1: 77–103.

Pierson, P. (1993), 'When Effects Become Cause: Policy Feedback and Political Change', *World Politics*, 45/4: 595–628.

Pierson, P. (1995a), 'The Creeping Nationalization of Income Transfers in the United States', in S. Leibfried and P. Pierson (eds.), *European Social Policy: Between Fragmentation and Integration* (Washington, DC: Brookings Institution), 301–28.

Pierson, P. (1995b), 'Federal Institutions and the Development of Social Policy', *Governance*, 8/4: 449–78.

Pierson, P. (1996), 'The Path to European Integration: A Historical Institutionalist Analysis', *Comparative Political Studies*, 29/2: 123–63.

Pierson, P. (2000), 'Increasing Returns, Path Dependence, and the Study of Politics', *American Political Science Review*, 94/2: 251–67.

Pierson, P. (2001) (ed.), *The New Politics of the Welfare State* (Oxford: Oxford University Press).

Pierson, P., and Leibfried, S. (1995), 'The Dynamics of Social Policy Integration', in S. Leibfried and P. Pierson (eds.), *European Social Policy: Between Fragmentation and Integration* (Washington, DC: Brookings Institution), 432–65.

Pinder, J. (1968), 'Positive Integration and Negative Integration: Some Problems of Economic Union in the EEC', *World Today*, 24/3: 88–110.

Pinder, J. (1991), *The European Community and Eastern Europe* (London: Pinter).

Pisani-Ferry, J. (2006), 'Only One Bed for Two Dreams: A Critical Retrospective on the Debate over the Economic Governance of the Euro Area', *Journal of Common Market Studies*, 44/4: 823–44.

Pochet, P. (2003), 'Pensions: The European Debate', in G. L. Clark and N. C. Whiteside (eds.), *Pension Security in the 21st Century: Redrawing the Public-Private Debate* (Oxford: Oxford University Press), 44–63.

Polanyi, K. (1994) [1944], *The Great Transformation* (New York, NY: Rinehart).

Pollack, M. A. (1995), 'Regional Actors in an Intergovernmental Play: The Making and Implementation of EC Structural Policy', in C. Rhodes and S. Mazey (eds.), *The State of the European Union*, vol. iii: *Building a European Polity?* (Boulder, CO: Lynne Rienner): 361–90.

Pollack, M. A. (1997), 'Delegation, Agency and Agenda Setting in the European Community', *International Organization*, 51/1: 99–134.

Pollack, M. A. (2003), *The Engines of European Integration: Delegation, Agency and Agenda Setting in the EU* (Oxford: Oxford University Press).

Pollack, M. A. (2004), 'The New Institutionalisms and European Integration', in A. Wiener and T. Diez (eds.), *European Integration Theory*, 1st edn. (Oxford: Oxford University Press), 137–56.

Pollack, M. A. (2009), 'The New Institutionalisms and European Integration', in A. Wiener and T. Diez (eds.), *European Integration Theory*, 2nd edn. (Oxford: Oxford University Press), 125–43.

Pollack, M. A., and Shaffer, G. S. (2010), 'Biotechnology Policy: Between National Fears and Global Disciplines', in H. Wallace, M. A. Pollack, and A. R. Young (eds.), *Policy-Making in the European Union*, 6th edn. (Oxford: Oxford University Press), 331–55.

Posner, E. (2009), 'Making Rules for Global Finance: Transatlantic Regulatory Cooperation at the Turn of the Millennium', *International Organization*, 63/4: 665–99.

Preston, C. (1997), *Enlargement and Integration in the European Union* (London: Routledge).

Price, R. (2003), 'Transnational Civil Society and Advocacy in World Politics', *World Politics*, 55/4: 579–606.

Pridham, G. (2005), *Designing Democracy: EU Enlargement and Regime Change in Post-Communist Europe* (Basingstoke: Palgrave Macmillan).

Pridham, G. (2008), 'The EU's Political Conditionality and Post-Accession Tendencies: Comparisons from Slovakia and Latvia', *Journal of Common Market Studies*, 46/2: 365–87.

Prosser, T. (2005), *The Limits of Competition Law* (Oxford: Oxford University Press).

Prügl, E. (2007), 'Gender and European Union Politics', in K. E. Jørgensen, M. A. Pollack, and B. Rosamond (eds.), *The Handbook of European Union Politics* (London: Sage), 433–48.

Puetter, U. (2006), *The Eurogroup: How a Secretive Circle of Finance Ministers Shape European Economic Governance* (Manchester: Manchester University Press).

Puetter, U. (2012), 'Europe's Deliberative Intergovernmentalism: The Role of the Council and the European Council in EU Economic Governance', *Journal of European Public Policy*, 19/2: 161–78.

Putnam, R. D. (1988), 'Diplomacy and Domestic Politics: The Logic of Two-Level Games', *International Organization*, 42/3: 427–60.

Quaglia, L., Eastwood, R., and Holmes, P. (2009), 'The Financial Turmoil and EU Policy Co-operation in 2008', *Journal of Common Market Studies*, 47/s1: 63–87.

Ramos Diaz, J., and Varela, A. (2012), 'From Opportunity to Austerity: Crisis and Social Policy in Spain', in M. Kilkey, G. Ramia, and K. Farnsworth (eds.), *Social Policy Review 24, Analysis and Debate in Social Policy, 2012* (Bristol: Policy Press), 231–56.

RAPID (European Commission press release service), various items.

Raunio, T. (2005), 'Holding Governments Accountable in European Affairs: Explaining Cross-National Variation', *Journal of Legislative Studies*, 11/3–4: 319–43.

Raunio, T. (2012), 'The European Parliament', in E. Jones, A. Menon, and S. Weatherill (eds.), *The Oxford Handbook of the European Union* (Oxford: Oxford University Press), 365–79.

Raustiala, K., and Slaughter, A.-M. (2002), 'International Law, International Relations and Compliance', in W. Carlsnaes, T. Risse, and B. A. Simmons (eds.), *Handbook of International Relations* (New York, NY: Sage), 538–58.

Recchi, E., and Favell, A. (2009) (eds.), *Pioneers of European Integration: Citizenship and Mobility in the EU* (Cheltenham: Edward Elgar).

Reh, C. (2014), 'Is Informal Politics Undemocratic? Trilogues, Early Agreements and the Selection Model of Representation', *Journal of European Public Policy*, 21/6: 822–41.

Reh, C., Héritier, A., Bressanelli, E., and Koop, C. (2013), 'The Informal Politics of Legislation: Explaining Secluded Decision-Making in the European Union', *Comparative Political Studies*, 46/9: 1112–42.

Rein, M., and Rainwater, L. (1986) (eds.), *Public–Private Interplay in Social Protection: A Comparative Study* (Armonk, NY: M. E. Sharpe).

Reinhart, C. M., and Rogoff, K. (2009), *This Time is Different: Eight Centuries of Financial Folly* (Princeton, NJ: Princeton University Press).

Reinicke, W. H. (1999–2000), 'The Other World Wide Web: Global Public Policy Networks', *Foreign Policy*, 117: 44–57.

Rhode, B. (2010), 'WMD Proliferation', *Adelphi Series*, 50/414–15: 149–75.

Rhodes, M. (1991), 'The Social Dimension of the Single European Market: National versus Transnational Regulation', *European Journal of Political Research*, 19/2–3: 245–80.

Rhodes, M. (1992), 'The Future of the "Social Dimension": Labour Market Regulation in Post-1992 Europe', *Journal of Common Market Studies*, 30/1: 23–51.

Rhodes, M. (1995), 'A Regulatory Conundrum: Industrial Relations and the Social Dimension', in S. Leibfried and P. Pierson (eds.), *European Social Policy: Between Fragmentation and Integration* (Washington, DC: Brookings Institution), 78–122.

Rhodes, M. (1999), 'An Awkward Alliance: France, Germany and Social Policy', in D. Webber (ed.), *The Franco-German Relationship in the European Union* (London: Routledge), 130–47.

Rhodes, M., and Visser, J. (2011), 'Seeking Commitment, Effectiveness and Legitimacy: New Modes of Socio-Economic Governance in Europe', in A. Héritier and M. Rhodes (eds.),

New Modes of Governance in Europe: Governing in the Shadow of Hierarchy (Basingstoke: Palgrave Macmillan), 104–34.

Rhodes, R. A. W. (1996), 'The New Governance: Governing without Government', *Political Studies*, 44/3: 652–7.

Rhodes, R. A. W. (1997), *Understanding Governance* (Buckingham: Open University Press).

Rhodes, R. A. W. (2006), 'Policy Network Analysis', in M. Moran, M. Rein, and R. E. Goodin (eds.), *The Oxford Handbook of Public Policy* (Oxford: Oxford University Press), 425–47.

Richardson, J. J. (1982) (ed.), *Policy Styles in Western Europe* (London: George Allen & Unwin).

Richardson, J. J. (2000), 'Government, Interest Groups and Policy Change', *Political Studies*, 48/5: 1006–25.

Richardson, J. J. (2006), 'Policy-Making in the EU: Interests, Ideas and Garbage Cans of Primeval Soup', in J. Richardson (ed.), *European Union: Power and Policy-Making*, 3rd edn. (London: Routledge), 3–30.

Rieger, E. (2005), 'The Common Agricultural Policy', in H. Wallace, W. Wallace, and M. A. Pollack (eds.), *Policy-Making in the European Union*, 5th edn. (Oxford: Oxford University Press), 161–90.

Rieger, E., and Leibfried, S. (2003), *Limits to Globalization: Welfare States in the World Economy* (Cambridge: Polity).

Riel, B. van, and Meer, M. van der (2002), 'The Advocacy Coalition for European Employment Policy: The European Integration Process after EMU', in H. Hegman and B. Neumaerker (eds.), *Die Europäische Union aus Politökonomischer Perspective* (Marburg: Metropolis Verlag), 117–37.

Riker, W. H. (1962), *The Theory of Political Coalitions* (New Haven, CT: Yale University Press).

Risse, T. (2000), '"Let's Argue!": Communicative Action in World Politics', *International Organization*, 54/1: 1–39.

Risse, T. (2002), 'Constructivism and International Institutions: Towards Conversations across Paradigms', in I. Katznelson and H. V. Milner (eds.), *Political Science: State of the Discipline* (New York, NY: W. W. Norton), 597–623.

Risse, T. (2009), 'Social Constructivism and European Integration', in A. Wiener and T. Diez (eds.), *European Integration Theory*, 2nd edn. (Oxford: Oxford University Press), 144–61.

Risse, T. (2010), *A Community of Europeans? Transnational Identity and Public Spheres* (Ithaca, NY: Cornell University Press).

Risse-Kappen, T. (1991), 'Public Opinion, Domestic Structure and Foreign Policy in Liberal Democracies', *World Politics*, 43/4: 479–512.

Risse-Kappen, T. (1996), 'Exploring the Nature of the Beast: International Relations Theory and Comparative Policy Analysis Meet the European Union', *Journal of Common Market Studies*, 34/1: 51–80.

Rittberger, B. (2005), *Building Europe's Parliament: Democratic Representation Beyond the Nation State* (Oxford: Oxford University Press).

Rittberger, B. (2006), '"No Integration Without Representation!" European Integration, Parliamentary Democracy, and Two Forgotten Communities', *Journal of European Public Policy*, 13/8: 1211–29.

Rittberger, B., and Wonka, A. (2011*a*) (eds.), 'Agency Governance in the EU and its Consequences', *Journal of European Public Policy*, 18/6 (special issue): 770–925.

Rittberger, B., and Wonka, A. (2011*b*), 'Introduction: Agency Governance in the European Union', *Journal of European Public Policy*, 18/6: 780–9.

Robertson, D. B. (1989), 'The Bias of American Federalism: The Limits of Welfare State Development in the Progressive Era', *Journal of Polity History*, 1/3: 261–91.

Roederer-Rynning, C. (2002), 'Farm Conflict in France and the Europeanization of Agricultural Policy', *West European Politics*, 25/3: 107–26.

Roederer-Rynning, C. (2003*a*), 'From "Talking Shop" to "Working Parliament"? The European Parliament and Agricultural Change', *Journal of Common Market Studies*, 41/1: 113–35.

Roederer-Rynning, C. (2003*b*), 'Impregnable Citadel or Leaning Tower? Europe's Common Agricultural Policy at Forty', *SAIS Review*, 23/1: 133–51.

Roederer-Rynning, C. (2004), 'Informal Governance in the Common Agricultural Policy', in T. Christiansen and S. Piattoni (eds.), *Informal Governance in the EU* (Cheltenham: Edward Elgar), 173–89.

Roederer-Rynning, C. (2011), 'The Paradigmatic Case: Beyond Emergency Exits in the CAP', in G. Falkner (ed.), *The EU's Decision Traps: Comparing Policies* (Oxford: Oxford University Press), 18–37.

Roederer-Rynning, C., and Schimmelfennig, F. (2012), 'Bringing Codecision to Agriculture: A Hard Case of Parliamentarization', *Journal of European Public Policy*, 19/7: 951–68.

Roederer-Rynning, C. (2014), 'The EP and the "CAP after 2013" Reform: In Search of a Collective Sense of Purpose', unpublished manuscript.

Romero, F. (1993), 'Migration as an Issue in European Interdependence and Integration: The Case of Italy', in A. S. Milward, F. M. B. Lynch, F. Romero, R. Ranieri, and V. Sørensen (eds.), *The Frontier of National Sovereignty: History and Theory, 1945–1991* (London: Routledge), 33–58, 205–8.

Ronnmar, M. (2008), *EU Industrial Relations versus National Industrial Relations* (The Hague: Kluwer Law International).

Rosamond, B. (2000), *Theories of European Integration* (Basingstoke: Palgrave Macmillan).

Rosati, J. A. (1981), 'Developing a Systematic Decision-Making Framework: Bureaucratic Politics in Perspective', *World Politics*, 33/2: 234–52.

Rosato, S. (2011*a*), *Europe United: Power Politics and the Making of the European Community* (Ithaca, NY: Cornell University Press).

Rosato, S. (2011*b*), 'Europe's Troubles: Power Politics and the State of the European Project', *International Security*, 35/4: 45–86.

Rosenau, J. N. (1992), 'Governance, Order and Change in World Politics', in J. N. Rosenau and E. O. Czempiel (eds.), *Governance without Government: Order and Change in World Politics* (Cambridge: Cambridge University Press), 1–29.

Rosenau, J. N., and Czempiel, E.-O. (1992) (eds.), *Governance Without Government: Order and Change in World Politics* (Cambridge: Cambridge University Press).

Rosenthal, G. G. (1975), *The Men Behind the Decisions: Cases in European Policy-Making* (Lanham, MD: Lexington Books).

Ross, G. (1995*a*), *Jacques Delors and European Integration* (Cambridge: Polity).

Ross, G. (1995b), 'Assessing the Delors Era in Social Policy', in S. Leibfried and P. Pierson (eds.), *European Social Policy: Between Fragmentation and Integration* (Washington, DC: Brookings Institution), 357–88.

Rothgang, H. (2007), *Differenzierung privater Krankenversicherungstarife nach Geschlecht* (Baden-Baden: Nomos).

Rothgang, H., Cacace, M., Frisina, L., Grimmeisen, S., Schmid, A. and Wendt, C. (2010), *The State and Health Care: Comparing OECD Countries* (Basingstoke: Palgrave Macmillan).

Saatcioglu, B. (2010), 'Unpacking the Compliance Puzzle: The Case of Turkey's AKP under EU Conditionality', *Kolleg-Forschergruppe Working Paper*, No. 14 (Berlin: Freie Universität Berlin).

Sabatier, P. A. (1998), 'The Advocacy Coalition Framework: Revisions and Relevance for Europe', *Journal of European Public Policy*, 5/1: 98–130.

Sabatier, P. A. (1999), 'The Need for Better Theories', in P. A. Sabatier (ed.), *Theories of the Policy Process* (Boulder, CO: Westview Press), 3–17.

Sabatier, P. A., and Jenkins-Smith, H. C. (1993), *Policy Change and Learning: An Advocacy Coalition Approach* (Boulder, CO: Westview Press).

Sabel, C., and Zeitlin, J. (2008), 'Learning from Difference: The New Architecture of Experimentalist Governance in the EU', *European Law Journal*, 14/3: 271–327.

Sabel, C., and Zeitlin, J. (2010) (eds.), *Experimentalist Governance in the European Union: Towards a New Architecture* (Oxford: Oxford University Press).

Sadeh, T., and Verdun, A. (2009), 'Explaining Europe's Economic and Monetary Union: A Survey of the Literature', *International Studies Review*, 11/2: 277–301.

Sandholtz, W., and Stone Sweet, A. (2012), 'Neo-Functionalism and Supranational Governance', in E. Jones, A. Menon, and S. Weatherill (eds.), *The Oxford Handbook of the European Union* (Oxford: Oxford University Press), 18–33.

Sandholtz, W., and Zysman, J. (1989), '1992: Recasting the European Bargain', *World Politics*, 42/1: 95–128.

Sapir, A., Aghion, P., Bertola, G., Hellwig, M., Pisani-Ferry, J., Rosati, D., Vinals, J., and Wallace, H. (2004), *An Agenda for a Growing Europe: Making the EU Economic System Deliver, Report of an Independent High Level Study Group* (Chairman: André Sapir) (Oxford: Oxford University Press; originally published online by the EU Commission, 2003).

Sasse, G. (2008), 'The Politics of EU Conditionality: The Norm of Minority Protection During and Beyond EU Accession', *Journal of European Public Policy*, 15/6: 842–60.

Saurugger, S. (2013), *Theoretical Approaches to European Integration* (Basingstoke: Palgrave).

Sbragia, A. (1992) (ed.), *Euro-Politics: Institutions and Policymaking in the 'New' European Community* (Washington, DC: Brookings Institution).

Sbragia, A. (1993), 'The European Community: A Balancing Act', *Publius*, 23/3: 23–38.

Sbragia, A. (1998), 'Institution-Building from Below and Above: The European Community in Global Environmental Politics', in A. Stone Sweet and W. Sandholtz (eds.), *European Integration and Supranational Governance* (Oxford: Oxford University Press), 283–303.

Sbragia, A. (2000), 'Environmental Policy: Economic Constraints and External Pressures', in H. Wallace and W. Wallace (eds.), *Policy-Making in the European Union*, 4th edn. (Oxford: Oxford University Press), 235–55.

Schalk, J., Torenvlied, R., Weesie, J., and Stokman, F. (2007), 'The Power of the Presidency in EU Council Decision-Making', *European Union Politics*, 8/2: 229–50.

Scharpf, F. W. (1988), 'The Joint-Decision Trap: Lessons From German Federalism and European Integration', *Public Administration*, 66/3: 239–78.

Scharpf, F. W. (1994), 'Community and Autonomy: Multi-level Policy-making in the European Union', *Journal of European Public Policy*, 1/2: 219–42.

Scharpf, F. W. (1997), *Games Real Actors Play: Actor-Centered Institutionalism in Policy Research* (Boulder, CO: Westview Press).

Scharpf, F. W. (1999), *Governing in Europe: Effective and Democratic?* (Oxford: Oxford University Press).

Scharpf, F. W. (2002), 'The European Social Model: Coping with the Challenges of Diversity', *Journal of Common Market Studies*, 40/4: 645–70.

Scharpf, F. W. (2006), 'The Joint-Decision Trap Revisited', *Journal of Common Market Studies*, 44/4: 845–64.

Scharpf, F. W. (2009), 'Legitimacy in the Multilevel Polity', *European Political Science Review*, 1/2: 173–204.

Scharpf, F. W. (2010), 'The Asymmetry of European Integration, or Why the EU Cannot be a "Social Market Economy"', *Socio Economic Review*, 8/2: 211–50.

Scharpf, F. W. (2011), 'Monetary Union, Fiscal Crisis and the Preemption of Democracy', LEQS Paper No. 36/2011 (London: London School of Economics).

Schelkle, W. (2006) (ed.), 'Economic Governance in EMU Revisited', *Journal of Common Market Studies*, 44/4: 669–864.

Schelkle, W., and Hassel, A. (2012), 'The Policy Consensus Ruling European Political Economy: The Political Attractions of Discredited Economics', *Global Policy*, 3/1: 16–27.

Schimmelfennig, F. (2001), 'The Community Trap: Liberal Norms, Rhetorical Action, and the Eastern Enlargement of the European Union', *International Organization*, 55/1: 47–80.

Schimmelfennig, F. (2008), 'EU Political Accession Conditionality after the 2004 Enlargement: Consistency and Effectiveness', *Journal of European Public Policy*, 15/6: 918–37.

Schimmelfennig, F. (2012), 'Constructivist Perspectives', in E. Jones, A. Menon, and S. Weatherill (eds.), *The Oxford Handbook of the European Union* (Oxford: Oxford University Press), 34–47.

Schimmelfennig, F., and Sedelmeier, U. (2002), 'Theorizing EU Enlargement: Research Focus, Hypotheses, and the State of Research', *Journal of European Public Policy*, 9/4: 500–28.

Schimmelfennig, F., and Sedelmeier, U. (2005a) (eds.), *The Europeanization of Central and Eastern Europe* (Ithaca, NY: Cornell University Press).

Schimmelfennig, F., and Sedelmeier, U. (2005b) (eds.), *The Politics of EU Enlargement: Theoretical Approaches* (London: Routledge).

Schimmelfennig, F., Engert, S., and Knobel, H. (2006), *International Socialization in Europe: European Organizations, Political Conditionality and Democratic Change* (Basingstoke: Palgrave Macmillan).

Schlachter, M. (2012), 'Equal Treatment for Transnational Temporary Agency Workers?', FORMULA Working Paper 32 (Oslo: University of Oslo).

Schmidt, S. K. (1998), 'Commission Activism: Subsuming Telecommunications and Electricity under European Competition Law', *Journal of European Public Policy*, 5/1: 169–84.

Schmidt, S. K. (2004a), *Die Folgen der europäischen Integration für die Bundesrepublik Deutschland: Wandel durch Verflechtung*, MPIfG Discussion Paper 02/4 (Cologne: Max Planck Institute for the Study of Societies).

Schmidt, S. K. (2004b), 'Rechtsunsicherheit statt Regulierungswettbewerb: die nationalen Folgen des europäischen Binnenmarkts für Dienstleistungen', habilitation thesis, FernUniversität Hagen, Hagen.

Schmidt, S. K., and Wonka, A. (2012), 'European Commission', in E. Jones, A. Menon, and S. Weatherill (eds.), *The Oxford Handbook of the European Union* (Oxford: Oxford University Press), 336–49.

Schmidt, V. (2002), *The Futures of European Capitalism* (Oxford: Oxford University Press).

Schmidt, V. (2008), 'Discursive Institutionalism: The Explanatory Power of Ideas and Discourse', *Annual Review of Political Science*, 11: 303–26.

Schmitter, P. C. (1996), 'Examining the Present Euro-Polity with the Help of Past Theories', in G. Marks, F. W. Scharpf, P. C. Schmitter, and W. Streeck (eds.), *Governance in the European Union* (London: Sage), 1–14.

Schneider, G., Steunenberg, B., and Widgrén, M. (2006), 'Evidence with Insight: What Models Contribute to EU Research', in R. Thomson, F. N. Stokman, C. H. Achen, and T. König (eds.), *The European Union Decides* (Cambridge: Cambridge University Press), 299–316.

Schneider, V., Fink, S., and Tenbücken, M. (2005), 'Buying out the State: A Comparative Perspective on the Privatization of Infrastructures', *Comparative Political Studies*, 38/6: 704–27.

Schreiber, K. (1991), 'The New Approach to Technical Harmonization and Standards', in L. Hurwitz and C. Lequesne (eds.), *The State of the European Community*, vol. i: *Politics, Institutions and Debates in the Transition Years* (Boulder, CO: Lynne Rienner), 97–112.

Schuler, M. (2005), 'Comments on Arts. 10a of Reg. 1408/71', in K.-J. Bieback and M. Fuchs (eds.), *Europäisches Sozialrecht: Nomos-Kommentar*, 4th edn. (Baden-Baden: Nomos), 151–3.

Schulte, B. (2012), 'Supranationales Recht', in B. Baron von Maydell and F. Ruland (eds.), *Sozialrechtshandbuch (SRH)*, 5th edn. (Baden-Baden: Nomos), 1434–500.

Schulz-Weidner, W. (1997), 'Die Konsequenzen des europäischen Binnenmarktes für die deutsche Rentenversicherung', *Deutsche Rentenversicherung*, 8: 445–73.

Schulz-Weidner, W. (2003), 'Die Öffnung der Sozialversicherung im Binnenmarkt und ihre Grenzen: zugleich eine Betrachtung zu der Entscheidung des Europäischen Gerichtshofs vom 3. Oktober 2002 in der Rechtssache "Danner" C 136/00', *Zeitschrift für europäisches Sozial- und Arbeitsrecht*, 2/2: 58–68.

Schulz-Weidner, W. (2004), 'Das europäische Beihilferecht und sein Einfluss auf die Sozialversicherung', *Deutsche Rentenversicherung*, 10: 592–613.

Schüssel, W. (2007), 'Europas Finanzen—Das alte System ist ausgereizt', *Spotlight Europe*, 2007/08 (Gütersloh: Bertelsmann Stiftung und Centrum für angewandte Politikforschung).

Schwark, P. (2003), 'Unisex-Tarife: Gebot der Gleichbehandlung oder Umverteilungsinstrument?', *Wirtschaftsdienst*, 83/10: 647–54.

Schwarze, J. (1998), 'Die Bedeutung des Territorialitätsprinzips bei mitgliedstaatlichen Preiskontrollen auf dem europäischen Arzneimittelmarkt', in J. Schwarze (ed.), *Unverfälschter Wettbewerb für Arzneimittel im europäischen Binnenmarkt* (Baden-Baden: Nomos), 59–74.

Scott, J. (1995), *Development Dilemmas in the European Community: Rethinking Regional Development Policy* (Buckingham and Philadelphia, PA: Open University Press).

Scott, J., and Trubek, D. (2002), 'Mind the Gap: Law and New Approaches to Governance in the European Union', *European Law Journal*, 8/1: 1–18.

Scully, R., Hix, S., and Farrell, D. M. (2012), 'National or European Parliamentarians? Evidence from a New Survey of the Members of the European Parliament', *Journal of Common Market Studies*, 50/4: 670–83.

Sedelmeier, U. (2005), *Constructing the Path to Eastern Enlargement: The Uneven Policy Impact of EU Identity* (Manchester: Manchester University Press).

Sedelmeier, U. (2007), 'The European Neighbourhood Policy: A Comment on Theory and Policy', in K. Weber, M. E. Smith, and M. Baun (eds.), *Governing Europe's Neighbourhood: Partners or Periphery?* (Manchester: Manchester University Press), 195–208.

Sedelmeier, U. (2008), 'After Conditionality: Post-Accession Compliance with EU Law in East Central Europe', *Journal of European Public Policy*, 15/6: 806–25.

Sedelmeier, U. (2011), 'Europeanisation in New Member and Candidate States', *Living Reviews in European Governance*, 6/1: 1–52.

Sedelmeier, U. (2012a), 'Europeanization', in E. Jones, A. Menon, and S. Weatherill (eds.), *The Oxford Handbook of the European Union* (Oxford: Oxford University Press), 825–39.

Sedelmeier, U. (2012b), 'Is Europeanization through Conditionality Sustainable? Lock-In of Institutional Change after EU Accession', *West European Politics*, 35/1: 20–38.

Sedelmeier, U. (2014), 'Anchoring Democracy from Above? The European Union and Democratic Backslide in Hungary and Romania after Accession', *Journal of Common Market Studies*, 52/1: 105–21.

Sedelmeier, U., and Wallace, H. (1996), 'Policies Towards Central and Eastern Europe', in H. Wallace and W. Wallace (eds.), *Policy-Making in the European Union*, 3rd edn. (Oxford: Oxford University Press), 353–87.

Seifert, J. (2011), 'Change and Stability in the EU Budget', Working Paper No. 3 (Singapore: EU Centre in Singapore).

Selin, H. (2007), 'Coalition Politics and Chemicals Management in a Regulatory Ambitious Europe', *Global Environmental Politics*, 7/3: 63–93.

Selznick, P. (1984) [1949], *TVA and the Grassroots: A Study of Politics and Organization* (Berkeley, CA: University of California Press; original edition, Berkeley, CA: University of California).

Senden, L. (2010), 'The OMC and its Patch in the European Regulatory and Constitutional Landscape', EUI Working Paper No. 2010/61 (Florence: European University Institute).

Shackleton, M. (1990), *Financing the European Community* (London: Pinter).

Shackleton, M. (1993a), 'The Community Budget After Maastricht', in A. W. Cafruny and G. G. Rosenthal (eds.), *The State of the European Community*, vol. II: *The Maastricht Debates and Beyond* (Boulder, CO: Lynne Rienner), 373–90.

Shackleton, M. (1993b), 'The Budget of the EC: Structure and Process', in J. Lodge (ed.), *The European Community and the Challenge of the Future* (London: Pinter).

Shapiro, M., and Stone, A. (1994), 'The New Constitutional Politics of Europe', *Comparative Political Studies*, 26/4: 397–420.

Shaw, J. (2000) (ed.), *Social Law and Policy in an Evolving European Union* (Oxford: Hart).

Shaw, J. (2007), 'EU-Citizenship and Political Rights in an Evolving European Union', *Fordham Law Review*, 75/5: 2549–78.

Sheingate, A. (2001), *The Welfare State for Farmers: Institutions and Interest Group Power in the United States, France, and Japan* (Princeton, NJ: Princeton University Press).

Shepsle, K. (1979), 'Institutional Arrangements and Equilibrium in Multidimensional Voting Models', *American Journal of Political Science*, 23/1: 27–60.

Shiller, R. J. (2008), *The Subprime Solution: How Today's Global Financial Crisis Happened, and What to Do about It* (Princeton, NJ: Princeton University Press).

Sievers, J., and Schmidt, S. (2014), 'Squaring the Circle with Mutual Recognition? *Demoi*-cratic Governance in Practice', *Journal of European Public Policy*, DOI: 10.1080/13501763.2014.881411

Simmons, B. A. (2010), 'Treaty Compliance and Violation', *Annual Review of Political Science*, 13: 273–96.

Sissenich, B. (2005), 'The Transfer of EU Social Policy to Poland and Hungary', in F. Schimmelfennig and U. Sedelmeier (eds.), *The Europeanization of Central and Eastern Europe* (Ithaca, NY: Cornell University Press), 156–77.

Sjursen, H. (2007) (ed.), *Civilian or Military Power? European Foreign Policy in Perspective* (London: Routledge).

Skjærseth, J. B., and Wettestad, J. (2007), 'Is EU Enlargement Bad for Environmental Policy? Confronting Gloomy Expectations with Evidence', *International Environmental Agreements*, 7/3: 263–80.

Skjærseth, J. B., and Wettestad, J. (2008), *EU Emissions Trading: Initiation, Decision-making and Implementation* (Farnham: Ashgate).

Skogstad, G. (1998), 'Ideas, Paradigms and Institutions: Agricultural Exceptionalism in the European Union and the United States', *Governance*, 11/4: 463–90.

Slaughter, A.-M. (2004), *A New World Order* (Princeton, NJ: Princeton University Press).

Slaughter, A.-M., Stone Sweet, A., and Weiler, J. H. H. (1997), *The European Court and National Courts* (Oxford: Hart).

Smaghi, L. B. (2006), 'Powerless Europe: Why is the Euro Area Still a Political Dwarf?', *International Finance*, 9/2: 261–79.

Smismans, S. (2008), 'The European Social Dialogue in the Shadow of Hierarchy', *Journal of Public Policy*, 26/1: 161–80.

Smith, E. W. (1999), 'Re-Regulation and Integration: The Nordic States and the European Economic Area', D.Phil. thesis, University of Sussex.

Smith, K. E. (2003), *European Union Foreign Policy in a Changing World* (Cambridge: Polity).

Smith, K. E. (2008), *European Union Foreign Policy in a Changing World*, 2nd edn. (Cambridge: Polity).

Smith, M. E. (2004), *Europe's Foreign and Security Policy: The Institutionalization of Cooperation* (Cambridge: Cambridge University Press).

Smith, M. J. (1986), *Realist Thought from Weber to Kissinger* (Baton Rouge, LA: Louisiana State University Press).

Smith, M. P. (2008), 'All Access Points are not Created Equal: Explaining the Fate of Diffuse Interests in the EU', *British Journal of Politics & International Relations*, 10/1: 64–83.

Spence, D. (2006) (ed.), *The European Commission*, 3rd edn. (London: John Harper).

Spendzharova, A. B., and Vachudova, M. A. (2012), 'Catching Up? Consolidating Liberal Democracy in Bulgaria and Romania after EU Accession', *West European Politics*, 35/1: 39–58.

Starke, P., Obinger, H., and Castles, F. G. (2008), 'Convergence Towards Where: In What Ways, If Any, Are Welfare States Becoming More Similar?', *Journal of European Public Policy*, 15/7: 975–1000.

Stern, N. (2006), *The Economics of Climate Change: The Stern Review* (London: HM Treasury).

Steunenberg, B. (2007), 'A Policy Solution to the European Union's Transposition Puzzle: Interaction of Interests in Different Domestic Arenas', *West European Politics*, 30/1: 23–49.

Stone Sweet, A. (2000), *Governing with Judges: Constitutional Politics in Europe* (Oxford: Oxford University Press).

Stone Sweet, A. (2010), 'The European Court of Justice and the Judicialization of EU Governance', *Living Reviews in European Governance*, 5/2, available at *http://www.livingreviews.org/lreg-2010-2*.

Stone Sweet, A., and Brunell, T. L. (1998a), 'The European Courts and National Courts: A Statistical Analysis of Preliminary References 1961–95', *Journal of European Public Policy*, 5: 66–97.

Stone Sweet, A., and Brunell, T. L. (1998b), 'Constructing a Supranational Constitution: Dispute Resolution and Governance in the European Community', *American Political Science Review*, 92/1: 63–81.

Stone Sweet, A., and Caporaso, T. (1998), 'From Free Trade to Supranational Policy', in W. Sandholtz and A. Stone Sweet (eds.), *European Integration and Supranational Governance* (Oxford: Oxford University Press), 92–133.

Streeck, W. (1995), 'From Market Making to State Building?', in S. Leibfried and P. Pierson, *European Social Policy: Between Fragmentation and Integration* (Washington, DC: Brookings Institution), 92–133.

Streeck, W. (1998), *The Internationalization of Industrial Relations in Europe: Prospects and Problems*, MPIfG Discussion Paper 98/2 (Cologne: Max Planck Institute for the Study of Societies).

Streeck, W. (2000), 'Competitive Solidarity: Rethinking the "European Social Model"', in K. Hinrichs, H. Kitschelt, and H. Wiesenthal (eds.), *Kontingenz und Krise: Institutionenpolitik in kapitalistischen und postsozialistischen Gesellschaften* (Frankfurt am Main: Campus), 245–61.

Streeck, W., and Schmitter, P. C. (1991), 'From National Corporatism to Transnational Pluralism: Organized Interests in the Single European Market', *Politics and Society*, 19/2: 133–64.

Streeck, W., and Thelen, K. (2005), 'Introduction: Institutional Change in Advanced Political Economies', in W. Streeck and K. Thelen (eds.), *Beyond Continuity: Institutional Change in Advanced Political Economies* (Oxford: Oxford University Press), 1–39.

Suda, Y. (2013), 'Transatlantic Politics of Data Transfer: Extraterritoriality, Counter-Extraterritoriality and Counter-Terrorism', *Journal of Common Market Studies*, 51/4: 772–88.

Swaan, A. de (1973), *Coalition Theories and Cabinet Formation* (Amsterdam: Elsevier).

Swaan, A. de (1992), 'Perspectives for a Transnational Social Policy', *Government and Opposition*, 27/1: 33–52.

Swinbank, A. (1989), 'The Common Agricultural Policy and the Politics of European Decision Making', *Journal of Common Market Studies*, 27/4: 303–22.

Syrpis, P. (2002), 'Legitimizing European Governance: Taking Subsidiarity Seriously within the Open Method of Coordination', Department of Law Working Papers 2002/10 (Florence: European University Institute).

Syrpis, P. (2007), *EU Intervention in Domestic Labour Law* (Oxford: Oxford University Press).

Syrpis, P. (2008), 'The Treaty of Lisbon: Much Ado … But About What?', *Industrial Law Journal*, 37/3: 219–35.

Syrpis, P. (2011), 'Reconciling Economic Freedom and Social Rights: The Potential of *Commission v. Germany* (Case C-271/08, Judgment of 15 July 2010)', *Industrial Law Journal*, 40/2: 222–9.

Szczerbiak, A., and Taggart, P. P. (2008), *Opposing Europe?: The Comparative Politics of Euroscepticism*, 2 vols. (Oxford: Oxford University Press).

Tallberg, J. (2000), 'The Anatomy of Autonomy: An Institutional Account of Variation in Supranational Influence', *Journal of Common Market Studies*, 38/5: 843–64.

Tallberg, J. (2002), 'Paths to Compliance: Enforcement, Management and the European Union', *International Organization*, 56/3: 609–43.

Tallberg, J. (2003), *European Governance and Supranational Institutions: Making States Comply* (London: Routledge).

Tallberg, J. (2006), *Leadership and Negotiation in the European Union* (Cambridge: Cambridge University Press).

Tallberg, J. (2007), 'Executive Politics', in K. E. Jørgensen, M. A. Pollack, and B. Rosamond (eds.), *The Handbook of European Union Politics* (London: Sage), 195–212.

Tallberg, J. (2008), 'The Power of the Chair: Formal Leadership by the Council Presidency', in D. Naurin and H. Wallace (eds.), *Unveiling the Council of the European Union: Games Governments Play in Brussels* (Basingstoke: Palgrave Macmillan), 187–202.

Tarschys, D. (2003), *Reinventing Cohesion: The Future of European Structural Policy*, Report No. 17 (Stockholm: Swedish Institute for European Policy Studies).

Tavistock Institute (1999), *The Thematic Evaluation of the Partnership Principle: Final Report* (London: Tavistock Institute).

Taylor, P. (1983), *The Limits of European Integration* (New York, NY: Columbia University Press).

Teichgraber, M. (2013), 'European Labour Force Summary—Annual Results 2012', Eurostat, available at *http://epp.eurostat.ec.europa.eu/statistics_explained/index.php/Labour_market_and_labour_force_statistics*.

Tenbücken, M. (2006), 'The Regulation of Network Infrastructures in the New European Union', Ph.D., University of Konstanz, available at *http://www.ub.uni-konstanz.de/kops/volltexte/2006/1736/index.html*.

Ténékidès, G. (1970), *Cours d'Organisations européennes* (Paris: Université de droit, d'Économie, et de Sciences Sociales Paris-V).

Thatcher, M. (1984), 'Europe: The Future', paper presented to the European Council, Fontainebleau, 25–26 June.

Thatcher, M., and Stone Sweet, A. (2002) (eds.), 'The Politics of Delegation: Non-Majoritarian Institutions in Europe', *West European Politics*, 25/1: 1–219 (special issue).

Thelen, K., and Steinmo, S. (1992), 'Introduction', in K. Thelen and S. Steinmo (eds.), *Structuring Politics: Historical Institutionalism in Comparative Politics* (Cambridge: Cambridge University Press), 1–32.

Thomas, D. C. (2006), 'Constitutionalization through Enlargement: The Contested Origins of the EU's Democratic Identity', *Journal of European Public Policy*, 13/8: 1190–210.

Thomson, R. (2007), 'The Impact of Enlargement on Legislative Decision Making in the European Union', paper presented at the General Conference of the European Consortium for Political Research, Pisa, Italy, 6–8 Sept.

Thomson, R. (2008), 'The Council Presidency in the European Union: Responsibility with Power', *Journal of Common Market Studies*, 46/3: 593–617.

Thomson, R. (2011), *Resolving Controversy in the European Union: Legislative Decision-Making Before and After Enlargement* (Cambridge: Cambridge University Press).

Thomson, R., and Hosli, M. (2006), 'Who Has Power in the EU? The Commission, Council and Parliament in Legislative Decision-Making', *Journal of Common Market Studies*, 44/2: 391–417.

Thomson, R., Stokman, F. N., Achen, C. H., and Konig, T. (2006), *The European Union Decides: Testing Theories of European Decision-Making* (Cambridge: Cambridge University Press).

Thomson, S., and Mossialos, E. (2007), 'Regulating Private Health Insurance in the European Union: The Implications of Single Market Legislation and Competition Policy', *Journal of European Integration*, 29/1: 89–107.

Tidow, S. (2003), 'The Emergence of a European Employment Policy', in H. Overbeek (ed.), *The Political Economy of European Employment* (London: Routledge), 77–98.

Timur, A., Picone, G., and DeSimone, J. (2011), 'Has the European Union Achieved a Single Pharmaceutical Market?', *International Journal of Health Care Finance and Economics*, 11/4: 223–44.

Tömmel, I., and Verdun, A. (2008) (eds.), *Innovative Governance in the European Union* (Boulder, CO: Lynne Rienner).

Toshkov, D. (2007), 'In Search of the Worlds of Compliance: Culture and Transposition Performance in the European Union', *Journal of European Public Policy*, 14/6: 933–59.

Toshkov, D. (2012), 'The Disaster that Didn't Happen: Compliance with EU Law in Central and Eastern Europe', *L'Europe En Formation*, 2: 91–109.

Townley, C. (2009), *Article 81 EC and Public Policy* (Oxford: Hart).

Townsend, M. (2007), *The Euro and Economic and Monetary Union: An Historical, Institutional and Economic Description* (London: John Harper).

Tracy, M. (1989), *Government and Agriculture in Western Europe* (New York, NY: Harvester Wheatsheaf).

Tranholm-Mikkelsen, J. (1991), 'Neo-Functionalism: Obstinate or Obsolete? A Reappraisal in Light of the New Dynamism of the EC', *Millennium: Journal of International Studies*, 20/1: 1–21.

Trauner, F., and Ripoll Servent, A. (2015) (eds.), *Policy Change in the Area of Freedom, Security and Justice: How EU Institutions Matter* (London: Routledge).

Treib, O. (2008), 'Implementing and Complying with EU Governance Outputs', *Living Reviews in European Governance*, 3/5, available at *http://www.livingreviews.org/lreg-2008-5*.

Trondal, J. (2007), 'The Public Administration Turn in Integration Research', *Journal of European Public Policy*, 14/6: 960–72.

Tsebelis, G. (1994), 'The Power of the European Parliament as a Conditional Agenda Setter', *American Political Science Review*, 88/1: 128–42.

Tsebelis, G. (1995), 'Decision Making in Political Systems: Veto Players in Presidentialism, Parliamentarism, Multicameralism and Multipartyism', *British Journal of Political Science*, 25/3: 289–325.

Tsebelis, G., and Garrett, G. (2000), 'Legislative Politics in the European Union', *European Union Politics*, 1/1: 9–36.

Tsebelis, G., and Garrett, G. (2001), 'The Institutional Foundations of Intergovernmentalism and Supranationalism in the European Union', *International Organization*, 55/2: 357–90.

Tsebelis, G., Jensen, C., Kalandrakis, A., and Kreppel, A. (2001), 'Legislative Procedures in the European Union: An Empirical Analysis', *British Journal of Political Science*, 31/4: 573–99.

Tsoukalis, L. (2011), 'The JCMS Annual Review Lecture: The Shattering of Illusions—And What Next?', *Journal of Common Market Studies*, 49/s1: 19–44.

Tugendhat, C. (1985), 'How to Get Europe Moving Again', *International Affairs*, 61/3: 421–9.

Uhl, S. (2008), 'Europe, the Nation State, and Taxation', in A. Hurrelmann, S. Leibfried, K. Martens, and P. Mayer (eds.), *Transforming the Golden Age Nation State* (Basingstoke: Palgrave Macmillan), 24–41.

UNICE, UEAPME, CEEP (2006), 'Implementation of the Framework Agreement on Telework. Report by the European Social Partners, adopted by the Social Dialogue Committee on 28 June 2006' (Brussels 2006), available at *http://ec.europa.eu/employment_social/news/2006/oct/telework_implementation_report_en.pdf*.

Utton, M. (2011), *Cartels and Economic Collusion* (Cheltenham: Edward Elgar).

Vachudova, M. A. (2005), *Europe Undivided: Democracy, Leverage and Integration after Communism* (Oxford: Oxford University Press).

Vachudova, M. A. (2008), 'Tempered by the EU? Political Parties and Party Systems Before and After Accession', *Journal of European Public Policy*, 15/6: 861–79.

Van Evera, S. (1990–1), 'Primed for Peace: Europe after the Cold War', *International Security*, 15/3: 7–57.

Vanhercke, B. (2013), 'Under the Radar? EU Social Policy in Times of Austerity', in D. Natali and B. Vanhercke (eds.), *Social Developments in the European Union 2012, 14th Annual Report* (Brussels: ETUI/OSE), 91–120.

Van Rompuy, H. (2012), 'Towards a Genuine Economic and Monetary Union', Brussels: European Council, 26 June, Presse 296.

Vaubel, R. (1986), 'A Public Choice Approach to International Organization', *Public Choice*, 51/1: 39–57.

Vaughan-Whitehead, D. (2003), *EU Enlargement versus Social Europe? The Uncertain Future of the European Social Model* (Cheltenham: Edward Elgar).

Vaughan-Whitehead, D. (2007), 'Work and Employment Conditions in New EU Member States: A Different Reality?', in P. Leisink, B. Steijn, and U. Veersma (eds.), *Industrial Relations in the New Europe: Enlargement, Integration and Reform* (Cheltenham: Edward Elgar), 41–62.

Vauhkonen, J., and Pylkkönen, P. (2004), 'Integration of European Banking and Insurance', in H. Koskenkylä (ed.), *Financial Integration*, Bank of Finland studies, A 108 (Helsinki: Suomen Pankki), 73–115.

Veljanovski, C. (2004), 'EC Merger Policy after *GE/Honeywell* and Airtours', *The Antitrust Bulletin*, Spring–Summer: 153–93.

Verdun, A. (1999), 'The Role of the Delors Committee in the Creation of EMU: An Epistemic Community', *Journal of European Public Policy*, 6/2: 308–28.

Versluis, E. (2007), 'Even Rules, Uneven Practices: Opening the "Black Box" of EU Law in Action', *West European Politics*, 30/1: 50–67.

Vickers, J. (2003), 'Competition Economics and Policy', *European Competition Law Review*, 24/3: 95–102.

Vogel, D. (1986), *National Styles of Regulation* (Ithaca, NY: Cornell University Press).

Vogel, D. (1995), *Trading Up: Consumer and Environmental Regulation in a Global Economy* (Cambridge, MA: Harvard University Press).

Vogel, D. (2003), 'The Hare and the Tortoise Revisited: The New Politics of Consumer and Environmental Regulation in Europe', *British Journal of Political Science*, 33/4: 557–80.

Vogel, D. (2012), *The Politics of Precaution: Regulating Health, Safety, and Environmental Risks in Europe and the United States* (Princeton, NJ: Princeton University Press).

Vogt, L. (2005), 'The EU's Single Market: At Your Service?', Economics Department Working Paper No. 449, ECO/WKP(2005)36 (Paris: Organization for Economic Cooperation and Development), 7 Oct.

Waarden, F. van, and Drahos, M. (2002), 'Courts and (Epistemic) Communities in the Convergence of Competition Policies', *Journal of European Public Policy*, 9/6: 913–34.

Walby, S. (2005) (ed.), 'Gender Mainstreaming', *Social Politics*, 12/3: 321–450 (special issue).

Wallace, H. (1973), *National Governments and the European Communities* (London: Chatham House).

Wallace, H. (1977), 'The Establishment of the Regional Development Fund: Common Policy or Pork Barrel?', in H. Wallace, W. Wallace, and C. Webb (eds.), *Policy-Making in the European Communities* (Chichester: Wiley), 136–64.

Wallace, H. (1983), 'Distributional Politics: Dividing up the Community Cake', in H. Wallace, W. Wallace, and C. Webb (eds.), *Policy-Making in the European Communities*, 2nd edn. (Chichester: Wiley), 81–113.

Wallace, H. (1984), 'Bilateral, Trilateral and Multilateral Negotiations in the European Community', in R. Morgan, and C. Bray (eds.), *Partners and Rivals in Western Europe: Britain, France and Germany* (Aldershot: Gower), 156–74.

Wallace, H. (1999), 'Whose Europe Is It Anyway?', *European Journal of Political Research*, 35/3: 287–306.

Wallace, H. (2001), 'The Changing Politics of the European Union: An Overview', *Journal of Common Market Studies*, 39/4: 581–94.

Wallace, H. (2007), 'Adapting to Enlargement of the European Union: Institutional Practice', TEPSA Working Paper (Brussels: TEPSA).

Wallace, W. (1982), 'Europe as a Confederation: The Community and the Nation-State', *Journal of Common Market Studies*, 20/1–2: 57–68.

Wallace, W. (1983), 'Less than a Federation, More than a Regime: The Community as a Political System', in H. Wallace, W. Wallace, and C. Webb (eds.), *Policy-Making in the European Community*, 2nd edn. (Chichester: John Wiley), 403–36.

Wallace, W. (1996), *Opening the Door: The Enlargement of NATO and the European Union* (London: Centre for European Reform).

Walt, S. M. (1998–9), 'The Ties that Fray: Why Europe and America are Drifting Apart', *The National Interest*, 54 (Winter): 3–11.

Waltz, K. N. (1979), *Theory of International Politics* (Reading, MA: Addison-Wesley).

Wapner, P. (1996), *Environmental Activism and World Civic Politics* (Albany, NY: SUNY Press).

Warntjen, A. (2008), 'The Council Presidency: Power Broker or Burden? An Empirical Analysis', *European Union Politics*, 9/3: 315–38.

Weale, A. (1992), *The New Politics of Pollution* (Manchester: Manchester University Press).

Weaver, R. E. (1986), 'The Politics of Blame Avoidance', *Journal of Public Policy*, 6/4: 371–98.

Webb, C. (1977), 'Introduction: Variations on a Theoretical Theme', in H. Wallace, W. Wallace, and C. Webb (eds.), *Policy-Making in the European Communities* (Chichester: Wiley), 1–32.

Weber, K., Smith, M. E., and Baun, M. (2007) (eds.), *Governing Europe's Neighbourhood: Partners or Periphery?* (Manchester: Manchester University Press).

Weiler, J. H. H. (1994), 'A Quiet Revolution: The European Court of Justice and its Interlocutors', *Comparative Political Studies*, 24/4: 510–34.

Weiler, J. H. H. (1995), 'Does Europe Need a Constitution? Reflections on Demos, Telos, and the German Maastricht Decision', *European Law Journal*, 1/2: 219–58.

Weiler, J. H. H. (1999), *The Constitution of Europe: 'Do the New Clothes Have an Emperor?' and Other Essays on European Integration* (Cambridge: Cambridge University Press).

Weishaupt, J. T., and Lack, K. (2011), 'The European Employment Strategy: Assessing the Status Quo', *German Policy Studies*, 7/1: 9–44.

Wendler, F. (2004), 'The Paradoxical Effects of Institutional Change for the Legitimacy of European Governance: The Case of EU Social Policy', European Integration online Papers, 8/7, available at *http://eiop.or.at/eiop*.

Westlake, M., and Galloway, D. (2005) (eds.), *The Council of the European Union*, 3rd edn. (London: John Harper).

Whish, R. (2008), *Competition Law*, 6th edn. (Oxford: Oxford University Press).

Whish, R., and Bailey, D. (2012), *Competition Law*, 7th edn. (Oxford: Oxford University Press).

Whitaker, R. (2011), *The European Parliament's Committees: National Party Control and Legislative Empowerment* (London: Routledge).

Wiener, A., and Diez, T. (2009) (eds.), *European Integration Theory*, 2nd edn. (Oxford: Oxford University Press).

Wigger, A. (2007), 'Towards a Market-Based Approach: The Privatization and Micro-economization of EU Antitrust Law Enforcement', in H. Overbeek, B. van Apeldoorn, and A. Nölke (eds.), *The Transnational Politics of Corporate Governance Regulation* (London: Routledge), 98–118.

Wigger, A., and Nölke, A. (2007), 'Enhanced Roles of Private Actors in EU Business Regulation and the Erosion of Rhenish Capitalism: The Case of Antitrust Enforcement', *Journal of Common Market Studies*, 45/2: 487–513.

Wilks, S. (2005*a*), 'Agency Escape: Decentralization or Dominance of the European Commission in the Modernization of Competition Policy?', *Governance*, 18/3: 431–52.

Wilks, S. (2005*b*), 'Competition Policy', in H. Wallace, W. Wallace, and M. A. Pollack (eds.), *Policy-Making in the European Union*, 5th edn. (Oxford: Oxford University Press), 113–40.

Wilks, S. (2007), 'Agencies, Networks, Discourses and the Trajectory of European Competition Enforcement', *European Competition Journal*, 3/2: 437–64.

Wilks, S. (2010), 'Competition Policy', in D. Coen, W. Grant, and G. Wilson (eds.), *The Oxford Handbook of Business and Government* (Oxford: Oxford University Press), 730–56.

Wilks, S., with Bartle, I. (2002), 'The Unanticipated Consequences of Creating Independent Competition Agencies', *West European Politics*, 25/1: 148–72.

Wilks, S., with McGowan, L. (1996), 'Competition Policy in the European Union: Creating a Federal Agency?', in G. B. Doern and S. Wilks (eds.), *Comparative Competition Policy: National Institutions in a Global Market* (Oxford: Clarendon Press), 225–67.

Williams, S. (1991), 'Sovereignty and Accountability in the European Community', in R. O. Keohane and S. Hoffmann (eds.), *The New European Community* (Boulder, CO: Westview), 155–76.

Wilson, J. Q. (1980), *The Politics of Regulation* (New York, NY: Basic Books).

Witney, N. (2008), *Re-Energising Europe's Security and Defence Policy* (Brussels: European Council on Foreign Relations).

Woll, C. (2009), 'Trade Policy Lobbying in the European Union: Who Captures Whom', in D. Coen and J. Richardson (eds.), *Lobbying in the European Union: Institutions, Actors and Issues* (Oxford: Oxford University Press), 268–89.

Woolcock, S. (1996), 'Competition among Rules in the Single European Market', in J. McCahery, W. W. Bratton, S. Picciotto, and C. Scott (eds.), *International Regulatory Competition and Coordination: Perspectives on Economic Regulation in Europe and the United States* (Oxford: Clarendon Press), 289–321.

Woolcock, S. (2008), 'The Potential Impact of the Lisbon Treaty on European Union External Trade Policy', Policy Papers (Stockholm: Swedish Institute for European Policy Studies).

Woolcock, S. (2010), 'Trade Policy: A Further Shift Towards Brussels", in H. Wallace, M. A. Pollack, and A. R. Young (eds.), *Policy-Making in the European Union*, 6th edn. (Oxford: Oxford University Press), 381–99.

Woolcock, S. (2012), *European Union Economic Diplomacy* (Farnham: Ashgate).

Woolcock, S. (2014), 'Differentiation within Reciprocity: the European Union Approach to Preferential Trade Agreements', *Comparative Politics*, 20/1: 36–48.

Woolcock, S., and Hodges, M. (1996), 'EU Policy in the Uruguay Round: The Story Behind the Headlines', in H. Wallace and W. Wallace (eds.), *Policy-Making in the European Union*, 3rd edn. (Oxford: Oxford University Press), 301–24.

Wright, G. (1953), 'Agrarian Syndicalism in Postwar France', *American Political Science Review*, 47/2: 402–16.

WTO (World Trade Organization) (2008), 'Thirteenth Annual Review of the Implementation and Operation of the TBT Agreement', G/TBT/23 (Geneva: World Trade Organization Committee on Technical Barriers to Trade), 20 Feb.

WTO (World Trade Organization) (2011), 'Trade Policy Review: European Union: Review by the Secretariat', WT/TPR/S/248 (Geneva: World Trade Organization), 1 June.

WTO (World Trade Organization) (2013), 'The Future of Trade: The Challenges of Convergence', Report of the Panel on Defining the Future of Trade convened by WTO Director General Pascal Lamy (Geneva: World Trade Organization), 24 Apr.

Wurzel, R. K. W. (2008), 'Environmental Policy: EU Actors, Leaders and Laggard States', in J. Hoyward (ed.), *Leaderless Europe* (Oxford: Oxford University Press), 66–88.

Wurzel, R. K. W., and Connelly, J. (2011) (eds.), *The European Union as a Leader in International Climate Change Politics* (London: Routledge).

Wurzel, R. K. W., Zito, A. R., and Jordan, A. J. (2013), *Environmental Governance in Europe: A Comparative Analysis of New Environmental Policy Instruments* (Cheltenham: Edward Elgar).

Yilmaz, G. (2012), 'From the Push of European Union Conditionality to Domestic Pull: Europeanization of Minority Rights in Turkey', PhD thesis, Free University Berlin.

Young, A. R. (1995), 'Ideas, Interests and Institutions: The Politics of Liberalisation in the EC's Road Haulage Industry', in D. Mayes (ed.), *The Evolution of Rules for a Single European Market, Part i: Industry and Finance* (Brussels: Office for Official Publications of the European Communities).

Young, A. R. (1997), 'Consumption without Representation? Consumers in the Single Market', in H. Wallace and A. R. Young (eds.), *Participation and Policy-Making in the European Union* (Oxford: Clarendon Press), 206–34.

Young, A. R. (1998), 'European Consumer Groups: Multiple Levels of Governance and Multiple Logics of Collective Action', in J. Greenwood and M. Aspinwall (eds.), *Collective Action in the European Union: Interests and the New Politics of Associability* (London: Routledge), 149–75.

Young, A. R. (2007), 'The Politics of Regulation and the Internal Market', in K. E. Jørgensen, M. A. Pollack, and B. Rosamond (eds.), *The Handbook of European Union Politics* (London: Sage), 373–94.

Young, A. R. (2008), 'Explaining EU Compliance with WTO Rules: A Research Project', paper to the UACES Conference, Edinburgh, 1–3 Sept.

Young, A. R. (2009), 'Analysing Compliance: The EU and the WTO', paper presented to the International Studies Association Conference, New York, 15–18 Feb.

Young, A. R. (2010), 'The Single Market: Deregulation, Reregulation, and Integration', in H. Wallace, M. A. Pollack, and A. R. Young (eds.), *Policy-Making in the European Union*, 6th edn. (Oxford: Oxford University Press), 107–31.

Young, A. R. (2012), 'Less Than You Might Think: The Impact of WTO Rules on EU', in O. Costa and K. E. Jørgensen (eds.), *The Influence of International Institutions on the EU: When Multilateralism Hits Brussels* (Basingstoke: Palgrave Macmillan), 23–41.

Young, A. R. (2014), 'Exporting Rules or Exporting Goods? The EU's Bilateral Regulatory Diplomacy in Comparative Perspective', paper to the Jean Monnet Chair Workshop 'Regulatory Power Europe? Assessing the EU's Efforts to Shape Global Rules', Georgia Institute of Technology, 18–19 Apr.

Young, A. R., and Peterson, J. (2014), *Parochial Global Europe: 21st Century Trade Politics* (Oxford: Oxford University Press).

Young, A. R., and Wallace, H. (2000), *Regulatory Politics in the Enlarging European Union: Weighing Civic and Producer Interests* (Manchester: Manchester University Press).

Young, O. R. (1999), *Governance in World Affairs* (Ithaca, NY: Cornell University Press).

Zeitlin, J. (2008), 'The Open Method of Co-ordination and the Governance of the Lisbon Strategy', *Journal of Common Market Studies*, 46/2: 436–50.

Zeitlin, J., and Pochet, P., with Magnusson L. (2005) (eds.), *The Open Method of Coordination in Action: The European Employment and Social Inclusion Strategies* (Brussels: PLE-Peter Lang).

Zito, A.R. (1999), 'Task Expansion: A Theoretical Overview', *Environment and Planning C: Government and Policy*, 17/1: 19–35.

Zito, A. R. (2001), 'Epistemic Communities, Collective Entrepreneurship and European Integration', *Journal of European Public Policy*, 8/4: 585–603.

Zürn, M. (2000), 'Democratic Governance Beyond the Nation-State', in M. T. Greven and L. Pauly (eds.), *Democracy Beyond the State? The European Dilemma and the Emerging Global Order* (Lanham, MD: Rowman & Littlefield), 91–114.

Zürn, M., and Checkel, J. T. (2005), 'Getting Socialized to Build Bridges: Constructivism and Rationalism, Europe and the Nation-State', *International Organization*, 59/4: 1045–79.

▌ INDEX

Note: page references for all legislation – decisions, directives, and regulations – and European court judgments are provided in the lists in the preliminary matter, pp. xxx-xxxvi.